Dreams
and
Inward
Journeys

A Rhetoric and Reader
for Writers

Seventh Edition

Marjorie Ford
Stanford University

Jon Ford
De Anza College

Longman

New York   Boston   San Francisco
London   Toronto   Sydney   Tokyo   Singapore   Madrid
Mexico City   Munich   Paris   Cape Town   Hong Kong   Montreal

Executive Editor: Lynn M. Huddon
Associate Editor: Rebecca Gilpin
Senior Marketing Manager: Sandra McGuire
Senior Supplements Editor: Donna Campion
Production Manager: Stacey Kulig
Project Coordination, Text Design, and Electronic Page Makeup: Pre-Press PMG
Cover Design Manager: John Callahan
Cover Designer: Maria Ilardi
Cover Art: © Estate of Pavel Kuznetsov/RAO, Moscow/VAGA, New York
Photo Researcher: Rebecca Karamehmedovic
Senior Manufacturing Buyer: Roy Pickering
Printer and Binder: R.R. Donnelley and Sons
Cover Printer: R.R. Donnelley and Sons

For permission to use copyrighted material, grateful acknowledgment is
made to the copyright holders on pp. 537–540, which are hereby made part of
this copyright page.

Library of Congress Cataloging-in-Publication Data
Ford, Marjorie (Marjorie A.)
   Dreams and inward journeys: a rhetoric and reader for writers/
   Marjorie Ford, Jon Ford.—7th ed.
      p. cm.
   Includes bibliographical references and index.
   ISBN 978-0-205-69935-3
   1. College readers.   2. Report writing—Problems, exercises, etc.
3. English language—Rhetoric—Problems, exercises, etc.   I. Ford, Jon.
II. Title.
   PE1417.F63 2009
   808'.0427—dc22

                                                    2009004930

2 3 4 5 6 7 8 9 10—DOC—12 11 10

**Longman
is an imprint of**

www.pearsonhighered.com

ISBN-13: 978-0-205-69935-3
ISBN-10: 0-205-69935-9

Contents

1 DISCOVERING OURSELVES IN WRITING AND READING 1

"For the person [writer] who follows with trust and forgiveness what occurs to him, the world remains always ready and deep, an inexhaustible environment, with the combined vividness of an actuality and flexibility of a dream."

"I think that dreams are a way that people's minds illustrate the nature of their problems. Or the answers to their problems in symbolic language."

"It will be a long time still, I think, before a woman can sit down to write a book without finding a phantom to be slain, a rock to be dashed against."

2 JOURNEYS IN MEMORY (NARRATIVE)   69

3   JOURNEYS AND REFLECTIONS (DESCRIPTION AND REFLECTION)   109

*"Afoot and light-hearted I take to the open road,
Healthy, free, the world before me,
The long brown path before me leading wherever I choose."*

*"'Vietnamese are Vietnamese if they believe they are,' he said by
way of explanation, and I liked him on the instant."*

*"The image of Grandpère and the mysteries of West Africa remain
intertwined. Embodied in his dancing eyes and quick wit is the
personification of the continent. Although he grew up in a land of
ossified custom and stupefying fatalism, he took control of his life and
was able to bend the fates to his will."*

*"Now at least we had hope—hope that we would never again feel
alien or foreign in any country or region so long as we continued to
keep the 'dreamland' of our upbringing alive."*

*"What had brought her to south Tucson was not merely the wish to
be entertained, but a desire to watch an affirmation of faith, of
ceremony, of belief in community and shared history—and in the
power of ritual to represent something admirable and enduring in
human nature."*

*"I was glad I'd contributed that much. And right there was
everything I knew, and I could not say what that was."*

"[After] its use as the set of the motion picture Field of Dreams
*[a cornfield] strangely became a refuge for those seeking the
embodiment of our perception of baseball and America."*

4 DREAMS, MYTHS, AND FAIRY TALES (COMPARISON)

*"Both the great and the lesser mythologies of mankind have, up to
the present, always served simultaneously, both to lead the young
from their estate in nature, and to bear the aging back to nature and
on through the last dark door."*

*"All cultures have attempted to provide an answer to the mystery of
creation, and our modern scientific model is no exception. Perhaps
more surprisingly, there is an intriguing correspondence between
answers suggested by mythic narratives and those suggested by
scientific research."*

"Genesis 1 and 2"
"How the Sun Was Made: Dawn, Noontide and Night"
   (Australian Aboriginal)
"The Pelasgian Creation Myth" (Ancient Greek)
"The Chameleon Finds" (Yao-Bantu, African)
"Spider Woman Creates the Humans" (Hopi,
   Native American)
"The Beginning of the World" (Japanese)

*"The comparison of different creation myths . . . represents a
reasoned approach to looking at God and creation and thus what
true religious conviction really is."*

*"A child conversant with the old tales accepts them with an ease
born of familiarity, fitting them into his own scheme of things,
endowing them with new meaning."*

6 JOURNEYS IN GENDER AND RELATIONSHIPS (CAUSAL ANALYSIS)

Contents by Strategies and Modes

Process Analysis

Example and Illustration

Comparison and Contrast

Classification

Definition

Causal Analysis

Argument

Interpretation and Evaluation

Research Writing

Poetry

To the Instructor

*D*reams and Inward Journeys began as an experiment; we wanted to create a textbook for students that would encourage them to explore their inner worlds of dreams, fantasies, and the unconscious mind as well as the way society influenced those worlds through various forms of art created within a cultural context such as poems, stories, and essays, as well as popular culture such as films, television, advertisements, and gaming. Our intention is to help students learn to become more engaged in the acts of reading and writing while feeling themselves empowered as agents of social change, which grows out of greater self-knowledge and understanding of the dynamic relationship between inner and outer worlds. Our commitment to this work has been rewarded through the success of *Dreams and Inward Journeys,* which is now entering its seventh edition, and by the enthusiastic response we have received from the many instructors and students who have used the book in their classes and in our own.

Gathering the new materials and writing this edition of *Dreams and Inward Journeys,* we have felt very fortunate to have the opportunity to continue following our dreams. In this new edition we have built on the pedagogical foundation put in place by the earlier editions. We continue to support a creative approach to teaching writing and reading that acknowledges the role and importance of the unconscious mind, of dreams, of the imagination, of the heart connected to the reasoning mind. We have seen our students' writing develop as they have experimented with different writing projects and genres, from reflective essays that are primarily based on personal experiences to essays based on the traditional modes such as comparison, causal analysis, and definition, to ambitious argument and research papers that involve synthesis of diverse perspectives on social issues.

As in previous editions of *Dreams,* we have enjoyed applying these assumptions in shaping the text around the theme of dreams, a topic that is intriguing, revealing, and challenging. *Dreams and Inward Journeys* presents a rich mixture of essays, stories, poems, and student writings thematically focused on dream-related topics such as writing, reading, nature, memory, myths, obsessions, the double, sexuality, gender roles, technology, popular culture, and spirituality. Each chapter features rhetorical advice and strategies for writing and critical thinking. All of the selections have personal and social meanings that encourage students to think about and develop new ways of seeing and understanding themselves in relation to fundamental social issues as well as universal human concerns.

Special features of the seventh edition include the following:

- Thirty-five new readings that continue to develop and update the text's thematic concept with more particular attention to social and political issues.
- A rhetorical and essay development advice section that opens each chapter and provides students with a particular writing and thinking strategy.
- Three chapters that take a very different direction and that contain many new readings: Chapter 3, "Journeys and Reflections (all new selections)"; Chapter 8, "Pop Dreams"; and Chapter 9, "Voyages in Spirituality."
- Classical artwork and photography that support the theme of each chapter, with related prompts that generate prewriting activities and informal and formal writing projects.
- One or two student essays in each chapter that present students' perspectives on the topics raised in the chapter and provide models of the rhetorical strategy outlined at the beginning of each chapter. Four of the student essays in the book are documented argumentative research papers. Eight of the student essays are new.
- Information on keeping a dream journal as well as journal writing prompts before each reading to encourage informal, expressive, and spontaneous thinking and writing.
- Poems that explore many chapter themes in a concrete, expressive, and literary form.
- New "Connection" questions as well as "Questions for Discussion" and "Ideas for Writing."
- "Topics for Research and Writing" questions at the end of each chapter. These questions give students suggestions for research and longer writing assignments, as well as film and URL suggestions for further viewing/reading/research.
- Web sites related to each selection to encourage students to do further research on the topics raised in the reading.

Supplements

An **Instructor's Manual** is available to teachers who adopt the seventh edition of *Dreams and Inward Journeys*. The Instructor's Manual presents instructors with possible course constructions as well as teaching suggestions and possible responses to the study questions for each reading.

PEARSON
mycomplab

The new **MyCompLab** Web site integrates the market-leading instruction, multimedia tutorials, and exercises for writing, grammar and research that users have come to identify with the program, along with a new online composing space and new assessment tools. The result is a revolutionary application that offers a seamless and flexible teaching and learning environment built specifically for writers. Created after years of extensive research and in partnership with composition faculty and students across the country, the new MyCompLab provides help for writers in the context of their writing, with instructor- and peer-commenting functionality; proven tutorials and exercises for writing, grammar, and research; an e-portfolio; an assignment-builder; a bibliography tool; tutoring services; and a gradebook and course management organization created specifically for writing classes. Visit www.mycomplab.com for more information.

Acknowledgments

First, we thank our reviewers around the country whose advice guided us in this revision: Cynthia Cox, Belmont University; Patricia Dodd, Brookhaven College; Jeff Lindemann, Houston Community College Southwest; Katie Marks, Ithaca College; Hildy Miller, Portland State University; Suzanne V. Shepard, Broome Community College; Cynthia L. Walker, Faulkner University; Vito Zdanys, Portland Community College.

Lynn Huddon, our editor, has helped us to interpret and apply the advice of the critics while continuing to support the creative vision of the book. Lindsay Bethoney carefully supervised the manuscript's proofreading and production, and Kavita Sreedhar contributed materials for the new Instructor's Manual. We thank our students at Stanford University and DeAnza College who have provided many valuable insights into ways that we could develop the manuscript's themes and keep the text lively. We are especially grateful to the eight students at De Anza College and Stanford University who wrote new essays for the seventh edition, spending much time outside of their required writing assignments to produce works that we think will inspire your student writers.

We thank our friends, particularly Catherine Young, who have provided countless hours of encouragement and love as we worked to finish this edition. Finally, we thank our loving children, Michael and Maya, whose lives bring us joy on a daily basis and make our own lives complete. Recently, we have been blessed with grandchildren, Elijah and Tahlia Ford. They brighten our lives and remind us of the magical power of unconditional love and the indispensable nature of play and the beauty that can be appreciated in our natural surroundings.

Marjorie Ford
Jon Ford

To the Student

Nothing said to us, nothing we can learn from others, reaches us so deep as that which we find in ourselves.
                                                              THEODORE REIK

Each person has a unique understanding of the role and importance of dreams. We may value and analyze the dreams we have while asleep, our daytime fantasies, our hopes and aspirations, our belief in the power of our own imagination and creativity. The lyrics of popular songs, the plots of movies and novels, advertisements, and travel literature—all speak of the power of dreams and promise fulfillment of fantasies, romance, success, or peace of mind. As you think more about the presence and importance of dreams in your personal life and culture, you will begin to discover even more subtle meanings. Just as everyone dreams while sleeping, each person has a personal dream or vision that guides his or her waking life. Perhaps it is a dream that one is just starting to explore, a dream that one has been working to accomplish, or a dream that has just "come true."

We have designed this text using the concept of the dream as a common meeting ground, one that we hope will encourage you to better understand yourself, your family, friends, college, and professional acquaintances—and the world in which you live. Dreams and the insights they bring from the inner self, with the universality of their patterns, imagery, and meaning, also present a central metaphor that can be likened to the writing process, which is often an inward journey that involves the imagination, creativity, and vision.

Dreams and Inward Journeys: A Reader for Writers, seventh edition, is composed of nine chapters. Each chapter presents an aspect of the book's theme as well as a writing strategy that we think will help you to understand yourself and your world while improving your writing fluency and skills. The earlier chapters ask you to reflect on your personal experiences as a reader and as a writer. As you progress through the book, you will be asked to relate your personal and imaginative experiences to the social and cultural realities that also help to shape your identity and values.

In Chapter 1, "Discovering Ourselves in Reading and Writing," you will explore the ways in which reading is an active process that encourages the reader to understand and clarify her or his inner resources and values in relation to the values and experiences that have been recorded in a text. The reading strategies introduced discuss techniques for activating and enriching your reading and language experience. We also emphasize how reading is closely related to writing, which is presented as a process that is often chaotic in its initial stages, but powerful and rewarding. Writing and revising help writers to better understand their thoughts and feelings, while at the same time communicating what is most important to their audience of readers. The writing techniques explained will help you to overcome writing-related anxieties and fears and get you started on your writing. The dream journal project introduced in this chapter will provide you with the opportunity to discover the similarities between the writing process and dreaming—to discover the concerns of your unconscious mind.

The readings in Chapter 2, "Memory," explore how early experiences and memories, especially those inner experiences that are rooted in dreams, fantasies, or even obsessions, influence one's sense of self. The readings included in this section also suggest that stories created and re-membered from childhood help to shape personal myths. At the same time, we include readings that examine what constitutes a person's store of memories, including both firsthand experiences as well as imagined scenes, stories we are told, and media intake. In this chapter, we discuss creative strategies for writing effective narratives. These strategies will help you when you write about your dreams and memories.

In Chapter 3, "Journeys and Reflections," the essays invite you to re-flect on the way travel and journeys within can inspire you to reflect on the "secrets" of nature as well as cultural and spiritual rituals experi-enced as they help us to feel and reflect upon essential connections be-tween human beings and the world around us. The selections in this chapter present a variety of journeys to a many unique places. These journeys contain revelations about the beauty and the power of the nat-ural world; they also remind us of the spiritual rituals that are a part of learning about a new culture as we watch, listen to, and recognize how each culture organizes and value their own worlds. The strategies that we focus on—observing and capturing details, using words and images (both literally as well as metaphorically), and the essential power of revi-sion through thinking about communicating with your audience—will help you to create striking descriptive accounts of what you see and how you have been affected by particular places in the natural world.

Chapter 4, "Myths and Fairy Tales," will help you develop perspective on your inward journey so that you can place it in a broader social and cultural context. Seeing how your self-concept and values have been in-fluenced by ancient and popular myths and fairy tales may encourage you to seek out new meanings in your life experiences. Because you will be asked to compare different versions of myths and tales, in this chap-ter we discuss strategies used in comparison writing as well as approaches to making clear evaluative statements.

The readings included in Chapter 5, "Obsessions and Transformation," explore situations and syndromes in which people are overwhelmed by negative and obsessive thoughts and behaviors. Readings also show how destructive obsessions can be transformed positively into greater self-understanding, through healing dreams and mental and physical guidance. The thinking and writing strategies discussed in this chapter will help you to define and draw distinctions among complex concepts such as dreams, myths, obsessions, and fantasies. We also explore some common misuses of words and some barriers to clear communication, as well as the difference between the private and public meanings and associations of words.

Chapter 6, "Gender and Relationships," explores issues of gender and sexuality as they influence an individual's self-concept and role in society. The readings also examine ways that sexuality is reflected in dreams and emotional life, as well as the ways that sexual feelings are channeled through myths and rituals. The chapter also focuses on issues of conflict between different genders, particularly in terms of family roles and responsibilities. The writing and thinking strategy presented in this chapter, causal analysis, will help you to analyze and interpret the readings and will provide you with a structure for composing the essays you will be asked to write in response to the readings.

Chapter 7, "The Double/The Other," begins with a discussion of the double-sided nature of the human personality and presents readings that include a variety of classic stories, many of which are based on dreams or fantasies. These essays and stories reflect different forms of the dualistic struggle within the human mind: the good self as opposed to the evil self, the rational self as opposed to the irrational self. The writing strategies in this chapter focus on how to create a balanced argument through exploring opposing viewpoints, empathizing with your audience, making decisions, and taking a final position of your own.

To what extent have your sense of community, self-image, and mental well-being been influenced by pop culture and digital technology? These thematic questions are considered in the readings included in Chapter 8, "Pop Dreams." The research writing strategies covered will help you to analyze social issues and to think critically about outside sources of opinion, while maintaining your own personal perspective and sense of voice.

Our final chapter is called "Voyages in Spirituality." Here you will read selections that remind us of how spiritual dreams and visions often come to us when least expected, and you will read essays by practitioners of active socially engaged spirituality, who seek to use their spiritual convictions to help other people in need of hope for a positive direction in life. Synthesis and problem solving, the writing strategies presented in this chapter, will help to reinforce your understanding of the chapter's readings and guide you in developing complex, creative essays.

Our experiences as writing teachers continue to confirm the importance of providing students with many opportunities to share their writing with their peers. We have included student essays for you to discuss in class. We hope, too, that you will share your own writing. We believe that you can gain confidence and motivation when you work on your writing with your peers and your instructor.

Demanding and challenging, writing is an invaluable and meaningful part of your discovery of issues and experiences that are vital, that are integrated into the core of your identity, that engage and enlarge your mind and your emotions. We believe that *Dreams and Inward Journeys* can provide opportunities for this type of engagement through the materials and activities we have included.

Marjorie Ford
Jon Ford

Discovering Ourselves in Writing and Reading 1

Fredrik Broden/Renee Rhyner
Untitled photograph (2002)

Write about a reading experience which stimulated your imagination and led you to see the world in a new way.

Writing itself is one of the great, free human activities. . . . For the person who follows what occurs to him with trust and forgiveness, the world remains always ready and deep, an inexhaustible environment, with the combined vividness of an actuality and flexibility of a dream.

WILLIAM STAFFORD
The Way of Writing

A dream which is not understood is like a letter which is not opened.
The Talmud

Looking back, it's clear to me that I was reading as a creator, myself . . . to a collaboration with the writer in the invention of an alternate world.

PETE HAMILL
D'Artagnan on Ninth Street:
A Brooklyn Boy at the Library

THEMATIC INTRODUCTION

Writing and reading can be described as inward journeys. Discovering what resides within your mind and your spirit begins anew each time you start a writing or reading project. Many people find it difficult to begin, wondering how they will be able to untangle all of their thoughts and feelings, and how they will finally decide on the most accurate words and sentence patterns to make their statement clear and compelling. You may feel overwhelmed by the possibilities of all that is waiting to be discovered within you, and, at the same time, you may feel a sense of wonder and excitement, anticipating the pleasures and rewards of uncovering and expressing new parts of your mind, imagination, and spirit.

The complex feelings often experienced at the beginning of the writing/reading process have been eloquently described by many authors whose language, images, and ideas can serve as your guides. They experience writing and reading as processes of self-discovery and self-understanding that are rooted in their unconscious and conscious minds, in their dreams and memories of childhood, and in their everyday lives and goals. At the same time, reading and writing are about communication with the public world as well as the inner world.

In our first selection, poet William Stafford, in his essay "A Way of Writing," presents writing as an inward, dreamlike process, "an inexhaustible environment" that requires the ability to draft freely and to forgive oneself for errors and false starts. In the essay that follows, "The Symbolic Language of Dreams," popular novelist Stephen King discusses the ways in which his dreams have helped him to solve various problems and "blocks" that he has had in writing. In contrast, Virginia Woolf, in her classic essay "Professions for Women," contextualizes the writing process by exploring ways that social, economic, and gender status have an impact on a person's ability to express herself openly and to write freely.

Reading can be a very active, intriguing, and creative process. Several of the authors in this chapter reflect on the ways that reading plays a part in the development of the reader's inner life and imagination. Frederick Douglass, in "Learning to Read and Write," shares his passion for reading from the perspective of a former slave; he speaks of his awakening to freedom through the knowledge he uncovers in the signs, books, and periodicals of his time. In her essay "Mother Tongue," bestselling novelist Amy Tan focuses on the importance of language and family culture in reading, and writing, revealing how she developed her writing talents by incorporating all that she and her mother, a nonnative speaker, knew about language and about life. Joyce Chang, in her essay "Drive Becarefully," a response to Amy Tan's "Mother Tongue," discusses Chang's inner struggle to accept her mother's language as fundamental to both of their identities.

In contrast, in "Don't Look Back," software entrepreneur and digital composer Steven Holtzman argues that we can't turn our backs on the new ways that reading is presented to us through technology. In a student essay, Molly Thomas responds to Steven Holtzman's "Don't Look Back" by pointing out some of the contradictions she sees in his position on the electronic media and its impact on our culture. In our final essay, Motoko Rich's "Literacy Debate: Online, R U Really Reading?", a *New York Times* book editor, examines ways that reading today is being redefined as an increasingly multimedia, Internet-based experience. Rich presents arguments on different sides of the debate over the impact of the Internet on reading ability and research skills.

Both writing and reading shape an individual's inner growth and identity. As you embark on your journey through the readings in this chapter, we hope that you will reflect on the universal yet changing nature of writing and reading. We know that these interrelated processes have the power to engage your mind in lively, imaginative, and provocative adventures.

A PROCESS VIEW OF WRITING AND READING

When people write and read, they are concerned with self-discovery, just as they are when they explore their dreams. Both writing and reading are complex processes that a reader controls consciously and also experiences unconsciously. These processes, for most of us, begin almost at the same time, although we may have experienced having our parents or preschool teachers read to us before we actually began to study our ABCs and learn to write and to read. In the act of writing, an internal conversation takes place between what we read and our own inner experiences and ideas that helps us to come up with the words we put down on the page. Similarly, in the act of reading, as in a conversation, a dialogue takes place between the voice of the inner self and the voice of the text being read. A good conversation with a text can lead to the development and clarification of the writer's and the reader's values and ideas. Both reading and writing require some formal understanding of literary conventions and language codes. To write well, we must have done some reading: the more the better. Likewise, writing down our responses to what we read helps to clarify our interpretations and evaluations of complex texts.

Because the processes are so interrelated, we could begin our discussion with either writing or reading. Since the course you are probably taking now is a writing class, we will start with writing and move outward to the more public, responsive dimension of reading and writing about what we read.

The Writing Process and Self-Discovery

William Stafford has said that "writing itself is one of the great, free human activities. There is scope for individuality, and elation, and discovery, in writing." At the same time, a good writer is also a patient craftsperson. Writing makes demands on both the creative and the rational sides of the mind. From the creative and intuitive mind, it summons forth details, images, memories, dreams, and feelings; from the rational and logical mind, it demands planning, development, evidence, rereading, rethinking, and revision.

Perhaps this basic duality associated with the act of writing can sometimes make it feel like a complex and overwhelming task. Practicing and studying particular writing strategies such as those presented in each chapter of *Dreams and Inward Journeys,* along with drafting, revising, and sharing your writing with your peers and instructor, will help you to develop your self-confidence. As a writer you need to be aware of the feelings and fears of your unconscious self as well as the expectations of your rational mind. Balancing these two sides of your mind—knowing when, for example, to give your creative mind license to explore while controlling and quieting your critical mind—is an important part of the challenge of developing self-confidence and learning to write well.

Stages of the Writing Process

Most professional and student writers benefit from conceptualizing writing as a process with a number of stages. Although these stages do not need to be rigidly separated, an awareness of the different quality of thoughts and feelings that usually occur in each of the stages of writing is useful. Having a perspective on your writing process will encourage you to be patient and help you create a finished piece of writing that speaks clearly about your own concerns, values, and opinions. The stages of the writing process include the prewriting, drafting, and revision phases. As you become a more experienced and skillful writer, you may find that you want to adapt this process to the goals of your writing assignment. Perhaps you will find that you need to spend more time in preliminary reading to collect background information for a research essay, or that you don't have as much time to spend on prewriting if you are working on an essay that must be completed in a shorter timeframe or during an in-class exam.

As preparation for writing the initial draft of an essay, prewriting allows you to pursue a variety of playful, creative activities that will help you to generate ideas and understand what you want to say about your subject. Drafting is your rapid first "take" on your topic and should be done after you have concentrated on your paper's subject and thought about the thesis or core concept around which you want to center the ideas and examples of your essay. You may find, however, that as you write your first draft, your thesis and focus shift or even change dramatically. Don't be concerned if this happens. Many professional writers have learned that although they begin drafting feeling that they have a focus and thesis, the actual process of writing the draft changes their initial plan. Rewriting is a natural part of the writing process. As you return to your draft and continue to work to shape your thoughts into clear sentences, they will better capture your inner feelings and ideas.

While you will need to rewrite to clarify your thinking and ideas, the process of revision can also be approached in stages. They include revising for your paper's overall shape and meaning, which may involve outlining the rough draft; rearranging whole paragraphs or ideas and examples; developing and cutting redundancy within paragraphs;

refining and clarifying sentences and individual words; and, finally, proofreading for grammar, spelling, and punctuation. The revision and editing stages of writing have become more exciting and less tedious since the invention of the computer and word processing software. Now your computer can help you because it includes commands for cutting and pasting text, outliners, spelling and grammar checkers, word and paragraph counters, and global search and replace functions that make it easier to correct any aspect of the entire essay. But revision is still a time-consuming and important element of the writing process, for it is through revision and editing that your essay moves from an approximate statement of a thought or insight into a well-crafted and moving verbal expression of your thoughts and purpose.

Strategies for Prewriting

Because writing begins with prewriting, we have chosen to focus on this stage here, at the beginning of your journey as a writer. The prewriting stage is enjoyable for those who enjoy creative expression and helpful for people who don't have much confidence in themselves as writers, who feel it is hard to get warmed up to the task. If you are apprehensive about writing and don't see yourself as a creative thinker, prewriting activities may help you to discover new or forgotten images, memories, and ideas, as well as to make connections you may never have anticipated. You may find yourself liberating a creative spirit hidden in the recesses of your mind. You are the only person who needs to read and evaluate your prewriting; at this stage, you determine what seems interesting and relevant.

Prewriting also makes the writing of later drafts easier because it helps you to clarify and organize your thoughts before they are put into a formal format. Drawing, freewriting, invisible writing, brainstorming, clustering, and journal keeping are all effective prewriting techniques that will help you to discover what you really want and need to say. Like the later stages of writing, all of these techniques can be practiced with a pencil, a pen, or sophisticated computer software. Although some students continue to feel more comfortable and natural when prewriting with pencil or pen, those who are familiar with the computer and have good keyboarding skills often find it helpful to do many of their prewritings on the computer so that they can save and possibly transform their initial ideas into details, images, and sentences for their drafts.

Drawing   Drawing a picture in response to a topic can help you understand what you think and feel. In the drawings in response to a topic included in this text, students used a computer program to capture their writing processes and responses to readings, but you may feel more comfortable using colored pencils, watercolors, charcoal, or ink.

A number of professional writers have spoken of the value of drawing as a way to develop ideas or understand a new text. In *The Nature and Aim of Fiction*, Flannery O'Connor maintains, "Any discipline can help your writing . . . particularly drawing. Anything that helps you to see, anything that makes you look." While drawing an image from a complex text you are reading, you will be able to focus your thoughts on the details that may have already unconsciously captured your imagination. This process of drawing about a piece of writing will increase your engagement with it and help you clarify your response as you make that response more tangible.

Freewriting A freewrite can start anywhere and usually lasts from 5 to 15 minutes. During these brief writing sessions, it is important to continue to write and not to censor any idea or feeling that comes to your mind. If you seem to run out of thoughts, just write, "I have no more to say," or anything you wish until a new thought emerges. After ten minutes of freewriting, read what you have written and try to sum up the central idea or feeling of the piece. You can then proceed to another freewrite, using the summary statement as a new starting point. Writers often do several freewrites before they decide how to focus their thoughts.

Invisible Writing With invisible writing, the writer creates "invisible" words, or words that can't be seen while the writer is working. Some writers never even look at the words generated in an invisible writing exercise but instead use the exercise as a rehearsal, a building of mental pathways that will make the actual writing of their paper less halting and painful. Many writers find new insights in their thoughts that were produced invisibly. Invisible writing can be done by writing on the back of a piece of carbon paper onto a piece of notebook paper or by keyboarding with a dimmed computer screen. While you are freewriting and doing invisible writing, do not consciously pay attention to central ideas, relationships between ideas, organizational patterns, or grammatical or spelling errors. Concentrate instead on getting your ideas and feelings out in words.

Brainstorming Brainstorming, which can be done effectively in groups or individually, involves writing a list of words, phrases, ideas, descriptions, thoughts, and questions that come to your mind in response to a topic or issue. As in freewriting, it is essential not to stop to censor, judge, or correct ideas or feelings. The process of listing will, itself, bring up new ideas and associations. Ideas will build on one another, leading to thoughts that are original and fresh, while creating a list will help you to see relationships between ideas that may have previously seemed disconnected. When your list is complete, normally in 15 to 20 minutes, go back to find patterns of thought or main ideas that you have uncovered. Bracketing or circling related ideas and details may help you form an organizational plan. Through brainstorming, you can formulate a rough outline for your essay that will guide you in the drafting phase of writing.

Clustering   Clustering, or mapping, closely reflects the way the mind functions in making nonlinear connections between ideas. Combined with brainstorming or freewriting, clustering can also help you to perceive relationships between ideas. Start your cluster by placing the topic to be explored in the center of the page. Draw a circle around it, and then draw lines out from your central circle in different directions to connect it with other circles containing additional ideas, phrases, or clues to experiences. The words in these circles will naturally develop their own offshoots as new associations emerge. The pattern being created by the clustering process continually changes in complex ways because any new idea will relate to all of the ideas already recorded. As in freewriting, clustering should be done without stopping. Once the cluster feels completed to you, write for a few minutes about what you have discovered. Completing a cluster and a related freewrite can help you understand how you want to focus your topic and organize the major relationships between ideas, examples, and details.

Journal Keeping   Daily writing in a notebook or journal will help you develop a record of your thoughts and feelings. Keeping a journal is similar to the type of prewriting assignments we have just discussed in that it allows you freedom to explore parts of your inner world, knowing that your writing will not be evaluated. Keeping a journal of your responses to the journal topics and study questions in a text, using either a small notebook or a computer, is one of the most effective ways to develop your confidence and skills as a writer. Both of the student essays included in this chapter were developed from journal entries that focused on strong inner experiences and images that initially seemed very private but were clarified and made public through drafting, revising, peer sharing, and more revision.

The Dream Journal   Because this text has been developed around the theme of dreams, and because the process of understanding your dreams may lead you to new insights and images that you may find useful in more formal writing, we recommend that you extend your journal keeping into the night world by writing down your dreams — a process used by many professional writers. Through keeping a dream journal, you can improve your ability to recall dreams, and you can capture unconscious images that intrigue or possibly disturb you. Perhaps, too, you will notice more similarities between your dream

images and some of the dreamlike stories in this text. Your appreciation of metaphors and symbols will increase.

By keeping your dream journal, you will also realize how understanding your writing process is similar to understanding your
dreams. The first written draft of your dream is like a prewrite of an
essay: a set of strong, if chaotic, images that you can work with
thoughtfully and creatively. As you bring form and meaning to a
dream through analysis and interpretation, you bring form and meaning to an essay through drafting and revising those first generative
ideas that begin the process of writing an essay, story, or poem.

Keep your dream journal at your bedside along with a pen or dark
pencil. The best time to write in your dream journal is in the early morning or immediately on awaking from a vivid dream. Some students have
even used a tape recorder to capture their "dream voice," its sounds and
rhythms. Try to write in your dream journal three or four times a week,
even if you have only a dim or fleeting image or impression to record.
Write down all the details you can remember, indicating a shift, jump in
time, or unclear portion of the dream with ellipses or a question mark.
Try not to censor or "clean up" the dream imagery, even if the thinking
seems illogical, chaotic, or even embarrassing to you. Avoid interpreting
your dream as you are recording it, although you might list in the margins any associations that immediately come to mind in relation to the
images as you record them. Later, as you reread your dream journal
entries over a period of several days, you may see patterns and more
complex associations emerging, and you may want to write about them.

Your Computer: Developing an Important Writing Partnership

Most students come to their college writing classes with basic computer skills. Your computer can help to facilitate and streamline your
writing process. Computers are not just keyboarding tools or drivers
for printing out text. In the later stages of revising and editing, computers are invaluable, making it possible for you to reorganize your
paper easily by moving around large sections of your essay, adding
concise examples and details, and fine-tuning grammar, syntax, and
word choice. The spell-checker on your computer will help you prepare your draft for final presentation, while an online dictionary and
thesaurus make it possible to find just the right word for precise and
powerful expression. Some students find that the flexibility that computers provide to generate new ideas; to experiment; to change sentences, paragraphs, details, and examples; and to refine major ideas
helps them overcome writing blocks.

In fact, all of the strategies for prewriting mentioned here, particularly the technique of invisible writing, can be completed and saved on

a computer. Other exploratory techniques work only on a computer, such as engaging in an online conversation on a subject for writing using a chat program or e-mail, and then saving the conversation for later use. You might decide to copy sections from any of your prewritings into the first or a later draft of your essay; this is much easier to do if you write them on a computer rather than on a piece of paper.

Prewriting strategies are more frequently used in the generative stage of the writing process, but we encourage you to use these techniques whenever you feel yourself getting blocked in your work. During the drafting stage of writing, or even after an instructor has returned your paper to you with corrections on it and you are working on a major revision, the exercises discussed above can continue to help you keep in touch with what you really want to say—with your own inner voice.

Discovering Ourselves in Reading: The Reading Process

Once absorbed in the complex mental process of reading, readers desire to identify with the characters, the ideas, the emotions, and the cultural and social assumptions of the text. Readers then are able to experience new and different realities vicariously; these encounters can contribute to the reader's personal growth as they present new intellectual and emotional experiences that help readers to build their inner resources. As a person becomes a better reader and develops a richer life through reading, his or her writing may also become more fluent and varied as the reader becomes more conscious of public values, opinions, and cultures that are different from his or her personal experiences.

Writing is one of the most valuable ways to respond to what you read. Writing about what you're reading will help you articulate and clarify your responses and will improve your writing as you develop your writer's voice through connecting to the words and thoughts of others. As with any form of writing, responses to reading can move through a series of phases or stages, each one building upon the next, moving gradually from prereading strategies to interpretation and evaluation.

Prereading/Early Reading

In the prereading phase, you examine what you plan to read, browsing through titles and subheadings, and noting epigraphs, topic sentences, headnotes, and footnotes, just as you probably did when you first picked up this textbook. Prereading can be a very helpful process if you combine it with writing down basic questions that you have during this initial browsing stage. Does this work seem like fact or fiction? Was it written recently or in the distant past? Is its style experimental or traditional? Is the writer American, or is he or she from a different culture and country? Is the writer male or female? Is the subject a familiar one? Do you need more background knowledge to understand the subject? Asking and answering such questions can help you become involved with the text and can help put you into a receptive frame of mind.

After previewing the work, proceed to the second part of the first stage in reading, the "early reading" phase. In this phase, as in writing a first draft, you simply plunge in, reading the work quickly to get an overall sense of its meaning, perhaps noting a few key passages or putting a question mark by an idea or detail that seems unfamiliar or confusing. At this stage of reading, avoid negative preconceptions about the content of the reading; don't tell yourself, "This is a subject in which I have no interest." Try instead to be open to the reading. Avoid evaluating the text before you give yourself a chance to become engaged with it.

Personal and Interpretive Response

In this second stage, the interpretive response phase, put the reading aside for a moment and write down a few immediate, personal reactions: Is this piece what I expected it to be? Did it make me angry? Sad? Elated? How did the piece challenge me? What didn't I understand after the first reading? Reread your notes and questions before attempting another reading. The second time, read more slowly and reflectively. Try to answer some of your initial questions as well as to move toward an overview and interpretation of the piece as a whole — its meaning, or your view of its meaning at this stage in your reading.

Look for those patterns that support an interpretation or view of the work: metaphors, plot and subplot, character relationships and conflicts, point of view, evolving personae, and narrative voice. Mark your book, placing circles around and drawing lines to connect ideas and images that you believe form a pattern of meaning. Ask yourself how much of the work is meant to be responded to literally, and how much is meant to be considered as ironic or symbolic. Record responses to this stage of the reading process in writing, including some particular quotations and references to the text. Also compare your reactions at this stage of reading with your written responses to the first reading of the text. You will probably find that your ideas have deepened considerably and that you have a more complete and interpretive view of the work than you did initially.

Critical and Evaluative Response

For the third stage in your reading/writing process, the "critical" phase, reread the story more rapidly, after reviewing your second written response and your textual references. Now write a final response, clarifying how this reading confirms, expands on, or causes you to question or revise your earlier readings. Using particular elements in the text that you noticed in your earlier readings as evidence, try to draw some larger evaluative conclusions about the work and your response to it: Is your overall response to the values, ideas, and emotions in the work positive or negative? How do you feel about the unity of the piece, its quality as writing? How do the values of this selection reflect or illuminate issues of concern to you and to your community? Was there something new about the experience of reading this work? Did it remind you of or seem to build upon other, similar works with which you are familiar? After finishing the text, did you want to read more by this writer or learn more about the theme of the work by reading related works by other writers? Would you recommend the work to other readers?

"Reading" Nonprint, Multimedia, and Online Texts

Although some theorists believe that the traditional act of reading is passé in this electronic age, the perceptual and critical thinking process for decoding, analyzing, interpreting, and evaluating materials that involve images along with printed words, or even with no words at all, is not as different from book reading as it might seem. Whether you are reading a book, watching a film, viewing a television show, or scrolling through Web pages, you need to pay close attention to all available clues for meaning. You will need to look for patterns of imagery, symbols, significant character interaction, plotlines, and crucial meaning statements, whether in the form of speeches by characters, key bits of dialogue, or voiceovers (in the case of a film).

Whether reading a book, viewing a film, or examining a Web page, you also need to know something about the author (director/screenwriter, in the case of a film; or, in the case of many Web pages, the organization that has produced the page and its objectives). You need to know how this work builds on other works by the same writer or organization, as well as what cultural assumptions and traditions (of writing, filmmaking, or multimedia) the work issues from.

Finally, whether you are reading a book, watching a film or TV show, or even surfing the Internet, you need the opportunity for a second reading/viewing, to get closer to the work through repeated exposure in order to grasp its full significance and to make interpretations and connections with other similar works. While this is easier to do with a book, you can always watch a film a second time and take notes, videotape a TV show, or, in the case of Web pages, bookmark the page or save the text for instant download later on. Note that in nonprint media or multimedia, you have to learn to read visual images for meaningful forms, symbols, intellectual suggestions, and emotional impact, just as you examine the words in a written text closely for their connotations or shadings of meaning. In multimedia, you need to be alert to a complex interplay between words, images, and even sounds.

What makes a person a good reader, interpreter, and judge of electronic media is precisely the kind of good study habits that an experienced reader brings to a book. You need to resist the passive mood many people sink into in front of TV sets or the "surfer" mentality that involves clicking rapidly and restlessly from one link to another on the Internet. When studying media, writing can be an especially helpful way to develop critical responses. Try keeping a journal of media you watch and listen to, responding actively by using the kind of entries suggested above in the section on keeping a reader's journal: preliminary responses and entries, interpretive entries, and evaluative entries for a repeated viewing of material that looks interesting. In this way, you can become a strong reader, sensitive to the world of books as well as an able critic of the electronic media that surround us daily, which at times overwhelm our abilities to respond or to take a position.

In reading and writing about the essays, stories, and poems selected for this textbook as well as the different media that you encounter, try to practice the slow, three-stage reading and written response process outlined above, taking time to write down questions and responses in your notebook and in the margins of the text. Give yourself enough time to absorb and think about what you have read and viewed. Your patience will yield you both heightened understanding and deeper pleasure in all your learning experiences.

William Stafford

A Way of Writing

William Stafford (1914–1993) was born and raised in Kansas, where he worked on farms and in oil refineries and, as a conscientious objector, served time in work camps during World War II. He earned his B.A. and M.A. at the University of Kansas and his Ph.D. at the University of Iowa. Stafford taught creative writing at the University of Iowa and at Lewis and Clark University in Oregon. He kept a daily journal, considered competitiveness corrupting, and retained his belief in pacifism as a way of life. He is best known for his personal lyric poetry that is complex in its perceptions of inner realities while in harmony with the social and environmental concerns of rural America. Stafford's "A Way of Writing" originally appeared in the Spring 1970 issue of the literary magazine Field. *The essay expresses Stafford's views on the need for receptivity to and trust of one's inner world in the act of writing.*

Develop an image that captures your creative process as a writer, a painter, a dancer, or a musician. Discuss the form of creativity that you find most rewarding.

A writer is not so much someone who has something to say as he is someone who has found a process that will bring about new things he would not have thought of if he had not started to say them. That is, he does not draw on a reservoir; instead, he engages in an activity that brings to him a whole succession of unforeseen stories, poems, essays, plays, laws, philosophies, religions, or—but wait!

Back in school, from the first when I began to try to write things, I felt this richness. One thing would lead to another; the world would give and give. Now, after twenty years or so of trying, I live by that certain richness, an idea hard to pin, difficult to say, and perhaps offensive to some. For there are strange implications in it.

One implication is the importance of just plain receptivity. When I write, I like to have an interval before me when I am not likely to be interrupted. For me, this means usually the early morning, before others are awake. I get pen and paper, take a glance out of the window (often it is dark out there), and wait. It is like fishing. But I do not wait very long, for there is always a nibble—and this is where receptivity comes in. To get started I will accept anything that occurs to me. Something always occurs, of course, to any of us. We can't keep from thinking. Maybe I have to settle for an immediate impression: it's cold, or hot, or dark, or bright, or in between! Or, well, the possibilities are endless. If I put down something, that thing will help the next thing come, and I'm off. If I let the process go on, things will occur to me that were not at all in my mind when I started. These things, odd or trivial as they may be, are somehow connected. And if I let them string out, surprising things will happen.

If I let them string out. . . . Along with initial receptivity, then, there is another readiness: I must be willing to fail. If I am to keep on writing, I cannot bother to insist on high standards. I must get into action and not let anything stop me, or even slow me much. By "standards" I do not mean "correctness"—spelling, punctuation, and so on. These details become mechanical for anyone who writes for a while. I am thinking about such matters as social significance, positive values, consistency, etc. . . . I resolutely disregard these. Something better, greater, is happening! I am following a process that leads so wildly and originally into new territory that no judgment can at the moment be made about values, significance, and so on. I am making something new, something that has not been judged before. Later others—and maybe I myself—will make judgments. Now, I am headlong to discover. Any distraction may harm the creating.

5   So, receptive, careless of failure, I spin out things on the page. And a wonderful freedom comes. If something occurs to me, it is all right to accept it. It has one justification: it occurs to me. No one else can guide me. I must follow my own weak, wandering, diffident impulses.

A strange bonus happens. At times, without my insisting on it, my writings become coherent; the successive elements that occur to me are clearly related. They lead by themselves to new connections. Sometimes the language, even the syllables that happen along, may start a trend. Sometimes the materials alert me to something waiting in my mind, ready for sustained attention. At such times, I allow myself to be eloquent, or intentional, or for great swoops (Treacherous! Not to be trusted!) reasonable. But I do not insist on any of that; for I know that back of my activity there will be the coherence of my self, and that indulgence of my impulses will bring recurrent patterns and meanings again.

This attitude toward the process of writing creatively suggests a problem for me, in terms of what others say. They talk about "skills" in writing. Without denying that I do have experience, wide reading, automatic orthodoxies and maneuvers of various kinds, I still must insist that I am often baffled about what "skill" has to do with the precious little area of confusion when I do not know what I am going to say and then I find out what I am going to say. That precious interval I am unable to bridge by skill. What can I witness about it? It remains mysterious, just as all of us must feel puzzled about how we are so inventive as to be able to talk along through complexities with our friends, not needing to plan what we are going to say, but never stalled for long in our confident forward progress. Skill? If so, it is the skill we all have, something we must have learned before the age of three or four.

A writer is one who has become accustomed to trusting that grace, or luck, or—skill.

Yet another attitude I find necessary: most of what I write, like most of what I say in casual conversation, will not amount to much. Even I will realize, and even at the time, that it is not negotiable. It will be like practice. In conversation I allow myself random remarks—in fact, as I recall, that is the way I learned to talk—so in writing I launch many expendable efforts. A result of this free way of writing is that I am not writing for others, mostly; they will not see the product at all unless the activity eventuates in something that later appears to be worthy. My guide is the self, and its adventuring in the language brings about communication.

10   This process-rather-than-substance view of writing invites a final, dual reflection:

1. Writers may not be special or talented in any usual sense. They are simply engaged in sustained use of a language skill we all have. Their "creations" come about through confident reliance on stray impulses that will, with trust, find occasional patterns that are satisfying.

2. But writing itself is one of the great, free human activities. There is scope for individuality, and elation, and discovery, in writing. For the person who follows with trust and forgiveness what occurs to him, the world remains always ready and deep, an inexhaustible environment, with the combined vividness of an actuality and flexibility of a dream. Working back and forth between experience and thought, writers have more than space and time can offer. They have the whole unexplored realm of human vision.

QUESTIONS FOR DISCUSSION

1. What do you think Stafford means when he says that a writer must be receptive? What image does he use to help the reader understand his concept of the creative process?
2. Is it difficult for you to allow yourself to write down your thoughts and feelings without censoring them as they flow through your mind? Why? How often do you give yourself the time to reflect and write alone in a peaceful place?
3. Have you ever used prewriting activities such as freewriting or invisible writing (composing on a computer with the screen dimmed) to encourage or allow yourself to write without editing? If you have tried such activities, what was their effect on your writing?
4. Why does Stafford feel that it is important for a writer to be willing to fail? Do you agree with him on this point? Is it hard for you to accept the imperfection and unpredictability of your early drafts? Do you ever experience writer's block or feel frustrated with your writing? Do you think that reading Stafford's essay will help you to overcome some of your anxiety about your writing skills?
5. Although Stafford's writing advice comes out of his experiences as a poet, it has application to other forms of writing, such as the classroom essay. Do you think that all writers, regardless of the genre in which they work, face the same basic issues and problems?
6. Stafford says, "Writing itself is one of the great, free human activities. There is scope for individuality, and elation, and discovery, in writing." Do you agree with his assertion? Develop several examples to support your point of view.

CONNECTION

Compare the ideas of Stafford and Stephen King on how a writer creates (see page 17).

IDEAS FOR WRITING

1. Write an essay that describes your writing process and discusses the internal barriers that make writing difficult for you. What

strategies have you developed to overcome writing blocks (inhibitions, fears, procrastination) that keep you from completing a piece of writing?

2. Develop an essay that uses comparisons or metaphors, such as Stafford does with his metaphor of writing as fishing, to describe your own writing process.

RELATED WEB SITES

Friends of William Stafford

www.williamstafford.org/

Created by a nonprofit organization that seeks to raise awareness on poetry and literature, this Web site provides links to resources, writings, and news pertaining to Stafford.

William Stafford

www.poets.org/poet.php/prmPID/224

Hosted by the Academy of American poets, poets.org provides a list of resources and links for each poet. The specific URL above gives links to poems, interviews, and tributes related to William Stafford.

Stephen King

The Symbolic Language of Dreams

Stephen King (b. 1947) is originally from Portland, Maine, where he continues to reside. After graduating from the University of Maine in 1970 with a B.A. in English, King taught high school and worked at odd jobs before finding time to write his first novel, Carrie *(1974), an immediate best seller that was made into a classic horror film. King has continued to be one of the most popular contemporary writers of horror novels. Some of his best-known works include* The Shining *(1977; film version 1980),* Firestarter *(1980; film version 1984),* Misery *(1987; film version 1990),* The Dark Half *(1989),* Desperation *(1996),* The Girl Who Loved Tom Gordon *(1999),* Hearts in Atlantis *(1999; film version 2001), and* The Dream Catcher *(2001). In the following essay, King describes some of the ways dreams have helped him with his writing.*

JOURNAL

Write about how one of your dreams or intuitions helped you to solve a writing problem or to better understand an issue in your life.

One of the things that I've been able to use dreams for in my stories is to show things in a symbolic way that I wouldn't want to come right out and say directly. I've always used dreams the way you'd use mirrors to look at something you couldn't see head-on—the way that you use a mirror to look at your hair in the back. To me that's what dreams are supposed to do. I think that dreams are a way that people's minds illustrate the nature of their problems. Or maybe even illustrate the answers to their problems in symbolic language.

When we look back on our dreams, a lot of times they decompose as soon as the light hits them. So, you can have a dream, and you can remember very vividly what it's about, but ten or fifteen minutes later, unless it's an extraordinarily vivid dream or an extraordinarily good dream, it's gone. It's like the mind is this hard rubber and you really have to hit it hard to leave an impression that won't eventually just erase.

One of the things that we're familiar with in dreams is the sense that familiar or prosaic objects are being put in very bizarre circumstances or situations. And since that's what I write about, the use of dreams is an obvious way to create that feeling of weirdness in the real world. I guess probably the most striking example of using a dream in my fiction was connected to the writing of *Salem's Lot*.

Now, I can think of only maybe five or six really horrible nightmares in the course of my life—which isn't bad when you think that that life stretches over 44 years—but I can remember having an extremely bad dream when I was probably nine or ten years old.

5   It was a dream where I came up a hill and there was a gallows on top of this hill with birds all flying around it. There was a hangman there. He had died, not by having his neck broken, but by strangulation. I could tell because his face was all puffy and purple. And as I came close to him he opened his eyes, reached his hands out and grabbed me.

I woke up in my bed, sitting bolt upright, screaming. I was hot and cold at the same time and covered with goosebumps. And not only was I unable to go back to sleep for hours after that, but I was really afraid to turn out the lights for weeks. I can still see it as clearly now as when it happened.

Years later I began to work on *Salem's Lot*. Now, I knew that the story was going to be about a vampire that came from abroad to the United States and I wanted to put him in a spooky old house. I got about that far in my thinking and, by whatever way it is that your mind connects things, as I was looking around for a spooky house, a guy who works in the creative department of my brain said, Well what about that nightmare you had when you were eight or nine years old? Will that work? And I remembered the nightmare and I thought, Yes, it's perfect.

I turned the dead man into a guy named Hubie Marston who owned a bad house and pretty much repeated the story of the dream in terms of the way he died. In the story, Hubie Marston hangs himself. He's some sort of black artist of the Aleister Crowley kind—some sort of a dark magician—and I kind of combined him with a stock character in American tabloidism—the wealthy guy who lives and dies in squalor.

For me, once the actual act of creation starts, writing is like this high-speed version of the flip books you have when you're a kid, where you mix and match. The cover of the book will say, "You Can Make Thousands of Faces!" You can put maybe six or seven different eyes with different noses. Except that there aren't just thousands of faces, there are literally billions of different events, personalities, and things that you can flip together. And it happens at a very rapid rate. Dreams are just one of those flip strips that you can flip in there. But they also work in terms of advancing the story.

10 Sometimes when I write I can use dreams to have a sort of precognitive effect on the story. Precognitive dreams are a staple of our supernatural folklore. You know, the person who dreamed that flight 17 was going to crash and changed his reservation and sure enough, flight 17 crashed. But it's like those urban fairy tales: you always hear somebody say, "I have a friend that this happened to." I've never actually heard anyone say, "This happened to *me.*"

The closest that I can come to a precognitive experience is that I can be in a situation where a really strong feeling of déjà vu washes over me. I'm sure that I've been there before. A lot of times I make the association that, at some point, I had a dream about this place and this series of actions, and forgot it with my conscious mind when I awoke.

Every now and then dreams can come in handy. When I was working on *It*—which was this really long book—a dream made a difference.

I had a lot of time and a lot of my sense of craft invested in the idea of being able to finish this huge, long book. Now, when I'm working on something, I see books, completed books. And in some fashion that thing is already there. I'm not really making it so much as I am digging it up, the way that you would an artifact, out of the sand. The trick is to get as much of that object as you possibly can, to get the whole thing out, so it's usable, without breaking it. You always break it somewhat—I mean you never get a complete thing—but if you're really careful and if you're really lucky, you can get most of it.

When I'm working I never know what the end is going to be or how things are going to come out. I've got an idea what direction I want the story to go in, or hope it will go in, but mostly I feel like the tail on a kite. I don't feel like the kite itself, or like the wind that blows on the kite— I'm just the tail of it. And if I know when I sit down what's happening or what's going to happen, that day and the next day and the day after, I'm happy. But with *It* I got to a point where I couldn't see ahead any more. And every day I got closer to the place where this young girl, who was one of my people—I don't think of them as good people or bad people, just my people—was going to be and they were going to find her.

15   I didn't know what was going to happen to her. And that made me extremely nervous. Because that's the way books don't get done. All at once you just get to a point where there is no more. It's like pulling a little string out of a hole and all at once it's broken and you don't get whatever prize there was on the end of it.

So I had seven, eight hundred pages and I just couldn't stand it. I remember going to bed one night saying, I've got to have an idea. I've got to have an idea! I fell asleep and dreamed that I was in a junk yard, which was where this part of the story was set.

Apparently, I was the girl. There was no girl in the dream. There was just me. And there were all these discarded refrigerators in this dump. I opened one of them and there were these things inside, hanging from the various rusty shelves. They looked like macaroni shells and they were all just sort of trembling in a breeze. Then one of them opened up these wings, flew out and landed on the back of my hand. There was a sensation of warmth, almost like when you get a subcutaneous shot of Novocain or something, and this thing started to turn from white to red. I realized it had anesthetized my hand and it was sucking my blood out. Then they all started to fly out of this refrigerator and to land on me. They were these leeches that looked like macaroni shells. And they were swelling up.

I woke up and I was very frightened. But I was also very happy. Because then I knew what was going to happen. I just took the dream as it was and put it in the book. Dropped it in. I didn't change anything.

In the story "The Body," there's an incident where several boys find themselves covered with leeches. That was something that actually happened to me. There's a lot of stuff in "The Body" that's just simply history that's been tarted up a little bit. These friends and I all went into this pond about a mile and half from the house where I grew up and when we came out we were just covered with those babies. It was awful. I don't remember that I had nightmares about the incident then but of course I had this leech dream years later.

20   I really think what happened with this dream was that I went to sleep and the subconscious went right on working and finally sent up this dream the way that you would send somebody an interoffice message in a pneumatic tube.

In the Freudian sense, I don't think there is any subconscious, any unconscious where things are going on. I think that consciousness is like an ocean. Whether you're an inch below the surface or whether you're down a mile and half deep, it's all water. All H_2O.

I think that our minds are the same nutrient bath all the way down to the bottom and different things live at different levels. Some of them are a little bit harder to see because we don't get down that deep. But whatever's going on in our daily lives, our daily thoughts, the things that the surface of our minds are concerned with eddy down—trickle down—and then they have some sort of an influence down there. And the messages that we get a lot of times are nothing more than symbolic reworkings of the things that we're concerned with. I don't think they're very prophetic or anything like that. I think a lot of times dreams are nothing more than a kind of mental or spiritual flatulence. They're a way of relieving pressure.

One way of looking at this water metaphor might be to talk about jumbo shrimp, everybody's favorite oxymoron. They're the big shrimp that nobody ate in restaurants until 1955 or 1960 because, until then, nobody thought of going shrimping after dark. They were there all the time, living their prosaic shrimp lives, but nobody caught them. So when they finally caught them it was, "Hello! Look at this. This is something entirely new." And if the shrimp could talk they'd say, "Shit, we're not new. We've been around for a couple of thousand years. You were just too dumb to look for us."

A slightly different way of looking at this is that there are certain fish that we get used to looking at. There are carp, goldfish, catfish, shad, cod—they're fish that are more or less surface fish. They go down to a depth of maybe fifty, sixty, or a hundred feet. People catch them, and we get used to seeing them. Not only do we see them in aquariums or as pictures in books, we see them on our plates. We cook them. We see them in the supermarket in the fish case. Whereas if you go down in a bathysphere, if you go down real deep, you see all these bright fluorescent, weird, strange things with membranous umbrellas and weird skirts that flare out from their bodies. Those are creatures that we don't see very often because they explode if we bring them up close to the surface. They are to surface fish what dreams are to our surface thoughts. Deep fish are like dreams of surface fish. They change shape, they change form.

25 There are dreams and there are deep dreams. There are dreams where you're able to tap sources that are a lot deeper. I'm sure that if you wanted to extend this metaphor you could say that within the human psyche, within human thought, there really are Mindanao trenches, places that are very very deep, where there are probably some extremely strange things floating around. And what the conscious mind brings up may be the equivalent of an exploded fish. It may just be a mess. It may be something that's gorgeous in its own habitat but when it gets up to the sun it just dries out. And then it's very gray and dull.

I remember about six months ago having this really vivid dream.

I was in some sort of an apartment building, a cheesy little apartment building. The front door was open and I could see all these black people going back and forth. They were talking and having a wonderful time. Somebody was playing music somewhere. And then the door shut.

In the dream I went back and got into bed. I think I must have shut the door myself. My brother was in bed with me, behind me, and he started to strangle me. My brother had gone crazy. It was awful!

I remember saying, with the last of my breath, "I think there's somebody out there." And he got up from the bed and went out. As soon as he was out I went up and closed the door and locked it. And then I went back to bed. That is, I started to lie down in this dream.

30   Then I began to worry that I hadn't really locked the door. This is the sort of thing that I'm always afraid of in real life. Did I turn off the burners on the stove? Did I leave a light on when I left the house? So, I got up to check the door and sure enough it was unlocked. I realized that he was still in there with me. Somewhere.

I screamed in the dream, "He's still in the house." I screamed so loud I woke myself up. Except I wasn't screaming when I woke up. I was just sort of muttering it over and over again: He's in the house, he's in the house. I was terrified.

Now, I keep a glass of ice water beside the bed where I sleep and the ice cubes hadn't melted yet, so it had happened almost immediately after I fell asleep. That's usually when I have the dreams that I remember most vividly.

Part of my function as a writer is to dream awake. And that usually happens. If I sit down to write in the morning, in the beginning of that writing session and the ending of that session, I'm aware that I'm writing. I'm aware of my surroundings. It's like shallow sleep on both ends, when you go to bed and when you wake up. But in the middle, the world is gone and I'm able to see better.

Creative imaging and dreaming are just so similar that they've got to be related.

35   In a story like "The Body" or *It,* which is set around the late fifties or the early sixties, I'm literally able to regress so that I can remember things that I'd forgotten. Time goes by and events pile up on the surface of your mind like snow, and it covers all these other previous layers. But if you're able to put yourself into that sort of semidreaming state— whether you're dreaming or whether you're writing creatively the brainwaves are apparently interchangeable—you're able to get a lot of that stuff back. That might be deep dreaming.

I'm aware, particularly in recent years, how precious that state is, I mean the ability to go in there when one is awake. I'm also aware, as an adult, of the vividness of my sleeping dreams when I have them. But I don't have any way of stacking up the number of dreams that I have as opposed to anybody else. My sense is I probably dream a little bit less at night because I'm taking off some of the pressure in the daytime. But I don't have an inherent proof of that.

I can remember finding that state for the first time and being delighted. It's a little bit like finding a secret door in a room but not knowing exactly how you got in. I can't remember exactly how I first found that state except that I would sit down to write every day, and I would pretty much do that whether the work went well or the work went badly. And after doing that for a while it was a little bit like having a posthypnotic suggestion.

I know that there are certain things that I do if I sit down to write: I have a glass of water or I have a cup of tea. There's a certain time I sit down around eight o'clock—or 8:15 or 8:30—somewhere within that half-hour every morning. I have my vitamin pill; I have my music; I have my same seat; and the papers are all arranged in the same places. It's a series of things. The cumulative purpose of doing those things the same way every day seems to be a way of saying to the mind: you're going to be dreaming soon.

It's not really any different than a bedtime routine. Do you go to bed a different way every night? Is there a certain side that you sleep on? I mean I brush my teeth. I wash my hands. Why would anybody wash their hands before they go to bed? I don't know. And the pillows: the pillows are supposed to be pointed a certain way. The open side of the pillowcase is supposed to be pointed *in* toward the other side of the bed. I don't know why.

40 And the sleeping position is the same: turn to the right, turn to the left. I think it's a way of your mind saying to your body, or your body saying to your mind—maybe they're communicating with each other saying—we're gonna go to sleep now. And probably dreaming follows the same pattern if you don't interrupt it with things like drug use, alcohol, or whatever.

The dreams that I remember most clearly are almost always early dreams. And they're not always bad dreams. I don't want to give you that impression. I can remember one very clearly. It was a flying dream. I was over the turnpike and I was flying along wearing a pair of pajama bottoms. I didn't have any shirt on. I'm just buzzing along under overpasses—*kazipp*—and I'm reminding myself in the dream to stay high enough so that I don't get disemboweled by car antennas sticking up from the cars. That's a fairly mechanistic detail but when I woke up from this dream my feeling was not fear or loathing but just real exhilaration, pleasure and happiness.

It wasn't an out of control flying dream. I can remember as a kid, having a lot of falling dreams but this is the only flying dream that I can remember in detail.

I don't have a lot of repetitive dreams but I do have an anxiety dream: I'm working very hard in a little hot room—it seems to be the room where I lived as a teenager—and I'm aware that there's a madwoman in the attic. There's a little tiny door under the eave that goes to the attic, and I have to finish my work. I have to get that work done or she'll come out and get me. At some point in the dream that door always bursts open and this hideous woman—with all this white hair stuck up around her head like a gone-to-seed dandelion—jumps out with a scalpel.

And I wake up.

45   I still have that dream when I'm backed up on my work and trying to fill all these ridiculous commitments I've made for myself.

Questions for Discussion

1. King says, "I think that dreams are a way that people's minds illustrate the nature of their problems. Or maybe even illustrate the answers to their problems in symbolic language." How does he develop this insight about dreams through the personal examples provided in the essay?

2. Discuss several different ways in which King uses his dreams in his writing. Which approach seems to have been most productive for him? Why?

3. King is known as a vivid and detailed writer, particularly in the construction of the fantasy scenes in his novels. Give examples of King's use of specific detail and effective choice of language in describing the dreams he refers to in this essay. Try to develop your own writing technique in a way that is similar to King's.

4. What conclusions about the way in which the mind functions does King develop through his metaphors of the mind as an ocean, as a nutrient bath, and as water? What different roles do the analogies he makes with jumbo shrimp and different kinds of fish play in his explanations?

5. What relationship does King find between his process of writing and his process of dreaming? Why does King believe that "creative imaging and dreaming are just so similar that they've got to be related"? Explain why you agree or disagree with him.

6. Although King is primarily a novelist, how will you be able to use his insights about the role of dreams in your own writing?

Connection

Compare and contrast King's and Woolf's use of their dreams and fantasies in their writing (see page 25).

Ideas for Writing

1. Write down a dream or nightmare you had that is vivid in your mind but that has never been recorded in words; then write an analysis of

the dream. Discuss what you have learned about yourself from recording the dream.

2. King gives us a good sense of the types of dreams that he has, the impact that his dreams have had on him, and the detailed fabric of his dreams. Write an essay in which you compare and contrast your dreams to King's dreams. What does this comparison and contrast suggest to you about how dreams might have a significant impact on waking life and your writing?

Related Web Sites

Stephen King

www.stephenking.com

This official site for author Stephen King provides the latest news about the author as well as relevant links. The site also includes information on Steven King's past and upcoming projects.

Online Symbolism Dictionary

www.umich.edu/~umfandsf/symbolismproject/symbolism. html/index.html

This online dictionary of symbols in dreams, literature, and the visual arts will serve as a helpful guide to readers, writers, or curious dreamers. Browse or search by keyword.

The Writer's Audience

www.boisestate.edu/wcenter/ww77.htm

These two online articles published by the Boise State University Writing Center examine the history of audience theory in the writing/reading process and make some practical suggestions for effective audience communication.

Virginia Woolf

Professions for Women

Virginia Woolf (1882–1941) grew up in London as the daughter of the eminent Victorian literary critic and agnostic Leslie Stephen. Since women were not sent to school at that time, Woolf educated herself in her father's extensive library. As a young woman, she was a member of the intellectual circle known as the Bloomsbury group. She is best known for her experimental, stream-of-consciousness novels Mrs. Dalloway *(1925),* To the Lighthouse *(1927), and* The Waves *(1931). Her extended essay,* A Room of One's Own *(1929), is considered one of the most important feminist texts of the twentieth*

*century. The essay that follows, "Professions for Women," reflects Woolf's deep
concern about the status of women writers in any society dominated by males.
The essay was first delivered in 1925 to a professional women's club and is
included in* Death of a Moth and Other Essays *(1942).*

Discuss what it would be like to have your own special writing room.
What would the room be like? How might you furnish it? Would it make a
social statement as well as a statement about how you value writing?

When your secretary invited me to come here, she told me that your
Society is concerned with the employment of women and she suggested that I might tell you something about my own professional experiences. It is true I am a woman: it is true I am employed; but what
professional experiences have I had? It is difficult to say. My profession is
literature; and in that profession there are fewer experiences for women
than in any other, with the exception of the stage—fewer, I mean, that
are peculiar to women. For the road was cut many years ago—by Fanny
Burney, by Aphra Behn, by Harriet Martineau, by Jane Austen, by
George Eliot—many famous women, and many more unknown and forgotten, have been before me, making the path smooth, and regulating
my steps. Thus, when I came to write, there were very few material obstacles in my way. Writing was a reputable and harmless occupation. The
family peace was not broken by the scratching of a pen. No demand was
made upon the family purse. For ten and sixpence one can buy paper
enough to write all the plays of Shakespeare—if one has a mind that way.
Pianos and models, Paris, Vienna and Berlin, masters and mistresses, are
not needed by a writer. The cheapness of writing is, of course, the reason
why women have succeeded as writers before they have succeeded in the
other professions.

But to tell you my story—it is a simple one. You have only got to figure to yourselves a girl in a bedroom with a pen in her hand. She had
only to move that pen from left to right—from ten o'clock to one. Then
it occurred to her to do what is simple and cheap enough for all—to slip
a few of those pages into an envelope, fix a penny stamp in the corner,
and drop the envelope into the red box at the corner. It was thus that
I became a journalist; and my effort was rewarded on the first day of the
following month—a very glorious day it was for me—by a letter from an
editor containing a cheque for one pound ten shillings and sixpence.
But to show you how little I deserve to be called a professional woman,
how little I know of the struggles and difficulties of such lives, I have to
admit that instead of spending that sum upon bread and butter, rent,
shoes and stockings, or butcher's bills, I went out and bought a cat—a

beautiful cat, a Persian cat, which very soon involved me in bitter disputes with my neighbours.

What could be easier than to write articles and to buy Persian cats with the profits? But wait a moment. Articles have to be about something. Mine, I seem to remember, was about a novel by a famous man. And while I was writing this review, I discovered that if I were going to review books I should need to do battle with a certain phantom. And the phantom was a woman, and when I came to know her better I called her after the heroine of a famous poem, The Angel in the House. It was she who used to come between me and my paper when I was writing reviews. It was she who bothered me and wasted my time and so tormented me that at last I killed her. You who come of a younger and happier generation may not have heard of her—you may not know what I mean by the Angel in the House. I will describe her as shortly as I can. She was intensely sympathetic. She was immensely charming. She was utterly unselfish. She excelled in the difficult arts of family life. She sacrificed herself daily. If there was a chicken, she took the leg; if there was a draught she sat in it—in short she was so constituted that she never had a mind or a wish of her own, but preferred to sympathize always with the minds and wishes of others. Above all—I need not say it—she was pure. Her purity was supposed to be her chief beauty—her blushes, her great grace. In those days—the last of Queen Victoria—every house had its Angel. And when I came to write I encountered her with the very first words. The shadow of her wings fell on my page; I heard the rustling of her skirts in the room. Directly, that is to say, I took my pen in hand to review that novel by a famous man, she slipped behind me and whispered: "My dear, you are a young woman. You are writing about a book that has been written by a man. Be sympathetic; be tender; flatter; deceive; use all the arts and wiles of our sex. Never let anybody guess that you have a mind of your own. Above all, be pure." And she made as if to guide my pen. I now record the one act for which I take some credit to myself, though the credit rightly belongs to some excellent ancestors of mine who left me a certain sum of money—shall we say five hundred pounds a year?—so that it was not necessary for me to depend solely on charm for my living. I turned upon her and caught her by the throat. I did my best to kill her. My excuse, if I were to be had up in a court of law, would be that I acted in self-defence. Had I not killed her she would have killed me. She would have plucked the heart out of my writing. For, as I found, directly I put pen to paper, you cannot review even a novel without having a mind of your own, without expressing what you think to be the truth about human relations, morality, sex. And all these questions, according to the Angel in the House, cannot be dealt with freely and openly by women; they must charm, they must conciliate, they must—to put it bluntly—tell lies if they are to succeed. Thus, whenever I felt the shadow of her wing or the radiance of her halo upon my page, I took up the inkpot and flung it at her. She died hard. Her fictitious nature was of great assistance to her. It is far harder to kill a phantom than a reality. She was always creeping back when I thought I had despatched her. Though I flatter myself that I killed her in the end, the struggle was severe; it took much time that had better have been spent upon learning Greek grammar; or in roaming the world in search of adventures. But it was a real experience; it was an experience that was bound to befall all women writers at that time. Killing the Angel in the House was part of the occupation of a woman writer.

But to continue my story. The Angel was dead; what then remained? You may say that what remained was a simple and common object—a young woman in a bedroom with an inkpot. In other words, now that she had rid herself of falsehood, that young woman had only to be herself. Ah, but what is "herself"? I mean, what is a woman? I assure you, I do not know. I do not believe that you know. I do not believe that anybody can know until she has expressed herself in all the arts and professions open to human skill. That indeed is one of the reasons why I have come here—out of respect for you, who are in process of showing us by your experiments what a woman is, who are in process of providing us, by your failures and successes, with that extremely important piece of information.

5   But to continue the story of my professional experiences. I made one pound ten and six by my first review; and I bought a Persian cat with the proceeds. Then I grew ambitious. A Persian cat is all very well, I said; but a Persian cat is not enough. I must have a motor car. And it was thus that I became a novelist—for it is a very strange thing that people will give you a motor car if you will tell them a story. It is a still stranger thing that there is nothing so delightful in the world as telling stories. It is far pleasanter than writing reviews of famous novels. And yet, if I am to obey your secretary and tell you my professional experiences as a novelist, I must tell you about a very strange experience that befell me as a novelist. And to understand it you must try first to imagine a novelist's state of mind. I hope I am not giving away professional secrets if I say that a novelist's chief desire is to be as unconscious as possible. He has to induce in himself a state of perpetual lethargy. He wants life to proceed with the utmost quiet and regularity. He wants to see the same faces, to read the same books, to do the same things day after day, month after month, while he is writing, so that nothing may break the illusion in which he is living—so that nothing may disturb or disquiet the mysterious nosings about, feelings round, darts, dashes and sudden discoveries of that very shy and illusive spirit, the imagination. I suspect that this state is the same both for men and women. Be that as it may, I want you to imagine

me writing a novel in a state of trance. I want you to figure to yourselves a girl sitting with a pen in her hand, which for minutes, and indeed for hours, she never dips into the inkpot. The image that comes to my mind when I think of this girl is the image of a fisherman lying sunk in dreams on the verge of a deep lake with a rod held out over the water. She was letting her imagination sweep unchecked round every rock and cranny of the world that lies submerged in the depths of our unconscious being. Now came the experience, the experience that I believe to be far commoner with women writers than with men. The line raced through the girl's fingers. Her imagination had rushed away. It had sought the pools, the depths, the dark places where the largest fish slumber. And then there was a smash. There was an explosion. There was foam and confusion. The imagination had dashed itself against something hard. The girl was roused from her dream. She was indeed in a state of the most acute and difficult distress. To speak without figure she had thought of something, something about the body, about the passions which it was unfitting for her as a woman to say. Men, her reason told her, would be shocked. The consciousness of what men will say of a woman who speaks the truth about her passions had roused her from her artist's state of unconsciousness. She could write no more. The trance was over. Her imagination could work no longer. This I believe to be a very common experience with women writers—they are impeded by the extreme conventionality of the other sex. For though men sensibly allow themselves great freedom in these respects, I doubt that they realize or can control the extreme severity with which they condemn such freedom in women.

These then were two very genuine experiences of my own. These were two of the adventures of my professional life. The first—killing the Angel in the House—I think I solved. She died. But the second, telling the truth about my own experiences as a body, I do not think I solved. I doubt that any woman has solved it yet. The obstacles against her are still immensely powerful—and yet they are very difficult to define. Outwardly, what is simpler than to write books? Outwardly, what obstacles are there for a woman rather than for a man? Inwardly, I think, the case is very different; she has still many ghosts to fight, many prejudices to overcome. Indeed it will be a long time still, I think, before a woman can sit down to write a book without finding a phantom to be slain, a rock to be dashed against. And if this is so in literature, the freest of all professions for women, how is it in the new professions which you are now for the first time entering?

Those are the questions that I should like, had I time, to ask you. And indeed, if I have laid stress upon these professional experiences of mine, it is because I believe that they are, though in different forms, yours also. Even when the path is nominally open—when there is nothing to prevent a woman from being a doctor, a lawyer, a civil servant—there are many phantoms and obstacles, as I believe, looming in her way. To discuss and define them is I think of great value and importance; for thus only can the labour be shared, the difficulties be solved. But besides this, it is necessary also to discuss the ends and the aims for which we are fighting, for which we are doing battle with these formidible obstacles. Those aims cannot be taken for granted; they must be perpetually questioned and examined. The whole position, as I see it—here in this hall surrounded by women practising for the first time in history I know not how many different professions—is one of extraordinary interest and importance. You have won rooms of your own in the house hitherto exclusively owned by men. You are able, though not without great labour and effort, to pay the rent. You are earning your five hundred pounds a year. But this freedom is only a beginning; the room is your own, but it is still bare. It has to be furnished; it has to be decorated; it has to be shared. How are you going to furnish it, how are you going to decorate it? With whom are you going to share it, and upon what terms? These, I think are questions of the utmost importance and interest. For the first time in history you are able to ask them; for the first time you are able to decide for yourselves what the answers should be. Willingly would I stay and discuss those questions and answers—but not tonight. My time is up; and I must cease.

QUESTIONS FOR DISCUSSION

1. In what way is Woolf's opening paragraph ironic? Is her use of irony effective? Explain.
2. Describe the angel-like phantom that torments Woolf when she tries to write reviews of men's work. What does the angel represent for Woolf? Do you ever think that you, too, have an angel-like figure that sometimes controls your thoughts and actions?
3. Why is it so difficult for Woolf to kill the phantom angel? Why was killing the phantom angel an important concern of any woman writer of Woolf's age? Do you think that women writers today still struggle against a phantom angel?
4. How does Woolf get into her writer's frame of mind? Why does she rely on her unconscious mind when she writes? What rouses Woolf from her artist's state of trance? Do women today still face this type of obstacle?
5. How does Woolf clarify her meaning through metaphors and images such as the phantom angel and the young girl who wants to write becoming "the image of a fisherman lying sunk in dreams on the verge of a deep lake with a rod held out over the water"? Are her metaphors and images persuasive and effective? Explain.
6. Why does Woolf believe that the inward obstacles women writers face are the hardest to overcome? In your own life as a writer, what are the most difficult challenges that you must overcome?

CONNECTION

Compare Woolf's advice to writers to Amy Tan's comments about the writer and her audience in "Mother Tongue." Whose advice do you find more useful? Which is most inspirational, and why (see page 39)?

IDEAS FOR WRITING

1. Write an essay that discusses the relevance of Woolf's ideas for modern men or women who are struggling to become writers. Develop several different ideas, and support each one with examples.
2. Create your own phantom angel, the visual and mental image that tries to keep you from expressing yourself in your writing. Begin by drawing (with pens and paper or on a computer program) this inner critic. Then write a dialogue between your inner critic and your creative self. In conclusion, write a paragraph that discusses what you learned from this activity.

RELATED WEB SITES

Virginia Woolf Resources
www.virginiawoolfsociety.co.uk/vw_resources.htm
Learn about Virginia Woolf at the Virginia Woolf Society of Great Britain's Web site of links to useful research materials about the author. It includes not only large collections of links but also chronologies, bibliographies, and books on Woolf.

Feminist Theory—An Overview
http://plato.stanford.edu/entries/feminism-topics/
Visit Stanford University's detailed entry about topics in feminism in the Stanford Encyclopedia of Philosophy. The informational Web site provides a history of feminism, descriptions of feminist theories and philosophies, as well a compilation of additional resources for the study of feminist theory and its subcategories.

Frederick Douglass

Learning to Read and Write

An important figure in the history of African American thought and writing, Frederick Douglass (1818–1895) was born in Maryland into slavery. After escaping to the North, he wrote of his journey to freedom in The Narrative Life of Frederick Douglass *(1845). He also became the publisher of two radical newspapers,* the North Star *and* The Frederick Douglass Paper, *which had a very significant impact on the antislavery movement. Douglass helped hundreds of slaves make their way to freedom on the Underground Railroad. During the Civil War, Douglass served as an advisor to President Abraham Lincoln, and after 1872, served as an international diplomat. In the short excerpt from his autobiography included below, Douglass describes how learning to read developed his intellect, pride, and resourcefulness.*

JOURNAL

How did you learn to read? What do you appreciate most about reading?

Very soon after I went to live with Mr. and Mrs. Auld, she very kindly commenced to teach me the A, B, C. After I had learned this, she assisted me in learning to spell words of three or four letters. Just at this point of my progress, Mr. Auld found out what was going on, and at once forbade Mrs. Auld to instruct me further, telling her, among other things, that it was unlawful, as well as unsafe, to teach a slave to read. To use his own words, further, he said, "If you give a nigger an inch, he will take an ell. A nigger should know nothing but to obey his master—to do as he is told to do. Learning would spoil the best nigger in the world. Now," said he, "if you teach that nigger (speaking of myself) how to read, there would be no keeping him. It would forever unfit him to be a slave. He would at once become unmanageable, and of no value to his master. As to himself, it could do him no good, but a great deal of harm. It would make him discontented and unhappy." These words sank deep into my heart, stirred up sentiments within that lay slumbering, and called into existence an entirely new train of thought. It was a new and special revelation, explaining dark and mysterious things, with which my youthful understanding had struggled, but struggled in vain.

I now understood what had been to me a most perplexing difficulty—to wit, the white man's power to enslave the black man. It was a grand achievement, and I prized it highly. From that moment, I understood the pathway from slavery to freedom. It was just what I wanted, and I got it at a time when I the least expected it. Whilst I was saddened by the thought of losing the aid of my kind mistress, I was gladdened by the invaluable instruction which, by the merest accident, I had gained from my master. Though conscious of the difficulty of learning without a teacher, I set out with high hope, and a fixed purpose, at whatever cost of trouble, to learn how to read. The very decided manner with which he spoke, and strove to impress his wife with the evil consequences of giving me instruction, served to convince me that he was deeply sensible of the truths he was uttering. It gave me the best assurance that I might rely with the utmost confidence on the results which, he said, would flow from teaching me to read. What he most dreaded, that I most desired. What he most loved, that I most hated. That which to him was a great evil, to be carefully shunned, was to me a great good, to be diligently sought; and the argument which he so warmly urged, against my learning to read, only served to inspire me with a desire and determination to learn. In learning to read, I owe almost as much to the bitter opposition of my master, as to the kindly aid of my mistress. I acknowledge the benefit of both . . .

I lived in Master Hugh's family about seven years. During this time, I succeeded in learning to read and write. In accomplishing this, I was compelled to resort to various stratagems. I had no regular teacher. My mistress, who had kindly commenced to instruct me, had, in compliance with the advice and direction of her husband, not only ceased to instruct, but had set her face against my being instructed by any one else. It is due, however, to my mistress to say of her, that she did not adopt this course of treatment immediately. She at first lacked the depravity indispensable to shutting me up in mental darkness. It was at least necessary for her to have some training in the exercise of irresponsible power, to make her equal to the task of treating me as though I were a brute.

My mistress was, as I have said, a kind and tenderhearted woman; and in the simplicity of her soul she commenced, when I first went to live with her, to treat me as she supposed one human being ought to treat another. In entering upon the duties of a slaveholder, she did not seem to perceive that I sustained to her the relation of a mere chattel, and that for her to treat me as a human being was not only wrong, but dangerously so. Slavery proved as injurious to her as it did to me. When I went there, she was a pious, warm, and tender-hearted woman. There was no sorrow or suffering for which she had not a tear. She had bread for the hungry, clothes for the naked, and comfort for every mourner that came within her reach. Slavery soon proved its ability to divest her of these heavenly qualities. Under its influence, the tender heart became stone, and the lamb-like disposition gave way to one of tiger-like fierceness. The first step in her downward course was in her ceasing to instruct me. She now commenced to practice her husband's precepts. She finally became even more violent in her opposition than her husband himself. She was not satisfied with simply doing as well as he had commanded; she seemed anxious to do better. Nothing seemed to make her more angry than to see me with a newspaper. She seemed to think that here lay the danger. I have had her rush at me with a face made all up of fury, and snatch from me a newspaper, in a manner that fully revealed her apprehension. She was an apt woman; and a little experience soon demonstrated, to her satisfaction, that education and slavery were incompatible with each other.

5   From this time I was most narrowly watched. If I was in a separate room any considerable length of time, I was sure to be suspected of having a book, and was at once called to give an account of myself. All

this, however, was too late. The first step had been taken. Mistress, in teaching me the alphabet, had given me the inch, and no precaution could prevent me from taking the ell.

The plan which I adopted, and the one by which I was most successful, was that of making friends of all the little white boys whom I met in the street. As many of these as I could, I converted into teachers. With their kindly aid, obtained at different times and in different places, I finally succeeded in learning to read. When I was sent of errands, I always took my book with me, and by going one part of my errand quickly, I found time to get a lesson before my return. I used also to carry bread with me, enough of which was always in the house, and to which I was always welcome; for I was much better off in this regard than many of the poor white children in our neighborhood. This bread I used to bestow upon the hungry little urchins, who, in return, would give me that more valuable bread of knowledge. I am strongly tempted to give the names of two or three of those little boys, as a testimonial of the gratitude and affection I bear them; but prudence forbids;—not that it would injure me, but it might embarrass them; for it is almost an unpardonable offence to teach slaves to read in this Christian country. It is enough to say of the dear little fellows, that they lived on Philpot Street, very near Durgin and Bailey's ship-yard. I used to talk this matter of slavery over with them. I would sometimes say to them, I wished I could be as free as they would be when they got to be men. "You will be free as soon as you are twenty-one, but I am a slave for life! Have not I as good a right to be free as you have?" These words used to trouble them; they would express for me the liveliest sympathy, and console me with the hope that something would occur by which I might be free.

I was now about twelve years old, and the thought of being a slave for life began to bear heavily upon my heart. Just about this time, I got hold of a book entitled *The Columbian Orator*. Every opportunity I got, I used to read this book. Among much of other interesting matter, I found in it a dialogue between a master and his slave. The slave was represented as having run away from his master three times. The dialogue represented the conversation which took place between them, when the slave was retaken the third time. In this dialogue, the whole argument in behalf of slavery was brought forward by the master, all of which was disposed of by the slave. The slave was made to say some very smart as well as impressive things in reply to his master—things which had the desired though unexpected effect; for the conversation resulted in the voluntary emancipation of the slave on the part of the master.

In the same book, I met with one of Sheridan's mighty speeches on and in behalf of Catholic emancipation. These were choice documents to me. I read them over and over again with unabated interest. They gave tongue to interesting thoughts of my own soul, which had frequently flashed through my mind, and died away for want of utterance. The moral which I gained from the dialogue was the power of truth over the conscience of even a slaveholder. What I got from Sheridan was a bold denunciation of slavery, and a powerful vindication of human rights. The reading of these documents enabled me to utter my thoughts, and to meet the arguments brought forward to sustain slavery; but while they relieved me of one difficulty, they brought on another even more painful than the one of which I was relieved. The more I read, the more I was led to abhor and detest my enslavers. I could regard them in no other light than a band of successful robbers, who had left their homes, and gone to Africa, and stolen us from our homes, and in a strange land reduced us to slavery. I loathed them as being the meanest as well as the most wicked of men. As I read and contemplated the subject, behold! that very discontentment which Master Hugh had predicted would follow my learning to read had already come, to torment and sting my soul to unutterable anguish. As I writhed under it, I would at times feel that learning to read had been a curse rather than a blessing. It had given me a view of my wretched condition, without the remedy. It opened my eyes to the horrible pit, but to no ladder upon which to get out. In moments of agony, I envied my fellow-slaves for their stupidity. I have often wished myself a beast. I preferred the condition of the meanest reptile to my own. Any thing, no matter what, to get rid of thinking! It was this everlasting thinking of my condition that tormented me. There was no getting rid of it. It was pressed upon me by every object within sight or hearing, animate or inanimate. The silver trump of freedom had roused my soul to eternal wakefulness. Freedom now appeared, to disappear no more forever. It was heard in every sound, and seen in every thing. It was ever present to torment me with a sense of my wretched condition. I saw nothing without seeing it, I heard nothing without hearing it, and felt nothing without feeling it. It looked from every star, it smiled in every calm, breathed in every wind, and moved in every storm.

I often found myself regretting my own existence, and wishing myself dead; and but for the hope of being free, I have no doubt but that I should have killed myself, or done something for which I should have been killed. While in this state of mind, I was eager to hear any one speak of slavery. I was a ready listener. Every little while, I could hear something about the abolitionists. It was some time before I found what the word meant. It was always used in such connections as to make it an interesting word to me. If a slave ran away and succeeded in getting clear, or if a slave killed his master, set fire to a barn, or did any thing very wrong in the mind of a slaveholder, it was spoken of as the fruit of abolition. Hearing the word in this connection very often, I set about learning what it meant. The dictionary afforded me little or no help. I found it was "the act of abolishing;" but then I did not know what was to be abolished. Here I was perplexed. I did not dare to ask any one about its meaning, for I was satisfied that it was something they wanted me to know very little about. After a patient waiting, I got one of our city papers, containing an account of the number of petitions from the north, praying for the abolition of slavery in the District of Columbia, and of the slave trade between the States. From this time I understood the words abolition and abolitionist, and always drew near when that word was spoken, expecting to hear something of importance to myself and fellow-slaves.

10   The light broke in upon me by degrees. I went one day down on the wharf of Mr. Waters; and seeing two Irishmen unloading a scow of stone, I went, unasked, and helped them. When we had finished, one of them came to me and asked me if I were a slave. I told him I was. He asked, "Are ye a slave for life?" I told him that I was. The good Irishman seemed to be deeply affected by the statement. He said to the other that it was a pity so fine a little fellow as myself should be a slave for life. He said it was a shame to hold me. They both advised me to run away to the north; that I should find friends there, and that I should be free. I pretended not to be interested in what they said, and treated them as if I did not understand them; for I feared they might be treacherous. White men have been known to encourage slaves to escape, and then, to get the reward, catch them and return them to their masters. I was afraid that these seemingly good men might use me so; but I nevertheless remembered their advice, and from that time I resolved to run away. I looked forward to a time at which it would be safe for me to escape. I was too young to think of doing so immediately; besides, I wished to learn how to write, as I might have occasion to write my own pass. I consoled myself with the hope that I should one day find a good chance. Meanwhile, I would learn to write. The idea as to how I might learn to write was suggested to me by being in Durgin and Bailey's ship-yard, and frequently seeing the ship carpenters, after hewing, and getting a piece of timber ready for use, write on the timber the name of that part of the ship for which it was intended. When a piece of timber was intended for the larboard side, it would be marked thus—"L." When a piece was for the starboard side, it would be marked thus—"S." A piece for the larboard side forward, would be marked thus—"L. F." When a piece was for starboard side forward, it would be marked thus—"S. F." For larboard aft, it would be marked thus—"L. A." For starboard aft, it would be marked thus—"S. A." I soon learned the names of these letters, and for what they were intended when placed upon a piece of timber in the ship-yard. I immediately commenced copying them, and in a short time was able to make the four letters named. After that, when I met with any boy who I knew could write, I would tell him I could write as well as he. The next word would be, "I don't believe you. Let me see you try it." I would then make

the letters which I had been so fortunate as to learn, and ask him to beat that. In this way I got a good many lessons in writing, which it is quite possible I should never have gotten in any other way. During this time, my copy-book was the board fence, brick wall, and pavement; my pen and ink was a lump of chalk. With these, I learned mainly how to write. I then commenced and continued copying the Italics in Webster's Spelling Book, until I could make them all without looking on the book. By this time, my little Master Thomas had gone to school, and learned how to write, and had written over a number of copy-books. These had been brought home, and shown to some of our near neighbors, and then laid aside. My mistress used to go to class meeting at the Wilk Street meetinghouse every Monday afternoon, and leave me to take care of the house. When left thus, I used to spend the time in writing in the spaces left in Master Thomas's copy-book, copying what he had written. I continued to do this until I could write a hand very similar to that of Master Thomas. Thus, after a long, tedious effort for years, I finally succeeded in learning how to write.

QUESTIONS FOR DISCUSSION

1. Why does the relationship between Frederick Douglass and his mistress change? What is the nature of their power struggle?
2. How did Douglass learn to read and finally to write?
3. Discuss several incidents from the selection that show Douglass's resourcefulness and understanding of human nature, as well as an ability to listen, think critically, and learn from his experience.
4. Why does Douglass grow more and more tormented by what he is reading and thinking? How does he combat his deep feelings of frustration and despair on his journey to becoming an educated and free man?
5. Why and how does Douglass finally join the abolitionists' cause?
6. What connections between education and freedom does Douglass make in this excerpt from his autobiography? What relationships have you seen between education and freedom in your own life?

CONNECTION

Compare Steven Holtzman's and Douglass's views on the importance of reading. Why do you think reading was more important to Douglass than it is for many young people today (see page 49)?

IDEAS FOR WRITING

1. Becoming educated through reading allowed Douglass to gain his freedom and helped many other slaves to gain theirs. Write an

essay that explores different ways in which your education through reading has helped you to gain more freedom and independence.

2. Using the resources at your college library and on the Internet, find out more about how slaves learned to read and write, and how their education helped them to gain their freedom.

RELATED WEB SITES

Frederick Douglass
`www.history.rochester.edu/class/douglass/home.html`
This biography of Frederick Douglass by Sandra Thomas will give you more insight into the struggles and challenges that Douglass overcame in his fight to gain his own freedom and the freedom of his people.

Frederick Douglass National Historic Site
`www.nps.gov/frdo/freddoug.html`
The Frederick Douglass National Historic Site is dedicated to preserving the legacy of the most famous African Americans of the nineteenth century. The museum is located at the final home that Douglass purchased in 1877, which he named Cedar Hill.

Frederick Douglass Papers
`www.iupui.edu/~douglass`
Housed at Indiana University–Purdue University at Indianapolis, the Frederick Douglass Papers project collects and publishes his speeches and writings.

Amy Tan

Mother Tongue

Born in Oakland, California, in 1952 to immigrant parents, Amy Tan received an M.A. (1974) from San Jose State University, where she studied linguistics. Her first best-selling novel, The Joy Luck Club *(1989), was inspired by the stories told by Chinese American women of her mother's generation. Tan has written three other novels—*The Kitchen God's Wife *(1991),* The One Hundred Secret Senses *(1995), and* The Bonesetter's Daughter *(2001)—as well as a number of essays in which she explores cultural and linguistic issues. As you read the following essay, notice how Tan uses her experiences growing up bilingual in a Chinese-American family to challenge the traditional expectations of academic writing achievement tests.*

In her essay, Amy Tan states that she is "fascinated by language in daily life." Discuss several striking examples of creative uses of language that you have noticed recently in your everyday life or in conversations with friends.

I am not a scholar of English or literature. I cannot give you much more than personal opinions on the English language and its variations in this country or others.

I am a writer. And by that definition, I am someone who has always loved language. I am fascinated by language in daily life. I spend a great deal of my time thinking about the power of language—the way it can evoke an emotion, a visual image, a complex idea, or a simple truth. Language is the tool of any trade. And I use them all—all the Englishes I grew up with.

Recently, I was made keenly aware of the different Englishes I do use. I was giving a talk to a large group of people, the same talk I had already given to half a dozen other groups. The nature of the talk was about my writing, my life, and my book, *The Joy Luck Club*. The talk was going along well enough, until I remembered one major difference that made the whole talk sound wrong. My mother was in the room. And it was perhaps the first time she had heard me give a lengthy speech, using the kind of English I have never used with her. I was saying things like, "The intersection of memory upon imagination" and "There is an aspect of my fiction that relates to thus-and-thus"—a speech filled with carefully wrought grammatical phrases, burdened, it suddenly seemed to me, with nominalized forms, past perfect tenses, conditional phrases, all the forms of standard English that I had learned in school and through books, the forms of English I did not use at home with my mother.

Just last week, I was walking down the street with my mother, and I again found myself conscious of the English I was using, the English I use with her. We were talking about the price of new and used furniture, and I heard myself saying this: "Not waste money that way." My husband was with us as well, and he didn't notice any switch in my English. And then I realized why. It's because over the twenty years we've been together, I've often used that same kind of English with him, and sometimes he even uses it with me. It has become our language of intimacy, a different sort of English that relates to family talk, the language I grew up with.

5   So you'll have some idea of what this family talk I heard sounds like I'll quote what my mother said during a recent conversation which I videotaped and then transcribed. During this conversation, my mother was talking about a political gangster in Shanghai who had the same last

name as her family's, Du, and how the gangster in his early years wanted
to be adopted by her family, which was rich by comparison. Later, the
gangster became more powerful, far richer than my mother's family, and
one day showed up at my mother's wedding to pay his respects. Here's
what she said in part:

"Du Yusong having business like fruit stand. Like off the street kind.
He is Du like Du Zong—but not Tsung-ming Island people. The local
people call putong, the near east side, he belong to that side local people. That man want to ask Du Zong father take him in like become own
family. Du Zong father wasn't look down on him, but didn't take seriously, until that man big like become a mafia. Now important person,
very hard to inviting him. Chinese way, came only to show respect, don't
stay for dinner. Respect for making big celebration, he shows up. Man
gives lots of respect. Chinese custom. Chinese social life that way. If too
important won't have to stay too long. He come to my wedding. I didn't
see, I heard it. I gone to boy's side, they have YMCA dinner. Chinese age
I was nineteen."

You should know that my mother's expressive command of English
belies how much she actually understands. She reads the *Forbes* report,
listens to *Wall Street Week,* converses daily with her stockbroker, reads all
of Shirley MacLaine's books with ease—all kinds of things I can't begin
to understand. Yet some of my friends tell me they understand 50 percent of what my mother says. Some say they understand 80 to 90 percent.
Some say they understand none of it, as if she were speaking pure Chinese. But to me, my mother's English is perfectly clear, perfectly natural.
It's my mother tongue. Her language, as I hear it, is vivid, direct, full of
observation and imagery. That was the language that helped shape the
way I saw things, expressed things, made sense of the world.

Lately, I've been giving more thought to the kind of English my
mother speaks. Like others, I have described it to people as "broken" or
"fractured" English. But I wince when I say that. It has always bothered
me that I can think of no way to describe it other than "broken," as if it
were damaged and needed to be fixed, as if it lacked a certain wholeness
and soundness. I've heard other terms used, "limited English," for example. But they seem just as bad, as if everything is limited, including people's perceptions of the limited English speaker.

I know this for a fact, because when I was growing up, my mother's
"limited" English limited *my* perception of her. I was ashamed of her
English. I believed that her English reflected the quality of what she had
to say. That is, because she expressed them imperfectly her thoughts
were imperfect. And I had plenty of empirical evidence to support me:
the fact that people in department stores, at banks, and at restaurants
did not take her seriously, did not give her good service, pretended not
to understand her, or even acted as if they did not hear her.

10   My mother had long realized the limitations of her English as well. When I was fifteen, she used to have me call people on the phone to pretend I was she. In this guise, I was forced to ask for information or even to complain and yell at people who had been rude to her. One time it was a call to her stockbroker in New York. She had cashed out her small portfolio and it just so happened we were going to go to New York the next week, our very first trip outside California. I had to get on the phone and say in an adolescent voice that was not very convincing, "This is Mrs. Tan."

And my mother was standing in the back whispering loudly, "Why he don't send me check, already two weeks late. So mad he lie to me, losing me money."

And then I said in perfect English, "Yes, I'm getting rather concerned. You had agreed to send the check two weeks ago, but it hasn't arrived."

Then she began to talk more loudly. "What he want, I come to New York tell him front of his boss, you cheating me?" And I was trying to calm her down, make her be quiet, while telling the stockbroker, "I can't tolerate any more excuses. If I don't receive the check immediately, I am going to have to speak to your manager when I'm in New York next week." And sure enough, the following week there we were in front of this astonished stockbroker, and I was sitting there red-faced and quiet, and my mother, the real Mrs. Tan, was shouting at his boss in her impeccable broken English.

We used a similar routine just five days ago, for a situation that was far less humorous. My mother had gone to the hospital for an appointment, to find out about a benign brain tumor a CAT scan had revealed a month ago. She said she had spoken very good English, her best English, no mistakes. Still, she said, the hospital did not apologize when they said they had lost the CAT scan and she had come for nothing. She said they did not seem to have any sympathy when she told them she was anxious to know the exact diagnosis, since her husband and son had both died of brain tumors. She said they would not give her any more information until the next time and she would have to make another appointment for that. So she said she would not leave until the doctor called daughter. She wouldn't budge. And when the doctor finally called her daughter, me, who spoke in perfect English—lo and behold—we had assurances the CAT scan would be found, promises that a conference call on Monday would be held, and apologies for any suffering my mother had gone through for a most regrettable mistake.

15   I think my mother's English almost had an effect on limiting my possibilities in life as well. Sociologists and linguists probably will tell you that a person's developing language skills are more influenced by peers. But I do think that the language spoken in the family, especially in immigrant families which are more insular, plays a large role in shaping the

language of the child. And I believe that it affected my results on achievement tests, IQ Tests, and the SAT. While my English skills were never judged as poor, compared to math, English could not be considered my strong suit. In grade school I did moderately well, getting perhaps B's, sometimes B-pluses, in English and scoring perhaps in the sixtieth or seventieth percentile on achievement tests. But those scores were not good enough to override the opinion that my true abilities lay in math and science, because in those areas I achieved A's and scored in the ninetieth percentile or higher.

This was understandable. Math is precise; there is only one correct answer. Whereas, for me at least, the answers on English tests were always a judgement call, a matter of opinion and personal experience. Those tests were constructed around items like fill-in-the-blank sentence completion, such as "Even though Tom was _____, Mary thought he was _____." And the correct answer always seemed to be the most bland combinations of thoughts, for example, "Even though Tom was shy, Mary thought he was charming," with the grammatical structure "even though" limiting the correct answer to some sort of semantic opposites, so you wouldn't get answers like, "Even though Tom was foolish, Mary thought he was ridiculous." Well, according to my mother, there were very few limitations as to what Tom could have been and what Mary might have thought of him. So I never did well on tests like that.

The same was true with word analogies, pairs of words in which you were supposed to find some sort of logical, semantic relationship—for example, "*Sunset* is to *nightfall* as _____ is to _____." And here you would be presented with a list of four possible pairs, one of which showed the same kind of relationship: *red* is to *stoplight, bus* is to *arrival, chills* is to *fever, yawn* is to *boring*. Well, I could never think that way. I knew what the tests were asking, but I could not block out of my mind the images already created by the first pair "*sunset* is to *nightfall*"—and I would see a burst of colors against a darkening sky, the moon rising, the lowering of a curtain of stars. And all the other pairs of words—red, bus, stoplight, boring—just threw up a mass of confusing images, making it impossible for me to sort out something as logical as saying: "A sunset precedes nightfall" is the same as "a chill precedes a fever." The only way I would have gotten that answer right would have been to imagine an associative situation, for example, my being disobedient and staying out past sunset, catching a chill at night, which turns into feverish pneumonia as punishment, which indeed did happen to me.

I have been thinking about all this lately, about my mother's English, about achievement tests. Because lately I've been asked, as a writer, why there are not more Asian-Americans represented in American literature. Why are there few Asian-Americans enrolled in creative writing programs?

Why do so many Chinese students go into engineering? Well, these are broad sociological questions I can't begin to answer. But I have noticed in surveys—in fact, just last week—that Asian students, as a whole, always do significantly better on math achievement tests than in English. And this makes me think that there are other Asian-American students whose English spoken in the home might also be described as "broken" or "limited." And perhaps they also have teachers who are steering them away from writing and into math and science, which is what happened to me.

Fortunately, I happen to be rebellious in nature and enjoy the challenge of disproving assumptions made about me. I became an English major my first year in college, after being enrolled as pre-med. I started writing nonfiction as a freelancer the week after I was told by my former boss that writing was my worst skill and I should hone my talents toward account management.

20   But it wasn't until 1985 that I finally began to write fiction. And at first I wrote using what I thought to be wittily crafted sentences, sentences that would finally prove I had mastery over the English language. Here's an example from the first draft of a story that later made its way into *The Joy Luck Club,* but without this line: "That was my mental quandary in its nascent state." A terrible line, which I can barely pronounce.

Fortunately, for reasons I won't get into today, I later decided I should envision a reader for the stories I would write. And the reader I decided upon was my mother, because these were stories about mothers. So with this reader in mind—and in fact she did read my early drafts—I began to write stories using all the Englishes I grew up with: the English I spoke to my mother, which for lack of a better term might be described as "simple"; the English she used with me, which for lack of a better term might be described as "broken"; my translation of her Chinese, which could certainly be described as "watered down"; and what I imagined to be her translation of her Chinese if she could speak in perfect English, her internal language, and for that I sought to preserve the essence, but neither an English nor a Chinese structure. I wanted to capture what language ability tests can never reveal: her intent, her passion, her imagery, the rhythms of her speech and the nature of her thoughts.

Apart from what any critic had to say about my writing, I knew I had succeeded where it counted when my mother finished reading my book and gave me her verdict: "So easy to read."

QUESTIONS FOR DISCUSSION

1. Tan discusses her awareness of using language differently when speaking with different audiences and on different occasions. Keep

a log for several days that records the situations when you change the way you use English for a specific group of friends, teachers, relatives, or a work situation. Share your observations and conclusions with your classmates.

2. Why is Tan critical of the descriptive term "limited English"? How did this term influence her perception of her own mother?

3. Why is the article entitled "Mother Tongue"? What do Tan's examples about how she would often speak for her mother suggest?

4. Why is Tan critical of the achievement tests she was given as an adolescent? Do you agree or disagree with her point of view and conclusions? Explain your perspective.

5. Do you believe like Tan that high school teachers encourage Asian students to study math and science rather than writing? How does she explain her success as a writer in spite of the evaluations provided by her teachers and former employer?

6. According to Tan, what is the real test of a writer? What advice does Tan offer to the person who aspires to be a successful writer?

CONNECTION

Compare Tan's views on the role of different "Englishes" in her writer's life and in her relationship with her mother with the views of Joyce Chang in her essay "Drive Becarefully" (see page 45).

IDEAS FOR WRITING

1. "I am a writer. And by that definition, I am someone who has always loved language. I am fascinated by language in daily life." Develop Tan's ideas on language into an essay, using personal experiences and examples from your reading that illustrate language's complexity and power.

2. Write an essay in which you discuss how your rebellion against a cultural or social myth helped you to develop a skill or talent that is both useful and rewarding.

RELATED WEB SITES

Amy Tan

www.luminarium.org/contemporary/amytan/

This extensive online resource on author Amy Tan includes interviews, book reviews, essays, links, and biographical information.

Asian American Studies Resources

http://sun3.lib.uci.edu/~dtsang/aas2.htm

This site contains hundreds of links to topics in Asian American studies, such as bibliographies, magazines, journals, audiovisual resources, research institutes, programs, and libraries.

Joyce Chang

Drive Becarefully

Student writer Joyce Chang (b. 1975) was raised in northern California. Living in a predominantly white neighborhood and growing up in a traditional, close-knit Asian family, Chang struggled to integrate her Chinese heritage with mainstream American culture. In the essay that follows, written originally for an introductory writing class, she explores the problem of coming to terms with her mother's nonstandard English after reading Amy Tan's essay, "Mother Tongue."

"**M**y mother's 'limited' English limited my perception of her. I was ashamed of her English." Amy Tan's self-evaluation in her essay, "Mother Tongue," clung to my conscience as I continued reading. I could have said those words myself. I have definitely thought those words a million times. Like Tan, I too used to be ashamed of my mother's English. I used to shudder whenever I heard an incorrect verb tense, misplaced adverb, or incorrect pronoun come from her lips. Like many people, I couldn't look beyond my mother's incorrect grammar to see the intent and beauty behind her words.

My mother immigrated to the United States in the 1970s, speaking only a few words of English. As time went on, she gradually learned more and more words, although her sentence structure remained very basic. As a young working woman and mother of two, my mother didn't have much of a chance to improve her grammar. Taking ESL courses was not one of her immediate concerns—trying to beat rush hour Chicago traffic to get home in time to make dinner was what she worried about. So my mother went on using phrases like "He go to the store."

Since I had the advantage of being born and raised in the United States, my English abilities quickly surpassed those of my mother by the time I was in grade school. I knew all about auxiliary verbs, the subjunctive, and plurals—my mother didn't. I could form sentences like "He treated her as if she were still a child." For my mother to convey that same idea, she could only say, "He treat her like child."

My mother's comprehension of the English language was comparable to her speaking abilities. When I was with her, I learned early on not to try any of the complicated, flowery, descriptive sentences that I had been praised for in school. Anything beyond a simple subject-verb-object construction was poorly received. When I was very young, I did not think much about having to use a different English with my mother. The two Englishes in my life were just different—one was not better than the other. However, that feeling quickly changed in third grade.

5   My young mind could not always switch between the two Englishes with ease. I usually knew which English belonged in which world, but sometimes my Englishes crossed over. I remember one day in third grade when I was supposed to bring something for a "cultural show-and-tell." It must have been sometime in winter—around Chinese New Year. My mother had given me a "red bag" for show-and-tell. A "red bag" is an envelope that contains money. Chinese people give and receive these envelopes of money as gifts for the new year. As my mother described it to me, "The bag for good fortune . . . you rich for New Year." When I tried to explain the meaning of the red envelope to my class, I used my mother's words, "The bag for good fortune. . . ." I do not think my classmates noticed my grammatical shortcomings, or maybe they did notice but chose not to comment. In any case, my teacher had an alarmed look on her face and sharply demanded, "What did you say?" She seemed to be in complete bewilderment at how one of her students who spoke "good English" could suddenly speak "bad English." Thinking that she just didn't hear me the first time, I innocently repeated the exact same phrase I had said before.

"Where did you learn *that* English?" she questioned. "It's wrong! Please speak correctly!" she commanded.

After her admonishment, it took me a while to continue speaking. When I finally opened my mouth to utter my first word, all I could think of was, "I hope this is correct." I was relieved when I finished with no further interruptions.

Hearing my teacher say that my mother's English was wrong had a lasting impression on me. When I went home that day, all I could think about when my mother spoke was the "wrongness" of her English, and the "wrongness" of her as a person. I took her awkward phrases, sentence fragments, and other incorrect phrases as a sign that she somehow was "incorrect." I became irritated with her when she made grammatical mistakes at home. I became ashamed of her when she made those same mistakes outside of the house.

By the time I entered high school I was tired of being ashamed of my mother's English. I thought I would do her a favor and take on a mission to improve her English. The mission turned out to be a lot more difficult than I thought it would be. No matter how many times I would tell her something that she said was wrong, she would still say the same phrase over and over again. For example, whenever I left the house, my mother would say, "Drive becarefully." After the first time she said that, I told her it was wrong. I would then add, "The correct way to say that is 'drive carefully' or 'be careful driving.'" She would then nod and say good-bye. However, the next day as I headed out the door, mother would come up to me and say "drive becarefully" again. I would get incredibly frustrated because she never seemed to learn. I was glad, however, that at least I was the only one to hear such an "incorrect" statement.

10   One day, however, a friend of mine was with me as we headed out the door. As usual my mother screamed out "drive becarefully" as we walked toward the car. I immediately rolled my eyes and muttered, "It's 'drive carefully.' Get it right."

Later, as I drove my friend back home, she asked me a question that I will never forget. "Is it your mom who wants to improve her English or is it you who wants to 'improve' her?" I was stunned at first by my friend's question. I had no response. After a lot of thinking, I realized my friend was right. My mom was satisfied with her English. She could convey her thoughts and didn't care that she did it in a way that was different from the standard. She had no problem with her use of language—I did.

After that conversation, I began to accept the idea that there are many different Englishes and that one is not necessarily better than the other. As long as a person is understood, it is not necessary to speak textbook perfect English. Presently, I am very concerned with how people treat others who speak "limited" English. I understand how easy it is to misperceive and mistreat people. In her essay "Mother Tongue," Tan also writes about how people are perceived differently just because of their "limited" English. She describes the problems her mother encounters day to day, "people in department stores, at banks, and at restaurants did not take her seriously, did not give her good service, pretended not to understand her, or even acted as if they did not hear her." Although I am very angry when I read about how a person with "limited" English is mistreated, I still understand how it is all too easy for a person not to take someone seriously when he/she does not speak the same English as that person. It is also easy to assume a person who speaks "broken" English wants someone to help him "fix" it.

Now, when I find myself talking with people who speak "another" English, I try to look for the meaning, the intent of what they say, and ignore the perhaps awkward structure of their statements. Also when I encounter someone who speaks an English different from my own, I try not to assume that he or she wants to "improve" it.

As Tan concludes her essay, the importance of what is spoken lies in a person's ". . . intent . . . passion . . . imagery . . . and the nature of . . . thoughts." These are the things I now look for when someone speaks to me. Incorrect verb tenses, misplaced adverbs, and incorrect pronouns are less significant issues. As I begin to realize this more, I feel more comfortable with not only my mom's different English but my own. My mom's English is the one I grew up with at home. It is one of the Englishes I speak.

15   The other day I went home to help my mom run errands.

"Go to store," she said.

"Buy what?"

"Juice and eggs. Drive becarefully!" my mom warned.

I couldn't help but to smile. I like hearing that now.

QUESTIONS FOR DISCUSSION

1. How has Chang applied the insights and experiences of Amy Tan in "Mother Tongue" to her own relationship with her mother?
2. Could you identify with any aspects of Chang's feelings and attitudes about her mother's English or with her struggle to accept her mother for who she is rather than to "fix" her?
3. Do you agree or disagree with Chang's teacher's attitude and her definition of correct English? Explain your point of view.
4. Do you agree or disagree with Chang's conclusion, "As long as a person is understood, it is not necessary to speak textbook perfect English"?

Steven Holtzman

Don't Look Back

Steven Holtzman (b. 1947) is interested in computers, philosophy, and creativity. He holds both an undergraduate degree in Western and Eastern philosophy and a Ph.D. in computer science from the University of Edinburgh. He is also founder and vice president of Optimal Networks in Palo Alto, California. Using computer techniques, he has composed a number of musical works that have been performed in Europe and the United States, some of which can be found on a CD he has produced, Digital Mantras *(Shriek! Records, 1994). He also has written two books that examine the new types of creative expression possible in the age of computers and cyberspace:* Digital Mantras: The Language of Abstract and Virtual Worlds *(1994), and* Digital Mosaics: The Aesthetics of Cyberspace *(1997). Holtzman's books are aesthetically appealing as well as intellectually provocative. In the following excerpt from* Digital Mosaics, *he argues that we can't turn our backs on today's digital technology, as it is already an inextricable part of our lives.*

JOURNAL

Write about your experience with reading books and other texts online. Have you found this kind of reading rewarding? Why or why not?

For centuries, the book has been the primary vehicle for recording, storing, and transferring knowledge. But it's hard to imagine that paper will be the preferred format in a hundred years. Digital media will marginalize this earlier form of communication, relegating it to a niche just as music CDs have replaced LPs. The book will be forced to redefine itself, just as TV forced radio to redefine itself, and radio and TV together transformed the newspaper's role. The process is survival of the fittest—competition in the market to be a useful medium. Whatever the book's future is, clearly its role will never be the same. The book has lost its preeminence.

The print medium of newspaper is also fading. Almost every major newspaper in the United States is experiencing significant declines in circulation. (The exception is *USA Today*—characterized by itself as "TV on paper.") More than 70 percent of Americans under the age of thirty don't read newspapers. And this trend isn't about to change.

The powers of the media business today understand this. As part of the frenzied convergence of media, communications, and the digital world, we're witnessing a dizzying tangle of corporate alliances and mega-mergers. Companies are jockeying for position for this epochal change. The list includes many multibillion-dollar companies—AT&T, Bertelsmann, Disney, Microsoft, Time Warner, Viacom—and many, many more small startup technology companies. They all want to position themselves as preeminent new media companies.

Clinging to the Past

Members of the literary establishment can also see this imminent change. Yet, for the most part, they take a dim view of these new digital worlds. Beyond the loss of their cherished culture, what disturbs many critics is that they find new digital media like CD-ROMs and the World Wide Web completely unsatisfying.

5   The literacy critic Sven Birkerts eloquently laments that the generation growing up in the digital age is incapable of enjoying literature. Teaching at college has brought Birkerts to despair because his students aren't able to appreciate the literary culture he so values. After only a proudly self-confessed "glimpse of the future" of CD-ROMs, he declares he is "clinging all the more tightly to my books."

The disillusionment with the digital experience is summed up by the *New York Times Book Review* critic Sarah Lyall. She complains that multimedia CD-ROMs

> still don't come close to matching the experience of reading a paper-and-print book while curled up in a chair, in bed, on the train, under a tree, in an airplane. . . . After all, the modern book is the result of centuries of trial

and error during which people wrote on bark, on parchment, on vellum, on clay, on scrolls, on stone, chiseling characters into surfaces or copying them out by hand.

Okay, I thought as I read Birkerts and Lyall, these are members of a dying cultural heritage who—like seemingly every generation—are uncomfortable with the new. Unable to shift their perspective, they'll be casualties of change. After all, Birkerts boasts that he doesn't own a computer and still uses only a typewriter.

Birkerts clings not to his books, but to the past. I was reminded of a comment by the cultural critic William Irwin Thompson, who is also wary of the consequences of digital technology:

> It is not the literary intelligentsia of *The New York Review of Books* [or *The New York Times,* as the case may be] that is bringing forth this new culture, for it is as repugnant to them as the Reformation was to the Catholic Church. . . . This new cyberpunk, technological culture is brought forth by Top and Pop, electronic science and pop music, and both the hackers and the rockers are anti-intellectual and unsympathetic to the previous Mental level expressed by the genius of European civilization.

This helped me dismiss the backlash from those looking in the rearview mirror. But then I came across a book by Clifford Stoll.

Muddier Mud

10 Stoll, who was introduced to computers twenty years ago, is a longtime member of the digerati. In his book *Silicon Snake Oil,* he claims to expose the true emptiness of the digital experience.

In opening, Stoll explains that "every time someone mentions MUDs [multi-user dungeons, a type of interactive adventure game] and virtual reality, I think of a genuine reality with muddier mud than anything a computer can deliver." Stoll then nostalgically recounts the story of the first time he went crawling through caves in his college days. "We start in, trailing a string through the muddy tunnel—everything's covered with gunk, as are the six of us crawling behind [the guide]. Not your ordinary slimy, brown, backyard mud, either. This is the goop of inner-earth that works its way into your hair, socks, and underwear."

Stoll's general theme: "You're viewing a world that doesn't exist. During that week you spend online, you could have planted a tomato garden. . . . While the Internet beckons brightly, seductively flashing an icon of knowledge-as-power, this nonplace lures us to surrender our time on earth."

I suppose this excludes any experience that might distract us from the real—a novel, a Beethoven symphony, a movie. (A tomato garden?)

And then we get the same theme that Birtkerts and Lyall hit on.

I've rarely met anyone who prefers to read digital books. I don't want my morning newspaper delivered over computer, or a CD-ROM stuffed with National Geographic photographs. Call me a troglodyte; I'd rather peruse those photos alongside my sweetheart, catch the newspaper on the way to work, and page through a real book. . . . Now, I'm hardly a judge of aesthetics, but of the scores of electronic multimedia productions I've seen, I don't remember any as being beautiful.

A CD-ROM Is Not a Book

15   These laments totally miss the point. No, a CD-ROM isn't a book. Nor is a virtual world—whether a MUD or a simulation of rolling in the mud— the same as the real experience. This is *exactly* the point! A CD-ROM isn't a book; it's something completely new and different. A MUD on the Internet isn't like mud in a cave. A virtual world isn't the real world; it offers possibilities unlike anything we've known before.

Birkerts, Lyall, and Stoll dismiss the digital experience to justify staying in the familiar and comfortable worlds of their past. Yet what's exciting to me about these digital worlds is precisely that they're new, they're unfamiliar, and they're our future.

It's not that I disagree with the literati's assertions. We will lose part of our literary culture and tradition. Kids today are so attuned to the rapid rhythms of MTV that they're unresponsive to the patient patterns of literary prose. They are indeed so seduced by the flickeringly powerful identifications of the screen as to be deaf to the inner voices of print. Literary culture—like classical music and opera—will become marginalized as mainstream culture pursues a digital path.

There never will be a substitute for a book. And today's multimedia CD-ROM—even surfing the World Wide Web—is still for the most part a static and unsatisfying experience. But it's rather early to conclude anything about their ultimate potential.

Patience Is a Virtue

It puzzles me that there are people who expect that, in almost no time at all, we'd find great works by those who have mastered the subtleties of such completely new digital worlds. We are seeing the first experiments with a new medium. It took a long time to master the medium of film. Or the book, for that matter. It will also take time to master new digital worlds.

20   It's challenging to create a multimedia digital world today. The enabling technologies that will make radically new digital worlds possible— Java, VRML, and a string of acronymic technologies—are still emerging. Artists, writers, and musicians must also be software programmers. Today, a rare combination of passion, artistry, and technical knowledge is

required. Yet, over time, these skills will become common. Even more important than the technical mastery of new digital media, a new conceptual framework and aesthetic must also be established for digital worlds.

When this conceptual and technical mastery is achieved, we'll discover the true possibilities of digital expression. In a few decades—or possibly in just five years—we'll look on today's explorations as primitive. Until then, we will continue to explore these new digital worlds and seek to learn their true potential.

Embracing the Digital

There will be nothing to replace the reading of a book or newspaper in bed. Curling up by a fireside to read a poem with an electronic tablet won't have the same intimacy as doing so with a book. But curling up by a fireside with an electronic tablet is itself simply an example of substituting electronic technology for an existing medium—extrapolating from today's flat-paneled handheld computers to an "electronic book." We need to develop a new aesthetic—a digital aesthetic. And the emerging backlash from the literati makes clear to me how urgently we need it.

When we've mastered digital media, we won't be talking about anything that has much to do with the antiquated form of the book. I imagine myself curled up in bed with laser images projected on my retinas, allowing me to view and travel through an imaginary three-dimensional virtual world. A story about the distant past flashes a quaint image of a young woman sitting and reading a book, which seems just as remote as the idea of a cluster of Navajo Indians sitting around a campfire and listening to a master of the long-lost tradition of storytelling. In a hundred years, we'll think of the book as we do the storyteller today.

Will we lose a part of our cultural heritage as we assimilate new media? No doubt. Is this disturbing? Absolutely. Today's traditional media will be further marginalized. Is there much value in decrying an inevitable future? Probably not. The music of *today* is written on electric instruments. Hollywood creates our theater. And soon digital media will be *our* media. Digital technology and new digital media—for better or worse—are here to stay.

25   That's not to say that all things digital are good. Perhaps, like the Luddites in Britain during the first half of the nineteenth century, the literati raise a flag of warning, raise awareness, and create debate, debunking some of the myths of a utopian digital future. But in the end, for better or for worse, the efforts of the Luddites were futile when it came to stopping the industrial revolution.

Likewise, today you can't turn off the Internet. Digital technology isn't going away. There are already thousands of multimedia CD-ROMs and hundreds of thousands of sites on the World Wide Web; soon there will be thousands of channels of on-demand digital worlds.

Digital technology is part of our lives, a part of our lives that we know will only continue to grow. We can't afford to dismiss it. Rather we must embrace it—not indiscriminately, but thoughtfully. We must seize the opportunities generated by the birth of a new medium to do things we've never been able to do before. Don't look back.

QUESTIONS FOR DISCUSSION

1. Why does Holtzman believe that the power and popularity of books and newspapers are fading? Do you agree?
2. According to William Thompson, why do the members of the "literary intelligentsia" find the "new culture" of CD-ROMs and the Internet to be repugnant? What other reasons for the rejection might there be?
3. What is computer scientist Cliff Stoll's primary reason for rejecting the Internet as a learning experience? How does Holtzman attempt to refute Stoll? Is he successful? With whose point of view do you agree?
4. What features of the book do the traditional critics such as Birkerts consider to be irreplaceable? Do these critics have valid arguments? Explain.
5. What do you think Holtzman means by his concluding statement that we must embrace digital media "not indiscriminately, but thoughtfully"? Do you think his essay is a good example of the thoughtful approach he recommends? Explain your point of view.

CONNECTION

Compare Holtzman's view of reading and its significance with those of Motoko Rich. How would Holtzman respond to Molly Thomas's critique of his position (see page 54)?

― IDEAS FOR WRITING

1. Write an essay in which you compare your own experience with the World Wide Web or a learning program on a multimedia CD-ROM disk to reading a regular book or textbook on the same subject. Which experience did you find more useful and worthwhile? Use examples to support your ideas.
2. Write an essay that predicts the changing roles that books and printed media will play in contrast to the roles of the Internet and other digital media in the next five years. Consider specific environments such as the home, schools, the workplace, and governmental agencies.

Molly Thomas

Response to "Don't Look Back"

*Student writer Molly Thomas wrote the following essay after reading "Don't
Look Back," included in this chapter. Notice how she writes using a number
of the response strategies suggested at the beginning of the chapter: giving
some background on the piece and its central debate, then moving to analyze
some of its strategies of refutation and audience, and finally taking her own
evaluative position on the piece itself and the larger debate over technology
and the book.*

Today the debate over the long-lasting effects of digital technology on
literacy and the culture of the book provoke many heated and widespread disputes that often pit different generations against one another.
In "Don't Look Back," a chapter from his book *Digital Mosaics,* Steven
Holtzman heralds the onset of the digital age and the opportunities it
will provide, dismissing the extreme negative critics of digital learning
and culture even as he expresses regret about its potential effects on the
high culture of books and print literacy. Holtzman's arguments are subtly contradictory enough to undermine some of his initial claims supporting technology.

In both the pro and antitechnology sides of the argument, there is an
impending feeling that the spread of digital technology is inevitable.
For Holtzman, this fact rests on the nature of the technology itself. He
writes, "For centuries, the book has been the primary vehicle for recording, storing, and transferring knowledge. But it's hard to imagine that
paper will be the preferred format in 100 years." In Holtzman's model,
technology takes the more active role, driven by sheer Darwinian evolution and a search for convenience. As is the case with most technological
developments, digital technology itself develops at a rate far faster than
the consideration of its moral and cultural implications. For Holtzman,
the argument seems to be simply over the technology itself, the
actual practical differences between writing information on a piece of

paper versus a computer. Later on in his argument, Holtzman goes on to compare the opponents of digital technology to the machine-smashing Luddites who rebelled against the rise of industrialization in nineteenth century Britain. The connotation today of a "Luddite" is of someone who appears antiquated in his or her approach to the world and as a result out of tune with reality. According to this view, people may have a say in how technology is created, but once it is in circulation it becomes self-propagating and as a result any opposition to its spread is futile.

In disqualifying opposition to his pro-digital argument, Holtzman quotes critic William Irwin Thompson who observes, "This new cyber-punk, technological culture is brought forth by . . . electronic science and pop music, and both the hackers and the rockers are anti-intellectual and unsympathetic to the previous Mental level expressed by the genius of European civilization." For Thompson, these digital advancements are less about the technology itself and instead are more defined by the community that fosters technological growth. This opinion is clearly very one-sided, and easy to refute as it only attributes digital creativity to those who have been traditionally classified as outlying, destructive and "anti-intellectual" deviants of modern culture such as hackers and rockers. From this perspective, the debate over digital technology versus books is less about the technology itself; it rather centers on how technology is fostered by a disinterest or aversion to learning and the intellectual.

Holtzman goes on to cite another dissenting opinion of technology from author Clifford Stoll who argues, "During that week you spend on-line, you could have planted a tomato garden. . . .While the Internet beckons brightly, seductively flashing an icon of knowledge-as-power, this nonplace lures us to surrender our time on earth." Holtzman is right to point out ironically that books and symphonies similarly deter us from direct, physical ways of acquiring knowledge through observation and action, although he could have developed his critique further. Stoll's imagery of the Internet seducing its youthful viewers is really a stereotype or cartoon image of evil technological tools that inevitably alienate youngsters from the world of experiential learning. Stoll is creating an either-or dilemma in response to technology: Why should manual labor provide more essential understanding than the Internet, rather than an equal and complementary insight into the world around us and the distant worlds of foreign cultures, geographies, and planetary systems?

5   Despite his deft refutation of Stoll, Holtzman's argument loses some of its power through the use of rhetorical strategies that suggest his audience is predominantly one that shares his point of view. For example,

after excerpting Thompson's quote on "cyberpunks" Holtzman states his response very briefly: "This helped me dismiss the backlash from those looking in the rearview mirror." Throughout the first half of his piece, Holtzman creates a distance between himself and those who espouse an anti-digital perspective by creating a casual dialogue-like tone between himself and the reader as he walks through the process of reaffirming his own beliefs. Again we see from the use of dismissive words like "rearview mirror" and "backlash" that those who are responding as antiquated "Luddites" are only protesting a technology that has and will inevitably spread.

However, Holtzman seems to draw back from fully supporting technology-based culture and learning by espousing some of the rhetoric associated with the opposing side of the debate. He writes, "There never will be a substitute for a book. And today's multimedia CD-ROM—even surfing the World Wide Web—is still for the most part a static and unsatisfying experience." It's true that no technology will be able to replicate a book exactly, but it's certainly an exaggeration to suggest that multimedia provides an "unsatisfying experience." Like the authors he criticizes, Holtzman seems to make a hierarchical distinction between reading and using the Internet. It might have helped for him to qualify this statement by specifying in what ways books *and* the Internet can be both rewarding and not. Holtzman goes on to inquire, "Will we lose part of our cultural heritage as we assimilate new media? No doubt. Is this disturbing? Absolutely." Here again, he fails to explain exactly what will be lost and what new culture might replace it. Although Holtzman begins his piece by suggesting that his argument is fundamentally one over the fated evolution of technology, he ends by conceding that books still give us insight into a world that will never be matched by technology.

Why is it, then, that books are unquestioningly associated with learning and intellectual growth while technology becomes defined as just the opposite? The answer lies in the fact that learning itself is frequently viewed as a tool of privilege; those who feel that the digital world is alien to them in turn cling to traditional means of learning that they do understand, means which are slowly becoming alien to today's youngest generations. As Holtzman concedes, "Kids today are so attuned to the rapid rhythms of MTV that they're unresponsive to the patient patterns of literary prose. . . . Literary culture—like classical music and opera—will become marginalized as mainstream culture pursues a digital path." Unlike the technological arguments that we saw earlier, the distinction he now makes seems more class-based. It would be sad indeed if books did meet the same fate that classical music and opera have met in modern culture, if they become part of a culturally elitist group that excludes its membership from mass culture. Holtzman cites one writer who prides himself in using only a typewriter and not even owning a computer. Many, like this writer, hide behind the façade of intellectualism to avoid integrating themselves into the digital world. In a sense, Holtzman seems to accept this position by similarly classifying books into a unique, unchanging and irreplaceable aspect of culture instead of seeing them as an evolving means of cultural communication. It's only when the cultures of readers and technology users become polarized that we really have to worry about one group having a superficial relationship with their surrounding world.

While opponents of the digital revolution claim that technology is "dumbing us down" and drawing us away from real learning, the reality is quite different. To the average person with access to an inexpensive home computer and a modem, the Internet alone has opened up doors to more sources of knowledge than anyone in history has ever had access to. For thousands of years, this type of access to vast knowledge contained previously only in world-class libraries has been limited by access to high-level literacy and quality education to a lucky few. Today the Internet has become the digital printing press of our generation. It's unfortunate, then, that there are those who still wish to deter the development of digital technology, and in turn maintain access to knowledge and learning as a privilege, not a right. Now that this privilege has become a widespread commodity, we shouldn't discourage its growth; rather we should help it to evolve into a universal tool for cultural expression.

QUESTIONS FOR DISCUSSION

1. In the first paragraph, how clearly does Thomas state both the subject of Holtzman's essay and his perspective on the debate between pro and antitechnology forces? Is her position on the essay clear?
2. In the second paragraph, how does Thomas use references to "Luddites" and Darwinian evolution theories to contrast the conflicting positions on technology of Holtzman and his opponents? Is her explanation of these terms clear?
3. Thomas uses both paraphrase and direct quoting from Holtzman's essay, as well as quoting and paraphrasing some of his critics. How effectively are these quotations and paraphrases used? Are there places where you would have liked to see quoting rather than paraphrasing, or more introduction or explanation of a quotation?
4. In the two paragraphs before the conclusion, Thomas criticizes Holtzman for conceding too much to the antitechnology argument, which comes from a "high culture," traditional perspective. Does her criticism seem justified? Why or why not?

Motoko Rich

Literacy Debate: Online, R U Really Reading?

New York Times July 27, 2008

Motoko Rich was born in Los Angeles and raised in Petaluma, California. She came East after high school to study at Yale, graduating in 1991 with a B.A. in history. She also received a Mellon Fellowship to study at Cambridge University, where she was awarded a degree in English in 1993. Rich was a reporter for the Financial Times *in London and at the* Wall Street Journal *before getting a job as a reporter for the* New York Times *in 2003. At the* Times *she first worked in the real estate area, becoming publishing beat reporter in 2006, covering corporate mergers, administrative and editorial changes in publishing, as well as new books and publishing scandals such as false memoirs. Rich has written several recent articles on reading, such as "A Good Mystery: Why We Read"(2007), as well as the following 2008 analysis of the debate over online reading and the decline of reading interest and ability among youth.*

JOURNAL

Do you think that reading on the Internet enhances reading skills? Why or why not?

Books are not Nadia Konyk's thing. Her mother, hoping to entice her, brings them home from the library, but Nadia rarely shows an interest.

Instead, like so many other teenagers, Nadia, 15, is addicted to the Internet. She regularly spends at least six hours a day in front of the computer here in this suburb southwest of Cleveland.

A slender, chatty blonde who wears black-framed plastic glasses, Nadia checks her e-mail and peruses myyearbook.com, a social networking site, reading messages or posting updates on her mood. She searches for music videos on YouTube and logs onto Gaia Online, a role-playing site where members fashion alternate identities as cutesy cartoon characters. But she spends most of her time on quizilla.com or fanfiction.net, reading and commenting on stories written by other users and based on books, television shows or movies.

Her mother, Deborah Konyk, would prefer that Nadia, who gets A's and B's at school, read books for a change. But at this point, Ms. Konyk said, "I'm just pleased that she reads something anymore."

5   Children like Nadia lie at the heart of a passionate debate about just what it means to read in the digital age. The discussion is playing out among educational policy makers and reading experts around the world, and within groups like the National Council of Teachers of English and the International Reading Association.

As teenagers' scores on standardized reading tests have declined or stagnated, some argue that the hours spent prowling the Internet are the enemy of reading—diminishing literacy, wrecking attention spans and destroying a precious common culture that exists only through the reading of books.

But others say the Internet has created a new kind of reading, one that schools and society should not discount. The Web inspires a teenager like Nadia, who might otherwise spend most of her leisure time watching television, to read and write.

Even accomplished book readers like Zachary Sims, 18, of Old Greenwich, Conn., crave the ability to quickly find different points of view on a subject and converse with others online. Some children with dyslexia or other learning difficulties, like Hunter Gaudet, 16, of Somers, Conn., have found it far more comfortable to search and read online.

At least since the invention of television, critics have warned that electronic media would destroy reading. What is different now, some literacy experts say, is that spending time on the Web, whether it is looking up something on Google or even britneyspears.org, entails some engagement with text.

Setting Expectations

10   Few who believe in the potential of the Web deny the value of books. But they argue that it is unrealistic to expect all children to read "To Kill a Mockingbird" or "Pride and Prejudice" for fun. And those who prefer staring at a television or mashing buttons on a game console, they say, can still benefit from reading on the Internet. In fact, some literacy experts say that online reading skills will help children fare better when they begin looking for digital-age jobs.

Some Web evangelists say children should be evaluated for their proficiency on the Internet just as they are tested on their print reading comprehension. Starting next year, some countries will participate in new international assessments of digital literacy, but the United States, for now, will not.

Clearly, reading in print and on the Internet are different. On paper, text has a predetermined beginning, middle and end, where readers focus for a sustained period on one author's vision. On the Internet, readers skate through cyberspace at will and, in effect, compose their own beginnings, middles and ends.

Young people "aren't as troubled as some of us older folks are by reading that doesn't go in a line," said Rand J. Spiro, a professor of educational psychology at Michigan State University who is studying reading practices on the Internet. "That's a good thing because the world doesn't go in a line, and the world isn't organized into separate compartments or chapters."

Some traditionalists warn that digital reading is the intellectual equivalent of empty calories. Often, they argue, writers on the Internet employ a cryptic argot that vexes teachers and parents. Zigzagging through a cornucopia of words, pictures, video and sounds, they say, distracts more than strengthens readers. And many youths spend most of their time on the Internet playing games or sending instant messages, activities that involve minimal reading at best.

15   Last fall the National Endowment for the Arts issued a sobering report linking flat or declining national reading test scores among teenagers with the slump in the proportion of adolescents who said they read for fun.

According to Department of Education data cited in the report, just over a fifth of 17-year-olds said they read almost every day for fun in 2004, down from nearly a third in 1984. Nineteen percent of 17-year-olds said they never or hardly ever read for fun in 2004, up from 9 percent in 1984. (It was unclear whether they thought of what they did on the Internet as "reading.")

"Whatever the benefits of newer electronic media," Dana Gioia, the chairman of the N.E.A., wrote in the report's introduction, "they provide no measurable substitute for the intellectual and personal development initiated and sustained by frequent reading."

Children are clearly spending more time on the Internet. In a study of 2,032 representative 8- to 18-year-olds, the Kaiser Family Foundation found that nearly half used the Internet on a typical day in 2004, up from just under a quarter in 1999. The average time these children spent online on a typical day rose to one hour and 41 minutes in 2004, from 46 minutes in 1999.

The question of how to value different kinds of reading is complicated because people read for many reasons. There is the level required of daily life—to follow the instructions in a manual or to analyze a mortgage contract. Then there is a more sophisticated level that opens the doors to elite education and professions. And, of course, people read for entertainment, as well as for intellectual or emotional rewards.

20   It is perhaps that final purpose that book champions emphasize the most.

"Learning is not to be found on a printout," David McCullough, the Pulitzer Prize-winning biographer, said in a commencement address at

Boston College in May. "It's not on call at the touch of the finger. Learning is acquired mainly from books, and most readily from great books."

What's Best for Nadia?

Deborah Konyk always believed it was essential for Nadia and her 8-year-old sister, Yashca, to read books. She regularly read aloud to the girls and took them to library story hours.

"Reading opens up doors to places that you probably will never get to visit in your lifetime, to cultures, to worlds, to people," Ms. Konyk said.

Ms. Konyk, who took a part-time job at a dollar store chain a year and a half ago, said she did not have much time to read books herself. There are few books in the house. But after Yashca was born, Ms. Konyk spent the baby's nap time reading the Harry Potter novels to Nadia, and she regularly brought home new titles from the library.

25   Despite these efforts, Nadia never became a big reader. Instead, she became obsessed with Japanese anime cartoons on television and comics like "Sailor Moon." Then, when she was in the sixth grade, the family bought its first computer. When a friend introduced Nadia to fanfiction.net, she turned off the television and started reading online.

Now she regularly reads stories that run as long as 45 Web pages. Many of them have elliptical plots and are sprinkled with spelling and grammatical errors. One of her recent favorites was "My absolutely, perfect normal life . . . ARE YOU CRAZY? NOT!," a story based on the anime series "Beyblade."

In one scene the narrator, Aries, hitches a ride with some masked men and one of them pulls a knife on her. "Just then I notice (Like finally) something sharp right in front of me," Aries writes. "I gladly took it just like that until something terrible happen. . . ."

Nadia said she preferred reading stories online because "you could add your own character and twist it the way you want it to be."

"So like in the book somebody could die," she continued, "but you could make it so that person doesn't die or make it so like somebody else dies who you don't like."

30   Nadia also writes her own stories. She posted "Dieing Isn't Always Bad," about a girl who comes back to life as half cat, half human, on both fanfiction.net and quizilla.com.

Nadia said she wanted to major in English at college and someday hopes to be published. She does not see a problem with reading few books. "No one's ever said you should read more books to get into college," she said.

The simplest argument for why children should read in their leisure time is that it makes them better readers. According to federal statistics, students who say they read for fun once a day score significantly higher on reading tests than those who say they never do.

Reading skills are also valued by employers. A 2006 survey by the Conference Board, which conducts research for business leaders, found that nearly 90 percent of employers rated "reading comprehension" as "very important" for workers with bachelor's degrees. Department of Education statistics also show that those who score higher on reading tests tend to earn higher incomes.

Critics of reading on the Internet say they see no evidence that increased Web activity improves reading achievement. "What we are losing in this country and presumably around the world is the sustained, focused, linear attention developed by reading," said Mr. Gioia of the N.E.A. "I would believe people who tell me that the Internet develops reading if I did not see such a universal decline in reading ability and reading comprehension on virtually all tests."

35   Nicholas Carr sounded a similar note in "Is Google Making Us Stupid?" in the current issue of the *Atlantic* magazine. Warning that the Web was changing the way he—and others—think, he suggested that the effects of Internet reading extended beyond the falling test scores of adolescence. "What the Net seems to be doing is chipping away my capacity for concentration and contemplation," he wrote, confessing that he now found it difficult to read long books.

Literacy specialists are just beginning to investigate how reading on the Internet affects reading skills. A recent study of more than 700 low-income, mostly Hispanic and black sixth through 10th graders in Detroit found that those students read more on the Web than in any other medium, though they also read books. The only kind of reading that related to higher academic performance was frequent novel reading, which predicted better grades in English class and higher overall grade point averages.

Elizabeth Birr Moje, a professor at the University of Michigan who led the study, said novel reading was similar to what schools demand already. But on the Internet, she said, students are developing new reading skills that are neither taught nor evaluated in school.

One early study showed that giving home Internet access to low-income students appeared to improve standardized reading test scores and school grades. "These were kids who would typically not be reading in their free time," said Linda A. Jackson, a psychology professor at Michigan State who led the research. "Once they're on the Internet, they're reading."

Neurological studies show that learning to read changes the brain's circuitry. Scientists speculate that reading on the Internet may also affect the brain's hard wiring in a way that is different from book reading.

40   "The question is, does it change your brain in some beneficial way?" said Guinevere F. Eden, director of the Center for the Study of Learning at Georgetown University. "The brain is malleable and adapts to its environment. Whatever the pressures are on us to succeed, our brain will try and deal with it."

    Some scientists worry that the fractured experience typical of the Internet could rob developing readers of crucial skills. "Reading a book, and taking the time to ruminate and make inferences and engage the imaginational processing, is more cognitively enriching, without doubt, than the short little bits that you might get if you're into the 30-second digital mode," said Ken Pugh, a cognitive neuroscientist at Yale who has studied brain scans of children reading.

But This Is Reading Too

Web proponents believe that strong readers on the Web may eventually surpass those who rely on books. Reading five Web sites, an op-ed article and a blog post or two, experts say, can be more enriching than reading one book.

    "It takes a long time to read a 400-page book," said Mr. Spiro of Michigan State. "In a tenth of the time," he said, the Internet allows a reader to "cover a lot more of the topic from different points of view."

    Zachary Sims, the Old Greenwich, Conn., teenager, often stays awake until 2 or 3 in the morning reading articles about technology or politics—his current passions—on up to 100 Web sites.

45   "On the Internet, you can hear from a bunch of people," said Zachary, who will attend Columbia University this fall. "They may not be pedigreed academics. They may be someone in their shed with a conspiracy theory. But you would weigh that."

    Though he also likes to read books (earlier this year he finished, and loved, *The Fountainhead* by Ayn Rand), Zachary craves interaction with fellow readers on the Internet. "The Web is more about a conversation," he said. "Books are more one-way."

    The kinds of skills Zachary has developed—locating information quickly and accurately, corroborating findings on multiple sites—may seem obvious to heavy Web users. But the skills can be cognitively demanding.

    Web readers are persistently weak at judging whether information is trustworthy. In one study, Donald J. Leu, who researches literacy and technology at the University of Connecticut, asked 48 students to look at a spoof Web site (http://zapatopi.net/treeoctopus/) about a mythical species known as the "Pacific Northwest tree octopus." Nearly 90 percent of them missed the joke and deemed the site a reliable source.

Some literacy experts say that reading itself should be redefined. Interpreting videos or pictures, they say, may be as important a skill as analyzing a novel or a poem.

50   "Kids are using sound and images so they have a world of ideas to put together that aren't necessarily language oriented," said Donna E. Alvermann, a professor of language and literacy education at the University of Georgia. "Books aren't out of the picture, but they're only one way of experiencing information in the world today."

A Lifelong Struggle

In the case of Hunter Gaudet, the Internet has helped him feel more comfortable with a new kind of reading. A varsity lacrosse player in Somers, Conn., Hunter has struggled most of his life to read. After learning he was dyslexic in the second grade, he was placed in special education classes and a tutor came to his home three hours a week. When he entered high school, he dropped the special education classes, but he still reads books only when forced, he said.

In a book, "they go through a lot of details that aren't really needed," Hunter said. "Online just gives you what you need, nothing more or less."

When researching the 19th-century Chief Justice Roger B. Taney for one class, he typed Taney's name into Google and scanned the Wikipedia entry and other biographical sites. Instead of reading an entire page, he would type in a search word like "college" to find Taney's alma mater, assembling his information nugget by nugget.

Experts on reading difficulties suggest that for struggling readers, the Web may be a better way to glean information. "When you read online there are always graphics," said Sally Shaywitz, the author of *Overcoming Dyslexia* and a Yale professor. "I think it's just more comfortable and—I hate to say easier—but it more meets the needs of somebody who might not be a fluent reader."

55   Karen Gaudet, Hunter's mother, a regional manager for a retail chain who said she read two or three business books a week, hopes Hunter will eventually discover a love for books. But she is confident that he has the reading skills he needs to succeed.

"Based on where technology is going and the world is going," she said, "he's going to be able to leverage it."

When he was in seventh grade, Hunter was one of 89 students who participated in a study comparing performance on traditional state reading tests with a specially designed Internet reading test. Hunter, who scored in the lowest 10 percent on the traditional test, spent 12 weeks learning how to use the Web for a science class before taking the Internet test. It was composed of three sets of directions asking the students to search for information online, determine which sites were reliable and explain their reasoning.

Hunter scored in the top quartile. In fact, about a third of the students in the study, led by Professor Leu, scored below average on traditional reading tests but did well on the Internet assessment.

The Testing Debate

To date, there have been few large-scale appraisals of Web skills. The Educational Testing Service, which administers the SAT, has developed a digital literacy test known as iSkills that requires students to solve informational problems by searching for answers on the Web. About 80 colleges and a handful of high schools have administered the test so far.

60   But according to Stephen Denis, product manager at ETS, of the more than 20,000 students who have taken the iSkills test since 2006, only 39 percent of four-year college freshmen achieved a score that represented "core functional levels" in Internet literacy.

Now some literacy experts want the federal tests known as the nation's report card to include a digital reading component. So far, the traditionalists have held sway: The next round, to be administered to fourth and eighth graders in 2009, will test only print reading comprehension.

Mary Crovo of the National Assessment Governing Board, which creates policies for the national tests, said several members of a committee that sets guidelines for the reading tests believed large numbers of low-income and rural students might not have regular Internet access, rendering measurements of their online skills unfair.

Some simply argue that reading on the Internet is not something that needs to be tested—or taught.

"Nobody has taught a single kid to text message," said Carol Jago of the National Council of Teachers of English and a member of the testing guidelines committee. "Kids are smart. When they want to do something, schools don't have to get involved."

65   Michael L. Kamil, a professor of education at Stanford who lobbied for an Internet component as chairman of the reading test guidelines committee, disagreed. Students "are going to grow up having to be highly competent on the Internet," he said. "There's no reason to make them discover how to be highly competent if we can teach them."

The United States is diverging from the policies of some other countries. Next year, for the first time, the Organization for Economic Cooperation and Development, which administers reading, math and science tests to a sample of 15-year-old students in more than 50 countries, will add an electronic reading component. The United States, among other countries, will not participate. A spokeswoman for the

Institute of Education Sciences, the research arm of the Department of Education, said an additional test would overburden schools.

Even those who are most concerned about the preservation of books acknowledge that children need a range of reading experiences. "Some of it is the informal reading they get in e-mails or on Web sites," said Gay Ivey, a professor at James Madison University who focuses on adolescent literacy. "I think they need it all."

Web junkies can occasionally be swept up in a book. After Nadia read Elie Wiesel's Holocaust memoir *Night* in her freshman English class, Ms. Konyk brought home another Holocaust memoir, *I Have Lived a Thousand Years,* by Livia Bitton-Jackson.

Nadia was riveted by heartbreaking details of life in the concentration camps. "I was trying to imagine this and I was like, I can't do this," she said. "It was just so—wow."

70   Hoping to keep up the momentum, Ms. Konyk brought home another book, *Silverboy,* a fantasy novel. Nadia made it through one chapter before she got engrossed in the Internet fan fiction again.

QUESTIONS FOR DISCUSSION

1. Why is Rich's lead-in an example of Nadia Konyk's pattern of reading novels and reading on the Internet an effective technique?
2. What questions focus this essay?
3. What do research and evidence suggest about the impact of youth's reading on the Internet? Why do experts offer a variety of answers to the questions that focus the essay? How do you think children and youth would answer these questions? For example, how would Nadia see the advantages of reading books and articles as opposed to reading online?
4. Why are neurologists concerned with how reading on the Internet affects the way that the brain develops?
5. What theories do tests about the impact of reading on the Internet reveal?
6. Why does Rich return to and conclude with Nadia's reading experiences?

CONNECTION

Compare Holtzman's ideas about reading in a digital age with Rich's and the individuals she interviewed (see page 48).

IDEAS FOR WRITING

1. Write an essay that explores the insights that you gained from reading Rich's article. Does the evidence she presents help you to draw

conclusions? Is the evidence confusing or effective? Give specific examples of research and evidence that confirm your ideas about digital literacy.

2. Write an argument that presents your point of view on the impact of digital literacy and reading on your future as a college student and a working professional. Which skills will you be able to apply to the profession you choose to pursue?

RELATED WEB SITES

Motoko Rich – The New York Times

`http://topics.nytimes.com/top/reference/timestopics/`
`people/r/motoko_rich/index.html?inline=nyt-per`

This Web site houses ten pages of links to articles written by Rich. Each article has a brief summary introducing the link.

TOPICS FOR RESEARCH AND WRITING

1. Drawing on evidence from the selections in this chapter such as the essays by King, Woolf, and Stafford, as well as outside research and your own experiences, write an essay that examines the role of dreams and the unconscious mind in the reading and writing processes.

2. Although several authors in this chapter discuss ways in which they have been influenced to become readers and writers, in contrast, Rich discusses reasons why people in today's society prefer to practice their reading and writing on the Internet and feel that digital literacy is an essential reading, writing, and critical-thinking skill. Taking into consideration the experiences of these writers, as well as those of others you have read about or interviewed, write an essay in which you discuss the advantages and disadvantages of both methods.

3. Tan, Woolf, and King value reading and writing as processes of self-discovery and healing. Write an essay in which you explore this perspective on reading and writing, taking into account these writers' ideas, those of other writers you read about, as well as your own experiences. Review the essays in Chapter Two, "Memory" for more ideas.

4. Woolf and Tan examine the social, ethical, and spiritual values involved in the art of writing. Taking into account their ideas and those of other authors that explore the same theme, write an essay that discusses several of the ways that reading and writing have a positive influence on beliefs, values, and social behavior.

5. Writers in the chapter such as Stafford, King, and Woolf present insights into the nature of creativity and the creative process. After doing some further research into this issue, write an essay in which you present and evaluate several current theories about creative thinking and the creative process in writing.

6. Holtzman and Rich suggest that the wide availability of computers, e-mail, and Internet chat groups is changing the way writers work and relate to their audience. After doing some research into new Web-based literary ideas, writers' groups, and online publications, write an essay about new directions for writing and interactions of writers and audiences that are arising as a direct result of the cyberspace revolution.

7. See one of the following films that approach the life of the writer and/or the reader: *The Postman, Naked Lunch, Misery, The Color Purple, Shakespeare in Love, Finding Forrester, Wonder Boys, Dead Poet's Society, The Swimming Pool, Sylvia, Adaptation, Neverland, Roman de Gare,* and *Atonement.* Making reference to such elements of the film as plot, theme, dialogue, voice over, characters, images, and visual symbolism, write an essay that discusses the ways in which the film explores the inner world of the writer and/or the reader.

Journeys in Memory

Peggie Mazziotta/Renee Rhyner
Untitled photograph (1961)

Write about and describe a memory or an old photograph from your childhood that captures how you saw and felt about yourself and your surroundings at the time.

In the New Age the Daughters of Memory shall become the Daughters of Inspiration.

          WILLIAM BLAKE

If I approach writing from memory with the assumption that I know what I wish to say, I assume that intentionality is running the show. Things are not that simple.

          PATRICIA HAMPL

Often I felt as though I was in a trance at my typewriter, that the shape of a particular memory was decided not by my conscious mind but by all that is dark and deep within me, unconscious but present.

          BELL HOOKS
          Writing Autobiography

THEMATIC INTRODUCTION

Self-concept, imagination, dreams, and memories — all are born in childhood. A person's identity as a writer begins there, too. Through writing about your memories, you will begin to rediscover yourself through places, people, events, and stories that are still alive in your mind. These formative memories may have kindled your dreams while creating the foundation of your self-concept. Because writing is a process of self-discovery that has its roots in childhood, some of the poems, essays, and stories that we have included address issues of childhood identity in relationship to dreams and fantasies, expectations, and goals. In many of the selections that follow, essayists and fiction writers create vividly narrated moments, some positive and some painful, from their earliest remembered experiences. Some of the selections present perspectives on the nature and the effects of memory itself.

The first chapter essay, bell hooks's "Writing Autobiography," explores psychological blocks leading to the author's difficulty in telling her own true story, the "secrecy and silence" that keep our painful memories locked inside us. The following two selections present traumatic, turning-point memories of family life. In "Silent Dancing," Judith Ortiz Cofer explores how her childhood memories of her native Puerto Rican culture and her immigrant relatives continue to have a powerful influence on her understanding and fears about her life in the United States. Finally, Saira Shah, in her memoir "The Storyteller's Daughter," narrates the attempts the author's father makes to re-create through literature and cuisine the feeling and sensations of their family's vanished homeland in prewar Afghanistan.

The three essays that follow reflect on the importance of grandparents and the legacy that they leave even after their death. In "The Best Seat in the House," Melissa Burns explores her poignant recollections of her grandfather, who helped to provide her with the motivation to succeed at the oboe and in life. Alberto Rios's poem "Nani" presents readers with still another portrait of a grandparent, a woman with whom the speaker in the poem shares a deep emotional reservoir of experience and memory but very little in the way of a common language. The second student essay in the chapter, by Julian Castro, interprets and reflects on Rios's poem after Castro notices strong similarities between his own relationship to his Mexican-born grandmother and Rios's reflections on his Nani.

Although most people mature and learn to function in the rational world, the dreams and ghosts of their childhoods continue to shape, haunt, and inspire their waking lives. Writing about the past can be one of the best ways to face and come to terms with the ghosts of memory. This type of writing can help us to formulate and construct realistic and positive dreams for the future.

NARRATION, MEMORY, AND SELF-AWARENESS

You will read a number of narrative accounts of childhood experiences in this chapter. Narratives serve two important functions for a writer: they can bring about a process of self-discovery, and they are fundamental sources and building blocks of both fiction and nonfiction writing. The brief stories or extended examples that develop, illustrate, and support points made in expository and argumentative essays are among the best resources writers have for presenting ideas in a clear, vivid, and convincing manner.

When you create a narrative, you draw on many inner resources and skills: memories of life experiences, dreams, your imagination, the ability to imitate the voices of others, and the skill required to develop a suspenseful plot that will hold your readers' attention. While not everyone can entertain friends with a natural storytelling ability, most of us can learn how to write a clear and engaging story.

Making Associations

As in other forms of writing, the first phase of narrative writing involves generating ideas and images to write about, experiences that come in part from your past and in part from your imagination that can later be shaped into a story with an overall theme. This marks an important distinction between personal narrative and the kind of close description of nature that we saw in some of the essays in the previous chapter.

How do you find ideas and events for your writing, however, if the only memories you have of your early years are vague or sketchy? Notice the following initial account of a student's childhood in Sacramento: "As a child, I lived for five years on B Street in Sacramento. It was always hot in the summer there." Writing strategies such as drawing, freewriting, invisible writing, brainstorming, and clustering can help you to generate details, images, and ideas associated with a particular time and place in your life. For example, you could start with a significant part of an address and do a cluster or ten-minute freewrite around it, letting one detail lead to another: "B Street, hot, barren, dusty, fire hydrant out front turned on in the summer, the ice cream wagon's jingle." If you follow this process long enough, you will begin to imagine and re-create a number of details you thought you had forgotten, and you will have begun to gather the words, thoughts, and images that you can later shape into an essay.

Focusing and Concentration: The Inner Screen

In developing your narrative, it is also important to try to focus on the most significant aspect of your memory. For example, you might visualize a particular room or the backyard of your house on a summer day when something significant happened to you: a fateful accident, a moment of serious conflict, an unexpected gift, a moment of friendship or intimacy. Close your eyes and try to visualize all the objects, colors, forms, people, and expressions associated with that place and a particular time there. Then try to visualize the movements within the scene, as movements in time and space are essential elements of narration. When did certain people arrive and leave? How did they walk? What gestures did they make? What activities did they perform? What did they say to one another? After visualizing and naming specific colors, try to recall other sensations: textures, warmth or coolness, smells, tastes, and sounds. Take notes as you begin to remember and imagine sensations, forms, and movements.

Dialogue and Characters

While not all people have vivid auditory memories, including some conversation in your narrative will help bring it to life. Focus on the way each person in your scene speaks; jot down some of the typical brief exchanges that the group could have had, and then try to understand each character more fully through role-playing. Imagine that you have become each person in the scene, one at a time. As you role-play, speak out loud in the voice of each person, then write down a paragraph in which you try to capture their typical concerns and rhythms of speech. Finally, try to construct a conversation between the people in the scene.

Main Idea or Dominant Impression

Now you should be ready to write about the strong ideas or feelings that underlie or dominate your scene. Brainstorm or cluster around key details in your notes. Which emotions does the remembered moment call up for you? What ideas, what "lessons," does it suggest? Develop a statement that you can later clarify and qualify: "That evening was one of waiting and apprehension"; "The morning was a joyful one for my family, yet tinged by regret." Writing this type of dominant impression statement will guide you in adding more details and bits of dialogue and in selecting and ordering your material. A central idea for your narrative will help you to achieve a sense of focus and purpose that will help you to engage your readers' interest; most importantly, it will help you clarify what you have gained from the experience. The process of writing the narrative will contribute to your personal growth and self-awareness.

Drafting and Shaping the Narrative

Using your central idea or dominant impression as a guide in selecting and ordering details and events, write a rapid first draft, including what is relevant from the notes you generated in your preliminary brainstorming. Leave out any details or events that introduce a tone or feeling that conflicts with or detracts from the impression you want to emphasize. Relevant but not particularly interesting events and periods of time do not need to be narrated in detail and can be summed up in a sentence or two: "For hours I played with my dog, waiting eagerly for my father to return from work."

Try to order the events of your narrative to emphasize your main idea as well. Although most writers use a chronological sequence in shaping a narrative, your dominant idea may demand withholding a key event for purposes of suspense or creating a powerful conclusion. You might also consider the use of flashbacks, beginning perhaps with a brief scene that occurs at the end of the action and then revealing the sequence of events leading up to the initially described event. Any order is acceptable as long as you clarify shifts of time for the reader with transitions and make sure that your order serves the overall purpose of your story.

While writing different drafts of your narrative, don't hesitate to experiment with rearranging the parts of the story or essay until you find a clear, comfortable fit between the structure and the meaning of your work. This rearrangement process is made much easier if you are revising on a computer, because the cut-and-paste functions of your word processor make it easy to see how different sequences work. You might try saving different versions of your narrative with different file names, each using a different sequence of events, then printing each out and reading them over to see more clearly what may be the advantages of each version.

Revising the Narrative: Point of View, Transition, and Style

Point of View and Transition   As you move from the early stages into the final drafting of your narrative, pay special attention to your point of view and style. Your narrative will probably use the first person "I" pronoun, unless you are writing about someone else's experience. As is the case with the essays in this chapter, narrative essays are most frequently told from the perspective of an adult looking back on the past and are known as "memoir narratives." Be sure to maintain a consistent point of view. If you decide to move into your mind as a young person, indicate this shift with a clear transition ("Then I thought to myself . . ."), after which you could write in language that is typical of the younger "you."

Word Choice and Transition   Like descriptions, narratives are seldom written in highly formal, abstract, or generalized language, so try to make your narrative voice down to earth, using common and concrete language as you try to capture the mood and feeling of the events being revealed and the characters involved. In refining the style of your narrative, ask yourself some questions about your word and sentence choices, questions similar to those you use in realistic descriptive writing, but with more emphasis on emotional tonality. For instance, have you used specific, concrete nouns, adjectives, verbs, and adverbs, and clear transitions indicating time lapses and movements, in order to capture the emotional feel of the experience you are describing? Always search for the word that best fits your meaning and mood. A thesaurus (paper or online) can be very helpful in finding specific replacements for tired, imprecise, general terms. When it seems as though no word exists to communicate your exact sensory impression or mood, try using literal or figurative comparisons as in descriptive writing, but with an imaginative twist. Always try for originality in your figurative comparisons, because clichés like "She looked like an angel" or "It was as dark as a dungeon" can tarnish the unique impression that you are trying to create.

Sentence Patterns   Your writing style is also created through the way you put words together. Thus your sentence patterns are a vital part of your narrative, as they should be in everything you write. Vary your sentence length for emphasis, using short sentences to slow down the action and to emphasize climactic moments. Try, too, to capture the voice rhythms of your characters through your punctuation. Remember that you can use a number of different sentence patterns (simple, compound, complex) as well as different ordering possibilities for the parts of your sentences. Again, in writing on your computer, try saving different versions of key sentences with different strategies for combination and punctuation; print them out and decide which works best in context. Consult your grammar text repeatedly to review the range of sentence patterns and punctuation strategies; experiment to heighten the dramatic effects of your writing.

Writing an engaging narrative is a challenge. It can also be a fulfilling writing experience that will bring you in touch with your past experiences, feelings, values, and identity.

bell hooks

Writing Autobiography

bell hooks is the pen name for Gloria Watkins (b. 1952) who was born in Hopkinsville, Kentucky. She graduated from Stanford University in English (1973) and earned her M.A. at the University of Wisconsin (1976). The author of more than 30 books, her ideas and books focus on feminism and on the interconnectivity of race, gender, and class, with their ability to perpetuate oppression and domination. Some of her most widely read works include the autobiographical Ain't I a Woman *(1981) and the essay collections* Talking Back, Thinking Feminist, Thinking Black *(1989) and* Yearning: Race, Gender, and Cultural Politics *(1990). In writing about cultural, gender, and ethnic issues, hooks reflects deeply upon her own experiences. As you read the following selection from* Talking Back, *notice how hooks emphasizes the role that pain and memory play in the writing process, as well as how writing can be a healing experience.*

JOURNAL

Write about a painful memory that you have avoided reflecting on. How did your writing help you to heal from the memory?

To me, telling the story of my growing up years was intimately connected with the longing to kill the self I was without really having to die. I wanted to kill that self in writing. Once that self was gone—out of my life forever—I could more easily become the me of me. It was clearly the Gloria Jean of my tormented and anguished childhood that I wanted to be rid of, the girl who was always wrong, always punished, always subjected to some humiliation or other, always crying, the girl who was to end up in a mental institution because she could not be anything but crazy, or so they told her. She was the girl who sat a hot iron on her arm pleading with them to leave her alone, the girl who wore her scar as a brand marking her madness. Even now I can hear the voices of my sisters saying "mama make Gloria stop crying." By writing the autobiography, it was not just this Gloria I would be rid of, but the past that had a hold on me, that kept me from the present. I wanted not to forget the past but to break its hold. This death in writing was to be liberatory.

Until I began to try and write an autobiography, I thought that it would be a simple task this telling of one's story. And yet I tried year after year, never writing more than a few pages. My inability to write out the story I interpreted as an indication that I was not ready to let go of the past, that I was not ready to be fully in the present. Psychologically, I considered the possibility that I had become attached to the wounds and sorrows of my childhood, that I held to them in a manner that blocked my efforts to be self-realized, whole, to be healed. A key message in Toni Cade Bambara's novel *The Salteaters,* which tells the story of Velma's suicide attempt, her breakdown, is expressed when the healer asks her "are you sure sweetheart, that you want to be well?"

There was very clearly something blocking my ability to tell my story. Perhaps it was remembered scoldings and punishments when mama heard me saying something to a friend or stranger that she did not think should be said. Secrecy and silence—these were central issues. Secrecy about family, about what went on in the domestic household was a bond between us—was part of what made us family. There was a dread one felt about breaking that bond. And yet I could not grow inside the atmosphere of secrecy that had pervaded our lives and the lives of other families about us. Strange that I had always challenged the secrecy, always let something slip that should not be known growing up, yet as a writer staring into the solitary space of paper, I was bound, trapped in the fear that a bond is lost or broken in the telling. I did not want to be the traitor, the teller of family secrets—and yet I wanted to be a writer. Surely, I told myself, I could write a purely imaginative work—a work that would not hint at personal private realities. And so I tried. But always there were the intruding traces, those elements of real life however disguised. Claiming the freedom to grow as an imaginative writer was connected for me with having the courage to open, to be able to tell the truth of one's life as I had experienced it in writing. To talk about one's life—that I could do. To write about it, to leave a trace—that was frightening.

The longer it took me to begin the process of writing autobiography, the further removed from those memories I was becoming. Each year, a memory seemed less and less clear. I wanted not to lose the vividness, the recall and felt an urgent need to begin the work and complete it. Yet I could not begin even though I had begun to confront some of the reasons I was blocked, as I am blocked just now in writing this piece because I am afraid to express in writing the experience that served as a catalyst for that block to move.

5   I had met a young black man. We were having an affair. It is important that he was black. He was in some mysterious way a link to this past that I had been struggling to grapple with, to name in writing. With him 1 remembered incidents, moments of the past that I had completely suppressed. It was as though there was something about the passion of contact that was hypnotic, that enabled me to drop barriers and thus enter fully, rather re-enter those past experiences. A key aspect seemed to be the way he smelled, the combined odors of cigarettes, occasionally alcohol, and his body smells. I thought often of the phrase "scent of memory," for it was those smells that carried me back. And there were specific occasions when it was very evident that the experience of being in his company was the catalyst for this remembering.

Two specific incidents come to mind. One day in the middle of the afternoon we met at his place. We were drinking cognac and dancing to music from the radio. He was smoking cigarettes (not only do I not smoke, but I usually make an effort to avoid smoke). As we held each other dancing those mingled odors of alcohol, sweat, and cigarettes led me to say, quite without thinking about it, "Uncle Pete." It was not that I had forgotten Uncle Pete. It was more that I had forgotten the childhood experience of meeting him. He drank often, smoked cigarettes, and always on the few occasions that we met him, he held us children in tight embraces. It was the memory of those embraces—of the way I hated and longed to resist them—that I recalled.

Another day we went to a favorite park to feed ducks and parked the car in front of tall bushes. As we were sitting there, we suddenly heard the sound of an oncoming train—a sound which startled me so that it evoked another long-suppressed memory: that of crossing the train tracks in my father's car. I recalled an incident where the car stopped on the tracks and my father left us sitting there while he raised the hood of the car and worked to repair it. This is an incident that I am not certain actually happened. As a child, I had been terrified of just such an incident occurring, perhaps so terrified that it played itself out in my mind as thought it had happened. These are just two ways this encounter acted as a catalyst breaking down barriers enabling me to finally write this long-desired autobiography of my childhood.

Each day I sat at the typewriter and different memories were written about in short vignettes. They came in a rush, as though they were a sudden thunderstorm. They came in a surreal, dreamlike style which made me cease to think of them as strictly autobiographical because it seemed that myth, dream, and reality had merged. There were many incidents that I would talk about with my siblings to see if they recalled them. Often we remembered together a general outline of an incident but the details were different for us. This fact was a constant reminder of the limitations of autobiography, of the extent to which autobiography is a very personal story telling—a unique recounting of events not so much as they had happened but as we remember and invent them. One memory that I would have sworn was "the truth and nothing but the truth" concerned a wagon that my brother and I shared as a child. I remembered that we played with this toy only at my grandfather's house, that we shared it, that I would ride it and my brother would push me. Yet one facet of the memory was puzzling, I remembered always returning home with bruises or scratches from this toy. When I called my mother, she said there had never been any wagon, that we had shared a red wheelbarrow, that it had always been at my grandfather's house because there were sidewalks on that part of town. We lived in the hills where there were no sidewalks. Again I was compelled to face the fiction that is a part of all retelling, remembering. I began to think of the work I was doing as both fiction and autobiography. It seemed to fall in the category of writing that Audre Lorde, in her autobiographically-based work *Zami,* calls biomythography. As I wrote, I felt that I was not as concerned with accuracy of detail as I was with evoking in writing the state of mind, the spirit of a particular moment.

The longing to tell one's story and the process of telling is symbolically a gesture of longing to recover the past in such a way that one experiences both a sense of reunion and a sense of release. It was the longing for release that compelled the writing but concurrently it was the joy of reunion that enabled me to see that the act of writing one's autobiography is a way to find again that aspect of self and experience that may no longer be an actual part of one's life but is a living memory shaping and informing the present. Autobiographical writing was a way for me to evoke the particular experience of growing up southern and black in segregated communities. It was a way to recapture the richness of southern black culture. The need to remember and hold to the legacy of that experience and what it taught me has been all the more important since I have since lived in predominately white communities and taught at predominately white colleges. Black southern folk experience was the foundation of the life around me when I was a child; that experience no longer exists in many places where it was once all of life that we knew. Capitalism, upward mobility, assimilation of other values have all led to rapid disintegration of black folk experience or in some cases the gradual wearing away of that experience.

10   Within the world of my childhood, we held onto the legacy of a distinct black culture by listening to the elders tell their stories. Autobiography was experienced most actively in the art of telling one's story. I can recall sitting at Baba's (my grandmother on my mother's side) at 1200 Broad Street—listening to people come and recount their life experience. In those days, whenever I brought a playmate to my grandmother's house, Baba would want a brief outline of their autobiography before we would begin playing. She wanted not only to know who their people were but what their values were. It was sometimes an awesome and terrifying experience to stand answering these questions or witness another playmate being subjected to the process and yet this was the way we would come to know our own and one another's family history. It is the absence of such a tradition in my adult life that makes the written narrative of my girlhood all the more important. As the years pass and these glorious memories grow much more vague, there will remain the clarity contained within the written words.

Conceptually, the autobiography was framed in the manner of a hope chest. I remembered my mother's hope chest, with its wonderful odor of cedar and thought about her taking the most precious items and placing them there for safekeeping. Certain memories were for me a similar treasure. I wanted to place them somewhere for safekeeping. An autobiographical narrative seemed an appropriate place. Each particular incident, encounter, experience had its own story, sometimes told from the first person, sometimes told from the third person. Often I felt as though I was in a trance at my typewriter, that the shape of a particular memory was decided not by my conscious mind but by all that is dark and deep within me, unconscious but present. It was the act of making it present, bringing it into the open, so to speak, that was liberating.

From the perspective of trying to understand my psyche, it was also interesting to read the narrative in its entirety after I had completed the work. It had not occurred to me that bringing one's past, one's memories together in a complete narrative would allow one to view them from a different perspective, not as singular isolated events but as part of a continuum. Reading the completed manuscript, I felt as though I had an overview not so much of my childhood but of those experiences that were deeply imprinted in my consciousness. Significantly, that which was absent, left out, not included also was important. I was shocked to find at the end of my narrative that there were few incidents I recalled that involved my five sisters. Most of the incidents with siblings were with me and my brother. There was a sense of alienation from my sisters present in childhood, a sense of estrangement. This was reflected in the narrative. Another aspect of the completed manuscript that is interesting to me is the way in which the incidents describing adult men suggest that I feared them intensely, with the exception of my grandfather and a few old men. Writing the autobiographical narrative enabled me to look at my past from a different perspective and to use this knowledge as a means of self-growth and change in a practical way.

In the end I did not feel as though I had killed the Gloria of my childhood. Instead I had rescued her. She was no longer the enemy within, the little girl who had to be annihilated for the woman to come into being. In writing about her, I reclaimed that part of myself I had long ago rejected, left uncared for, just as she had often felt alone and uncared for as a child. Remembering was part of a cycle of reunion, a joining of fragments, "the bits and pieces of my heart" that the narrative made whole again.

Questions for Discussion

1. "To me, telling the story of my growing up years was intimately connected with the longing to kill the self I was without really having to die." What was your initial response to this opening sentence? After reading the entire essay, go back and reinterpret the meaning of the statement. Does hooks change her original perspective on writing about her past? How?

2. Why is it difficult for hooks to write her autobiography? What helps her to get beyond her writer's block? Do you think that her technique might help you? Will you try it?

3. How does hooks experience the recollection of her memories? What specific events, sensations, and images in the present helped her to recall past memories? Have you experienced the recall of memories in similar ways? What helps you to get in touch with your memories?

4. Why does hooks believe that autobiography involves invention and imagination as well as the reporting of events? Do you agree with her? Why or why not?

5. Hooks writes, "Often I felt as though I was in a trance at my typewriter, that the shape of a particular memory was decided not by my conscious mind but by all that is dark and deep within me, unconscious but present." Have you ever experienced writing in this way?

6. Hooks describes the influence that the legacy of African American oral storytelling had on her ability to frame her past experiences in writing. Was there a similar type of legacy in your own family? If so, do you think that you could draw upon it as source for your writing?

CONNECTION

Compare bell hooks's and Judith Ortiz Cofer's writing about traumatic memories (see page 81).

IDEAS FOR WRITING

1. Write about an incident from your past about which you still have mixed feelings, a part of the past you still don't understand or to which you don't yet feel reconciled. Compare your experience of self-understanding to those that hooks experienced in writing her autobiography. How did your feelings toward the material you were writing about change in the course of doing the writing? What did you learn about the event and yourself in the writing process?
2. Hooks discusses her writer's block and how she works through it. Develop an essay that explores the topic of writer's block, presenting some strategies for overcoming the problem that have worked for you or for other writers in this text.

RELATED WEB SITES

Metroactive: For Whom The bell Tolls
**www.metroactive.com/papers/metro/02.15.96/
hooks-9607.html**
Metroactive, Silicon Valley's Weekly Newspaper, not only provides a literary review of one of bell hooks's books, *Killing Rage: Ending Racism*, but also shares links to a biography of hooks and the first chapter of this book.

The e-Journal Website: bell hooks Resources
www.synaptic.bc.ca/ejournal/hooks.htm
The e-Journal Web site is a self-proclaimed "critical thinks resource" site. This specific eJournal entry shares over a dozen resources on bell hooks, as well as other feminists and feminist topics.

Judith Ortiz Cofer

Silent Dancing

Born in Puerto Rico in 1952, Judith Ortiz Cofer came to New Jersey with her family when she was a child. After receiving an M.A. from Florida Atlantic University, Cofer taught English and Spanish at the University of Miami and currently teaches at the University of Georgia. Cofer's works include Silent Dancing: A Partial Remembrance of a Puerto Rican Childhood *(1990);* Latin Deli: Prose and Poetry *(1993);* Island Like You: Stories of the Barrio *(1995);* Women In Front of the Sun *(2000); and* Call Me Maria *(2004). In the following selection from* Silent Dancing, *Cofer recalls memories of a childhood spent in two strikingly different cultures.*

JOURNAL

Write about a photograph or a home movie that evokes memories of your childhood.

We have a home movie of this party. Several times my mother and I have watched it together, and I have asked questions about the silent revellers coming in and out of focus. It is grainy and of short duration but a great visual aid to my first memory of life in Paterson at that time. And it is in color—the only complete scene in color I can recall from those years.

We lived in Puerto Rico until my brother was born in 1954. Soon after, because of economic pressures on our growing family, my father joined the United States Navy. He was assigned to duty on a ship in Brooklyn Yard, New York City—a place of cement and steel that was to be his home base in the States until his retirement more than twenty years later. He left the Island first, tracking down his uncle who lived with his family across the Hudson River, in Paterson, New Jersey. There he found a tiny apartment in a huge apartment building that had once housed Jewish families and was just being transformed into a tenement by Puerto Ricans overflowing from New York City. In 1955 he sent for us. My mother was only twenty years old, I was not quite three, and my brother was a toddler when we arrived at *El Building,* as the place had been christened by its new residents.

My memories of life in Paterson during those first few years are in shades of gray. Maybe I was too young to absorb vivid colors and details, or to discriminate between the slate blue of the winter sky and the darker hues of the snow-bearing clouds, but the single color washes over the whole period. The building we lived in was gray, the streets were gray with slush the first few months of my life there, the coat my father had bought for me was dark in color and too big. It sat heavily on my thin frame.

I do remember the way the heater pipes banged and rattled, startling all of us out of sleep until we got so used to the sound that we automatically either shut it out or raised our voices above the racket. The hiss from the valve punctuated my sleep, which has always been fitful, like a nonhuman presence in the room—the dragon sleeping at the entrance of my childhood. But the pipes were a connection to all the other lives

neighbors smokin' crack

being lived around us. Having come from a house made for a single family back in Puerto Rico—my mother's extended-family home—it was curious to know that strangers lived under our floor and above our heads, and that the heater pipe went through everyone's apartment. (My first spanking in Paterson came as a result of playing tunes on the pipes in my room to see if there would be an answer.) My mother was as new to this concept of beehive life as I was, but had been given strict orders by my father to keep the doors locked, the noise down, ourselves to ourselves.

5   It seems that Father had learned some painful lessons about prejudice while searching for an apartment in Paterson. Not until years later did I hear how much resistance he had encountered with landlords who were panicking at the influx of Latinos into a neighborhood that had been Jewish for a couple of generations. But it was the American phenomenon of ethnic turnover that was changing the urban core of Paterson, and the human flood could not be held back with an accusing finger.

"You Cuban?" the man had asked my father, pointing a finger at his name tag on the Navy uniform—even though my father had the fair skin and light brown hair of his northern Spanish family background and our name is as common in Puerto Rico as Johnson is in the U.S.

"No," my father had answered looking past the finger into his adversary's angry eyes, "I'm Puerto Rican."

"Same shit." And the door closed. My father could have passed as European, but we couldn't. My brother and I both have our mother's black hair and olive skin, and so we lived in El Building and visited our great-uncle and his fair children on the next block. It was their private joke that they were the German branch of the family. Not many years later that area too would be mainly Puerto Rican. It was as if the heart of the city map were being gradually colored in brown—*café-con-leche* brown. Our color.

The movie opens with a sweep of the living room. It is "typical" immigrant Puerto Rican decor for the time: the sofa and chairs are square and hard-looking, upholstered in bright colors (blue and yellow in this instance, and covered in the transparent plastic) that furniture salesmen then were adept at making women buy. The linoleum on the floor is light blue, and if it was subjected to the spike heels as it was in most places, there were dime-sized indentations all over it that cannot be seen in this movie. The room is full of people dressed in mainly two colors: dark suits for the men, red dresses for the women. I have asked my mother why most of the women are in red that night, and she shrugs, "I don't remember. Just a coincidence." She doesn't have my obsession for assigning symbolism to everything.

10   *The three women in red sitting on the couch are my mother, my eighteen-year-old cousin, and her brother's girlfriend. The "novia" is just up from the Island, which is apparent in her body language. She sits up formally, and her dress is carefully pulled over her knees. She is a pretty girl but her posture makes her look*

insecure, lost in her full skirted red dress which she has carefully tucked around her to make room for my gorgeous cousin, her future sister-in-law. My cousin has grown up in Paterson and is in her last year of high school. She doesn't have a trace of what Puerto Ricans call "la mancha" (literally, the stain: the mark of the new immigrant—something about the posture, the voice, or the humble demeanor making it obvious to everyone that that person has just arrived on the mainland; has not yet acquired the polished look of the city dweller). My cousin is wearing a tight red-sequined cocktail dress. Her brown hair has been lightened with peroxide around the bangs, and she is holding a cigarette very expertly between her fingers, bringing it up to her mouth in a sensuous arc of her arm to her as she talks animatedly with my mother, who has come up to sit between the two women, both only a few years younger than herself. My mother is somewhere halfway between the poles they represent in our culture.

It became my father's obsession to get out of the barrio, and thus we were never permitted to form bonds with the place or with the people who lived there. Yet the building was a comfort to my mother, who never got over yearning for *la isla*. She felt surrounded by her language: the walls were thin, and voices speaking and arguing in Spanish could be heard all day. *Salsas* blasted out of radios turned on early in the morning and left on for company. Women seemed to cook rice and beans perpetually—the strong aroma of red kidney beans boiling permeated the hallways.

Though Father preferred that we do our grocery shopping at the supermarket when he came home on weekend leaves, my mother insisted that she could cook only with products whose labels she could read, and so, during the week, I accompanied her and my little brother to *La Bodega*—a hole-in-the-wall grocery store across the street from *El Building*. There we squeezed down three narrow aisles jammed with various products. Goya and Libby's—those were the trademarks trusted by her Mamá, and so my mother bought cans of Goya beans, soups and condiments. She bought little cans of Libby's fruit juices for us. And she bought Colgate toothpaste and Palmolive soap. (The final *e* is pronounced in both those products in Spanish, and for many years I believed that they were manufactured on the Island. I remember my surprise at first hearing a commercial on television for the toothpaste in which Colgate rhymed with "ate.") We would linger at La Bodega, for it was there that mother breathed best, taking in the familiar aromas of the foods she knew from Mamá's kitchen, and it was also there that she got to speak to the other women of El Building without violating outright Father's dictates against fraternizing with our neighbors.

But he did his best to make our "assimilation" painless. I can still see him carrying a Christmas tree up several flights of stairs to our apartment, leaving a trail of aromatic pine. He carried it formally, as if it were a flag in a parade. We were the only ones in El Building that I knew of who got presents on both Christmas Day and on *Día de Reyes,* the day when the Three Kings brought gifts to Christ and to Hispanic children.

Our greatest luxury in El Building was having our own television set. It must have been a result of Father's guilty feelings over the isolation he had imposed on us, but we were one of the first families in the barrio to have one. My brother quickly became an avid watcher of Captain Kangaroo and Jungle Jim. I loved all the family series, and by the time I started first grade in school, I could have drawn a map of Middle America as exemplified by the lives of characters in "Father Knows Best," "The Donna Reed Show," "Leave It to Beaver," "My Three Sons," and (my favorite) "Bachelor Father," where John Forsythe treated his adopted teenage daughter like a princess because he was rich and had a Chinese houseboy to do everything for him. Compared to our neighbors in El Building, we were rich. My father's Navy check provided us with financial security and a standard of life that the factory workers envied. The only thing his money could not buy us was a place to live away from the barrio—his greatest wish and Mother's greatest fear.

15 *In the home movie the men are shown next, sitting around a card table set up in one corner of the living room, playing dominoes. The clack of the ivory pieces is a sound familiar. I heard it in many houses on the Island and in many apartments in Paterson. In "Leave It to Beaver," the Cleavers played bridge in every other episode; in my childhood, the men started every social occasion with a hotly debated round of dominoes: the women would sit around and watch, but they never participated in the games.*

Here and there you can see a small child. Children were always brought to parties and, whenever they got sleepy, put to bed in the host's bedrooms. Babysitting was a concept unrecognized by the Puerto Rican women I knew: a responsible mother did not leave her children with any stranger. And in a culture where children are not considered intrusive, there is no need to leave children at home. We went where our mother went.

Of my preschool years I have only impressions: the sharp bite of the wind in December as we walked with our parents towards the brightly lit stores downtown, how I felt like a stuffed doll in my heavy coat, boots and mittens; how good it was to walk into the five-and-dime and sit at the counter drinking hot chocolate.

On Saturdays our whole family would walk downtown to shop at the big department stores on Broadway. Mother bought all our clothes at Penney's and Sears, and she liked to buy her dresses at the women's specialty shops like Lerner's and Diana's. At some point we would go into Woolworth's and sit at the soda fountain to eat.

We never ran into other Latinos at these stores or eating out, and it became clear to me only years later that the women from El Building shopped mainly at other places—stores owned either by other Puerto

Ricans, or by Jewish merchants who had philosophically accepted our presence in the city and decided to make us their good customers, if not neighbors and friends. These establishments were located not downtown, but in the blocks around our street, and they were referred to generically as *La Tienda, El Bazar, La Bodega, La Botánica.* Everyone knew what was meant. These were the stores where your face did not turn a clerk to stone, where your money was as green as anyone else's.

20   On New Year's Eve we were dressed up like child models in the Sears catalogue—my brother in a miniature man's suit and bow tie, and I in black patent leather shoes and a frilly dress with several layers of crinolines underneath. My mother wore a bright red dress that night, I remember, and spike heels; her long black hair hung to her waist. Father, who usually wore his Navy uniform during his short visits home, had put on a dark civilian suit for the occasion: we had been invited to his uncle's house for a big celebration. Everyone was excited because my mother's brother, Hernán—a bachelor who could indulge himself in such luxuries—had bought a movie camera which he would be trying out that night.

Even the home movie cannot fill in the sensory details such a gathering left imprinted in a child's brain. The thick sweetness of women's perfume mixing with the ever-present smells of food cooking in the kitchen: meat and plantain *pasteles,* the ubiquitous rice dish made special with pigeon peas—*gandules*—and seasoned with the precious *sofrito* sent up from the Island by somebody's mother or smuggled in by a recent traveler. *Sofrito* was one of the items that women hoarded, since it was hardly ever in stock at La Bodega. It was the flavor of Puerto Rico.

The men drank Palo Viejo rum and some of the younger ones got weepy. The first time I saw a grown man cry was at a New Year's Eve party. He had been reminded of his mother by the smells in the kitchen. But what I remember most were the boiled *pasteles*—boiled plantain or yucca rectangles stuffed with corned beef or other meats, olives, and many other savory ingredients, all wrapped in banana leaves. Everyone had to fish one out with a fork. There was always a "trick" pastel—one without stuffing—and whoever got that one was the "New Year's Fool."

There was also the music. Long-playing albums were treated like precious china in these homes. Mexican recordings were popular, but the songs that brought tears to my mother's eyes were sung by the melancholic Daniel Santos, whose life as a drug addict was the stuff of legend. Felipe Rodríguez was a particular favorite of couples. He sang about faithless women and broken-hearted men. There is a snatch of a lyric that has stuck in my mind like a needle on a worn groove: "De piedra ha de ser mi cama, de piedra la cabecera . . . la mujer que a mí me quiera . . . ha de quererme de veras. Ay, Ay, corazón, ¿por qué no amas . . .?" I must have heard it a thousand times since the idea of a bed made of stone, and its connection to love, first troubled me with its disturbing images.

The five-minute home movie ends with people dancing in a circle. The creative filmmaker must have asked them to do that so that they could file past him. It is both comical and sad to watch silent dancing. Since there is no justification for the absurd movements that music provides for some of us, people appear frantic, their faces embarrassingly intense. It's as if you were watching sex. Yet for years, I've had dreams in the form of this home movie. In a recurring scene, familiar faces push themselves forward into my mind's eye, plastering their features into distorted close-ups. And I'm asking them: "Who is she? Who is the woman I don't recognize? Is she an aunt? Somebody's wife? Tell me who she is. Tell me who these people are."

25   "No, see the beauty mark on her cheek as big as a hill on the lunar landscape of her face—well, that runs in the family. The women on your father's side of the family wrinkle early; it's the price they pay for that fair skin. The young girl with the green stain on her wedding dress is *La Novia*—just up from the island. See, she lowers her eyes as she approaches the camera like she's supposed to. Decent girls never look you directly in the face. *Humilde*, humble, a girl should express humility in all her actions. She will make a good wife for your cousin. He should consider himself lucky to have met her only weeks after she arrived here. If he married her quickly, she will make him a good Puerto Rican-style wife; but if he waits too long, she will be corrupted by the city, just like your cousin there."

"She means me. I do what I want. This is not some primitive island I live on. Do they expect me to wear a black *mantilla* on my head and go to mass every day? Not me. I'm an American woman and I will do as I please. I can type faster than anyone in my senior class at Central High, and I'm going to be a secretary to a lawyer when I graduate. I can pass for an American girl anywhere—I've tried it—at least for Italian, anyway. I never speak Spanish in public. I hate these parties, but I wanted the dress. I look better than any of these *humildes* here. My life is going to be different. I have an American boyfriend. He is older and has a car. My parents don't know it, but I sneak out of the house late at night sometimes to be with him. If I marry him, even my name will be American. I hate rice and beans. It's what makes these women fat."

"Your *prima* is pregnant by that man she's been sneaking around with. Would I lie to you? I'm your great-uncle's common-law wife—the one he abandoned on the Island to marry your cousin's mother. I was not invited to this party, but I came anyway. I came to tell you that story about your cousin that you've always wanted to hear. Remember that comment your mother made to a neighbor that has always haunted you? The only thing you heard was your cousin's name and then you saw your mother pick up your doll from the couch and say: 'It was as big as this doll when they flushed it down the toilet.' This image has bothered you for years, hasn't it? You had nightmares about babies being flushed down the toilet, and you wondered why anyone would do such a horrible thing. You didn't dare ask your mother about it. She would only tell you that you had not heard her right and yell at you for listening to adult conversations. But later, when you were old enough to know about abortions, you suspected. I am here to tell you that you were right. Your cousin was growing an *Americanito* in her belly when this movie was made. Soon after she put something long and pointy into her pretty self, thinking maybe she could get rid of the problem before breakfast and still make it to her first class at the high school. Well, Niña, her screams could be heard downtown. Your aunt, her Mamá, who had been a midwife on the Island, managed to pull the little thing out. Yes, they probably flushed it down the toilet, what else could they do with it—give it a Christian burial in a little white casket with blue bows and ribbons? Nobody wanted that baby—least of all the father, a teacher at her school with a house in West Paterson that he was filling with real children, and a wife who was a natural blond.

"Girl, the scandal sent your uncle back to the bottle. And guess where your cousin ended up? Irony of ironies. She was sent to a village in Puerto Rico to live with a relative on her mother's side: a place so far away from civilization that you have to ride a mule to reach it. A real change in scenery. She found a man there. Women like that cannot live without male company. But believe me, the men in Puerto Rico know how to put a saddle on a woman like her. *La Gringa,* they call her. ha, ha. ha. *La Gringa* is what she always wanted to be. . . ."

The old woman's mouth becomes a cavernous black hole I fall into. And as I fall, I can feel the reverberations of her laughter. I hear the echoes of her last mocking words: *La Gringa, La Gringa!* And the conga line keeps moving silently past me. There is no music in my dream for the dancers.

30   When Odysseus visits Hades asking to see the spirit of his mother, he makes an offering of sacrificial blood, but since all of the souls crave an audience with the living, he has to listen to many of them before he can ask questions. I, too, have to hear the dead and the forgotten speak in my dream. Those who are still part of my life remain silent, going around and around in their dance. The others keep pressing their faces forward to say things about the past.

My father's uncle is last in line. He is dying of alcoholism, shrunken and shriveled like a monkey, his face is a mass of wrinkles and broken arteries. As he comes closer I realize that in his features I can see my whole family. If you were to stretch that rubbery flesh, you could find my father's face, and deep within *that* face—mine. I don't want to look into those eyes ringed in purple. In a few years he will retreat into silence, and take a long, long time to die. *Move back, Tío,* I tell him. *I don't want to hear what you have to say. Give the dancers room to move, soon it will be midnight. Who is the New Year's Fool this time?*

Questions for Discussion

1. Which cultural and lifestyle differences affect Cofer most strikingly when she first arrives in Paterson? What types of prejudice does her family encounter there?
2. What do the television programs that she watches teach Cofer about American family life and how to adapt to it?
3. How do Cofer's father and mother relate differently to their neighborhood environment? With whose values does Cofer identify?
4. How does Cofer respond to the "La Gringa" story? What dream continues to haunt Cofer?
5. What dreamlike images and symbols does Cofer use in her narrative? How do these images contribute to the story and its power?
6. Interpret the meaning of the title, "Silent Dancing." In what ways is the dancing "silent"?

Connection

Compare and contrast Cofer's way of adjusting to life to Saira Shah's in the selection that follows. What difficulties do each of them face, and how do they integrate their past into the present?

Ideas for Writing

1. Write an essay that explores a conflict that you or a close friend experienced because one of you was not a member of the dominant cultural group in your community. What did you learn from this conflict, and how did it help to shape your perceptions and expectations of the world?
2. Develop your journal entry into an essay. You might discuss a series of photographs or two or three films or videos made over a period of years. What do these images reveal to you about you and your family's evolving values and concerns?

Related Web Sites

Puerto Rican Immigrants
`www.latinamericanstudies.org/pr-us.htm`
The Latin American Studies Web site features photographs of Puerto Rican immigrant life from the period described in Cofer's essay as well as links to articles on issues related to the immigrants.

Judith Ortiz Cofer Web Site
`www.english.uga.edu/~jcofer/`
This personal Web site contains a biography, bibliography, and links to articles by and about Judith Ortiz Cofer.

Saira Shah

The Storyteller's Daughter

Saira Shah was born in Britain into an Afghan family. Her father, Idries Shah, was a famous Sufi writer, translator, and storyteller. Saira Shah has said, "Stories were a part of my childhood—and never considered just for children. This was a family tradition and a very Afghan one." She first visited Afghanistan at age 21 and worked there for three years covering the guerilla war against the Soviet occupiers; later, she reported stories for Britain's Channel 4 News about the NATO action in Kosovo, massacres in Algeria, the fall of President Mobutu Sésé Seko in Zaire, the Palestinian-Israeli conflict, and bombings in Northern Ireland. Her reporting for Channel 4 News won her awards from Amnesty International, the New York Film Festival, and the Royal Television Society. She has produced two award-winning documentaries about Afghanistan: Beneath the Veil *and* Unholy War. *Her memoir,* The Storyteller's Daughter: Return to a Lost Homeland *(2003), is an account of her search for a cultural identity. The selection included here is from the beginning of her memoir; in it, Shah explores her protected yet alienated childhood living in England as an Afghani in exile.*

JOURNAL

Write a family story about a place of family origin in another area or country.

I am three years old. I am sitting on my father's knee. He is telling me of a magical place: the fairytale landscape you enter in dreams. Fountains fling diamond droplets into mosaic pools. Coloured birds sing in the fruitladen orchards. The pomegranates burst and their insides are rubies. Fruit is so abundant that even the goats are fed on melons. The water has magical properties: you can fill to bursting with fragrant *pilau,* then step to the brook and drink—and you will be ready to eat another meal.

On three sides of the plateau majestic mountains tower, capped with snow. The fourth side overlooks a sunny valley where, gleaming far below, sprawls a city of villas and minarets. And here is the best part of the story: it is true.

The garden is in Paghman, where my family had its seat for nine hundred years. The jewel-like city it overlooks is the Afghan capital, Kabul. The people of Paghman call the capital Kabul *jan:* beloved Kabul. We call it that too, for this is where we belong.

"Whatever outside appearances may be, no matter who tells you otherwise, this garden, this country, these are your origin. This is where you are truly from. Keep it in your heart, Saira *jan*. Never forget."

5   Any western adult might have told me that this was an exile's tale of a lost Eden: the place you dream about, to which you can never return. But even then, I wasn't going to accept that. Even then, I had absorbed enough of the East to feel I belonged there. And too much of the West not to try to nail down dreams.

My father understood the value of stories: he was a writer. My parents had picked Kent as an idyllic place to bring up their children, but we were never allowed to forget our Afghan background.

Periodically during my childhood, my father would come upon the kitchen like a storm. Western systematic method quickly melted before the inspiration of the East. Spice jars tumbled down from their neat beechwood rack and disgorged heaps of coloured powder on to the melamine sideboard. Every pan was pressed into service and extra ones were borrowed from friends and neighbours. The staid old Aga wheezed exotic vapours—*saffran, zeera, gashneesh;* their scents to this day are as familiar to me as my own breath.

In the midst of this mayhem presided my father, the alchemist. Like so many expatriates, when it came to maintaining the traditions, customs and food of his own country he was *plus royaliste que le roi*. Rather than converting lead into gold, my father's alchemical art transported our English country kitchen to the furthest reaches of the Hindu Kush.

We children were the sorcerer's apprentices: we chopped onions and split cardamom pods, nibbling the fragrant black seeds as we worked. We crushed garlic and we peeled tomatoes. He showed us how to steep saffron, to strain yoghurt and to cook the rice until it was *dana-dar,* possessing grains—that is, to the point where it crumbles into three or four perfect round seeds if you rub it between your fingers.

10   In the kitchen, my father's essential *Afghaniyat*, Afghanness, was most apparent. The Afghan love of *pilau* is as fundamental to the national character as the Italian fondness for spaghetti. The Amir Habibullah, a former ruler of Afghanistan, would demolish a vast meal of *pilau,* meatballs and sauce for lunch, then turn to his courtiers and ask: "Now, noblemen and friends, what shall we cook tonight?"

We knew to produce at least three times more *pilau* than anyone could ever be expected to eat. Less would have been an insult to our name and contrary to the Afghan character. As my great-great-great-grandfather famously roared: "How dare you ask me for a *small* favour?"

If, at any point, my father found himself with an unexpected disaster— rice that went soggy or an overboiling pan that turned the Aga's hotplate into a sticky mess—he would exclaim: "Back in Afghanistan, we had cooks to do this work!"

He would tell us, with Afghan hyperbole: "We are making a *Shahi pilau*, a *pilau* fit for kings. This recipe has been handed down through our family since it was prepared for up to four thousand guests at the court of your ancestors. It is far better than the *pilau* you will find when you visit homes in Afghanistan today."

On one notable occasion, my father discovered the artificial food colouring, tartrazine. A *pilau*-making session was instantly convened. Like a conjurer pulling off a particularly effective trick, he showed us how just one tiny teaspoon could transform a gigantic cauldron of *pilau* to a virulent shade of yellow. We were suitably impressed. From that moment on, traditional saffron was discarded for this intoxicating substance.

15   Years later, I learned that all of the Afghan dishes my father had taught me diverged subtly from their originals. His method of finishing off the parboiled rice in the oven, for example, was an innovation of his own. Straining yoghurt through cheesecloth turned out to be merely the first stage in an elaborate process. In Kent, rancid sheep's fat was hard to come by, so he substituted butter. Cumin was an Indian contamination. And so it went on.

Yet although his methods and even his ingredients were different, my father's finished dishes tasted indistinguishable from the originals. He had conveyed their essential quality; the minutiae had been swept away.

During these cookery sessions, we played a wonderful game. We planned the family trip to Afghanistan that always seemed to be just round the corner. How we would go back to Paghman, stroll in the gardens, visit our old family home and greet the relatives we had never met. When we arrived in the Paghman mountains, the men would fire their guns in the air—we shouldn't worry, that was the Afghan way of welcome and celebration. They would carry us on their shoulders, whooping and cheering, and in the evening we would eat a *pilau* that eclipsed even the great feasts of the court of our ancestors.

My mother's family background, which is Parsee from India, rarely got a look in. As far as my father was concerned, his offspring were pure Afghan. For years, the mere mention of the Return was enough to stoke us children into fits of excitement. It was so much more alluring than our mundane Kentish lives, which revolved round the family's decrepit Land Rover and our pet Labrador, Honey.

"Can we take the Land Rover?" asked my brother Tahir.

20   "We shall take a fleet of Land Rovers," said my father grandly.

My sister Safia piped up: "Can we take Honey?"

There was an uncomfortable pause. Even my father's flight of fantasy balked at introducing to Afghans as a beloved member of our family that unclean animal, the dog.

When I was fifteen, the Soviet Union invaded and occupied Afghanistan. During a *pilau*-making session quite soon after that, I voiced an anxiety that had been growing for some time now. How could my father expect us to be truly Afghan when we had grown up outside an Afghan community? When we went back home, wouldn't we children be strangers, foreigners in our own land? I expected, and possibly hoped for, the soothing account of our triumphant and imminent return to Paghman. It didn't come. My father looked tired and sad. His answer startled me: "I've given you stories to replace a community. They are your community."

"But surely stories can't replace experience."

25 He picked up a packet of dehydrated onion. "Stories are like these onions—like dried experience. They aren't the original experience but they are more than nothing at all. You think about a story, you turn it over in your mind, and it becomes something else." He added hot water to the onion. "It's not fresh onion—fresh experience—but it is something that can help you to recognize experience when you come across it. Experiences follow patterns, which repeat themselves again and again. In our tradition, stories can help you recognize the shape of an experience, to make sense of and to deal with it. So, you see, what you may take for mere snippets of myth and legend encapsulate what you need to know to guide you on your way anywhere among Afghans."

"Well, as soon as I'm eighteen I'm going to go to see for myself," I said, adding craftily: "Then perhaps I'll have fresh experiences that will help me grow up."

My father had been swept along on the tide of his analogy. Now, he suddenly became a parent whose daughter was at an impressionable age and whose country was embroiled in a murderous war.

"If you would only grow up a little in the first place," he snapped, "then you would realize that you don't need to go at all." . . .

For many years, in the secret cubbyhole where precious things were stored, my father kept a dusty file containing two pieces of paper. The first was the crumbling title deed to our estate in Paghman. The other was our family tree, stretching back before the Prophet Muhammad, two thousand years back, to the time before my family had even heard of Afghanistan.

30 The title deed was no longer worth the paper it was written on. In Afghanistan, if you are not present to defend your property, you had better be prepared to take it back by the gun. As for our family tree, we didn't need a piece of paper to tell us who we were. My father, and his father before him, saw to it that our lineage was etched on our hearts.

Our family traces its descent through Fatima, the daughter of the Prophet Muhammad. The man who, during his lifetime, founded one of the world's great monotheistic religions, who united the feuding tribes of Arabia, and who could have accumulated wealth beyond compare, but died in poverty. On his deathbed he left this bequest: "I have nothing to leave you, except my family." Since then, his descendants have been revered throughout the Muslim world. They are entitled to use the honorific Sayed.

My grandfather maintained that ancestry was something to try to live up to, not to boast about. As an old man, his hooded, faintly Mongolian eyes, his hooked nose and his tall *karakul* lambskin hat made him look like an inscrutable sage from a Mughal miniature. I remember this venerable figure telling me a joke: "They asked a mule: 'What kind of creature are you?' He replied: 'Well, my mother was a horse!'"

The old man laughed, enjoying the punch-line, and so did I, though I barely understood it. "Do you understand? He was only a mule, but he boasted of the horse, his ancestor! So, you see, Saira *jan,* it is less important who your forebears were than what you yourself become."

Islam, as I absorbed it, was a tolerant philosophy, which encouraged one to adopt a certain attitude to life. The Qur'an we studied taught: "There is no compulsion in religion." The Prophet we followed said: "The holy warrior is he who struggles with himself."

35   Many of the sayings of the Prophet that I was raised on are from a compilation by the Afghan authority Baghawi of Herat. In the orthodox Muslim world it is eclipsed by the monumental collection of Imam Bokhari. Bokhari set out to preserve the literal words and traditions of the Prophet as an act of pious scholasticism. He investigated six hundred thousand sayings, passing only around five thousand as incontestably authentic.

The purpose of Baghawi's collection, on the other hand, is instrumental, rather than scholastic. It was revered by the classical Persian poets, and is widely used in dervish mystical communities to this day. Sayings are included for content. The distinction between these two great Islamic figures is a matter of emphasis: the literal or the spiritual.

Probably because Afghans were thin on the ground in Tunbridge Wells, my father hired an Iranian Qur'an teacher for us. We didn't like him. He felt that, when it came to the Holy Word of God, rote learning was more important than understanding. He slapped my six-year-old sister for failing to memorize in Arabic the mystical verse from the Qur'an known as the Niche for Lights:

Allah is the light of the heavens and of the earth.
His light is like a niche, wherein there is a lamp:
The lamp within a glass, the glass like unto a pearly star.
It is lit from a blessed olive tree
Neither of the East, nor of the West
The oil of which itself shines, although fire has touched it not:
Light upon light!

Outside our sealed bubble of tolerant Muslim culture, the Islamic world was changing. Some years before the Iranian revolution, our Qur'an teacher became fascinated by the ideas of Ayatollah Khomeini. He was hurriedly dismissed, and he eventually returned to Iran to study in a religious seminary. When the thirst for Islamic revolution had stirred his heart sufficiently, he decided he had been brought to our household for a purpose: to witness the depravity and error into which our branch of the family of the Prophet had sunk. For a while, we children were hurried past the thick laurel bushes in the driveway, in case our erstwhile Qur'an instructor was lurking there, ready to attack us.

What unacceptable religious ideas had he encountered in our home? What teachings did he find so detrimental to the hearts of the faithful? Perhaps Baghawi of Herat's sayings of the Prophet, which adjured one to think for oneself rather than conform to externals without question:

"One hour's teaching is better than a whole night of prayer."
"Trust in God, but tie your camel first."
"The ink of the learned is holier than the blood of the martyr."
"You ask me to curse unbelievers, but I was not sent to curse."
"I order you to help any oppressed person, whether they are Muslim or not."
"Women are the twin halves of men."

QUESTIONS FOR DISCUSSION

1. What descriptive details and magical comparisons are used in the father's story of the garden in Paghman? What is the purpose of this elegant description and its impact on Saira?
2. How does her father's cooking help to bring back the distant past and the culture of Afghanistan? Although the ingredients have been adapted to what is available in Kent, England, how is the food able to "conve[y] th[e] essential quality" of the original dishes?
3. Why does the father compare his stories about the family's past in Afghanistan to dried onions? Do you agree with him that such stories can help one to develop a sense of one's original community without actually returning physically to a place of origin?
4. Why does the father keep the "crumbling title deed" and the record of the family tree in a secret place? According to Saira's grandfather, what are the importance and responsibility of ancestry? How does his story of the mule help to illustrate his viewpoint?
5. What philosophical concept of Islam does Saira learn? How do the Qur'an sayings from the collection of Baghawi of Herat differ from those of the orthodox Muslim world? Discuss examples in the text that illustrate both traditions, then draw some conclusions about the values inherent in both of them.
6. Why is the Iranian Qur'an teacher dismissed? What values does he represent?

CONNECTION

Compare Shah's memories of her childhood as an exile or immigrant with those of Judith Ortiz Cofer in her memoir "Recollections of a Puerto

Rican Childhood" (see page 81). How do both writers recall rituals designed to keep the homeland culture alive in a new environment?

IDEAS FOR WRITING

1. Develop your journal entry into an essay about childhood stories
   told to you about another place or country. Indicate the impact such
   stories had on you as you were growing up. If you were able to visit
   the place where your family first lived, how did your expectations
   differ from your experiences?
2. Do some research into the conflict between "orthodox," or fundamentalist, Muslim beliefs and the philosophy and beliefs emphasized by the Baghawi of Herat compilation or another, less
   absolutist, branch of the faith.

RELATED WEB SITES

Interview with Saira Shah
`www.identitytheory.com/interviews/birnbaum133.html`
In this interview, Saira Shah discusses the formative experiences that
led her to travel from her protected home environment to Afghanistan
and to become a journalist and documentary filmmaker.

Asia Source Interview with Saira Shah
`www.asiasource.org/news/special_reports/shah.cfm`
The Asia Source interview focuses on the audience for Shah's memoir
and the East/West dichotomy the book emphasizes.

Melissa Burns

The Best Seat in the House

*Melissa Burns wrote this essay for her freshman writing class. As the essay
suggests, Melissa is an accomplished bassoonist. Always active in dorm life
and engaged in campus activities, Melissa Burns finds community life
rewarding and is always willing to accept roles of leadership.*

On my bookshelf at college sits a beautiful oak box, about six inches
long by three inches wide and high. Its four sides, each with two tri-
angular end pieces, are masterfully flush; they fit together so as to unfold
fully into a flattened green, felt-lined surface. Well-placed brass hinges
and tight fittings guarantee a smooth alignment when the box is latched

shut. The top panel is stamped with a hot-iron oval and reads "PATENTED 1889 FEBRUARY." I have been told that my grandfather, Poppy, constructed this treasure box from a kit. My mother, a young girl at the time, remembers her father carefully gluing the velvet upholstery fabric, now faded and fraying, to the box's interior. For decades, it sat undisturbed on Poppy's dresser, the keeper of his rarely worn cufflinks. When Poppy passed away, my grandmother handed the box to my mother, who subsequently placed it into my hands. It is a memory of the grandfather I never knew, a man who loved me with all his heart. Today, this cherished oak box is known as the "reed graveyard," the place where good bassoon reeds go to die.

Poppy was a master craftsman, a WWII statistical officer in Italy, a peace-maker, a member of a bombardier squadron in the European Theater, a fighter pilot, a looker, a gentleman, a joke-teller. He traveled the globe, swam Lake Erie from Buffalo to Toronto, and constructed ornate and pre-cision grandfather clocks, among numerous other works of art. Poppy fixed all things broken—electrical appliances, furniture, hearts. He was a gentle German giant: six foot four and slender, with an olive complexion and dark but graying hair. He wore a wicked grin, as if to forewarn all whom he met of his mischievous pranks, funny sayings, and unique brand of sarcasm. My grandfather awoke one freezing morning, concerned that the razor-sharp icicles dangling from the awning of his Amherst, New York, home might in-jure his family and friends. Instead, it was Poppy himself who succumbed to nature's wrath. While diligently chipping away at the deadly spikes, he suf-fered a massive coronary heart attack, dying immediately and painlessly. There were no good-byes. Poppy left my physical world on January 10, 1986, just four days after his 72nd birthday. I was two and a half years old.

My mother has shown me so many photographs of her father and me that sometimes I believe I can conjure the contours of his long, hollowed face and cheeks or his warm embrace as we snuggled in a lawn chair in the tall green grass of summertime in upstate New York. On other occa-sions, I realize that I possess no actual recollection of Poppy; I've simply deceived myself into believing false, picture-induced memories, all the while praying to God that I should someday reunite with my grandfather. Poppy is gone from the earth, but not from my soul. I embrace him through stories, maxims, and possessions. Over the years, I have learned to take comfort in his status as my guardian angel, protecting and shel-tering me from the atrocities of this world.

Matt, my older brother and only sibling, bears an eerily striking re-semblance to Poppy—he shares the height, the charm, the gait, and most of all, that devilish, cock-eyed smile. Growing up, however, it was I who captured my grandfather's precious attention. Poppy was well known to occupy our living room rocking chair, listening anxiously for the soft cries signaling that I had awoken from an afternoon nap. He would race upstairs, sweep me from my crib, and hold me soothingly against his broad chest. That was our special time together, my only grandfather and me.

5   When I was in a playful, alert mood, Poppy would lay me down on the family room floor and conduct a series of "tests." Very much the mathematician, calculating the release of bombs and their ensuing catastrophic destruction, Poppy transformed his wartime accuracy into tender, delicate, and methodical child rearing. He concealed my toys behind his back—Would I perceive their continued existence? He raided the kitchen for pots and pans and walked circles around the room, clanging them loudly in different locations while watching my tiny head move frantically from side to side. I have a vivid mental image of a photograph in which Poppy has placed colorful plastic rings around my arms to gauge my strength. Poppy's premature testing was often dismissed as playtime nonsense by the rest of the family, yet he was seriously equipping his only granddaughter with the resources necessary to grow up strong, healthy, independent, resourceful, smart, and intuitive. Poppy was preparing my two-year-old self for a life of struggles and achievements, failures and triumphs. He took great pride in his beautiful baby granddaughter, but he never felt the satisfaction or the joy of witnessing her metamorphosis into a little girl, a teenager, and now, a woman—a woman with a talent of which Poppy was entirely unaware.

I began to play the bassoon, an extremely difficult and intricate double-reed instrument, at the unprecedented age of ten. My decision to play this instrument was prompted by words of encouragement from family friends who recognized my musical aptitude for the piano, as well as the great orchestral demand for young bassoonists. This musical decision was to become perhaps the most consequential, life-altering choice of my life. My bassoon journeys have carried me from Williams College to New York City to Germany to Prague, and most recently, to Stanford University. Because of my musical performances, I have experienced the world's most amazing sights and sounds while interacting with extraordinarily talented and kindhearted members of society.

My story begins with a stroke of luck. I established contact with a renowned bassoon performer and instructor named Stephen Walt, a Williams College teacher in high demand, who had never before considered working with a beginning pupil. Instantaneously, I could tell that our personalities were well-suited, and he became my bassoon coach for the seven years I studied the instrument until moving to California. Mr. Walt is an inspiration, a musical virtuoso, and the most warm, encouraging, demanding instructor I can possibly imagine. My success as a musician is due in great part to his dedication and guidance. Every other weekend, my father drove me from Niskayuna, New York, to

Williamstown, Massachusetts. Mr. Walt's lessons were worth every second of the hour-and-twenty-minute car ride along oftentimes slippery, snow-covered mountain roads.

As my years of practice accumulated, I steadily increased my skill level, becoming a proficient high school bassoonist. The summer before my sophomore year, I auditioned for, and gained acceptance to, one of America's premier youth orchestras, the Empire State Youth Orchestra. Although I was at first intimidated by the phenomenally talented musicians surrounding me in the orchestra, lengthy bus rides together, nights spent in hotels in foreign countries, and a sense of mutual admiration soon created an atmosphere in which these musicians became several of my closest friends. I will never forget the day our revered and beloved conductor, Francisco Noya, stood imposingly before us at the podium and announced in a thick Venezuelan accent, "Are you prepared to work extremely hard? Jes or no? Dis year, we play Carnegie Hall." I momentarily lost my grip on reality. Life for an orchestral musician does not reach a zenith more meaningful, more overwhelming, or more spectacular, than the opportunity to perform at *Carnegie Hall.*

For months, the idea of my orchestra's concert at Carnegie Hall constantly intruded on my thoughts. When I wasn't practicing the musical selections, my hands rehearsing complicated fingering passages, I imagined the sights and the sounds of the hall, and I stared at my monthly planner, scratching off each slowly passing day. One such day a week or so before the performance, I sat in my practice chair in the den trying to relax my aching mouth muscles, and I turned to look at the reed graveyard. Every reed I had used over the years, meticulously handcrafted from raw cane by Mr. Walt, inevitably found its way to the graveyard when it was worn-down, broken, cracked, weak, or simply no longer reliable. I carefully unfolded Poppy's box to examine its contents: hundreds of reeds, varying slightly in size, shape, cane discoloration, and string color—red, green, blue, even multi-hued—stuffed the box's interior. As I carefully lifted the reeds and let them sift through my fingers, each one evoked memories of a particular concert, practice session, summer camp, quintet, lesson, rehearsal, or pit orchestra. To this day, every tiny wooden relic, unique, beautiful, and delicate, tells a different, unforgettable story. The reed graveyard, I realized, is a metaphor for Poppy's undying love; it is representative of his personal contribution to my achievements. My greatest accomplishments, I now understood, were housed in this creation, crafted by his strong but gentle hands. Feeling revived, I closed the precious box, placed it on the shelf beside me, and resumed my practice.

10   My dream, from the moment that I began my avocation as a musician, was now materializing. I was standing in the wings of Carnegie Hall, placing my black patent leather shoes where all "the greats" had placed theirs. I peered around the velvet curtain, trembling slightly and sweating profusely.

Scanning the sea of faces for a few seconds, I finally located my large cohort of immediate family and close friends. I found them sitting in the upper left-hand balcony in a private box protruding far from the wall. Matt, appropriately, was directly in front and practically falling over the railing, grinning with a true pride that I'd never seen before, and have not seen since. Poppy, I'm quite certain, was witnessing the entire scene from above. He undoubtedly had the best seat in the house. As Poppy's presence filled the air above my head, he beamed his joy through Matt, who served as a surrogate physical representation for a grandfather who would have loved, more than anyone else, to hug and hold his granddaughter on that emotional afternoon.

From the time I found my seat on the stage until the concert was over, my memories are blurred. I have been told that the show ran its entirety without a single hitch; I, for one, was too nervous, excited, ecstatic, and satisfied, to have known what was going on. Thankfully, my musical bodily functions—lungs, heart, fingers, and muscles—took over for a severely wandering mind. I simply cannot describe the fantastic, all-encompassing feeling of earning and achieving one's greatest goal.

I regained mental composure after the last note of our program finished resonating in Carnegie Hall. My attention was called immediately to my support group, cheering and clapping above all others. Beneath it all was the underlying essence of my grandfather's love. I breathed a sigh of relief, took my bows, and, bassoon clutched close to my heart, walked off the stage of the world-renowned Carnegie Hall. What happens to the dreamer when her dream becomes a reality? Is a new dream born? I currently attend Stanford University in northern California, a place I consider to be an ideal launching pad for the discovery of fresh and thrilling ambitions. I am searching for my calling, yet again.

As for Poppy, he resides in the heavens, continuing to protect his baby granddaughter as she matures, becoming stronger and more independent. Late on the night of the concert, when I arrived at my home in Niskayuna, I walked into the den and cradled the reed graveyard in my hands. I opened Poppy's box and placed the most absolutely perfect reed I had ever known inside, where it would retire among the masses that had come before. I latched the box shut as I positioned it in its resting place on the shelf, thus signifying the end to one marvelous chapter of my life. With Poppy as my copilot, I flew off in search of uncharted horizons.

QUESTIONS FOR DISCUSSION

1. What did Melissa learn from Poppy? Why was he her first "teacher"? Why has he remained such an important role model and source of support for her? What details are used to characterize him?

2. What personal and family qualities do you think led Melissa to become a successful bassoonist? What did playing at Carnegie Hall mean for her? What examples best reveal her dedication?
3. Why is the essay entitled "The Best Seat in the House"? How does this phrase help to clarify her ongoing relationship with "Poppy"?
4. Discuss the writer's central symbol of the reed box. Why does Melissa value her "reed graveyard"? How does her description of the box make it compelling to the reader?

Alberto Alvaro Rios

Nani

Alberto Alvaro Rios (b. 1952) was born in the border town of Nogales, Arizona. His father, originally from Guatemala, was a justice of the peace. Rios earned his B.A. (1974) and an M.F.A. in Creative Writing (1979) from the University of Arizona. Since 1994, Rios has been Regents Professor of English at Arizona State University, where he began teaching in 1982. His most widely read books include Stories of the Heart: Pig Cookies and Other Stories *(1995), and* Capirotada: A Nogales Memoir and Curtain of Trees *(1999). Rios looks for the "unheard of" aspects of his heritage in his poetry and stories, examining the culturally diverse stories of his family through a magical realism that incorporates the literary styles of great Mexican and South American writers such as Pablo Neruda, Jorge Luiz Borges, and Isabel Allende. The selection that follows, "Nani," is representative of Rios' poetry—beginning as it does with an ordinary family event and exploring its personal, cultural, and imaginative complexity.*

JOURNAL

Discuss a family member who expressed his or her love and concern for your well-being in ways other than words.

Sitting at her table, she serves
the sopa de arroz to me
instinctively, and I watch her,
the absolute mamá, and eat words
5 I might have had to say more

out of embarrassment. To speak,
now-foreign words I used to speak,
too, dribble down her mouth as she serves
me albóndigas. No more
10 that a third are easy to me.
By the stove she does something with words
and looks at me only with her
back. I am full. I tell her
I taste the mint, and watch her speak
15 smiles at the stove. All my words
make her smile. Nani never serves
herself, she only watches me
with her skin, her hair. I ask for more.

I watch the mama warming more
20 tortillas for me. I watch her
fingers in the flame for me.
Near her mouth, I see a wrinkle speak
of a man whose body serves
the ants like she serves me, then more words
25 from more wrinkles about children, words
about this and that, flowing more
easily from these other mouths. Each serves
as a tremendous string around her,
holding her together. They speak
30 nani was this and that to me
and I wonder just how much of me
will die with her, what were the words
I could have been, was. Her insides speak
through a hundred wrinkles, now, more
35 than she can bear, steel around her,
shouting, then, What is this thing she serves?

She asks me if I want more.
I own no words to stop her.
Even before I speak, she serves.

QUESTIONS FOR DISCUSSION

1. What do you think the poem's speaker means by his description of
   Nani as the "absolute mama"? In what sense is she absolute or
   mythical in her presence or activities?
2. Rios develops the image of Nani's wrinkles. Analyze what they represent in the poem. In what way do Nani's wrinkles help the speaker
   in the poem? Refer to specific lines to support your interpretation.

3. What does the speaker mean when he wonders, "just how much of me/will die with her"?
4. In what ways does Nani help the speaker to be part of a larger community?
5. Why does Nani serve "instinctively"? How would you answer the question that the speaker poses at the poem's conclusion, "What is this thing she serves"?
6. How does Rios' repeated use of the line ending words (*me, words, speak, more, serves,* and *her*) strengthen the poem?

CONNECTION

Compare Rios' poem and his sense of sadness over the loss of his culture to that of the father and daughters in Saira Shah's story (see page 90).

IDEAS FOR WRITING

1. Write an essay that discusses a changing relationship that you have had with an older family member who kept the traditions of your family alive. In what ways was your family community changed? How will you share with your own children the traditions, rituals, and sense of community that have been passed down through your family?
2. Interview several elderly members of your family to learn more about your family's traditions. Write an essay that tells the story of your family as you have learned more about it. What have you gained from learning more about your family and its traditions?

RELATED WEB SITES

Alberto Alvaro Rios
www.public.asu.edu/~aarios/
Arizona State University's Web site for Alberto Rios gives links to numerous informational resources on the author. These include biographical information, updated news on Rios, interviews, and publications.

Online Extra . . . An Interview with Alberto Ríos
**www.aarpsegundajuventud.org/english/entertainment/
2007-ON/07ON_rios.html**
AARP Segunda Juventud is a bilingual magazine that features articles on current and past issues. This specific article provides an interview with Alberto Rios and gives insight into his relationship with the Spanish language.

Julian Castro

An Interpretation of "Nani"

Julian Castro (b. 1974) wrote this essay for his first year writing class at Stanford University. He went on to earn his law degree at Harvard Law School and became involved in Mexican-American politics in San Antonio, Texas, where he was born. Castro served on the San Antonio City Council from 2001 to 2005, where he sought to establish himself as a leader on issues of economic development, education, and environmental protection. Castro campaigned to be Mayor of San Antonio in 2005.

"Nani": An Analysis

Alberto Ríos has achieved success and acclaim as a writer and scholar. However, his good fortune sharply contrasts with the experiences of most first generation Mexican-American immigrants. In his poem "Nani," the speaker, an assimilated Mexian-American, acknowledges the distance between his life and the life of his grandmother, Nani. As the speaker reflects on his separation from her, his questions turn inward, and his words uncover confusion about his bicultural heritage.

The poem begins at a dinner table, where the speaker is being served by "the absolute mama," Nani. Right away the language of the poem indicates the presence of a second culture. She serves him sopa de arroz, the Spanish term for rice soup. His use of the term "sopa de arroz" instead of the English term gives a clue that he understands at least some words of Spanish and that Nani is probably a Spanish speaker as well. However, the next line is a perplexing one. "I watch her/the absolute mama and eat words/I might have had to say more out of embarrassment." Immediately, the reader wonders why the speaker would be embarrassed by being served by Nani. Just as quickly, the speaker explains why he feels uncomfortable.

In lines six through ten the speaker reveals his inability to fully understand Nani's language, for when he speaks of her words he says, "No more than a third are easy to me." But he also mentions that he did understand her once. When he says, "To speak/now foreign words I used to speak," we know that he once felt a part of the ritual Nani is performing at the dinner table. The speaker intensifies the separation by using contrasting references. First, he describes how the words "dribble down her mouth." That image makes her speech seem like babbling, for it might as well be to him. But then he uses a second Spanish term. ". . . as she serves me albondigas," he states. His use of the Spanish term reveals how language used to unite them through the eating ritual. Little bits of dialogue remain in his vocabulary, but the language is now "foreign" to him.

In lines eleven through eighteen the speaker changes his focus and his perception on Nani. He uses imagery that puts her in a mythical light: "By the stove she does something with her words and looks at me only with her back," and "Nani never serves/herself, she only watches me/with her skin, her hair. . . ." These images illustrate how powerful, almost magical Nani appears to the speaker. She serves him unselfishly and takes nothing for herself. As his images liken her to a supernatural being, a question arises about the past relationship between Nani and the speaker. The speaker gives hints. He says that "All my words/make her smile." Nani's every gesture expresses feelings of great warmth and affection. Even though the speaker is grown up, Nani continues to spoil him with her kindness.

5   In line thirteen, when the speaker says "I am full," the meaning is ambiguous, suggesting the speaker's confusion—is his stomach full, is he full of guilt, or is he full of love for Nani? The next section of the poem, lines nineteen through thirty-six, offer a tentative answer to the question of fullness, although not a complete one. Here the speaker elaborates on his relationship with Nani. She fills him with love, having apparently given him everything that she ever could, surviving others whom she has previously loved and served as well: "I see a wrinkle speak/of a man whose body serves/the ants like she serves me. . . ." Could that man be the speaker's grandfather, or his own father? The speaker equates Nani's life experiences and her fond memories of the past with her numerous wrinkles, each of which "serves/as a crucial string around her,/holding her together." He suggests here that those experiences are what keep her going, and what she wants is to pass her wisdom on to him, to "fill him up" in a far more meaningful way than merely serving him a meal.

Herein lies the central theme of the poem. It becomes obvious that the speaker is separated from Nani and from part of himself. He has assimilated into the mainstream American culture, and like so many second and third generation Mexican-Americans, he has lost the ability to speak Spanish well. This is the base of his separation from Nani. He no longer possesses that knowledge of his culture, while Nani has lived her life by its traditions. Thus, he ponders the consequences of Nani's death: "I wonder just how much of me/will die with her. . . ." She knows everything about his past, and his future will be a sad one if he cannot regain what he has lost, his culture. Already he only speaks Spanish when he is with her; when will he use it after she is gone?

The Spanish language here implies more than just a set of sounds, words, and symbols for communication; it represents the Mexican customs and traditions that contribute to the character of an individual. He stands to lose part of his identity. Therefore, when Nani speaks to him "through a hundred wrinkles, now, more/than she can bear, steel around her,/shouting then," he realizes, as she does, that she may not have long to live, that their conversation is perhaps a final opportunity for her to teach him about that other side of him that he has lost, the Mexican side. This may explain why it seems to him like Nani is frantically "shouting" through her wrinkles. Because she is doing so, the speaker has to ask himself, "What is this thing she serves?" In that phrase alone it is evident that the speaker knows Nani has given him more than just a home and good food. She has given him his identity. From her he has learned about his past and his present. She probably has helped him learn to read and write, and now she teaches him about who he really is.

When the speaker realizes how removed his life is from Nani's, he becomes confused and feels guilty. Throughout the poem he contrasts his life with hers. When he states ". . . what were the words/I could have been, was," he reveals his curiosity about what might have become of him if he had not assimilated. Nani has given him all that she possibly could, and his words reflect a great respect for the way she has lived her life. Perhaps she doesn't speak English or have much formal education, but she did the best she could, and even in her old age, she continues to provide him with love and stability. Because of this, he feels guilty.

He does not know if he has done the right thing by separating himself from his native culture. He must ask himself what his life would have been like if he had lived as Nani has. Could he have been unselfish enough to live such a life? Because he realizes that he cannot be as giving, he is embarrassed in line six when she serves him. After all, Nani is an old woman, but he is an able-bodied young man.

10   In lines thirty-seven through thirty nine ("She asks me if I want more. /I own no words to stop her/Before I speak, she serves"), the speaker reveals his dilemma. Here is a man, probably in the prime of his life, who continues to take and take without giving back much. He must be confused about how he can repay her for everything she has given him. Money means little to her, but what else does he have to give? Is his company enough for her? Although he may never be completely comfortable because of what he cannot give back, I think he believes that Nani wants only his company and attention. Therefore, he can accept how generous she is and just enjoy regaining part of his identity.

The structure of the poem, a sestina form that involves the repetition of six key words at the end of the lines, emphasizes the character of Nani and the conflict of the speaker. At every sixth line throughout much of the poem, one of the words is repeated at the end of consecutive lines. This form adds to the speaker's mythical portrayal of Nani, and it reveals something about her personality. The poem is split into two sections, lines one through eighteen and nineteen through thirty-nine. Words like "serves," "me," "more," "words," "her," and "speak" indicate that Nani is benevolent. Special attention should be paid to the word "serves" which occurs at the end of the first and last lines of the poem. The speaker clearly wants to emphasize how much Nani has given him, and the impact on him of her constant, selfless service. Other key words, like "speak," indicate what Nani does for him in terms of language. Her love keeps him close to her and to his culture of origin.

Alberto Ríos puts his subject in familiar surroundings to have him realize how far he has drifted from them. That can be taken as a message to the children and grandchildren of immigrants, many of whom, like the speaker, have assimilated and lost much of their native heritage. Identity is made up of more than one part. Thus, the speaker's self-questioning is an invitation to these people to consider what they are giving up and at what price. To those of us who have experienced Mexican customs, Nani is a common figure. The way the poem presents her with dignity and pride illustrates a special respect for the women, who, although often unacknowledged, are our nurturers. What can we give back to them?

QUESTIONS FOR DISCUSSION

1. What is Castro's thesis? What rhetorical devices does he use in speaking about the first four lines of the poem?
2. Castro points to ambiguous questions in the poem, such as "I watch her/the absolute mama and eat words/I might have had to say more out of embarrassment." Why is Castro's technique of pointing his readers to questions raised in the poem effective?
3. In what other ways do words become central issues in Castro's interpretation of the poem?
4. Do you agree with Castro that Nani is a "mythical" figure? Explain.
5. What does Castro identify as the central theme of the poem? Do you agree with his analysis and conclusion?

TOPICS FOR RESEARCH AND WRITING

1. Write an essay in which you discuss how readings such as those by Cofer, Angelou, and Shah in this chapter, as well as outside readings and research, have affected your understanding of the importance of memories as a rich source for writing material.

2. After reading the essays by Saira Shah and Judith Ortiz Cofer, do some further research and write an essay about the relation between memories of discrimination in minority and/or immigrant groups and the writing that comes out of their communities.

3. Explore the way that historical memory often is a mixture of personal remembered events and larger events that we learn about from reading or exposure to the media. Do some research into an event such as 9/11, the war in Iraq, or another recent historical conflict of which you have secondhand knowledge. Write an essay that explores the ways that the secondhand knowledge of the event created a sense of "memory" and emotional impact of the event for you.

4. After examining essays in this chapter, do some reading about the quality and improvability of memory. Can we improve our memories of recent and past events, or is memory simply a "given" ability that we can do nothing about? Write an essay that presents your findings and conclusions on this topic.

5. Explore the reliability of memories of the past, questioning the extent to which the past and "history" are said to truly exist outside of what we recall and re-create through memory and imagination. Do some further research into the reliability of early memories, and draw some conclusions. Is there an "objective" past, or does each person or group of people invent a version of history? If so, what are our "versions" most often based upon? Write your conclusions in an essay.

6. Write an essay that explores your family's legacy by giving an account of several memories that have been crucial to its sense of identity and values. If possible, interview different family members, including extended family such as grandparents, uncles, aunts, and cousins.

7. Write about a film that focuses on the importance of memories and/or the reliability of memory, referring to elements such as dreams of characters, flashback sequences, and other cinematic devices for showing remembered scenes. Films to consider include *Cries and Whispers, Cinema Paradiso, The Joy Luck Club, Memento, The Sixth Sense, Titanic, The Piano Lesson, The English Patient, The Butterfly Effect, I Know Why the Caged Bird Sings, The Eternal Sunshine of the Spotless Mind, The Butterfly and the Diving Bell, Forrest Gump, The Namesake,* and *Angela's Ashes.*

Journeys and Reflections

Jon Ford (b.1943)
Pokhara Bus, Nepal (2008)

JOURNAL

Reflect on and write about a bus trip or other journey you have taken where you encountered unfamiliar people, customs, and physical environments.

The world is a book, and those who do not travel read only a page.
                                                        ST. AUGUSTINE

Travel is fatal to prejudice, bigotry, and narrow-mindedness.
                                                        MARK TWAIN

I met a lot of people in Europe. I even encountered myself.
                                                        JAMES BALDWIN

THEMATIC INTRODUCTION

As James Baldwin suggests in the quote above, many who travel realize that the journeys they have taken to new cultures and new continents have opened their minds and senses to deeper psychological, cultural, and sometimes spiritual understandings. Travel, in this sense, can be understood as an inward journey that helps one to understand more about his or her identity and values as well as those in the public world. Travel enriches and expands the knowledge we learn from reading about culture, history, spirituality, and identity.

Journeys, like dreams, can be exhilarating and inspiring or confusing or disturbing. In travel we find ourselves in close contact with aspects of ourselves we may have not examined in years — or perhaps never examined. People travel for many reasons — some to rereturn to a place that has held deep memories, some to learn more about a culture that they have studied and want to understand better, some out of curiosity. Travel can be a joyous experience that opens our hearts and minds to people and experiences that we could never have imagined. Perhaps Walt Whitman puts it best in the powerful opening verse to his long poem, "Song of the Open Road": "Afoot and light-hearted I take to the open road,/Healthy, free, the world before me."

The first reading in this chapter focuses on a journey of return. In a travel narrative that has its origins in the Vietnam-War era, "Viet Kieu" (foreigner or "overseas Vietnamese"), Andrew Pham explores his journey from his home in San Jose, California, where he grew up with his refugee family, back to Viet Nam. Pham discovers more than he expected as he is troubled by images of racism and abuse from his youth in San Jose that come unexpectedly to his mind on the journey.

Torn between two worlds, he meets a young Vietnamese tour-guide whose envious and unrealistic attitude towards over-seas Vietnamese disturbs him.

In another story featuring a tour-guide, Ken Matusow's "Grand-père," the author also is deeply touched, but in a positive way, by his encounter with a tour guide on a boat trip down the Niger River in West Africa, a wise and warm-hearted man and a natural leader who has taken control of his life, protecting and nurturing the tourists whom he introduces to his world in a way that is unique and memorable. Next, in another story of return, a student writer from Bangladore, India, Kavita Sreedhar, writes about her visit back to India, after five years in the United States, to help her mother recover from an illness. In her essay "Traveling Home" Sreedhar considers the changes she notices in her home town and reflects upon its rapidly changing environment, architecture, and interpersonal relations, as well as the implications of these changes on her own sense of belonging as a native of India.

The next group of selections examines travel as a spiritual experience, a search for enduring values and ritual observances not easily found in our own rapidly changing culture. In the following selection, Francine Prose, in "Ritual Tourist," begins by questioning the motivations of those who travel to watch spiritual ritual practices that are unlike those in their own culture. While Prose seems critical of the tourist industry, at one of the gatherings she attends her resistance breaks down as she feels empathy for the emotions of those around her. Her compassion for the other tourists helps her to understand more deeply the need to find meaning through travel. In contrast, American writer and Buddhist, Natalie Goldberg explores her feelings of alienation and disillusionment when she visits in their homeland the Japanese Buddhist monks who have inspired her spirituality. Her journey helps her to rethink her own beliefs.

An essay about travel to a destination in a manufactured environment follows. Joan M. Thomas, in "The Field of Dreams Mystique: Quest for an American Ideal," examines the psychology and values of those tourists who look for the spirit of America through visiting the Iowa baseball field, home, and cornfield that were the settings for the popular movie *Field of Dreams*. Each journey, even to seemingly ordinary places, can become a life lesson that deepens our understanding and ignites our dreams. From travel, too, we sometimes realize that life itself is "dream-like," requiring us to constantly redefine what for us is real and what is illusion.

WRITING DESCRIPTIONS

When we describe, we try to create powerful impressions of our experiences so that others can share our visions, feeling what we have felt, seeing through our eyes, and sharing other senses as well— hearing, taste, smell, and touch. Descriptions need to be written with great attention to detail, in specific language, and with much thought as to the choice of material in order to communicate your meaning to your audience.

Observing

The more awake and alert your senses are to the world around you, the more fully you experience your world, and the more likely it is that you will be able to collect the relevant, unique, and interesting details needed to create an evocative and expressive description. To train your senses to be receptive to your surroundings and to help you write a vivid description, spend some time in quiet observation of a particular object or place you want to describe. Try observing your subject from various perspectives, walking around it, looking at it in different lights, and experiencing it through your senses. Can you listen to it? Touch it? Smell it? While you observe, try asking yourself these questions: Why am I doing this observation? How do I feel about my subject? How do my feelings influence the way I perceive the subject? Spend ten minutes or so in quiet observation before you begin to write; then jot down as many details as you can about your subject. Read your list over to see if you can add more sensory details. Share your list of details with a classmate who may be able to help you to think about details you had forgotten.

Words and Images

Writer Annie Dillard has noted that "Seeing is . . . verbalization." When describing a person, place, thing, or even something so seemingly imprecise as an emotion, it is important to verbalize your response using specific, carefully chosen words. When you use words effectively, you can create a series of images, or sensory clusters of detail, which, taken together, convey to your readers an intimate or intense description of your experiences. Notice how in the following example from her travel memoir *Russian Journal*, Andrea Lee used a series of images that evoke specific colors ("gold," "yellow"), a sense of touch ("stuck," "cold"), a concrete impression of textures and forms ("decayed," "grotesque," "peeling front"), and a specific place or area ("a mansion in the Arbat"): "In Moscow I found more demanding pleasures of nature and architecture: rain on the gold domes inside the Kremlin walls, yellow leaves stuck to a wet pavement; a decayed stone grotesque on the peeling front of a mansion in the Arbat; a face in a subway crowd."

An image may be clarified by a comparison (a simile or a metaphor) that helps to explain more fully the quality of an experience by linking it imaginatively or literally to other, related experiences or things. This is a technique Farley Mowat uses in his essay "Learning to See" to capture his confusion as he notices something mysterious and white that looks like a feather boa at first, yet turns out to be the tails of two huge, playful wolves: "Without warning, both boas turned toward me; began rising higher and higher, and finally revealed themselves as the tails of two wolves beginning to top the esker." A reader of such a comparison is imaginatively drawn into the image and the author's attempt to create meaning for it. Use specific images and comparisons in your writing in order to invite your readers to become imaginatively engaged in your thoughts and descriptions.

Revising Initial Descriptions

Look back through a first draft of one of your essays to find several descriptive passages of physical objects, places, people, or moods. Try to replace observations or descriptions, in particular any words that now seem too general, generic, or imprecise, with specific, concrete, words or with imaginative images and comparisons that will involve your readers' minds and emotions.

Establishing Vantage Point and Tone

A descriptive writer, like a painter or a photographer, is interested in establishing a coherent, unified impression. To create this impression, it is necessary to focus the description from a particular vantage point, to let the reader see the scene from one special window as well as to establish tone. Student writer Kavita Sreedhar in her essay "Traveling Home" focuses her description tightly and establishes a tone of shock and indignation in the opening sentences: "Just as I was setting foot into the country at one of the immigration counters, I had my first taste of how alienated I was to feel in my own homeland. The police officers in Khaki uniforms brandished the *lathi* (a form of stick like weapon), hitting it on the floor by the red lines behind which people had to wait. In my enthusiasm at being Indian and belonging among my shoving and pushing brethren, I stepped on the red line. 'Crack!' A loud noise almost made me jump out of my skin, as the *lathi* came down, landing in front of me. I looked up at a pot-bellied constable in an ill-fitting khaki uniform. He looked at me screaming '*Lime ke Peeche!*' 'Back of the line, back of the line!' I looked around to see if he were talking to someone else, and all I saw were scores and scores of eyes staring at me." Sreedhar's re-introduction to India was certainly not what she had expected. We feel her outrage, her disappointment, her confusion.

Thinking About Your Purpose and Audience

Although descriptions are often written for the pleasure of capturing an experience with accuracy, description serves other purposes in writing, depending in part upon the occasion for and intended audience of the piece. Now that you have had some practice in observing unfamiliar places or objects and in selecting a purpose and tone, audience, and vantage point, you are ready to write a precise, imaginative, and expressive description of a place that holds strong meaning for you. Finding the words to describe what you see and selecting the pertinent details, images, and comparisons to clarify and support your ideas and opinions are skills that you will need to master as you continue to improve your ability to describe. As you become more adept at using these strategies, you will discover that powerful writing is also writing that reveals what lights up the darkness around you.

As you read the selections in this chapter, consider how travel can enrich our lives and bring meaning and perspective to day-to-day concerns, illuminating what we take for granted through contrast with other types of encounters and different cultures. Travel can provide alternative suggestions for how we can live more fully and intensely through what we have learned on our journeys.

Walt Whitman

From "Song of the Open Road"

Walt Whitman (1819-1892) was born in Long Island, lived in Brooklyn, New Orleans, Washington D.C., and in Camden, New Jersey for the last 18 years of his life. Whitman ended his formal education at age 12 and became a self-educated man, working at various jobs that included typesetter, school teacher, journalist, nurse, and housebuilder. His life's work, Leaves of Grass, *was self-published in 1855. Whitman continued to revise* Leaves of Grass, *which was published in its final form in 1891–1892. Whitman's poem became an American classic, known as a declaration of literary independence with its broad, bold, and comprehensive affirmation of freedom, democracy, and celebration of life in the New World. Known as the father of free verse, Whitman's collection of poetry made him one of the most influential American poets. The selection that follows from "Song of the Open Road" (1856) asks readers to reflect on how travel changes us.*

JOURNAL

Write about your feelings as you prepared to embark on a hike into the forest or into an open space.

Song of the Open Road

1

Afoot and light-hearted, I take to the open road,
Healthy, free, the world before me,
The long brown path before me, leading wherever I choose.

Henceforth I ask not good-fortune—I myself am good fortune;
5   Henceforth I whimper no more, postpone no more, need nothing,
Strong and content, I travel the open road.

The earth—that is sufficient;
I do not want the constellations any nearer;
I know they are very well where they are;
10   I know they suffice for those who belong to them.

(Still here I carry my old delicious burdens;
I carry them, men and women—I carry them with me wherever I go;
I swear it is impossible for me to get rid of them;
I am fill'd with them, and I will fill them in return.)

QUESTIONS FOR DISCUSSION

1. What meaning does the title of the poem suggest to you?
2. What is the speaker's attitude and mood as he begins his journey on the open road? How has the speaker had to change to gain his freedom? What is the symbolism of the road being brown?
3. How is living in the moment on the open road different from his previous lifestyle? What is he learning? Does he seem to regret choosing freedom?

4. Why does the speaker savor the fact that he carries "my old burdens"? Who are his burdens and why must he hold on to them? Is he still free, carrying his burdens with him?
5. Summarize the meaning in this poem. Do you think that you would want to embark on a journey that is similar to the speaker's? Why or why not?
6. Explain what "living in the moment" means to you. How have you experienced living in the moment? Do you value this type of experience? Why?

CONNECTION

Compare the motivation for travel in "Song of the Open Road" to Andrew Pham's in "Viet-Kieu" (see page 117).

IDEAS FOR WRITING

1. Read the entire "Song of the Open Road." Summarize the main ideas in the poem and discuss which of Whitman's ideas or concepts make most sense to you. Refer to specific lines or stanzas to give the reader a better idea of what you value about the poem's ideas. If you do not agree with the ideas in this poem, explain why.
2. Write a research paper that includes background information about Walt Whitman and his life. Then interpret "Song of the Open Road" using this biographical data. Refer to scholars who have commented on the poem to support your point of view.

RELATED WEB SITES

The Walt Whitman Archive
www.whitmanarchive.org/
This Web site provides links to published works, manuscripts, criticism, and other resources regarding Walk Whitman and his writing. Also included are links to pictures and audio clips, as well as news and updates.

Browse the Whitman Collection—Electronic Text Center
http://etext.virginia.edu/whitman/
Created by the University of Virginia Library, this Web site contains a complete e-collection of all of Whitman's works, both prose and poetry. Find out about faculty and student projects regarding Whitman's writing.

Andrew Pham

Viet-Kieu

Andrew Pham (b. 1967) was born in Vietnam, and fled with his family at the age of ten to California, worked hard, went to UCLA, landed a good technical job at United Airlines—and always carried a letter of resignation in his briefcase. Much to his parents' displeasure Pham quit his job and set off on bicycle excursions through Mexico, Japan, and, finally, Vietnam. "I have to do something unethnic," he said. "I have to go. Make my pilgrimage." He sold all his possessions to embark on the year-long bicycle journey that took him through the Mexican desert, from Narita to Kyoto in Japan, and 2,357 miles to Saigon. Catfish and Mandala (1998), from which "Viet Kieu" is excerpted, presents a vibrant, picaresque memoir of that bicycle journey, which documents an unforgettable search for cultural identity.

JOURNAL

Discuss a time when you were aware of being an outsider in a community that had been your home. How did you feel?

The closer I come to Nha Trang the more frequently I see group tours busing to local points of interest. The locals are familiar with the tourist traffic and don't shout *"Oy! Oy!"* at foreigners. The main road loops around a mountain and enters the outskirts of the city from the south side. There is a shortcut, some high school kids point out to me, up the mountain and along the cliff. It's a good sporting ride, they say. I'm about to bag 120 miles today and have no wish to climb a mountain. I come into the city the easy way.

Although the outlying area is a mirror image of all the other dusty little towns, the city center is far more developed than anything I've seen. I limp the battered bike through town, heading toward the water where the locals have told me there is lodging. Shady lanes unroll between banks of sprawling buildings set back behind brick fences. There's a nice flavor here predating the Liberation of '75. I was just a kid then, but I remember Mom being very hip with her bellbottoms and buggy sunglasses. She must have wasted scores of film rolls in Nha Trang, her favorite city. The breeze is fresh, sweet, not salty like Phan Thiet. Out on the beachfront boulevard, I am suddenly in Waikiki! Someone has ripped it out of Hawaii and dropped it in downtown Nha Trang. A colossal skeleton of the Outrigger Hotel is being framed on the beach practically in the surf line. Tall, gleaming towers of glass and steel are already taking residence a stone's throw from the water. The sandy stretch of beach is jammed with fancy restaurants, bars hopping with modern rock, jazz, and Vietnamese pop. Aromas of grilled food turn heads and sharpen appetites. Along the avenue, fat Europeans and Australians pad about in thong bikinis, sheer sarongs, and Lycra shorts, dropping wads of dollars for seashells, corals, lacquered jewelry boxes, and bad paintings, loot, mementos, evidence.

I take the cheapest room available to a Viet-kieu at a government-run hotel (for some reason, Danes and Germans get lower rates), jump through a cold shower, then get back on my bike to head to the Vietnamese part of Nha Trang, where the food is cheaper and better. I am ravenous. Diarrhea be damned. Tonight I'm going to eat anything I want. After nearly three months of sporadic intestinal troubles, I'm still hoping that my system will acclimatize. I'm Vietnamese after all, and these microorganisms once thrived in my gut as thoroughly as in any Vietnamese here.

I eat dinner at an alley diner, nine tables crammed between two buildings lit with a couple of bare light bulbs. The family running the place says they are happy to have me, although they generally don't like foreigners. Eat too little, drink too little, but talk too much, they complain. Foreigners like to sit and sit and talk. Vietnamese eat and get out. Lounging is done in coffeehouses and beer halls. No problem. I prove to them I'm Vietnamese. I down two large bottles of Chinese beer and gorge myself on a monstrous meal of grilled meat served with a soy-and-pork-fat gravy, wrapping the meat in rice paper, cucumber, mint, pickled daikon, sour carrot, fresh basil, lettuce, chili pepper, cilantro, and rice vermicelli. Then I clear out quickly. I go to a hotel to check on a friend who might be in town. As a tour guide, he is a regular at the hotel. The concierge confirms that my friend Cuong and his tour are in town. I leave him a note and wait for him at an ice-cream parlor down the street.

5   "Hello! Andrew!"

"Cuong!"

I met him a few weeks after I arrived in Saigon. We bummed around the city several times with his girlfriends. I like him. We both agreed to check on each other when in Nha Trang or Vung Tau, both major cities on his itinerary.

He skips across the street, penny-loafing around the dog shit as he dodges motorbikes. Cuong doesn't wear sandals. No more. Not ever again. He told me, You can tell a Vietnamese by the way he wears his sandals. Is the stem firmly held between the toes? Or does the ball of the heel drag beyond the sandal? Do the sandals flap like loose tongues when he walks? Does he know there is mud between his toes? All this from a man who—in his own words—"*dribbled away [his] youth as a roadside petrol-boy selling gasoline out of glass bottles, wiping down motorbikes, hustling for dimes, and playing barefoot soccer in the dirt.*"

He smoothes his shirt, fingers the ironed pleats of his gray slacks, straightens his pin-striped blue tie with red polka dots. Then, grinning, he steps closer and pumps my hand enthusiastically. "Calvin," he corrects me. "I'm sticking with your suggestion: Calvin. It's easier for the foreigners to pronounce." I'd come up with the name at his request. He wanted something that started with a "C" and was short and sharp and American.

10   "You made it! You're not hurt? No?" he says, patting me on the arm and looking me over. "A little thinner and darker, yes. Incredible. You biked all that way? Yes, yes, of course you did."

"You got my message?"

"Of course. May I join you?" he queries, forever the Vietnamese gentleman. I fill him in on all that happened since I last saw him nearly two months ago. When a waitress brings him his chilled Coke—no ice, just like the way foreigners drink their soda—he thanks her. She looks at him, a little startled to hear a Vietnamese man uttering platitudes like Westerners. Calvin has picked up the habit because he finds it more genteel and civilized.

I first made his acquaintance at a sidewalk café. He took me for a Japanese and wanted to practice his English. When I told him I was a Vietnamese from California, he was very uncomfortable using the term Viet-kieu, explaining that people said it with too many connotations. Sometimes, it was just a word, other times an insult or a term of segregation. *"Vietnamese are Vietnamese if they believe they are,"* he had said by way of explanation, and I liked him on the instant.

By Saigon standards, Calvin is a yuppie who came into his own by the most romantic way possible—by the compulsion of a promise made to his mother on her deathbed. One afternoon, when we were touring the outer districts of Saigon on his motorbike, Calvin pointed to a pack of greyhound-lean young men, shirtless, volleying a plastic bird back and forth with their feet. *"That was me. That's how I was until I was twenty-two. Can you believe it? I threw away all my young years, working odd jobs and messing around. I just didn't care."* His mother bequeathed him, her only child, a small sum, which he spent on English classes, not bothering to finish up high school. With what little remained, he bribed his way into a job as a hotel bellhop and worked his way up. He entered a special school for tour guides. After three years of intense training, he makes four hundred dollars a month plus two hundred in tips. Now, twenty-nine, single, and rich even by Saigon standards, he fares better than college grads who are blessed if they can command two hundred dollars a month. His biggest regret: *"I wish my mother could see me now."*

15   Calvin sips his Coke and plucks a pack of Marlboros from his shirt pocket, the American cigarette one of his main props for marking himself one of the upwardly mobile. "I'm down to half a pack a day," he mumbles apologetically, offering me a smoke. I decline. He puts his

cigarette down saying: "Dirty, dirty, Vietnamese habit." Calvin keeps a list of "dirty Vietnamese habits" and steels himself against them.

I tell him that Americans used to call cigarettes "white slavers." He considers that for a moment then smirks. *"That has a double meaning for us, doesn't it."* He counts the cigarettes remaining in the pack. *"Last one today,"* he announces. He seems to want my approval so I nod. Vindicated, he ignites the last of his daily nicotine allowance. He sighs the smoke downwind. *"Tell me. Tell me everything about your trip."*

As I recount the events since I last saw him, Calvin grows increasingly excited, digging me more for the details of Vietnam than for the actual mechanics of bike touring. How did the police treat you? Hanoi people are more formal than Southerners, aren't they? You think Uncle Ho's body is a hoax? What's the countryside like? Is it pretty like the Southern country? He flames another cigarette and orders us a round of beer. By our third round, he has chain-smoked into a second pack of Marlboros.

Late in the night, when I am sapped of tales from the road, Calvin, who is beer-fogged, leans back in his chair and asks, *"America is like a dream, isn't it?"*

After all I've seen, I agree. *"Sure."*

20   We contemplate the beer in our glasses. I ask him, *"Do you want to go there?"* I don't know why I ask him this. Maybe, believing that he is my equivalent in Vietnam, I want him to say that he really loves the country and that it is magical, wonderful in ways I have yet to imagine. More powerful, more potent than the West.

Calvin sounds annoyed. *"Of course. Who wouldn't?"* He pauses, taking long, pensive drags on his cigarette. *"But perhaps only to visit. To see, understand-no?"*

"Why?"

"Simple. Here . . . here, I am a king." He leans over the table, shaking the cigarette at me. *"In America you, I mean all you Viet-kieu, are guests. And guests don't have the same rights as hosts."* He sits back, legs crossed at the knees, and throws a proprietary arm over the city. *"At least, here, I am king. I belong. I am better than most Vietnamese."*

"No, we're not guests. We're citizens. Permanent. Ideally we are all equal. Equal rights," I insert lamely, the words, recalled from elementary school history lessons, sounding hollow.

25   *"Right, but do you FEEL like an American? Do you?"*

Yes! Yes! Yes, I do. I really do, I want to shout it in his face. Already, the urge leaves a bad taste in my mouth. *"Sometimes, I do. Sometimes, I feel like I am a real American."*

I wish I could tell him. I don't mind forgetting who I am, but I know he wouldn't understand. I don't mind being looked at or treated just like another American, a white American. No, I don't mind at all. I want it. I like it. Yet every so often when I become really good at tricking myself, there is always that inevitable slap that shocks me out of my shell and prompts me to reassess everything.

How could I tell him my shame? How could I tell him about the drive-bys where some red-faced white would stick his head out of his truck, giving me the finger and screaming, "Go home, Chink!" Could I tell him it chilled me to wonder what would happen if my protagonist knew I was Vietnamese? What if his father had died in Vietnam? What if he was a Vietnam vet? Could I tell Calvin about the time my Vietnamese friends and I dined in a posh restaurant in Laguna Beach in Southern California? A white man at the next table, glaring at us, grumbled to his wife, "They took over Santa Ana. And now they're here. This whole state is going to hell." They was us Vietnamese. Santa Ana was now America's Little Saigon.

Could I tell Calvin I was initiated into the American heaven during my first week Stateside by eight black kids who pulverized me in the restroom, calling me Viet Cong? No. I grew up fighting blacks, whites, and Chicanos. The whites beat up the blacks. The blacks beat up the Chicanos. And everybody beat up the Chinaman whether or not he was really an ethnic Chinese. These new Vietnamese kids were easy pickings, small, bookish, passive, and not fluent in English.

30 So, we congregate in Little Saigons, we hide out in Chinatowns and Japantowns, blending in. We huddle together, surrounding ourselves with the material wealth of America, and wave our star-spangled banners, shouting: "We're Americans. We love America."

I cannot bring myself to confront my antagonists. Cannot always claim my rights as a naturalized citizen. Cannot, for the same reason, resist the veterans' pleas for money outside grocery stores. Cannot armor myself against the pangs of guilt at every homeless man wearing army fatigues. Sown deep in me is a seed of discomfort. Maybe shame. I see that we Vietnamese Americans don't talk about our history. Although we often pretend to be modest and humble as we preen our successful immigrants stories, we rarely admit even to ourselves the circumstances and the cost of our being here. We elude it all like a petty theft committed ages ago. When convenient, we take it as restitution for what happened to Vietnam.

Calvin senses my discomfort. It is his talent, a marked skill of his trade. He looks away, reaching for yet another cigarette to cover the silence I opened. He asks me the question that Vietnamese throughout Vietnam have tried to broach obliquely: *"Do they look down on Vietnamese in America? Do they hate you?"*

I don't want to dwell on that. Vietnamese believe that white Americans are to Viet-kieu as Viet-kieu are to Vietnamese, each one a level above the next, respectively. And, somehow, this shames me, maybe because I cannot convince myself that it is entirely true or false. I divert the thrust and ask him, *"You are Westernized. You know how different foreigners are from Vietnamese. How do you feel showing them around the country?"*

"I like the work. Many of them are very nice. Curious about our culture. I like the Australians most. Rowdy and lots of trouble, but they respect Vietnamese."

35   *"But don't you see the reactions on their faces when they see our squalor? Don't you hear the things they say about us? Don't tell me you've never heard it."*

He looks uncomfortable, drawing deep from his nicotine stick, sighing the smoke to the stars. Then to his credit and my everlasting respect for him, he says quietly, facing the sky, *"I do. I can't help it but I do. I take them out on the Saigon streets, you know, the poor parts because they ask me. They want pictures. I see them flinch at the beggars, the poverty of Vietnamese. The chicken-shacks we live in."*

A wordless lull falls between us. We're both drunk. I am irritated at having to delve into a subject I avoid, and feeling mean-spirited I have goaded him onto equally disconcerting ground.

"It's very hard being a tour guide. Sometimes I feel like a pimp." He switches into his tour-guide English: "Here, look at this, sir. Yes, ma'am, these are the average Vietnamese. Yes, they are poor. Yes, sir. Here is our national monument. Very big. Very important to Vietnamese. You impressed? No, not so big?" He shrugs, saying, *"I know they've got bigger monuments in their countries. Older, more important. What do our little things mean to them?"*

The silence tells me we are moving too far into no-man's-land. One more cigarette. More beer. Tusking the smoke out of his nostrils, he seems to brace himself, gathering force like a wave, building before cresting white. As his beliefs come barreling out, I know the crushing impact of his words will stay with me, for in them I catch a glimpse of myself and of the true Cuong, the Cuong that came before and is deeper than the suave Calvin facing me. *"Vietnamese aren't ashamed of our own poverty. We're not ashamed of squatting in mud huts and sleeping on rags. There is no shame in being poor. We were born into it just as Westerners are born white. The Westerners are white as we are yellow. There is already a difference between us. Our poverty is minor in the chasm that already exists. A small detail. The real damning thing is the fact that there are Viet-kieu, our own brothers, skin of our skin, blood of our blood, who look better than us, more civilized, more educated, more wealthy, more genteel. Viet-kieu look kingly next to the average Vietnamese. Look at you, look at me. You're wearing old jeans and I'm wearing a suit, but it's obvious who . . . who is superior. Can't you see? We look like monkeys because you make us look like monkeys just by your existence."*

40   *"Is this truly how Vietnamese see us Viet-kieu?"*

"Some call you the lost brothers. Look at you. Living in America has lightened your skin, made you forget your language. You have tasted Western women and you're probably not as attracted to Vietnamese women anymore. You eat nutritious

Western food and you are bigger and stronger than us. You know better than to smoke and drink like Vietnamese. You know exercise is good so you don't waste your time sitting in cafés and smoking your hard-earned money away. Someday, your blood will mix so well with Western blood that there will be no difference between you and them. You are already lost to us."

I listened with dismay as his observations fall on me like a sentence, but I can tell in the back of his mind he is saying: And I want to be more like you because that's where the future is. He must suspect I am doubting what he has told me the first time our paths crossed: *"Vietnamese are Vietnamese if they believe they are."*

Calvin and I bid each other good night, each going his own way. He has to resolve a fracas of intoxicated Australians in his charge back at the hotel. In our drunkenness, our conversation crossed forbidden boundaries and we were both depressed. Maybe it is just the beer wearing off. I pedal down to the beach for some sea air. As I coast along the ocean boulevard, a gorgeous girl, unusually tall for a Vietnamese, dressed in the traditional *ao dai* like a college student, tails me on her expensive motorbike, a Honda Dream, the Vietnamese Cadillac. Hello, she says in English. Hello, I smile. She thinks I'm Japanese or Korean. How are you, she asks me. Good, I say—always glad to talk to students eager to practice their English. And you, I say to keep the conversation going, how are you? You are very pretty, she tells me. No, I chuckle, standing now with her on the dark sidewalk, you are pretty. Very pretty. Pretty enough, I fancy silently to myself, for me to fall madly in love with. My heart dances ahead of me with improbable possibilities. Wild schemes streak through my head ratting out ways for me to stay in Nha Trang longer to make her acquaintance. Maybe get a job here. There are so many foreign companies, it should be easy. And on and on. Hopeful. I am smiling.

Then she says, "You go with me?"

45   "Yes, sure. Where? Anywhere! Let's go!"

"You go with me very cheap. You go. Me very cheap, very good. You go with me very cheap. Very, very cheap. I make you happy."

My smile feels waxy. I turn away, looking at the surf rolling on the white sand, the moon pearling us all. She parrots it over and over.

No, yes, maybe, later, I must meet a friend now, see you soon, bye, I blurt for the sake of blurting and I ride away from the tourist boardwalk with my money, my opportunities, my privileges, my life. I look back once and see her glossy cherry lips mouthing those words to me, a red wound in the neon night of Nha Trang.

QUESTIONS FOR DISCUSSION

1. How did Calvin and Andrew meet? How does each of them feel about the label "Viet-Kieu"? Why do they remain friends?

2. Why does Calvin value his job as a tour guide in Vietnam? What does Andrew do in the United States? Compare and contrast their challenges and responsibilities.
3. Who do you think is happier with his life, Andrew or Calvin? Why wasn't Andrew completely honest with Calvin about how he is treated in the United States?
4. As Andrew is walking along the beach, he sees a pretty Vietnamese woman with "glossy cherry lips." Why does he think of them as "a red wound in the neon night of Nha Trang"? Why do you think Andrew is appalled and saddened about the woman's appearance and her role?
5. What does Andrew learn from his trip? How is he changed by revisiting his home country? How do you think his life in the United States will be affected?
6. Talk with your friends and do some research into the meaning and connotations of Viet-Kieu. What are the connotations of the term?

CONNECTION

Compare Pham's views of change and alienation from his former homeland with Kavita Sreedhar's return to Bangalore (see page 131).

IDEAS FOR WRITING

1. Write an essay that explores one of the issues raised in the conversation between Andrew and Calvin.
2. Write an essay that explores some of the problems and issues that a particular immigrant group in your community has encountered in adjusting to American culture.

RELATED WEB SITES

Andrew X. Pham
www.andrewxpham.com
This personal and professional homepage about author Andrew X. Pham features a biography, information on current projects, and recommended books.

Constitutional Rights Foundation: Refugees from Vietnam and Cambodia
www.crf-usa.org/immigration/lesson-8.html
The Constitutional Rights Foundation provides information on Vietnamese-American history, the Vietnamese refugee experience, and the Asian American population in the United States as per the 2000 Census Bureau.

Ken Matusow

Grandpère

Ken Matusow earned a B.A. in mathematics from the University of Wisconsin and an M.S. in General Systems Theory from SUNY-Binghamton, New York. He has worked in the computer industry for over 20 years, founding and for ten years running a large systems software consulting firm, Détente Technology. Currently he works in Silicon Valley as an entrepreneur, investor, and mentor. He has helped a number of startup companies in the wireless and broadband areas, sometimes taking an operational role, and has advised technology companies in developing countries in Eastern Europe, Africa, and northern Asia. Frequently, Ken Matusow travels in the developing world for months at a time, learning more about other cultures and the different ways in which people relate to one another abroad. The essay below, "Grandpère", about Matusow's tour guide on a journey down the Niger River in the West African country of Mali to the fabled city of Timbuktu, was published in Best Travel Writing of 2007.

JOURNAL

Write about what you think it would be like to visit West Africa.

The secret to navigating West Africa is its people.

The first time I saw Grandpère he was sitting on a stoop inside the courtyard of a dilapidated hotel in the suburbs of Bamako, the capital of the West African country of Mali. My first impression was one of surprise. He looked young, with chiseled features colored in dark chocolate. His sharp, intelligent eyes exhibited nothing of the wizened and sympathetic visage usually associated with the term *grandpère*, French for grandfather. He was dressed in Western clothes, blue jeans with an open-necked button-down shirt, hiking boots, and baseball cap. Next to Grandpère sat a more traditional West African man, an overweight moneychanger clad in a sweat-stained parody of a leisure suit. With Grandpère translating between English and French, the moneychanger counted out piles of tattered, filthy notes of Malian currency known as CFA. Grandpère carefully audited the transaction as I offered four crisp hundred-dollar bills to the ersatz banker in return for the black-market money. I had never before met Grandpère. I knew nothing of his history or his character. Yet I somehow felt relieved that my interests were being looked after. . . .

I was traveling with about twenty Westerners on an overland journey through the heart of West Africa, from Senegal in the west to Ghana in the south. Nestled between these two coastal countries lies the sub-Saharan nation of Mali. For many travelers Mali is the focus of a West African visit. Famed for its music and art, Mali is home to a variety of unique indigenous tribes and cultures, contemporary remnants of a thousand-year-old empire. While Europe struggled through its Dark Ages, Mali's most famous city, Timbuktu, lured North Africans to a cosmopolitan metropolis known for its wealth and respected as a center of learning and sophistication. Today, Timbuktu is an isolated and forlorn fossil, inhabited by the ghosts of its glorious past and the trickle of tourists that wander into the town from its newly-built international airport. Timbuktu was once a major port on the Niger River. But even that esteemed watercourse abandoned Timbuktu, leaving the city an orphan, cut off from its umbilical, which now flows fifteen miles south of the town.

In Mali, anything or anyone cut off from the Niger withers and eventually dies. The Niger irrigates the history and the culture of Mali, as surely as it irrigates its crops. It is the dominant geographic feature of the country, the bringer of life, a ribbon of water that provides transportation and communication for most of the nation. In a very real sense, the Niger is to Mali what the Nile is to Egypt, albeit with a French accent.

5   For most of our trip through Mali we would be following the immense arcing loop sketched on the West African savannah by the river. Entering Mali in the southwest, the great river meanders to Bamako, continues northeast to Mopti, past the Bandiagara Escarpment of the Dogon people, eventually approaching the Saharan town of Timbuktu. After tasting the Sahara there, the river makes a great turn to the southeast, eventually flowing into the Atlantic Ocean in southern Nigeria. As with most things in Mali, my group of travelers would be dependent on the Niger. It would be our nurturer, our mother. Unknown to me at the time, we would also have a father. The father was Grandpère.

Grandpère was a quiet man. He was invariably courteous, happy to answer questions about Mali or details of our trip, but he rarely initiated a conversation. Despite having an easy laugh, he was not the kind of person who invited inane discussion or idle chat. Although he appeared young, perhaps in his thirties, Grandpère was able to assert his authority effortlessly, with the easy grace of one who has no doubt in his ability. He was a serious man, but one who wore the mantle of responsibility lightly, as if the possibility of things going seriously wrong were so remote as to not warrant undue consideration. His attitude was exceptional, as Mali was a country where things going seriously wrong were the norm, not the exception.

We drove north, by truck, from Bamako to the port city of Mopti, situated on a tributary of the Niger. Ancient wooden boats, painted in an explosion of brilliant reds, greens, and yellows were moored on the river. Hand-made signs advertising Djenne, Gao, or Timbuktu as destinations provided hints to where the boats might be headed. Hawkers ambled along the docks selling hats or shirts, food and cigarettes. The quiet bustle created an atmosphere that seemed to mimic the flow and rhythm of the river. This rhythm quickly changed once we climbed down from our truck. Our presence in Mopti distorted the flow of the town the way a rock in a rapidly flowing river creates eddies and turbulence. Pestering locals surrounded me asking for gifts or offering illicit goods. *"Bonjour mon ami,* where are you from" poured from multiple mouths, each trying to outdo the others. I tried to smooth the cacophony, offering up simple greetings with a smile and disarming gestures. I tried to explain that I didn't need any friends as I merely needed to do a bit of shopping. I spoke in English and in French. My efforts were futile. Visitors were rare in Mopti and were often viewed either as potential marks for absurd scams or benevolent missionaries of a rich idyllic country.

In a fit of exasperation I growled *"Je suis avec Grandpère,"* a bastardized French phrase indicating that I was traveling with Grandpère. The world changed immediately. Aggressive young punks became solicitous. The pleading eyes of the women hawkers, eyes used to squeeze a sale, were transformed into soft orbs that communicated kindness and caring. A young tough grabbed my hand and led me across the street saying that he would accompany me to the store to make sure the owner did not rip me off. The incantation of the phrase "Grandpère" had been powerful and immediate, and to me, the results were extraordinary.

We were in Mopti to begin a three-day trip on the Niger. We would motor upstream by day and camp on the shore at night. In the late afternoon of the third day, if all went well, we would arrive in Timbuktu. Grandpère owned the boat. It was a pirogue, perhaps forty feet long and six wide. Helpers loaded up the boat with coolers of food provided by Grandpère, and we climbed aboard. This day Grandpère was dressed West African style in a grand *boubou,* a riotously colored robe-like shift. As we poled away from the wharf, he sat cross-legged on the roof towards the stern of the boat waving his arms and shouting directions to his staff in a mix of English, French, and Bambara, the local language of Mali.

10   I got to know Grandpère a little better during our voyage. He told me how he grew up in Timbuktu. He described a life with no future, only a past. The past was shadowed by the lives of his parents, and his parents' parents. The future was something no one had any control over. One merely endured. We discussed the world of the *marabouts,* the Islamic rulers of the numerous clans of Mali, the true men of power in the country. I learned how he came to see the tourists of Timbuktu as a potential way out of the fatalistic and overbearing world of West Africa. In his quiet

undulating voice he told me how he had approached tour groups as a teenager and offered to carry luggage for less than a dollar a day. He became a guide and led tours through the old Islamic universities of Timbuktu. His keen mind quickly understood the need to move to the next level of the tour business, and so he started making agreements directly with tour companies and travel agencies. He gradually became known in central Mali as the "go to" guy. Local businesses tried to solicit his business, and more importantly, the business of the tourists who were under his guidance and protection. Wielding his newfound power like a stiletto, he created alliances among community business and clan leaders. He became a man to be respected. He became Grandpère.

As we slowly chugged down the Niger it became clear that our group lived within a world of West African patronage. Grandpère created a corona of security, a transparent sphere of isolation that afforded us a view of West African life while insulating us from the realities of the land. A couple of times a day we would pull into a village on the banks of the Niger. We would spend a few hours exploring, talking, and trading stories with the locals. The villages were invariably attractive, the people friendly. We took pictures and left. There were no arguments, no altercations. Grandpère was everywhere, explaining village life, translating, overseeing his minions, making sure that nothing unpleasant took place. When pressed, Grandpère would explain that the Niger was in flood and that most of the villages we visited were economically devastated. If not questioned, he left us on our own, offering little in the way of political or economic commentary.

Only once did he falter. That was when we inadvertently left the Canadian, Tino, behind after one of our village visits. An hour after leaving the village we put in for the night on a deserted stretch of beach. Tino was missing. How had we forgotten him? He had no money or passport. There were no roads to the village. The river was the only connection between the village and the rest of the planet. We immediately ran to Grandpère. Startled, he quickly turned and spoke in Bambara to one of his helpers. After a brief conversation with his aide, his smile quickly returned. "No problem," he said in English. "He will be here soon." Twenty minutes later Tino turned up in an outrigger paddled by two villagers.

Timbuktu was our final stop on the Niger. Although the town will be forever linked with mystery and isolation, Timbuktu is in reality an ugly village perched on the southern rim of the Sahara Desert. Its streets are unpaved, covered with four or five inches of fine powdered dust. The dust seeped into my shoes. When the wind blew, swirls of dust enveloped me, coating my face in a patina of gray. It got into my eyes and into my mouth. When I sipped some water to try to wash away the grit, the only effect was to transform the dust into mud, mud that slowly dripped down my throat. My fondest wish was to take a shower and wash my clothes. I bundled up my river garb and gave them to a local to launder before diving into a luxurious shower in preparation for a farewell banquet organized by Grandpère.

Dinner was a magnificent outdoor affair. Grandpère was dressed in casual Western business clothes. A Malian feast, augmented with local beer, enlivened the retelling of our trip to Timbuktu. For a few hours the gritty realities of West Africa drifted away in the smoky evening air of the Sahel. For the first time in weeks I felt I could completely relax, let down my guard, and absorb the exotic flavors of Saharan Africa. As I went to pay for the meal, I reached into my pocket to extract the grimy CFA I had purchased from Grandpère and the black marketer so many days before. Instead I found nothing. There was no bundle of notes. Nearly two hundred dollars worth of CFA was missing. In a panic I realized that when I handed my clothes to the cleaner, I had forgotten to remove my money. The amount of cash I had lost was the equivalent of a years' salary for the average Timbuktuan.

15   I ran over to my guardian, Grandpère, and explained the situation. He listened carefully and said, "Do not worry. The man found the money and took it home for safekeeping. He will bring it to town tomorrow with the rest of your clothes." Problem solved. It never occurred to me that Grandpère might have been lying, or that the man might not return. I was in Timbuktu, on the edge of the Sahara Desert, one of the most isolated towns on earth. It was an area noted for its lawlessness and banditry. A stranger had walked away with all of my cash. His home was nearly an hour's walk from town. Yet when Grandpère almost casually assured me there was not a problem, I believed him. Such was his power.

The laundry man returned with both my clothes and my money. As I thanked Grandpère and wished him well, I reflected on the journey from Bamako to Timbuktu. The story was now complete. Our relationship began when I changed money, chaperoned by his trusting nature. Our relationship ended when the same money was lost, then found, under his watchful eyes. We both promised we would keep in touch, but both of us knew this was a fiction. Grandpère would begin his next cycle with a new group of tourists. I would continue my travels to Ghana. Our paths were now separate. Yet I did not forget him. The image of Grandpère and the mysteries of West Africa remain intertwined. Embodied in his dancing eyes and quick wit is the personification of the continent. Although he grew up in a land of ossified custom and stupefying fatalism, he took control of his life and was able bend the fates to his will.

Whenever I reflect on West Africa, the smiling face of Grandpère invariably emerges from the mists of my mind. And when it does, a little smile creeps across my own face, a tacit and silent greeting.

QUESTIONS FOR DISCUSSION

1. How was Matusow's expectation of Grandpère different from the man he meets? What positive qualities does Grandpère possess?
2. Why is Grandpère leading the tour of 20 Westerners to Mali? Does Matusow give you a good sense of what the travelers might be up against?
3. How does Grandpère help the tour group? Why is the Niger River the nurturer and Grandpère the father?
4. How is life in the port city of Mopti different than life on the river? How does Grandpère assert his authority and show his responsibility to his tour group? How would you describe the source and effectiveness of Grandpère's leadership?
5. What does Matusow learn about Grandpère's character on the way down the Niger to Timbuktu? Grandpère seems like more than a tour guide. Why?
6. When Matusow looks back on his trip, what do you think he will remember?

CONNECTION

Compare and contrast Grandpère and Calvin as tour guides (see page 117).

IDEAS FOR WRITING

1. Do research into the area of West Africa that the tour visited. Integrate the journey as told by Matusow as well as what the group learned about the ways of the culture and the land with the factual information presented in an encyclopedia, perhaps *Wikipedia*. Try to make this essay both a character sketch of Grandpère's expertise as well as a factual account of the area.
2. Explain the meaning of Matusow's concluding comments about Grandpère and West Africa: "The image of Grandpère and the mysteries of West Africa remain intertwined. Embodied in his dancing eyes and quick wit is the personification of the continent. Although he grew up in a land of ossified custom and stupefying fatalism, he took control of his life and was able to bend the fates to his will."

RELATED WEB SITES

Ken Matusow Archives
`http://travelerstales.com/carpet/cat_ken_matusow.shtml`
Travelers' Tales, a Web site created by two travel writers, provides archives for other travel writers and tales. This specific URL provides the works of Ken Matusow.

World History Archives: The History of West Africa
`www.hartford-hwp.com/archives/34/index.html`

Hartford Web Publishing presents a list of links to historical articles on West Africa. The links are categorized by African country or region.

Kavita Sreedhar

Travelling Home

Kavita Sreedhar was born in Karnataka state in Southern India, which is now the "Silicon Valley" of India. Born into a traditional and orthodox Brahmin family, Kavita's parents encouraged her to be creative and open-minded. They taught her the importance of Indian culture and its values and yet encouraged her to always think for herself and not be bogged down by dogma. Her passion for writing began when she was a child. Her mother encouraged her to write stories and to keep a journal. By the age of 8, her poetry and stories had been published in Indian children's magazines such as Target *and* Chanda Mama. *Kavita moved to the United States about nine years ago and has settled in Santa Clara County, California. She returned to school to complete additional credits in education in order to pursue a master's degree in Business Administration. Among her many goals, the one that remains most important to her is writing the life story of her mother.*

The sudden blare of the artificially sweetened voice over the intercom jolted me out of my slumber. As I struggled to adjust to the blistering sunlight from the window that my co-passenger had opened up, I realized that I had slept all the way from Seoul to Mumbai—the Tylenol PM had finally worked! It had been a stressful week; what with the sudden news of mother's hospitalization, finding a replacement, handing over work, finding reasonably priced last minute tickets to travel back home, coordinating travel arrangements with my brother and the stress of the 32 hour long journey with so many stopovers at the oddest hours and the oddest places (at least they seemed odd to me). But here I was finally, "Home Sweet Home," back in India after five long years; time had just flown by—and even that artificial, insincere tone of voice of the air-hostess that announced, "*Bharat mein apka swagat hai*" ("Welcome to India"), seemed like the warmest and kindest thing I had heard in ages. The familiarity of the kind and courteous language, the sarees worn by the women greeting us with a *namaste* (a folded salutational hand-gesture) filled me with a warm sense of pride and joy at being back in my homeland, a land steeped in values, cultures, tradition and spirituality. The smiles that did not reach the eyes of these women welcoming me did not deter or even prepare me for what I would experience being back in my motherland over the next two months during this vacation.

This forced vacation to visit my mother in the hospital was a much-needed one, despite her health problems; just the fact that our small family of three was re-uniting after almost a decade, in the land where we had been born and raised, was enough to make me feel good about being home.

As I stepped out of the aircraft, the unmistakable musty smell and hot humid air of Mumbai hit my face. Phew! It was hot—probably in the 100s. As I shielded my eyes from the glare of the sun and squinted to see the exit doors to the main airport, a burly old man brushed past me along with several women who had been behind me. Whatever happened to lines and asking for people to make way? I picked up my bag that had been knocked over by the rushing passengers and reminded myself that I was now back in Mumbai where there were too many people and too little space. People were in too much of a hurry to indulge in unnecessary formalities such as lines, waiting their turn etc. The Darwinian mantra of "survival of the fittest" is what reigns supreme in the minds of people in this highly competitive, severely overcrowded city; so I hurried along too, without a care for who I was brushing against, bumping into or knocking over in the process—after all, I was in a hurry too: I had to leave the international airport, go to the domestic airport, about 20 kilometers away, and then make the earliest connection possible to Bangalore, my hometown, where my mother was hospitalized. So off I went, scurrying through, bags, passport, ticket and all, racing for the Immigration counter, feeling utterly important since here I didn't have to go through any other grueling lines and questions for non-citizens and visitors, like in the USA; here I was a citizen who enjoyed all the privileges of coasting right through these counters; I was one of their own.

Just as I was setting foot into the country at one of these immigration counters, I had my first taste of how alien I was to feel in my own homeland. The police officers in khaki uniforms brandished the *lathi* (a form of stick like weapon), hitting it on the floor by the red lines behind which people had to wait. In my enthusiasm at being Indian and belonging among my shoving and pushing brethren, I had stepped on the red line. "Crack!" A loud noise almost made me jump out of my skin, as the *lathi* came down, landing in front of me. I looked up at a pot-bellied constable in an ill-fitting khaki uniform. He looked at me screaming—*"Line ke Peeche!"*: "Back of the line, back of the line!" I looked around to see if he were talking to someone else, and all I saw were scores and scores of eyes staring at me. I looked back at the *havaldar* (constable) as he brought the *lathi* close to my shoes and tapped the floor hard again, pointing to where I was standing on the line, rather than behind it. I retreated half in fear of his *lathi* and half in fear of his lack of personal boundaries, as he had stepped very close to me. I muttered a feeble apology and was shocked by the remark he then made—*"Ye log amreeka jaake, apne aap ko firang samajte hain . . . inko aise hi dikhana padta hai*," which translates to "These people go to America and think they are Whites [supreme]—they ought to be put in their place just like this." What had brought on such hostility? How did he know I was returning from the US? Was it the blond highlights? Was it the SFO tag on my purse? Did he know that I could have understood him? And did the people around him actually agree with him and laugh because of the fear of authority, or did they actually think I was a *firang* (a foreigner)? "Foreigner" in my homeland—a land that prides itself in its hospitality and generosity—welcoming one of their own with a *lathi*—I was mortified.

I was glad to get to the immigration counter where the officer spoke with me only in English and I responded to him in Hindi. The constable who was supposedly guarding the red line stepped close to the counter where I was standing to peer over at my passport and other details. When the officer asked me why I was traveling to India, I responded in fluent Hindi, explaining my situation and reason for travel. The lecherous gaze of the constable changed into one of horror and embarrassment when he heard me speaking in Hindi. It was sheer joy to see him retreat to the red line, just the way he had made me retreat behind it with his silly *lathi*. The officer stamped my passport with the cold-hearted professionalism that only authority can offer, without as much as a sympathetic smile or pleasantry. I could almost feel the eyes of the lecherous *havaldar* and the other people whom he was now snickering with blazing through my back. I turned around and sure enough, they all looked away suddenly, some just blankly staring at a wall, while peeking to see if I was still looking.

5   It was hot, I needed water and I needed to feel the warmth of my homeland. And there it was—the beaming, smiling face of my darling brother towering over the hundreds of faces on his six and a half feet frame, waving a bottle of water at me, screaming, "*Didi . . . Didi . . .*" (elder sister). Now, I knew I was home. He made way for me and we hugged among the thousands of people at Mumbai airport. I heard a few gasps as I planted a huge slobbery kiss on his forehead. I could almost hear the "*hai, hai*" (Oh my!), but I didn't care. It had been years since I had seen my baby brother, and I did not care that I was in a public place kissing a grown man. We chatted like we had never been apart, just picking up where we had left off. Time had frozen for us when we had left India, and here we were again, thawing out every memory, every moment, and every place that we had left so many years ago.

Memories started to come unthawed as we stepped out of Mumbai airport to get to our taxi that would take us to the domestic airport almost 20 miles away; my ears started to become accustomed to the noise-level around me. Car horns were blaring, people were speaking at decibel levels that no one in the United States would even dream of; taxi drivers were yelling for customers while auto-rickshaw drivers were also doing their share of soliciting passengers. Again I was almost knocked over by a scurrying group of women who pushed me aside to get ahead in the taxi line. Thankfully, Kishan had already made arrangements for our ride and we just had our luxury cab pull right up in front of us—a white Maruti minivan which put the other Fiat and Premier Padmini yellow and black taxis to shame. Again, I could feel the eyes boring into us as we got into the van— the same eyes that were averted from our friendly, acknowledging glances.

It was reassuring that we were moving closer to home, towards Bangalore, and some three and half hours later we were back in friendly territory where everything looked so familiar. Our prepaid taxi picked us up at Bangalore Airport which was thankfully pleasantly welcoming and not as crowded as Mumbai's had been. The weather was cooler, and we were probably a little more relaxed after the nap on the flight, secure in the knowledge that we were heading home. There were still those eyes that followed me, but this time, it was different; these were the glances and stares that I was used to as a young girl growing up in Bangalore—the appreciative glances, the shameless ogling that most Indian men carried on irrespective of their surroundings. Surprisingly, it did not feel as sickening or as bad as had the stares at Mumbai. I pointed it out to Kishan, and he simply remarked jokingly, "Welcome home, Didi," humming the famous Bollywood song and dance number, "It Happens Only in India." We rushed directly to the hospital since visiting hours were going to end by seven pm and we had barely an hour to spend with mother with all the traffic and the commute time.

"Miss Kavita—" A friendly voice belonging to an equally friendly face appeared at the deserted front desk of the hospital. I scrambled up from the seat that I had again dozed off in while awaiting clearance to see my mother in the hospital lobby. The front desk clerk turned out to be the Patient Relations Executive (PRE) at the hospital who had come to take us to see our mother. She was asleep, and they were not sure if it was a good idea for us to visit her that evening as there was only an hour remaining before visiting hours ended. Kishan and I put to use our persuasive marketing skills, requesting to visit her even if she were asleep and to be given an extension of normal visiting hours. It helped that I had mentioned that I was "American returned," as some of the local staff called it; we were treated with the utmost courtesy, respect and regard.

Ironic as it was that I had to tout my "non-resident" status to be treated well in my own hometown, it worked to our advantage. More questions popped up in my mind, though: Was it not standard policy at the hospital that all patients and their families be treated the same? My brother eased my conscience by zeroing in on the fact that it worked out for the benefit of our family, and that I should simply enjoy the privilege of being an NRI

(Non Resident Indian). As the PRE led us up to the room in which our mother was resting, we followed close on her heels, with great anticipation and excitement. The angst and worry about mother's health had suddenly given way to the excitement of seeing her again after so many years. As I straightened my T-shirt, I could see Kishan smoothing out his shirt as well—we both wanted to look our best for mother. The eyes were back again, darting accusing and questioning glances from those of the patients and their departing visitors who wondered how we were being allowed to go in when they were all being led out.

10   As we approached the room, a patient in a wheelchair with an I/V stopped us short. He began questioning the PRE regarding us, complaining in the same breath about how his grandson who had come to visit him had been rushed to leave by the nurse who gave the patient his medication early because she was ending her shift. The PRE dismissed his queries and simply stated that we were being allowed to see my mother because we had just landed from America, unashamedly lying to him in Kannada, the local dialect, that we had connections higher up in the hospital, hence the favor. Both Kishan and I gulped at the sheer audacity of the PRE for lying so blatantly in front of us and then rolling her eyes meaningfully at the old man, suggesting that we were given undue privilege because of connections. As I began to protest, she simply turned around and shush me; we were at mother's room. We tiptoed in behind her, wave after wave of excitement flowing through my veins and as I stepped into the dimly lit room, I felt I would drown in the anxiety, worry, and pain that filled my being upon seeing my mother's exceptionally calm and pale face. Suddenly, I felt a strong hand grasp mine. I turned and looked at my brother and I saw the little boy who always held my hand, whenever we went out into the strange, big world, just as mother had diligently taught us. Instinctively, I knew that this was far from the homecoming that I expected. Gone was the excitement, gone were the plans of holidaying and vacationing after checking mother out of the hospital, gone were her impish, twinkling eyes that lit up and sparkled whenever she saw us. Instead of her youthful and healthy frame, there lay a limp, thin, aging lady with the dark circles around her eyes the only color on her pale face. Instinctively, I firmed my grip on my brother's hand and we asked the PRE to leave us there for a few minutes. She told us that we could take as long as we liked and that we could leave the same way she had walked us in.

   The hour we spent there seemed like an eternity. We sat on the cold steel chairs for visitors in the room, more uncomfortable in our worry than in the dreariness of the surroundings. Kishan had dozed off on my shoulder, and eventually I did too. Suddenly, I felt a pair of eyes looking at me. It was mother gazing at us with the warmth that only she could generate. She had awakened a little after the PRE had left and had not wanted to disturb us, since we were both so tired and fast asleep. "Nice highlights," she said, smiling—and in that instant, all the worries, all the steely coldness and dreariness of the room disappeared. I just knew things would work out fine, like they always did whenever we were around her. I was safely back home secure in the warmth of my mother's presence and my brother's support. Now all we had to do was nurse her back to health so that we could pick up where we left off the last time we were all together in India.

For the first three weeks we were in India, we spent almost every waking hour traveling between the hospital and the hotel, and then the apartment. Since we had made it our mission to eat healthy meals with mother, we ate every meal at the hospital. The "American returned" brand was definitely paying off—we were treated like royalty, food was sent to the room even for us "guests," which was something that was never done—or at least that's what Seena the ward-boy told us. Seena always made certain that he was assigned to our room, and actually worked on his own time (at least that's what he told my brother), and attended to us with the utmost regard and courtesy during the time that mother was in the hospital. With his broken English, ever-ready smiles and "yessir's," Seena tried his best to worm his way into our hearts. Little did we realize that all that hospitality was being generated by his greedy anticipation of "American-size" tips. It had gotten quite tiresome that he always expected to be tipped fifty or hundred rupees each day. On the morning that mother was going to be discharged, Seena hung around the room, hoping for a final generous gratuity. Kishan was helping mother into the wheelchair; in his attempt to get our attention, Seena grabbed the wheelchair as if trying to help, almost knocking both Kishan and mother down. Instead of apologizing for his mistake, Seena insisted on wheeling her down to the lobby, refusing to let go. Kishan relented, and when we were all ready to take off, Seena ran around to Kishan's side of the car and reminded him shamelessly about the tip. When Kishan pulled out a twenty rupee note, the disgust on Seena's face undid everything good he had done over the past few weeks: "Saar . . . You make Dollar money. What, saar—you are so *kanjoos marwadi* [tight fisted]." Kishan reminded him that he had tipped him over four thousand rupees ($100), more than Seena's monthly salary in the past few weeks, and that we worked hard for a living as well. Seena replied, "*Che, Che . . . America ante . . . duddillvante . . . ha che . . .*" ("These people claim they are from America and they say they don't have money, shame on them."). Once again I felt conflicting emotions and questions about modern India: Whatever had happened to the cherished Indian values of hospitality, kindness, gratitude and respect for fellow human beings?

As we drove away from the hospital, the dark exhaust fumes of traffic from the highly congested Palace Road seemed to mirror the pollution in the minds of the people in this town. I used to walk down this road from college and now there was no pavement, only potholes, and traffic had increased ten-thousand fold. What had happened to all the trees of this garden city? Where there were once little bungalows were now mini high-rises, and those dark clouds we had noticed were clouds of smoke. Mother explained that people were all in for a quick buck. The call-centers, offshore software development, and the transcription companies had provided the youth of the city with a lot of disposable income. American companies paid 1/3 what they would pay here, but it was still a lot of money in India. One could easily afford a bike, a car, an apartment even—hence the overpopulation and overcrowding of our streets. Obviously nature had to move out to make way for the rising capitalist builders and promoters who tempted homeowners with free condos and part share of the high-rise if they let them build on their land, no matter how small the lot. This was not the city that I had left behind, the city that I had frolicked in as a child, the place that the child in me always longed to go back to. Things were very different. Maybe I had changed; maybe I had developed a more idealistic view of my homeland and its culture after being away for so long—maybe it was just all in my mind.

The following day revealed so much more than I ever wanted to learn, convincing me that things had indeed changed and that it was not necessarily for the better. After weeks of eating healthy food, Kishan and I decided to head out upon mother's insistence to our favorite Indo-Chinese place on Residency Road. The traffic was mind-numbing even on a weekday afternoon. With great difficulty we reached the restaurant after taking an hour and a half to drive less than 15 miles. Parking was a huge issue near the restaurant, especially with the rampant theft rate, so we parked in a Government parking lot and decided to take a stroll down Brigade Road— a road that we had fond memories of from our school years. However, now there were no more of those nice little mom-and-pop shops run by local merchants; instead, there were Dominoes, MacDonald's, KFC and other international brands; also along that two mile stretch of the road were countless pubs and cyber cafés. As we walked down Brigade, we saw teenage boys and girls in school uniforms whose skirts were far shorter than those of the outfits we remembered. These kids were hanging around outside the pubs. Girls and boys alike stood outside smoking cigarettes, holding hands and one another. I gulped down my embarrassment at being caught staring at two Cottonians (Bishop Cotton school students) making out right in front of us in broad daylight outside the street corner of NASA (a local pub). The girl was probably fourteen at the most and the boy looked about sixteen. They didn't seem to care about the attention they drew and continued their overly explicit display of affection even after the slight interruption that I caused by almost bumping into them.

15   I could have dismissed the school kids as a chance incident, but as I walked down the streets, I realized that there were many more such kids,

indulging in behavior that left little to the imagination. Kishan laughed at my question about whether it was a school holiday and how these kids got the money to frequent these pricey places. At Underground, one of our favorite pubs, not for its alcohol but for its fun environment and its pool tables, I felt I had seen enough. These were kids, school-going kids, some even in uniform, not much younger than I was when I left Bangalore, who were sitting at the bar, downing beers and hard liquor, undressing in public, and indulging in acts that would put even the porn stars of the Western World to shame. At 24, I was not a prude; I had been considered a rebel five years ago for leaving the country all on my own, without being married or even engaged, much against the wishes of the elders in my family. Kishan was only 22 and he was in shock as well at the utter grossness that surrounded us. The subtleties of Indian values and culture seemed to be lost somewhere between the guilt that the parents from the double income families felt at perhaps neglecting their children in pursuit of their own self-interest, and the affluence that came with the excessive disposable income and overindulgence of these children who desperately tried to emulate so-called "Westernized" values of free love and free sex. As in everything else, India was riding this wave of "liberation" a few decades too late.

While the Western world is opening its eyes to subtlety, to spirituality, and to a rejection of materialism, leaning towards the ancient teachings of yoga, meditation and spirituality that India has to offer, delving into its history of being the land of mysticism, of ancient heritage and of a rich culture that prides itself in its conservative, spiritual values and ways, here was our country, sitting in a complete antithesis of its own classical ideals. One old friend whom we bumped into dismissed our concerns at the school kids being served alcohol with a simple remark: "Of course things have changed! Bangalore is more westernized now, more sophisticated and progressive. Where have you been? This should be commonplace for you—you live in America!" I had no answer and neither did Kishan. This certainly was not commonplace for me, and it certainly did not seem progressive. When the West was looking to the East for spiritual guidance and returning to the core values of human nature, India, or at least her youth, were blindly imitating the West, completely caught up in superficiality and materialism, without respect for the cultural values of the society that they hailed from. Five years ago, the attitudes we witnessed in Bangalore and Mumbai would have been considered sacrilege. There was enough fear and respect for hardworking parents that children would not indulge in such behavior. There was also possibly less money, more parenting and more intact, extended families five years ago to keep cultural values alive. If so much had changed in less than half a decade, I dreaded to think about how much more "progress" the youth of India would make before they realized that they were headed in the wrong direction morally and spiritually.

Kishan and I talked about how we felt that night over dinner at home. We felt like misfits in our own society. How could that be when we valued everything that we cherished as being Indian, and when we were in our homeland, there was so little left to value? Perhaps, we had frozen our nation in our minds when we left the country five years ago, but India had moved on, just like everyone and everything else. We sought to recapture the land that we had left behind when, in fact, all of that past seemed to have vanished. We came upon a harsh realization that aside from being "legal aliens" in America or Oman, we were now aliens in our own country. We had no place that we could call "home"—what we so fondly referred to as home was for us now just a fantasy, a dream world that was fast losing its occupants.

There was no more disconcerting a feeling than not knowing where we belonged. In a world of global shifts and global cultures, our values were being submerged and washed away by the tsunamis of capitalism, consumerism and materialism. It was extremely distressing for me especially since I had believed that I would raise my children in India with its spiritual, conservative, and humanistic values. Mother was surprisingly silent throughout the entire deliberation between Kishan and me about how we did not know what was "home" anymore. Her answer, as clichéd as it may have been, rang true and made perfect sense to both of us. "Home is where the heart is," she murmured. She went on to explain that tradition and values do not lie buried in the land or permeate the air as we had romanticized; they lay in our spirits, within our hearts, and in our families. She threw us a reality check, noting that she had raised us in conflicting and changing times as well. Like so many of Bangalore's parents today, she too had worked full-time, side by side with our father—but they had made certain that we were raised in a family that valued relationships, humanism, and spirituality above everything else. It took a lot of trouble, a lot of time and effort on their part, but they kept the Indian tradition alive in our lives by keeping it alive in their hearts and thus in ours. Those values that we cherished so dearly were not restricted by land, boundaries, or people, so there was no need to worry about where we belonged—we belonged so long as our hearts belonged. She pointed out that when we were agonizing over how much things had changed, things were changing in different parts of the world for the better, and things would continue to change forever. It was up to us to keep up with change by not losing ourselves to it.

She had done it again—in her own optimistic and idealistic view of the world, she had once again explained something lofty and profound in such simple and real terms. Now at least we had hope, hope that we would never feel alien or foreign in any man-made land or region, so long as we continued to keep the "dreamland" of our upbringing alive in our hearts.

1. What was the author's feeling about going back to her country and why? How did the *havaldar* at the airport influence her feelings at being home?
2. "Memories started to come unthawed"—what was the author referring to with this statement? Discuss the events and surroundings that prompted the "unthawing" of memories.
3. How does the author feel about her "non-resident Indian" status? Discuss the similarities, contrasts, and significance in the "NRI"/"Firang" status that the hospital workers and the Havaldar attribute to her.
4. Why did the author and her brother feel like "misfits"? What had changed?
5. Discuss the significance of the author's mother in the story. What is her final advice?.
6. What role do values, upbringing, and culture play in our lives? Discuss your opinions of how justified the author is to have felt the way she did about the "progress" youth in her country were making.

Francine Prose

Confessions of a Ritual Tourist

Francine Prose, born in 1947 in Brooklyn, New York, graduated from Radcliffe College in 1968 and dropped out of a Ph.D. program to devote herself to writing. She has taught literature and creative writing at Harvard, Bard College, Sarah Lawrence, the Iowa Writers' Workshop, and the Bread Loaf and Sewanee Writers Conferences, and is a fellow of the New York Institute for the Humanities. The author of 15 novels, three collections of short stories, and several books of non-fiction, Prose has been awarded a Guggenheim fellowship, a Fulbright fellowship, and two NEA grants. Her stories, essays, and reviews have been published in leading magazines and journals. Her recent works include Blue Angel *(2001),* The Lives of the Muses: Nine Women and the Artists They Inspired *(2003),* A Changed Man *(2005), and the non-fiction work,* Reading Like a Writer *(2007). The following essay by Francine Prose on observing rituals as a tourist appeared in* The Best Women's Travel Writing *(2006).*

JOURNAL

Where do you like to travel? What "rituals" have you observed in your travels?

I fell in love with Swami Sandcastle on my second trip to India in the late 1970s. My husband and I happened to stop at a small South Indian beachside town, where, as it turned out, people from the surrounding area came to toss packets of food into the sea: meals for the departed, offerings to keep their dead from going hungry. Every morning, we watched this holy man—tall, bearded, with flowing orange robes and a strikingly handsome face—making designs and mounds in the sand and dispensing food packets to the pilgrims in exchange for small sums of money. We watched him, and he saw us watching him. By the end of a few days, we had what I guess you could call a relationship. In fact, we had a huge crush on him, and, in a way, I think he knew it.

We were thrilled when eventually he beckoned to us and, using the little English he knew, made it clear that he would allow us to take him to a nearby tea house. We bought tea for everyone in the tea house, all of whom seemed to know him and to be giving us odd looks as we ourselves drank cup after cup of the hot (well, actually, rather tepid) milky liquid.

The next morning, we awoke with the fiercest cases of dysentery we'd ever had in all our travels. At our hotel, the receptionist told us that no one in the town—in fact, no one except pilgrims from distant villages who didn't know any better—went to the tea house, which was famous locally for its filthiness and for the variety of diseases you could catch there.

It was among the low points of my life as a ritual tourist, by which I mean a traveler drawn to the rites and ceremonies of other cultures— the more unlike mine, the better. My ritual tourism had always had a sort of freeform, improvisational nature. If I happened to be somewhere that a ceremony was in progress, or living in a place where I knew they celebrated a particular holiday, so much the better. Only rarely have I purposely coordinated my travels to correspond with some local celebration.

5　　But I have known people who have gone on journeys of this sort in a more organized, official way—pilgrims who go long distances to observe pilgrimages, you might say. For many years, I had a neighbor whose vocation involved taking groups of New Age goddess-worshipers on trips to holy sites, tours timed to coincide with important astronomical events and exotic fertility rituals. Together, my neighbor and her traveling companions celebrated the solstice at Machu Picchu, ushered in the equinox amid the red rocks of Sedona, and traveled through the Brazilian jungle to watch their Amazonian sisters perform some sort of secret ceremony involving the ghost of a dead jaguar.

As a novelist, every instinct I had made me want to join them to watch these innocents abroad offering incense to the deities and spitting mouthfuls of potent local homebrew into the roaring bonfires. But every instinct I had as a human warned me away from a situation that I feared I might find uncomfortable, embarrassing, and certainly disingenuous as I conducted my own private, voyeuristic study of the ritual tourists. Hesitant to join these trips, I did what every novelist would do, I wrote a book about it instead.

It probably goes without saying that the things we're drawn to satirize are, in many cases, the things we're most wary of, and suspicious about, in ourselves. So perhaps one reason I had so much fun subjecting the fictional travelers in my novel *Hunters and Gatherers* to a succession of highly comic misadventures was that I knew, in my heart of hearts, I was a ritual tourist. The truth was that often I was the traveler you could spot—if not in the front row, then certainly somewhere in the crowd—as the Holy Week procession passed by in the streets of some Mexican village, the one trekking to the cemetery in Oaxaca to watch people picnic on their loved ones' well-tended graves in honor of the Day of the Dead. I was the one in the last pew at the Church of St. Anne de Beaupre in Quebec, watching the worshipers who arrive on crutches, rattling their bottles of pills, in the hopes of being cured and made whole again through the saint's intercession.

I suppose that my career as a ritual tourist began, like many people's on the shores of the Ganges, in Benares, or Varanasi, where pious Hindus come to die or to burn their dead and scatter their ashes in the holy river. I can still recall how thrilling it was to wake up before dawn to reach the banks of the river in time for the sunrise, to watch the crowds of faithful come to wash in the sacred waters, and to hire a boatman to take me past the burning ghats where the wrapped-up corpses smoldered. The crowds, the color and variety of the scene, the sheer sensory stimulation, was so intense, so utterly transfixing that, on that first visit, a sacred cow pissed all over my foot and I didn't even notice. Everything about the city and the ceremonies I was observing fascinated me so much that I remember wanting to stay there, to spend weeks or months, however long it took for me to begin to understand the mysteries I was seeing.

At the same time, I felt sort of guilty. I understood that this was not some performance, some Indian version of the hula and flamenco shows staged to entertain tourists in Hawai'i and Andalusia. Someone's loved one had died, someone was in mourning, someone believed that total immersion in the waters of the river would speed up the long and painful cycle of suffering and rebirth. So what exactly was I doing there with my little guidebook and my little camera, taking notes on my impressions of an event that was, for the people I was observing, nothing less than a matter of life and death?

10   Over the years, I heard stories about tourists who'd crossed boundaries of privacy and respect, who'd had their cameras seized and smashed for rudely photographing the wrong secret rite. Not until I received my own lesson about the dangers of ritual tourism, courtesy of Swami Sandcastle, did I realize how culpable I had been.

Still, my attraction to ritual tourism persisted. It flourished when I lived with my family in Tucson, Arizona. There, from time to time, we would drive out to the Mission San Xavier del Bac, the beautiful "white dove of the desert," where pilgrims, mostly Yaqui Indians and Mexicans from across the nearby border, performed the ritual of filing past—and lifting— the heavy wooden statue of Saint Francis that lay on the altar in a side chapel. According to the legend, only the sinless and pure of heart could lift the statue, while sinners couldn't budge it, no matter how hard they tried. I myself was always afraid to try—hesitant to subject myself to this instant and public spiritual diagnosis.

Every year at Easter we would go to south Tucson where the Yaqui community enacted an elaborate Easter ceremony representing the victory of light over darkness and good over evil. And every year I found myself in tears when light and goodness won.

That was where I discovered one remedy for my guilt about the voyeuristic aspects of my ritual tourism, which was to look down upon my fellow ritual tourists. What were these crude interlopers doing, trying to get between me and my enjoyment of a solemn ceremony? Many of these travelers happened to be Germans, loaded with cameras, traveling in large groups, shouting to one another, eagerly muscling their way to the front of the crowd. I glared at them. I sighed and rolled my eyes. I did everything in my power to make it obvious that these were real people performing real ceremonies, that this was not some circus being staged for these onlookers' benefit. I wondered why they had spent so much money and traveled so far to see the rites of others when they could have seen their own culture's ceremonies—say, the local Oktoberfest. Was it the desire to see something in others that looked closer to a purer, more compelling sort of faith? Or was it, as I suspected, a kind of romanticism which made the tourists feel as if the people they were watching were closer to some secret knowledge that had been lost in more industrialized cultures? These reflections interested me, but not enough to stop me from wishing that all the ritual tourists—that is, except me—would give it up and go home.

Then, one year, a strange thing happened.

15   It was just at the crucial moment in the ceremony. The masked figures representing the soldiers and the Pharisees had twice tried to storm the little structure decorated with streamers and paper flowers that symbolized the church. Each time they were rebuffed—pelted with flowers—by our heroes, the dancers. Finally, the soldiers were defeated. There was a storm of flowers, the masks of the villains came off, and the masks and an effigy of Judas were thrown into a roaring bonfire.

That was the moment at which, every year, I burst into tears. But this time, for some reason, I looked to the side and saw that one of the German tourists, in fact the woman who'd been especially annoying to me all through the ceremony, had likewise erupted in wrenching sobs. Suddenly, I realized that she'd been affected in the same way I had, that she was probably there for the same reason I was. What had brought her to south Tucson was not merely the wish to be entertained, but a desire to watch an affirmation of faith, of ceremony, of belief in community and shared history—and in the power of ritual to represent something admirable and enduring in human nature.

QUESTIONS FOR DISCUSSION

1. How does Prose define a ritual tourist? Why does she scorn them?
2. Which incident made Prose realize that she was a ritual tourist? Why does Prose write about ritual tourists?
3. In the context of the essay, interpret the meaning of Prose's claim: "The things we're drawn to satirize are, in many cases, the things we're most wary about in ourselves"? Explain your understanding of Prose's insights through the use of your travel experiences and reflections.
4. Which of the examples of ritual tourists helped you to understand her concept?
5. How does Prose finally come to understand that ritual tourists can be connected to others through ritual ceremonies? How does Prose experience her connection, compassion, and faith while attending a ritual ceremony?
6. According to Prose, why is being a ritual tourist not necessarily a form of voyeurism, "but a desire to watch an affirmation of faith, of ceremony, of belief in community and shared history"? Explain why you agree or disagree with her—if possible through one of your own tourist adventures.

CONNECTION

According to Prose's definition, is Goldberg's experience at the Zen monastery a form of ritual tourism? Why or why not (see page 145)?

IDEAS FOR WRITING

1. Write an essay in which you explore the following questions: Do you think that Prose's negative and positive definitions of a ritual tourist help you to understand the concept of a ritual tourist? What do you think could be done to further clarify the two kinds of ritual tourists? What have you learned about the value of travel from reading this essay? Do you think the concept of ritual travel will change the way that you choose to travel?

2. Do research into tourism and travel. Then write an essay that explores how tourist packages may or may not affect the quality of a trip to a ceremonial, religious, or historical site or monument. Include your thoughts about the rise of the tourism industry and its impact on the meaning that travel can have for an individual.

RELATED WEB SITES

Francine Prose, Novelist & Essayist
`www.blueflowerarts.com/fprose.html`
The Blue Flower Arts Agency gives a biography on Francine Prose as well as excerpts and discussions regarding some of her works.

Francine Prose News: The New York Times
`http://topics.nytimes.com/top/reference/timestopics/`
`people/p/francine_prose/index.html`
The *New York Times* Web site contains the above archive of articles relating to Francine Prose.

Natalie Goldberg

On the Shores of Lake Biwa

Natalie Goldberg (b. 1948) is an author of fiction, poetry, and non-fiction; a long-time painter; a teacher of creative writing; and a student of Zen Buddhism and meditation for over 24 years. She teaches writing workshops and retreats around the United States and near her home in Taos, New Mexico, often at the Mabel Dodge Luhan House, an historical artists' retreat in Taos. Her teaching and retreats are modeled on her Zen training; she believes that writing is "a way to help you penetrate your life and become sane." Her eleven books include Writing Down the Bones: Freeing the Writer Within *(1986),* Wild Mind: Living the Writer's Life *(1990),* Long Quiet Highway: Waking Up in America *(1993), and* Old Friend From Far Away: The Practice of Writing Memoir *(2008). The following essay about her travel experiences in Japan and her stay at the Bukkokuji monastery on Lake Biwa, appeared in* The Best Buddhist Writing 2007 *(2007).*

JOURNAL

Write about a time when you went on a trip to expand your understanding of a subject that you had studied. How were your expectations different from the reality of the trip?

I wanted to go to Japan to see the country that produced my teacher. But Japan was far away. I'm terrible with languages. When I tried to learn short Japanese phrases, it sounded like I was shredding coleslaw with my tongue and not budging one inch from Brooklyn. And all the words of that island country are written in kanji. I wouldn't even be able to decipher signs.

People assured me that everyone in Japan learned English in school. "No problem," they said. I didn't believe them. Hadn't I studied French for eight years? and all I could do was conjugate the verb "to be." Better to just spend my days on Coney Island—I knew where the hot dogs were.

But I had a writing student who had lived in Japan for several years and generously contacted a Japanese couple; they agreed to take me around Kyoto. They spoke good English, so I could ask questions. I talked my partner Michele into coming along.

We'd been there a week when Kenji and Tomoko picked us up at the hotel. I already felt isolated, walking down crowded streets, peering into unknown temples. I found myself several times towering over a young man or woman, asking something and receiving giggles behind polite hands. The Japanese might have learned English in school but they were too shy to speak it.

5   "They grind their own beans here," Kenji said as he drove us to a coffee shop.

Just the smell cleared my sinuses. I never drink coffee—I have enough trouble sleeping and fear chugging that dark brew would send me running at 100 m.p.h. But at this moment, I was so elated to speak to a native, not to feel so alone, that I too ordered a shot.

The four of us sat at a small square table, elbow to elbow. "So how do you know English so well?" I asked.

The white cups were placed in front of us. I took a sip. The black blend cut off the top of my head, hair and all. My eyes darted around the room. No tea, cookies, buns, rolls, rice cakes. Zen purity had been translated into a single-taste caffeine shop.

"We lived in England for four years. I was getting a Ph.D. in philosophy," Kenji explained.

10   "Really? Who did you study over there?" I'd done my master's in Western philosophy in my early twenties. But soon after I'd discovered Zen, I never thought of Bergson or Heidegger again.

"Immanuel Kant."

"You're kidding." My mouth fell open. "I did my thesis on him. You went all the way over to Europe for Kant?" I was incredulous. "In America we want to study Dogen."

It was Kenji's turn to be dumbstruck. "Ugh, no one understands Dogen. He's much too difficult." His nose crunched up.

Then I let the bomb drop. "I've been a Zen student for over two decades."

15   Now Tomoko grimaced. "That's awful. No one here likes Zen."

I had suddenly become peculiar to this Japanese couple.

Kenji injected, "Zen monks all die young."

I already knew, but asked, anyway, "Why?" I swallowed another gulp of coffee. I was never able to admit the answer through years of knee-aching, backbreaking sitting on little sleep.

"The training's too hard for a human being," he said.

20   My teacher had died in his early sixties. I could name several other Zen masters who had died too early. I had hoped it was the difficult shift they had made to America.

The conversation slid into pleasantries. Yes, I was a writer. Yes, my first book had been translated into Japanese.

Michele offered to meet them in New York the next time they visited. She described her family's apartment in that favorite of cities. I was watchful for my next opportunity to gather another crumb of information, a morsel of understanding, to slip in another question about my old practice.

My cup was almost empty. If I took one more sip I'd buzz out the window. I threw care to the neon lights above the entrance and put liquid to mouth. I leaned in close. "Can I ask you a question?" They both nodded simultaneously. Michele rolled her eyes. She knew where this was going. That morning in bed I had had a realization. Maybe I did know a little Japanese after all. In the zendo we chanted from cards that translated Japanese sounds into English syllables.

"Does this sound familiar?" I asked and then belted out the first line of the early morning chant that preceded putting on our rakusus. At this moment in the zendo our hands would be clasped in front of us with the lay ordination cloth on top of our heads. I saw the whole scene unfold as I chanted Dai Sai Ge Da Pu Ku in the coffee shop.

25   "Never heard of it," both Kenji and Tomoko shook their heads. They must have learned that head shake in England. When I shook my head No here, everyone looked at me blankly.

"You're kidding." What had I been studying all these years?

"What does it mean?" Tomoko asked.

I was too disappointed to be embarrassed. "Great robe of liberation."
They both stared at me.

30   "This coffee is delicious," Michele quickly interjected and downed
her cup.

They explained where they were going to take us. All I caught was
"famous temples." I was templed out. Everyplace Michele and I went no
one was meditating—just beautiful buildings, ornate altars, highly
waxed, fine wood floors. I hadn't realized it, but what I'd come for was
sixteenth-century Japan. I was looking for the descendants of Linji and
Hakuin. Where were the kick-ass practitioners, like the wild Americans
back in the States who were imitating the monks we thought were over
here? We woke at four a.m., meditated all day, sewed robes, ate in formal
style with three enamel bowls, even had miso soup for breakfast.

I let Michele do the socializing as I sat looking out the car window in
the backseat next to Tomoko. Michele shifted the conversation from the
dot-com explosion to a list of Japanese authors we'd been reading since
we arrived. I perked up. "Yeah, we're reading these prize-winning novels
and it's a surprise how often the plot is around a homosexual or a lesbian.
I thought the Japanese were more uptight than that?"

Kenji lifted a hand off the steering wheel, "Oh, no, we're used to it—
from the monasteries. The boys go in young."

I gulped. Is that what goes on in monasteries?

35   They drove us from one ancient shrine to another, all with indis-
cernible names. I was young again, dragged to one art museum after
another. The afternoon was a blur and my eyes teared. I wanted to lie
down and take a deep nap.

"I'm sorry," Kenji said. "We only have one more, but this one is important. You have to see it. Very famous."

Two young girls in navy-blue school uniforms explained the significance
of the temple. All of the other visitors were Japanese. Michele and I politely
stood with our hands shading our eyes. We didn't understand a word.

My mind was zinging out in the stratosphere, rejoicing that this was
the last temple, when one word snapped through my daydream. Hold
everything! Did that ingénue on the left say a familiar name?

"Excuse me, Tomoko," I whispered. "Who lived here in ancient days?
What's his name?"

40   She shrugged. Even though she spoke the language this world was foreign to her.

"Please, help me," I took her hand. "I have to find out."

The student didn't know what I was talking about even through translation. She handed me the sheet she read from.

"Is the name 'Ikkyu' here?" I turned the paper over to Tomoko.
"What's the name of this temple?"

Tomoko slowly pronounced, "Daitokuji."

45 My eyebrows jumped off my face. "Daitokuji. Did this temple burn down in the fifteenth century? Who rebuilt it? Does it say?"

Tomoko looked back at the paper and translated to the young hosts what I was asking. "Hai, hai," in unison they nodded.

"Oh my god." I threw my hand over my mouth.

The thinner girl pointed to a square white building over the high stuccoed wall we were standing near. This time Kenji translated. "She says Ikkyu is in there."

"Ikkyu in there," my eyes widened, the eccentric Zen monk with a wild spirit whose poetry I loved. I imagined him preserved in zazen position in his ragged, brown monk's robe, the one he wore when hanging out with drunks under the bridge.

50 My hands curled into fists. I wanted to leap the wall, burst into the tomb, bow at his feet, tell him how I'd spent a cold winter and dark spring reading his poems. They never failed me.

When a friend having a hard time would call, I'd say, "Hold on a minute," and grab Crow with No Mouth. "Listen to this," and I'd read them Ikkyu.

People were horrified by Ikkyu's unconventional life—he alternated between practicing hard, then frequenting brothels and bars with prostitutes and hoboes. But when he was eighty-two, he was asked to be head of Daitokuji. It was a great honor. He did not refuse. With his tremendous energy, he rebuilt the temple.

The intensity of having Ikkyu nearby was overwhelming. I was afraid I disappointed this great practitioner. He would have leaped over the barrier. He was waiting for me. I think he is still waiting.

I left Michele in Kyoto to travel north by train to Bukkokuji, one of the few Japanese monasteries that were willing to take Westerners and women. I thought, if I was going to be in this country, I had to experience their monasteries, even if for a short time. Michele and I went over my route many times in the hotel before I departed. The train moved fast and I was alert to hear the Obama stop announced, even though I

55 knew it wouldn't be for quite a while.

To my right out the window was a great gray lake, reflecting the overcast sky. I heard, "Biwa."

"Biwa?" I poked the man next to me. This was very un-Japanese, but the train moved so quickly I had to act fast.

He nodded briskly, not glancing my way. "Hai."

At twenty-seven, Ikkyu, meditating alone at midnight out in a rowboat on this very lake, heard the caw caw caw of a crow overhead and was turned inside out, becoming totally realized.

He was a poet. It made sense that awakening would enter his body through sound. For a cook the ax might fall while tasting a particularly pungent lemon: She would drop to the ground, savoring bitter lemon in all things.

60   My stop was finally called and I jumped off, clutching my knapsack. I followed a path through weeds and empty lots into the monastery cemetery. Often at night monks sat at the gravestones and meditated. It was mid-afternoon. I was nervous. I kept repeating, You'll be okay. You've sat six three-month difficult practice periods and this time it's just a few days.

The small building complex was a hundred yards away, built right up against a hill. I stepped into the courtyard. No one was there. A beefily built monk appeared and spoke to me in Japanese.

I shook my head. I understood not a word.

He continued to talk and motion with his hands. At this point Tangen—I recognized his face from a photo—the Zen master of the monastery, who was in his seventies and had rarely left in the last thirty-five years, glided into the courtyard and he and the head monk (I figured out who the beefily built man was) grunted at each other. The head monk then grabbed my pack and I followed him.

Near twin sinks he stopped and pointed, holding out my sack. I took it and walked alone through a set of doors. Ten thin mattresses were on the floor and five Japanese nuns with shaved heads were lying on them. Near the entrance was a small, spare woman—the only other Western female at the monastery—who introduced herself and pointed to a rolled bed. I nervously set out my few things, unrolled the mattress, and laid down. I didn't know what the routine would be, but I knew it would be in silence. I tried to rest. How did the saying go? Rest when you rest, sleep when you sleep, cry when you cry. Et cetera, et cetera. I could have made the list go on: be nervous when you're nervous, feel your tight chest when you feel your tight chest, want to go home when you want to go home. I noticed how hot and humid it was. My straight hair was curling. No one else around me had any hair. I remembered my friend who'd been to Japan saying, there is nothing like the humidity. For emphasis he repeated himself: Trust me, Natalie, in all the world, your clothes will not get wetter than in Japan. Obama was on the sea. I was in for it.

65   Bells rang. All seven of us in the dormitory sprang up. They put on their robes; I put on my black long-sleeved tee-shirt and black long pants and we sat through two periods of zazen in the upstairs zendo across the court. I had no idea how long each sitting was. It could have been twenty-five minutes or forty. I was just happy to know how to do something and proud at the end to recognize the Heart Sutra as it was shot through at a speed no American could follow.

At dinner we ate cross-legged in the dining room in a ritualized style, with three oryoki bowls, chopsticks, napkin, and drying cloth. The actual meal was a mush of colors. What hadn't been eaten from breakfast and lunch was consumed at night. What hadn't been eaten from the meals of the days before were also in there. If mold was forming from a week ago, a high boil took care of it all.

At the end of the meal, we fingered thin slices of pickles to clean our bowls, ate the pickle slices, and drank the washing water. The bowls were then wrapped again in the lap cloth with a formal knot. I could do all this and the Japanese nuns clucked in surprise.

We sat zazen again and went to bed. I hadn't spoken a word to anyone. I didn't know what time we would wake the next morning, but I could rely on the tight structure. Don't think, I told myself. Take care of your life—connected to all life—moment by moment.

I did not sleep for one moment the entire night. I was drenched in sweat. I think it was three a.m. when the bells rang and everyone popped out of bed. I ran the brush one time over my teeth. We were in the zendo fifteen minutes later.

70 The zendo was a comfort, but not for long. The bell quickly rang again and people ran down the stairs. Where were they going? I turned around and everyone was gone. I bolted after them and saw the monks running out the gate. I put on my shoes and dashed after them.

The streets of Obama were quiet. I heard only the swish of my rubber soles. Thank god I hadn't worn flip-flops. I chugged along, but way behind. Suddenly they turned a corner and I lost them. We were the Japanese Marx brothers. I headed east on one block, I saw them passing west on another; I darted north at the lamppost, I caught sight of them sprinting south at the turn. I was panting hard. I hadn't run like this in ten years. The sea was to my right as I galloped up an incline. Just as they neared the gate I caught up. My lungs were burning. My breath was heaving. I was soaked, hair dripping, pants and shirt stuck to my body.

I followed the monks into an empty room, where less than twenty-four hours ago the head monk had grunted at me. Another monk called out a command and everyone hit the ground flat-out; another shout and everyone was on their feet. Then we were slammed on the floor again, doing push-ups. I was already one command behind. They were down; I was up. They were up; I was down. Finally, the exercise stopped. I was a dishrag.

People stood around. Sunlight was creeping across the gravestones. I sidled over to the Irishwoman and whispered so softly—the sound could have fit under a saltine cracker—"Can we take showers now?"

She replied with a single line: "There are no showers here."

75 Uh huh, I nodded. I'd heard a rumor years ago back in the comfort of the Minneapolis zendo that baths in Japanese monasteries were taken once a week at public bath houses.

I sat on a stone step and waited for the next activity. Exhaustion allowed surrender.

The bell rang. We piled up to the zendo and sat for one period. Another bell rang and off everyone dashed down the stairs again. This time I walked. I didn't care if the fires of hell leaped at me. I found the monks in seiza, kneeling with their legs tucked under them, on the hard, wooden floor in a single row. A bell rang in another room and the first person in line jumped up and disappeared. The row of people on their knees slid up to the next place.

I knelt at the end, the last person, the longest wait. My knees felt as though they were about to snap, but I didn't change positions. I crawled behind everyone else each time the first person left. I knew what was happening. This was our chance to talk to the Roshi, face to face, in his small dokusan room. I had heard he was clear, that just to watch him walk across a room was inspiring, that he took joy in the smallest things.

What was I doing here with this resounding pain? No one said I had to stay in this position, but everyone else was doing it and I was a stubborn person. Dedication no longer mattered, only animal will. What could I say to this man from another world? I had already had my true teacher. He'd died eight years ago.

80 My turn came. I did the three prostrations and sat in front of Tangen Roshi. He tilted his head to peer at me. I was hopeless. I knew it. He said three English words: Not long enough.

I thought, thank god. I was fifty years old. Too old. Too tired. Too dirty.

The gesture was made for me to leave. The meeting was over. I had the urge to put my hand on his knee, to assure him I would be okay. After all, here was a man who was dedicated to waking us up. I didn't want to disappoint him but right then I wanted to go to sleep.

That afternoon after a work period when we beat mattresses and rolled blankets and towels, we had tea—and doughnuts, wrapped in cellophane, bought at a local store. I could tell this was a real treat and I abstained so the monks could have more.

Each day was long. I had no illusions that something big or deep would happen. I just wanted to make it through each day running, walking, sitting, eating in that single pair of black pants and shirt.

85 Young monks pounded big bells that hung from eaves and ran in the halls. Even the army knows to take boys early. Only me, only I don't know I'm not young. That is what these days taught me: I was no longer young. How easy it was for me at twenty-six, at thirty-one—but even then I complained. Now I had only a few days left in a Japanese monastery and I was thankful I would get to leave.

That day did come and there was no formality. No one said, "Oh, Natalie, we loved having you." I rolled up my mattress, deposited my scant towel and bedding in the laundry room and slung my pack on my back.

I was thinking how I couldn't wait to return to Kyoto and take a shower when I passed the altar room. I noticed a big Buddha statue and a small inconspicuous donation box, but it wasn't necessary to pay anything for your stay.

I turned to head out. "C'mon, Nat, you can give a little something, even though these days were no fun."

I counted out yen. I was not good at figuring out the equivalent in dollars, a hundred and ten to one, too many zeros. I left what I thought was twenty-five dollars. I followed the path through weeds back to the railroad station. I was a bit early for the next train. I wandered over to the concession stand and eyed the bags of M & M's. A great compulsion overcame me. I bought two. I ripped one open; they were already melted. I shoved the colored chocolates into my mouth and they smeared over my right hand and around my lips. I had nothing to wipe them with but my dirty black sleeve.

90   Suddenly I looked up: one of the monks from the monastery had just entered the station, recognized me, and was walking over. He was dressed immaculately in formal traveling attire. I tried to hide my chocolate-covered hand, having already wiped my mouth. He stood in front of me in his platform sandals. He noticed my hand and flashed a warm smile. I felt the color come to my face. He reached into the front of his robe. He pulled out some kind of bar and held it up. My eyes focused. Almond Joy. We both burst out laughing.

My train pulled up. I threw myself into a seat near the window and waved. The scenery zoomed by.

All at once, yens popped into my head. I hadn't left 2,750—I left 27,500. Two hundred and fifty American dollars. I gasped, my stomach tightened. Then completely let go. It was fine, just fine. I was glad I'd contributed that much. And right there was everything I knew and I could not say what that was.

QUESTIONS FOR DISCUSSION

1. What does Goldberg hope to learn on her trip to Japan?
2. During the first week in Kyoto, what is Goldberg's reaction to the modern Japanese way of life? How does she feel about her meeting with Kenji and Tomoko? What are the differences in her expectations and the reality of the tour that she takes with Kenji and Tomoko?
3. What expectations do you think Goldberg has as she takes the train to the monastery at Lake Biwa? Do you think that her prior experiences in Japan may have influenced her expectations?
4. What makes Goldberg apprehensive when she sees the monastery and then recognizes the Zen master, Tangen, whose work she admires? How do the monks treat her? Describe the routine at the monastery.

5. What is Goldberg's reaction to the monastery's ritual? What does Goldberg come to understand during her stay at the monastery? How is her "reverence" for Zen Buddhism changed as a consequence of the trip?

6. Why does Goldberg leave too much money at the monastery? Why does she run to find chocolate as soon as she arrives at the train station? What is ironic about both incidents? Why does the monk who comes to see her off reveal his own candy? Why does the essay end here?

CONNECTION

To which travel experience in this chapter is Goldberg's most similar? Be clear about why you chose the selection and also discuss the differences between the experiences of the travelers in the two situations.

IDEAS FOR WRITING

1. Write an essay that explores Goldberg's major realizations, how they affected her, and speculate on how her ideas about Japan and Zen monasteries might have changed. Considering your own knowledge of Japan and Zen monasteries, how do you relate to Goldberg's experiences? What have you learned?

2. Write an essay that develops your journal writing about a trip in depth. Consider that your trip may have been more (or less) enjoyable than Goldberg's and how you may have gained perspective, self-understanding, and knowledge from travel.

RELATED WEB SITES

Natalie Goldberg

www.nataliegoldberg.com

This personal and professional homepage for Natalie Goldberg gives information regarding her workshops, books, tapes, paintings, and other news about Goldberg.

Lake Biwa – A Global Ecoregion

www.panda.org/about_wwf/where_we_work/ecoregions/ lake_biwa.cfm

The World Wildlife Fund provides ecological and demographic information about Lake Biwa in Japan.

Joan M. Thomas

The Field of Dreams Mystique: Quest for the American Ideal

Joan Thomas, a freelance writer and scholar of baseball history, received her B.S. in Mass Communications from Lindenwood University in St. Charles in 1989. She has published articles (usually baseball related) in Progressive Woman; Gateway: the Quarterly Magazine of the Missouri Historical Society; the St. Louis Post-Dispatch; the Encyclopedia of Women and Baseball; *and the anthologies* Baseball/Literature/Culture Essays *(1995–2001, 2002–2003, 2004–2005). Thomas has also delivered many papers at the Conference on Baseball in Literature and Culture at Indiana State University, Terre Haute, Indiana. She has written a book,* St. Louis' Big League Ballparks *(2004), and in that year won First Place Award for Research from the National Federation of Press Women. The following researched essay, published in* Baseball/Literature/Culture: Essays 1995–2001, *examines the popularity as a tourist destination of the Iowa site of the film* Field of Dreams.

JOURNAL

Write about a monument or theme park you have visited that reminded you of the dreams and values of your culture or country.

A fantasy born of the imagination of a baseball-loving writer and brought to life on the big screen by a Hollywood producer inadvertently created an American shrine to the national sport. A mere cornfield, near the small town of Dyersville, in eastern Iowa, only one of thousands of cornfields in that farm state—after its use as the set of the motion picture *Field of Dreams*—strangely became a refuge for those seeking the embodiment of our perception of baseball and America. A relatively simple yet fantastic story based on W. P. Kinsella's 1982 novel *Shoeless Joe,* the film unashamedly spins a yarn about Ray Kinsella, a 1960s college radical turned Iowa farmer whose seeming hallucination while working in his cornfield convinces him to plow under some of the valuable crop in order to build a baseball field there. The plot thickens even more fantastically from that point on. In the end—after the ghosts of White Sox baseball player Shoeless Joe Jackson and his teammates, banished from baseball after being accused of throwing the 1919 World Series, emerge from the surrounding cornfield—Ray meets up with the spirit of his own father, who died before the two could settle a dispute stemming from Jackson's alleged involvement in the scandal. Silently reconciled, the two men play catch, something Ray refused the last time he saw his father alive.

Since the film's release in 1989, the site in Dyersville reportedly attracts upwards of 50,000 visitors annually. Early in the story, a mysterious voice tells the farmer "If you build it, he will come." In twelve years following the movie's release, some 740,000 visitors have come. Upon examination, this relentless throng of pilgrims would seem to be something of a phenomenon in a rural community, far from anything that meets with our concept of a big city. The town's chief attraction before the film was the National Farm Toy Museum.

Primarily a farm state, Iowa produces 24% of the nation's pork. It ranks first in the nation in grain harvested. Corn grows taller and more abundantly there than any other place on earth. These aspects alone, however, rarely serve as a lure for sightseers. Though points of historical interest and museums of various types dot this agricultural paradise, named Iowa for the American Indian word meaning "the land," most travelers would not regard it as a vacation Mecca. One can consider it the ideal setting for wholesome family life but certainly not as a high-ranking choice for a pleasure trip. Iowa does, however, serve well as a backdrop for a romantic or mystical story, possibly owing to its relative obscurity and pristine beauty. Another movie, *Bridges of Madison County,* filmed on location near the town of Winterset, in south central Iowa, created a huge increase in visitors to that area. Before that film's premiere, Winterset boasted of its six covered bridges listed in the National Register of Historic Places. It also maintains the birthplace of American film icon John Wayne. Yet *Bridges,* with Clint Eastwood and Meryl Streep, boosted the town's guest register from 8,000 in 1994 to 37,000 in 1995. That figure did not include the thousands of additional visitors drawn by the film that traveled there by motor coach for day trips.

The curiosity about the set of *Field of Dreams* in Dyersville is that there is nothing of the historic value comparable to the actual bridges of Winterset. The ballfield was built just for the movie. The only shred of actual fact in the story is the legend of Joe Jackson. His return as a ghost in that bucolic setting, pure fabrication to satisfy a deep-rooted desire for vindication, does not logically explain the fascination with the movie set.

5　　A more plausible mania, a rise in the number of visitors to Jackson's gravesite at Woodlawn Memorial Park in Greenville, South Carolina, came after the films *Field of Dreams* and *Eight Men Out* revived interest in the outcast ballplayer. Following the success of the latter that depicted the 1919 White Sox scandal, the city of Greenville reconstructed the ballfield near Brandon Cotton Mill, where the real life Jackson once played as a textile leaguer. Using land donated by the cotton mill's owner for a community park, the city named it Shoeless Joe Park. The national media attention focusing on Jackson caused county court house officials to take action; they put Jackson's will, bearing his rare, scratched signature, under lock and key, protecting it from autograph seeking predators. Well into 2001, Greenville continued receiving calls regarding the park, and visitors to Woodlawn now leave baseballs and even bats at Shoeless Joe's grave. But Jackson probably never even heard of Dyersville, much less emerged from a cornfield there.

The story portrayed in the film *Field of Dreams* and its Iowa cornfield setting remain the keys to the enigma of why thousands of vacationers continue to embark on a pilgrimage to that remote ball field. A fantasy made credible under the broad, clear sky in a simple field, the story appeals to our desire for order and sanity. Hal Erickson, in his *Baseball in the Movies*, quotes director Philip Alden Robinson's comment, appearing in a *Time* magazine article, in which he describes the film as tapping into a communal desire for "more innocent times" as a curative to the cynicism of today: "A lot of our heroes have turned out to have clay feet. I don't believe in Astrology, crystals, reincarnation, heaven, hell! I don't believe in dreams come true. But it's primal emotion to want to make the bad good—to hope things will turn out in the end" (151).

What better location to stage such a story than a place seemingly unadulterated by the social problems beset by most of the country—the kind of place Grant Wood depicted in his regionalist paintings in the 1930s, a land once farmed by people like the sober man and woman in Wood's most famous work *American Gothic*. The artist lived and worked most of his life in Cedar Rapids, in east central Iowa, not far from Dyersville. In Wanda Corn's biography of Wood, she notes that:

> American Gothic embodies many traditional values and is more important for what it symbolizes than as a work of art. . . . A simple pictograph—one house, two people and a pitchfork—reminds so many Americans of their own ancestral photographs and triggers association with a wide range of celebrated American experiences: our Puritan beginnings, life on the frontier, free enterprise, self-reliance, the Protestant work ethic, agrarianism, the nuclear family, and the common man (206–207).

In a sense, *Field of Dreams* joins *American Gothic* and John Wayne as American icons.

The spiritual vision of baseball in American life frequently surfaces in Hollywood productions with the game serving to represent the wholesome side of American life or as a vehicle to describe the collective American character. Baseball movies, such as *Angels in the Outfield, Damn Yankees, The Natural,* and *It Happens Every Spring* deal with the fantastic, religious or occult. Combining the beloved sport of baseball with a strong desire to return it to its original form—erasing its scandals and corruption—the story of *Field of Dreams* in the foreground of Grant

Wood's Iowa reaches beyond conscious desires to people's deepest, inarticulated needs and wishes.

10   Don and Becky Lansing live in the house used in the film *Field of Dreams*. Don was actually born in that house, which has been in his family for 95 years. The Lansings believe Kinsella's story achieves credibility because "many people *want* to believe and so come to stand at the intersection of reality and fantasy" ("Field" 11). Perhaps their explanation makes more sense than any high-toned treatise. The famous dialogue between Joe Jackson and farmer Ray when Jackson asks, "Is this Heaven?" and Ray answers "No, it's Iowa" plainly describes Mrs. Lansing's theory. Iowa is reality. Iowa is the land. Jackson is a phantom, a vision. A comparable exchange in the film *Star Trek 4: The Voyage Home* points to the same conclusion. A twentieth-century woman befriended by Captain Kirk, a visitor from a future century, says incredulously "You mean to tell me you're from outer space!" Kirk responds by saying "No, actually I'm from Iowa. I just work in outer space." That somehow makes his story believable. Nobody would lie about being from Iowa.

Hal Erickson describes the movie's audience most affected by its story as men "on the fringes of middle age with most of their youthful aspirations and hopes of creating a better world either compromised or forgotten" (152). Since the main character is a man seeking reconciliation with his father, Erickson's conclusion sounds cogent. However, the people flocking to Dyersville come in all ages and both genders. The film's appeal touches on much more than middle age and baseball. All of its characters follow their own chosen path in life to an ethereal place in time that allows them the chance to take another path. The viewer can vicariously answer the eternal question, *What if?* The speech by the Terrence Mann character, a reclusive writer representing J. D. Salinger handily woven into the plot and so marvelously portrayed by James Earl Jones, best describes the mysterious something that grabs viewers' emotions and validates their hopes. He says "This field, this game, is part of all that once was good, and can be again."

Mann resurrects all the best vision of the American Dream. He reminds the viewer that with all the nation's noble ideals, things just have not always turned out as hoped. So in the dark of the theatre, viewers can believe, maybe not in Santa Claus or the tooth fairy but in possibility. And who could make it more convincing than that magnificent recognizable voice we also know as Darth Vader.

Hopefully, the shrine to a lost dream in Dyersville will never fall prey to the predictable corporate greed. The surrounding land there still gets farmed as usual. Because the filmmakers needed part of the land situated on two separate farms due to the direction of the sunlight on the house, the baseball field remains the property of two families. Don and Becky Lansing own the house as well as the property where the movie producers carved the infield, right field and part of center field. The Al and Rita Ameskamp family, who live just up the road, own left field and part of center field.

Originally the Ameskamps plowed under their part of the field. They didn't anticipate any reaction. Don Lansing, in contrast, always wanted to keep the ball field. In 1996 the Ameskamps turned management of their part of the field over to GS2, a Milwaukee banking firm. The firm hired Keith Rahe, a local farmer who originated the Ghost Players, as its manager of the left and center field. The Ghost Players, consisting of a group of local men, re-enact the movie's ghost ball players emerging from the bordering cornfield, playing ball with visitors. Their presence naturally enhances the experience of the tourist. The group also travels all over the world, entertaining people unable to "go the distance" to Iowa.

15   GS2 proposed putting in batting cages and an 1800 square-foot concession and souvenir stand, replacing the smaller, utilitarian stand that accommodates visitors of the Ameskamp's land. The county Board of Adjustments turned down the plan, much to the relief of the Lansings. An article in the *Wall Street Journal* in July 1996 quotes Mrs. Lansing as saying that there "has even been talk of using the site for corporate motivation seminars." The piece goes on to say that it all strikes the Lansings as inappropriate. "This place is not about making money . . . ," Mrs. Lansing says. "We want it to remain small, simple and serene . . . .We feel their vision (GS2's) is the generation of the dollar" (Gibson B3a).

But in 1999, the local county board granted a zoning change, permitting a new attraction on the Ameskamp property. A tunnel-like path, or maze, cut through the corn stalks behind left field now allows visitors to wind through the cornfield. Adults pay six dollars for the privilege of making an imaginary disappearance on the same grounds where in the film they saw the evaporation of the White Sox ghosts, James Earl Jones, and Burt Lancaster (the latter seasoned veteran played an aging doctor who gave up the majors years earlier before getting an at-bat. The ghosts give him his shot). So like American League and the National League fans at odds about the DH, the two owners remain divided over what is appropriate and what is not.

There are even separate web sites for the dream field. The Lansing site is titled Field of Dreams, and the other is Left and Center Field of Dreams. In addition, each faction has its own souvenir stand on its respective property. Visitors can purchase tee shirts, caps, and other souvenirs such as one might buy at any baseball park. There is still no charge for parking or admission at the field. It stands to reason that the loss of crop revenue and the upkeep of the property would necessitate some kind of income producing activity. So when does it become too commercial? We Americans know all about free enterprise and exploitation.

This question then leads back to the primary reason that fans are so enamored with this improbable tourist draw. There are still no gargantuan neon signs, casinos or luxury hotels. It's not likely that such things will ever come to Dyersville. Iowa is not like Nevada, where entertainment ensures economic success. Iowa's black fertile soil is capable of producing food for the world. Keith Rahe, the ghost player who works for the Left and Center Field of Dreams faction, once expressed his need for simplicity. *The Cedar Rapids Gazette,* in a September 1996 article about the Ghost Players, quotes him: "It's not like a dream come true for me because I love farming. It's nice to see you do have an idea and see it . . . come to reality. It's gratifying." He went on to say that he missed the solitude of "being on a tractor and driving for hours" (Boar).

Angie Wessels, Dyersville tourism director in 1997, claimed that intrusion by outsiders on the town had not been a problem. She said that the attraction of the Field of Dreams in the community had changed nothing. They take pride in the fact that Dyersville is the "farm toy capitol of the world." Keith Rahe, in a telephone interview in April of 1997, agreed with Wessels. He suggested that not only has the field not altered the town's lifestyle but that it has been a "godsend" to the community. The local residents are glad that they have a "wholesome, family oriented place" for people to go. So far, it remains the unspoiled place the film sets forth and visitors envision.

20   Nevertheless, why would such large crowds continually flock to the Field of Dreams more than ten years after the release of the film? Attendance at the sport's shrine, the National Baseball Hall of Fame in Cooperstown, New York, has fluctuated with baseball's tenuous popularity in recent years. Following the last baseball strike it experienced a plummeting decline in visitors. Figures obtained from Hall of Fame officials show that from 407,000 in 1993, attendance fell to a low of 285,000 in '97. By the year 2000 it climbed up to 344,008. Museum librarian John Bobnick in 1997 said that people associate the museum with Major League Baseball.

While Major League Baseball continues on its seemingly reckless path, constantly looking for new and inventive ways to lure fans, people visit Dyersville hoping it remains a constant. Major League owners must notice this fascination with the basic baseball field. Into the twenty-first century, the trend moves toward building new "retro" parks, fashioned to resemble the old-time parks seen in photos and in the movies. In 1996, St. Louis Cardinals owners replaced the Astroturf with natural grass at Busch Stadium. The following year they introduced a novel "hand operated" scoreboard. One quintessential baseball purist, Robert J. Thomas, Jr., pointed out that the ultimate absurdity would arrive when fans at the park could view behind-the-scenes operation of the manually operated scoreboard on the stadium's modern electronic video screen.

In 2001, local backers proposed replacing the stadium with a "baseball village" featuring an old-style ballpark—supposedly like the Cardinal's former home, Sportsman's Park.

Perhaps the people closest to the place understand the mystique of the Field of Dreams best. Becky Lansing says, "People visit for many different reasons. Baseball is just one of them. . . . There are many different facets of the movie. Spirituality, reconciliation, life, death, dreams, etc. Baseball is the venue" ("Field" 11). Keith Rahe captures the reason people come in one word. He says that they come for the "magic." He has been all over the world with his Ghost Players and says that the film fascinates people everywhere. Apparently the same holds true with Major League ballplayers, despite how pampered and oblivious they often seem to fans. In Rahe's interview with *Cedar Rapids Gazette* reporter Ann Boar, he comments that he has given up bringing entertainers to the field. He says that he has found that they don't keep their word. But baseball players are different. "The field means something to them and the movie means something to them." It means "something" to each of us. What that something is that elicits such an emotional reaction depends on each individual's life experience. Like a haunting classical music composition, the idea of the field draws on each person's inner convictions and aspirations.

Although the film *Field of Dreams* garnered three Academy Award nominations, for Best Picture, Best Screenplay Adaptation, and Best Original Score, it drew mixed reviews when first released in 1989. More cynical critics condemned it as shamelessly sentimental, using words like *maudlin, mawkish, sugary,* and *treacle.* Some critics qualified their contempt for what they considered a ridiculous premise by admitting its ability to tug at the heartstrings. Others, including Roger Ebert, liked the film, buying into its premises and pointing out the fine performances and stylish direction.

Despite the mixed reviews, the film is more popular at video stores than those that surpassed it at the Oscars. In a hectic and often callous world, many viewers likely value the film's ability to draw on emotions, even to evoke a flood of tears. A writer for the *Baltimore Sun* in 1989 claimed that *Field of Dreams* made Brooks Robinson cry. The well-known baseball figure claimed he rarely went to movies but went to see *Field* on Jim Palmer's advice. The scene where the farmer's little girl first sees Joe Jackson on her dad's newly built baseball field drew the first tears to the baseball veteran's eyes (Murray F1).

25   Baseball aficionados of a realist bent enjoyed pointing out the film's most obvious error: Joe Jackson batting right-handed. The Sox outfielder batted from the left. But then, the film *is a fantasy.* So far as we know, Jackson never really came back to life in a cornfield just so he could play baseball again. The film never pretends to explain any of the story's miraculous occurrences. If viewers could buy the mystical voice in the cornfield,

why not a right-handed Shoeless Joe? Early in the film, while watching a baseball game on television, the little girl asks her father "What's a south-paw?" Could her question be taken as a hint that such mundane realities as left and right are not important in the world of the film?

And whose voice did farmer Ray hear anyway? The whispering voice told Ray to build the field, and after he obeyed, it said to "Ease his pain." So he complied, not only giving Jackson a second chance but also recuperating Terrance Mann and permitting a second chance for both Ray and his dad. While the voice may seem supernatural, far-fetched, anyone from an Iowa farm will attest that the rows of tall corn on a breezy day create a sort of whis-pering noise. This strange sound results from the long leaves of the corn-stalks rubbing against one another. Another significant point about Iowa's topography is that there are very few trees or tall buildings, especially out-side of the towns. In the country, an unobstructed sky seems to go on for-ever. With no large cities anywhere nearby, there is very little traffic, and virtually no pollution, just the pungent aroma of livestock manure pollution. But that distinctly rural feature is natural, and not harmful to one's health. On a summer's day, one might hear only the insect-like song of a red winged blackbird, perhaps the chugging of a tractor, the tinkling of a cow bell, or the barking of a single dog—and the human-like murmuring sounds cre-ated by a breeze rustling through the corn stalks. To some that might seem like "heaven," or at least a place where strange things can happen.

Some call it magic; others point to the elements of faith, hope and redemption. Whatever draws folks to the real piece of Iowa earth to try to live out the fantasy of a film, the land will always remain. As far as it is possible, contamination by materialistic endeavors will never change the reality that the field is still just an Iowa farm. In an interview with writer Steve Murray in 1989, James Earl Jones made the observation that "with every pure movement, corruption follows very fast. Freedom lets every-thing in" (F1). But one can also consider a line uttered by Scarlett O'Hara's father in the classic film *Gone with the Wind.* When lecturing her about the importance of the land he says, "Land is the only thing that matters . . . it's the only thing that lasts." Perhaps visitors want to believe that when they are gone from this life, they can return as ghosts and play ball with Shoeless Joe and his pals—on real soil.

In the final analysis, faith restored is the lure. In *Field of Dreams,* Terrance Mann is a disillusioned liberal. The farmer is a disillusioned radical. The White Sox ballplayers are disillusioned themselves and have disillusioned their ardent fans. Despite their ideals, Americans often resist stories seen as "schmaltz," hardening themselves against too much display of sentiment. But the success of another, now classic, Hollywood film provides some idea of when a story ceases to be "corny." In *Casablanca,* based on a story originally considered overly sentimental, the mercenary American, Rick Blaine, and the corrupt French prefect, Captain Renault, both ultimately fall on the side of right, walking off into the uncertain future with their patriotism rediscovered and "a beautiful friendship" born. Like the stern man and woman portrayed in *American Gothic,* Americans tend to disdain emotion. But after the tragic events of September 11, 2001, our need to renew our idyllic vision of America prompted a dramatic resurgence in patriotic fervor. We need to cling to some kind of a belief in ourselves. In order to do that, we must cherish and find strength in our origins. *Field of Dreams* and a cornfield in Dyersville can inspire us to seek that end.

WORKS CITED

Associated Press. "Field of Dreams Owners Questioned About Land." *St. Louis Post-Dispatch* 28 July 1996: Sec. F, 11.

Boar, Ann Scholl. "Build It and They Will Come" *Cedar Rapids Gazette* 18 September 1996, microfilm record number 00313* 19960918*08588.

Casablanca. Dir. Michael Curtiz. Perf. Humphrey Bogart and Ingrid Bergman. Warner Brothers, 1942.

Corn, Wanda. *Grant Wood, The Regionalist Vision.* Minneapolis: University of Minnesota UP, 1983.

Erickson, Hal. *Baseball in the Movies: A Comprehensive Reference, 1915–1991.* Jefferson, NC: McFarland, 1992.

Field of Dreams. Dir. Philip Alden Robinson. Perf. Kevin Costner and James Earl Jones. Universal, 1989.

Gibson, Richard. "Field of Dreams Hosts Owners' Tiff, Leading to Lockout of 'Ghost Players'" *Wall Street Journal* 12 July 1996, B3a.

QUESTIONS FOR DISCUSSION

1. How does Thomas use comparison and contrast to other historical sites in Iowa and elsewhere in the country to emphasize her central argument about why tourists are attracted to Dyersville, Iowa, site of the filming of the movie *Field of Dreams?*

2. Thomas discusses the symbolism inherent to the Dyersville site and the state of Iowa, as well as the symbolism within the film, to help the reader understand the site's appeal. What symbols does she discuss, and how do these symbols help to create a mythic reality for visitors?

3. Most historical tourist sites and theme parks are highly commercialized. Why does the lack of commercialism of the Dyersville field appeal to visitors? What is particularly ironic about the site's continuing mass appeal?

4. Thomas uses quotations from several sources: *Field of Dreams* director Philip Alden Robinson, a biography of the Iowa artist Grant Wood (famous for his painting "American Gothic"), and Don and Becky Lansing, owners of the Dyersville home where the film was shot. What do these quotations add to the interpretation Thomas makes of the film and site for viewers and visitors alike?

5. Thomas uses references to several other classic films, as well as a number of baseball films, to help make her points about the appeal of *Field of Dreams* and the Dyersville site. What common film themes does she emphasize? What do these film references and themes add to the essay?

6. Why has the *Field of Dreams* mystique become more popular after September 11, 2001?

CONNECTION

Compare and contrast Thomas's and Prose's views on "ritual tourism (see page 140).

IDEAS FOR WRITING

1. After researching Web sites about Dyersville and the *Field of Dreams* site, write a travel essay in which you take an imagined trip to the Field of Dreams. What descriptive details might enrich your portrait of the cornfields, the Lansing home, and the small community of Dyersville? What fantasies about the past would your visit evoke for you? How might you be moved or changed by your visit?

2. Develop the journal entry above relative to a place you have actually visited that reminded you of the dreams and values of your culture or country.

RELATED WEB SITES

Field of Dreams Movie Site—Tourism Info
www.fieldofdreamsmoviesite.com
This official Web site for the *Field of Dreams* movie provides behind-the-scenes background to the making of the film, as well as information regarding the tourist attractions.

Topics for Research and Writing

1. Do some research into the rise of tourism and its impact on places of natural beauty that could never be replaced. Also research the ways that environmentalists are working to preserve the natural beauty of these regions all over the world. Pick one natural area to research, and write a paper about how it is being protected by environmentalists. What are your thoughts and feelings about one nature area, and what is your reaction to its beauty?

2. As we travel, we project values, fears, and stereotypical beliefs onto the people we encounter, which, at times, prevents us from seeing and appreciating them as they are. Do some research into this tendency to see others through a limited cultural lens; then write an essay in which you evaluate the problems such stereotyping might cause.

3. The authors in this chapter present a skilled ability to observe and write about in precise and metaphorical detail unfamiliar cultures and environments; apply the ideas in this chapter to a travel essay based on your own experiences.

4. Travel to a place where you grew up or that you knew well. Then, write an essay about your memories of your travels. Compare and contrast what you remembered the community to be like with the way it is now. Be sure to choose a community that you not only know well but that is not too large to write about in a brief essay.

5. Today, more and more people are travelling alone or in organized tourist groups. Which of the essays in this chapter discuss tourism, and how are these different perspectives explored? Can you draw any conclusions about why people like to travel?

6. Do some research into the tourist industry. Write an essay that discusses the major advantages of travelling in a big group as a tourist, where all of your decisions have been made for you. Then, examine the contrasting point of view. What are the draw backs of the tourist industry?

7. After reading the articles in this chapter, write about what you learned from the issues raised and from the use of style in the essay. What was the most intriguing travel essay? After reading this chapter, how have your feelings about traveling changed? Where would you like to go and how would you like to travel? You will need to do research to support where you would like to go and how you would like to travel.

8. Each of the films listed below is about a journey. Select one of the films to write about. Consider in what ways the film captures the mood, time period, and ambience of the journey. Are the characters persuasive? Does the structure of the plot help to reinforce the themes of the film? What are the major themes of the movie? Conclude with an evaluation of the film. You can choose from the following films: *A Passage to India, Roman Holiday, Under the Tuscan Sun, Before Sunrise, My House in Umbria, The Lord of the Rings trilogy, Titanic, Out of Africa, Easy Rider, O Brother, Where Art Thou?, Into the Wild, Before the Rains, The Visitor, Babel, Little Miss Sunshine, Blueberry Nights, Borat,* and *The Darjeeling Limited.*

4 Dreams, Myths, and Fairy Tales

Tommy Lowry Tjapaltjarri
Warrmala the Serpent (1986) (Australian Aboriginal creator and rain-god)

JOURNAL

Write a creation story or myth that tells how some aspect of the world came into being—water, land, the sun, an animal or people, or the earth itself.

Myths are public dreams, dreams are private myths.
                    JOSEPH CAMPBELL
                    Hero with a Thousand Faces

*Fantasy is the core of all writing for children, as I think it is for the writing
of any book, for any creative act, perhaps for the act of living.*
                    MAURICE SENDAK

THEMATIC INTRODUCTION

Once you understand how your memories of particular childhood events have shaped and continue to influence your identity and the direction of your life, you may enjoy comparing your personal history to myths and fairy tales. These universal stories have helped to connect humans to larger patterns of history, to their own cultures, and to one another, despite their historical and cultural differences. Myths are patterned stories that present the reader with ideal heroes and heroines acting through dreamlike plots and settings, representing the fundamental values of a culture and a society. Fairy tales satisfy the needs of younger people and adults as well, for dangerous adventures where evil is ultimately banished and happiness and justice ultimately prevail. Both forms provide ethical lessons that help readers to discriminate between creative and destructive or good and evil behavior.

From Greek myths to nursery rhymes and fairy tales, images of heroism and of creation have marked our developing understanding of the cultural values and the workings of the human mind. The fundamental adventure and quest patterns of stories and legends are continually being transformed and adapted according to the values of each new age. Today's popular myths provide readers with revised values and reflections on changing cultural norms.

We begin by presenting an essay by Joseph Campbell on the social and psychological function of myths, followed by physicist Marcelo Gleiser's "The Myths of Science—Creation" in which he compares creation myths to scientific narratives of creation. Next, a portfolio of creation myths from around the world provides concrete examples of imaginatively charged mythical explanations of creation that embody the core values and beliefs of the cultures that produced the stories. We have included myths from the Book of Genesis as well as from ancient Australian, Greek, African, Native American, and Japanese traditions. The section on myths ends with a student essay by Joshua Groban in which he compares two creation myths from radically different cultures and examines the religious and social values that underlie each.

Just as dreams and myths give us clues to our unconscious selves and our connections to universal human concerns, fairy tales, a particular class of mythic stories, have been created for children to help them to understand the complexity of human nature. Jane Yolen in her essay in this chapter "How Basic is Shazam?" emphasizes the importance of fairy tales in helping children develop a sense of civilization, cultural history, and the resonance of language.

To help you understand the different ways in which a fairy tale can be interpreted and transformed by particular cultures and historical periods, we have included four versions of the Cinderella myth: "Aschenputtel" by the Brothers Grimm; Charles Perrault's "Cendrillon"; a Native American version of the tale, "The Algonquin Cinderella"; and a Vietnamese Cinderella story, "Tam and Cam." A student essay concludes the readings selected for this chapter: Anne Levitsky, in "Classic Cinderella in Today's World," examines ways that the Disney Cinderella story can have a negative influence on young girls growing up in the modern world.

Comparing myths and fairy tales from different cultures can help you gain new insights into your own culture as you see your world in a broader perspective of diverse values, emotional needs, and spiritual concerns. Drawing comparisons between versions of myths and fairy tales will help you to see how these universal forms can change and endure. Perhaps they will help you make sense of your contemporary world and see its connection to the past. Reflecting on and writing about the implications of your dreams and myths as well as the dreams and myths of others can create an essential path to your inward journey and provide a deeper appreciation of the world in which you live.

COMPARING AND CONTRASTING: STRATEGIES FOR THINKING AND WRITING

The readings selected for this chapter encourage you to think comparatively. You will find that dreams are compared to myths, myths to fairy tales, and traditional tales to modern forms of literature. Also included are different versions of the same basic myths from various cultures. We have designed the chapter in this way because comparing and contrasting are related and essential aspects of reading and writing and are crucial as well to the way the mind thinks and organizes experiences.

When you compare and contrast, you explore relationships between subjects that, despite apparent distinctions, have qualities in common. Comparative writing demands sophisticated, analytical thinking and organization of ideas. Although everyone naturally makes comparisons while thinking, the structure of comparative writing is more balanced and complex than what one normally does when making comparisons in daily life. Prewriting is especially useful for gathering insights and details to use for comparison.

Prewriting for Comparison

You can do prewriting for a comparison paper using any of the techniques discussed in Chapter 1, such as freewriting or clustering. For example, to use brainstorming, begin by dividing a piece of paper down the middle, then create brainstorming lists of points or qualities you perceive in the subjects of your analysis. A student who wanted to develop a comparison between fairy tales and elementary school readers took the following notes:

Fairy Tales	*Elementary School Readers*
imaginative	seem written by "formula"
engage interest and feelings	don't involve students deeply
teach living skills and heroism	teach "basic reading skills"
encourage imagination	encourage conformity
raise some disturbing issues	avoid controversial issues

You can see some striking contrasts in the lists above. After eliminating some items and grouping the related points, the student could move from the list to a general, clearly worded thesis statement such as the following: "Fairy tales engage the feelings and mind of the child, while primary school texts often fail to attract the interests of children, and thus may actually turn children off to reading." In a very short time, this student writer has found several major points of contrast for possible development and a good central idea to unify a paragraph or essay.

Outlining and Transition

Use of an outline helps to structure extended comparison/contrast papers. An outline will help you to achieve a balanced treatment of each subject and major point in your paper. In preparing an outline, consider the kind of organization you want to use. Comparisons can be structured around points of similarity or difference. Use details to clarify and add interest to the comparison. In subject-by-subject comparing, points are made about two subjects in separate paragraphs or sections of a paper, and the two subjects are brought together in the conclusion for a final evaluation or summary of major points. In writing your comparison essay, make the basic points of your comparison clear to your readers through transitional statements. As you move from one comparative issue to another, use expressions such as "in comparison to," "similarly," and "likewise." If the differences between your subjects seem more striking than the similarities, use contrast as your major strategy for examining and noting distinctions, emphasizing your points with transitional expressions such as "in contrast to" and "another point of distinction." As student writer Joshua Groban does in this chapter in his comparison essay between the Yao myth of creation and the story of Genesis in the Bible, order and develop your points with care, distinguishing between similarities and differences to retain a clear sense of the overall purpose of your comparison, to understand complex realities, and to evaluate.

Evaluation

Evaluating involves making a judgment based on a standard that you hold about a subject or issue. In the prewriting exercise above, the student who contrasted fairy tales with elementary school textbooks made an evaluation of each based on personal likes and dislikes: the student liked fairy tales and disliked textbooks. Although the student writer didn't discuss her standards for judging children's literature, we can assume that she likes reading that is entertaining and engaging and is bored by writing that exists simply as a tool for learning. The student might have even thought more critically about the standards that are appropriate for school readers. If she had, she might have considered the problems that schools have in selecting and judging materials for different types of learners. Regardless of your subject of comparison, you can come closer to seeing whether your values are realistic guides for belief and behavior by establishing guidelines for comparing your standards with those of other people.

Logical Fallacies of Comparison and Contrast

When you think and write comparatively, you may find yourself falling into misleading patterns of thought. A common problem involving comparison and contrast is drawing rigid distinctions that force a choice between artificially opposed positions. Often a contrastive statement will imply that one position is a bad choice: "America, love it or leave it"; "A person is either a God-fearing Christian or a sinful atheist"; or "You're either a real he-man or a spineless coward." Such statements employ both an incorrect use of contrast and an inappropriate use of evaluation by setting up an either/or dilemma. There are occasions when any comparison oriented toward evaluating may seem inappropriate. In comparing and contrasting the myths from different cultures included in this chapter, you may note that each myth of creation involves very different sets of images and values relative to the act and purpose of creation. When thinking about radically different cultures and values, it is more useful simply to make relevant distinctions than to attempt to evaluate one culture as superior or inferior to another.

In the faulty analogy, another common error in comparing, a person attempts to create a connection between two subjects when there are insufficient strong points of similarity. For example, a writer could argue that because life is dreamlike in certain ways, a person should go through life passively, accepting whatever happens just as one might in a dream. Analogies and imaginative, nonliteral comparisons, known as metaphors and similes, can be useful in writing, giving a sense of unexpected and imaginative connections, making descriptions clearer, and generating new insights. On the other hand, taking a metaphorical statement, such as "Life is a dream," and applying it too literally as a standard for conduct ignores real distinctions between the waking world and the sleeping world.

The section on dialogic argument in Chapter 7 discusses ways in which flexible stances in argument can allow you to move beyond rigid, unexamined standards of comparison and evaluation. For now, you should feel ready to use the strategy of comparison more systematically and productively to help you to perceive clear relationships between the public world and your inner world.

Joseph Campbell

The Four Functions of Mythology

Joseph Campbell (1904–1987) was born in New York and studied Medieval Literature at Columbia University. He dropped out of the doctoral program there when informed that mythology was not an acceptable subject for his dissertation. Campbell taught mythological studies at Sarah Lawrence

College for many years before retiring to Hawaii and pursuing his interests in writing and lecturing. In later life he became a popular figure in contemporary culture, inspiring George Lucas's Star Wars films and doing a number of interviews with Bill Moyers on public television. Campbell shared Carl Jung's belief in the archetypal patterns of symbolism in myths and dreams. He was author and editor of many books on world mythology, including The Hero With a Thousand Faces *and the four-volume* The Masks of God. *In the following selection from* "Mythological Themes in Creative Literature and Art," *an essay included in the collection* Myths, Dreams, and Religion *(1970), Campbell explores what he considers to be the major functions of mythology in the lives of individuals, cultures, and societies.*

JOURNAL

Write a definition of "myth" or "mythology" based on your own personal association with the term. List as many qualities and functions of myths or mythology as you can.

Traditional mythologies serve, normally, four functions, the first of which might be described as the reconciliation of consciousness with the preconditions of its own existence. In the long course of our biological prehistory, living creatures had been consuming each other for hundreds of millions of years before eyes opened to the terrible scene, and millions more elapsed before the level of human consciousness was attained. Analogously, as individuals, we are born, we live and grow, on the impulse of organs that are moved independently of reason to aims antecedent to thought—like beasts: until, one day, the crisis occurs that has separated mankind from the beasts: the realization of the monstrous nature of this terrible game that is life, and our consciousness recoils. In mythological terms: we have tasted the fruit of the wonder-tree of the knowledge of good and evil, and have lost our animal innocence. Schopenhauer's scorching phrase represents the motto of this fallen state: "Life is something that should not have been!" Hamlet's state of indecision is the melancholy consequence: "To be, or not to be!" And, in fact, in the long and varied course of the evolution of the mythologies of mankind, there have been many addressed to the aims of an absolute negation of the world, a condemnation of life, and a backing out. These I have termed the mythologies of "The Great Reversal." They have flourished most prominently in India, particularly since the Buddha's time (sixth century B.C.), whose First Noble Truth, "All life is sorrowful," derives from the same insight as Schopenhauer's rueful dictum.

However, more general, and certainly much earlier in the great course of human history, have been the mythologies and associated rites of redemption through affirmation. Throughout the primitive world, where direct confrontations with the brutal bloody facts of life are inescapable and unremitting, the initiation ceremonies to which growing youngsters are subjected are frequently horrendous, confronting them in the most appalling, vivid terms, with experiences—both optically and otherwise—of this monstrous thing that is life: and always with the requirement of a "yea," with no sense of either personal or collective guilt, but gratitude and exhilaration.

For there have been, finally, but three attitudes taken toward the awesome mystery in the great mythological traditions; namely, the first, of a "yea"; the second, of a "nay"; and the last, of a "nay," but with a contingent "yea," as in the great complex of messianic cults of the late Levant: Zoroastrianism, Judaism, Christianity, and Islam. In these last, the well-known basic myth has been, of an originally good creation corrupted by a fall, with, however, the subsequent establishment of a supernaturally endowed society, through the ultimate world dominion of which a restoration of the pristine state of the good creation is to be attained. So that, not in nature but in the social order, and not in all societies, but in this, the one and only, is there health and truth and light, integrity and the prospect of perfection. The "yea" here is contingent therefore on the ultimate world victory of this order.

The second of the four functions served by traditional mythologies—beyond this of redeeming human consciousness from its sense of guilt in life—is that of formulating and rendering an image of the universe, a cosmological image in keeping with the science of the time and of such kind that, within its range, all things should be recognized as parts of a single great holy picture, an icon as it were: the trees, the rocks, the animals, sun, moon, and stars, all opening back to mystery, and thus serving as agents of the first function, as vehicles and messengers of the teaching.

The third traditional function, then, has been ever that of validating and maintaining some specific social order, authorizing its moral code as a construct beyond criticism or human emendation. In the Bible, for example, where the notion is of a personal god through whose act the world was created, that same god is regarded as the author of the Tablets of the Law; and in India, where the basic idea of creation is not of the act of a personal god, but rather of a universe that has been in being and will be in being forever (only waxing and waning, appearing and disappearing, in cycles ever renewed), the social order of caste has been traditionally regarded as of a piece with the order of nature. Man is not free, according to either of these mythic views, to establish for himself the social aims of his life and to work, then, toward these through institutions of his own devising; but rather, the moral, like the natural order, is fixed for all time, and if times have changed (as indeed they have, these past six hundred years), so that to live according to the ancient law and to believe according to the ancient faith have become equally impossible, so much the worse for these times.

5   The first function served by a traditional mythology, I would term, then, the mystical, or metaphysical, the second, the cosmological, and the third, the sociological. The fourth, which lies at the root of all three as their base and final support, is the psychological: that, namely, of shaping individuals to the aims and ideals of their various social groups, bearing them on from birth to death through the course of a human life. And whereas the cosmological and sociological orders have varied greatly over the centuries and in various quarters of the globe, there have nevertheless been certain irreducible psychological problems inherent in the very biology of our species, which have remained constant, and have, consequently, so tended to control and structure the myths and rites in their service that, in spite of all the differences that have been recognized, analyzed, and stressed by sociologists and historians, there run through the myths of all mankind the common strains of a single symphony of the soul. Let us pause, therefore, to review briefly in sequence the order of these irreducible psychological problems.

The first to be faced derives from the fact that human beings are born some fourteen years too soon. No other animal endures such a long period of dependency on its parents. And then, suddenly, at a certain point in life, which varies, according to the culture, from, say, twelve to about twenty years of age, the child is expected to become an adult, and his whole psychological system, which has been tuned and trained to dependency, is now required to respond to the challenges of life in the way of responsibility. Stimuli are no longer to produce responses either of appeal for help or of submission to parental discipline, but of responsible social action appropriate to one's social role. In primitive societies the function of the cruel puberty rites has been everywhere and always to effect and confirm this transformation. And glancing now at our own modern world, deprived of such initiations and becoming yearly more and more intimidated by its own intransigent young, we may diagnose a neurotic as simply an adult who has failed to cross this threshold to responsibility: one whose response to every challenging situation is, first, "What would Daddy say? Where's Mother?" and only then comes to realize, "Why gosh! *I'm* Daddy, I'm forty years old! Mother is now my wife! It is *I* who must do this thing!" Nor have traditional societies ever exhibited much sympathy for those unable or unwilling to assume the roles required. Among the Australian aborigines, if a boy in the course of his initiation seriously misbehaves, he is killed and eaten[*]— which is an efficient way, of course, to get rid of juvenile delinquents, but deprives the community, on the other hand, of the gifts of original thought. As the late Professor A. R. Radcliffe-Brown of Trinity College, Cambridge, observed in his important study of the Andaman Island pygmies: "A society depends for its existence on the presence in the minds of its members of a certain system of sentiments by which the conduct of the individual is regulated in conformity with the needs of the society. . . . The sentiments in question are not innate but are developed in the individual by the action of the society upon him."[†] In other words: the entrance into adulthood from the long career of infancy is not, like the opening of a blossom, to a state of naturally unfolding potentialities, but to the assumption of a social role, a mask or "persona," with which one is to identify. In the famous lines of the poet Wordsworth:

Shades of the prison-house begin to close
Upon the growing Boy.[‡]

A second birth, as it is called, a social birth, is effected, and, as the first had been of Mother Nature, so this one is of the Fathers, Society, and the new body, the new mind, are not of mankind in general but of a tribe, a caste, a certain school, or a nation.

Whereafter, inevitably, in due time, there comes a day when the decrees of nature again break forth. That fateful moment at the noon of life arrives when, as Carl Jung reminds us, the powers that in youth were in ascent have arrived at their apogee and the return to earth begins. The claims, the aims, even the interests of society, begin to fall away and, again as in the lines of Wordsworth:

Our noisy years seem moments in the being
Of the eternal Silence: truths that wake,
    To perish never:
Which neither listlessness, nor mad endeavour,
    Nor Man nor Boy,
Nor all that is at enmity with joy,
Can utterly abolish or destroy!

---

[*]Géza Róheim, *The Eternal Ones of the Dream* (New York: International Universities Press, 1945), p. 232, citing K. Langloh Parker, *The Euahlayi Tribe* (London: A. Constable & Co., 1905), pp.72–73.

[†]A. R. Radcliffe-Brown, *The Andaman Islanders* (Cambridge: The University Press, 1933), pp. 233–234.

[‡]William Wordsworth, *Intimations of Immorality from Recollections of Early Childhood*, ll. 64–65.

Hence in a season of calm weather
　　Though inland far we be,
Our Souls have sight of that immortal sea
　　Which brought us hither,
Can in a moment travel thither,
And see the Children sport upon the shore,
And hear the mighty waters rolling evermore.[§]

　　Both the great and the lesser mythologies of mankind have, up to the present, always served simultaneously, both to lead the young from their estate in nature, and to bear the aging back to nature and on through the last dark door. And while doing all this, they have served, also, to render an image of the World of nature, a cosmological image as I have called it, that should seem to support the claims and aims of the local social group; so that through every feature of the experienced world the sense of an ideal harmony resting on a dark dimension of wonder should be communicated. One can only marvel at the integrating, life-structuring force of even the simplest traditional organization of mythic symbols.

QUESTIONS FOR DISCUSSION

1. As the title indicates, Campbell describes four functions of mythology. What are the functions, and how do they differ from one another? Do you agree with this division? Would you have included other functions?

2. Why does Campbell believe that "our consciousness recoils" at the awareness of the "terrible game" of life? What is terrible or sorrowful about life? How does this awareness involve a loss of innocence similar to the tasting of the apple in the Book of Genesis? How does Christianity offer an answer to the sorrow and loss of innocence that is the nature of life? How is the Christian answer a "nay" with a contingent "yea"?

3. Campbell believes that traditional mythology presents us with "an image of the universe," a sense of the order of created things. What image of the universe does traditional Judeo-Christian religion present us with, in the Book of Genesis, for example?

4. Why do the mythic views of both the Bible and the tradition of India tell us that humans are not free? What prevents individual freedom from occurring, according to these traditional mythological views? Can you give examples of other mythic stories and classical works which contain a moral or pattern that implies that there is no individual freedom of choice and action?

[§]Ibid, II. 158–171.

5. How do traditional religions and mythological systems pattern our psychological growth and development as we move toward adulthood, reducing the kind of "neurotic" fixations at a certain maturity level that are so common in our own society? How do mythologies help one to create a "persona" as a social being and prepare us emotionally to come to terms with aging and death?

6. Although Campbell approaches his topic from a general perspective, he makes his ideas more concrete through the use of quotations and references to mythologies familiar to his readers, such as the Book of Genesis from the Bible. What other examples might he have used?

CONNECTION

Analyze one of the myths or fairy tales in this chapter using Campbell's criteria in "The Four Functions of Mythology."

IDEAS FOR WRITING

1. Elsewhere in the longer essay from which this selection is excerpted, Campbell states that both the cosmological and social functions of mythology have been weakened through modern advances in science and technology. Write an essay in which you present several examples that either support or refute Campbell's assertion that the reliance on science and technology has diminished the power of the human spirit that myths embody.

2. Write an essay in which you discuss a myth that you are familiar with which fulfills one of the four functions that Campbell discusses in his essay. Include a copy or detailed description of the myth with your essay. In what ways is this myth woven into the cultural and social assumptions and values that form the basis of your beliefs and lifestyle?

Marcelo Gleiser

The Myths of Science—Creation

Marcelo Gleiser was born in 1959 in Rio de Janeiro, Brazil, and received an M.Sc. in Rio de Janeiro in 1981. After completing his Ph.D. at the University of London in 1986, he immigrated to the United States, where he continued to study astronomy and physics. In 1995 he was hired as an associate professor of astrophysics at Dartmouth College, where he currently is the Appleton Professor of Physics. He has contributed articles to many professional journals and is widely known for his books The Dancing Universe: From Creation Myths to the Big Bang *(English translation, 1997), and* The Prophet and the Astronomer: A Scientific Journey to the End of Time *(2002). In the following article, Gleiser explores parallels between scientific and mythical accounts of the "creation" of the universe.*

JOURNAL

Write about your idea of creation. Where did the world come from? How long did creation take? How did you come to these conclusions?

Myth, religion and science have more often than not proved inseparable in addressing the eternal imponderable: why something rather than nothing?

Since the dawn of civilization, humankind has marvelled at the skies and at Nature's myriad creations. This sense of wonder was deeply interwoven with a sense of fear: Nature's dual role as creator and destroyer has puzzled and polarized our perceptions of the cosmos. As a way of establishing a degree of control over the apparent unpredictability of natural phenomena, gods were held responsible for these conflicting manifestations. In short, Nature was deified.

The question of why there is something rather than nothing was a crucial part of this process. All cultures have attempted to provide an answer to the mystery of creation, and our modern scientific tradition is no exception. Perhaps more surprisingly, there is an intriguing correspondence between answers suggested by mythic narratives and those suggested by scientific research. The crucial difference, of course, is that the scientific process is capable of weeding out explanations which do not measure up to observations, while those based on myth are held true on the basis of faith alone.

Greece and Reason

Creation myths can be divided conveniently into two kinds: either the cosmos appeared at a specific moment in time marking the beginning of history, or it has always been "there." Myths with a creation event describe time in a linear fashion, with a beginning, middle and, as in the Christian narrative, an end. Myths without a creation event may consider time to be either unimportant or cyclic. Within these two sets, we encounter an enormous variety. Starting with the "no creation myths," the two possibilities are: an eternal, uncreated cosmos, as in the narrative of the Jains of India, or a cyclic cosmos, continuously created and destroyed, as beautifully represented in the Hindu tradition by the dance of Shiva.

5   The first and by far the most common "myth with creation" invokes a deity or deities who create the world, as in the Judaeo-Christian myth of Genesis. A second possibility is that the world was created out of nothing, without the interference of a god; this is what the Maori people of New Zealand have in mind when they sing, "from nothing the begetting, from nothing the increase. . . . " A final possibility is that the world appeared spontaneously from a primordial Chaos, where order coexists with disorder, Being with Non-Being.

The religious nature of the creation event has permeated scientific thought since its origins in Ancient Greece in the sixth century B.C. As the Greek philosophers pondered the physical mechanisms that created the world and controlled its motions, many assumed an organizational principle based on rational design, attributed to a "Demiurge" by Plato or to the "Unmoved Mover" by Aristotle. Plato was a true heir of the Pythagorean tradition, which saw the world as a manifestation of Number, arranged and combined to create the harmonies perceived by the senses. The emphasis on a creation event was somewhat left aside, being substituted by the importance of reason in understanding the workings of Nature. The philosopher, in his search for rational meaning, was in effect elevating himself to a higher level of existence or that of the Demiurge's mind. To understand Nature was to understand God, or, in an oftquoted aphorism, to understand the mind of God.

This tradition reappeared in the West during the birth of modern science in the Renaissance. The great natural philosophers that spearheaded the so-called Copernican Revolution were all, to a greater or lesser degree, deeply religious men, who saw their scientific work as an integral part of their religious beliefs. Thus, Copernicus himself was a canon of the cathedral in Frauenberg, a reluctant revolutionary who sought to reconcile the arrangement of the celestial spheres with the Platonic ideal of circular motions with constant velocities. His model of the solar system was an elegant compromise between the old and the new, looking back at Plato and forward at the aesthetic principles of his time. His great opus, On the Revolutions of the Heavenly Orbs, was dedicated to Pope Paul III, in the hope that the Church would recognize the need for a reinterpretation of the Scriptures based on the new astronomical thought.

It was through the work of Giordano Bruno and, more importantly, Johannes Kepler and Galileo Galilei, that the Copernican Revolution was enacted. Kepler was deeply influenced by the Pythagorean tradition, a number mystic who believed geometry to be the key to the cosmic harmony. His three laws of planetary motion are a powerful illustration of how the scientific output of a great mind can be a byproduct of a belief system tempered by the analysis of data.

No Final Truths

Galileo's now famous tribulations with the Church were also a product of his beliefs. A pious (and overconfident) man, Galileo took as his personal mission to reset the course of Christian theology, preaching to the Church leaders the importance of accepting the new cosmic design. The clash was unavoidable, and in 1633 Galileo was forced to abjure his conviction in the Copernican system. Not for long, though, for soon after Isaac Newton put forward his three laws of motion and his universal theory of gravity in 1687, the sun-centered cosmos became widely accepted. To Newton, the cosmos was a manifestation of God's glory, infinite in extent and sublime in design.

10   During the twentieth century, the Newtonian universe was substituted by a curved Einsteinian universe; Einstein showed how matter and energy can bend space and alter the flow of time, endowing them with an unprecedented plasticity. Nowhere is this more spectacularly displayed than in the expansion of the universe itself, discovered by Edwin Hubble in 1929. Once again, the question of origins came back to haunt scientists: if the universe is expanding, there was a moment in time when all matter was squeezed into a very small volume. Astronomy was proclaiming that the universe did have an origin, after all. A cry of dissent emerged from Cambridge University via the proposal of the "steady-state model," where the universe never had a beginning in time. With the discovery that the whole cosmos is immersed in a bath of microwave radiation in the 1960s, the steady-state model was abandoned by most cosmologists; the "big-bang model" has since been accepted as the one which best fits the data.

Can science "explain" the age-old question of Creation? Certainly, physical models describing the origin of the cosmos can and have been proposed, at least since the 1970s. But these models face a serious technical obstacle: the lack of a proper theory to describe physical processes at the enormous energy scales prevalent during the first moments of cosmic history. They could be called scientific creation narratives, at least until they can be placed on more solid theoretical ground. We see old themes coming back, dressed in scientific jargon. In some models the universe was born out of "nothing," a quantum vacuum populated by all sorts of ephemeral energy fluctuations; others see the beginning as essentially chaotic, with an ordered cosmos emerging homogeneously in three dimensions.

Some of these models of creation make predictions about measurable properties of the universe, which can be used to test and refine them. Yet it may be hard to rule out all alternative models, which may also be compatible with these measurements. The best that we can hope for is a workable model of cosmic origins, compatible with observations but open to changes. Scientific inquiry is after all an ongoing process—there is no final truth, only approximations to the truth. Furthermore, science, at least as it is formulated at present, cannot answer questions concerning its own origin: we do not know why the universe operates according to the laws we have uncovered and not others. This essential incompleteness of science suggests a new form of complementarity between science and religion; religion does not exist to cover the holes of our scientific knowledge, but as a driving force behind scientific inspiration. Through our search for knowledge we uncover our true nature, fuelled by the same sense of mystery which filled our ancestors with awe.

QUESTIONS FOR DISCUSSION

1. Why does Gleiser believe that "Nature was deified" in the mythical age? What is the chief similarity and the chief difference between mythical narratives of creation and scientific explanations?

2. What does Gleiser believe are the two main types of creation myths and the different possibilities of each? Based on the readings in the "Portfolio of Creation Myths" later in this chapter, what other types and possibilities might there be?

3. According to Gleiser, how have religion-based notions of creation "permeated scientific thought" since long before the Christian era? How does Plato's idea of the "Demiurge" serve as an example of "rational design" in the universe? How was Copernicus a "reluctant revolutionary," in Gleiser's view? How did Copernicus attempt to reconcile his radical scientific views with traditional Christianity?

4. Although Newton managed to advance a sun-based center for the cosmos, how was his design still based on religious faith in "God's glory"?

5. How did the twentieth century move beyond religious-based theories of the origin of life and matter?

6. What is missing in contemporary scientific theories of origins of the cosmos? Why does Gleiser call these theories "scientific creation narratives"? What is the "new form of complementarity between science and religion" that Gleiser refers to in his final paragraph?

CONNECTION

Compare Gleiser's idea of the purpose and possibilities of creation myths to one of the myths in the "Portfolio of Creation Myths" later in this chapter in order to determine how well the myth you have chosen fits into Gleiser's view of such myths.

IDEAS FOR WRITING

1. Write an essay in which you compare a particular scientific explanation of the origin and/or structure of the world such as those discussed in Gleiser's essay and a similar religious creation narrative/myth, such as one found in the "Portfolio of Creation Myths" or in a book or Internet site containing a variety of such myths.

2. Write an essay that explains your theory of creation. Draw on your own ideas and experiences as well as reading and research that you have done.

RELATED WEB SITES

Marcelo Gleiser
`www.dartmouth.edu/~physics/faculty/gleiser.html`
This Dartmouth College site includes information on research, lectures, and books by Marcelo Gleiser, professor of Physics and Astronomy since 1991.

Science and Creation: The Riddle in the Skies
`www.unesco.org/courier/2001_05/uk/doss22.htm`
This issue of the *Unesco Courier* features several articles by Marcelo Gleiser and other scientists concerning the relationship between scientific and religious concepts of creation.

Portfolio of Creation Myths

We have selected the following myths from cultures around the world to encourage you to compare different fundamental beliefs and assumptions about reality. Preceding each myth is a note about the culture that produced it; following the portfolio is a set of questions for thought and writing.

Genesis 1–2 (Old Testament of the Hebrew Bible)

The following contains two accounts of creation in the Book of Genesis. Genesis 1 *details the creation of the world and, briefly, that of man, while* Genesis 2 *is thought to come from a different, less formal writing tradition (the "J," or Jehovah, tradition) from that of* Genesis 1. Genesis 2 *reveals a more intimate relationship between God and his natural and human creation and introduces the tree of life and the knowledge of good and evil. As you read the selection, consider the impact that the* Book of Genesis *has had on Western cultural assumptions and traditions.*

Genesis 1

<u>1</u> In the beginning God created the heaven and the earth. <u>2</u> And the earth was without form, and void; and darkness was on the face of the deep. And the Spirit of God moved on the face of the waters. <u>3</u> And God said, "Let there be light": and there was light. <u>4</u> And God saw the

light, that it was good: and God divided the light from the darkness. 5 And God called the light Day, and the darkness he called Night. And the evening and the morning were the first day.

6 And God said, "Let there be a firmament in the middle of the waters, and let it divide the waters from the waters." 7 And God made the firmament, and divided the waters which were under the firmament from the waters which were above the firmament: and it was so. 8 And God called the firmament Heaven. And the evening and the morning were the second day.

9 And God said, "Let the waters under the heaven be gathered together to one place, and let the dry land appear": and it was so. 10 And God called the dry land Earth; and the gathering together of the waters called He Seas: and God saw that it was good. 11 And God said, "Let the earth burst forth with growth, the plants yielding seed, and the fruit trees yielding fruit with seed in it, on the earth": and it was so. 12 And the earth brought forth grass, and plants yielding seed, and the tree yielding fruit, whose seed was in itself: and God saw that it was good. 13 And the evening and the morning were the third day.

14 And God said, "Let there be lights in the firmament of the heaven to divide the day from the night; and let them be for signs, and for seasons, and for days, and years: 15 And let them be for lights in the firmament of the heaven to give light on the earth": and it was so. 16 And God made two great lights; the greater light to rule the day, and the lesser light to rule the night: he made the stars also. 17 And God set them in the firmament of the heaven to give light on the earth, 18 and to rule over the day and over the night, and to divide the light from the darkness: and God saw that it was good. 19 And the evening and the morning were the fourth day.

5   20 And God said, Let the waters bring forth abundantly the moving creature that has life, and birds that may fly above the earth in the open firmament of heaven. 21 And God created great whales, and every living creature that moves, which the waters brought forth abundantly, after their kind, and every winged bird after his kind: and God saw that it was good. 22 And God blessed them, saying, "Be fruitful, and multiply, and fill the waters in the seas, and let birds multiply in the earth." 23 And the evening and the morning were the fifth day.

24 And God said, "Let the earth bring forth the living creature after his kind, cattle, and creeping thing, and beast of the earth after his kind: and it was so." 25 And God made the beasts of the earth after his kind, and cattle after their kind, and every thing that creeps on the earth after his kind: and God saw that it was good.

26 And God said, "I will make man in my image, after my likeness: and let them have dominion over the fish of the sea, and over the birds of the

air, and over the cattle, and over all the earth, and over every creeping thing that creeps on the earth." 27 So God created man in His own image, in the image of God created He him; male and female created He them. 28 And God blessed them, and God said to them, "Be fruitful, and multiply, and replenish the earth, and subdue it: and have dominion over the fish of the sea, and over the birds of the air, and over every living thing that moves on the earth. 29 And God said, "Behold, I have given you every plant bearing seed, which is on the face of all the earth, and every tree in which is the fruit yielding seed; to you it shall be for food. 30 And to every beast of the earth, and to every fowl of the air, and to every thing that creeps on the earth, wherein there is life, I have given every green plant for food": and it was so. 31 And God saw every thing that He had made, and, behold, it was very good. And the evening and the morning were the sixth day.

Genesis 2

1 Thus the heavens and the earth were finished, and all the host of them. 2 And on the seventh day God ended his work which he had made; and He rested on the seventh day from all his work. 3 And God blessed the seventh day, and sanctified it: because that in it He had rested from all his work which God created and made.

4 These are the generations of the heavens and of the earth when they were created, in the day that the Lord God made the earth and the heavens, 5 and every plant of the field before it was in the earth, and every herb of the field before it grew: for the Lord God had not caused it to rain on the earth, and there was not a man to till the ground. 6 But there went up a mist from the earth, and watered the whole face of the ground. 7 And the Lord God formed man of the dust of the ground, and breathed into his nostrils the breath of life; and man became a living being. 8 And the Lord God planted a garden eastward in Eden; and there He put the man whom he had formed. 9 And out of the ground made the Lord God to grow every tree that is pleasant to the sight, and good for food; the tree of life was also in the middle of the garden, and the tree of knowledge of good and evil.

10   10 And a river rose in Eden to water the garden; and from there it was parted, and became four branch streams. 11 The name of the first is Pishon: that is it which compasses the whole land of Havilah, where there is gold; 12 And the gold of that land is good: there is bdellium and the onyx stone. 13 And the name of the second river is Gihon: the same is it that compasses the whole land of Ethiopia. 14 And the name of the third river is Tigris: it goes toward the east of Assyria. And the fourth river is the Euphrates..

15 And the Lord God took the man, and put him into the garden of Eden to till it and to tend it. 16 And the Lord God commanded the man, saying, "Of every tree of the garden you may freely eat: 17 But of the tree

of the knowledge of good and evil, you shall not eat: for in the moment that you eat thereof you shall be doomed to death."

<u>18</u> And the Lord God said, "It is not good that the man should be alone; I will make him a helper suited to him." <u>19</u> And out of the ground the Lord God formed every beast of the field, and every fowl of the air; and brought them to Adam to see what he would call them: and whatever Adam called every living creature, that was the name thereof. <u>20</u> And Adam gave names to all cattle, and to the birds of the air, and to every beast of the field; but for Adam there was not found a helper fit for him. <u>21</u> And the Lord God caused a deep sleep to fall on Adam, and as he slept: God took one of his ribs, and closed up the flesh instead thereof; <u>22</u> And the rib, which the Lord God had taken from man, He fashioned into a woman, and brought her to the man.

<u>23</u> And Adam said, "This one is now bone of my bones and flesh of my flesh: she shall be called Woman, for she was taken out of Man."

<u>24</u> Therefore shall a man leave his father and his mother, and shall join to his wife: and they shall be one flesh. <u>25</u> And they were both naked, the man and his wife, and were not ashamed.

How the Sun Was Made: Dawn, Noontide and Night (Australian Aboriginal)

This aboriginal story of the sun's creation was adapted by W. J. Thomas, author of The Welsh Fairy-Tale Book *(1908), and appeared (using the flowery diction of his earlier anthology) in his collection* Some Myths and Legends of the Australian Aborigines *(1923).*

When the emu egg was hurled up to the sky it struck a great pile of wood which had been gathered by a cloud man named Ngoudenout. It hit the wood with such force that the pile instantly burst into flame, and flooded the earth with the soft, warm light of dawn. The flowers were so surprised that they lifted their sleepy heads to the sky and opened their petals so wide that the glistening dewdrops which night had given them fell to the ground and were lost. The little birds twittered excitedly on the trees, and the fairies, who kept the snow on the mountain tops, forgot their task, and allowed it to thaw and run into the rivers and creeks.

And what was the cause of this excitement? Away to the east, far over the mountains, the purple shadows of night were turning grey; the soft, pink-tinted clouds floated slowly across the sky like red-breasted birds winging their way to a far land. Along the dim sky-line a path of golden fire marked the parting of the grey shadows, and down in the valley the white mist was hiding the pale face of night.

Like a sleeper stirring softly at the warm touch of a kiss, all living things of the bush stirred at the caress of dawn. The sun rose with golden splendor in a clear blue sky, and, with its coming, the first day dawned. At first the wood pile burned slowly, but the heat increased, until at noonday it was thoroughly ablaze. But gradually it burnt lower and lower, until at twilight only a heap of glowing embers remained. These embers slowly turned cold and grey. The purple shadows and white mists came from their hiding-places, and once again the mantle of night was over the land.

When Ngoudenout saw what a splendid thing the sun was, he determined to give it to us for ever. At night, when the fire of the sun has burnt out, he goes to a dark forest in the sky and collects a great pile of wood. At dawn he lights it, and it burns feebly until noonday is reached, then it slowly burns away until twilight and night falls. Ngoudenout, the eternal wood gatherer, then makes his lonely way to the forest for the wood that lights the fire of the sun.

The Pelasgian Creation Myth (Ancient Greek)

This myth is the earliest known Greek creation myth. The Pelasgian stories were gathered in rural areas of Greece by a British scholar of mythology, Robert Graves, and published in his book The Pelasgian Myth *(1955). The following brief selection from the book describes the creation of all things out of the ritual dancing and coupling of the primal Eurynome, the "Goddess of All Things," with the snake Ophion.*

In the beginning, Eurynome, the Goddess of All Things, rose naked from Chaos, but found nothing substantial for her feet to rest upon, and therefore divided the sea from the sky, dancing lonely upon its waves. She danced towards the south, and the wind set in motion behind her seemed something new and apart with which to begin a work of creation.

Wheeling about, she caught hold of this north wind, rubbed it between her hands, and behold! the great serpent Ophion. Eurynome danced to warm herself, wildly and more wildly, until Ophion, grown lustful, coiled about those divine limbs and was moved to couple with her. Now, the North Wind, who is also called Boreas, fertilizes; which is why mares often turn their hind-quarters to the wind and breed foals without aid of a stallion. So Eurynome was likewise got with child.

Next, she assumed the form of a dove, brooding on the waves and, in due process of time, laid the Universal Egg. At her bidding, Ophion coiled seven times about this egg, until it hatched and split in two. Out tumbled all things that exist, her children: sun, moon, planets, stars, the earth with its mountains and rivers, its trees, herbs, and living creatures.

Eurynome and Ophion made their home upon Mount Olympus, where he vexed her by claiming to be the author of the Universe. Forthwith she bruised his head with her heel, kicked out his teeth, and banished him to the dark caves below the earth.

5   Next, the goddess created the seven planetary powers, setting a Titaness and a Titan over each. Theia and Hyperion for the Sun; Phoebe and Atlas for the Moon; Dione and Crius for the planet Mars; Metis and Coeus for the planet Mercury; Themis and Eurynmedon for the planet Jupiter; Tethys and Oceanus for Venus; Rhea and Cronus for the planet Saturn. But the first man was Pelasgus, ancestor of the Pelasgians; he sprang from the soil of Arcadia, followed by certain others, whom he taught to make huts and feed upon acorns and sew pig-skin tunics such as poor folk still wear in Euboea and Phocis.

The Chameleon Finds (Yao-Bantu, African)

"The Chameleon Finds" is a creation myth of the Yao, a Bantu tribe living by Lake Nyasa in Mozambique, Africa. Expressive of a close relationship with nature, this Yao myth, with a clever Chameleon and a helper Spider as the creator god's assistants, takes a critical view of human beings.

At first there were no people. Only Mulungu and the decent peaceful beasts were in the world. One day Chameleon sat weaving a fish-trap, and when he had finished he set it in the river. In the morning he pulled the trap and it was full of fish, which he took home and ate. He set the trap again. In the morning he pulled it out and it was empty: no fish.

"Bad luck," he said, and set the trap again.

The next morning when he pulled the trap he found a little man and woman in it. He had never seen any creatures like this.

"What can they be?" he said. "Today I behold the unknown." And he picked up the fish-trap and took the two creatures to Mulungu.

5   "Father," said Chameleon, "see what I have brought."

Mulungu looked. "Take them out of the trap," he said. "Put them down on the earth and they will grow."

Chameleon did this. And the man and woman grew. They grew until they became as tall as men and women are today.

All the animals watched to see what the people would do. They made fire. They rubbed two sticks together in a special way and thus made fire. The fire caught in the bush and roared through the forest and the animals had to run to escape the flames. The people caught a buffalo and killed it and roasted it in the fire and ate it. The next day they did the same thing. Every day they set fires and killed some animal and ate it.

"They are burning up everything!" said Mulungu. "They are killing my people!"

10   All the beasts ran into the forest as far away from mankind as they could get. Chameleon went into the high trees.

"I'm leaving!" said Mulungu. He called to Spider. "How do you climb on high?" he said.

"Very nicely," said Spider. And Spider spun a rope for Mulungu and Mulungu climbed the rope and went to live in the sky.

Thus the gods were driven off the face of the earth by the cruelty of man.

Spider Woman Creates the Humans (Hopi, Native American)

The following myth from Frank Waters' Book of the Hopi *is only a brief selection from the much longer Hopi Emergence Story that uses birth imagery to explain a complex sequence of transformations in the act of creation. In the Hopi culture, the Emergence Story is told to the tribal initiates on the last evening of the year, after which the young men ascend a ladder to emerge from the kiva (Hopi dwelling) as full-fledged adult members of the Hopi community.*

So Spider Woman gathered earth, this time of four colors, yellow, red, white, and black; mixed with tuchvala, the liquid of her mouth; molded them; and covered them with her white-substance cape which was the creative wisdom itself. As before, she sang over them the Creation Song, and when she uncovered them these forms were human beings in the image of Sotuknang. Then she created four other beings after her own form. They were wuti, female partners, for the first four male beings.

When Spider Woman uncovered them the forms came to life. This was at the time of the dark purple light, Qoyangnuptu, the first phase of the dawn of Creation, which first reveals the mystery of man's creation.

They soon awakened and began to move, but there was still a dampness on their foreheads and a soft spot on their heads. This was at the time of the yellow light, Sikangnuqua, the second phase of the dawn of Creation, when the breath of life entered man.

In a short time the sun appeared above the horizon, drying the dampness on their foreheads and hardening the soft spot on their heads. This was the time of the red light, Talawva, the third phase of the dawn of Creation, when man, fully formed and firmed, proudly faced his Creator.

5   "That is the Sun," said Spider Woman. "You are meeting your Father the Creator for the first time. You must always remember and observe these three phases of your Creation. The time of the three lights, the dark purple, the yellow, and the red reveal in turn the mystery, the

breath of life, and warmth of love. These comprise the Creator's plan of life for you as sung over you in the Song of Creation:

Song of Creation

The dark purple light rises in the north,
A yellow light rises in the east.
Then we of the flowers of the earth come forth
To receive a long life of joy.
We call ourselves the Butterfly Maidens.

Both male and female make their prayers to the east,
Make the respectful sign to the Sun our Creator.
The sounds of bells ring through the air,
Making a joyful sound throughout the land,
Their joyful echo resounding everywhere.

Humbly I ask my Father,
The perfect one, Taiowa, our Father,
The perfect one creating the beautiful life
Shown to us by the yellow light,
To give us perfect light at the time of the red light.

The perfect one laid out the perfect plan
And gave to us a long span of life.
Creating song to implant joy in life.
On this path of happiness, we the Butterfly Maidens
Carry out his wishes by greeting our Father Sun.

The song resounds back from our Creator with joy,
And we of the earth repeat it to our Creator.
At the appearing of the yellow light,
Repeats and repeats again the joyful echo,
Sounds and resounds for times to come.

The Beginning of the World (Japanese)

Like the other myths in this section, this Japanese story describes the process of creation (in this selection, of the islands of Japan) and focuses on issues such as the proper social role of the sexes. The myth is from Genji Shibukawa's Tales from the Kojiki *(712 C.E.), translated by Yaichiro Isobe. The* Kojiki *or* Records of Ancient Matters *is the oldest work written in the Chinese kanji characters introduced to Japan through Korea in the sixth century. These were the original symbols used to record the Japanese language.*

Before the heavens and the earth came into existence, all was a chaos, unimaginably limitless and without definite shape or form. Eon followed eon: then, lo! out of this boundless, shapeless mass something light and transparent rose up and formed the heaven. This was the Plain of High Heaven, in which materialized . . . three divine beings are called the Three Creating Deities.

In the meantime what was heavy and opaque in the void gradually precipitated and became the earth, but it had taken an immeasurably long time before it condensed sufficiently to form solid ground. In its earliest stages, for millions and millions of years, the earth may be said to have resembled oil floating, medusa-like, upon the face of the waters. Suddenly like the sprouting up of a reed . . . many gods were thus born in succession, and so they increased in number, but as long as the world remained in a chaotic state, there was nothing for them to do.

Whereupon, all the Heavenly deities summoned the two divine beings, Izanagi and Izanami, and bade them descend to the nebulous place, and by helping each other, to consolidate it into terra firma. "We bestow on you," they said, "this precious treasure, with which to rule the land, the creation of which we command you to perform." So saying they handed them a spear . . . embellished with costly gems. The divine couple received the sacred weapon respectfully and ceremoniously and then withdrew from the presence of the Deities, ready to perform their august commission. Proceeding forthwith to the Floating Bridge of Heaven, which lay between the heaven and the earth, they stood awhile to gaze on that which lay below. What they beheld was a world not yet condensed, but looking like a sea of filmy fog floating to and fro in the air, exhaling the while an inexpressibly fragrant odor.

They were, at first, perplexed just how and where to start, but at length Izanagi suggested to his companion that they should try the effect of stirring up the brine with their spear. So saying he pushed down the jeweled shaft and found that it touched something. Then drawing it up, he examined it and observed that the great drops which fell from it almost immediately coagulated into an island, which is, to this day, the Island of Onokoro. Delighted at the result, the two deities descended forthwith from the Floating Bridge to reach the miraculously created island. In this island they thenceforth dwelt and made it the basis of their subsequent task of creating a country. Then wishing to become espoused, they erected in the center of the island a pillar, the Heavenly August Pillar, and built around it a great palace called the Hall of Eight Fathoms.

5   Thereupon the male Deity turning to the left and the female Deity to the right, each went round the pillar in opposite directions. When they again met each other on the further side of the pillar, Izanami, the female Deity, speaking first, exclaimed: "How delightful it is to meet so handsome a youth!" To which Izanagi, the male Deity, replied: "How

delightful I am to have fallen in with such a lovely maiden!" After having spoken thus, the male Deity said that it was not in order that woman should anticipate man in a greeting. Nevertheless, they fell into connubial relationship, having been instructed by two wagtails which flew to the spot. Presently the Goddess bore her divine consort a son, but the baby was weak and boneless as a leech. Disgusted with it, they abandoned it on the waters, putting it in a boat made of reeds. Their second offspring was as disappointing as the first.

The two Deities, now sorely disappointed at their failure and full of misgivings, ascended to Heaven to inquire of the Heavenly Deities the causes of their misfortunes. The latter performed the ceremony of divining and said to them: "It is the woman's fault. In turning round the Pillar, it was not right and proper that the female Deity should in speaking have taken precedence of the male. That is the reason."

The two Deities saw the truth of this divine suggestion, and made up their minds to rectify the error. So, returning to the earth again, they went once more around the Heavenly Pillar. This time Izanagi spoke first saying: "How delightful to meet so beautiful a maiden!" "How happy I am," responded Izanami, "that I should meet such a handsome youth!" This process was more appropriate and in accordance with the law of nature. After this, all the children born to them left nothing to be desired. First, the island of Awaji was born, next, Shikoku, then, the island of Oki, followed by Kyushu; after that, the island Tsushima came into being, and lastly, Honshu, the main island of Japan. The name of . . . the Country of the Eight Great Islands was given to these eight islands. After this, the two Deities became the parents of numerous smaller islands destined to surround the larger ones.

QUESTIONS FOR DISCUSSION

1. What different images of the creator gods are presented in the various myths? Is the primary god in each clearly described? What powers and limits does the god have? Does the god operate alone or with other helping beings? What conclusions about the culture that produced each myth can you draw from these differences?

2. In the myths that present a clear picture of the physical world of the creation, how is the world described? How orderly and sequential is the act of creating the different elements and beings of the world? What conclusions can you draw from the varied presentation in these creation myths about the values of the culture that produced each myth?

3. Creation myths make significant comments on the roles and status of the sexes in various cultures. Compare and contrast the roles of sex and gender in the different creation myths included.

4. Another issue presented in some creation myths is the relationship of men and women to their creator. How do the humans in the various myths relate to the creator gods? How worshipful of God are the humans in the various myths?

5. Compare the ways that the different myths show the relationship between humans and nature. How harmonious a part of nature or how much at odds with nature do humans seem in the various myths? How are animals involved in the act of creation? Does part of the natural world need to be destroyed for creation to be completed?

6. Creation myths differ in tone. They can be imaginative and dream-like, solemn and serious, philosophical, or even comical and mocking in tone. Compare the tone and attitude toward creation presented in each of the myths, then draw some conclusions about the values of each culture.

IDEAS FOR WRITING

1. Write your own creation myth, using characters, descriptions, and narration to illustrate the relationship between different aspects of creation: gods, animals, people, and the earth. At the end of your myth, comment on the values and ideas about the creative process and the world that your myth is designed to illustrate.

2. Develop an essay in the form of an extended comparison between two or three creation myths, each of which illustrates fundamental values and beliefs about gods, humans, and the natural world.

RELATED WEB SITES

Creation Myths—"Mything Links"
www.mythinglinks.org/ct~creation.html
Learn about creation myths from around the world at this Web site. Here you will find an annotated and illustrated collection of worldwide links to mythologies, fairy tales and folklore, sacred arts, and sacred traditions.

Joshua Groban

Two Myths

Joshua Groban, who grew up in an artistic and literary family, has always been interested in mythology and issues related to creativity. In his freshman English class, Groban wrote a research paper comparing a number of different Native American accounts of the creation and was fascinated by the imagination and diversity of the visions he encountered in his reading. The following essay is Groban's comparative response to the two accounts of creation (the Genesis version and that of the Yao people) from the portfolio of myths presented in this chapter (see pages 182 and 187).

An individual growing up in today's society is quickly indoctrinated into believing the predominant myth about creation. Our church, our parents, our teachers, and the media all reinforce such concepts as Adam and Eve and the Garden of Eden. However, every culture has its own unique myth to explain the birth of the planet and its inhabitants. By comparing the Bible's depiction of creation to that of the Yao myth, "The Chameleon Finds," one is reminded of the many different and imaginative ways people have presented such fundamental issues as gender relations, our connection with and responsibility to the environment, and the relationship of human beings to God.

First, we are struck by the different views of women in the two accounts of creation; the Bible's narration of creation depicts women as secondary to and subservient to men. In the Book of Genesis, "all cattle," "the birds of the air," and "every beast of the field" are created before women. This order of creation gives the impression that the beasts are more central to life on earth than women, and thus are created first. But, despite the abundance of these beasts, "there was not found a helper fit for him [man]." Genesis makes it clear that women are given life not as man's equal, but as his "helper" or assistant. When God finally creates females, they are divested from any sense of individuality; they are not created in the image of God, as man is, but from the rib of man. Thus, women are presented as owing their very existence to men. Genesis 2:4 concludes by emphasizing this idea, explaining that "she shall be called Woman, because she was taken out of Man." The Bible ties not only a woman's existence, but even her name to men. In this way, this creation myth clearly establishes women as subservient to men and lacking an equivalent sense of identity.

The Yao creation myth presents a different and more favorable portrayal of women. Women are not created as an afterthought in "The Chameleon Finds," to function as a helper to men, as they are in the Bible. Instead, men and women come into the world together, as companions. Males and females are given life when the Creator plucks them from the river in his trap. The myth says, "The next morning when he pulled the trap he found a little man and woman in it. He had never seen any creatures like this." In this way, the two sexes begin their existence in equality. Females do not come from males and are not granted life after men, cattle, birds, and beasts. The myth creates men and women together, and thus suggests that the two sexes should live their lives in this state of equality as well.

A juxtaposition of the Genesis and Yao stories in regard to their view of nature reveals a similar divergence. In the Bible, man dominates nature in much the same way as he dominates women. Both the environment and females are presented in Genesis as subservient "helpers" to man. Genesis 2:9 professes, "And out of the ground the Lord God made to grow every tree that is pleasant to the sight and good for food." Nature exists to serve and to help man; trees have life only to serve mankind by being "pleasant to the sight and good for food." Like women, the role of nature is to serve man rather than exist in equality with him. The Bible reads, "The Lord God took the man and put him in the Garden of Eden to till it and keep it." Man does not exist in the garden to coexist with the plants and animals of the garden. Instead, he is to "keep it," as if the earth were a possession.

5   The Yao story of creation sees humans as irresponsible and destructive in their relation to the earth. In the Yao tale, the first man and woman set fire to the vegetation and kill animals that inhabit the earth. Their creator is appalled by this behavior: "'They are burning up everything'" he exclaims. "'They are killing my people!'" He is so disturbed by the way humans treat the earth that He decides to leave the planet. A spider makes him a ladder and He goes to live in the sky. The story ends, "Thus the gods were driven off the face of the earth by the cruelty of man." This myth, in contrast to the Bible, sets clear expectations about the consequences of man's mistreatment of the earth. In "The Chameleon Finds," nature, like women, has rights that should never be usurped. Genesis ignores these universal rights, affording them only to God and to man.

This contrast also exists in the way the two myths portray man's relationship to God. In Genesis, God is a distant, autocratic deity; he speaks and the act is performed. In this story, God "took" the man and "put him" in the Garden of Eden. Later, He "commands" man never to eat from the tree of good and evil. Humans are pawns controlled by this distant deity. They make no decisions in Genesis 2:4–23, but are instead "taken," "put," and "commanded." The Bible's God is one that controls humans and merely speaks in order to create.

The Yao Creator is an entirely different, more human sort of figure. This God is not presented as an all-powerful deity that merely speaks to create life. He unknowingly discovers humans in his trap, and no indication is given that He created them at all. This Creator does not command humans to do as He wants them to do. When humans destroy the earth, no punishment comes from a distant deity, as in the Bible. Instead, the Creator leaves the earth, leaving humans free to make their own decisions and choose their own destiny. This contrast impacts both man's relationship with God and his view of himself. In the Bible, The Creator is a force that has complete control over humans. He creates by merely speaking, commands humans, and punishes them. In contrast, the Yao Creator does not control every human action. He creates people not by speaking, but by discovering them. He does not command or punish, but leaves people to make their own choices about life on earth. This divergent approach functions to empower humans. The Yao myth enables people to feel in control of their life because no distant, supreme being controls them. Consequently, this fosters a heightened sense of morality and responsibility. "The Chameleon Finds" does not allow the individual to blame God or rely upon him. Instead, this creator deity, having set the world in motion and established His ideology, now leaves the decisions in the hands of humans, whose punishment for their crimes against nature is abandonment by the creator.

It would be misguided to contend that the discrepancy between the Bible and other myths on gender issues, the environment, and man's relationship with God proves that the Bible is responsible for the social ills of today. Religion does not create society; rather society creates religion. The Bible did not cause sexism or environmental disaster, and is not at the root of today's societal evils. However, comparing the account of the Creation in Genesis to similar myths from other cultures is of value in reminding the individual that there are no absolute truths. Every society has to define its origins and values as it sees fit. The dominance of Judeo-Christian thinking in our society does not make it more correct. There are alternative stories, such as "The Chameleon Finds," that present different visions of creation. This process of comparison can lead to an appreciation of a contrasting ideology; however, the appreciation of other religions and their view of creation comes only when someone begins to think about the validity of their own religion rather than blindly accepting it. The comparison of different creation myths is not antithetical to religion; it represents a reasoned approach to looking at God and creation and thus defines what true religious conviction really is.

QUESTIONS FOR DISCUSSION

1. What are the main points of comparison and contrast around which Groban structures his essay? Do they seem appropriate to the myths he studied, or would you have selected others?

2. How effectively does Groban use details and references to the two myths he contrasts to support his conclusions about their differences? Are there other details he might have used or different inferences he might have drawn based on the details he selects?

3. Although Groban states in some parts of his essay that all creation myths have validity, since "there are no absolute truths," he seems quite critical of the Biblical version. Do you think that some views of creation are better than others, or is each version a product of the culture that produced it?

4. What are the criteria that Groban uses in his evaluation of the two myths he is comparing? Do his criteria seem appropriate, or would you substitute others? How would you set up criteria for evaluating myths of creation, if you believe that it is possible to do so?

Jane Yolen

How Basic is Shazam?

Jane Yolen was born in New York in 1937 and earned her B.A. at Smith College in 1960 and her M.Ed. at the University of Massachusetts in 1976, where she also completed course work for a doctorate in children's literature. Yolen has taught creative writing and Children's Literature at Smith College and has written over 200 children's books. She has received many awards for her writing including the Caldecott children's book award for Owl Moon *(1988), as well as the Parents' Choice Gold Medal for* Sword of the Rightful King *(2004). In "How Basic is Shazam?" from her essay collection* Touch Magic, *Yolen warns against the dangers today's youth face in failing to be exposed to traditional myths, folklore, and fairy tales of the past.*

JOURNAL

What myths and fairy tales do you remember from your early years? Have you ever been assigned or taught such imaginative material in a school setting?

If one were preparing a slide show to represent children in a mythless age, it might go something like this:

CLICK. A hundred thousand boys and girls in front of their TV sets shouting "Shazam!"

CLICK. An advertisement in a serious teachers' magazine for "Phonics Comix" with a picture of Spider Man on the top.

CLICK. Three children in a car by a gas station under the sign of the "Flying A" horse, a red horse with wings.

CLICK. A classroom full of children watching a movie about Apollo—the space program.

CLICK. A class of freshmen at Boston College taking an identification test, measuring their ability to recall names from the great religions and mythologies of the past. Well over half miss the name "King David."

CLICK. A class at the prestigious women's college, Smith, listening to a paper on Keats's "La Belle Dame Sans Merci." Asking for a reference explanation, one senior asks, "Did you make up that Lilith?"

No. Nor would these pictures be "made up" either. They and hundreds of others just as telling are part of a growing body of anecdotes that point to the fact that we are well on the way to the de-mythologizing of our human existence. Our children are growing up without their birthright; the myths, fairy tales, fantasies and folklore that are their proper legacy. It is a serious loss.

Who was Lilith? King David? Pegasus? Anansi the Spider? Apollo? Or the six whose names originally formed the acronym SHAZAM in the "Captain Marvel" spell: Solomon, Hercules, Atlas, Zeus, Achilles, Mercury?

In fact, *Shazam* itself has become a mnemonic for instant change and nothing more; this transformation is perhaps the deepest, sharpest metaphor for what is happening to our children today.

5   Mythology, legend, the lore of the folk, those tales that were once as real to their believers as a sunrise, hardly exist today even as reference points. In our haste to update educational standards, we have done away with the older gods, so that now all that we have left are names without faces, mnemonics without meaning.

Over the last few years there have been many educational councils and conferences, papers and presentations about the need to return to the Basics—to the teaching of the fundamental skills of reading, writing and arithmetic. But they are not the only subjects that are vital to our intellectual and human growth. An understanding of, a grounding in, a familiarity with the old lores and wisdoms of the so-called dead worlds is also a basic developmental need. Folklorist Charles Potter has written that "Folklore is a lively fossil that refuses to die." If children are invited to meet the great stories, to shake hands with the lively fossil, they will soon discover—as did their parents before them—that the well-kept bones are indispensable to the life of the mind. Myth and legend and folklore can serve four very basic functions in the education of Everychild.

One of the basic functions of myth and folk literature is to provide a landscape of allusion. With the first story a child hears, he or she takes a step toward perceiving a new environment, one that is filled with quests and questers, fated heroes and fetid monsters, intrepid heroines and trepidant helpers, even incompetent oafs who achieve competence and wholeness by going out and trying. As the child hears more stories and tales that are linked in both obvious and subtle ways, that landscape is broadened and deepened, and becomes more fully populated with memorable characters. These are the same folk that the child will meet again and again, threading their archetypal ways throughout the cultural history of our planet.

Stories lean on stories, art on art. This familiarity with the treasure-house of ancient story is necessary for any true appreciation of today's literature. A child who has never met Merlin—how can he or she really recognize the wizards in Earthsea? The child who has never heard of Arthur—how can he or she totally appreciate Susan Cooper's *The Grey King?* The child who has never known dryads or fauns will not recognize them in Narnia, or find their faces on museum walls or in the black silhouettes on Greek vases. Never to have trod the stony paths of Mount Pelion with Chiron and to have seen only the sexually precocious centaurs of *Fantasia* is to be diminished, narrowed, condemned to live in a cultural landscape that is dry as dust.

The second function of folklore is to provide a way of looking at another culture from the inside out. If a child becomes familiar with the pantheon of Greek gods, who toy with human lives as carelessly as children at play, then the Greek world view begins to come into focus. If a child learns about the range of Norse godlings who wait for heroic companions to feast with them at Valhalla, then the Vikings' emphasis on battle derring-do makes more sense. The study of the myth-making process, of those things which come together in a culture and propel a folk towards a coherent mythology, may be a very sophisticated one indeed, but its beginnings are back in the tales themselves.

10   Stories lean on stories, cultures on cultures. Just as any great city is built upon the bones and stones of its ancestors, so too is any mythology. And if our children can look at their own modern folklore within a broader context, they will see some very surprising shadows indeed. Spiderman and the Incredible Hulk, Fonzie and the Bionic Woman do not spring from a void but from needs within our own culture. And those needs lean on past needs.

Maureen Duffy writes in *The Erotic World of Fqery:*

> We remake our mythology in every age out of our own needs. We may use ideas lying around loose from a previous system or systems as part of the fabric. The human situation doesn't radically alter and therefore certain myths are constantly reappearing.

Thus, for example, in the adaptable Spiderman who helps the poor, the vulnerable, and the helpless we see Prometheus and Robin Hood, though his abilities also echo the African Anansi the Spider. In the rage and strength of the Incredible Hulk we see Atlas and Hercules and Paul Bunyan. Sly, vain, heroic Fonzie is both Loki and Achilles crossed with Lancelot du Lac. The Bionic Woman springs directly from Diana the Huntress and the Amazons, propelled by the electronic revolution and feminist rage.

This is mythic archeology, probing now for then, splitting the present to find the past. It works because humans have always had, in folklorist Joseph Campbell's fine phrase, "a long backward reach."

Providing a landscape of allusion and a knowledge of ancestral cultures are the two most obvious functions of mythology in the intellectual development of the child. But the next two functions are more complex and also more important.

15   According to Albert Lavin, "Myth conceived of as symbolic form . . . [is] a way of organizing the human response to reality . . . [and is] a fundamental aspect of the way we 'process' experience." By extension, in Lavin's view and also in the view of Dr. Bruno Bettelheim, the noted child psychologist whose book *The Uses of Enchantment* exploded onto the literary scene in 1976, myth becomes a marvelously adaptable tool of therapy.

Like a kaleidoscope, a folktale is made up of large and small units—motifs—incidents that, like bits of colored glass, are picked up as the tale travels from story to story, from country to country, from culture to culture. Shake up the folktale kaleidoscope, and these motifs rearrange themselves in an infinite variety of usable and attractive forms. Stith Thompson's monumental *Motif Index of Folk Literature* gives a view of the range of these forms. If the therapists need an archetypal evil stepmother or wicked natural mother, they can simply shake the folkloroscope and find one in a variant of a Cinderella story or a Medea myth. If a heroic conquest of a giant parent-figure is called for, they can shake and take Jack and his beanstalk or the story of Polyphemus or Beowulf. If the problem centers around a downtrodden, seemingly simpleton son, they can use the Fool-of-the-World story or any of its variations.

The idea of folklore as a tool for psychotherapy found its best articulation in Bettelheim's books, in which he wrote: "The fairy tale is a verification of the interior life of the child." The emphasis, in this case, is on immediate *applicability,* on the *use* of the archetypes in these stories to mold a mentally stable individual.

The fourth function of myth and fantasy, while related to this one, is much subtler and much more important. The great archetypal stories provide a framework or model for an individual's belief system. They are, in Isak Dinesen's marvelous expression, "a serious statement of our existence." The tales and stories handed down to us from the cultures that preceded us were the most serious, succinct expressions of the accumulated wisdom of those cultures. They were created in a symbolic, metaphoric story language and then honed by centuries of tongue-polishing to a crystalline perfection.

Symbolic language is something that a young child seems to understand almost viscerally; metaphoric speech is the child's own speech, though it is without analytic thought: a black cat is called "Midnight," a white dog named "Snowball"—immediate metaphors. Thus even very young children can absorb the meanings and wisdom of these symbolically expressed ancient tales and use them as tools for interpreting their own day-to-day experiences.

20   Myth as serious statement plays an important role in the life of the child. It can be the child's key to understanding his or her own existence. It can also be the key to our understanding of the child. William

Butler Yeats has written, "There is some one myth for every man which, if we but knew it, would make us understand all he did and thought."

These four functions of myth and folklore should establish the listening to and learning of the old tales as being among the most basic elements of our education: creating a landscape of allusion, enabling us to understand our own and other cultures from the inside out, providing an adaptable tool of therapy, and stating in symbolic or metaphoric terms the abstract truths of our common human existence.

And if we deny our children their cultural, historical heritage, their birthright to these stories, what then? Instead of creating men and women who have a grasp of literary allusion and symbolic language, and a metaphorical tool for dealing with the serious problems of life, we will be forming stunted boys and girls who speak only a barren language, a language that accurately reflects their equally barren minds. Language helps develop life as surely as it reflects life. It is most important part of our human condition.

Our children today face a serious deprivation—the loss of the word, of words. For as stories depend on stories, lives depend on lives. Contact and continuity are essential links in the long chain of human culture. One should not be seduced by the idea of the noble savage. The feral child deprived of all human contact does not become a Mowgli or a Tarzan, conversant with the animals. Lacking human language, he lacks true memory and thus lacks the ability to learn. Without mythology or art he cannot generalize or interpret his experience. Running on four limbs, he is slower than the beasts he follows, less agile than the humans he flees. His lifespan is diminished, his mental span likewise. In reality, the feral child does not live as a god in the jungle, but as a being rather less than human and not as well adapted as a beast.

We are in danger of creating our own feral children when we deny them access to their inheritance of story. When we let them run free with only their minimal animal demands on language, or deprive them of the insights and poetic visions expressed in words that humans have produced throughout human history, we deny them—in the end—their own humanity.

25   A child conversant with the old tales accepts them with an ease born of familiarity, fitting them into his own scheme of things, endowing them with new meaning. That old fossil, those old bones, walk again, and sing and dance and speak with a new tongue. The old stories bridge the centuries.

QUESTIONS FOR DISCUSSION

1. What point does Yolen make with the "slideshow" that begins her essay? Is her presentation convincing?
2. What was the original significance of the acronym "SHAZAM" versus its modern significance? What does this meaning-shift signify

about our changing views of mythical characters and knowledge, according to Yolan? Do you agree?

3. What are the four functions of myth and folk literature in the life of the growing child, in Yolan's view? Which of these functions seems most important to you, or does each seem equally significant to children and to society as a whole?

4. In what sense are myths and fairy tales "a marvelously adaptable tool of therapy," as child therapist Bruno Bettelheim presents them in his book *The Uses of Enchantment?*

5. According to Yolen, how can the metaphoric and symbolic language of myths, tales, and fantasy writing provide a "framework or model for an individual's belief system"?

6. Why does Yolen warn that the child deprived of myths and stories becomes not a "noble savage" but a "feral child . . . lacking true memory and . . . the ability to learn"? Do you agree?

CONNECTION

Compare Yolen's view of the social and cultural functions of myths and fairy tales with the view of Joseph Campbell on these themes in his essay in this chapter (see page 172).

IDEAS FOR WRITING

1. Write about the myths and fairy tales, ancient or modern, that made the greatest impression on your imagination as you were growing up. How (if at all) did these stories have an impact in shaping your personal belief system?

2. Do some research into the ways myths and fairy tales have been used in psychotherapy and its theories of child development by Bettelheim and/or other psychologists. Write up your conclusions in a brief research essay with quotations and formal citations.

RELATED WEB SITES

Jane Yolen Web Site

www.janeyolen.com/

The official website for Jane Yolen contains a bibliography of books by Yolen, a biography, a set of links for teachers on how to use children's books in the classroom, and extensive links for writers.

Surlalune Fairy Tales Web Site

www.surlalunefairytales.com/

Maintained by children's literature scholar and librarian Heidi Anne Heiner, this site includes an extensive introduction to folk and fairy tales, essays by professionals in the field, many annotated fairy tales, links to other related sites, and a number of complete fairy tale e-books.

Four Versions of Cinderella

Common tales are shared throughout the world in similar yet subtly distinct versions and are retold, generation after generation, over a period of many centuries. Following are four versions of the popular Cinderella fairy tale: the classic Brothers Grimm fairy tale, "Aschenputtel"; Charles Perrault's "Cendrillon"; the Native American "Algonquin Cinderella"; and "Tam and Cam," a Vietnamese folk version of Cinderella.

JOURNAL

Write down a fairy tale that you remember from your childhood. Why was this story an important one to you when you were a child? What meaning does the story have for you today?

The Brothers Grimm

Aschenputtel

Jacob Grimm (1785–1863) and his brother Wilhelm Grimm (1786–1859) were scholars of the German language and of folk culture; they collected oral narratives that embodied the cultural values of the German peasant and reflected on universal human concerns. The Grimms' tales have been translated into more than seventy different languages. "Aschenputtel," a version of the Cinderella story, appears here in a version translated by Lucy Crane.

There was once a rich man whose wife lay sick, and when she felt her end drawing near she called to her only daughter to come near her bed, and said, "Dear child, be pious and good, and God will always take care of you, and I will look down upon you from heaven, and will be with you."

And then she closed her eyes and expired. The maiden went everyday to her mother's grave and wept, and was always pious and good. When the winter came the snow covered the grave with a white covering, and when the sun came in the early spring and melted it away, the man took to himself another wife.

The new wife brought two daughters home with her, and they were beautiful and fair in appearance, but at heart were black and ugly. And then began very evil times for the poor stepdaughter.

"Is the stupid creature to sit in the same room with us?" said they; "those who eat food must earn it. Out upon her for a kitchen-maid!"

5 They took away her pretty dresses, and put on her an old gray kirtle, and gave her wooden shoes to wear.

"Just look now at the proud princess, how she is decked out!" cried they laughing, and then they sent her into the kitchen. There she was obliged to do heavy work from morning to night, get up early in the morning, draw water, make the fires, cook, and wash. Besides that, the sisters did their utmost to torment her—mocking her, and strewing peas and lentils among the ashes, and setting her to pick them up. In the evenings, when she was quite tired out with her hard day's work, she had no bed to lie on, but was obliged to rest on the hearth among the cinders. And as she always looked dusty and dirty, they named her Aschenputtel.

It happened one day that the father went to the fair, and he asked his two stepdaughters what he should bring back for them.

"Fine clothes!" said one.

"Pearls and jewels!" said the other.

10 "But what will you have, Aschenputtel?" said he.

"The first twig, father, that strikes against your hat on the way home; that is what I should like you to bring me."

So he bought for the two stepdaughters fine clothes, pearls, and jewels, and on his way back, as he rode through a green lane, a hazel-twig struck against his hat; and he broke it off and carried it home with him. And when he reached home he gave to the stepdaughters what they had wished for, and to Aschenputtel he gave the hazel-twig. She thanked him, and went to her mother's grave, and planted this twig there, weeping so bitterly that the tears fell upon it and watered it, and it flourished and became a fine tree. Aschenputtel went to see it three times a day, and wept and prayed, and each time a white bird rose up from the tree, and if she uttered any wish the bird brought her whatever she had wished for.

Now it came to pass that the king ordained a festival that should last for three days, and to which all the beautiful young women of that country were bidden, so that the king's son might choose a bride from among them. When the two stepdaughters heard that they too were bidden to appear, they felt very pleased, and they called Aschenputtel, and said,

"Comb our hair, brush our shoes, and make our buckles fast, we are going to the wedding feast at the king's castle."

15 Aschenputtel, when she heard this, could not help crying, for she too would have liked to go to the dance, and she begged her stepmother to allow her.

"What, you Aschenputtel!" said she, "in all your dust and dirt, you want to go to the festival! you that have no dress and no shoes! you want to dance!"

But as she persisted in asking, at last the stepmother said,

"I have strewed a dish-full of lentils in the ashes, and if you can pick them all up again in two hours you may go with us."

Then the maiden went to the back-door that led into the garden, and called out,

"O gentle doves, O turtle-doves,
And all the birds that be,
The lentils that in ashes lie
Come and pick up for me!
The good must be put in the dish,
The bad you may eat if you wish."

20   Then there came to the kitchen-window two white doves, and after them some turtle-doves, and at last a crowd of all the birds under heaven, chirping and fluttering, and they alighted among the ashes; and the doves nodded with their heads, and began to pick, peck, pick, peck, and then all the others began to pick, peck, pick, peck, and put all the good grains into the dish. Before an hour was over all was done, and they flew away. Then the maiden brought the dish to her stepmother, feeling joyful, and thinking that now she should go to the feast; but the stepmother said,

"No, Aschenputtel, you have no proper clothes, and you do not know how to dance, and you would be laughed at!"

And when Aschenputtel cried for disappointment, she added,

"If you can pick two dishes full of lentils out of the ashes, nice and clean, you shall go with us," thinking to herself, "for that is not possible." When she had strewed two dishes full of lentils among the ashes the maiden went through the backdoor into the garden, and cried,

"O gentle doves, O turtle-doves,
And all the birds that be,
The lentils that in ashes lie
Come and pick up for me!
The good must be put in the dish,
The bad you may eat if you wish."

So there came to the kitchen-window two white doves, and then some turtle-doves, and at last a crowd of all the other birds under heaven, chirping and fluttering, and they alighted among the ashes, and the doves nodded with their heads and began to pick, peck, pick, peck, and then all the others began to pick, peck, pick, peck, and put all the good grains into the dish. And before half-an-hour was over it was all done, and they flew away. Then the maiden took the dishes to the stepmother, feeling joyful, and thinking that now she should go with them to the feast; but she said "All this is of no good to you; you cannot come with us, for you have no proper clothes, and cannot dance; you would put us to shame."

25   Then she turned her back on poor Aschenputtel, and made haste to set out with her two proud daughters.

And as there was no one left in the house, Aschenputtel went to her mother's grave, under the hazel bush, and cried,

"Little tree, little tree, shake over me,
That silver and gold may come down and cover me."

Then the bird threw down a dress of gold and silver, and a pair of slippers embroidered with silk and silver. And in all haste she put on the dress and went to the festival. But her stepmother and sisters did not know her, and thought she must be a foreign princess, she looked so beautiful in her golden dress. Of Aschenputtel they never thought at all, and supposed that she was sitting at home, and picking the lentils out of the ashes. The King's son came to meet her, and took her by the hand and danced with her, and he refused to stand up with any one else, so that he might not be obliged to let go her hand; and when any one came to claim it he answered,

"She is my partner."

And when the evening came she wanted to go home, but the prince said he would go with her to take care of her, for he wanted to see where the beautiful maiden lived. But she escaped him, and jumped up into the pigeon-house. Then the prince waited until the father came, and told him the strange maiden had jumped into the pigeon-house. The father thought to himself,

30   "It cannot surely be Aschenputtel," and called for axes and hatchets, and had the pigeon-house cut down, but there was no one in it. And when they entered the house there sat Aschenputtel in her dirty clothes among the cinders, and a little oil-lamp burnt dimly in the chimney; for Aschenputtel had been very quick, and had jumped out of the pigeon-house again, and had run to the hazel bush; and there she had taken off her beautiful dress and laid it on the grave, and her bird had carried it away again, and then she had put on her little gray kirtle again, and had sat down in the kitchen among the cinders.

The next day, when the festival began anew, and the parents and stepsisters had gone to it, Aschenputtel went to the hazel bush and cried,

"Little tree, little tree, shake over me,
That silver and gold may come down and cover me."

Then the bird cast down a still more splendid dress than on the day before. And when she appeared in it among the guests every one was astonished at her beauty. The prince had been waiting until she came, and he took her hand and danced with her alone. And when any one else came to invite her he said,

"She is my partner."

And when the evening came she wanted to go home, and the prince followed her, for he wanted to see to what house she belonged; but she broke away from him, and ran into the garden at the back of the house. There stood a fine large tree, bearing splendid pears; she leapt as lightly as a squirrel among the branches, and the prince did not know what had become of her. So he waited until the father came, and then he told him that the strange maiden had rushed from him, and that he thought she had gone up into the pear-tree. The father thought to himself, "It cannot surely be Aschenputtel," and called for an axe, and felled the tree, but there was no one in it. And when they went into the kitchen there sat Aschenputtel among the cinders, as usual, for she had got down the other side of the tree, and had taken back her beautiful clothes to the bird on the hazel bush, and had put on her old gray kirtle again.

35   On the third day, when the parents and the stepchildren had set off, Aschenputtel went again to her mother's grave, and said to the tree,

"Little tree, little tree, shake over me,
That silver and gold may come down and cover me."

Then the bird cast down a dress, the like of which had never been seen for splendour and brilliancy, and slippers that were of gold.

And when she appeared in this dress at the feast nobody knew what to say for wonderment. The prince danced with her alone, and if any one else asked her he answered,

"She is my partner."

And when it was evening Aschenputtel wanted to go home, and the prince was about to go with her, when she ran past him so quickly that he could not follow her. But he had laid a plan, and had caused all the steps to be spread with pitch, so that as she rushed down them the left shoe of the maiden remained sticking in it. The prince picked it up, and saw that it was of gold, and very small and slender. The next morning he went to the father and told him that none should be his bride save the one whose foot the golden shoe should fit. Then the two sisters were very glad, because they had pretty feet. The eldest went to her room to try on the shoe, and her mother stood by. But she could not get her great toe into it, for the shoe was too small; then her mother handed her a knife, and said,

40   "Cut the toe off, for when you are queen you will never have to go on foot." So the girl cut her toe off, squeezed her foot into the shoe, concealed the pain, and went down to the prince. Then he took her with him on his horse as his bride, and rode off. They had to pass by the grave, and there sat the two pigeons on the hazel bush, and cried,

"There they go, there they go!
There is blood on her shoe;
The shoe is too small,
—Not the right bride at all!"

Then the prince looked at her shoe, and saw the blood flowing. And he turned his horse round and took the false bride home again, saying she was not the right one, and that the other sister must try on the shoe. So she went into her room to do so, and got her toes comfortably in, but her heel was too large. Then her mother handed her the knife, saying, "Cut a piece off your heel; when you are queen you will never have to go on foot."

So the girl cut a piece off her heel, and thrust her foot into the shoe, concealed the pain, and went down to the prince, who took his bride before him on his horse and rode off. When they passed by the hazel bush the two pigeons sat there and cried,

"There they go, there they go!
There is blood on her shoe;
The shoe is too small,
—Not the right bride at all!"

Then the prince looked at her foot, and saw how the blood was flowing from the shoe, and staining the white stocking. And he turned his horse round and brought the false bride home again.

"This is not the right one," said he, "have you no other daughter?"

45   "No," said the man, "only my dead wife left behind her a little stunted Aschenputtel; it is impossible that she can be the bride." But the King's son ordered her to be sent for, but the mother said,

"Oh no! she is much too dirty, I could not let her be seen."

But he would have her fetched, and so Aschenputtel had to appear.

First she washed her face and hands quite clean, and went in and curtseyed to the prince, who held out to her the golden shoe. Then she sat down on a stool, drew her foot out of the heavy wooden shoe, and slipped it into the golden one, which fitted it perfectly. And when she stood up, and the prince looked in her face, he knew again the beautiful maiden that had danced with him, and he cried,

"This is the right bride!"

50   The stepmother and the two sisters were thunderstruck, and grew pale with anger; but he put Aschenputtel before him on his horse and rode off. And as they passed the hazel bush, the two white pigeons cried,

"There they go, there they go!
No blood on her shoe;
The shoe's not too small,
The right bride is she after all."

And when they had thus cried, they came flying after and perched on Aschenputtel's shoulders, one on the right, the other on the left, and so remained.

And when her wedding with the prince was appointed to be held the false sisters came, hoping to curry favour, and to take part in the festivities. So as the bridal procession went to the church, the eldest walked on the right side and the younger on the left, and the pigeons picked out an eye of each of them. And as they returned the elder was on the left side and the younger on the right, and the pigeons picked out the other eye of each of them. And so they were condemned to go blind for the rest of their days because of their wickedness and falsehood.

RELATED WEB SITES

The Brothers Grimm

`www.pitt.edu/~dash/grimm.html`

Biographical information, studies of specific tales, electronic tales, and links to more resources on the Brothers Grimm can be found at this simple but informative URL.

Grimm Brothers @ NationalGeographic.com

`www.nationalgeographic.com/grimm/`

This attractive and entertaining Web site from *National Geographic* shares texts from many of Grimms' original fairy tales. It also includes audio samples of some of the stories, beautiful images, and interactive learning tools.

Charles Perrault

Cendrillon

This classic version of the Cinderella story, which is similar to the version Walt Disney used as the basis for his famous animated cartoon film, was written (based on earlier folk sources) by French author Charles Perrault (1628–1703) and collected in his Mother Goose Tales *(1697). "Cendrillon" was translated and adapted in an English version as "Cinderella, or the Little Glass Slipper" by English writer Andrew Lang for* The Blue Fairy Book *(1889).*

Once there was a gentleman who married, for his second wife, the proudest and most haughty woman that was ever seen. She had, by a former husband, two daughters of her own, who were, indeed, exactly like her in all things. He had likewise, by another wife, a young daughter, but of unparalleled goodness and sweetness of temper, which she took from her mother, who was the best creature in the world.

No sooner were the ceremonies of the wedding over but the step-mother began to show herself in her true colors. She could not bear the good qualities of this pretty girl, and the less because they made her own daughters appear the more odious. She employed her in the meanest work of the house. She scoured the dishes, tables, etc., and cleaned madam's chamber, and those of misses, her daughters. She slept in a sorry garret, on a wretched straw bed, while her sisters slept in fine rooms, with floors all inlaid, on beds of the very newest fashion, and where they had looking glasses so large that they could see themselves at their full length from head to foot.

The poor girl bore it all patiently, and dared not tell her father, who would have scolded her; for his wife governed him entirely. When she had done her work, she used to go to the chimney corner, and sit down there in the cinders and ashes, which caused her to be called Cinder-wench. Only the younger sister, who was not so rude and uncivil as the older one, called her Cinderella. However, Cinderella, notwithstanding her coarse apparel, was a hundred times more beautiful than her sisters, although they were always dressed very richly.

It happened that the king's son gave a ball, and invited all persons of fashion to it. Our young misses were also invited, for they cut a very grand figure among those of quality. They were mightily delighted at this invitation, and wonderfully busy in selecting the gowns, petticoats, and hair dressing that would best become them. This was a new diffi-culty for Cinderella; for it was she who ironed her sister's linen and pleated their ruffles. They talked all day long of nothing but how they should be dressed.

5 "For my part," said the eldest, "I will wear my red velvet suit with French trimming."

"And I," said the youngest, "shall have my usual petticoat; but then, to make amends for that, I will put on my gold-flowered cloak, and my dia-mond stomacher, which is far from being the most ordinary one in the world."

They sent for the best hairdresser they could get to make up their headpieces and adjust their hairdos, and they had their red brushes and patches from Mademoiselle de la Poche.

They also consulted Cinderella in all these matters, for she had excel-lent ideas, and her advice was always good. Indeed, she even offered her services to fix their hair, which they very willingly accepted. As she was do-ing this, they said to her, "Cinderella, would you not like to go to the ball?"

"Alas!" said she, "you only jeer me; it is not for such as I am to go to such a place."

10　　"You are quite right," they replied. "It would make the people laugh to see a Cinderwench at a ball."

Anyone but Cinderella would have fixed their hair awry, but she was very good, and dressed them perfectly well. They were so excited that they hadn't eaten a thing for almost two days. Then they broke more than a dozen laces trying to have themselves laced up tightly enough to give them a fine slender shape. They were continually in front of their looking glass. At last the happy day came. They went to court, and Cinderella followed them with her eyes as long as she could. When she lost sight of them, she started to cry.

Her godmother, who saw her all in tears, asked her what was the matter.

"I wish I could. I wish I could." She was not able to speak the rest, being interrupted by her tears and sobbing.

15　　This godmother of hers, who was a fairy, said to her, "You wish that you could go to the ball; is it not so?"

"Yes," cried Cinderella, with a great sigh.

"Well," said her godmother, "be but a good girl, and I will contrive that you shall go." Then she took her into her chamber, and said to her, "Run into the garden, and bring me a pumpkin."

Cinderella went immediately to gather the finest she could get, and brought it to her godmother, not being able to imagine how this pumpkin could help her go to the ball. Her godmother scooped out all the inside of it, leaving nothing but the rind. Having done this, she struck the pumpkin with her wand, and it was instantly turned into a fine coach, gilded all over with gold.

She then went to look into her mousetrap, where she found six mice, all alive, and ordered Cinderella to lift up a little the trapdoor. She gave each mouse, as it went out, a little tap with her wand, and the mouse was that moment turned into a fine horse, which altogether made a very fine set of six horses of a beautiful mouse colored dapple gray.

Being at a loss for a coachman, Cinderella said, "I will go and see if 20　　there is not a rat in the rat trap that we can turn into a coachman."

"You are right," replied her godmother, "Go and look."

Cinderella brought the trap to her, and in it there were three huge rats. The fairy chose the one which had the largest beard, touched him with her wand, and turned him into a fat, jolly coachman, who had the smartest whiskers that eyes ever beheld.

After that, she said to her, "Go again into the garden, and you will find six lizards behind the watering pot. Bring them to me."

She had no sooner done so but her godmother turned them into six footmen, who skipped up immediately behind the coach, with their liveries all bedaubed with gold and silver, and clung as close behind each other as if they had done nothing else their whole lives. The fairy then said to Cinderella, "Well, you see here an equipage fit to go to the ball with; are you not pleased with it?"

"Oh, yes," she cried; "but must I go in these nasty rags?"

25   Her godmother then touched her with her wand, and, at the same instant, her clothes turned into cloth of gold and silver, all beset with jewels. This done, she gave her a pair of glass slippers, the prettiest in the whole world. Being thus decked out, she got up into her coach; but her godmother, above all things, commanded her not to stay past midnight, telling her, at the same time, that if she stayed one moment longer, the coach would be a pumpkin again, her horses mice, her coachman a rat, her footmen lizards, and that her clothes would become just as they were before.

She promised her godmother to leave the ball before midnight; and then drove away, scarcely able to contain herself for joy. The king's son, who was told that a great princess, whom nobody knew, had arrived, ran out to receive her. He gave her his hand as she alighted from the coach, and led her into the hall, among all the company. There was immediately a profound silence. Everyone stopped dancing, and the violins ceased to play, so entranced was everyone with the singular beauties of the unknown newcomer.

Nothing was then heard but a confused noise of, "How beautiful she is! How beautiful she is!"

The king himself, old as he was, could not help watching her, and telling the queen softly that it was a long time since he had seen so beautiful and lovely a creature.

All the ladies were busied in considering her clothes and headdress, hoping to have some made next day after the same pattern, provided they could find such fine materials and as able hands to make them.

30   The king's son led her to the most honorable seat, and afterwards took her out to dance with him. She danced so very gracefully that they all more and more admired her. A fine meal was served up, but the young prince ate not a morsel, so intently was he busied in gazing on her.

She went and sat down by her sisters, showing them a thousand civilities, giving them part of the oranges and citrons which the prince had presented her with, which very much surprised them, for they did not know her. While Cinderella was thus amusing her sisters, she heard the clock strike eleven and three-quarters, whereupon she immediately made a courtesy to the company and hurried away as fast as she could.

Arriving home, she ran to seek out her godmother, and, after having thanked her, she said she could not but heartily wish she might go to the ball the next day as well, because the king's son had invited her.

As she was eagerly telling her godmother everything that had happened at the ball, her two sisters knocked at the door, which Cinderella ran and opened.

"You stayed such a long time!" she cried, gaping, rubbing her eyes and stretching herself as if she had been sleeping; she had not, however, had any manner of inclination to sleep while they were away from home.

35   "If you had been at the ball," said one of her sisters, "you would not have been tired with it. The finest princess was there, the most beautiful that mortal eyes have ever seen. She showed us a thousand civilities, and gave us oranges and citrons."

Cinderella seemed very indifferent in the matter. Indeed, she asked them the name of that princess; but they told her they did not know it, and that the king's son was very uneasy on her account and would give all the world to know who she was. At this Cinderella, smiling, replied, "She must, then, be very beautiful indeed; how happy you have been! Could not I see her? Ah, dear Charlotte, do lend me your yellow dress which you wear every day."

"Yes, to be sure!" cried Charlotte; "lend my clothes to such a dirty Cinderwench as you are! I should be such a fool."

Cinderella, indeed, well expected such an answer, and was very glad of the refusal; for she would have been sadly put to it, if her sister had lent her what she asked for jestingly.

The next day the two sisters were at the ball, and so was Cinderella, but dressed even more magnificently than before. The king's son was always by her, and never ceased his compliments and kind speeches to her. All this was so far from being tiresome to her, and, indeed, she quite forgot what her godmother had told her. She thought that it was no later than eleven when she counted the clock striking twelve. She jumped up and fled, as nimble as a deer. The prince followed, but could not overtake her. She left behind one of her glass slippers, which the prince picked up most carefully. She reached home, but quite out of breath, and in her nasty old clothes, having nothing left of all her finery but one of the little slippers, the mate to the one that she had dropped.

40   The guards at the palace gate were asked if they had not seen a princess go out. They replied that they had seen nobody leave but a young girl, very shabbily dressed, and who had more the air of a poor country wench than a gentlewoman.

When the two sisters returned from the ball Cinderella asked them if they had been well entertained, and if the fine lady had been there.

They told her, yes, but that she hurried away immediately when it struck twelve, and with so much haste that she dropped one of her little glass slippers, the prettiest in the world, which the king's son had picked up; that he had done nothing but look at her all the time at the ball, and that most certainly he was very much in love with the beautiful person who owned the glass slipper.

What they said was very true; for a few days later, the king's son had it proclaimed, by sound of trumpet, that he would marry her whose foot this slipper would just fit. They began to try it on the princesses, then the duchesses and all the court, but in vain; it was brought to the two sisters, who did all they possibly could to force their foot into the slipper, but they did not succeed.

Cinderella, who saw all this, and knew that it was her slipper, said to them, laughing, "Let me see if it will not fit me."

45   Her sisters burst out laughing, and began to banter with her. The gentleman who was sent to try the slipper looked earnestly at Cinderella, and, finding her very handsome, said that it was only just that she should try as well, and that he had orders to let everyone try.

He had Cinderella sit down, and, putting the slipper to her foot, he found that it went on very easily, fitting her as if it had been made of wax. Her two sisters were greatly astonished, but then even more so, when Cinderella pulled out of her pocket the other slipper, and put it on her other foot. Then in came her godmother and touched her wand to Cinderella's clothes, making them richer and more magnificent than any of those she had worn before.

And now her two sisters found her to be that fine, beautiful lady whom they had seen at the ball. They threw themselves at her feet to beg pardon for all the ill treatment they had made her undergo. Cinderella took them up, and, as she embraced them, said that she forgave them with all her heart, and wanted her always to love her.

She was taken to the young prince, dressed as she was. He thought she was more charming than before, and, a few days after, married her. Cinderella, who was no less good than beautiful, gave her two sisters lodgings in the palace, and that very same day matched them with two great lords of the court.

Moral: Beauty in a woman is a rare treasure that will always be admired. Graciousness, however, is priceless and of even greater value. This is what Cinderella's godmother gave to her when she taught her to behave like a queen. Young women, in the winning of a heart, graciousness is more important than a beautiful hairdo. It is a true gift of the fairies. Without it nothing is possible; with it, one can do anything.

50   Another moral: Without doubt it is a great advantage to have intelligence, courage, good breeding, and common sense. These and similar talents come only from heaven, and it is good to have them. However, even these may fail to bring you success, without the blessing of a godfather or a godmother.

RELATED WEB SITES

Charles Perrault's Mother Goose Tales
www.pitt.edu/~dash/perrault.html
This site provides biographical information and useful links on Charles Perrault and his *Mother Goose Tales*.

The Algonquin Cinderella

*This Native American version of the Cinderella story was anthologized by
Idries Shah, father of Saira Shah and a student of world folklore and
Sufism, in* World Tales *(1979). As you read the tale, notice its emphasis
on the spiritual power of beauty and vision.*

There was once a large village of the MicMac Indians of the Eastern
Algonquins, built beside a lake. At the far end of the settlement
stood a lodge, and in it lived a being who was always invisible. He had a
sister who looked after him, and everyone knew that any girl who could
see him might marry him. For that reason there were very few girls who
did not try, but it was very long before anyone succeeded.

This is the way in which the test of sight was carried out: at evening-
time, when the Invisible One was due to be returning home, his sister
would walk with any girl who might come down to the lakeshore. She, of
course, could see her brother, since he was always visible to her. As soon
as she saw him, she would say to the girls:

"Do you see my brother?"

"Yes," they would generally reply—though some of them did say "No."

5   To those who said that they could indeed see him, the sister would say:

"Of what is his shoulder strap made?" Some people say that she would
enquire:

"What is his moose-runner's haul?" or "With what does he draw his sled?"
And they would answer:

"A strip of rawhide" or "a green flexible branch," or something of that
kind.

10   Then she, knowing that they had not told the truth, would say:

"Very well, let us return to the wigwam!"

When they had gone in, she would tell them not to sit in a certain
place, because it belonged to the Invisible One. Then, after they had
helped to cook the supper, they would wait with great curiosity, to see
him eat. They could be sure that he was a real person, for when he took
off his moccasins they became visible, and his sister hung them up. But
beyond this they saw nothing of him, not even when they stayed in the
place all the night, as many of them did.

Now there lived in the village an old man who was a widower, and his
three daughters. The youngest girl was very small, weak and often ill: and
yet her sisters, especially the elder, treated her cruelly. The second
daughter was kinder, and sometimes took her side: but the wicked sister
would burn her hands and feet with hot cinders, and she was covered
with scars from this treatment. She was so marked that people called her
Oochigeaskw, the Rough-Faced-Girl.

When her father came home and asked why she had such burns, the bad sister would at once say that it was her own fault, for she had disobeyed orders and gone near the fire and fallen into it.

15   These two elder sisters decided one day to try their luck at seeing the Invisible One. So they dressed themselves in their finest clothes, and tried to look their prettiest. They found the Invisible One's sister and took the usual walk by the water.

When he came, and when they were asked if they could see him, they answered: "Of course." And when asked about the shoulder strap or sled cord, they answered: "A piece of rawhide."

But of course they were lying like the others, and they got nothing for their pains.

The next afternoon, when the father returned home, he brought with him many of the pretty little shells from which wampum was made, and they set to work to string them.

That day, poor Little Oochigeaskw, who had always gone barefoot, got a pair of her father's moccasins, old ones, and put them into water to soften them so that she could wear them. Then she begged her sisters for a few wampum shells. The elder called her a "little pest," but the younger one gave her some. Now, with no other clothes than her usual rags, the poor little thing went into the woods and got herself some sheets of birch bark, from which she made a dress, and put marks on it for decoration, in the style of long ago. She made a petticoat and a loose gown, a cap, leggings and a handkerchief. She put on her father's large old moccasins, which were far too big for her, and went forth to try her luck. She would try, she thought, to discover whether she could see the Invisible One.

20   She did not begin very well. As she set off, her sisters shouted and hooted, hissed and yelled, and tried to make her stay. And the loafers around the village, seeing the strange little creature, called out "Shame!"

The poor little girl in her strange clothes, with her face all scarred, was an awful sight, but she was kindly received by the sister of the Invisible One. And this was, of course, because this noble lady understood far more about things than simply the mere outside which all the rest of the world knows. As the brown of the evening sky turned to black, the lady took her down to the lake.

"Do you see him?" the Invisible One's sister asked.

"I do, indeed—and he is wonderful!" said Oochigeaskw.

The sister asked:

25   "And what is his sled-string?"

The little girl said:

"It is the Rainbow."

"And, my sister, what is his bow-string?"

"It is The Spirit's Road—the Milky Way."

30   "So you *have* seen him," said his sister. She took the girl home with her and bathed her. As she did so, all the scars disappeared from her body. Her hair grew again, as it was combed, long, like a blackbird's wing. Her eyes were now like stars: in all the world there was no other such beauty. Then, from her treasures, the lady gave her a wedding garment, and adorned her.

Then she told Oochigeaskw to take the *wife's* seat in the wigwam: the one next to where the Invisible One sat, beside the entrance. And when he came in, terrible and beautiful, he smiled and said:

"So we are found out!"

"Yes," said his sister. And so Oochigeaskw became his wife.

RELATED WEB SITES

Cinderella Stories
www.ucalgary.ca/~dkbrown/cinderella.html
Lists of variations on the Cinderella story can be found at this URL from the University of Calgary. Links to teaching ideas, articles, and essays will also be found here.

Tam and Cam (Vietnam)

"Tam and Cam" is a Vietnamese folk story that demonstrates how universal the Cinderella story is, as well as how unique each version is to the particular culture out of which it grew. The sensitive and resourceful Tam is similar in many ways to the Western Cinderella, yet she is very much a product of a strongly Buddhist, nature-oriented society. She is willing to use violence to attain her revenge, and she is reborn several times during the story as a different sort of being. "Tam and Cam" is retold by Vo Van Thang and Jim Larson in a bilingual version included in Vietnamese Folktales *(1993).*

There were once two stepsisters named Tam and Cam. Tam was the daughter of their father's first wife. She died when the child was young so her father took a second wife. Some years later the father died and left Tam to live with her stepmother and stepsister.

Her stepmother was most severe and treated the girl harshly. Tam had to labor all day and long into the night. When there was any daylight she had to care for the buffalo, carry water for the cooking, do the washing and pick vegetables and water-fern for the pigs to eat. At night she had to spend a lot of time husking the rice. While Tam worked hard her sister did nothing but play games. She was given pretty clothes to wear and always got the best food.

Early one morning the second-mother gave two creels to Tam and Cam and told them to go to the paddy fields to catch tiny shrimp and crab. "I will give a *yêm* of red cloth to the one who brings home a full creel," she promised.

Tam was very familiar with the task of finding shrimp and crab in the paddy fields, and by lunchtime she had filled her creel. Cam walked and waded from field to field but she could not catch anything. She looked at Tam's full creel and said to her, "Oh, my dear sister Tam, your hair is covered in mud. Get into the pond to wash it, or you will be scolded by mother when you return home."

5   Believing what her sister told her, Tam hurried to the pond to wash herself. As soon as her stepsister entered the water, Cam emptied the shrimp and crab into her own creel, and hurried home to claim the *yêm* of red cloth.

When she had finished washing and saw her empty creel Tam burst into tears.

A Buddha who was sitting on a lotus in the sky heard her sobs and came down beside her. "Why are you crying?" asked the Buddha.

Tam told him all that had happened and the Buddha comforted her. "Do not be tearful. Look into your creel and see if anything is left."

Tam looked into the creel and said to the Buddha, "There is only one tiny *bông* fish."

10   "Take the fish and put it in the pond near your home. At every meal you must save a bowl of rice with which to feed it. When you want the fish to rise to the surface to eat the rice you must call like this:

Dear *bông,* dear *bông,*
Rise only to eat my golden rice,
For that of others will not taste nice.

"Goodbye child, I wish you well." After saying this the Buddha disappeared.

Tam put the fish in the pond as she had been bidden, and every day, after lunch and the evening meal, she took some rice to feed it. Day by day the *bông* fish grew, and the girl became great friends with it.

Seeing Tam take rice to the pond after each meal the second-mother became suspicious, and bade Cam go to spy on her stepsister. Cam hid in a bush near the pond. When Tam called the *bông* fish the hidden girl listened to the words, and rushed to her mother to tell her of the secret.

That evening, the second-mother instructed Tam that on the following day she must take the buffalo to the far field.

15   "It is now the season for vegetables. Buffalo cannot graze in the village. Tomorrow you have to take the buffalo to the far field. If you graze in the village it will be taken by the notables."

Tam set off very early the next morning to ride the buffalo to the far field. When she was gone, Cam and her mother took rice to the pond and called the *bông* fish. It rose to the surface and the woman caught it. She then took it to the kitchen where she cooked and ate it.

Tam returned in the evening, and after eating her meal took rice to the pond to feed her friend. She called and called, again and again, but she saw only a drop of blood on the surface of the water. Tam knew that something terrible had happened to the *bông* fish and began to weep.

The Buddha appeared by her side again. "Why do you weep this time, my child?"

Tam sobbed out her story and the Buddha spoke. "Your fish has been caught and eaten. Now, stop crying. You must find the bones of the fish and put them in four jars. After doing this you must bury the jars. Put one under each of the legs of your bed."

20 Tam searched and searched for the bones of her beloved friend but could not find them anywhere. As she looked even further a rooster came and called to her.

Cock-a-doodle-do, cock-a-doodle-do,
A handful of rice,
And I'll find the bones for you.

Tam gave rice to the rooster, and when it had eaten it strutted into the kitchen. In no time at all the elegant fowl returned with the bones and laid them at Tam's feet. The girl placed the bones into four jars and buried one under each of the legs of her bed.

Some months later the king proclaimed that there would be a great festival. All the people of Tam's village were going to attend, and the road was thronged with well dressed people making their way to the capital. Cam and her mother put on their finest clothes in readiness to join them. When the woman saw that Tam also wanted to attend the gala day she winked at Cam. Then she mixed a basketful of unhusked rice with the basket of clean rice Tam had prepared the previous evening. "You may go to the festival when you have separated this grain. If there isn't any rice to cook when we return home you will be beaten."

With that, she and her daughter joined the happy people on their way to the festival, and left Tam to her lonely task. She started to separate the rice, but she could see that it was hopeless and she began to weep.

Once again the Buddha appeared by her side. "Why are there tears in your eyes?" he asked.

25 Tam explained about the rice grains that had to be separated, and how the festival would be over by the time she had finished.

"Bring your baskets to the yard," said the Buddha. "I will call the birds to help you."

The birds came and pecked and fluttered until, in no time at all, they had divided the rice into two baskets. Not one single grain did they eat, but when they flew away Tam began to weep again.

"Now why are you crying?" asked the Buddha.

"My clothes are too poor," sobbed Tam. "I thank you for your help, but I cannot go dressed like this."

30 "Go and dig up the four jars," ordered the Buddha. "Then you will have all you need."

Tam obeyed and opened the jars. In the first she found a beautiful silk dress, a silk *yêm* and a scarf of the same material. In the second jar she found a pair of embroidered shoes of a cunning design which fitted her perfectly. When she opened the third jar great was her surprise when she saw a miniature horse. It neighed once, and grew to become a noble steed. In the fourth jar there was a richly ornamented saddle and bridle which grew to fit the horse. She washed herself and brushed her hair until it shone. Then she put on her wonderful new clothes and rode off to the festival.

On the way she had to ride through a stream flowing over the road. As she did so, one of her embroidered shoes fell into the water and sank beneath the surface. She was in such a hurry that she could not stop to search for it, so she wrapped the other shoe in her scarf and rode on.

Shortly afterwards, the king and his entourage, led by two elephants, arrived at the same spot. The elephants refused to enter the water and lowered their tusks, bellowing and trumpeting. When no amount of goading would force them on, the king ordered his followers to search the water. One of them found the embroidered shoe and brought it to the king, who inspected it closely.

Finally he said, "The girl who wore a shoe as beautiful as this must herself be very beautiful. Let us go on to the festival and find her. Whoever it fits will be my wife."

35 There was great excitement when all the women learned of the king's decision, and they eagerly waited for their turn to try on the shoe.

Cam and her mother struggled to make it fit, but to no avail, and when they saw Tam waiting patiently nearby the woman sneered at her. "How can someone as common as you be the owner of such a shoe? And where did you steal those fine clothes? Wait till we get home. If there isn't any rice to cook I am going to beat you severely."

Tam said nothing, but when it came her turn to try on the shoe it fitted perfectly. Then she showed the other one that was wrapped in the scarf, and everyone knew that she was the future queen.

The king ordered his servants to take Tam to the palace in a palanquin, and she rode off happily under the furious and jealous gazes of her stepsister and stepmother.

Tam was very happy living in the citadel with the king, but she never forgot her father. As the anniversary of his death came nearer she asked the king if she could return to her village to prepare the offering.

40 When Cam and her mother saw that Tam had returned, their jealous minds formed a wicked plan. "You must make an offering of betel to your father," said the stepmother. "That areca tree over there has the best nuts. You are a good climber, so you must go to the top of the tree and get some."

Tam climbed the tree and when she was at the top her stepmother took an axe and began to chop at the trunk. The tree shivered and shook and Tam cried out in alarm. "What is happening? Why is the tree shaking so?"

"There are a lot of ants here," called her stepmother. "I am chasing them away."

She continued to chop until the tree fell. Its crown, with Tam in it, toppled into a deep pond and the beautiful young woman was drowned. The wicked murderer gathered Tam's clothes, gave them to Cam, and led her to the citadel. She explained about the terrible "accident" to the king and offered Cam as a replacement wife. The king was very unhappy, but he said nothing.

When Tam died she was transformed into a *vang anh* bird. The bird flew back to the palace gardens and there she saw Cam washing the king's clothes near the well. She called out to her. "Those are my husband's clothes. Dry the clothes on the pole, not on the fence, lest they be torn."

45 Then she flew to the window of the king's room, singing as she went. The bird followed the king everywhere and he, who was missing Tam greatly, spoke to it, "Dear bird, dear bird, if you are my wife, please come to my sleeve."

The bird sat on the king's hand and then hopped onto his sleeve. The king loved the bird so much that he often forgot to eat or sleep, and he had a golden cage made for it. He attended to it day and night and completely ignored Cam.

Cam went to her mother and told her about the bird. The woman advised that she must kill it and eat it, and make up a story to tell the king. Cam waited until the king was absent, then she did, as her mother had instructed. She threw the feathers into the garden afterwards.

When the king returned he asked about the bird and Cam answered, "I had a great craving for bird meat so I had it for a meal." The king said nothing.

The feathers grew into a tree. Whenever the king sat beneath it the branches bent down and made a parasol to shade him. He ordered a hammock to be placed under the tree and every day he rested there.

50 Cam was not happy about this, and once again she sought her mother's counsel.

"You must cut down the tree in secret. Use the wood to make a loom and tell the king you will weave some cloth for him."

On a stormy day Cam had the tree felled and made into a loom. When the king asked her about it she said that the wind had blown it over, and that now she would weave cloth for him on the loom made from its timber. When she sat down at the loom it spoke to her, "Klick klack, klick klack, you took my husband. I will take your eyes."

The terrified Cam went to her mother and told her of the loom's words. "Burn the loom and take the ashes far away from the palace," she told her daughter.

Cam did as she was bidden and threw the ashes at the side of the road a great distance from the king's home. The ashes grew into a green *thi* tree, and when the season came it bore one piece of fruit, with a wonderful fragrance that could be smelled from far away.

55   An old woman, who sold drinking water at a nearby stall, was attracted by the scent and she stood beneath the tree. She looked at the fruit, opened her pocket and called longingly, "Dear *thi,* drop into my pocket. I will only smell you, never eat you."

The fruit fell into her pocket, and she loved and treasured it, keeping it in her room to look at and to smell its fragrance.

Each day, when the old woman went to her stall, a small figure stepped from the *thi* fruit and grew into the form of Tam. She cleaned the house, put things in order, cooked the rice and made soup out of vegetables from the garden. Then she became tiny again and went back inside the *thi* fruit.

The old woman was curious and decided to find out who was helping her. One morning she pretended to go to her stall and hid behind a tree near the back door. She watched through a crack and saw Tam emerge from the *thi* fruit and grow into a beautiful girl. The old woman was very happy and rushed into the house and embraced her. She tore apart the skin of the fruit and threw it away. Tam lived happily with the old woman and helped her with the housework every day. She also made cakes and prepared betel to sell on the stall.

One day the king left his citadel and rode through the countryside. When he came to the old woman's stall he saw that it was neat and clean, so he stopped. The old woman offered him water and betel, and when he accepted it he saw that the betel had been prepared to look like the wings of an eagle. He remembered that his wife had prepared betel exactly in this fashion.

60   "Who prepared this betel?" he asked.

"It was done by my daughter," replied the old woman.

"Where is your daughter? Let me see her."

The old woman called Tam. When she came the king recognized his beloved wife, looking even younger and more beautiful. The king was very happy, and as the old woman told him the story he sent his servants to bring a rich palanquin to carry his wife back to the citadel.

When Cam saw that Tam had returned she was most fearful. She did her best to ingratiate herself and asked her stepsister the secret of her great beauty.

65   "Do you wish to be very beautiful?" asked Tam. "Come, I will show you how." Tam had her servants dig a hole and prepare a large jar of boiling water. "If you want to be beautiful you must get into this hole," Tam told her wicked stepsister.

When Cam was in the hole Tam ordered the servants to pour in the boiling water, and so her stepsister met her death. Tam had the body made into *mam,* a rich sauce, and sent it to her stepmother, saying that it was a present from her daughter.

Each day the woman ate some of the *mam* with her meals, always commenting how delicious it was. A crow came to her house, perched on the roof ridge and cawed, "Delicious! The mother is eating her own daughter's flesh. Is there any left? Give me some."

The stepmother was very angry and chased the bird away, but, on the day when the jar of *mam* was nearly empty, she saw her daughter's skull and fell down dead.

RELATED WEB SITES

Women In Vietnamese Folklore
www.geocities.com/chtn_nhatrang/women.html
This paper by Cong Huyen Trang was presented for the panel discussion *Southeast Asian Women Then and Now: A View from the Folklore of the Philippines, Thailand, and Vietnam,* at the University of Hawaii at Manoa in 1992.

QUESTIONS FOR DISCUSSION

1. What aspects of each tale help you to identify it as a Cinderella story? What would you consider to be the minimum set of motifs or key details to qualify as a Cinderella variant? (Note that the "glass slipper" in the Perrault story came from a mistranslation of a common French word that actually means "fur.")

2. How do you feel about rereading the "Cendrillon" ("Cinderella") tale, which is so much like the Disney version, as an adult? Does the Cinderella story hold a different meaning for you today than it did when it was first told to you? Why or why not?

3. Contrast the tone and theme of the four versions of the story. What different attitudes toward nature and the material world are expressed in each tale?

4. Were you surprised or shocked by the violent and punitive endings of the Grimms' version and "Tam and Cam"? Do you think these versions are suitable for children? Why do you think the popular fairy tales that most parents today read to their children are less violent than some of the older tales? Is this a positive development?

5. Comment on the themes of alienation and class exploitation in the various versions of Cinderella and the endings for each. What set of social values is implied in each story?

6. Comment on the use of supernatural or spiritual values implicit in each version of the tale. How are these values typical of the culture that produced each story?

IDEAS FOR WRITING

1. Write an essay that discusses how the Cinderella story helps to shape values for young women. Do you consider this story in its classic version to be sexist, or do you think it still has relevant meanings to convey? Explain your response.

2. Do a close comparison of any two of the Cinderella versions. You can consider such issues as nature, materialism, class dominance, and feminism.

Anne Adele Levitsky

Classic Cinderella in Today's World

Anne Levitsky wrote the essay that follows for her first-year writing course. Anne is the musical director of an all-female A Cappella group on her campus and is in the University singers group. In high school, she participated in the Stanford Opera Society's production of "Hansel and Gretel." Her engagement with music and fairy tales inspired her response to the older Cinderella stories included in Dreams and Inward Journeys. *Feeling strongly that Disney had distorted and stripped away the values of the classic Cinderella, Levitsky expresses her point of view, including her changing personal reactions to Disney's Cinderella, in the from of an extended comparison between Parrault's Cinderella and Disney's.*

I grew up with the Disney Princesses. My first idols were cartoon heroines, all alike in their beauty and ability to snag the prince at the end. As a little girl, I watched *The Little Mermaid* repeatedly, drawn in by Ariel's flowing red hair and beautiful voice. It was only later I realized that

Disney's princesses were based on folklore and fairy tales from countries around the world and not simply the creations of screenwriters at Disney. As a four-year-old, I was enchanted by attractive young women who found happiness after overcoming disadvantages with seeming ease. Disney's verson of Cinderella led me to believe that all one needed for a happy life was to be pretty; then small animals and fairies would be the guides to finding the prince of one's dreams.

As I grew older, reading the glossy pages of teen magazines only reinforced the same ideals. While there were no talking animals, the message was the same: beauty, fashion, and a slender body would lead to a happy life. These magazines became my new fairy tales, and I studied the pages with their glamorous layouts and rail-thin models. Although the articles emphasized the importance of loving yourself and staying healthy, the contradictory pictures said everything the text did not. The message seemed clear: External beauty is more important than being yourself. External beauty is what gets a woman what she wants—a perfect prince charming.

This idea is not new to our modern society. Disney's Cinderella was transformed from the classic Cinderella fairytale, Charles Perrault's "Cendrillon" (or Cinderwench, as Perrault's stepsisters call her). Both Disney's and Perrault's Cinderellas are very beautiful and win the prince over at the ball with beauty. The prince in Perrault's classic tale does not remember the girl for her wit or personality (although one of Perrault's "morals" tacked on at the end of the story praises her for her "graciousness," while providing no concrete examples). In fact, although Cinderella dances with the prince very well, she is not shown actually speaking to him during the course of the evening, nor does she put her smarts to use in getting to the ball; instead she stays at home as she has been told to do. Her magic fairy grandmother does arrive just in time to dress her for the ball and arrange for her transportation, but it is reasonable to conclude that without a considerable push in the right direction, Cinderella would never have made it to the ball, met her prince, and/or lived happily ever after.

Some young women today might say, "What a drip. Really—If she can't even get her head together enough to do something about her ashy predicament, does she really deserve the hand of the prince? She does put up with a lot from her awful stepsisters and hellish stepmother, but couldn't all that criticism and endless work serve as motivation for her to get up and do something about it? It would definitely motivate me." In today's fast-paced world, Cinderella would lose out on the prince if she just sat around and waited. Another girl with more strength and spirit would sweep into the ball and steal the prince from Cinderella with her scintillating wit. While Perrault's and Disney's Cinderellas rely on their beauty and devotion, today's more daring girls often use their brains to come up with the solutions to their problems. Indeed, modern Cinderella stories abound in the news, detailing rags-to-riches stories that the classic Cinderellas would never dream of. Princes take the form of Olympic teams, college scholarships and record deals, and the girls who rise from firepits to chase them are as varied as their dreams.

5   Perhaps I am being too hard on Disney's Cinderella. After all, today's fairy tales are stories handed down through the centuries. Cinderella might not have felt able to speak out for herself, as today's girls can. Disney did little to change her story. Disney's Cinderella seems to have a more limited skills-set than Perrault's heroine, and she does not lift a finger to help herself succeed. However, in defense of Disney, the company's story book and films are made for a very young audience that would be likely to enjoy the use of comical singing and dancing animals in their cartoon films, and the magical rodents in the French fairy tale do lend themselves easily to Disney's screenplay. The colorful pictures and figures in Disney's film are crucial to creating the magic for Disney's child audience and in capturing the myth of "prince charming." Yet while Perrault and earlier storytellers describe Cinderella as "the most beautiful that mortal eyes have ever seen," they say nothing of her delicate size or slender waist. Disney's illustrators of storybooks and cartoonists have imprinted Cinderella with modern society's standard of beauty: a slim waistline, helping to perpetuate the societal pressure to be thin and beautiful. Teenage girls face enough scrutiny in the eye of fashion models and beauty magazines, and they do not need additional pressure from their childhood favorites.

To little girls, bedecked in glitter and fairy wings, Cinderella is more than just a fairytale character: she is a real person, a play companion, and a fast friend. As these girls grow, she becomes yet another slender model of beauty to aspire to. My friends and I have had many Disney movie marathons, often accompanied by the sigh, "Disney movies ruined real life for me." The magical worlds of story land are perfect places where lives end happily ever after, and they ruin our expectations of adult life with their magical events. Growing up with these tales makes young girls believe that they can live happily ever after if only they can attract "the prince," when in reality the modern world is nothing like Cinderella's storybook town.

Unlike Disney's fairytale, Perrault's "Cendrillon" does support some positive values because the heroine is "of unparalleled goodness and sweetness of temper," and takes after her mother, who was "the best creature in the world." Perrault augments Cinderella's superficial physical beauty with beauty and grace of soul, making her an inherently good human being as well as a lovely one. Perrault's tale becomes a story of the triumph of good over evil instead of simply promoting Cinderella's good looks in order to win the prince's affection.

However, this goodness is nowhere to be found in Disney's movie. Cinderella waltzes across the animated screen looking beautiful and thin, dancing right into the heart of the prince. The Disney film washes all the meaning from the Cinderella story and creates a shallow film with brightly colored people that will appeal to young audiences while making more sophisticated viewers shake their heads in disbelief. Perhaps Disney is attempting to simplify the story for young children, but in doing so all the redeeming qualities of the original fairy tale have been diluted past recognition; what is left of the story is a superficial shell, empty of any "graciousness" or real depth of character.

In contrast, the classic Cinderella tale comes from a tradition of moral values. Cinderella may be externally beautiful, but Perrault and other storytellers emphasize both the evil of the haughty stepmothers and the lazy step-sisters, as well as Cinderella's good fashion sense, gracious goodness of heart, and unblemished character as at least part of the solution to her problems. The beauty found in Perrault's tale is neither materialistic nor elitist. It is found within Cinderella, and she has complete control over the goodness of her heart. She receives help from her fairy godmother because she is an inherently good person, proving that good people do not need to channel evil to survive.

10   Cinderella's victory over her stepsisters helps to prove that good people can be independent of evil in the world. The stepsisters are vain and conceited, thinking only of themselves as they belittle and mock Cinderella. These women reflect the materialistic, external values present in Disney's movie as they preen and prepare for the prince's ball, making sure to wear the most elaborate clothing and hairstyles. The stepsisters appear as a Regan and Goneril to Cinderella's Cordelia, and they hide their inner selves to gain the love of the prince at the ball. Their vanity only highlights Cinderella's internal beauty, as she is still the most beautiful of the three girls even though she is dressed in rags and dirt. In the classic tales, external appearance does not matter nearly as much as do internal qualities. Disney has reversed this moral in its films, turning the Cinderella fairy tale into a shallow children's film. External beauty is the end for Disney, not just a part of the larger picture of her grace as it is for Perrault's heroine.

Although modern day Cinderellas seem helpless and too focused on their external beauty to fight their own battles, this is hardly true in the world of fairly tales. The classic Cinderella's inherent sense of right and wrong guides her along the path to her reward, ensuring that she discovers the way to true happiness. In today's depictions of Cinderella, the heroine flutters her eyelashes until someone comes to her aid, and external beauty wins the day. Disney's portrayal of a Cinderella without intelligence leads an audience of young girls to place less importance on their intellect and more importance on perfect hair, a side effect of Disney's materialistic, commercial goals.

The contrast to the Perrault story is unavoidable—the beauty found there comes from within and is not commercial or branded in any way. As with most oral traditions, the details of the Cinderella story have changed over time, but up until Perrault's rendition, the moral values remained essentially the same. Disney's modern version, while popular for its beautiful pictures and accessible storyline, has diluted the values and changed the essence of the fairy tale. The Disney Corporation has looked at its heroine through the perspective of a modern world, squeezing and pushing Cinderella to fit into a twentieth-century slipper, confusing little girls of today who aren't yet old enough to understand how they too are being squeezed and pushed into a tight slipper: a narrow and confining world view and self-image.

QUESTIONS FOR DISCUSSION

1. Did you have "Cinderella dreams" when you were a young girl? As a young boy how did you feel about "prince charming"?

2. Do you agree with feminists' criticism of the Disney version of Cinderella? Why or why not?

3. If you are or became a parent, would you be critical of Disney's popularity among young girls? How would you change the values and plot line of the Disney version of Cinderella and still keep the story magical?

4. Discuss Levitsky's use of comparison between the "classic Cinderella" of Charles Perrault and the modern Disney version. After reading the Perrault version included above, do you agree with the distinctions drawn between these two versions, or do they seem essentially the same? Explain your position.

Topics for Research and Writing

1. Write an essay that presents your own definition of a myth. Draw on your personal experiences and the readings in this chapter, as well as outside research into the nature of myths and mythology. Do some research into the differences between a myth and a fairy tale before drawing your final conclusions. Would you consider a fairy tale like Cinderella, a myth? Why or why not?

2. Write your own myth, based on your view of yourself as a hero or heroine. Then write an analysis of your myth, comparing the "ideal" self that emerges in the story you have written to your "real" self. How does your myth reflect the concerns of your generation and your own values? Make connections between your myth and the hero/heroine myths that you have read about in your research.

3. There are over 500 different versions of the Cinderella myth told in cultures around the world. Do some research to find several unique versions from particular cultures. Then write a comparison paper of two versions. What did you learn about the Cinderella story from studying each culture's tale? Which of the two versions do you prefer, and why? Have either of these myths or fairy tales helped to shape your identity?

4. Compare and contrast a traditional myth or tale with its modern retelling—perhaps in a popular culture format such as a TV show or comic book. Reflect on how and why the original myth or tale has been changed. Which of the two versions do you prefer, and why?

5. Write an essay that explores how several myths function in our culture. Select the myths that you know best. Support each myth with an example from your own life. Do some research to support your insights.

6. Many myths and fairy tales have been revised to acknowledge changing gender roles and values. Write a modern version of a traditional myth or fairy tale. If you wish, you can illustrate the tale. The illustrations will bring further meaning to your work.

7. See one of the following films that explores the role of myth. Analyze the aspects of the film that are connected to mythical qualities. Choose from the following list: *Excalibur, Black Orpheus, Star Wars* (any episode), *Ever After, The Lion King, Harry Potter* (any episode), *Lord of the Rings* (any episode), *Batman Begins, The Dark Knight, Spiderman, Pan's Labyrinth, O Brother, Where Art Thou?, A Cinderella Story, Troy,* and *300*.

Obsessions and Transformation 5

Vincent Van Gogh (1853–1890)
Starry Night (Saint-Remy, June 1889)

JOURNAL

Describe a place or setting, urban or rural, interior or exterior, trying to show how the mind can distort reality according to inner pressures and concerns.

*Yes indeed, I realized, looking into the mirror. There was a world in my eye.
And I saw that it was possible to love it: that in fact, for all it had taught
me of shame and anger and inner vision, I did love it.*
ALICE WALKER

*Even more than our experiences, our beliefs became our prisons. But we
carry our healing with us even into the darkest of our inner places.*
RACHEL NAOMI REMEN

*These dreams refuse to go quietly, for they mean to change us utterly. If we
look into their depths, we may behold a unique destiny struggling from its
chrysalis, and watch, astonished and not a little afraid, as our
unsuspected selfhood unfolds a new, wetly glistening wing.*
MARC IAN BARASCH

THEMATIC INTRODUCTION

Dreams and fantasies can be healthy; they can serve as a means
for escape from trivial or tedious routines and demands. Popular entertainment, for example, often provides us with simple es-
capist fantasies that encourage us to identify with an idealized hero
or heroine. We can become strong, beautiful, courageous, or very
wise, and, for a moment, we may be able to forget the realities of our
own lives. When our minds return from a fantasy, we may feel more
refreshed, more capable of handling daily responsibilities. Often
fantasies provide more than just possibilities of short-term escape;
they can also offer insights that will lead to deeper self-understanding
as well as psychological and/or spiritual transformation. Each individual has unique dreams and fantasies. When these messages from
our unconscious minds and from our dream worlds are understood
and interpreted, they can help us have more fulfilling and rewarding lives.

Some people suffer from personal obsessions and compulsions
that can lead to behavior that can be limiting, repetitive, and sometimes even destructive to self or others. In such cases, the obsession
controls the individual rather than the individual controlling the
goal. Why do some people become possessed by their fantasies and
obsessions, whereas others can maintain their psychological equilibrium and learn about themselves through their preoccupations,
their unconscious dreams? How do people's unconscious obsessions
influence their day-to-day life and decision-making processes? The

essays, story, and poem included in this chapter provide you with a range of perspectives that will help you consider these and other issues related to how our inner lives, our unconscious, our dreams, nightmares, fantasies, and obsessions have a impact on political and social life.

In this chapter's first selection, "Fog-Horn" by W. S. Merwin, the poem's speaker reflects on the power of a forgotten, unconscious world of feelings that, if heeded, can serve as a valuable warning for people. Addictions are closely related to depression, which, as Andrew Solomon notes in his essay "Depression," if left untreated can lead to the decay of the inner self.

The next selections show how depressive frames of mind can be lived through and result in a transformation of personality. In her essay about a troubled patient, "Remembering," therapist Naomi Remen points out how crippling obsessions and depression born of childhood trauma can be eased by retelling stories of shame and through sharing positive dreams that allow sufferers to get in touch with hope and a new outlook on their lives. In her powerful personal essay, "Hunger," Anne Lamott reveals how she transformed her addiction to alcohol and bulimia through learning to value herself and her own sensory world. In contrast, in their essays, student writers Lexie Spiranac ("Working it Out") and Sharon Slayton ("The Good Girl") write of how obsessions with being competitive, well-behaved, and "perfect" led them to focus so much energy on being "good" that it caused them to reject their own inner needs for many years.

The last three professional selections examine holistic approaches to physical and psychological healing. Maressa Orzack's "Computer Addiction" reveals the way failure to stay in touch with our inner worlds can lead us into the repetitive, limiting behavior of addiction to technological modes of experience, while Carrie Demer's "Chaos or Calm" reveals ways that meditation, yogic breathing, and other relaxation techniques can improve health and reduce the stress of hectic modern life. In our final selection, "What Is a Healing Dream?" Jungian analyst Marc Ian Barasch defines a healing dream while giving many examples of how individuals have used their dreams to enrich and improve their sense of physical and mental well-being.

The works in this chapter ask readers to look within, to listen to the questions and fears in their hearts and spirits. Through reading and reflecting on the selections in this chapter, we hope that you can recognize obsessive types of behavior and at the same time realize that they can be potential sources of creative inspiration, transformation, and love.

DEFINITION: WORD BOUNDARIES OF THE SELF

Definition involves clarifying a term's meaning through precise use of language and through distinguishing among several words that may be difficult to use appropriately because they have similar or overlapping meanings. Definitions, both short and expanded, can be used not only as a way of clarifying the denotative or dictionary meanings of the crucial words and abstract terminology that you use in your writing but also as a way of exploring personal definitions of terms based on feelings, values, and language.

Public Meanings and Formal Definition

In essay writing, definition is most often used as a method for clarifying meaning for your readers. If, for example, you are writing an essay on obsessions, you would first want to define what is meant by "obsession." Although you would first turn to a dictionary, an encyclopedia, or another reliable authority for a definition of this basic term, you would also need to use your own words to create your statement of meaning. Your own words will help you to develop control over the direction of your paper and capture your reader's interest. Begin by placing the term within a formal pattern. First, state the word you will be defining—in this case, "obsession"—then put the term in a larger class or group: "An obsession is a strong emotional response." Next, you will need one or more details or qualifying phrases to distinguish your term from others in the larger group of strong emotions: "An obsession is an emotional response or preoccupation that is compulsive and highly repetitive, a response over which a person often has little or no control and that can have destructive consequences." If this definition still seems inadequate, you could add more details and develop the definition further with a typical example: "Overeating can be an obsessive form of behavior."

In writing an extended definition of a key term, carefully construct the initial definition. If you place the term in too large a class, fail to distinguish it from others in the class, or merely repeat your original term or a form of the term, you will have difficulty developing your ideas clearly and will confuse your reader. You also need to decide how you plan to use your definition: what will its purpose be?

Once you have created the initial definition, you can proceed to develop your paragraph or essay using other analytical writing strategies such as process analysis, discussion of cause and effect, or comparative relationships. For example, you could discuss several of the qualities of a typical obsession, provide an ordered exploration of the stages of the obsession, or examine the kinds of human growth and interactions with which the obsession can interfere, as Sharon Slayton does in her essay on the obsession with being good. For clarity, reader interest, and essay development, examples and illustrations can be used effectively with any of the larger analytical structures that you might wish to take advantage of in your essay: examples from personal experience, friends, or your reading of fictional or factual sources.

Stipulative and Personal Definitions

Sometimes writers decide to develop a personal definition. This form of definition, referred to as a "stipulative definition," is based on the writer's personal ideals and values. In this case, you still need to be clear in making crucial distinctions. For example, if you are writing a paper on your own personal dream, you might begin with a dictionary definition of "dream" to contrast the qualities of your personal dream to the traditional connotations associated with the term as stated in the dictionary.

Freewriting and clustering will help you define what the term means to you and discover the term's deeper personal levels of meaning. Comparative thinking can also be useful. Write a series of sentences beginning with the words "My dream is . . ." or "My dream is like . . ." and make as many different associations with concrete objects or events as you can. Examine the associations you have made and construct a personal definition qualified with expressions such as "my," "to me," or "in my opinion," and include several personal distinguishing qualities.

A stipulative definition is often supported by personal experiences that help the reader understand the origins and basis of your views. Provide contrasts with qualities that others may associate with the term. For example, other people may believe that a dream as you have defined it is just "wishful thinking," an exercise in escapism. You could argue that, to the contrary, it is necessary to have a dream as a high ideal or aspiration; otherwise, one may too readily accept a version of reality that is less than what it could be and lose faith in the imagination that is necessary to solve problems and to move confidently into the future. Thus a stipulative definition can become a type of argument, an advocacy of one's perspective on life.

Contradiction

In developing your definition, be careful not to create contradictions. Contradiction or equivocation occurs when you define a term in one way and then shift the definition to another level of meaning. To base an argument intentionally on a contradiction is at best confusing and at worst dishonest and propagandistic. For example, if you begin your paper with a definition of "myth" as the cultural and social stories that bind a people together and then shift to a discussion of private dreams and personal mythology, you will confuse your reader by violating the logic of your definition, and your essay will lose much of its credibility. A better strategy for dealing with the real complexity of certain words is to concede from the start (in your thesis) that this is an expression with seemingly contradictory or ironic shades of meaning—as in the case of the word "good" in Slayton's essay in this chapter—and then spell out the complexity clearly in your definition. Read your paper carefully before turning it in, checking to see that your definition and your arguments and examples are consistent. If not, your paper needs a revision, and you may want to modify your initial definition statement.

Writing objective and personal definitions will help you clarify your thoughts, feelings, and values. As you work to find the qualities, distinctions, and personal experiences that give a complex concept a meaning that reflects your inner self as well as the consensus of the public world, you will also be moving forward on your inward journey.

W. S. Merwin

Fog-Horn

W. S. Merwin (b. 1927) was raised in Pennsylvania. After graduating from Princeton University in 1947, he lived for several years in London, translating French and Spanish classics for the British Broadcasting Corporation (BBC). Merwin, who has published many collections of poems and translations, explores myths, cultural contrasts, and ecology. His style is often discontinuous and mysterious—wavering between waking and sleeping states and creating a dialogue between the conscious and the unconscious mind. Merwin's writing often creates strong emotional responses. His books include Opening the Hand *(1983),* The Vixen *(1996),* The River Sound Poems *(2000), and* The Pupil *(2001). His recent essays appear in* Ends of the Earth: Essays *(2005). The poem "Fog-Horn" was included in Merwin's* The Drunk in the Furnace *(1958). As you read the poem, try to re-create the sound and image of the foghorn in your own imagination.*

JOURNAL

Write about a warning that came to you from your unconscious, a warning that might have taken the form of a dream, a fantasy, a minor accident, or a psychosomatic illness.

Surely that moan is not the thing
That men thought they were making, when they
Put it there, for their own necessities.
That throat does not call to anything human
5   But to something men had forgotten,
That stirs under fog. Who wounded that beast
Incurably, or from whose pasture
Was it lost, full grown, and time closed round it
With no way back? Who tethered its tongue
10 So that its voice could never come
To speak out in the light of clear day,
But only when the shifting blindness
Descends and is acknowledged among us,
As though from under a floor it is heard,
15 Or as though from behind a wall, always
Nearer than we had remembered? If it
Was we that gave tongue to this cry
What does it bespeak in us, repeating
And repeating, insisting on something
20 That we never meant? We only put it there
To give warning of something we dare not
Ignore, lest we should come upon it
Too suddenly, recognize it too late,
As our cries were swallowed up and all hands lost.

QUESTIONS FOR DISCUSSION

1. How does Merwin personify the foghorn, making it more than just an object? Refer to specific details that you think are particularly effective.
2. What does the cry of the foghorn signify? What is its warning?
3. What words, images, and phrases make the poem seem like a dream or a nightmare?
4. Why can't the voice of the foghorn "speak out in the light of clear day"?
5. Why does the voice of the foghorn call to something "forgotten"? What parts of ourselves are we most likely to forget or ignore? What helps us to remember what we want to forget?
6. What is your interpretation of the poem? What state of mind is the poet attempting to define?

Compare and contrast the symbolism of the foghorn in Merwin's poem with the symbolism of the eagle's talons in Lamott's "Hunger" (see page 252).

IDEAS FOR WRITING

1. Write an essay in which you define and clarify with examples and comparisons the positive role that you think the unconscious mind can play in helping one to create a balanced and fulfilling life. Refer to the poem in shaping your response.
2. Write a narrative or a poem in which you use an object or an animal as a comparison to or as a way of defining and understanding the unconscious mind. Try to emphasize how the unconscious mind communicates with the conscious mind.

RELATED WEB SITES

W. S. Merwin
`www.poets.org/poet.php/prmPID/123`
Learn more about the American poet W. S. Merwin at the Web site for The Academy of American Poets. Find related poetry, related prose, and translations by Merwin.

The Unconscious in Clinical Psychology
`www.guidetopsychology.com/ucs.htm`
This thorough Web site on psychological terms, issues, and problems gives a brief history of the idea of the unconscious mind and links to other sites and articles on the subject.

Andrew Solomon

Depression

Andrew Solomon was born in 1963. He grew up in New York and received a B.A. from Yale University as well as a B.A. and M.A. from Cambridge University. He has written for the New Yorker, Art Forum, *and the* New York Times Magazine. *His books include* The Irony Tower: Soviet Artists in a Time of Glasnost *(1991) and the novel* A Stone Boat *(1994). The following selection is drawn from his recent work,* The Noonday Demon: An Atlas of Depression *(2001).*

Write about a time when you felt "down" or mildly depressed. Describe your feelings and how you coped with them.

Depression is the flaw in love. To be creatures who love, we must be creatures who can despair at what we lose, and depression is the mechanism of that despair. When it comes, it degrades one's self and ultimately eclipses the capacity to give or receive affection. It is the aloneness within us made manifest, and it destroys not only connection to others but also the ability to be peacefully alone with oneself. Love, though it is no prophylactic against depression, is what cushions the mind and protects it from itself. Medications and psychotherapy can renew that protection, making it easier to love and be loved, and that is why they work. In good spirits, some love themselves and some love others and some love work and some love God: any of these passions can furnish that vital sense of purpose that is the opposite of depression. Love forsakes us from time to time, and we forsake love. In depression, the meaninglessness of every enterprise and every emotion, the meaninglessness of life itself, becomes self-evident. The only feeling left in this loveless state is insignificance.

Life is fraught with sorrows: no matter what we do, we will in the end die; we are, each of us, held in the solitude of an autonomous body; time passes, and what has been will never be again. Pain is the first experience of world-helplessness, and it never leaves us. We are angry about being ripped from the comfortable womb, and as soon as that anger fades, distress comes to take its place. Even those people whose faith promises them that this will all be different in the next world cannot help experiencing anguish in this one; Christ himself was the man of sorrows. We live, however, in a time of increasing palliatives; it is easier than ever to decide what to feel and what not to feel. There is less and less unpleasantness that is unavoidable in life, for those with the means to avoid. But despite the enthusiastic claims of pharmaceutical science, depression cannot be wiped out so long as we are creatures conscious of our own selves. It can at best be contained—and containing is all that current treatments for depression aim to do.

Highly politicized rhetoric has blurred the distinction between depression and its consequences—the distinction between how you feel and how you act in response. This is in part a social and medical phenomenon, but it is also the result of linguistic vagary attached to emotional vagary. Perhaps depression can best be described as emotional pain that forces itself on us against our will, and then breaks free of its externals. Depression is not just a lot of pain; but too much pain can compost itself into depression. Grief is depression in proportion to circumstance; depression is grief out of proportion to circumstance. It is tumbleweed distress that thrives on thin air, growing despite its detachment from the nourishing earth. It can be described only in metaphor and allegory. Saint Anthony in the desert, asked how he could differentiate between angels who came to him humble and devils who came in rich disguise, said you could tell by how you felt after they had departed. When an angel left you, you felt strengthened by his presence; when a devil left, you felt horror. Grief is a humble angel who leaves you with strong, clear thoughts and a sense of your own depth. Depression is a demon who leaves you appalled.

Depression has been roughly divided into small (mild or disthymic) and large (major) depression. Mild depression is a gradual and sometimes permanent thing that undermines people the way rust weakens iron. It is too much grief at too slight a cause, pain that takes over from the other emotions and crowds them out. Such depression takes up bodily occupancy in the eyelids and in the muscles that keep the spine erect. It hurts your heart and lungs, making the contraction of involuntary muscles harder than it needs to be. Like physical pain that becomes chronic, it is miserable not so much because it is intolerable in the moment as because it is intolerable to have known it in the moments gone and to look forward only to knowing it in the moments to come. The present tense of mild depression envisages no alleviation because it feels like knowledge.

5   Virginia Woolf has written about this state with an eerie clarity: "Jacob went to the window and stood with his hands in his pockets. There he saw three Greeks in kilts; the masts of ships; idle or busy people of the lower classes strolling or stepping out briskly, or falling into groups and gesticulating with their hands. Their lack of concern for him was not the cause of his gloom; but some more profound conviction—it was not that he himself happened to be lonely, but that all people are." In the same book, *Jacob's Room,* she describes how "There rose in her mind a curious sadness, as if time and eternity showed through skirts and waistcoats, and she saw people passing tragically to destruction. Yet, heaven knows, Julia was no fool." It is this acute awareness of transience and limitation that constitutes mild depression. Mild depression, for many years simply accommodated, is increasingly subject to treatment as doctors scrabble to address its diversity.

Large depression is the stuff of breakdowns. If one imagines a soul of iron that weathers with grief and rusts with mild depression, then major depression is the startling collapse of a whole structure. There are two models for depression: the dimensional and the categorical. The dimensional posits that depression sits on a continuum with sadness and represents an extreme version of something everyone has felt and known. The categorical describes depression as an illness totally separate from other emotions, much as a stomach virus is totally different from acid indigestion. Both are true. You go along the gradual path or the sudden trigger of emotion and then you get to a place that is genuinely different. It takes time for a rusting iron-framed building to collapse, but the rust is ceaselessly powdering the solid, thinning it, eviscerating it. The collapse, no matter how abrupt it may feel, is the cumulative consequence of decay. It is nonetheless a highly dramatic and visibly different event. It is a long time from the first rain to the point when rust has eaten through an iron girder. Sometimes the rusting is at such key points that the collapse seems total, but more often it is partial: this section collapses, knocks that section, shifts the balances in a dramatic way.

It is not pleasant to experience decay, to find yourself exposed to the ravages of an almost daily rain, and to know that you are turning into something feeble, that more and more of you will blow off with the first strong wind, making you less and less. Some people accumulate more emotional rust than others. Depression starts out insipid, fogs the days into a dull color, weakens ordinary actions until their clear shapes are obscured by the effort they require, leaves you tired and bored and self-obsessed—but you can get through all that. Not happily, perhaps, but you can get through. No one has ever been able to define the collapse point that marks major depression, but when you get there, there's not much mistaking it.

Major depression is a birth and a death: it is both the new presence of something and the total disappearance of something. Birth and death are gradual, though official documents may try to pinion natural law by creating categories such as "legally dead" and "time born." Despite nature's vagaries, there is definitely a point at which a baby who has not been in the world is in it, and a point at which a pensioner who has been in the world is no longer in it. It's true that at one stage the baby's head is here and his body not; that until the umbilical cord is severed the child is physically connected to the mother. It's true that the pensioner may close his eyes for the last time some hours before he dies, and that there is a gap between when he stops breathing and when he is declared "brain-dead." Depression exists in time. A patient may say that he has spent certain months suffering major depression, but this is a way of imposing a measurement on the immeasurable. All that one can really say for certain is that one has known major depression, and that one does or does not happen to be experiencing it at any given present moment.

The birth and death that constitute depression occur at once. I returned, not long ago, to a wood in which I had played as a child and saw an oak, a hundred years dignified, in whose shade I used to play with my brother. In twenty years, a huge vine had attached itself to this confident tree and had nearly smothered it. It was hard to say where the tree left off and the vine began. The vine had twisted itself so entirely around the scaffolding of tree branches that its leaves seemed from a distance to be the leaves of the tree; only up close could you see how few living oak branches were left, and how a few desperate little budding sticks of oak stuck like a row of thumbs up the massive trunk, their leaves continuing to photosynthesize in the ignorant way of mechanical biology.

10   Fresh from a major depression in which I had hardly been able to take on board the idea of other people's problems, I empathized with that tree. My depression had grown on me as that vine had conquered the oak; it had been a sucking thing that had wrapped itself around me, ugly and more alive than I. It had had a life of its own that bit by bit asphyxiated all of my life out of me. At the worst stage of major depression, I had moods that I knew were not my moods: they belonged to the depression, as surely as the leaves on that tree's high branches belonged to the vine. When I tried to think clearly about this, I felt that my mind was immured, that it couldn't expand in any direction. I knew that the sun was rising and setting, but little of its light reached me. I felt myself sagging under what was much stronger than I; first I could not use my ankles, and then I could not control my knees, and then my waist began to break under the strain, and then my shoulders turned in, and in the end I was compacted and fetal, depleted by this thing that was crushing me without holding me. Its tendrils threatened to pulverize my mind and my courage and my stomach, and crack my bones and desiccate my body. It went on glutting itself on me when there seemed nothing left to feed it.

I was not strong enough to stop breathing. I knew then that I could never kill this vine of depression, and so all I wanted was for it to let me die. But it had taken from me the energy I would have needed to kill myself, and it would not kill me. If my trunk was rotting, this thing that fed on it was now too strong to let it fall; it had become an alternative support to what it had destroyed. In the tightest corner of my bed, split and racked by this thing no one else seemed to be able to see, I prayed to a God I had never entirely believed in, and I asked for deliverance. I would have been happy to die the most painful death, though I was too dumbly lethargic even to conceptualize suicide. Every second of being alive hurt me. Because this thing had drained all fluid from me, I could not even cry. My mouth was parched as well. I had thought that when you feel your worst your tears flood, but the very worst pain is the arid pain of total violation that comes after the tears are all used up, the pain that stops up every space through which you once metered the world, or the world, you. This is the presence of major depression.

I have said that depression is both a birth and a death. The vine is what is born. The death is one's own decay, the cracking of the branches that support this misery. The first thing that goes is happiness. You cannot gain pleasure from anything. That's famously the cardinal symptom of major depression. But soon other emotions follow happiness into oblivion: sadness as you had known it, the sadness that seemed to have led you here; your sense of humor; your belief in and capacity for love. Your mind is leached until you seem dim-witted even to yourself. If your hair has always been thin, it seems thinner; if you have always had bad skin, it gets worse. You smell sour even to yourself. You lose the ability to trust anyone, to be touched, to grieve. Eventually, you are simply absent from yourself.

Maybe what is present usurps what becomes absent, and maybe the absence of obfuscatory things reveals what is present. Either way, you are less than yourself and in the clutches of something alien. Too often, treatments address only half the problem: they focus only on the presence or only on the absence. It is necessary both to cut away that extra thousand pounds of the vines and to relearn a root system and the techniques of photosynthesis. Drug therapy hacks through the vines. You can feel it happening, how the medication seems to be poisoning the parasite so that bit by bit it withers away. You feel the weight going, feel the way that the branches can recover much of their natural bent. Until you have got rid of the vine, you cannot think about what has been lost. But even with the vine gone, you may still have few leaves and shallow roots, and the rebuilding of your self cannot be achieved with any drugs that now exist. With the weight of the vine gone, little leaves scattered along the tree skeleton become viable for essential nourishment. But this is not a good way to be. It is not a strong way to be. Rebuilding of the self in and after depression requires love, insight, work, and, most of all, time.

Diagnosis is as complex as the illness. Patients ask doctors all the time, "Am I depressed?" as though the result were in a definitive blood test. The only way to find out whether you're depressed is to listen to and watch yourself, to feel your feelings and then think about them. If you feel bad without reason most of the time, you're depressed. If you feel bad most of the time with reason, you're also depressed, though changing the reasons may be a better way forward than leaving circumstance alone and attacking the depression. If the depression is disabling to you, then it's major. If it's only mildly distracting, it's not major. Psychiatry's bible—the *Diagnostic and Statistical Manual,* fourth edition *(DSM-IV)*—ineptly defines depression as the presence of five or more on a list of nine symptoms. The problem with the definition is that it's entirely arbitrary. There's no particular reason to qualify five symptoms as constituting depression; four symptoms are more or less depression; and five symptoms are less severe than six. Even one symptom is unpleasant. Having slight versions of all the symptoms may be less of a problem than having severe versions of two symptoms. After enduring diagnosis, most people seek causation, despite the fact that knowing why you are sick has no immediate bearing on treating the sickness.

15　　　　Illness of the mind is real illness. It can have severe effects on the body. People who show up at the offices of their doctors complaining about stomach cramps are frequently told, "Why, there's nothing wrong with you except that you're depressed!" Depression, if it is sufficiently severe to cause stomach cramps, is actually a really bad thing to have wrong with you, and it requires treatment. If you show up complaining that your breathing is troubled, no one says to you, "Why, there's nothing wrong with you except that you have emphysema!" To the person who is experiencing them, psychosomatic complaints are as real as the stomach cramps of someone with food poisoning. They exist in the unconscious brain, and often enough the brain is sending inappropriate messages to the stomach, so they exist there as well. The diagnosis—whether something is rotten in your stomach or your appendix or your brain—matters in determining treatment and is not trivial. As organs go, the brain is quite an important one, and its malfunctions should be addressed accordingly.

Chemistry is often called on to heal the rift between body and soul. The relief people express when a doctor says their depression is "chemical" is predicated on a belief that there is an integral self that exists across time, and on a fictional divide between the fully occasioned sorrow and the utterly random one. The word *chemical* seems to assuage the feelings of responsibility people have for the stressed-out discontent of not liking their jobs, worrying about getting old, failing at love, hating their families. There is a pleasant freedom from guilt that has been attached to *chemical.* If your brain is predisposed to depression, you need not blame yourself for it. Well, blame yourself or evolution, but remember that blame itself can be understood as a chemical process, and that happiness, too, is chemical. Chemistry and biology are not matters that impinge on the "real" self; depression cannot be separated from the person it affects. Treatment does not alleviate a disruption of identity, bringing you back to some kind of normality; it readjusts a multifarious identity, changing in some small degree who you are.

Anyone who has taken high school science classes knows that human beings are made of chemicals and that the study of those chemicals and the structures in which they are configured is called biology. Everything that happens in the brain has chemical manifestations and sources. If you close your eyes and think hard about polar bears, that has a chemical effect on your brain. If you stick to a policy of opposing tax breaks for capital gains, that has a chemical effect on your brain. When you remember some episode from your past, you do so through the complex chemistry of memory. Childhood trauma and subsequent difficulty can alter brain chemistry. Thousands of chemical reactions are involved in deciding to read this book, picking it up with your hands, looking at the shapes of the letters on the page, extracting meaning from those shapes, and having intellectual and emotional responses to what they convey. If time lets you cycle out of a depression and feel better, the chemical changes are no less particular and complex than the ones that are brought about by taking antidepressants. The external determines the internal as much as the internal invents the external. What is so unattractive is the idea that in addition to all other lines being blurred, the boundaries of what makes us ourselves are blurry. There is no essential self that lies pure as a vein of gold under the chaos of experience and chemistry. Anything can be changed, and we must understand the human organism as a sequence of selves that succumb to or choose one another. And yet the language of science, used in training doctors and, increasingly, in nonacademic writing and conversation, is strangely perverse.

The cumulative results of the brain's chemical effects are not well understood. In the 1989 edition of the standard *Comprehensive Textbook of Psychiatry*, for example, one finds this helpful formula: a depression score is equivalent to the level of 3-methoxy-4-hydroxyphenylglycol (a compound found in the urine of all people and not apparently affected by depression); minus the level of 3-methoxy-4-hydroxymandelic acid; plus the level of norepinephrine; minus the level of normetanephrine plus the level of metanepherine, the sum of those divided by the level of 3-methoxy-4-hydroxymandelic acid; plus an unspecified conversion variable; or, as *CTP* puts it: "D-type score = C_1 (MHPG) − C_2 (VMA) + C_3 (NE) − C_4 (NMN + MN)/VMA + C_0." The score should come out between one for unipolar and zero for bipolar patients, so if you come up with something else—you're doing it wrong. How much insight can such formulae offer? How can they *possibly* apply to something as nebulous as mood? To what extent specific experience has conduced to a particular depression is hard to determine; nor can we explain through what chemistry a person comes to respond to external circumstance with depression; nor can we work out what makes someone essentially depressive.

Although depression is described by the popular press and the pharmaceutical industry as though it were a single-effect illness such as diabetes, it is not. Indeed, it is strikingly dissimilar to diabetes. Diabetics produce insufficient insulin, and diabetes is treated by increasing and stabilizing insulin in the bloodstream. Depression is *not* the consequence of a reduced level of anything we can now measure. Raising levels of serotonin in the brain triggers a process that eventually helps many depressed people to feel better, but that is *not* because they have abnormally low levels of serotonin. Furthermore, serotonin does *not* have immediate salutary effects. You could pump a gallon of serotonin into the brain of a depressed person and it would not in the instant make him feel one iota better, though a long-term sustained raise in serotonin level has some effects that ameliorate depressive symptoms. "I'm depressed but it's just chemical" is a sentence equivalent to "I'm murderous but it's just chemical" or "I'm intelligent but it's just chemical." Everything about a person is just chemical if one wants to think in those terms. "You can say it's 'just chemistry,'" says Maggie Robbins, who suffers from manic-depressive illness. "I say there's nothing 'just' about chemistry." The sun shines brightly and that's just chemical too, and it's chemical that rocks are hard, and that the sea is salt, and that certain springtime afternoons carry in their gentle breezes a quality of nostalgia that stirs the heart to longings and imaginings kept dormant by the snows of a long winter. "This serotonin thing," says David McDowell of Columbia University, "is part of modern neuromythology." It's a potent set of stories.

20   Internal and external reality exist on a continuum. What happens and how you understand it to have happened and how you respond to its happening are usually linked, but no one is predictive of the others. If reality itself is often a relative thing, and the self is in a state of permanent flux, the passage from slight mood to extreme mood is a glissando. Illness, then, is an extreme state of emotion, and one might reasonably describe emotion as a mild form of illness. If we all felt up and great (but not delusionally manic) all the time, we could get more done and might have a happier time on earth, but that idea is creepy and terrifying (though, of course, if we felt up and great all the time we might forget all about creepiness and terror).

Influenza is straightforward: one day you do not have the responsible virus in your system, and another day you do. HIV passes from one person to another in a definable isolated split second. Depression? It's like trying to come up with clinical parameters for hunger, which affects us all several times a day, but which in its extreme version is a tragedy that kills its victims. Some people need more food than others; some can function under circumstances of dire malnutrition; some grow weak rapidly and collapse in the streets. Similarly, depression hits different people in different ways: some are predisposed to resist or battle through it, while others are helpless in its grip. Willfulness and pride may allow one person to get through a depression that would fell another whose personality is more gentle and acquiescent.

Depression interacts with personality. Some people are brave in the face of depression (during it and afterward) and some are weak. Since personality too has a random edge and a bewildering chemistry, one can write everything off to genetics, but that is too easy. "There is no such thing as a mood gene," says Steven Hyman, director of the National Institute of Mental Health. "It's just shorthand for very complex gene-environment interactions." If everyone has the capacity for some measure of depression under some circumstances, everyone also has the capacity to fight depression to some degree under some circumstances. Often, the fight takes the form of seeking out the treatments that will be most effective in the battle. It involves finding help while you are still strong enough to do so. It involves making the most of the life you have between your most severe episodes. Some horrendously symptom-ridden people are able to achieve real success in life; and some people are utterly destroyed by the mildest forms of the illness.

Working through a mild depression without medications has certain advantages. It gives you the sense that you can correct your own chemical imbalances through the exercise of your own chemical will. Learning to walk across hot coals is also a triumph of the brain over what appears to be the inevitable physical chemistry of pain, and it is a thrilling way to discover the sheer power of mind. Getting through a depression "on your own" allows you to avoid the social discomfort associated with psychiatric medications. It suggests that we are accepting ourselves as we were made, reconstructing ourselves only with our own interior mechanics and without help from the outside. Returning from distress by gradual degrees gives sense to affliction itself.

Interior mechanics, however, are difficult to commission and are frequently inadequate. Depression frequently destroys the power of mind over mood. Sometimes the complex chemistry of sorrow kicks in because you've lost someone you love, and the chemistry of loss and love may lead to the chemistry of depression. The chemistry of falling in love can kick in for obvious external reasons, or along lines that the heart can never tell the mind. If we wanted to treat this madness of emotion, we could perhaps do so. It is mad for adolescents to rage at parents who have done their best, but it is a conventional madness, uniform enough so that we tolerate it relatively unquestioningly. Sometimes the same chemistry kicks in for external reasons that are not sufficient, by mainstream standards, to explain the despair: someone bumps into you in a crowded bus and you want to cry, or you read about world overpopulation and find your own life intolerable. Everyone has on occasion felt disproportionate emotion over a small matter or has felt emotions whose origin is obscure or that may have no origin at all. Sometimes the chemistry kicks in for no apparent external reason at all. Most people have had moments of inexplicable despair, often in the middle of the night or in the early morning before the alarm clock sounds. If such feelings last ten minutes, they're a strange, quick mood. If they last ten hours, they're a disturbing febrility, and if they last ten years, they're a crippling illness.

25   It is too often the quality of happiness that you feel at every moment its fragility, while depression seems when you are in it to be a state that will never pass. Even if you accept that moods change, that whatever you feel today will be different tomorrow, you cannot relax into happiness as you can into sadness. For me, sadness always has been and still is a more powerful feeling; and if that is not a universal experience, perhaps it is the base from which depression grows. I hated being depressed, but it was also in depression that I learned my own acreage, the full extent of my

soul. When I am happy, I feel slightly distracted by happiness, as though it fails to use some part of my mind and brain that wants the exercise. Depression is something to do. My grasp tightens and becomes acute in moments of loss: I can see the beauty of glass objects fully at the moment when they slip from my hand toward the floor. "We find pleasure much less pleasurable, pain much more painful than we had anticipated," Schopenhauer wrote. "We require at all times a certain quantity of care or sorrow or want, as a ship requires ballast, to keep on a straight course."

There is a Russian expression: if you wake up feeling no pain, you know you're dead. While life is not only about pain, the experience of pain, which is particular in its intensity, is one of the surest signs of the life force. Schopenhauer said, "Imagine this race transported to a Utopia where everything grows of its own accord and turkeys fly around ready-roasted, where lovers find one another without any delay and keep one another without any difficulty: in such a place some men would die of boredom or hang themselves, some would fight and kill one another, and thus they would create for themselves more suffering than nature inflicts on them as it is . . . the polar opposite of suffering [is] boredom." I believe that pain needs to be transformed but not forgotten; gainsaid but not obliterated.

Questions for Discussion

1. Solomon begins his definition of depression by claiming, "Depression is the flaw in love." What does he mean by this compelling statement, and how does he develop it further in his opening paragraphs?

2. In his third paragraph, Solomon contrasts grief with depression. What distinction does he draw, and how does this help to clarify his definition of depression?

3. How does Solomon contrast mild and major depression? How does his example from Virginia Woolf's *Jacob's Room* help to clarify the point he is making about mild depression? Could you clarify his point in another way?

4. How does Solomon use rust as a metaphor to explain how major depression can overcome an individual? Is his metaphor effective? Explain your response.

5. How does Solomon use his personal observation of an oak tree choked by a vine to explain both depression's process and its cure through drug therapy?

6. Solomon has a complex opinion of the value of chemical therapy in treating depression. How does he explain its benefits, its limitations, and its misapplications?

7. According to Solomon, what valuable insights can grow out of depression? How do the quotations he uses from Schopenhauer help to reinforce his point at the end of the essay?

CONNECTION

Compare Solomon's and Remen's views of the therapy for the treatment of depression (see page 248).

IDEAS FOR WRITING

1. Using a series of metaphors and comparisons as Solomon does in the first part of his essay, write a definition of depression or some other type of mental or physical illness that reflects obsessive behavior.
2. Write an essay arguing for or against the concept that Solomon presents at the end: pain and suffering are positive because they relieve complacency, help us to understand ourselves more deeply, and develop in us a stronger appreciation of beauty. According to Solomon, how is the struggle to get through a depression a form of transformation?

RELATED WEB SITES

Depression
`www.nimh.nih.gov/publicat/depression.cfm`
Information on symptoms, biochemical makeup, treatment, and other issues relating to depression will be found at this governmental URL. The site also offers information about medications for depression and who to contact for help or more facts on the subject.

Healing Depression
`www.upliftprogram.com/index.html`
This site, created by a psychologist and a psychotherapist, offers many resources and much useful information about clinical depression. Its purpose is to "help thousands of people to become happier and more optimistic and to heal from depression and anxiety."

Rachel Naomi Remen

Remembering

Nationally known for her leadership in the mind-body health movement, Rachel Naomi Remen, M.D., is the cofounder and medical director of the Commonweal Cancer Help Program in Bolinas, California. She is currently a clinical professor of family and community medicine at the University of California, San Francisco, School of Medicine. Her books include Humanistic Medicine *(1975),* The Human Patient *(1980),* Kitchen

Table Wisdom *(1996), and* My Grandfather's Blessings *(2000). In her private practice, she has worked as a psycho-oncologist for more than 20 years. Her particular blend of caring and wisdom has developed through her professional life as a physician and her experience of living with a chronic illness. In the following selection for* Kitchen Table Wisdom, *Remen reflects on the power of memory to shape identity and to heal.*

JOURNAL

Write about whether or not writing and talking about issues from your past helped you to put those memories behind you and forgive yourself.

What we do to survive is often different from what we may need to do in order to live. My work as a cancer therapist often means helping people to recognize the difference, to get off the treadmill of survival, and to refocus their lives. Of the many people who may have confronted this issue, one of the most dramatic was an Asian woman of remarkable beauty and style. Through our work together I realized that some things which can never be fixed can still heal.

She was about to begin a year of chemotherapy for ovarian cancer, but this is not what she talked about in our first meeting. She began our work together by telling me she was a "bad" person, hard, uncaring, self-ish, and unloving. She delivered this self-indictment with enormous poise and certainty. I watched the light play across her perfect skin and the polish of her long black hair and thought privately that I did not believe her. The people I had known who were truly selfish were rarely aware of it—they simply put themselves first without doubt or hesitation.

In a voice filled with shame, Ana began to tell me that she had no heart, and that her phenomenal success in business was a direct result of this ruthlessness. Most important, she felt that it was not possible for her to become well, as she had earned her cancer through her behavior. She questioned why she had come seeking help. There was a silence in which we took each other's measure. "Why not start from the beginning?" I said.

It took her more than eight months to tell her story. She had not been born here. She had come to this country at ten, as an orphan. She had been adopted by a good family, a family that knew little about her past. With their support she had built a life for herself.

5   In a voice I could barely hear, she began to speak of her experiences as a child in Vietnam during the war. She began with the death of her parents. She had been four years old the morning the Cong had come, small enough to hide in the wooden box that held the rice in the kitchen. The soldiers had not looked there after they had killed the others. When at last they had gone and she ventured from hiding

she had seen that her family had been beheaded. That was the beginning. I was horrified.

She continued on. It had been a time of brutality, a world without mercy. She was alone. She had starved. She had been brutalized. Hesitantly at first, and then with growing openness, she told story after story. She had become one of a pack of homeless children. She had stolen, she had betrayed, she had hated, she had helped kill. She had seen things beyond human endurance, done things beyond imagination. Like a spore, she had become what was needed to survive.

As the weeks went by, there was little I could say. Over and over she would tell me that she was a bad person, "a person of darkness." I was filled with horror and pity, wishing to ease her anguish, to offer comfort. Yet she had done these things. I continued to listen.

Over and over a wall of silence and despair threatened to close us off from each other. Over and over I would beat it back, insisting that she tell me the worst. She would weep and say, "I do not know if I can," and hoping that I would be able to hear it, I would tell her that she must. And she would begin another story. I often found myself not knowing how to respond, unable to do anything but stand with her here, one foot in this peaceful calm office on the water, the other in a world beyond imagination. I had never been orphaned, never been hunted, never missed a meal except by choice, never violently attacked another person. But I could recognize the whisper of my darkness in hers and I stood in that place in myself to listen to her, to try to understand. I wanted to jump in, I wanted to soothe. I wanted to make sense, yet none of this was possible. Once, in despair myself, I remember thinking, "I am her first witness."

Over and over she would cry out, "I have such darkness in me." At such times it seemed to me that the cancer was actually helping her make sense of her life, offering the relief of a feared but long-awaited punishment.

10   At the close of one of her stories, I was overwhelmed by the fact that she had actually managed to live with such memories. I told her this and added, "I am in awe." We sat looking at each other. "It helps me that you say that. I feel less alone." I nodded and we sat in silence. I *was* in awe of this woman and her ability to survive. In all the years of working with people with cancer, I had never met anyone like her. I ached for her. Like an animal in a trap that gnaws off its own leg, she had survived—but only at a terrible cost.

Gradually she began to shorten the time frame of her stories, to talk of more recent events: her ruthless business practices, how she used others, always serving her own self-interest. She began to talk about her contempt, her anger, her unkindness, her distrust of people, and her competitiveness. It seemed to me that she was completely alone. "Nothing has really changed," I thought. Her whole life was still organized around her survival.

Once, at the close of a particularly painful session, I found myself reviewing my own day, noticing how much of the time I was focused on surviving and not on living. I wondered if I too had become caught in survival. How much had I put off living today in order to do or say what was expedient? To get what I thought I needed. Could survival become a habit? Was it possible to live so defensively that you never got to live at all?

"You have survived, Ana," I blurted out. "Surely you can stop now." She looked at me, puzzled. But I had nothing further to say.

One day, she walked in and said, "I have no more stories to tell."

15   "Is it a relief?" I asked her. To my surprise she answered, "No, it feels empty."

"Tell me." She looked away. "I am afraid I will not know how to survive now." Then she laughed. "But I could never forget," she said.

A few weeks after this she brought in a dream, one of the first she could remember. In the dream, she had been looking in the mirror, seeing herself reflected there to the waist. It seemed to her that she could see through her clothes, through her skin, through to the very depths of her being. She saw that she was filled with darkness and felt a familiar shame, as intense as that she had felt on the first day she had come to my office. Yet she could not look away. Then it seemed to her as if she were moving, as if she had passed through into the mirror, into her own image, and was moving deeper and deeper into her darkness. She went forward blindly for a long time. Then, just as she was certain that there was no end, no bottom, that surely this would go on and on, she seemed to see a tiny spot far ahead. As she moved closer to it, she was able to recognize what it was. It was a rose. A single, perfect rosebud on a long stem.

For the first time in eight months she began to cry softly, without pain. "It's very beautiful," she told me. "I can see it very clearly, the stem with its leaves and its thorns. It is just beginning to open. And its color is indescribable: the softest, most tender, most exquisite shade of pink."

I asked her what this dream meant to her and she began to sob. "It's mine," she said. "It is still there. All this time it is still there. It has waited for me to come back for it."

20   The rose is one of the oldest archetypical symbols for the heart. It appears in both the Christian and Hindu traditions and in many fairy tales. It presented itself now to Ana even though she had never read these fairy tales or heard of these traditions. For most of her life, she had held her darkness close to her, had used it as her protection, had even defined herself through it. Now, finally, she had been able to remember. There was a part she had hidden even from herself. A part she had kept safe. A part that had not been touched.

Even more than our experiences, our beliefs became our prisons. But we carry our healing with us even into the darkest of our inner places. *A Course in Miracles* says, "When I have forgiven myself and remembered who I am, I will bless everyone and everything I see." The way to freedom often lies through the open heart.

QUESTIONS FOR DISCUSSION

1. Why does Ana believe that she is a bad person and that her cancer is a punishment? Do you think Ana recovers from her cancer? Why doesn't Remen tell us if Ana does or does not recover from her cancer?
2. Why do you think that Remen values memory? What is unique about her perspective on memory?
3. How and why is Remen able to help Ana? What has Remen learned from listening to Ana's struggle? What have you learned?
4. What is the significance of Ana's dream and the symbolism of the rose?
5. Why does Remen believe that "some things which can never be fixed can still heal"? Explain why you agree or disagree with her.
6. How does Remen's discussion of Ana support her conclusion that freedom can begin only after one can forgive oneself and have an open heart? Do you agree with Remen?

CONNECTION

Compare Remen's insights into the need to integrate traumatic memories through dreams rather than to deny the past with Barasch's insights in "The Healing Dream" (see page 280).

IDEAS FOR WRITING

1. Explain Remen's claim, "What we do to survive is often different from what we may need to do in order to live." Develop the idea into an essay, using examples drawn from personal experience and observation to support your main ideas.
2. Write an essay that supports or refutes Remen's implied premise that people's beliefs about themselves affect their ability to live a healthy life and recover from an illness. Research this issue on the Internet and the library as well as examples from your own experience and observations of others to support your main ideas.

RELATED WEB SITES

Rachel Naomi, Remen, M.D.

www.rachelremen.com

This Web Site is an excellent introduction to the work and life of Naomi Remen, a pioneer in the mind-body holistic health movement.

Trauma and Disease: The Sidran Traumatic Stress Institute

www.sidran.org

This organization provides online links and articles devoted to "education, advocacy and research related to the early recognition and treatment of trauma-related stress in children and the understanding and treatment of adults suffering from trauma-generated disorders."

Anne Lamott

Hunger

Anne Lamott (b. 1954) grew up in Marin County, north of San Francisco, where she still lives. After attending two years of Goucher College from 1971 to 1973, Lamott began her career as a writer. To help support herself, she has also worked as an editor, a restaurant critic, a lecturer, and a writing teacher. Hard Laughter *(1980), about her father's struggle with brain cancer, was her first widely acclaimed book. Her prose works include* Operating Instructions: A Journal of My Son's First Year *(1993) and* Bird by Bird *(1994), in which Lamott explores the crucial human connections between writing and life. In 1997 Lamott's novel,* Crooked Little Heart, *became a best-seller immediately after its publication. The following selection, "Hunger," about her personal obsession with food and eating, is from her collection of essays,* Traveling Mercies *(1998).*

JOURNAL

Explore your thoughts and feelings about eating disorders. You might want to write about the causes or the effects of the condition or your observations of people who have or have had an eating disorder.

This is the story of how, at the age of thirty-three, I learned to feed myself. To begin with, here's what I did until then: I ate, starved, binged, purged, grew fat, grew thin, grew fat, grew thin, binged, purged, dieted, was good, was bad, grew fat, grew thin, grew thinner.

I had been a lean and energetic girl, always hungry, always eating, always thin. But I weighed 100 pounds at thirteen, 130 at fourteen. For the next ten years, I dieted. It is a long, dull story. I had lots of secrets and worries about me and food and my body. It was very scary and obsessive, the way it must feel for someone who is secretly and entirely illiterate.

One week after my father was diagnosed with brain cancer, I discovered bulimia. I felt like I'd discovered the secret to life, because you could eat yourself into a state of emotional numbness but not gain weight. Then I learned how to do it more effectively by reading articles in women's magazines on how to stop doing it. I barfed, but preferred laxatives. It was heaven: I lost weight.

All right, OK: there were some problems. I was scared all the time, full of self-loathing, and my heart got funky. When you've lost too much water and electrolytes, your muscular heart cramps up; it races like a sewing machine. Sometimes it would skip beats, and other times there would be a terrible feeling of vacuum, as if there were an Alhambra water tank in my heart and a big bubble had just burbled to the surface.

5   I would try to be good, in the puritanical sense, which meant denying my appetites. Resisting temptation meant I was good—strong, counter-animal—and I'd manage to resist fattening foods for a while. But then the jungle drums would start beating again.

I looked fine on the outside: thin, cheerful, even successful. But on the inside, I was utterly obsessed. I went into a long and deep depression after seeing some photos of people on a commune, working with their hands and primitive tools and workhorses, raising healthy food. I could see that they were really tuned to nature, to the seasons, to a direct sense of bounty, where you plant something and it grows and you cut it down or pick it and eat it, savoring it and filling up on it. But I was a spy in the world of happy eating, always hungry, or stuffed, but never full.

Luckily I was still drinking at the time.

But then all of a sudden I wasn't. When I quit in 1986, I started getting healthier in almost every way and I had all these women helping me, and I told them almost every crime and secret I had, because I believed them when they said that we are as sick as our secrets. My life got much sweeter right away, and less dramatic; the pond inside me began to settle, and I could see through the water, which was the strangest sensation because for all those years I'd been taking various sticks—desperate men, financial drama, impossible deadlines—and stirring that pond water up. So now I was noticing beautiful little fish and dreamy underwater plants, and shells lying in the sand. I started getting along with myself pretty well for the first time in my life. But I couldn't or wouldn't tell anyone that for the last ten years I had been bingeing and purging, being on a diet, being good, getting thin, being bad, getting fat.

I remember hanging out with these people, letting their stories wash over me, when all of a sudden the thing inside would tap me on the shoulder and whisper, "OK, honey, let's go." And I'd cry out inwardly, No! No! "Sorry," it would say, "time to go shopping." And silently I'd cry out, Please don't make me go shopping! I'm not even hungry! "Shh, shh," it would whisper, "Let's go."

10   I felt that when I got sober, God had saved me from drowning, but now I was going to get kicked to death on the beach. It's so much hipper to be a drunk than a bulimic. Drunks are like bikers or wrestlers; bulimics are baton twirlers, gymnasts. The voice would say how sorry it was, but then glance down at its watch, tap its foot and sigh, and I'd sigh loudly too, and get up, and trudge behind it to the store.

It was actually more painful than that. It reminded me of the scene in Kazantzakis's *The Last Temptation of Christ,* when Jesus is walking along in the desert, really wanting to spend his life in a monastery praying, secluded and alone with God. Only of course God has different plans for him and, to get his attention, sends eagles down to wrap their talons around Jesus' heart, gripping him so that he falls to the sand in pain.

I did not feel eagle talons, but I felt gripped in the heart by a presence directing me to do exactly what it said. It said it was hungry and we had to go to the store.

So that voice and I would go buy the bad things—the chocolates, the Cheetos, the Mexican food—and big boxes of Epsom salts and laxatives. I grew weaker and more desperate until finally, one day in 1987, I called a woman named Rita Groszmann, who was listed in the Yellow Pages as a specialist in eating disorders. I told her what was going on and that I had no money, and she said to come in anyway, because she was afraid I was going to die. So I went in the next day.

I sat in her office and explained how I'd gotten started and that I wasn't ready to stop but that I was getting ready to be ready to stop. She said that was fine. I said that in fact I was going to go home that very night and eat chocolates and Mexican food and then purge. She said fine. I said, "Don't try to stop me." She said, "OK." I said, "There's nothing you can do to stop me, it's just the way it is," and we did this for half an hour or so, until she finally said very gently that she was not going to try to take my bulimia away from me. That she in fact was never going to take anything away from me, because I would try to get it back. But she said that I had some choices.

15   They were ridiculous choices. She proposed some, and I thought, This is the angriest person I've ever met. I'll give you a couple of examples. If I was feeling lonely and overwhelmed and about to binge, she said I could call someone up and ask them if they wanted to meet me for a movie. "Yeah," I said, "right." Or here's another good one: If I was feeling very *other*, sad and scared and overwhelmed, I could invite someone over for a meal, and then see if he or she felt like going for a walk. It is only because I was raised to be Politeness Person that I did not laugh at her. It was like someone detoxing off heroin, who's itching to shoot up, being told to take up macramé.

She asked if I was willing to make one phone call after I ate and buy time. I could always purge if I needed to, but she wanted me to try calling one person and see what happened. Now I'm not stupid. I knew she was up to something.

But I was really scared by the power the bad voice had over me, and I felt beaten up and out of control, scared of how sick I had somehow become, how often my pulse raced and my heart skipped beats, scared that one time when the eagle talons descended, they would grip too hard and pop me open. So I agreed. I got home, ate a more or less regular meal, called a friend, made contact, and didn't purge. The next day, I ate a light breakfast and lunch, and then a huge dinner, rooting around the fridge and cupboards like a truffle pig. But then I called my younger brother. He came over. We went for a walk.

Several weeks later, during one of our sessions, Rita asked me what I'd had for breakfast. "Cereal," I said.

"And were you hungry when you ate?"

20   "What do you mean?" I asked.

"I mean, did you experience hunger, and then make breakfast?"

"I don't really understand what you're asking," I said.

"Let me put it this way," she said. "Why did you have breakfast?"

"Oh! I see," I said. "I had breakfast because it was breakfast time."

25   "But were you hungry?"

I stared at her a moment. "Is this a trick question?" I asked.

"No," she said. "I just want to know how you know it's time to eat."

"I know it's time to eat because it's mealtime," I said. "It's morning, so I eat breakfast, or it's midday, so I eat lunch. And so on."

To make a long story ever so slightly shorter, she finally asked me what it felt like when I was hungry, and I could not answer. I asked her to explain what it felt like when she was hungry, and she described a sensation in her stomach of emptiness, an awareness of appetite.

30   So for the next week, my assignment was to notice what it felt like when I was hungry. It was so strange. I was once again the world's oldest toddler. I walked around peering down as if to look inside my stomach, as if it was one of those old-fashioned front-loading washing machines with a window through which you could see the soapy water swirling over your clothes. And I paid attention until I was able to isolate this feeling in my stomach, a gritchy kind of emptiness, like a rat was scratching at the door, wanting to be let in.

"Wonderful," Rita said, and then gave me my next assignment: first, to notice when I was hungry, and then—this blew my mind—to feed myself.

I practiced, and all of a sudden I was Helen Keller after she breaks the code for "water," walking around touching things, learning their names. Only in my case, I was discovering which foods I was hungry for, and what it was like to eat them. I felt a strange loneliness at first, but then came upon a great line in one of Geneen Roth's books on eating, which said that awareness was about learning to keep yourself company. So I'd feel the scratchy emptiness in my belly, and I'd mention to myself that I seemed hungry. And then I'd ask myself, in a deeply maternal way, what I felt like eating.

"Well, actually, I feel like some Cheetos," I might say. So I'd go and buy a bag of Cheetos, put some in a bowl, and eat them. God! It was amazing. Then I'd check in with myself: "Do you want some more?" I'd ask.

"No," I'd say. "But don't throw them out."

35   I had been throwing food out or wetting it in the sink since I was fourteen, ever since my first diet. Every time I broke down and ate forbidden
foods, I would throw out or wet what I'd left uneaten, because each time
I was about to start over and be good again.

"I'm hungry," I'd say to myself. "I'd like some frosting."

"OK."

"And some Cheetos."

So I'd have some frosting and some Cheetos for breakfast. I'd eat for
a while. Then I'd check in with myself, kindly: "More?"

40   "Not now," I'd say. "But don't wet them. I might want some more later."

I ate frosting and Cheetos for weeks. Also, cookies that a local bakery
made with M&M's instead of chocolate chips. I'd buy half a dozen and
keep them on the kitchen counter. It was terrifying; it was like knowing
there were snakes in my kitchen. I'd eat a little, stop when I was no
longer hungry. "Want one more cookie?" I'd ask.

"No, thanks," I'd say. "But maybe later. Don't wet them."

I never wet another bag of cookies. One day I woke up and discovered
that I also felt like having some oranges, then rice, then sautéed bell pep-
pers. Maybe also some days the random pound of M&M's. But from then
on I was always able at least to keep whatever I ate down—or rather, in
my case, up. I went from feeling like a Diane Arbus character, viewed
through the lens of her self-contempt, to someone filmed by a friendly
cousin, someone who gently noted the concentration on my face as I
washed a colander of tiny new potatoes.

Over the years, my body has not gotten firmer. Just the opposite in fact.
But when I feel fattest and flabbiest and most repulsive, I try to remember
that gravity speaks; also, that no one needs that plastic-body perfection
from women of age and substance. Also, that I do not live in my thighs or
in my droopy butt. I live in joy and motion and cover-ups. I live in the nourishment of food and the sun and the warmth of the people who love me.

45   It is, finally, so wonderful to have learned to eat, to taste and love what
slips down my throat, padding me, filling me up, that I'm not uncomfortable calling it a small miracle. A friend who does not believe in God says,
"Maybe not a miracle, but a little improvement," but to that I say, Listen!
You must not have heard me right: I couldn't *feed* myself! So thanks for
your input, but I know where I was, and I know where I am now, and you
just can't get here from there. Something happened that I had despaired
would ever happen. It was like being a woman who has despaired of ever
getting to be a mother but now who cradles a baby. So it was either a
miracle—Picasso said, "Everything is a miracle; it's a miracle that one
does not dissolve in one's bath like a lump of sugar"—or maybe it was
more of a gift, one that required some assembly. But whatever it was,
learning to eat was about learning to live—and deciding to live; and it is
one of the most radical things I've ever done.

QUESTIONS FOR DISCUSSION

1. Lamott writes in the first person. How does this impact the essay's meaning?
2. After Lamott stops drinking, she says that "the pond inside me began to settle, and I could see through the water." What can she see? Why is she still unable to reveal her secret eating disorder?
3. What do the eagle talons symbolize? Why does Lamott finally call Rita Grossman to ask for help with her eating disorder? How do Rita and the choices she offers help Lamott?
4. What might Lamott's food-wetting ritual represent?
5. Why does she need to relearn what it feels like to be hungry and feed herself? How is she finally able to take this responsibility for herself? Why does Lamott conclude that deciding to feed herself and live was "one of the most radical things I've ever done"?
6. Would a more scientific approach to this topic have been more persuasive? Why or why not?

CONNECTION

Compare Lamott's obsession with her eating disorder with the depressed state of mind described by Andrew Solomon (see page 236).

IDEAS FOR WRITING

1. Write an essay in which you discuss the positive aspects of Lamott's struggle to overcome her eating disorder. Consider how her obsession and struggle transform her life.
2. Write a paper about blogs that discuss eating disorders. Use testimonies on the blogs to support or refute Lamott's transformation.

RELATED WEB SITES

Anne Lamott
`www.barclayagency.com/lamott.html`
Anne Lamott's life and work are presented at this URL through a brief text, links of interest, a schedule of her appearances, and an "Anne Lamott FAQ" section.

Eating Disorders Awareness and Prevention
`www.nationaleatingdisorders.org/`
The National Eating Disorders Association hosts this Web site to provide information, referrals, support, prevention, and conferences for individuals with eating disorders or people interested in learning about the issue.

Lexie Spiranac

Working It Out

Lexie Spiranac is a student at Stanford University who enjoys participating in sports related activities and has been a member of the Stanford track team. She studied Chinese in Beijing during the summer Olympics in 2008 and is currently majoring in communications with a special interest in psychology. Spiranac wrote "Working It Out" for her first-year English Composition and Rhetoric class in an effort to understand and effectively channel her own competitive drive which has always led her to want to give "one hundred and ten percent" to any activity she has embarked on.

Every day, deep in my mind, someone is urging me to get up and go work out. The continual nagging voice makes off-hand remarks like, "Oh, so you're *not* going to the gym then?" and "Hmm, do what you want, but I heard it's best to exercise in the morning." My subconscious easily rolls out the kind of comments that you can't pinpoint as being aggressive, but which nevertheless succeed at producing a tightening of my chest, what feels like the beginnings of an anxiety attack. No matter how hard I try to tell myself that it's okay to finish my REM cycle in lieu of that early-bird spin class, I can't seem to shake the impulse to put exercise above all else. After years of living a workout-driven life, I decided I needed to dig deep and discover the cause of my fixation.

My effort to discover the cause of this obsession began when I decided to quit track and field competition. After five long years of training at an elite level, I was completely burned out. Following the toughest decision of my nineteen-year-old life, I called up my coaches and said goodbye to them all. Finally, I was free of the worries of being fit, and not only fit to complete grueling four hour workouts and to be able to adequately compete at the Division I collegiate level, but also free from worrying about having the ideal body. For no matter which event, whether it be sprinting or high jump, it is very important to look the part; a body typical of the event in almost every situation leads to improved performance. Now I had no coach constantly scrutinizing my body, telling me what should be bigger, what should be smaller, and continually asking me which foods I was eating.

Because of my concerns about the coaches' opinions on maintaining perfect body image, track and field team meals caused me some of the greatest anxiety. Team meals are usually a chance for celebration, with plenty of free food and team bonding; however, my excitement was always quelled after I remembered the sequence of events that usually occurred. I'd walk over to the food line; and after grabbing my plate and looking at the buffet style choices, I'd lick my lips in anticipation, starved from a day of competition. Then a pang of disappointment would shoot through my body as I'd see my coach out of the corner of my eye. *Oh, here it goes,* I'd think, *another session of question and answer.* As the way down the buffet line ensued, I'd mentally battle with myself, willing my hand not to take too much of this, to pour less of that, trying to remember which dishes upset my coach the most. As a person who knows a lot about nutrition, I was positive that I made healthy and appropriate meal choices, but whether my coach agreed with me or not was a different story. After compiling what I thought was an adequate plate for dinner, I'd nevertheless notice where my coach sat and proceed to skirt the entire room in an attempt to get to my seat without his judging eyes spying me. However, my efforts were always in vain. He would somehow find me, and much like that obnoxious voice that nags at me to be more productive, he would make little quips such as "Oh, are you actually going to eat *that?*" and "Hmm, didn't you already eat today?" Anger and shame would flood through my body, embarrassed that not only did my coach think I was overweight, but that my peers had heard his comments. Would they now be analyzing my figure, scanning my body to assess the damages? I'd cautiously laugh it off, struggling to find replies that didn't include some choice four letter words. After I quit, I was obviously excited to leave this team dinner situation behind. My body was no longer dedicated to the track, so I could look how I wanted and do what I pleased. If my problem truly was an obsession with attaining the perfect figure, this relief of external pressures should resolve the issue.

With the days of running in circles behind me, I was now looking forward to what my coach used to call "housewife workouts." These workouts consist of those group cardio classes where it must be a rule to wear brightly colored 80's style spandex, with lots of walking around the gym equipment, spending more time evaluating the machines rather than sweating on them. Gone were the days of running until someone puked and weight training until I could barely lift my arms to wash my hair. I could finally pick up yoga, instead of sprinting my heart out on the track, the burning hot rubber searing a hole through my running spikes.

5   However, I soon realized that even though I no longer had the pressures of competition or coaches' expectations, I couldn't stop myself from going to the gym. Everyday, sometimes twice a day, I'd find myself in a tangle of exercise equipment. Even though no one was yelling at me to go faster or to run further, even though I no longer had a coach telling me to lose weight, I found myself glancing over at the cardio machines next to me, trying to push myself harder than everyone else around me. There I was, in the middle of the cardio jungle, realizing

that I didn't compulsively run to the gym simply because I thought I needed to lose weight, but rather because I craved competition, the thrill of being the best and pushing it to the limit. Certainly my coaches had an influence on my thoughts and decisions, but if that was truly the only reason I worked myself to the bone, the problem should have been solved. Furthermore, I began to realize that this is more than a simple obsession with working out. This isn't a simple affinity for the weight room; this is a full on obsession with giving 110 percent that permeates each facet of my life.

The cliché "give 110 percent" is used in many arenas of life, from the office to the football field, to motivate and encourage the best possible performance. Giving 110 percent is to put your heart and soul into each and every action. But what happens when giving 110 percent becomes an obsession? After the realization that my obsession with working out was a result of my need to have every detail in my life performed to the best of my ability, I finally understood why I was miserable in track as well as in several other aspects of my life. To me, giving my all was less about what I wanted, and more about my expectations of what everyone else wanted. I didn't get up extra early because I actually wanted to work out; I did it because I knew other people were working out, too. I didn't push myself because I wanted to see how far I could go; I did it so that everyone around me would also know how much further I could go than the others. Certainly this affinity for pushing myself to the limit isn't all bad, and it's not all a result of external motivations. Yes, other people influenced what I thought and did, but it was only because I *allowed* them to, because deep down inside I had a need to achieve the best and their comments simply fueled the fire. To a certain extent I enjoy the competition and I like how I feel after a good hard workout. However, there are many times that I contemplate staying home or doing a lighter workout only to hear that internal voice scream in protest. Sometimes this can act as an excellent source of motivation, as activities such as working out and completing homework are best done when done intensely; however, when desire to give 110 percent acts as an inhibitor, narrowing one's choices in life, it becomes an issue of concern for one's own freedom and health.

Now, in hindsight, I know what my obsession is and how it works. It can actually be very positive when applied to the right situation, situations which demand intense attention and perfection, but I now know I must be careful. When making decisions, I constantly ask myself "Am I doing this because I want to? Or am I continuing the activity because I feel I *need* to?" By asking these questions I can now filter my effort and attention towards the activities that I will most enjoy or that will benefit me the most.

Sharon Slayton

The Good Girl

After growing up in Florida and spending several years in Denver working in the computer field, Sharon Slayton moved to California to complete her education. When she wrote this essay, she was a part-time student in psychology with plans to transfer to a four-year university and to become a lawyer. Slayton enjoys writing and has contributed several articles to small business newsletters. The following essay was written in response to a question posed in her critical thinking class that asked her to define a form of obsessive or addictive behavior about which she had personal knowledge.

Most people who meet me today see a very strong and confident individual. They see a young woman who has accomplished a great deal in a short time. They see a very responsible and reliable person who can be counted on to get a job done with skill and competency. Typically, I am spokesperson for any group of which I become part. I am looked to for leadership and guidance among my friends and colleagues. I am quite proud of my reputation; however, I wish that I had come by it through some other means. You see, all of these admirable characteristics were developed over the past twenty-five years through an obsession with being good.

Maybe I should rephrase that, because merely being "good" has never quite been "good" enough for me—not since I was six years old and my parents failed to believe me about the most important issue in my life. I went to them for protection against a child molester, and they refused to believe that such a thing could be happening in their world. Those things do not happen to "nice" people, to "good" people. Those things could not happen to *their* child. My parents defended themselves the only way they knew how, by denying the reality of my perceptions and telling me that I was "bad" for telling such stories. Their choice of the word "bad" affected everything I was ever to do afterwards. From that time on I understood only one thing, that I must be "good."

"Good" soon came to encompass everything in my world: school, friends, home, work, society. I had to be good; and, if at all possible, I had to be great. Every deed at which I excelled, every recognition I received, every honor bestowed meant that I was one step closer to no longer being "bad." As the years passed, I forgot why I was trying so hard and lost touch with the reasoning that had started this quest—yet I pursued my goal with a diligence and devotion that can only be termed as obsessive.

I knew just about everyone at school, but I never made many friends. I didn't have time to be bothered with people, except superficially, because I was totally preoccupied with my grades; I had to get all "A's." Nothing less would do. When I wasn't studying, I was deeply involved in clubs and organizations. I decided, while still in elementary school, when I saw my first high school yearbook, that I would have the longest senior listing in my high school class when I graduated. Out of a class of almost eight hundred students, I got what I wanted. I had hoped my parents would be proud, but they hardly seemed to notice.

5   By the time I was fifteen I was looking for more ways to show "them" that I could do anything, and do it well. I was a junior in high school and started working full time while attending classes all day. My day began at 7:20 A.M. when the first bell rang and ended around 1:00 A.M. when I arrived home from work. Neither I nor my family needed extra money, but for me, there was no other way: I always had to do more. I kept this schedule up until I graduated. Of course, I was an honor student; I was also a student council representative, vice president of two clubs, treasurer of one. I attended and received top awards in state foreign language competitions in two languages and was a member of two choral groups which gave concerts statewide and which participated in state-level competitions. No one ever seemed to notice or to care.

What I didn't notice was that my parents were immensely proud of me. They often bragged about me to their friends and relatives, but I wasn't paying attention. I was after something that they could never give. My "badness" no longer existed for them, and probably had not since about an hour after that episode when I was six—but it was very much a part of me. I picked everything apart, thinking that everything could always use improvement, that nothing was "good" enough as it was. My grades were good, but some of the subjects weren't as "easy" for me as I wished. I was popular, but there were always some people I didn't know. I was working, but I had to be the best at my job, the fastest, the most knowledgeable. I actually learned stock numbers and prices to over two hundred items of inventory by heart so I could impress my manager with how good I was.

Was I getting tired? Maybe. But I was also getting plenty of recognition for my accomplishments. I fed off of it; I lived for it; I required it. I needed every reward or approval I got to reinforce me in my feeling that I was on the right track, that I was getting better and better. I was no longer consciously aware of what I was seeking. The obsession had taken over my behavior, almost completely; being constantly challenged was now a way of life. Never resting, never relaxing, always striving, always achieving—these things were second nature to me by the time I was twenty.

My relationships were disastrous. My constant need for approval and recognition was very difficult for anyone to supply. Likewise, no matter how much praise I was given, I never felt like it was enough. I felt that people patronized me, so I had to prove to them that I could always do more than anyone else. I criticized anyone who was willing to settle for less than I. If someone told me that they loved me, I would pick it apart, frequently arguing with the people I was involved with: "How can you say you love me? If you loved me, then you would stop making me feel like nothing I ever do is good enough."

When I was twenty-three I started my own business, which was quite successful for a time. I had moved two thousand miles away from my family, determined that I would be a great success. I was really going to make them proud this time, but my plans went awry as moving away from my family helped dim the constant need to impress them. Because of distance, they were no longer privy to my life and to daily events. Lacking the "audience" for my constant efforts to prove myself, I began to lose the motivation to excel, to be the "good one." Slowly, I began to lose interest in my business, lacking the drive to devote myself utterly to something that was unrecognized by my family. I began to realize what I might never have discovered if I had stayed close to home. Without parental recognition and approval, my business success meant little.

10   In fact, I began to realize that I had been so damned "good" all my life that I had missed out on a great deal of fun. Suddenly my life began to change. I was involved in many things, but I derived little pleasure now from activities I had thoroughly enjoyed in the past. At twenty-seven years of age I knew nothing about myself. I had no idea what I really liked and had no concept of happiness. I only knew what I was capable of accomplishing. I set about enjoying myself with the same devotion that I had given to everything else, and for the next few years my life became a set of extremes. Struggling constantly with a desire to be good and a need to be "bad," I would go out drinking with friends and get very drunk, but I was always the one who forced myself to try to act

sober. I was always the one responsible for making sure that everyone else got home. I thought I was enjoying the first freedom that I had ever experienced in my life, but I had really only broadened my obsession to include being bad as well. Whatever mood I was in, whatever my particular focus was for the hour, whether being good or being bad, I accomplished either with an abandon and passion hard to match. And I was very, very unhappy.

What was the point? Did I really enjoy anything I was doing? No. I had no idea what I wanted, yet I demanded attention and recognition. If I couldn't get enough recognition from my family, then I would get it from everyone else. But that had proved unsatisfying as well. What could I do now? What was I after and what did I want? The only thing I really knew was that I didn't want to go on living like I was anymore. With the help of one of the few friends I had managed to make along the way, I started psychiatric counseling. The results of that counseling you see in what you have just read.

So, here I am today, thirty-two years old and just beginning to discover myself as a person who exists outside of the obsession to be good. Actually, I think I have an advantage over a lot of people my age in that I covered a lot of ground when I was young. Driven by an obsession for goodness, I tested my limits and discovered what many people never learn: that I really could accomplish anything to which I put my mind. In going from one subject to another to prove I could do it all, I was exposed to a wide variety of experiences and activities, some of which I have rejected, some of which I have made a part of my current lifestyle. Either way, the experiences I have picked up along the way have made my life rich and varied. My obsessive past has given me a strength with which to confront the future; I just wish I had arrived here by some other way.

QUESTIONS FOR DISCUSSION

1. Despite feeling proud of her achievements, why does Slayton now wish she "had arrived here by some other way"? Do you agree with her?

2. How did Slayton's parents respond to her story about a molestation? Does their response seem understandable? Would modern parents be as likely to respond as did her parents?

3. This essay is an example of what is known as an extended definition. What qualities make up Slayton's definition of the "good girl" obsession? Is her definition of the essay's key terms a clear one?

4. To develop her definition essay, Slayton uses her own case history and a number of examples from her life at different stages. What are the key incidents that Slayton emphasizes? Are there any that seem to need more development or detail? Do all of the incidents she mentions seem relevant to her definition?

Maressa Hecht Orzack, Ph.D.

Computer Addiction: What Is It?

Maressa Hecht Orzack, a Massachusetts-licensed psychologist, is a faculty member with the Cognitive Behavior Therapy Program at Boston's McLean Hospital and a lecturer in the Department of Psychiatry at the Harvard Medical School. Dr. Orzack specializes in the treatment of addictive and impulsive behavioral problems such as gambling, substance and alcohol abuse, eating disorders, and sex addiction. In 1996 she founded and continues to serve as coordinator of the Computer Addiction Service at McLean Hospital. This program offers comprehensive evaluation and treatment services for individuals suffering from computer addiction and for people who are close to the computer addict. Orzack has described computer addiction as a "disorder suffered by people who find the virtual reality on computer screens more attractive than everyday reality." Notice how Orzack defines computer addiction by comparing it to other forms of "addictive" behavior.

JOURNAL

Write about your computer/Internet use or that of a friend. Do you think that the usage you have observed/experienced could be considered a form of addiction? Why or why not?

In 1995, I noticed that I was spending more and more time playing solitaire on my computer. I was trying to learn a new computer program and was very frustrated by it. My anger and inability to decipher the manuals led me to escape to solitaire. I became aware that I started my game program at an earlier time each evening, and at times I would avoid my primary reasons for using the computer. I was not alone.

Some of my patients told me about their computer use and how they were unable to stop spending time online or arranging electronic files.

I decided that these patterns might indicate a form of dysfunctional behavior associated with a new technology, and was worth investigating. I found support for my idea from colleagues, friends and reports in the media (Murray, 1996). As a trained cognitive behavior therapist, I often treat gamblers, alcoholics and people with obsessive-compulsive disorder, and have also studied mood changes resulting from the recreational use of psychotropic medication. I concluded that this inappropriate and excessive use of the computer might be a distinct disorder (Orzack et al., 1988).

This behavior has variously been called Internet addiction, pathological Internet use, problematic Internet use, and a mere symptom of other disorders. I am often asked why I call it computer addiction. I was not the first to use this term. Shotton (1989) coined the term in her book *Computer Addiction*. After searching the literature about alcoholism, gambling and other addictive behaviors, Shotton decided that she was witnessing computer addiction in a very specialized group of men who were developing hardware and software for computers. According to Shotton, these men were completely focused on their activities in the laboratory to the point of neglecting both family and friends.

5 The information superhighway did not exist when Shotton wrote her book. Few ordinary citizens outside of academia, the military and the computer industry had their own PCs, and fewer still had access to the Internet. Since then we have moved into the Information Age. The computer industry is now the fastest growing industry in the world. In 1997, the population of Internet users in the United States was estimated at 50 million to 80 million, and is projected to increase to 150 million to 200 million by the year 2000 (Pohly, 1995).

Any new technology requires a shakedown period in which the flaws and its effects on both society and individuals become evident. This is also true of the computer. As this rapidly evolving technology develops, so do the opportunities for negative consequences from its use. It is for these reasons that we must examine the phenomenon.

No epidemiological studies on computer addiction have been done. There have been online studies (Brenner, 1997; Young, 1998) and targeted group studies (Anderson, 1998; Scherer, 1997; Shotton, 1989), but to my knowledge no one has either interviewed a randomized sample of people about their computer use or recorded usage directly.

We have no idea what levels or kinds of computer usage are "normal." Therefore, we cannot state which behavior is always pathological. There have been heated and contentious arguments about these issues in an online forum devoted to research on the Internet (see *http://www.cmhc.com/mlists*). Discussions include topics such as the validity of scales to measure Internet addiction, with exact indicators defining a pathological or addictive behavior.

What is it about using computers that makes some people behave in ways in which they would not ordinarily? Is it the technology itself, or is it the way people interact with that technology? Is the behavior pathological or creative? Why are some people so connected to life on the screen that they have difficulty coming back to reality? Who are the people who act this way, and if they come to your office for help, how do you treat them?

Signs and Symptoms

10 Based on contact with my own patients, numerous requests for referrals from other therapists, and many online requests for help, I have designed a behavior list based on an impulse control model very similar to one used for gambling. These are the signs and symptoms of computer addiction, or, as I now prefer to call it, impulse-control disorder, not otherwise specified. I make no other claim for the validity of this diagnostic paradigm, since it is based on a highly selected population.

Tolerance, withdrawal and compulsive use are requisites for any diagnosis of dependency (American Psychiatric Association, 1994). Psychological tolerance is indicated by the need to spend increasing amounts of time on computer activities such as playing games, arranging files or participating in online discussion groups. Even though computer users are aware of problem behavior, they continue to use the computer compulsively. They often blame others for the problem. Withdrawal symptoms are indicated by an increase in irritability and anxiety when a person is unable to access a computer. Even though one investigator (Anderson, 1998) used a three-day abstinence as an indicator of problems, at least one patient has said that it is a matter of only hours before he starts to feel irritable, depressed or anxious.

The physical symptoms associated with computer addiction can have serious consequences. For instance, resulting carpal tunnel syndrome often requires months of care and may result in surgery. Eating habits change so that some people eat while at the computer and never exercise. Others may skip meals altogether. One patient has told me that she sometimes does not get to the bathroom in time. Failure to blink can cause migraines. Optometrists and ophthalmologists often prescribe special lenses for computer use because patients spend so much time looking at the screen.

The following cases illustrate the signs and symptoms described above:

Patient A, a recovering substance abuser, stated that she craved participating in an online chat and that she returned to it at earlier and earlier hours each day. She had such an intense relationship with a cyber friend that she lost her sobriety when that person suddenly disappeared from her screen.

15 Patient B also has a history of substance abuse, and compared his feelings when he was on a chat line to an amphetamine high.

Patient C said he feels an intense power and excitement when he plays interactive power games.

Patient D turned to a computer game for comfort after she wrecked her car.

A therapist who treats paraphilias tells me that a good proportion of his patients download pornography at their workplaces as well as at home (Kafka, personal communication, 1998). Other technologies have been considered addictive, including the telephone, television, pinball machines and video games. All these activities initially provide positive rewards for their use. Once someone is addicted to a behavior, however, the positive rewards are diminished. Gambling, for example, requires an early win to catch the player. Without a win, the gambler will leave in frustration. If the gambler wins and then loses, he or she will continue to play, taking more risks by raising the ante. The gambler chases losses by expecting to win on the next play.

For the Web surfer, satisfaction must come early, or the user will leave the site. Web pages are aptly named because of the many links attracting the computer user to new experiences, causing him or her to lose track of time. Patient D, who complained about the amount of time she spent online, said she could not leave the Web because the next connection might be just what she was looking for.

Socialization Online

20   The newest lure is Internet gambling. Shaffer (1996) points out that it is not the addictive quality of the games or program, but rather their capacity to influence the human experience that is the important element to be studied.

Buzzell (1997), who describes the effects in some children who have had seizures watching a TV screen, asks whether the same effect might occur in children who play computer games by the hour. Eastman (1998) goes even further, suggesting that the activity of watching a screen may be hypnotic, and may therefore contribute to the addictive process by maintaining the exposure for longer time periods.

What is it that makes participation in activities like MUD (multi-user domains), Internet relay chat groups, Internet support groups and surfing the Web so compelling? It is a combination of factors which are balanced in nondependent individuals who can surf the Net, enter data, play games or engage in an online forum without it interfering with their other real life obligations. Those who cannot do this can be classified as dependent or addicted.

In the online world, people can become anyone they wish to be. Furthermore, they believe that they are part of a group. Being part of a MUD allows a participant to play a prescribed role that would be impossible in real life. As an example, a young patient fell asleep in class from staying up at night for hours directing a power game.

In addition to the actual activity there is a social connection with other players, which is highly reinforcing. Another patient, in recovery from several problems, described the sense of belonging he feels at a poker table. It is this same sense of belonging that I have heard expressed by people who belong to chat groups. A depressed patient continues to participate in chat groups even though she has had several traumatic experiences with men she arranged to meet offline.

25   One of the dormitory counselors at a major university reported that sports gambling on the Internet is a very popular group activity. Although gambling on the Internet is illegal in the United States, it thrives because it is hosted on offshore sites over which the U.S. has no regulatory authority. The other highly controversial topic is the number of sex and pornography sites that exist directly on the Internet and on CD-ROMs. How to regulate this is a subject of concern to many people.

Another view of computer addiction suggests that excessive and inappropriate computer use is a new symptom of other psychiatric problems. Shapira (1998) found that 14 self-selected Internet users who had problematic Internet use fit the *DSM-IV* criteria for a mean of five different psychiatric disorders. This data may suggest that this technology presents a new way to express affect.

One final consideration is treatment of this addiction. Whether or not this addiction is similar to substance dependency, impulse control disorder or a symptom of other disorders, its treatment cannot require abstinence. Computers are present in workplaces, schools, universities and households. Treatment must be similar to that given for an eating disorder where the aim is to help the patient normalize their behavior in order to survive. A combination of cognitive behavior therapy and motivational interviewing are the most helpful to the patient. Treating the depression and anxiety with antidepressants is also recommended. Shapira (1998) has had excellent results in prescribing serotonin reuptake inhibitors or other antidepressants for his patients.

Computer addiction is a combination of signs and symptoms that fit a dependency model, an impulse control disorder model, and are often comorbid with other psychiatric diagnoses. The treatment, therefore, must be for all three classifications. My hope is that an epidemiological study can be done which will define the limits of normal computer usage. Then we can decide what is pathological.

REFERENCES

American Psychiatric Association. 1994. *Diagnostic and statistical manual of mental disorders,* 4th ed. Washington, DC: American Psychiatric Association.

Anderson, K. 1998. Internet dependency among college students: Should we be concerned? Paper presented at the American College Personnel Association, March, St. Louis, Missouri.

Brenner, V. 1997. Psychology of computer use: XLVII. Parameters of Internet use, abuse, and addiction: The first 90 days of the Internet Usage Survey. *Psychological Reports* 80 (3, pt. 1): 879–82.

Buzzell, K. A. 1997. *The human brain and the influences of television viewing: An inquiry into meaning in the post-quantum world.* Denmark, ME: Cardinal Printing Company.

Eastman, G. 1998. The effect of electronic imaging on our experience of reality. Paper presented at the Eastern Psychology Association meeting, February, Boston.

Murray, J. B. 1996. Computer addictions entangle students. *APA Monitor* 27 (6): 38–39.

Orzack, M. H., L. Friedman, E. Dessain, et al. 1998. Comparative study of the abuse liability of alprazolam, lorazepam, diazepam, methaqualone, and placebo. *Int J Addict* 23 (5): 449–67.

Pohly, D. 1995. Selling in cyberspace. http://www.demographics.com/publications/mt/95_mt/9511_mt/mt368.htm (accessed July 7, 1998).

Scherer, K. 1997. College life online: Healthy and unhealthy Internet use. *J College Student Development* 38 (6): 655–64.

Shaffer, H. J. 1996. Understanding the means and objects of addiction, technology, the Internet and gambling. *J Gambling Studies* 12:461–69.

Shapira, N. A. 1998. Problematic Internet use. Paper presented at the annual meeting of the American Psychiatric Association, May, Toronto.

Shotton, M. A. 1989. *Computer addiction? A study of computer dependency.* New York: Taylor & Francis.

Young, K. S. 1989. *Caught in the net: How to recognize the signs of Internet addiction and a winning strategy for recovery.* New York: John Wiley & Sons.

QUESTIONS FOR DISCUSSION

1. What led Orzack to investigate the "dysfunctional behavior" associated with excessive computer use? How does she define this type of behavior?

2. What are the symptoms and withdrawal effects of computer addiction, in Orzack's view? Why does she define computer addiction as a compulsion?

3. What are the negative physical consequences of computer addiction? What cases and examples does Orzack use to support her discussion of consequences of computer addiction? Provide examples from your own experiences or those from relatives or friends.

4. How do computer-addicted individuals misuse the computer world as a source of socialization? What negative consequences can come from the artificial socialization that occurs in computer chat groups and MUDs?

5. How is gambling, despite its illegality, a particularly difficult type of obsessive activity to control when it is played by computer? How is Internet addiction similar to gambling addiction?

6. Orzack concludes by speculating on possible therapies for computer addiction. What might work, and why is it necessary to determine what "normal" computer usage is before we can begin to define and properly treat "pathological" usage?

CONNECTION

Compare the description of symptoms and psychological interventions for addictions to compulsive drinking and overeating/bulimia in Anne Lamott's "Hunger" (see page 252) with the symptoms and interventions for computer addiction provided by Orzack.

IDEAS FOR WRITING

1. Do some research into Orzack's treatment methods and those of other therapists for individuals who have difficulties controlling their computer use, and draw some conclusions about how effective their strategies might be.
2. Do you agree with Orzack that "addiction" is an accurate description of what goes on when people spend large amounts of time working on computers or online? Write an essay in which you argue your position on this controversial subject.

RELATED WEB SITES

Computer Addiction Services
www.computeraddiction.com
Maressa Orzack's site includes advice on recognizing computer addiction, its symptoms, and questions and answers on the issue, as well as a bibliography of articles by and about Orzack, her ideas, and her work with computer addicts.

The Psychology of Cyberspace
www.rider.edu/~suler/psycyber/psycyber.html
This site, created and maintained by John Suler, a psychology professor at Rider College, covers all aspects of the psychological impact of computers and cyberspace, including computer addiction. The site contains an extensive collection of links to relevant online articles.

Carrie Demers, M.D.

Chaos or Calm: Rewiring the Stress Response

Carrie Demers (b. 1961) is a holistically-oriented physician who blends modern medicine with traditional approaches to health such as yoga and meditation. Board certified in internal medicine, she received her medical degree from the University of Cincinnati and completed a residency at Michael

Reese Hospital in Chicago. She has been director of the Himalayan Institute's Center for Health and Living and was on the faculty at the Institute's main campus in Honesdale, Pennsylvania. Dr. Demers has been interviewed by numerous newspapers and magazines about her holistic approaches to health and is a frequent lecturer and guest on radio shows nationwide. She has written articles for Yoga International *and other magazines. The following article describes some of the health benefits of yoga and meditation in response to stress-related disorders.*

JOURNAL

Write about a time when you felt "stressed out." What helped you to relieve your sense of being overwhelmed?

Remember the tale "The Lady or the Tiger"? As it ends, the hero is standing before two identical doors: one conceals a beautiful maiden; the other, a ferocious tiger. The hero must open one of these doors—the choice is his—but he has no way of knowing which will bring forth the lady and which will release the tiger.

I'm sometimes reminded of this story when a patient is describing one of the symptoms of chronic stress: headaches, indigestion, ulcers, tight muscles, high blood pressure or some combination of these. When I point out that the symptom is stress-related, the patient seems resigned—stress is such a constant in most people's lives that all the doors seem to have tigers lurking behind them. Most of the people who find their way to my office know the fight-or-flight response is hardwired into our nervous system and many have come to accept a constant feeling of tension as normal, even inevitable.

It isn't. Like the hero in the story, we have a choice. There is another door, another response to the challenges of everyday living that is also hardwired into our nervous system. And unlike the hero, whose destiny rests with chance, we can discover which door is which. A general understanding of the nervous system and how it responds to stress, coupled with training in three fundamental yoga techniques, make it possible for us to distinguish one door from the other. Practicing these techniques gives us the power to choose the lady while leaving the door that unleashes the tiger firmly closed.

Releasing the Tiger

The autonomic nervous system controls all the body's involuntary processes: respiratory rate, heart rate, blood pressure, gastric juice secretion, peristalsis, body temperature, and so on. It has two main components or branches—the sympathetic and the parasympathetic. When we feel stressed, our brain activates the sympathetic nervous system, which has come to be known as the fight-or-flight response. This causes the adrenal medulla to secrete adrenaline (also called epinephrine), a hormone that circulates through the bloodstream, affecting almost every organ. Adrenaline revs up the body to survive a threat to life and limb: The heart pumps faster and harder, causing a spike in blood pressure; respiration increases in rate and moves primarily into the chest; airways dilate to bring more oxygen into the body; blood sugar rises to provide a ready supply of fuel; some blood vessels constrict to shunt blood away from the skin and the core of the body, while others dilate to bring more blood to the brain and limbs. The result? A body pumped up to fight or run, and a mind that is hyper alert.

5   This response is a crucial reaction to a life-threatening event: when we find ourselves face-to-face with a mountain lion, the stress response dramatically increases our chances of surviving. And we've all heard stories of fantastic feats: the mom lifting a car off her trapped child, the firefighter carrying a man twice his size from a burning building. These are the benefits of the sympathetic nervous system. Any time we respond quickly and decisively when a life is at stake, this is the system to thank.

The fight-or-flight response is meant to be triggered sporadically, in those rare moments when we are actually in peril. Ideally, it remains dormant until the next close call (weeks, months, or even years later!). But in many of us this response is triggered daily, even hourly. Some people— soldiers, tightrope walkers, members of a SWAT team, for example—do find themselves in life-or-death situations frequently. But for most of us, such situations are rare: a mugging, a traffic accident, a close-up with a bear in the backcountry. Once the threatening event is over, hormonal signals switch off the stress response, and homeostasis is reestablished.

The problem is that for many of us the fight-or-flight response rarely switches off, and stress hormones wash through the body almost continuously. The source of our stress is psychological rather than physical—a perception that something crucial to us is threatened. Fear of the unknown, major changes in our circumstances, uncertainty about the future, our negative attitudes—all these are sources of stress. Today we worry more about our jobs, our relationships or getting stuck in traffic than we do about fighting off a wild animal, but even though the perceived threat is psychological, it still triggers the archaic survival response.

The upshot is that our bodies are in a constant state of tension, ready to fight or flee, and this causes a host of physical problems. You can see what some of these are if you look again at what happens when adrenaline courses through the body: elevated blood pressure, rapid shallow breathing, high blood sugar and indigestion. What is more, adrenaline makes our platelets stickier, so our blood will clot quickly if we are wounded. This increases our chances of surviving a physical injury—but chronically sticky platelets are more apt to clot and create blockages in our arteries. And this sets the stage for a heart attack or a stroke.

The damage doesn't end there. When we are constantly in fight-or-flight mode, the adrenal cortex begins to secrete cortisol, a steroid whose job it is to help us adapt to a prolonged emergency by ensuring that we have enough fuel. Cortisol acts on the liver and muscle tissues, causing them to synthesize sugars (glucose) and fats and release them into the bloodstream. From the body's viewpoint, this is a reasonable response—dumping fat and sugar into the blood will help us survive a shipwreck, for example. But when this fuel is not metabolized in response to prolonged physical duress, disease results. Excess sugar in the bloodstream leads to diabetes, and excess fat to high cholesterol/high triglycerides. Both conditions boost our chances of developing heart disease.

10   The steroids cortisol and cortisone quell inflammation in auto-immune diseases and asthma, and so are useful when used infrequently and for brief periods, but their constant presence in the bloodstream suppresses immune function. This causes the white blood cells—those hardy defenders against bacteria, viruses, cancer cells, fungi, and other harmful microorganisms—to become sluggish. And this makes us more prone to disease, especially cancer and chronic infections like Lyme disease, hepatitis, and the Epstein-Barr virus.

Sounds grim, doesn't it? It is. It's a tiger. A chronically activated sympathetic nervous system keeps the body under constant pressure. If we ignore early warning symptoms—tight shoulders, digestive upset, recurring headaches, an increasing tendency to lose our temper or become easily upset—sooner or later the tiger will tear us up. But we can make another choice. The autonomic nervous system has another component, the parasympathetic nervous system. Rather than living under the tyranny of a ramped-up sympathetic nervous system, we can learn to trigger the parasympathetic system, the rest-and-digest response, instead.

Just as the fight-or-flight response automatically kicks in at the threat of danger, the rest-and-digest response automatically responds to our sense of equilibrium. When it is activated, the heart rate drops, blood pressure falls, and respiration slows and deepens. Blood flow to the core of the body is reestablished—this promotes good digestion, supports the immune system and infuses us with a sense of well-being.

We unconsciously achieve this state on vacation, in the throes of a hearty laugh, or in deep sleep. It feels good, and it offers a much needed respite from the hectic pace we set for ourselves. But we have come to accept stress as the norm and to expect the feeling of relaxed well-being to come about only sporadically—and so it does. We release the tiger a dozen times a day, even though the other door is also there in every moment. Once we learn to open it at will, we can override the harmful habit of triggering our stress response by activating the rest-and-digest component of our nervous system instead.

Greeting the Lady

I use a variety of natural therapies in my medical practice, but the basic treatments are drawn from yoga—stretching, breathing, relaxation and meditation—and these techniques are especially effective when it comes to managing stress. You already know from personal experience that aerobic exercise is excellent for dissipating stress-created tension, and that sugar, caffeine and spicy food contribute to jangling your nervous system and shortening your temper. You are probably also familiar with the relaxing effects of practicing yoga postures—they teach us to move and stretch our tense, strained bodies and to focus on the breath. But do you know that breathing slowly and deeply is the easiest way to activate the rest-and-digest system? That is one reason yoga classes are so popular—they soothe frazzled nerves and quiet anxious minds. But yoga also works at an even deeper level: it reestablishes healthy breathing patterns, teaches us to relax consciously and systematically, and gives us the opportunity to explore the inner workings of our minds through meditation. These techniques, both separately and in combination, nourish and strengthen the parasympathetic nervous system so that the relax-and-digest response becomes our normal mode. The fight-or-flight response is then reserved for emergencies, as nature intended. So let's take a look at some ways we can open Door Number Two.

15 ***Diaphragmatic Breathing*** Babies and young children breathe deeply and fully, using the dome shaped diaphragm that separates the chest and abdominal cavities to move air in and out of their lungs. Their bellies are relaxed and move in concert with their breath. This is the natural, healthy way to breathe. But as we grow up we are taught to constrict the abdomen (Pull your stomach in and stand up straight!), and that training, coupled with an unconscious tendency to tighten the belly when we experience stress, disrupts the natural flow of our breath. With the abdomen pulled in, the breath is confined to the upper portion of the lungs (from about the nipple line up). And because this breathing pattern is perceived by the body to be a stress response, it reinforces the fight-or-flight reaction.

Diaphragmatic breathing, on the other hand, activates the relax-and-digest response by stimulating the primary mediator of the parasympathetic nervous system, the vagus nerve. This nerve travels from the brain to nearly all the thoracic and abdominal organs ("vagus" comes from the same root as "vagabond"), and triggers a cascade of calming effects. Most of the time we wait for it to be activated by something pleasant and hope for a trickle-down effect, not realizing that the nerve (and hence the entire parasympathetic nervous system) can be turned on from the bottom up by diaphragmatic breathing.

The fight-or-flight response is meant to be triggered sporadically, in those rare moments when we are actually in peril.

Of all the processes regulated by the autonomic nervous system (heart rate, blood pressure, secretion of gastric juices, peristalsis, body temperature, etc.), only breathing can be controlled consciously. And in doing so, we stimulate the branch of the vagus nerve that innervates the diaphragm (which carries a message to the other vagus branches and the brain) to activate the entire rest-and-digest response. This is why the first step in reversing our chronic stress response is to learn to breathe again the way we were born to breathe.

If you haven't been trained in diaphragmatic breathing, find an experienced teacher and practice every day until it once again becomes a habit. Then, as you develop the skill of breathing from the diaphragm in the course of your daily activities, you will begin to experience your breath as a barometer for the nervous system. As long as you are breathing deeply and from the diaphragm, you will find that you can access a feeling of calm and balance even when you are confronted with an unpleasant situation. And you will also notice that if you allow your breath to become shallow by breathing from your chest, anxiety creeps in, your muscles tighten, and your mind begins to race and spin. When this agitated breathing is prolonged, it creates an unsettled and defensive outlook on life. Once you know this from your own experience, you can make a different choice.

20 ***Systematic Relaxation*** To activate the parasympathetic nervous system, diaphragmatic breathing makes an excellent beginning. But we need to do more, particularly when we have spent years unconsciously flinging open the door to the tiger's cage. Daily periods of relaxation are a must. When I tell my patients this, many of them say they relax while they watch TV or read or knit or socialize. The problem is that while these activities distract the mind from its usual worries (and so provide some relief), they do little to relieve the stress we hold in the form of muscular contraction and tension.

To reverse well-established habits of holding tension in our bodies, we need to work with what the yogis call the energy body (pranamaya kosha). Systematic relaxation practices offer a precise, orderly technique for releasing tension from head to toe. There are a number of these techniques, and like all yoga practices, they are best learned from an experienced teacher, and then honed through patient practice. They range in complexity from simple tension/relaxation exercises and point-to-point breathing practices to techniques that require making fine distinctions among various points in the energy body. But all involve moving our attention through the body in a methodical fashion, usually while resting in shavasana (corpse pose). And all require that we withdraw our attention—from the drama of our lives. For the duration of the practice, we let go of our memories, plans, worries, and fantasies, and focus on what we are doing here and now as we move our awareness calmly and quietly from one part of the body to another.

Breathing from the diaphragm, while systematically bringing our full attention to one point in the body after another, not only releases tension and fatigue in the places where we rest our attention, it also augments the energy flow among those points. This promotes both healing and cleansing. Further, because full engagement with a systematic relaxation practice requires that we clear our minds and attend fully to the present moment, we are also refining a skill that opens the door to meditation.

Meditation Since stress begins with the perception that our lives (or at least our sense of wellbeing) are in danger, working with the mind to alter our perceptions is the most powerful technique for quieting our stress response. Most of what activates our fight-or-flight response is not a matter of life or death. We may feel pressured to accomplish a certain task or worried about what will happen at tomorrow's meeting—but our lives don't depend upon the outcome. With rare exceptions, the habitual thought patterns that create the experience of stress for us are overreactions to events in our lives. Instead of responding in a way that floods the body with adrenaline, however, we can reframe the experience to make it not only less stressful, but also more accurate in reflecting what is really happening ("I'm only in a traffic jam, I'm not at death's door." "I want to please this person, but if I don't, I'm not going to be fired"). This goes a long way toward quieting the fight-or-flight response, and it is a skill that comes with experience in meditation.

Meditation helps us understand our mental habits by giving us the opportunity to observe them from a neutral vantage point. This is why I often prescribe meditation to my patients as a way to manage stress.

25   If we ignore early warning symptoms, sooner or later the tiger will tear us up.

I don't mean to minimize meditation as a means of spiritual transformation, but in its early stages, one of the most delicious benefits of meditation practice is seeing that it is possible to avoid getting sucked into the banter and hysteria of our mental chatter. Meditation allows us to witness that banter—to observe it impartially—without being smack in the middle of it. It's like watching a rainstorm from a warm, dry room. The peace we feel when we are watching our minds rather than identifying with our thoughts is the peace at our core.

When you are fast learning to meditate, the mind will wander away from the object of meditation to dwell on some other thought. This will happen again and again. Your job is to gently and repeatedly bring your attention back to your object of meditation, and to do it patiently, without judgment. Sometimes it may seem as if the distracting thoughts are like movie images projected onto a personal viewing screen in your mind. And some may be strange and wild. But you are in the rest-and-digest mode, and as strange as they are, your projections don't trigger the fight-or-flight response. The ability to simply observe them is evidence that they aren't you. And the ability to distinguish between the inner observer in you and the chaotic jumble in your mind means that you can respond with equanimity, rather than react and flood your body with stress hormones.

The more we practice meditation, the more we will be able to discriminate between what is real and what is not—between what is truly life-threatening and what is just a habitual overreaction. And once we begin to see that almost everything that triggers our sympathetic nervous system is merely a habitual overreaction, we can begin to make different choices. Instead of reacting to an unpleasant event, we can cushion the jarring effect on our nervous system by observing it in the same way that we observe our mental chatter in meditation and by consciously breathing from the diaphragm.

This is likely to prove challenging in the beginning. When your spouse or a coworker snaps at you, you may find yourself halfway into an angry retort before you notice that you have switched to chest breathing. Then you need to remind yourself to breathe from the diaphragm and to find a neutral vantage point. But this skill comes with time, particularly when you are sitting for meditation regularly, practicing diaphragmatic breathing, and punctuating your day with a systematic relaxation practice. And as you choose to activate your rest-and-digest response consciously and continuously, you will find yourself in fight-or-flight mode only when your car skids on a patch of ice or the cat knocks over a candle and sets the curtains on fire. Your health will improve, to say nothing of your outlook on life. You have learned to choose the right door.

QUESTIONS FOR DISCUSSION

1. How does Carrie Demers use the story "The Lady or the Tiger" to structure her essay? Point out examples where this strategy is used effectively. What do the "tiger" and the "lady" represent in the essay? What is the "other door" that Demers provides for us?
2. What is the autonomic nervous system? How does Demers define it and describe its functions? How does she make her definition clear?
3. What is problematic about the "fight-or-flight response" in the modern world? What physical problems does it create for us? What are

the advantages of the naturally accruing steroids cortisol and corti-sone? What can happen if they are always in the bloodstream?

4. What is the "rest-and-digest" response, and what happens when we learn to control it?

5. Describe the techniques Demers uses in her practice to help her clients open the "door" of the parasympathic nervous system. How do meditation and controlled breathing assist in this process?

6. How does yogic practice help people to become less anxious and more relaxed? Why is relaxing while doing activities such as watching television or socializing not often successful in achieving these ends?

CONNECTION

Compare the program for holistic healing presented in Demers's essay with the ideas on healing explored in Marc Barasch's "Healing Dream" in this chapter (see page 280).

IDEAS FOR WRITING

1. Do some research into different programs that assist in stress reduc-tion. Do any of these programs seem to be particularly effective in improving patient health and well-being? Have any scientific stud-ies been performed to demonstrate the positive effects? Write up your findings in the form of a documented essay.

2. Try using some form of systematic relaxation, meditation, and breath control or a beginning yoga CD/DVD daily for a week or more, and keep track of your responses to this program in a journal. Write up your findings in the form of an essay that is supported by references to your journal. Alternatively, interview a person who has used a similar program over a significant period of time. Write up your findings in the form of an essay that is supported by references to your interview.

RELATED WEB SITES

Stress Management and Emotional Wellness Links
www.optimalhealthconcepts.com/Stress
This site from Optimal Health Concepts contains links and information on many stress reduction strategies, including meditation, biofeedback, emotive therapy, humor, breathing, and hypnosis.

Yoga Online Mind and Body
http://yoga.org.nz/index.htm
Yoga Online's site contains extensive information on yoga as a means for stress reduction, including definitions and types of yoga, as well as the exercise and spiritual dimensions of yoga.

Marc Ian Barasch

What Is a Healing Dream?

Marc Ian Barasch attended Yale University, where he studied literature, psychology, anthropology, and film. He was a founding member of the psychology department at Naropa University in Boulder, Colorado. Barasch has been editor-in-chief of New Age *Journal (which won a National Magazine Award under his tenure), and a contributing editor to* Psychology Today *and* Natural Health *magazines. He is an award-winning documentary producer and writer, and the founder of an environmental charity, the Green World Campaign. His most widely read books include* The Healing Path: A Soul Approach to Illness *(1992),* Remarkable Recovery *(1995),* Field Notes on the Compassionate Life *(2005), and* Healing Dreams: Exploring the Dreams That Can Transform Your Life *(2000), from which the following selection is excerpted:*

JOURNAL

Write about an unusual, especially memorable, or repeated dream that you have had, one that "stopped you in your tracks" and made you think about your life from a new perspective.

I have had a most rare vision. I have had a dream, past the wit of man to say what dream it was: man is but an ass, if he go about to expound this dream. . . . The eye of man hath not heard, the ear of man hath not seen, man's hand is not able to taste, his tongue to conceive, nor his heart to report, what my dream was.

—Bottom, in Shakespeare's *A Midsummer Night's Dream*

Most of us have had (or, inevitably, will have) at least one dream in our lives that stops us in our tracks. Such dreams tell us that we're not who we think we are. They reveal dimensions of experience beyond the everyday. They may shock us, console us, arouse us, or repulse us. But they take their place alongside our most memorable life events because they're so vivid and emblematic. Some are like parables, setting off sharp detonations of insight; others are like gripping mystery tales; still others are like mythic dramas, or horror stories, or even uproarious jokes. In our journey from childhood to age, we may count them on one hand. Yet once they have flared in the soul, they constellate there, emitting a steady, pulsarlike radiance.

The number of people I have discovered grappling with these powerful inner experiences has astounded me. In a time when the individual psyche is increasingly colonized by mass culture, when media images seem ever more intent on replacing dreams wholesale, here is an unvoiced parallel existence dreamers sometimes do not share with even their loved ones.

People often describe such striking dreams in a self-devised lexicon: "deep" dreams; "vibrational" dreams; "strong" dreams; "flash" dreams; "TV" dreams (a South African priestess); "lucky-feeling dreams" (a dog breeder in Quebec); "true" dreams (a Salish Indian healer in Oregon). A folk artist named Sultan Rogers, famous for his fancifully erotic woodcarvings, refers to his most powerful dreams as "futures," so filled are they with the urgency to be manifest in the world. (He makes a point of carving them immediately upon waking, while the sensuous images are still fresh.) Yet many I spoke with displayed a genuine reticence about discussing their dreams, as if exposing them to daylight might stunt some final germination still to come. Famed Jungian analyst Marion Woodman declined to share a dream she believed helped heal her of a serious physical illness, because, she told me, "I cannot let others into my holy of holies." Some said they feared the professional consequences of being seen as overly attentive to dreams. "I'm in the midst of putting together a multimillion-dollar deal based on a dream I had ten years ago," one man confided. His vision had become the polestar of his life. "But it wouldn't do," he said, "for my partners to think I'm relying on invisible consultants."

In the fifteen years since I began my exploration, a nascent field of research has arisen, along with a host of terms—*impactful, transformative, titanic, transcendent*—to differentiate big dreams from ordinary ones. I have coined the term *Healing Dreams,* because they seem to have a singular intensity of purpose: to lead us to embrace the contradictions between flesh and spirit, self and other, shadow and light in the name of wholeness. The very word for "dream" in Hebrew—*chalom*—derives from the verb meaning "to be made healthy or strong." With remarkable consistency, such dreams tell us that we live on the merest outer shell of our potential, and that the light we seek can be found in the darkness of a yet-unknown portion of our being.

5   Jung labeled them numinous (from the Latin *numen,* meaning "divine command"), but often just used the succinct shorthand, big. While most dreams, he wrote, were "nightly fragments of fantasy," thinly veiled commentaries on "the affairs of the everyday," these significant dreams were associated with major life passages, deep relationship issues, and spiritual turning points.

Many cultures have had a terminology for such dreams of surpassing power. The Greek New Testament seems to contain more words for inner experience than Eskimos have for snow: *onar* (a vision seen in sleep as opposed to waking); *enypnion* (a vision seen in sleep that comes by surprise); *horama* (which could refer to visions of the night, sleeping visions, or waking visions); *horasis* (a supernatural vision); *optasia* (a supernatural vision that implies the Deity revealing Himself); and so on. By and large the English language has been impoverished of a working vocabulary; we have little at hand beyond *dream* and *nightmare*. Given our cultural paucity, it can be a struggle to define these signal occurrences.

"How do you know when you've had a special dream?" I once asked a Choctaw Indian acquaintance named Preston. A humorous man with rubbery features—his role in his tribe, he told me, was as a "backwards person," a trickster and comedian—he grew uncharacteristically serious at my question.

"These vision dreams are things that you follow," he said. "Things that you do. They show you a situation that needs to be taken care of, and a way to turn it around."

"But *how* do you know?" I pressed him.

10 "It's the way you feel. That kind of dream wakes you up very sudden-like. Maybe you wake up really, really happy." He looked at me, eyebrow cocked. "Or maybe you wake up with your bed so soaking wet you'da thought you'd peed on yourself!"

His ribald comment points to a universally reported attribute of Healing Dreams—what we might call ontological weight, the heft and immediacy of lived experience. Remarks from various dreamers return often to a common theme of "realer than real." They often comment on the acuity of the senses—taste, touch, sight, smell, and hearing. I, too, can recall awakening with my ears still ringing from a dream gunshot, or waking up momentarily blinded by a dream's burst of light.

There is often a depth of emotion that beggars normal waking life. The sixteenth-century rabbi and physician Solomon Almoli wrote: "If one dreams of powerful fantasy images that cause him to be excited or to feel anger or fear during the dream itself, this is a true dream; but if the images are insipid and arouse no strong feelings, the dream is not true." Such dreams are filled not with simple anxiety, but terror; not mere pleasantness, but heart-bursting joy. People report waking up on tear-soaked pillows, or laughing in delight. (The Bantu people of Africa have a specific term for the latter—*bilita mpatshi,* or blissful dreaming.)

Healing Dreams are analogous to ancient Greek theater, where actors in colorful, oversized costumes presented stories contrived to put an audience through the emotional wringer; to make it feel, viscerally, the heroes' agonies and ecstasies. Indeed, some Healing Dreams feature larger-than-life settings and personages—palatial buildings, sweeping landscapes, beings of supernatural goodness or terrible malignancy. Healing Dreams seem designed to produce a catharsis, to lead their "audience" to a metanoia, a change of heart.

Like drama, such dreams often have an unusually coherent narrative structure. Islamic dream texts refer to the ordinary dream as *azghas*—literally, "handful of dried grass and weeds," signifying a lack of arrangement—in contrast to the more coherent messages of *akham* ("genuine inspiration from the Deity, warning from a protecting power, or revelation of coming events"). The Healing Dream's story-telling tends to be more artful, often containing a rich array of literary or cinematic devices—subplots, secondary characters, sudden reversals and surprise endings, flashbacks and flashforwards, adumbration, even voice-over narration and background music.

15   Healing Dreams often involve a sense of the uncanny or paranormal. Within the dream, one may find one has special powers to telekinetically move objects; receive information as if via telepathy; levitate; transform oneself into other creatures; visit heavens or hells. Dreamers report of out-of-body experiences; actual events foreseen; talking with the departed; having a near-identical dream to that of a friend or loved one; and other strange synchronicities. Healing Dreams hum with so much energy that, like a spark from a Van de Graaf generator, they seem to leap the gap between the visible and invisible worlds.

In such dreams, symbols tend to be extraordinarily multilayered—exaggerated cases of what Freud referred to as "over-determination," where an image seems to be "chosen" by the unconscious for its multiplicity of associations. Language itself reveals a dense richness. A key dream-word may yield half a dozen definitions, each with a different or even opposing nuance. There is often a powerful aesthetic component—such dreams may depict dances and rituals, music and song, poetry, photos, paintings, and other art forms. There is frequently a collective dimension—the dream seems to transcend the dreamer's personal concerns, reaching into the affairs of family, clan, community, or the world at large.

Such dreams also have a peculiar persistence. People report waking up with the images still before their eyes. The dream lingers in memory long after common ones fade. New meanings emerge over time. One lives, as it were, into the dream. "The *findout*," the Native American sage Lame Deer told one researcher, "has taken me all my life."

Most important, Healing Dreams, if heeded, can be transformational—creating new attitudes toward ourselves and others, magnifying our spiritual understanding, deepening the feeling side of life, producing changes in careers and relationships, even affecting society itself. After a Healing Dream, one may never be the same again.

The Dream Uses You

Many people wonder why they should bother with their dreams at all. A common answer is that they will help us with our lives, and this is certainly true. Even the most extraordinary dream, properly investigated, will have much to say about bread-and-butter issues like work, love, and

health. But the Healing Dream is less a defender of our waking goals—
material achievement, perfect romance, a modest niche in history—than
an advocate-general for the soul, whose aims may lay athwart those of the
ego. Dreams are often uninterested in the self-enhancement stratagems
we mistake for progress. "It's vulgarizing to say that we can use dreams as
tools—like shovels!—to get ahead, or be more assertive, like a kid who
prays his little sister will drop dead so he can have her candy," a dream-
worker once told me with some passion. "It's more like"—and here he
seemed to fluoresce with certainty—"the dream uses *you*."

20   Such dreams "use" us only if we are willing to dwell for a time within
their ambiguities without resolving them. The Jungian psychologist
Robert Johnson tells of the time he had a dreamlike vision of a "spirit
man" with burning orange fire coursing through his veins. The man
plunged to the bottom of an indigo lake, but the fire was miraculously
unquenched. Then the spirit man took Johnson by the hand and flew
him to a great nebula coruscating like a diamond at the center of the
universe. Standing on the very threshold of divine majesty, before vast,
dazzling whorls of light eternal, Johnson tugged at the man's sleeve and
asked impatiently, "This is fine, but *what is it good for?*"

"The spirit man looked at me," wrote Johnson, "in disgust: 'It isn't
good for *anything*.'" Still, Johnson wondered for a long while afterward
how his experience might tangibly change his life. Then he had a key insight: *He would never know.* "This magnificent power," he wrote "is trans-
muted into small things, day-to-day behavior, attitudes, the choices that
we make in the ordinariness of daily human life."

Johnson's experience emphasizes that, contrary to a slew of popular
works (starting with the dream manuals of the early Egyptians), there
may be no surefire, direct method to utilize the power of dreams. We
may be astonished by a bolt of lightning, but that doesn't mean we can
harness it to flash down upon the grill to cook our steak. Healing
Dreams offer few outright prescriptions. They often require us to live
our questions rather than furnish instant answers.

How, then, should we see a Healing Dream? We might think of it as a
window that enlarges our perspective, freeing us of a certain tunnel vision. It frames our daily concerns in a context beyond the confines of
our room. The view from this dream window opens onto what we may
think the exclusive province of mystics and philosophers—conundrums
like the meaning of the sacred, the problem of evil, the nature of time,
the quest for a true calling, the mysteries of death and love—making
these issues intimately our own.

Or we might see the dream as a worthy opponent. It is often said that spiritual work is an *opus contra naturam*, going against the grain of what seems
natural, normal, or even good. The unconscious is not just the repository

of beauty and light, or the issuer of benign, firm-handed guidance, but the home of the trickster. The dream figure that bears the denied powers of the self often appears sinister and antithetical. Yet he may also be our secret ally: in spiritual life, what is merely pleasant can become the ego's friction-free way of sliding by without learning much of anything. By rubbing us the wrong way, the Healing Dream kindles an inner heat, forcing us to include our obstacles and adversaries in our process of growth.

25   We might regard a Healing Dream as a work of art, something that evokes a feeling of meaningfulness that cannot be put into words. Like the glowing Vermeer painting of a simple woman with a pitcher, it is the extraordinary thing that sheds light on the ordinary. Like art, dreams create a shift in perspective in the very act of beholding them. Seeing things in a way we have not seen before—taking the stance of the appreciator rather than the analyst—changes us, as suggested by the remark by the phenomenologist Merleau-Ponty: "Rather than seeing the painting, I see according to or with it."

Healing Dreams might be conceived as visits to another world with its own geography and inhabitants. From this perspective, we are explorers visiting a foreign land whose citizens have customs, beliefs, and language that are not entirely familiar. Dream images thus are experienced in their own right, not just as self-fabricated symbols. Through this sort of living encounter, dreams become the proverbial travel that broadens the mind.

Or we might regard the Healing Dream as a wise teacher, one who instructs us in the most personal way—embarrassingly so, for she knows our forbidden desires and deepest fears, our secret hopes and unexpressed gifts. This teacher tells us stories about ourselves, about our relationships to others, about our place in the larger schema. This approach may require a humility the ego finds discomforting. Jung told one dreamer: "Look here, the best way to deal with a dream is to think of yourself as a sort of ignorant child, ignorant youth, and to come to the two-million-year-old man or to the old mother of days and ask, 'Now, what do you think of me?'"

What *does* the dream think? Or is a Healing Dream itself more a question posed to *us*? If so, the most reasonable-seeming answer is often the wrong one. Such dreams play by rules that confound the waking mind. But at the heart of Healing Dreams are certain consistent, if challenging, attitudes. Before we set out to understand the big dream, it would be helpful to consider some of the principles and perspectives that will recur on the journey:

▪ *Nonself:* Dreams show us we are not who we think we are: "We walk through ourselves," wrote James Joyce, "meeting robbers, ghosts, giants, old men, young men, wives, widows, brothers-in-love." Dreams de-center us from our everyday identity, pushing us toward a richer multiplicity of being. Thus in dreams we may be startled to find, as one dream researcher puts it, that we are "a woman and not a man, a dog not a person, a child not an adult . . . [even] two people at once." As Alice in Wonderland says: "I know who I *was* this morning, but since then I have changed several times." What Healing Dreams attempt to cure is nothing less than the ego's point of view—that habitual "I" that clings to rigid certainties of what "I want," "I fear," "I hate," "I love." What is sometimes called the ego-self or the "I" figure in our dreams may be a mere side character, reacting or observing but not in control of events. We may experience the diminution of what in waking life we most prize in ourselves, and the elevation of what we find belittling. One sign of a healthy personality is the ability to acknowledge other selfhoods and inhabit other skins.

■ *Nonsense:* From the ego's standpoint, dream logic is an oxymoron. It is a sure bet that whatever we deem most ridiculous upon waking is the fulcrum point of what the dream wants to tell us. Indeed, when we find ourselves disparaging an image as meaningless, it is a signal to retrieve it from the scrap heap and place it on the table. Like a magician, the dream may confuse us through misdirection, but only because we are paying too much attention to the right hand and not enough to the left. Like a fool in the court of a king, dreams use absurdity to tell the truth when none else dare; but the king must realize the joke is on him in order to get the punch line.

■ *Balance:* A Healing Dream often comes to redress imbalance—something in the personality is askew, awry, not right (or perhaps, *too* right). If we have become inflated, it cuts us back down to human scale; if we wander in a dark vale, lost, it suddenly illumines the mountaintop. The psyche, Jung suggests, "is a self-regulating system that maintains its equilibrium just as the body does. Every process that goes too far immediately and inevitably calls forth compensations." The quickest way to the heart of a dream is to ask what one-sided conscious attitude it is trying to offset.

■ *Reversal of value:* In dreams, our fixed reference points—our opinions, values, and judgments—may be revealed as mere tricks of perspective. What the conscious mind believes to be a precious gem may be a beach pebble to the spirit, while what it tosses aside may be the pearl of great price. Alice, on her journey through Wonderland's dreamscape, first drinks a potion that makes her large, and she weeps in misery. Then when another elixir makes her shrink, she finds herself literally drowning in her own tears. A few small tears, usually a matter of little import, suddenly become a matter of life or death—as indeed they may be to the dreaming soul.

■ *Wholeness:* Healing Dreams point to the relatedness of all things, reveling in the union of opposites. They show us a vision of the divine that encompasses both growth and decay, horror and delight. We may crave a world of either/or, but the Dream says, *Both/and.* We build a wall between our social persona and our inner selves; the Dream bids us, *Demolish it.* We wish to believe we're separate from one another, but the Dream insists, *We are in this together.* We believe time to be a one-way river, flowing from past to present to future, yet the Dream reveals, *All three times at once.* We wish to be virtuous and free of taint, but the Dream insists, *The dark and the light are braided and bound.*

The Way of the Healing Dream

We live in a practical era, one that stresses the productive usage of things. Yet Healing Dreams are not easily reduced to the utilitarian. Although they may offer practical revelation, they have more in common with the realm of art, poetry, and music, where what you do with an experience is not the overriding issue. Such dreams open up a gap in the ordinary, allowing something new, and often indefinable, to enter our lives. We can work with our dreams, "unpack" them, analyze them, learn from them. But it is their residue of mystery that gives them enduring power, making them touchstones we return to again and again.

30   When we take our dreams seriously, their images and feelings subtly begin to alter our waking lives. Meaning seeps in through a kind of osmosis. We begin to glimpse the principle that connects each to all. Any sincere attention (and commitment) to our dreams renders us spiritually combustible. What was once inert now strikes sparks.

Healing Dreams seem to *want* something of us, and often will not let go until they receive it. But few of us pay them serious mind. Their images dissipate into air, dissolve like snowflakes on water. We dive back into the slipstream of our dailiness with something akin to relief. We sense that if we were to draw too near, the gravitational field of dreams might perturb, forever, the fixed orbit of our lives.

For this reason, I've chosen to focus as much as possible on these dreams that won't allow themselves to be tossed aside; the ones that yank off the bedclothes, spook us, amaze us, drag us below, lift us above, damn us, save us—in terms so strong, in presence so palpable, we simply can't ignore them. *These* dreams refuse to go quietly, for they mean to change us utterly. If we look into their depths, we may behold a unique destiny struggling from its chrysalis, and watch, astonished and not a little afraid, as our unsuspected selfhood unfolds a new, wetly glistening wing.

QUESTIONS FOR DISCUSSION

1. How does Barasch use similes in the first paragraph to reinforce some of the qualities of the "Healing Dream"? Why would it be (as Bottom says in the quotation from *A Midsummer Night's Dream*) so difficult to "conceive" and "report" what such a dream is about?
2. Why did some of the people Barasch interviewed express "reticence" to share and discuss their healing dreams?
3. Why does the author compare healing dreams to Greek theater and other dramatic forms of art?
4. In what sense are healing dreams "transformational"? How do they "use" us, changing our lives in subtle ways?

5. How do healing dreams "enlarge our perspective," serving as an opponent, a teacher, or an artwork?
6. Explain the five bulleted "attitudes" and "principles and perspectives" of the healing dream. How might these five attitudes help in the dreamer's healing process?

CONNECTION

Compare and contrast Stephen King's views on the significance of dreams (see page 17) with Barasch's views.

IDEAS FOR WRITING

1. Analyze the dream you narrated in your journal entry above from the perspective of the five attitudes presented at the end of the essay. How did examining the dream using the attitudes delineated by Barasch help you to understand it better?
2. Write a definition of another type of dream than the healing dream, using some of the same techniques as Barasch does, listing qualities, principles, attitudes, similes, and analogies. You can also use examples of such dreams that you have had or read about.

RELATED WEB SITES

Marc Ian Barasch
www.healingdreams.com/author.htm
At this Web site you will find information about the author, Marc Ian Barasch; his book, *Healing Dreams;* and his work surrounding the subject of harnessing the power of dreams to heal.

The International Center for the Study of Dreams
www.asdreams.org
This organization maintains a Web site with a large archive of professional articles on all aspects of dreams and dream research from their journal and magazine; there are also many useful educational materials available online through the site.

TOPICS FOR RESEARCH AND WRITING

1. Select one of the following terms: "nightmare," "obsession," "addiction," "depression." Research the term, and write an extended definition of it. Quote from the selections that helped you with your definition. How have the readings in this chapter helped you to better understand the meaning of the word that you are defining? Give examples of how you can apply the definition to your own life, to issues in the media, or to issues that your friends have.

2. After reading the essay by Maressa Ozack in this chapter, do some research into different types of potentially obsessive and destructive behavior associated with overuse of computers and cyberspace—online gambling, video game play, avatar role-playing, social networking sites, and so on. Write an essay about your findings and indicate what might be done to control some of these "computer abuses." Or, argue for the positive impact of computers and cyberspace.

3. Solomon defines depression as being related to obsessive behavior. Although not as extreme, what forms of addiction presented in this chapter are rooted in less serious forms of depression? Write an essay that relates several of the obsessive forms of behavior discussed in this chapter to Solomon's definition of depression.

4. Using Lamott's essay "Hunger" as a point of departure, do some research and write an essay defining the nature and origins of eating disorders such as anorexia and bulimia. What social, psychological, or chemical factors can lead to an eating disorder? What solutions have worked in helping people recover from their eating disorders?

5. Marc Barasch writes about escape from depression and obsession through a form of spiritual transformation that comes from a "healing dream." Do some research into ways that strongly charged dreams can lead to mental healing and draw some conclusions about the efficacy of such approaches in contrast to more traditional forms of therapy or medications.

6. Write a short story that captures a sense of an addiction that you have.

7. Write an essay on one of the types of obsessive behavior discussed in this chapter. Do research on the topic, and then integrate the research into your personal understanding of the obsessive behavior. By integrating your personal experience and your research, you will be better able to help your readers understand the type of obsessive behavior you are defining.

8. See one of the following films that explores the relationship between nightmares, obsessions, and addictions. Write a paper that analyzes how the film presents the obsession. What did you learn about the obsession from watching the film? Here are some choices: *Field of Dreams, The Piano, House of Games, Jacob's Ladder, A Beautiful Mind, Tom and Viv, Moulin Rouge, Beloved, Traffic, What Dreams May Come, Insomnia, The Cell, Girl, Interrupted, The Virgin Suicides, Shine, Amadeus, Leaving Las Vegas, The Hours, Adaptation, Juno, Requiem For a Dream, The Machinist, There Will Be Blood, No Country For Old Men,* and *Definitely Maybe.*

6 Journeys in Gender and Relationships

Marc Chagall (1887–1985)
Birthday (1915)

Write about a romantic relationship so joyous that it might make a couple feel the world was topsy-turvy, with all the normal rules of gravity, logic, and time suspended.

*No one who accepts the view that censorship is the chief reason for dream
distortion will be surprised to learn from the results of dream interpretation
that most of the dreams of adults are traced back by analysis to* erotic wishes.
                    SIGMUND FREUD
                    Erotic Wishes and Dreams

She obeyed him; she always did as she was told.
                    MAXINE HONG KINGSTON
                    No Name Woman

*No, it wasn't easy for any of us, girls and boys, as we forced our beautiful,
free-flowing child-selves into those narrow, constricting cubicles labeled
female and male.*

                    JULIUS LESTER
                    Being a Boy

THEMATIC INTRODUCTION

People in all cultures define themselves in relationship to gender roles and sexuality. Individuals develop a sense of their gender role through observation and participation in the values and rituals of their family, peer group, culture, and spiritual heritage. The shifting social definitions of acceptable gender-role behavior have led many people today to feel confused about their gender identity and about what constitutes appropriate sexual behavior: How do we meet somebody we should spend our entire life with when in more traditional times "arranged" relationships and marriages were the norm? Should a sexual relationship be casual or only available within a stable, loving relationship? What if our gender orientation is other than mainstream heterosexual? What responsibility does each partner in a relationship have for birth control, for making decisions about child bearing and child care responsibilities? Given the growing openness of modern society, people can feel confused about their gender identity and some rebel consciously against their culture's gender roles. As much as we think about gender relationships as being a part of social and cultural values, each individual's gender and sexuality is an unconscious aspect that is often revealed in dreams and fantasies, as well as in daily life.

Each of the readings selected for this chapter relates to a particular issue of controversy about relationships, gender roles, and sexuality. We begin with a poem, Pablo Neruda's "The Dream," which explores the question of what we learn in a loving sexual relationship through conflict, struggle, and reaffirmation. The next reading, Sigmund Freud's "Erotic Wishes and Dreams," presents his classic theories of dream symbols as reflecting repressed sexual desire and erotic wish fulfillment. The selection by Mary Pipher, "Saplings in the Storm," explores how gender role and the sexual feelings of puberty transform young girls. Pipher argues against traditional gender roles and encourages readers to consider the importance of allowing maturing girls to retain independent minds and self-made roles and goals.

Almost every teenager today plays computer games at home and at school. These games play an important role in establishing friendships and gender identity. In Bonnie Ruberg's "Games for Girls," she questions the lack of challenge in games designed for girls in contrast to those designed for boys, a reflection of traditional gender roles.

The next selections present examples of how youth today experience nontraditional gender roles. In "The Real Boy Code," William Pollack discusses a number of situations in which young men are moving away from traditional expectations of men towards expectations more often associated with women, such as expressing feelings, showing emotion, and more willingness to create equality within relationships. David Sedaris's "I Like Guys" presents a tragicomic memoir of growing up gay in the late 1950s, pointing out how school integration did little to alleviate the sexual oppression experienced by gay youth of the period. Finally, college student Jakki Martinez writes frankly about the striking changes in relationships between the genders in "The College 'Hook Up' Scene." Relying both on her research and observation, Martinez defines "hooking up," a ritual widely practiced in college communities all over our country. She distances herself from the practice, believing that it makes women less than equal to men, both in regard to their emotional well-being and their reputation.

In an essay on youth and college student socializing that goes beyond the casual hook-up, student writer Gilberto Jimenez in "It's Complicated: Facebook and Modern Youth Relationships" examines the way popular social networking sites like Facebook are changing the way young men and women today present one another and maintain viable relationships as well as the computer applications and social etiquette involved in modern dating.

The final essay in this chapter is about new perspectives of father–daughter relations in an urban African-American family. In "Loving a One-armed Man," Tajamika Paxton examines the struggles that men face in a world where they are "being torn apart by the traditional demands of one dimensional manhood." In the new millennium, the issues of gender identity and sexuality only promise to become more complex, particularly with the increasing social, cultural, and political differences between traditional family values and the values of today's youth culture. We hope that the readings in this chapter will give you insights into the customs of the past as well as some provocative points of view about changing gender roles and nontraditional relationships.

CAUSALITY AND THE INWARD JOURNEY

What causes people to have certain kinds of dreams or to remember a particular dream? Do people's gender concerns influence their dreams? How do dreams and sexual fantasies influence an individual's waking life and personal relationships? Why can certain people use their dreams to make their lives richer while others are overwhelmed by their unconscious fears? All of these questions, central to the issues raised in *Dreams and Inward Journeys*, are also issues of causality.

As you reflect on your dreams and emotions, working to understand what you read and to create clear, focused arguments, causal analysis will be a fundamental part of your thinking process. Causal analysis can help you to understand your inner life, to interpret your relationship to the public world, and to explain how and why things happen the way they do. Finding connections that exist between two events, understanding how one event led to or produced another event, and speculating about the consequences of earlier events—all involve causal reasoning.

Observing and Collecting Information

People naturally search for solutions to mental dilemmas and physical problems, wanting to explain why something occurred and how they can improve the situation. In most cases, the more confident we are about our explanations of any event, the better we feel. Observing and collecting information about both your inner and outer worlds will increase your chances of making accurate causal connections and inferences about the sources and meanings of your dreams and the public events that are influencing you. For example, if you are keeping a dream journal, you may find that after writing down your dreams for a while, you notice repeated images or situations that reflect your psychological concerns and may help you to draw more accurate inferences about your inner needs. Similarly, keeping a media journal of newspaper clippings or stories downloaded from the Internet will help you become more alert to issues of cause and effect in the external world: immediate and long-term causes for our country's attack on another nation, for instance, or the effects of a series of "strategic" bombing raids on the ecological system, the rate of global pollution and disease, and the flow of refugees out of and into various countries in a region of the world.

Whether you are studying dreams, literature, or current events, be sure that the causal connections you make are sound ones. Observe carefully and consider all possible causes, not simply the obvious, immediate ones. For example, consider all of the complex causes and effects that are raised in the essays that consider nontraditional sexual relationships: Jakki Martinez's "The College 'Hook-Up' Scene" and David Sedaris's narrative "I Like Guys."

In writing a causal analysis, whether of a dream, a short story, or a social issue, it is essential that you provide adequate evidence, both factual and logical, for the conclusions that you draw. You may believe that you understand the causes involved quite clearly, but perceiving these connections for yourself is not enough; you must re-create for your reader, in clear and specific language, the mental process you went through to arrive at your conclusions. Methodically and carefully questioning your own thought process will help you to clarify your insights, to generate new ideas and evidence that can be used to support your analysis, and to avoid logical fallacies.

Causal Logical Fallacies

People create connections between events or personal issues about which they feel strongly, often rushing their thinking process to a hasty conclusion. One of the most common errors, the post hoc fallacy ("after this, therefore because of this"), mistakenly attempts to create a causal connection between unrelated events that follow each other closely in time. But a sequence in time is not necessarily a causal sequence. In fact, most magical or superstitious thinking relative to dreams and daily life is based on faulty causal analysis of sequential events. For instance, people may carry a burden of guilt because of coincidences between their inner thoughts and outer events, such as a dream of the death of a loved one and that person's subsequent death or injury.

Another common problem in thinking and writing about causality is causal oversimplification, in which a person argues that one thing caused something to happen, when in fact a number of different elements worked together to produce a major effect or outcome. For example, one's dream of flying may have been inspired in part by watching a television program about pilots the night before, yet other causes may also be present: one's love for performing or showing off or one's joy about a recent accomplishment. When trying to apply a broad theory to explain many individual cases, thinkers often become involved in causal oversimplification. We can ask, for example, if Freud's theories about the sexual content and sources of dreams really explain the entire range of dream stories and imagery. What other causes and sources might he have neglected to consider? Asking about other possible causal relations not covered by a causal thesis will help you to test the soundness of your analysis.

The slippery slope fallacy is also of particular relevance to the issues explored in this text. In the slippery slope fallacy, a reasoned analysis of cause and effect is replaced by a reaction of fear in which a person might argue that if one seemingly insignificant event is allowed to happen, there will be serious consequences. Of course, in some cases this may be true: if one isn't careful about sexually transmitted diseases, there is the possibility that a person may get AIDS and eventually die. In many cases, however, theorizing about dreadful future events can become a way of validating irrational fears or can become a way of providing an excuse for maintaining the status quo. Recognizing the slippery slope fallacies both in others' thinking and within your own thinking can help you to free yourself from irrational anxiety and to develop better critical thinking skills.

Good causal reasoning can lead you closer to understanding and developing theories and explanations for the multiple causes and effects of the issues and events you encounter in your reading and in your own life. With an awareness of the complexities of causal thinking, you will be able to think and write more critically, clearly, and persuasively.

Pablo Neruda

The Dream

Pablo Neruda (1904–1973) was born and educated in Chile. When he was 25, he began a long career in politics as a Chilean consul in Ceylon and East Asia and went on to serve at the Chilean Embassy in Mexico City. He was a member of the World Peace Council from 1950 to 1973 and received many international peace prizes. Neruda is considered one of the greatest poets of the twentieth century, and his work has been translated into 20 different languages. In 1971 he received the Nobel Prize in Literature. Critics have noted that Neruda's poetry "structures itself on emotive association like the subconscious, and worlds in the flux of sensation and thought." These qualities are apparent in "The Dream" (from The Captain's Verses, *1972), a poem that can be read as an account of a turning point in a relationship.*

Write about a time when you felt like ending a relationship that was becoming too all-involving or too stressful. Did you find a way to save or
transform the relationship? If so, how?

Walking on the sands
I decided to leave you.

I was treading a dark clay
that trembled
5   and I, sinking and coming out,
decided that you should come out
of me, that you were weighing me down
like a cutting stone,
and I worked out your loss
10 step by step:
to cut off your roots,
to release you alone into the wind.

Ah in that minute,
my dear, a dream
15 with its terrible wings
was covering you.

You felt yourself swallowed by the clay,
and you called to me and I did not come,
you were going, motionless,
20 without defending yourself
until you were smothered in the quicksand.

Afterwards
my decision encountered your dream,
and from the rupture
25 that was breaking our hearts
we came forth clean again, naked,
loving each other
without dream, without sand,
complete and radiant,
30 sealed by fire.

QUESTIONS FOR DISCUSSION

1. What is the significance of the sands and the trembling "dark clay"
   that the speaker treads on in the first part of the poem? How do the

speaker and the "you" in the poem change and gain power over the clay and sand as the poem progresses? How does this change comment on the central relationship in the poem?

2. What leads the "I" in the poem to decide to leave the "you"? What kind of a crisis in a relationship might this decision suggest?

3. What is the meaning of the dream with "terrible wings" that covers the "you?"

4. What seems to cause the "I" to have a change of heart toward the "you"? What might be the "rupture" that cleanses and renews the couple's relationship?

5. What new definition of love emerges as the speaker comments on the lovers as "naked,/loving each other/without dream, without sand"? Does the kind of love suggested here seem erotic, spiritual, or something else entirely?

CONNECTION

Compare the portrayal of struggle, rejection, and acceptance in a close relationship in Neruda's poem with the father–daughter relationship in Paxton's "Loving a One-armed Man" in this chapter (see page 346).

IDEAS FOR WRITING

1. Write an essay in which you define an ideal love capable of overcoming obstacles in its path. Use personal examples as well as references to Neruda's poem.

2. Write an essay in which you analyze the poem from the perspective of gender roles. Argue which gender a reader would be most likely to assign to the "I" and which to the "you" in the poem and explain your choices, making specific references to the poem. What criticism and/or acceptance of traditional gender roles does the poem make or imply, and how does it make such points?

RELATED WEB SITES

Academy of American Poets: Pablo Neruda
`www.poets.org/poet.php/prmPID/279`
This page on Neruda contains a biography, translations of poems, and links to other sites and materials relevant to his work.

Interview with Martin Espada on Pablo Neruda
`www.democracynow.org/article.pl?sid=04/07/16/1442233`
This interview for *Democracy Now!* on NPR highlights Neruda's contributions to twentieth-century poetry and emphasizes his importance in Chilean history and culture.

Sigmund Freud

Erotic Wishes and Dreams

Known as the founder of the psychoanalytic method and the originator of concepts such as the unconscious mind and the Oedipus complex, Sigmund Freud (1856–1939) was also a pioneer in the scientific study of dreams and human sexuality. Freud spent most of his life in Vienna, where he practiced psychoanalysis and published many important studies on psychology and dream interpretation as well as cultural studies that focus on psychological interpretations of art and history. His works include Interpretation of Dreams *(1900),* Totem and Taboo, *and* Leonardo da Vinci: A Study in Psychosexuality. *In "Erotic Wishes and Dreams," from his explanation of dream theory,* On Dreams *(1901), Freud presents his ideas on dream symbolism and expresses his conviction that dreams focus on erotic wishes and fantasies, although sometimes in a disguised form.*

JOURNAL

Write about a dream you have had that you consider explicitly or implicitly sexual in its content. Did you consider the dream to be a form of wish fulfillment, or could there have been some other explanation for the dream and its images?

No one who accepts the view that censorship is the chief reason for dream distortion will be surprised to learn from the results of dream interpretation that most of the dreams of adults are traced back by analysis to *erotic wishes*. This assertion is not aimed at dreams with an *undisguised* sexual content, which are no doubt familiar to all dreamers from their own experience and are as a rule the only ones to be described as "sexual dreams." Even dreams of this latter kind offer enough surprises in their choice of the people whom they make into sexual objects, in their disregard of all the limitations which the dreamer imposes in his waking life upon his sexual desires, and by their many strange details, hinting at what are commonly known as "perversions." A great many other dreams, however, which show no sign of being erotic in their manifest content, are revealed by the work of interpretation in analysis as sexual wish fulfillments; and, on the other hand, analysis proves that a great many of the thoughts left over from the activity of waking life as "residues of the previous day" only find their way to representation in dreams through the assistance of repressed erotic wishes.

There is no theoretical necessity why this should be so; but to explain the fact it may be pointed out that no other group of instincts has been submitted to such far-reaching suppression by the demands of cultural education, while at the same time the sexual instincts are also the ones which, in most people, find it easiest to escape from the control of the highest mental agencies. Since we have become acquainted with infantile sexuality, which is often so unobtrusive in its manifestations and is always overlooked and misunderstood, we are justified in saying that almost every civilized man retains the infantile forms of sexual life in some respect or other. We can thus understand how it is that repressed infantile sexual wishes provide the most frequent and strongest motive forces for the construction of dreams.

There is only one method by which a dream which expresses erotic wishes can succeed in appearing innocently nonsexual in its manifest content. The material of the sexual ideas must not be represented as such, but must be replaced in the content of the dream by hints, allusions and similar forms of indirect representation. But, unlike other forms of indirect representation, that which is employed in dreams must not be immediately intelligible. The modes of representation which fulfill these conditions are usually described as "symbols" of the things which they represent. Particular interest has been directed to them since it has been noticed that dreamers speaking the same language make use of the same symbols, and that in some cases, indeed, the use of the same symbols extends beyond the use of the same language. Since dreamers themselves are unaware of the meaning of the symbols they use, it is difficult at first sight to discover the source of the connection between the symbols and what they replace and represent. The fact itself, however, is beyond doubt, and it is important for the technique of dream interpretation. For, with the help of a knowledge of dream symbolism, it is possible to understand the meaning of separate elements of the content of a dream or separate pieces of a dream or in some cases even whole dreams, without having to ask the dreamer for his associations. Here we are approaching the popular ideal of translating dreams and on the other hand are returning to the technique of interpretation used by the ancients, to whom dream interpretation was identical with interpretation by means of symbols.

Although the study of dream symbols is far from being complete, we are in a position to lay down with certainty a number of general statements and a quantity of special information on the subject. There are some symbols which bear a single meaning almost universally: thus the Emperor and Empress (or the King and Queen) stand for the parents, rooms represent women and their entrances and exits the openings of the body. The majority of dream symbols serve to represent persons, parts of the body and activities invested with erotic interest; in particular, the genitals are represented by a number of often very surprising symbols, and the greatest variety of objects are employed to denote them symbolically. Sharp weapons, long and stiff objects, such as tree trunks and sticks, stand for the male genital; while cupboards, boxes, carriages or ovens may represent the uterus. In such cases as these the *tertium comparationis,* the common element in these substitutions, is immediately intelligible; but there are other symbols in which it is not so easy to grasp the connection. Symbols such as a staircase or going upstairs, representing sexual intercourse, a tie or cravat for the male organ, or wood for the female one, provoke our unbelief until we can arrive at an understanding of the symbolic relation underlying them by some other means. Moreover a whole number of dream symbols are bisexual and can relate to the male or female genitals according to the context.

5   Some symbols are universally disseminated and can be met with in all dreamers belonging to a single linguistic or cultural group; there are others which occur only within the most restricted and individual limits, symbols constructed by an individual out of his own ideational material. Of the former class we can distinguish some whose claim to represent sexual ideas is immediately justified by linguistic usage (such, for instance, as those derived from agriculture, e.g., "fertilization" or "seed") and others whose relation to sexual ideas appears to reach back into the very earliest ages and to the most obscure depths of our conceptual functioning. The power of constructing symbols has not been exhausted in our own days in the case of either of the two sorts of symbols which I have distinguished at the beginning of this paragraph. Newly discovered objects (such as airships) are, as we may observe, at once adopted as universally available sexual symbols.

It would, incidentally, be a mistake to expect that if we had a still profounder knowledge of dream symbolism (of the "language of dreams") we could do without asking the dreamer for his associations to the dream and go back entirely to the technique of dream interpretation of antiquity. Quite apart from individual symbols and oscillations in the use of universal ones, one can never tell whether any particular element in the content of a dream is to be interpreted symbolically or in its proper sense, and one can be certain that the *whole* content of a dream is not to be interpreted symbolically. A knowledge of dream symbolism will never do more than enable us to translate certain constituents of the dream content, and will not relieve us of the necessity for applying the technical rules which I gave earlier. It will, however, afford the most valuable assistance to interpretation precisely at points at which the dreamer's associations are insufficient or fail altogether.

Dream symbolism is also indispensable to an understanding of what are known as "typical" dreams, which are common to everyone, and of "recurrent" dreams in individuals.

If the account I have given in this short discussion of the symbolic mode of expression in dreams appears incomplete, I can justify my neglect by drawing attention to one of the most important pieces of knowledge that we possess on this subject. Dream symbolism extends far beyond dreams: it is not peculiar to dreams, but exercises a similar dominating influence on representation in fairy tales, myths and legends, in jokes and in folklore. It enables us to trace the intimate connections between dreams and these latter productions. We must not suppose that dream symbolism is a creation of the dream work; it is in all probability a characteristic of the unconscious thinking which provides the dream work with the material for condensation, displacement and dramatization.

QUESTIONS FOR DISCUSSION

1. Why does Freud believe that "repressed infantile sexual wishes" are the strongest motivation behind dreams and their primary content? Does he provide convincing evidence for this belief?
2. How might a dream express erotic wishes and also appear innocent of sexual content? What might cause this apparent contradiction?
3. How does Freud define "symbols" as they appear in dreams? What examples does he provide? Do these seem like sexual symbols to you?
4. How does Freud compare traditional, culturally universal dream symbols with more modern symbols based on technological inventions? Can you think of modern dream symbols that have sexual implications?
5. According to Freud, why is it always a mistake to create dream interpretations without investigating the dreamer's own associations with the symbols from his or her dreams? Do you agree with Freud that popular books that list the meanings of dream symbols are basically worthless? Explain your position.
6. What is the relationship between dream symbolism, the unconscious mind, and more literary works such as fairy tales, myths, and legends? Do you agree with Freud's comparison and analysis?

CONNECTION

Apply Freud's view of sexuality, gender, dreams, and fantasy to Judith Ortiz Cofer's "The Other" (see page 362).

IDEAS FOR WRITING

1. Apply Freud's theory about the content and symbolism of dreams to a dream of your own. Write an interpretive essay about your dream. Did Freud's ideas help you to understand the dream and its causes more clearly? What else might have influenced the imagery and events involved?

2. Because Freud's theories about the repressed erotic content and symbolism in dreams can also be applied to fantasy literature such as myths and fairy tales, many critics have attempted "Freudian" analyses of imaginative literature. Using a "Freudian" or sexual-symbol approach, try to interpret the characters, symbolism, and events of one of the stories or myths in this text. Did you find this approach satisfactory? Why or why not?

RELATED WEB SITES

Sigmund Freud
www.freudfile.org
This Web site is dedicated to the life and work of Sigmund Freud. It offers information about his biography, self-analysis, and work, as well as about the personalities who interacted with his ideas and with the development of psychoanalysis. Bibliographical notes, quotations, and references concerning Freud and his activity in the psychoanalytical field will also be found here.

The American Psychoanalytic Association
www.apsa.org
Learn about psychoanalysis at this large Web site devoted to the subject. It also includes many relevant links, essays, news, and information on upcoming conferences.

An Erotic Table D'hôte
www.haverford.edu/psych/ddavis/ftable.html
Psychology professor Doug Davis presents a brief analysis of one of Freud's own dreams. The site contains links to others of Freud's dreams and of modern analyses of his work, which provide a clear sense of how Freud approached gender issues and the erotic dream.

Mary Pipher

Saplings in the Storm

Mary Pipher was born in 1947 and grew up in Springfield, Missouri. She earned a B.A. in cultural anthropology at the University of California, Berkeley in 1969 and, at the University of Nebraska–Lincoln, completed her Ph.D. in clinical psychology in 1977. Pipher has a private practice and is a faculty member at the University of Nebraska. Her recent books include Another Country: Navigating the Emotional Terrain of Our Elders *(1999) and* Letters to a Young Therapist *(2003). She is best known for*

her writing on adolescent girls; her book Reviving Ophelia: Saving the
Selves of Adolescent Girls *(1994) became an international best-seller
and was awarded the American Psychological Association Presidential Ci-
tation for excellence. In the following selection from* Reviving Ophelia,
*Pipher describes some of the difficulties that girls today have in making a
satisfactory transition from childhood to adolescence.*

JOURNAL

Write about a time in your early adolescent years when you felt you were
losing your identity and self-confidence. What factors led to your confusion and sense of loss?

When my cousin Polly was a girl, she was energy in motion. She danced,
did cartwheels and splits, played football, basketball and baseball with
the neighborhood boys, wrestled with my brothers, biked, climbed trees and
rode horses. She was as lithe and as resilient as a willow branch and as
unrestrained as a lion cub. Polly talked as much as she moved. She yelled
out orders and advice, shrieked for joy when she won a bet or heard a good
joke, laughed with her mouth wide open, argued with kids and grown-ups
and insulted her foes in the language of a construction worker.

We formed the Marauders, a secret club that met over her garage. Polly
was the Tom Sawyer of the club. She planned the initiations, led the spying expeditions and hikes to haunted houses. She showed us the rituals to
become blood "brothers" and taught us card tricks and how to smoke.

Then Polly had her first period and started junior high. She tried to
keep up her old ways, but she was called a tomboy and chided for not acting more ladylike. She was excluded by her boy pals and by the girls, who
were moving into makeup and romances.

This left Polly confused and shaky. She had temper tantrums and
withdrew from both the boys' and girls' groups. Later she quieted down
and reentered as Becky Thatcher. She wore stylish clothes and watched
from the sidelines as the boys acted and spoke. Once again she was accepted and popular. She glided smoothly through our small society. No
one spoke of the changes or mourned the loss of our town's most
dynamic citizen. I was the only one who felt that a tragedy had transpired.

5   Girls in what Freud called the latency period, roughly age six or seven
through puberty, are anything but latent. I think of my daughter Sara during those years—performing chemistry experiments and magic tricks,
playing her violin, starring in her own plays, rescuing wild animals and bik-
ing all over town. I think of her friend Tamara, who wrote a 300-page novel
the summer of her sixth-grade year. I remember myself, reading every children's book in the library of my town. One week I planned to be a great

doctor like Albert Schweitzer. The next week I wanted to write like Louisa May Alcott or dance in Paris like Isadora Duncan. I have never since had as much confidence or ambition.

Most preadolescent girls are marvelous company because they are interested in everything—sports, nature, people, music and books. Almost all the heroines of girls' literature come from this age group—Anne of Green Gables, Heidi, Pippi Longstocking and Caddie Woodlawn. Girls this age bake pies, solve mysteries and go on quests. They can take care of themselves and are not yet burdened with caring for others. They have a brief respite from the female role and can be tomboys, a word that conveys courage, competency and irreverence.

They can be androgynous, having the ability to act adaptively in any situation regardless of gender role constraints. An androgynous person can comfort a baby or change a tire, cook a meal or chair a meeting. Research has shown that, since they are free to act without worrying if their behavior is feminine or masculine, androgynous adults are the most well adjusted.

Girls between seven and eleven rarely come to therapy. They don't need it. I can count on my fingers the girls this age whom I have seen: Coreen, who was physically abused; Anna, whose parents were divorcing; and Brenda, whose father killed himself. These girls were courageous and resilient. Brenda said, "If my father didn't want to stick around, that's his loss." Coreen and Anna were angry, not at themselves, but rather at the grown-ups, who they felt were making mistakes. It's amazing how little help these girls needed from me to heal and move on.

A horticulturist told me a revealing story. She led a tour of junior-high girls who were attending a math and science fair on her campus. She showed them side oats grama, bluestem, Indian grass and trees—redbud, maple, walnut and willow. The younger girls interrupted each other with their questions and tumbled forward to see, touch and smell everything. The older girls, the ninth-graders, were different. They hung back. They didn't touch plants or shout out questions. They stood primly to the side, looking bored and even a little disgusted by the enthusiasm of their younger classmates. My friend asked herself, What's happened to these girls? What's gone wrong? She told me, "I wanted to shake them, to say, 'Wake up, come back. Is anybody home at your house?'"

10   Recently I sat sunning on a bench outside my favorite ice-cream store. A mother and her teenage daughter stopped in front of me and waited for the light to change. I heard the mother say, "You have got to stop blackmailing your father and me. Every time you don't get what you want, you tell us that you want to run away from home or kill yourself. What's happened to you? You used to be able to handle not getting your way."

The daughter stared straight ahead, barely acknowledging her mother's words. The light changed. I licked my ice-cream cone. Another mother approached the same light with her preadolescent daughter in tow.

They were holding hands. The daughter said to her mother, "This is fun. Let's do this all afternoon."

Something dramatic happens to girls in early adolescence. Just as planes and ships disappear mysteriously into the Bermuda Triangle, so do the selves of girls go down in droves. They crash and burn in a social and developmental Bermuda Triangle. In early adolescence, studies show that girls' IQ scores drop and their math and science scores plummet. They lose their resiliency and optimism and become less curious and inclined to take risks. They lose their assertive, energetic and "tomboyish" personalities and become more deferential, self-critical and depressed. They report great unhappiness with their own bodies.

Psychology documents but does not explain the crashes. Girls who rushed to drink in experiences in enormous gulps sit quietly in the corner. Writers such as Sylvia Plath, Margaret Atwood and Olive Schreiner have described the wreckage. Diderot, in writing to his young friend Sophie Volland, described his observations harshly: "You all die at 15."

Fairy tales capture the essence of this phenomenon. Young women eat poisoned apples or prick their fingers with poisoned needles and fall asleep for a hundred years. They wander away from home, encounter great dangers, are rescued by princes and are transformed into passive and docile creatures.

15   The story of Ophelia, from Shakespeare's *Hamlet,* shows the destructive forces that affect young women. As a girl, Ophelia is happy and free, but with adolescence she loses herself. When she falls in love with Hamlet, she lives only for his approval. She has no inner direction; rather she struggles to meet the demands of Hamlet and her father. Her value is determined utterly by their approval. Ophelia is torn apart by her efforts to please. When Hamlet spurns her because she is an obedient daughter, she goes mad with grief. Dressed in elegant clothes that weigh her down, she drowns in a stream filled with flowers.

Girls know they are losing themselves. One girl said, "Everything good in me died in junior high." Wholeness is shattered by the chaos of adolescence. Girls become fragmented, their selves split into mysterious contradictions. They are sensitive and tenderhearted, mean and competitive, superficial and idealistic. They are confident in the morning and overwhelmed with anxiety by nightfall. They rush through their days with wild energy and then collapse into lethargy. They try on new roles every week— this week the good student, next week the delinquent and the next, the artist. And they expect their families to keep up with these changes.

My clients in early adolescence are elusive and slow to trust adults. They are easily offended by a glance, a clearing of the throat, a silence, a lack of sufficient enthusiasm or a sentence that doesn't meet their immediate needs. Their voices have gone underground—their speech is more tentative and less articulate. Their moods swing widely. One week they love their world and their families, the next they are critical of everyone. Much of their behavior is unreadable. Their problems are complicated and metaphorical—eating disorders, school phobias and self-inflicted injuries. I need to ask again and again in a dozen different ways, "What are you trying to tell me?"

Michelle, for example, was a beautiful, intelligent seventeen-year-old. Her mother brought her in after she became pregnant for the third time in three years. I tried to talk about why this was happening. She smiled a Mona Lisa smile to all my questions. "No, I don't care all that much for sex." "No, I didn't plan this. It just happened." When Michelle left a session, I felt like I'd been talking in the wrong language to someone far away.

Holly was another mystery. She was shy, soft-spoken and slow-moving, pretty under all her makeup and teased red hair. She was a Prince fan and wore only purple. Her father brought her in after a suicide attempt. She wouldn't study, do chores, join any school activities or find a job. Holly answered questions in patient, polite monosyllables. She really talked only when the topic was Prince. For several weeks we talked about him. She played me his tapes. Prince somehow spoke for her and to her.

20   Gail burned and cut herself when she was unhappy. Dressed in black, thin as a straw, she sat silently before me, her hair a mess, her ears, lips and nose all pierced with rings. She spoke about Bosnia and the hole in the ozone layer and asked me if I liked rave music. When I asked about her life, she fingered her earrings and sat silently.

My clients are not different from girls who are not seen in therapy. I teach at a small liberal arts college and the young women in my classes have essentially the same experiences as my therapy clients. One student worried about her best friend who'd been sexually assaulted. Another student missed class after being beaten by her boyfriend. Another asked what she should do about crank calls from a man threatening to rape her. When stressed, another student stabbed her hand with paper clips until she drew blood. Many students have wanted advice on eating disorders.

After I speak at high schools, girls approach me to say that they have been raped, or they want to run away from home, or that they have a friend who is anorexic or alcoholic. At first all this trauma surprised me. Now I expect it.

Psychology has a long history of ignoring girls this age. Until recently adolescent girls haven't been studied by academics, and they have long baffled therapists. Because they are secretive with adults and full of contradictions, they are difficult to study. So much is happening internally that's not communicated on the surface.

Simone de Beauvoir believed adolescence is when girls realize that men have the power and that their only power comes from consenting to become submissive adored objects. They do not suffer from the penis envy Freud postulated, but from power envy.

25   She described the Bermuda Triangle this way: Girls who were the subjects of their own lives become the objects of others' lives. "Young girls slowly bury their childhood, put away their independent and imperious selves and submissively enter adult existence." Adolescent girls experience a conflict between their autonomous selves and their need to be feminine, between their status as human beings and their vocation as females. De Beauvoir says, "Girls stop being and start seeming."

    Girls become "female impersonators" who fit their whole selves into small, crowded spaces. Vibrant, confident girls become shy, doubting young women. Girls stop thinking, "Who am I? What do I want?" and start thinking, "What must I do to please others?"

    This gap between girls' true selves and cultural prescriptions for what is properly female creates enormous problems. To paraphrase a Stevie Smith poem about swimming in the sea, "they are not waving, they are drowning." And just when they most need help, they are unable to take their parents' hands.

    Olive Schreiner wrote of her experiences as a young girl in *The Story of an African Farm*. "The world tells us what we are to be and shapes us by the ends it sets before us. To men it says, work. To us, it says, seem. The less a woman has in her head the lighter she is for carrying." She described the finishing school that she attended in this way: "It was a machine for condensing the soul into the smallest possible area. I have seen some souls so compressed that they would have filled a small thimble."

    Margaret Mead believed that the ideal culture is one in which there is a place for every human gift. By her standards, our Western culture is far from ideal for women. So many gifts are unused and unappreciated. So many voices are stilled. Stendhal wrote: "All geniuses born women are lost to the public good."

30   Alice Miller wrote of the pressures on some young children to deny their true selves and assume false selves to please their parents. *Reviving Ophelia* suggests that adolescent girls experience a similar pressure to split into true and false selves, but this time the pressure comes not from parents but from the culture. Adolescence is when girls experience social pressure to put aside their authentic selves and to display only a small portion of their gifts.

    This pressure disorients and depresses most girls. They sense the pressure to be someone they are not. They fight back, but they are fighting a "problem with no name." One girl put it this way: "I'm a perfectly good carrot that everyone is trying to turn into a rose. As a carrot, I have good color and a nice leafy top. When I'm carved into a rose, I turn brown and wither."

    Adolescent girls are saplings in a hurricane. They are young and vulnerable trees that the winds blow with gale strength. Three factors make young women vulnerable to the hurricane. One is their developmental level. Everything is changing—body shape, hormones, skin and hair. Calmness is replaced by anxiety. Their way of thinking is changing.

Far below the surface they are struggling with the most basic of human questions: What is my place in the universe, what is my meaning?

Second, American culture has always smacked girls on the head in early adolescence. This is when they move into a broader culture that is rife with girl-hurting "isms," such as sexism, capitalism and lookism, which is the evaluation of a person solely on the basis of appearance.

Third, American girls are expected to distance from parents just at the time when they most need their support. As they struggle with countless new pressures, they must relinquish the protection and closeness they've felt with their families in childhood. They turn to their none-too-constant peers for support.

35   Parents know only too well that something is happening to their daughters. Calm, considerate daughters grow moody, demanding and distant. Girls who loved to talk are sullen and secretive. Girls who liked to hug now bristle when touched. Mothers complain that they can do nothing right in the eyes of their daughters. Involved fathers bemoan their sudden banishment from their daughters' lives. But few parents realize how universal their experiences are. Their daughters are entering a new land, a dangerous place that parents can scarcely comprehend. Just when they most need a home base, they cut themselves loose without radio communications.

Most parents of adolescent girls have the goal of keeping their daughters safe while they grow up and explore the world. The parents' job is to protect. The daughters' job is to explore. Always these different tasks have created tension in parent-daughter relationships, but now it's even harder. Generally parents are more protective of their daughters than is corporate America. Parents aren't trying to make money off their daughters by selling them designer jeans or cigarettes, they just want them to be well adjusted. They don't see their daughters as sex objects or consumers but as real people with talents and interests. But daughters turn away from their parents as they enter the new land. They befriend their peers, who are their fellow inhabitants of the strange country and who share a common language and set of customs. They often embrace the junk values of mass culture.

This turning away from parents is partly for developmental reasons. Early adolescence is a time of physical and psychological change, self-absorption, preoccupation with peer approval and identity formation. It's a time when girls focus inward on their own fascinating changes.

It's partly for cultural reasons. In America we define adulthood as a moving away from families into broader culture. Adolescence is the time for cutting bonds and breaking free. Adolescents may claim great independence from parents, but they are aware and ashamed of their parents' smallest deviation from the norm. They don't like to be seen with them and find their imperfections upsetting. A mother's haircut or a father's joke can ruin their day. Teenagers are furious at parents who say the wrong things or do not respond with perfect answers. Adolescents claim not to hear their parents, but with their friends they discuss endlessly all parental attitudes. With amazing acuity, they sense nuances, doubt, shades of ambiguity, discrepancy and hypocrisy.

Adolescents still have some of the magical thinking of childhood and believe that parents have the power to keep them safe and happy. They blame their parents for their misery, yet they make a point of not telling their parents how they think and feel; they have secrets, so things can get crazy. For example, girls who are raped may not tell their parents. Instead, they become hostile and rebellious. Parents bring girls in because of their anger and out-of-control behavior. When I hear about this unexplainable anger, I ask about rape. Ironically, girls are often angrier at their parents than at the rapists. They feel their parents should have known about the danger and been more protective; afterward, they should have sensed the pain and helped.

40   Most parents feel like failures during this time. They feel shut out, impotent and misunderstood. They often attribute the difficulties of this time to their daughters and their own failings. They don't understand that these problems go with the developmental stage, the culture and the times.

Parents experience an enormous sense of loss when their girls enter this new land. They miss the daughters who sang in the kitchen, who read them school papers, who accompanied them on fishing trips and to ball games. They miss the daughters who liked to bake cookies, play Pictionary and be kissed goodnight. In place of their lively, affectionate daughters they have changelings—new girls who are sadder, angrier and more complicated. Everyone is grieving.

Fortunately adolescence is time-limited. By late high school most girls are stronger and the winds are dying down. Some of the worst problems— cliques, a total focus on looks and struggles with parents—are on the wane. But the way girls handle the problems of adolescence can have implications for their adult lives. Without some help, the loss of wholeness, self-confidence and self-direction can last well into adulthood. Many adult clients struggle with the same issues that overwhelmed them as adolescent girls. Thirty-year-old accountants and realtors, forty-year-old homemakers and doctors, and thirty-five-year-old nurses and schoolteachers ask the same questions and struggle with the same problems as their teenage daughters.

Even sadder are the women who are not struggling, who have forgotten that they have selves worth defending. They have repressed the pain of their adolescence, the betrayals of self in order to be pleasing. These women come to therapy with the goal of becoming even more pleasing to others. They come to lose weight, to save their marriages or to rescue their children. When I ask them about their own needs, they are confused by the question.

Most women struggled alone with the trauma of adolescence and have led decades of adult life with their adolescent experiences unexamined. The lessons learned in adolescence are forgotten and their memories of pain are minimized. They come into therapy because their marriage is in trouble, or they hate their job, or their own daughter is giving them fits. Maybe their daughter's pain awakens their own pain. Some are depressed or chemically addicted or have stress-related illnesses—ulcers, colitis, migraines or psoriasis. Many have tried to be perfect women and failed. Even though they followed the rules and did as they were told, the world has not rewarded them. They feel angry and betrayed. They feel miserable and taken for granted, used rather than loved.

45   Women often know how everyone in their family thinks and feels except themselves. They are great at balancing the needs of their co-workers, husbands, children and friends, but they forget to put themselves into the equation. They struggle with adolescent questions still unresolved: How important are looks and popularity? How do I care for myself and not be selfish? How can I be honest and still be loved? How can I achieve and not threaten others? How can I be sexual and not a sex object? How can I be responsive but not responsible for everyone?

As we talk, the years fall away. We are back in junior high with the cliques, the shame, the embarrassment about bodies, the desire to be accepted and the doubts about ability. So many adult women think they are stupid and ugly. Many feel guilty if they take time for themselves. They do not express anger or ask for help.

We talk about childhood—what the woman was like at ten and at fifteen. We piece together a picture of childhood lost. We review her own particular story, her own time in the hurricane. Memories flood in. Often there are tears, angry outbursts, sadness for what has been lost. So much time has been wasted pretending to be who others wanted. But also, there's a new energy that comes from making connections, from choosing awareness over denial and from the telling of secrets.

We work now, twenty years behind schedule. We reestablish each woman as the subject of her life, not as the object of others' lives. We answer Freud's patronizing question "What do women want?" Each woman wants something different and particular and yet each woman wants the same thing—to be who she truly is, to become who she can become.

Many women regain their preadolescent authenticity with menopause. Because they are no longer beautiful objects occupied primarily with caring for others, they are free once again to become the subjects of their own lives. They become more confident, self-directed and energetic. Margaret Mead noticed this phenomenon in cultures all over the world and called it "pmz," postmenopausal zest. She noted that some cultures revere these older women. Others burn them at the stake.

Questions for Discussion

1. What point does Pipher make through the narrative about her cousin Polly? What specific details does Pipher use to make Polly's adolescent transformation vivid and disturbing?
2. Why and how does Pipher disagree with Freud about the "latency period"? What personal examples does she use to make her point about this important stage in a girl's life? Why do girls in this period of their lives seldom begin therapy?
3. How does the horticulturist's story about two different age groups of girls on a campus tour support Pipher's argument about the difference between preadolescent and adolescent girls? What other contrasting stories does Pipher use persuasively?
4. How does Pipher use the story of Ophelia and narratives from her own patients to support her argument about adolescent transformation?
5. What is Simone de Beauvoir's view of adolescent female power envy? How do adolescent girls become "female impersonators"? Why does culture pressure them to "assume false selves," in Pipher's view? Do you agree? Explain your point of view.
6. According to Pipher, what three factors make girls vulnerable to the "hurricane" of adolescence? How have the traditional pressures on girls increased in recent years? Why is the "reality of discrimination" even more confusing for modern girls than in the past?

Connection

Compare Pipher's examples of the pressures and confusion of adolescent females today with Lamott's narrative of her own experiences as a young woman from her essay "Hunger" in Chapter 5 (see page 252).

Ideas for Writing

1. Write an essay in which you argue whether girls entering adolescence today have greater pressures and difficulties than young women in previous generations. Do some research into this subject; try doing interviews with older women about problems they encountered in adolescence; contrast their views with those of young women you interview.
2. In an essay based on personal experience and research, present some possible solutions for the gender-based pressure adolescent girls experience today.

Related Web Sites

Reading Group Guide to *Reviving Ophelia*

`www.readinggroupguides.com/guides_R/reviving_`
`ophelia2.asp`

This reading guide contains an interview with Mary Pipher, study questions, a biography, and an excerpt from the text.

Girl Power!

`http://mentalhealth.samhsa.gov/publications/allpubs/`
`ca-0038/default.asp`

Girl Power is a Web site for the national public education campaign sponsored by the U.S. Department of Health and Human Services to help encourage and motivate 9 to 13-year-old girls to make the most of their lives. The site contains health messages and statistics related to typical problems encountered by this age group.

Bonnie Ruberg

Games for Girls

Bonnie Ruberg graduated from Bard College in 2007 with a degree in creative writing, literature, and sexuality and gender. Along with being the editor-in-chief for the literary magazine Verse Noire, *Ruberg is a professional sex writer who now lives in San Francisco, where she blogs about video games for the* Voice *and writes a weekly cybersex column,* Click Me. *She is also a freelance writer and has published articles in* Forbes.com *and* Gamasutra. *Ruberg enjoys researching online about popular culture, game designs, and images of academia. Her interest in sexuality is linked to gender concerns, as you will realize through reading her critique of girl games in "Games for Girls."*

JOURNAL

From your experiences and those of your friends, are girls and young women as involved in game playing as adolescent boys and young men?

You've seen them in the stores. You've walked the aisles of your favorite gaming retailer and sighed, wondering, Why are these here? You've skimmed the wall of GBA boxes, searching for a new release, and noticed their brightly-colored presence among the normal, better titles. You've started to ignore them. You don't even consider them real games anymore. After all, they're just for kids. Or even worse, for girls.

Girl games. Where did they go wrong?

There's a plethora of bad girl games floating around right now. As far as Nintendo products are concerned, most of them are for the GBA. Take, for example, the Mary-Kate and Ashley line from Acclaim. *Girls Night Out* seems to have worked its way into the realm of acceptable mediocrity, but

Sweet 16, which received a 45% review average on *IGN* says *Sweet 16* "arrives
as a clear *Mario Party* clone with the Olsen twins license slapped on for
good measure." Disney's *That's SO Raven* offers only more of the same:
girly (sometimes insulting) objectives, awkward controls, and shallow
gameplay. Top that all off with the fact that the game itself isn't even fun.

A few recent girl games have begun the upstream battle toward quality.
A2M's *Lizzie McGuire 2: Lizzie Diaries,* the sequel to a stereotypically poor
original, shows serious signs of improvement, including clear graphics and
actually enjoyable mini-games. Stifled by extremely short play time, and
the almost total lack of replay value, *Lizzie McGuire 2* still manages to have
a leg up on the other titles in its genre. *Kim Possible 2,* another sequel from
A2M, seems to even have legitimate, non-girl-game promise. IGN has
named it their sleeper hit of the year. With more complicated gameplay
and a strong plot, it hasn't just moved to the top of the girl game class, it's
proved itself worthy of entering a different category all together.

5   Which brings up an important point about girl games: a really good
girl game isn't a girl game anymore. It's just a game.

"Funny thing is" says IGN, "this deserving sleeper might actually find
a second fanbase. You've got a platformer with polished design, tight
control, plenty of replayability, and a hot gal in the lead role as the butt-
kicking, high-flying, belly-shirt-sporting hero chick. Think Castlevania set
in So-Cal, or Catwoman with some class. It's certainly a game that you
gamer boys shouldn't be ashamed of picking up . . . if you think you can
keep up with her."

But what exactly defines a girl game in the first place? Female characters? Girly missions? Slapdash designs? In my mind, a girl game is one that
has been specifically created for and marketed to girls. The primary concern of those in charge of its production is not quality gaming, but picking
up on sales from a profitable niche market. Not that every game publisher
doesn't have money on the mind, but in the case of girl games, that desire
for profit is rarely followed up by the healthy market competition that
forces production teams to put out a worthwhile product in order to stay
afloat. It's a widely accepted element of the industry: girl games suck.

Or, if it's unfair to say they outright "suck," it's obvious that they receive
considerably less development care than other, non-girl titles. An overwhelming number of them, instead of deriving from original concepts,
are based off of movies and television shows. Girls, the industry seems to
be saying, don't need originality. They don't need nuanced gameplay,
well-rendered graphics, or interesting sound. Girls don't want innovation;
they want mini-games and flashy puzzles. Why waste time in development
that will go unappreciated? Girls want what's girly. They want what sucks.

Who, exactly, are these girls? College students? Stay-at-home moms?
Grandmothers in rockers cradling their GBAs? No, in the case of girl
games, when the industry says "girls", the word is synonymous with

"children" (an issue ridiculous enough to warrant an entirely different editorial). So maybe these games are justified in their over-simplicity because they are made for kids.

10   Maybe. But if little girls get crummy girls games, why don't little boys get crummy boy games? Sure there are other poor, but less "girly," TV and movie-based titles. But we don't call these boy games. We just call them bad.

What do young girls really want? Could it be the industry actually has female kids pegged with these (usually) at best luke-warm games? If it seems that way, it's only because girls aren't exposed to other types of gaming. They try out the things the media tells them they'll like. They watch other girls, ones just like themselves, enjoying these games in the ads on TV. They can't see themselves in *Halo 2* advertisements. Why would they? From all that they've been told, from what they've seen, girls don't play those sorts of games.

What about older girls, women—should they get their own games too? How many sales is the industry missing out on by not putting out equally shoddy titles for female adults? The only reason they haven't taken advantage of the opportunity like they have with girl games is that they think women wouldn't buy. Even designing crummy games would be waste of money. Women don't game. For now, and for the sake of holding back a swarm of bad "women's games," let's not tell them the truth.

And how much of a difference would it make if these games were good? If girl games got just as much time and attention in development as normal games, would they be morally ok? There's no answer to that question, because such an approach could never actually happen. Girl games are designed for "peripheral" gamers. They are, as such, peripheral games. If they were not, if they were good, as mentioned before, they would cease to be girl games. They might continue to be "girly," but they would not be girl games.

In the end, the idea of creating gender-specific games, whether for girls or for boys, is just demeaning. By putting out these titles, game makers are implying that girls can't, and don't want to, handle real games. Sometimes that might seem right, but only because it's an accepted (by both sexes) preconception, and not because it's innately true.

15   Many people, game publishers and female gamers alike, stand up for girls games, claiming they serve as a necessary entry-point for many girls into the world of gaming—a gateway to more legitimate games. But do the girls who play girl games really ever move on to better, more complicated titles? Is this gateway really a gateway, or is it more like a cul-de-sac?

In my opinion, playing girl games has none of the desired effects. That is, girls who play them do not continue to game. For plenty of consumers, girl games and their primary platform (the GBA) are separate from the rest of the gaming market. As noted on *Game Spot,* according to a recent Club Nintendo survey, 22 percent of Japanese DS owners are female. It's become acceptable, in fact somewhat normal, for girls to own handheld systems, but not consoles. The girls I know who are into gaming (and I mean actual, dedicated gamers) certainly did not come in through girl's games. In fact, the majority of girls I've met who used to or still do play girl games foster the expected dislike for normal gaming that already-established gamers find so frustrating.

What the industry needs to do, both to help out with issues of gender-equality and to make things more money, is to change the face of general, quality, non-gender-specific gaming. If little boys can like real games, so can little girls; it's just a question of perspective, marketing, and (please!) a little more equal representation in the games themselves. If reluctant, potential girl gamers need gateway games, then Nintendo should be pushing titles like *Animal Crossing* and *Pikmin,* quality games with some girl-attractive aspects. Don't start newbies out by showing them what's bad and sexist in gaming; show them the cool stuff. Then they'll be no more need for girl games, just good ones.

QUESTIONS FOR DISCUSSION

1. What is Ruberg's thesis? What reasons does she give to support her thesis?
2. What qualities define the "plethora of bad girl games"? What attitudes about girls' capabilities or intelligence are implied by the analysis of these games? If you have ever played girl games, what was your opinion of them? What games does Ruberg think are more challenging for girls?
3. By the fifth paragraph, do you know who Ruberg's audience is? Define the knowledge level of the audience for whom she is writing. How much do you assume that they know about games for boys and girls? If you aren't in Ruberg's target audience, how much of her argument can you absorb?
4. Why is Ruberg opposed to girl games? What kinds of games does she think should be designed for both boys and girls? How does she define a good game?
5. Why do you think that gender discrimination against girls is embedded in the idea of a girl game? Since the 1970s, feminists have argued that men and women are capable of performing similar intellectual and physical activities. Why then does this discrimination against women still prevail?
6. What is Ruberg's solution to creating games that are less gender specific? Are you satisfied with her solutions? Can you think of other ways to lessen the gap between girls' and boys' games?

CONNECTION

Discuss how William Pollack in "Revising the Boy Code" would respond to the thesis of "Games for Girls" (see page 317).

1. Ruberg says, "In the end, the idea of creating gender-specific games, whether for girls or boys, is just a meaning. By putting out these titles, game makers are implying that girls can't, and don't want to, handle real games. Sometimes that might seem right, but only because it's an accepted (by both sexes) preconception, and not because it's innately true." Write an argument that supports or refutes Ruberg's claim. Remember to consider the opposing point of view.

2. Do research on girl and boy games. Then, write an essay from the research you did, as well as your own experiences, that supports your point of view on why the differences between boy and girl games exist. Do not feel obligated to support or refute Ruberg's argument.

Heroine Sheik

www.heroine-sheik.com

Heroine Sheik is Bonnie Ruberg's blog, which discusses gender issues in video games as well as cultural analysis. Also included are links to Ruberg's articles, as well as links to other Web sites that cover gender issues in video-game culture.

William Pollack

Revising the Boy Code

William S. Pollack, Ph.D. directs the Centers for Men and Young Men at McLean Hospital and is also Assistant Clinical Professor in psychology at Harvard Medical School. He is founder and director of the REAL BOYS® Educational Programs and has consulted on safe schools for the U.S. Secret Service and The National Campaign Against Youth Violence. His research and writings are directed towards freeing boys from the legacy of male violence and the repressive punishments that are society's response to it—what Pollack refers to as the "Columbine Syndrome." His work on youth violence has appeared widely in the national (and international) print periodical and broadcast media, and his books include Real Boys: Rescuing Our Sons from the Myths of Boyhood *(1998);* Real Boys' Voices *(2000), with Todd Shuster; and* Real Boys Workbook: The Definitive Guide to Understanding and Interacting with Boys of All Ages, *with Kathleen Cushman (2001). The following selection from Pollack's first book provides an encouraging case study and analysis indicating ways that the traditional "code" of emotionally repressed "tough" behavior for boys is gradually changing to create new, more caring models for masculine identity.*

JOURNAL

Do you think that males are becoming more able to express their feelings, admit to weaknesses, and compete with other males less frequently? why or why not?

For me, one of the most heartwarming experiences in listening closely to boys is hearing one of them share a thought or tell a story that reflects his resistance to the Boy Code—an unconscious and almost imperceptible rebellion against the gender straitjacketing that most of our sons experience every day. Often arising from what seems to be his gut sense that "I've just got to do what's right" or "I'm just going to have to be myself," these touching moments seem to surface when the boy—despite society's rigid gender-based expectations and his own years of stoic suppression of real emotion—finally connects with a new voice within.

When a boy utters these words to assert himself, when he takes on the old Boy Code, he is engaging in an act of heroism, a first attempt to dismantle our society's double standards and toxic views about the male gender. He may be blazing the path for a far more expansive, far less oppressive set of guidelines and expectations—a New Boy Code that respects what today's boys and men are really about—one that will be based upon honesty rather than fear, communication rather than repression, connection rather than disconnection.

My recent conversation with Chris revealed one such boy, one such hero.

Towering over me at nearly six feet, Chris Jackson, with his shock of red hair and intense greenish-brown eyes, seemed unusually self-confident for his seventeen years. Though at first he seemed somewhat shy and reserved, as he began speaking to me I was impressed by his candor and guileless manner. Chris, I had been told, was a top athlete at his school, an able pupil, and one of his school's most respected student leaders. Our conversation covered a range of issues, but Chris seemed most interested in talking about his friends and about the ups and downs of his relationships with them.

5   "I've got a good group of friends," he boasted with a proud smile. "I've never had any major problems with them."

"No conflicts whatsoever?" I asked.

"Well," he confessed, "now that you mention it, there was that whole scene with Dan that started out as just a hassle but really upset me."

Chris explained to me that Dan Norton had been his friend since kindergarten, that they had lived in the same working-class suburb of Chicago for as long as he could remember. The two had been T-ball teammates and soccer team cocaptains, and now they were varsity co-captains of the high school football team. "We were pretty close for a long time," Chris volunteered, "We went through a lot together. Dan's parents got divorced, and my mother had breast cancer recently, although she's doing fine now."

"It sounds like a pretty important friendship," I offered.

10   "Well, we used to spend a lot of our free time together," Chris continued, "and, yes, we were good friends, actually very close friends."

Chris seemed relaxed when talking about his feelings and comfortable about sharing with me how much he had cared for Dan. But apparently things had recently changed between the two childhood buddies.

"I guess I should say that we *were* good friends. I used to really like the guy until he started to have this one big problem that just completely annoyed me."

"And what was that?" I asked Chris.

"Well," he answered, "Dan would always be late and keep me waiting, like when we were supposed to meet up in the morning to take the bus to school. It took me a while to say anything to him—you know, I sort of needed time to sort things out in my own mind."

15   "So, did you confront him?" I asked.

"Yep. And when I did, he was really mean, really negative in response. He said some awful things like 'Who do you think *you* are?' and that kind of thing. I didn't want to react right then, so I walked away and tried to think about it—to let it blow over."

But Chris found that the more he puzzled about this incident the more upset he became. "Somehow I couldn't let go of it in my head, and then it dawned on me why. It wasn't just the stuff he was doing to me. You see, he was also starting to pull pranks and hassle the younger kids at our school. Like, ever since he made varsity, he'd rank on the freshmen, hide stuff from their lockers—and sometimes he'd just rough them up. He didn't do anything real bad, but I could see he was, like, terrorizing these younger kids."

"So what did you do about it?"

"That's when I told him he was becoming a jerk, that he was going too far. These kids didn't deserve to be ranked on or beat up. You know, I asked how he would feel if one of the seniors started giving *him* a hard time."

20   "And how did Dan respond to that?"

"Well, he was like: 'C'mon, Chris. What's gotten into you? Have you become a little wimp or something? Don't you remember what those seniors used to do to us when we came up from junior high? It's just part of being a guy.'" Chris, in fact, did remember all the hazing, even some of the roughhousing that—though never physically harmful—always left him with a deep sense of shame. He even remembered one kid who teased him when his mother had to go through a mastectomy.

"It sounds like going to your high school can be pretty rough," I suggested.

"Yeah. Back then, my older brother, who was a junior at the time, was like, 'Chris, just act tough and ignore them, and they'll lay off you.'"

"Did his advice work well for you?"

25 "Well, yes and no. I mean, yes, it kept the other guys from hassling me. But, you know, it's stupid to have to act tough all the time. You get all wound up inside, like maybe you're going to have a heart attack or something. You feel awful about yourself, like you're just a big dopey loser. And now that I'm on the other side and I see what these little kids have to go through, I don't really think it's worth it. So, when I see Dan roughing up the little guys, I'm like, 'No way.' I told Dan, 'Why don't you just cut the shit—all it does is screw kids up, like it did us. It's just not right.'"

"So what did Dan say to that?" I asked.

"Well, Dan and I were still friendly for a while, even though the way he treated the other kids—almost like a bully—bothered me a lot. But then Allison moved to town."

"Allison?"

"Yeah. She was this really neat girl, kind of funky, artistic, and real smart. You know in English class, when the teacher would ask all those tough questions, she always had the right answer. I liked her right away."

30 "She was a friend of yours?"

"Well, she wasn't like a girlfriend or anything. I mean she was just a friend, more like a sister. We started to spend some time together. Unfortunately this wasn't the cool thing to do."

"Why not?"

"First of all, she was new, and kids weren't sure they liked her. But she was 'different'—her clothes, the music she listened to, and that stutter she had. You see, when Allie was a little girl, she was real shy and would stutter when she talked in front of the class. She told me that she used to be like, 'That, that, that's right.' Her parents got her help for this, speech therapy I think it was, and it mostly went away. But even these days, if she gets real nervous, sometimes it comes back. And when we started at high school with the older kids and everything—she had some bad days, with a lot of stuttering."

"So Dan wasn't too supportive of Allison?" I asked.

35 "For some reason," Chris explained, "He seemed to really hate her, and I knew he ranked on her behind her back. But then one day in math when she was trying to answer a question the stutter came out and it was real hard for her to stop. 'The ger . . . the ger . . .' Finally the teacher realized it and just tried to change the subject. But from the back of the class I could hear this big old horse laugh. I knew that laugh. It was Dan's. I wanted to do something right then and there, but I knew Allie wanted to fight her own battles and so I respected that—I kept quiet. I didn't want to make her feel even worse than she probably already did."

"Good for you," I offered.

"But after class," Chris continued, "it got worse. After the teacher had left, Dan and a couple of other guys surrounded Allie and were saying: 'GERR . . . GERR . . . what's the matter Allie, cat got your tongue?'"

"Was everyone involved in the teasing?"

"Some of the other kids were giggling, but most just seemed pretty angry and so they took off. Funny thing, all the girls and other guys mostly left and it was only Dan and a couple of other boys who hung around and teased her. Allie started to defend herself, but the stutter wouldn't stop. She started crying and ran from the room, with Dan laughing the whole time. It was pretty awful."

40   "What did you do about it?"

"I just couldn't stand it anymore. I walked right up to Dan and said. 'Dan, cut this crap out! I've told you before to stop the bullying. Can't you see you're hurting Allie?'"

"How did Dan respond to that?"

"He stepped real close to me—you know, his face right into mine—and said real loudly, 'What you going to do about it, you wuss?' It was a direct challenge. He was shouting at me. I knew he was looking for a fight. I don't really know what I would have done, and maybe never will. Because just when he was trying to pick a stupid fight with me, these other kids came up to us and were like, 'What the hell?' A bunch of guys from the football team were there and they were just shouting: 'Hey, back the hell off, Dan.' My friend Kevin was shouting: 'Chill out, Dan' and pulled him away. Then Greg said something like 'Hey, Chris is right—why are you bullying her? She's a nice kid, so lay off.' And then, four of the guys went up to Dan and said, 'You lay off Chris and you leave Allie alone. And if you lay a hand on either of them, we know just where to find you.'"

"How did you feel about that?" I asked Chris.

45   "I was really happy that they sided with me. Me and Allie were sort of the underdogs—and the other guys were taking our side. Like maybe my older brother would have told me to just stick with Dan and act cool and tough. But here were four of the other guys from our team defending me and Allie, sticking up for her rights. And my parents told me I handled it well too."

"So, how did it turn out?"

"Well, Dan never bothered Allie again and I think he got a little less rough with the other kids too. I'd known him for a long time, though. So, after a while, I tried to talk to him, to explain my feelings, and he just went, 'Well, Chris, I guess we're in different worlds now.' You know I felt bad for a couple of days but then I kept thinking—OK, why did I finally stand up to the guy? And the thought that kept coming to mind was: *It just isn't right—somebody's got to try to change these things.*"

"What things do you mean exactly?"

"Like that guys have to act mean and rank on other people. Or that kids like Allie who have problems get teased. It just seems like a big waste. I think everybody's human so everyone should be treated the same. This year when I was going for class president, my campaign message was 'At Hickman High, there's a place for everyone.' I thought some people might think I was a nerd or whatever, but I decided that I just don't mind anymore. It's a good thing, because now I'm class president and Dan seems to be coming around too. I think I know why he felt pressured to act like such a jerk, and so maybe now we can just let the past be the past and someday even be friends again."

50   As this story reflects, it's quite possible for a boy today to break out of the gender straitjacket, buck the old Boy Code, and still win the approval and love of family, friends, and society at large. Despite the pressure on him to behave otherwise, Chris stood up for himself and for his friend Allie and triumphed in the end. Unbeknownst to Chris, he was acting like something of a pioneer, rebelling against our old rules about masculinity, and thus breaking new ground for boys and for men.

About forty years ago, society began the process of discarding its old rules about girls and women that tied them down to traditional feminine and maternal obligations, required them to forfeit higher education (and then depend financially on men), and barred them from participating in the many professions, activities, and pursuits once thought to be either "unladylike" or "for men only." While we've hardly finished the process, we've come a long way in opening a broad range of opportunities to girls and women and in helping them feel comfortable sounding their true voices and being their true selves without fear of being seen as anything less than a hundred percent "feminine." We've come a long way in liberating girls and women from the gender straitjacket that for years they've been forced to wear.

Boys like Chris show us that society seems to be ready to begin as equivalent process of liberation for boys and men. We are starting to revise the old Boy Code that for ages has cut our boys and men in two, calling upon them to suppress their loving, sensitive, emotionally expressive sides, and then bemoaning the lack of these qualities in them as adults especially in their relationships with women.

Boys like Chris are beginning to question the double standard of masculinity that has pushed boys and men to feel they must choose between being the kind of tough, competitive, unfeeling, uncommunicative man traditionally celebrated as "masculine" and being the kind of open, expressive egalitarian man now heralded as ideal by much of contemporary society.

Boys like Chris show us that, yes, boys can have some or all of there qualities without having to choose between them arbitrarily, that there is way for boys to be at once tough and gentle, vulnerable and courageous dependent and independent. Like Chris, they can handle some tough situations on their own, but decide to lean on their peers without being shamed. Like him, they can play a rugged sport like football and yet steer clear of unnecessary physical fighting. Perhaps at last we're beginning to cherish all the emotions and qualities that boys naturally have inside themselves. Love, fear, empathy, guilt, anger, sadness, bravado, loyalty, courage—all of these are normal, healthy parts of the real boy.

55   It seems we're getting ready for a second gender revolution. The boys we've met in this book all seem to be telling us, some directly and some more subtly, "I want out of the old Boy Code," "I'm sick of hiding important parts of who I really am," and "I want to be able to be myself."

Today it would be virtually unheard of to require a girl to stick to old rules about being a "good little girl," refrain from showing qualities historically celebrated as "masculine," such as assertiveness or independence, or restrict herself to expressing only half of the person she genuinely is. I believe that boys like Chris are finally catching on that, in a very similar way, it's simply no longer acceptable for boys to have to follow the old Boy Code rules, stuff away feelings and behaviors once labeled "feminine," and suppress half of themselves to avoid being shamed.

I hear boys telling us "Enough already" and "Let's move on." Boys seem eager to unite their private and public selves, to feel proud of who they really are, to be freed of the shackles of shame that have held them back for centuries.

Chris teaches us that boys do care; they do love; they do nourish; they can be tough; they do flex their muscles; and, they greatly value their friendships. Boys like Chris are helping us to codify a new set of rules for boys and men, a code for the Real Boy. Here at last will be a set of rules, much like those we've been striving to enforce for girls and women, that say "Every door is open to you," "There's not just one right way of doing things," and "You are good just the way you are."

I believe the time has come for us to allow boys to craft this new, far more flexible code of manhood. As we've seen, boys are not biologically wired to act in just one "boylike" way; they are not mean-spirited, violent, or "toxic"; there is not one single way of acting or being that is more "masculine" than the next; boys are simply not the stoic, self-confident loners of procrustean myths.

60   As tough, cool, independent as they may sometimes seem, boys yearn desperately for friendships and relationships. Despite the bragging and bravado, boys like Chris, just like most girls and women, may feel devastated when these friendships or relationships suffer or fail. They too can become sad, frightened, and lonely, suffer low-self-esteem, and tumble toward serious depression.

And as we've seen, boys may actually become traumatized if emotionally they're pushed away from their closest loved ones before they're truly ready. In spite of all of society's messages to the contrary, parents cannot love their boys too much or somehow spoil them with too much caring or affection. In fact, boys with parents who remain emotionally connected to them do better in school, are more healthy psychologically, and, when they become adults, achieve greater success in their careers and relationships.

Unless they are conditioned not to be, boys are eminently loving and caring human beings. Like Chris, today's real boy sincerely wants to help others. He's sensitive to what other people feel and he does not want to hurt them. He takes action not only because he knows that it's right or just, but because he feels genuine empathy. But as we've seen, if this empathy is to stay alive, a boy must feel that others will reciprocate. If we withhold our love and affection, our boy feels ashamed and then hardens himself. If we don't stay active in his emotional life and listen to his feelings well, he comes to believe that his emotions are not welcomed. In sum, if we don't give him our empathy, he won't give empathy to us.

Real boys need people to be with who allow them to show *all* of their emotions, including their most intense feelings of sadness, disappointment, and fear. Real boys need to hear that these feelings are normal, good, and "masculine." They need to know that there really isn't any feeling, activity, or behavior that is forbidden to them as boys (other than those that could end up seriously hurting them or somebody else). They need to be taught connection rather than disconnection. They need to treated with the same kind of caring and affection we hope they'll be able to express when they become men in the next century. They need to be convinced, above all, that both their strengths and their vulnerabilities are good, that all sides of them will be celebrated, that we'll love them through and through for being just the boys they really are.

QUESTIONS FOR DISCUSSION

1. Why is it extremely difficult for boys to break away from the Boy Code? According to Pollack, why does a boy who asserts himself, refusing to follow the Boy Code, a hero? Do you agree with Pollack? Why do you think that boys need a "New Boy Code"? Or, do you think that the current Boy Code works?

2. How does Chris Jackson embody a male hero? What issues does Chris struggle with as he "follows his hero path"?

3. What begins the breakdown of the friendship between Chris and Dan, which had been especially strong since they had been best friends since childhood? Which of Dan's behaviors infuriate Chris? Why does he think Dan is acting inappropriately?

4. How does Allison's move to the school bring up new issues between Dan and Chris? How does Chris try to protect Allison from Dan's treatment of her as he follows the Boy Code?

5. Why does Chris continue to act considerately and no longer follow the Boy Code?

6. Is Chris's election as Class President a testimony to the students' acceptance of the need for a New Boy Code, or is it a sign of his general popularity? How do you think the Boy Code should be revised after reflecting on this article and thinking about how "guys" bully women just to prove that they are "tough"?

CONNECTION

Compare and contrast Sedaris's and Pollack's ideas about the extreme limitations of the Code (see page 325).

IDEAS FOR WRITING

1. Like Pollack does in this article, narrate an event or series of related events that explore and illustrate the issues, struggles, and conflicts that are happening as gender roles, and specifically the Boy Code change. Use a style similar to Pollack's in which you include quotes from your characters and significant details to make your story persuasive. Select a situation that you felt deeply about that will help you to write a better story.

2. Write an essay that compares and contrasts the New Boy Code and the Boy Code. Begin by defining both codes and then give several examples to help the reader get a better sense of what you mean by each code.

RELATED WEB SITES

Dr. William Pollack
www.williampollack.com
This personal Web site of Dr. William Pollack provides links to some of his articles regarding the psychological issues of manhood. In addition, The Center for Men at McLean Hospital

David Sedaris

I Like Guys

David Sedaris was born in 1957 in Raleigh, North Carolina. He completed his degree from the Art Institute of Chicago in 1987. Sedaris has worked as a radio commentator and diarist for National Public Radio (NPR); has written short stories; and has worked as an apartment cleaner, moving company worker, and office worker. In 2000, Sedaris won the Lambda Literary Award in the humor category. Sedaris's books include Barrel Fever: Stories and Essays *(1994);* Naked *(1997);* Holidays on Ice *(short stories, 1997);* Me Talk Pretty One Day *(2000); and* Dress Your Family in Corduroy and Denim *(2004).*

JOURNAL

How were gay students treated at the high school or middle school that you attended? Were they accepted by the other students and the teachers?

Shortly before I graduated from eighth grade, it was announced that, come fall, our county school system would adopt a policy of racial integration by way of forced busing. My Spanish teacher broke the news in a way she hoped might lead us to a greater understanding of her beauty and generosity.

"I remember the time I was at the state fair, standing in line for a Sno-Kone," she said, fingering the kiss curls that framed her squat, compact face. "And a little colored girl ran up and tugged at my skirt, asking if she could touch my hair. 'Just once,' she said. 'Just one time for good luck.'

"Now, I don't know about the rest of you, but my hair means a lot to me." The members of my class nodded to signify that their hair meant a lot to them as well. They inched forward in their seats, eager to know where this story might be going. Perhaps the little Negro girl was holding a concealed razor blade. Maybe she was one of the troublemakers out for a fresh white scalp.

I sat marveling at their naiveté. . . . Like all her previous anecdotes, this woman's story was headed straight up her ass.

5 "I checked to make sure she didn't have any candy on her hands, and then I bent down and let this little colored girl touch my hair." The teacher's eyes assumed the dewy, faraway look she reserved for such Hallmark moments. "Then this little fudge-colored girl put her hand on my cheek and said, 'Oh,' she said, 'I wish I could be white and pretty like you.'" She paused, positioning herself on the edge of the desk as though she were posing for a portrait the federal government might use on a stamp commemorating gallantry. "The thing to remember," she said, "is that more than anything in this world, those colored people wish they were white."

I wasn't buying it. This was the same teacher who when announcing her pregnancy said, "I just pray that my firstborn is a boy. I'll have a boy and then maybe later I'll have a girl, because when you do it the other way round, there's a good chance the boy will turn out to be funny."

"'Funny,' as in having no arms and legs?" I asked.

"That," the teacher said, "is far from funny. That is tragic, and you, sir, should have your lips sewn shut for saying such a cruel and ugly thing.

When I say 'funny,' I mean funny as in . . . " She relaxed her wrist, allowing her hand to dangle and flop. "I mean 'funny' as in *that* kind of funny." She minced across the room, but it failed to illustrate her point, as this was more or less her natural walk, a series of gamboling little steps, her back held straight, giving the impression she was balancing something of value atop her empty head. My seventh-period math teacher did a much better version. Snatching a purse off the back of a student's chair, he would prance about the room, batting his eyes and blowing kisses at the boys seated in the front row. "So fairy nice to meet you," he'd say.

Fearful of drawing any attention to myself, I hooted and squawked along with the rest of the class, all the while thinking, *That's me he's talking about.* If I was going to make fun of people, I had to expect a little something in return, that seemed only fair. Still, though, it bothered me that they'd found such an easy way to get a laugh. As entertainers, these teachers were nothing, zero. They could barely impersonate themselves. "Look at you!" my second-period gym teacher would shout, his sneakers squealing against the basketball court. "You're a group of ladies, a pack of tap-dancing queers."

10   The other boys shrugged their shoulders or smiled down at their shoes. They reacted as if they had been called Buddhists or vampires; sure, it was an insult, but no one would ever mistake them for the real thing. Had they ever chanted in the privacy of their backyard temple or slept in a coffin, they would have felt the sting of recognition and shared my fear of discovery.

I had never done anything with another guy and literally prayed that I never would. As much as I fantasized about it, I understood that there could be nothing worse than making it official. You'd seen them on television from time to time, the homosexuals, maybe on one of the afternoon talk shows. No one ever came out and called them a queer, but you could just tell by their voices as they flattered the host and proclaimed great respect for their fellow guests. These were the celebrities never asked about their home life, the comedians running scarves beneath their toupees or framing their puffy faces with their open palms in an effort to eliminate the circles beneath their eyes. "The poor man's face lift," my mother called it. Regardless of their natty attire, these men appeared sweaty and desperate, willing to play the fool in exchange for the studio applause they seemed to mistake for love and acceptance. I saw something of myself in their mock weary delivery, in the way they crossed their legs and laughed at their own jokes. I pictured their homes: the finicky placement of their throw rugs and sectional sofas, the magazines carefully fanned just so upon the coffee tables with no wives or children to disturb their order. I imagined the pornography hidden in their closets and envisioned them powerless and sobbing as the police led them away in shackles, past the teenage boy who stood bathed in the light of the television news camera and shouted, "That's him! He's the one who touched my hair!"

It was my hope to win a contest, cash in the prizes, and use the money to visit a psychiatrist who might cure me of having homosexual thoughts. Electroshock, brain surgery, hypnotism—I was willing to try anything. Under a doctor's supervision, I would buckle down and really change, I swore I would.

My parents knew a couple whose son had killed a Presbyterian minister while driving drunk. They had friends whose eldest daughter had sprinkled a Bundt cake with Comet, and knew of a child who, high on spray paint, had set fire to the family's cocker spaniel. Yet, they spoke of no one whose son was a homosexual. The odds struck me as bizarre, but the message was the same: this was clearly the worst thing that could happen to a person. The day-to-day anxiety was bad enough without my instructors taking their feeble little potshots. If my math teacher were able to subtract the alcohol from his diet, he'd still be on the football field where he belonged; and my Spanish teacher's credentials were based on nothing more than a long weekend in Tijuana, as far as I could tell. I quit taking their tests and completing their homework assignments, accepting Fs rather than delivering the grades I thought might promote their reputations as good teachers. It was a strategy that hurt only me, but I thought it cunning. We each had our self-defeating schemes, all the boys I had come to identify as homosexuals. Except for a few transfer students, I had known most of them since the third grade. We'd spent years gathered together in cinder-block offices as one speech therapist after another tried to cure us of our lisps. Had there been a walking specialist, we probably would have met there, too. These were the same boys who carried poorly forged notes to gym class and were the first to raise their hands when the English teacher asked for a volunteer to read aloud from *The Yearling* or *Lord of the Flies*. We had long ago identified one another and understood that because of everything we had in common, we could never be friends. To socialize would have drawn too much attention to ourselves. We were members of a secret society founded on self-loathing. When a teacher or classmate made fun of a real homosexual, I made certain my laugh was louder than anyone else's. When a club member's clothing was thrown into the locker-room toilet, I was always the first to cheer. When it was my clothing, I watched as the faces of my fellows broke into recognizable expressions of relief. *Faggots*, I thought. *This should have been you.*

Several of my teachers, when discussing the upcoming school integration, would scratch at the damp stains beneath their arms, pulling back their lips to reveal every bit of tooth and gum. They made monkey noises, a manic succession of ohhs and ahhs meant to suggest that soon our school would be no different than a jungle. Had a genuine ape been seated in the room, I guessed he might have identified their calls as a cry of panic. Anything that caused them suffering brought me joy, but I doubted they would talk this way come fall. From everything I'd seen on television, the Negros would never stand for such foolishness. As a people, they seemed to stick together. They knew how to fight, and I hoped that once they arrived, the battle might come down to the gladiators, leaving the rest of us alone.

15   At the end of the school year, my sister Lisa and I were excused from our volunteer jobs and sent to Greece to attend a month-long summer camp advertised as "the Crown Jewel of the Ionian Sea." The camp was reserved exclusively for Greek Americans and featured instruction in such topics as folk singing and something called "religious prayer and flag." I despised the idea of summer camp but longed to boast that I had been to Europe. "It changes people!" our neighbor had said. Following a visit to Saint-Tropez, she had marked her garden with a series of tissue-sized international flags. A once discreet and modest woman, she now paraded about her yard wearing nothing but clogs and a flame-stitched bikini. "Europe is the best thing that can happen to a person, especially if you like wine!"

I saw Europe as an opportunity to re-invent myself. I might still look and speak the same way, but having walked those cobblestoned streets, I would be identified as Continental. "He has a passport," my classmates would whisper. "Quick, let's run before he judges us!"

I told myself that I would find a girlfriend in Greece. She would be a French tourist wandering the beach with a loaf of bread beneath her arm. Lisette would prove that I wasn't a homosexual, but a man with refined tastes. I saw us holding hands against the silhouette of the Acropolis, the girl begging me to take her accordion as a memento of our love. "Silly you," I would say, brushing the tears from her eyes, "just give me the beret, that will be enough to hold you in my heart until the end of time."

In case no one believed me, I would have my sister as a witness. Lisa and I weren't getting along very well, but I hoped that the warm Mediterranean waters might melt the icicle she seemed to have mistaken for a rectal thermometer. Faced with a country of strangers, she would have no choice but to appreciate my company.

Our father accompanied us to New York, where we met our fellow campers for the charter flight to Athens. There were hundreds of them, each one confident and celebratory. They tossed their complimentary Aegean Airlines tote bags across the room, shouting and jostling one another. This would be the way I'd act once we'd finally returned from camp, but not one moment before. Were it an all-girl's camp, I would have been able to work up some enthusiasm. Had they sent me alone to pry leeches off the backs of blood-thirsty Pygmies, I might have gone bravely—but spending a month in a dormitory full of boys, that was asking too much. I'd tried to put it out of my mind, but faced with their boisterous presence, I found myself growing progressively more hysterical. My nervous tics shifted into their highest gear, and a small crowd gathered to watch what they believed to be an exotic folk dance. If my sister was anxious about our trip, she certainly didn't show it. Prying my fingers off her wrist, she crossed the room and introduced herself to a girl who stood picking salvageable butts out of the standing ashtray. This was a tough-looking Queens native named Stefani Heartattackus or Testicockules. I recall only that her last name had granted her a lifelong supply of resentment. Stefani wore mirrored aviator sunglasses and carried an oversized comb in the back pocket of her hiphugger jeans. Of all the girls in the room, she seemed the least likely candidate for my sister's friendship. They sat beside each other on the plane, and by the time we disembarked in Athens, Lisa was speaking in a very bad Queens accent. During the long flight, while I sat cowering beside a boy named Seamen, my sister had undergone a complete physical and cultural transformation. Her shoulder-length hair was now parted on the side, covering the left half of her face as if to conceal a nasty scar. She cursed and spat, scowling out the window of the chartered bus as if she'd come to Greece with the sole intention of kicking its dusty ass. "What a shithole," she yelled. "Jeez, if I'd knowed it was gonna be dis hot, I woulda stayed home wit my headdin da oven, right, girls!"

20   It shamed me to hear my sister struggle so hard with an accent that did nothing but demean her, yet I silently congratulated her on the attempt. I approached her once we reached the camp, a cluster of whitewashed buildings hugging the desolate coast, far from any neighboring village.

"Listen, asshole," she said, "as far as this place is concerned, I don't know you and you sure as shit don't know me, you got that?" She spoke as if she were auditioning for a touring company of *West Side Story*, one hand on her hip and the other fingering her pocket comb as if it were a switchblade.

"Hey, Carolina!" one of her new friends called.

"A righta ready," she brayed. "I'm comin', I'm comin'."

That was the last time we spoke before returning home. Lisa had adjusted with remarkable ease, but something deep in my stomach suggested I wouldn't thrive nearly as well. Camp lasted a month, during which time I never once had a bowel movement. I was used to having a semiprivate bathroom and could not bring myself to occupy one of the men's room stalls, fearful that someone might recognize my shoes or, even worse, not see my shoes at all and walk in on me. Sitting down three times a day for a heavy Greek meal became an exercise akin to packing a musket. I told myself I'd sneak off during one of our field trips, but those toilets were nothing more than a hole in the floor, a hole I could have filled with no problem whatsoever. I considered using the Ionian Sea, but for some unexplained reason, we were not allowed to swim in those waters. The camp had an Olympic-size pool that was fed from the sea and soon grew murky with stray bits of jellyfish that had been pulverized by the pump. The tiny tentacles raised welts on campers' skin, so shortly after arriving, it was announced that we could photograph both the pool *and* the ocean but could swim in neither. The Greeks had invented democracy, built the Acropolis, and then called it a day. Our swimming period was converted into "contemplation hour" for the girls and an extended soccer practice for the boys.

25   "I really think I'd be better off contemplating," I told the coach, massaging my distended stomach. "I've got a personal problem that's sort of weighing me down."

Because we were first and foremost Americans, the camp was basically an extension of junior high school except that here everyone had an excess of moles or a single eyebrow. The attractive sports minded boys ran the show, currying favor from the staff and ruining our weekly outdoor movie with their inane heckling. From time to time the rented tour buses would carry us to view one of the country's many splendors, and we would raid the gift shops, stealing anything that wasn't chained to the shelf or locked in a guarded case. These were cheap, plated puzzle rings and pint-size vases, little pompommed shoes, and coffee mugs reading SPARTA IS FOR A LOVER. My shoplifting experience was the only thing that gave me an edge over the popular boys. "Hold it like this," I'd whisper. "Then swivel around and slip the statue of Diana down the back of your shorts, covering it with your T-shirt. Remember to back out the door while leaving and never forget to wave good-bye."

There was one boy at camp I felt I might get along with, a Detroit native named Jason who slept on the bunk beneath mine. Jason tended to look away when talking to the other boys, shifting his eyes as though he were studying the weather conditions. Like me, he used his free time to curl into a fetal position, staring at the bedside calendar upon which he'd x-ed out all the days he had endured so far. We were finishing our 7:15 to 7:45 wash-and-rinse segment one morning when our dormitory counselor arrived for inspection shouting, "What are you, a bunch of goddamned faggots who can't make your beds?"

I giggled out loud at his stupidity. If anyone knew how to make a bed, it was a faggot. It was the others he needed to worry about. I saw Jason laughing, too, and soon we took to mocking this counselor, referring to each other first as "faggots" and then as "stinking faggots." We were "lazy faggots" and "sunburned faggots" before we eventually became "faggoty faggots." We couldn't protest the word, as that would have meant acknowledging the truth of it. The most we could do was embrace it as a joke. Embodying the term in all its clichéd glory, we minced and pranced about the room for each other's entertainment when the others weren't looking. I found myself easily out-performing my teachers, who had failed to capture the proper spirit of loopy bravado inherent in the role. *Faggot*, as a word, was always delivered in a harsh, unforgiving tone befitting those weak or stupid enough to act upon their impulses. We used it as a joke, an accusation, and finally as a dare. Late at night I'd feel my bunk buck and sway, knowing that Jason was either masturbating or beating eggs for an omelette. *Is it me he's thinking about?* I'd follow his lead and wake the next morning to find our entire iron-frame unit had wandered a good eighteen inches away from the wall. Our love had the power to move bunks.

Having no willpower, we depended on circumstances to keep us apart. *This cannot happen* was accompanied by the sound of bedsprings whining, *Oh, but maybe just this once.* There came an afternoon when, running late for flag worship, we found ourselves alone in the dormitory. What started off as name-calling escalated into a series of mock angry slaps. We wrestled each other onto one of the lower bunks, both of us longing to be pinned. "You kids think you invented sex," my mother was fond of saying. But hadn't we? With no instruction manual or federally enforced training period, didn't we all come away feeling we'd discovered something unspeakably modern? What produced in others a feeling of exhilaration left Jason and me with a mortifying sense of guilt. We fled the room as if, in our fumblings, we had uncapped some virus we still might escape if we ran fast enough. Had one of the counselors not caught me scaling the fence, I felt certain I could have made it back to Raleigh by morning, skittering across the surface of the ocean like one of those lizards often featured on television wildlife programs.

30   When discovered making out with one of the Greek bus drivers, a sixteen-year-old camper was forced to stand beside the flagpole dressed in long pants and thick sweaters. We watched her cook in the hot sun until, fully roasted, she crumpled to the pavement and passed out.

"That," the chief counselor said, "is what happens to people who play around."

If this was the punishment for a boy and a girl, I felt certain the penalty for two boys somehow involved barbed wire, a team of donkeys, and the nearest volcano. Nothing, however, could match the cruelty and humiliation Jason and I soon practiced upon each other. He started a rumor that I had stolen an athletic supporter from another camper and secretly wore it over my mouth like a surgical mask. I retaliated, claiming he had expressed a desire to become a dancer. "That's nothing," he said to the assembled crowd, "take a look at what I found on David's bed!" He reached into the pocket of his tennis shorts and withdrew a sheet of notebook paper upon which were written the words I LIKE GUYS. Presented as an indictment, the document was both pathetic and comic. Would I supposedly have written the note to remind myself of that fact, lest I forget? Had I intended to wear it taped to my back, advertising my preference the next time our rented buses carried us off to yet another swinging sexual playground?

I LIKE GUYS. He held the paper above his head, turning a slow circle so that everyone might get a chance to see. I supposed he had originally intended to plant the paper on my bunk for one of the counselors to find. Presenting it himself had foiled the note's intended effect. Rather than beating me with sticks and heavy shoes, the other boys simply groaned and looked away, wondering why he'd picked the thing up and carried it around in his pants pocket. He might as well have hoisted a glistening turd, shouting, "Look what he did!" Touching such a foul document made him suspect and guilty by association. In attempting to discredit each other, we wound up alienating ourselves even further.

Jason—even his name seemed affected. During meals I studied him from across the room. Here I was, sweating onto my plate, my stomach knotted and cramped, when *he* was the one full of shit. Clearly he had tricked me, cast a spell or slipped something into my food. I watched as he befriended a girl named Theodora and held her hand during a screening of *A Lovely Way to Die,* one of the cave paintings the head counselor offered as a weekly movie.

35   She wasn't a bad person, Theodora. Someday the doctors might find a way to transplant a calf's brain into a human skull, and then she'd be just as lively and intelligent as he was. I tried to find a girlfriend of my own, but my one possible candidate was sent back home when she tumbled down the steps of the Parthenon, causing serious damage to her leg brace.

Jason looked convincing enough in the company of his girlfriend. They scrambled about the various ruins, snapping each other's pictures while I hung back fuming, watching them nuzzle and coo. My jealousy stemmed from the belief that he had been cured. One fistful of my flesh and he had lost all symptoms of the disease.

Camp ended and I flew home with my legs crossed, dropping my bag of stolen souvenirs and racing to the bathroom, where I spent the next several days sitting on the toilet and studying my face in a hand mirror. *I like guys.* The words had settled themselves into my features. I was a professional now, and it showed.

I returned to my volunteer job at the mental hospital, carrying harsh Greek cigarettes as an incentive to some of the more difficult patients.

"Faggot!" a woman shouted, stooping to protect her collection of pinecones. "Get your faggoty hands away from my radio transmitters."

40   "Don't mind Mary Elizabeth," the orderly said. "She's crazy."

Maybe not, I thought, holding a pinecone up against my ear. She's gotten the faggot part right, so maybe she was onto something.

The moment we boarded our return flight from Kennedy to Raleigh, Lisa re-arranged her hair, dropped her accent, and turned to me saying, "Well, I thought that was very nice, how about you?" Over the course of five minutes, she had eliminated all traces of her reckless European self. Why couldn't I do the same?

In late August my class schedule arrived along with the news that I would not be bused. There had been violence in other towns and counties, trouble as far away as Boston; but in Raleigh the transition was peaceful. Not only students but many of the teachers had been shifted from one school to another. My new science teacher was a black man very adept at swishing his way across the room, mocking everyone from Albert Einstein to the dweebish host of a popular children's television program. Black and white, the teachers offered their ridicule as though it were an olive branch. "Here," they said, "this is something we each have in common, proof that we're all brothers under the skin."

Questions for Discussion

1. Why does Sedaris introduce his selection with the fact that the school district will implement racial integration with forced busing? What does the Spanish teacher's anecdote about the "colored girl" at the state fair who wanted to touch the teacher's hair reflect about common attitudes of the time regarding racial integration in the schools?
2. Why is Sedaris critical of his teachers and especially their sense of humor? What does Sedaris fear? Why does Sedaris believe that he is a member of a secret society founded on self-loathing?
3. How and why does Sedaris identify with the African American students who will be coming to his school in the fall? Why does he welcome their arrival and feel that they have more power than he does?
4. Why is Sedaris anxious about his one-month trip to summer camp in Greece? Why is it easier for his sister Lisa to adjust to camp?
5. Why are Jason and Sedaris frightened by their sexual experience? Why does Sedaris become jealous of Jason?
6. Why does Sedaris end the essay with the observation of his new science teacher, "a black man very adept at swishing his way across the room, mocking everyone from Albert Einstein to the dweebish host of a popular children's television program"? What does he mean when he says, "Black and white, the teachers offered their ridicule as though it were an olive branch"?

Connection

Compare Sedaris's recollections of conflicts in school with the attitudes portrayed in "Revising the Boy Code" (see page 317).

Ideas for Writing

1. Write an essay in which you discuss Sedaris's most important points. While he does reveal his homosexuality, the essay brings up more issues. Include your reaction to "I Like Guys."
2. Write an essay that compares the ways students and teachers dealt with the issue of homosexuality at your own high school with Sedaris's experiences and insights. How were the comments and activities sanctioned at Sedaris's junior high both similar and different from what was happening at your high school? How do you feel about the way homosexuals were treated at your high school?

David Sedaris
`http://home.pacifier.com/~paddockt/sedaris.html`
Learn about David Sedaris at this Web site dedicated to the author and
comedian. Read articles about Sedaris, read or listen to his work and
interviews, view his bibliography, talk to other fans, and find out where
the author will speak next.

Gay Literature
`www.gayliterature.com/biblios.htm`
This Web site is devoted to sharing the works of the world's gay writers.
One can also find several relevant links to other sites that discuss gay
literature and its influence on society.

Jakki Martinez

The College "Hook Up" Scene

*Jakki Martinez (b. 1987) was born and raised in Brownsville, Texas.
In 2005, Martinez graduated as high school valedictorian and is currently
an undergraduate pre-medical student at Stanford University, majoring in
Biological Sciences. She maintains aspirations in forensic pathology and
medical examination, as well as interests in gender studies, fetish culture,
and horror culture. The following paper was inspired by topics and issues
discussed in a Stanford University sociology course taught by Paula England,
titled "Sex and Love in Modern Society."*

JOURNAL

Describe a time when social expectations and standards left you in a
negative, unfair position, while your peers seemed to benefit from the
situation.

I danced to the electronic music, hands in the air, eyes closed, my mood
uplifted by the fact that final exams were over. My limbs occasionally
made contact with other sweating bodies on the steamy dance floor. As I
began to lose myself in the digital syncopations of the music, my arm was
suddenly grabbed aggressively by a boy I had never seen in my life, who
gazed wildly into my eyes, his own bloodshot and glazed over. Barely
audible over the music, he yelled at me, "What's your name?" I returned

his shout-out with a curt answer. As he wrapped his arms around my still moving waist, he continued his small-talk, making sure to maintain eye contact with me.

Determined to rid myself of this grabby, drunken boy, I moved ever so slowly in the direction of my friend. Smoothly, she came towards me and whispered in my ear, "Are you hooking up with him tonight?" The look in my eyes answered *no.* She understood, easing her body in between mine and the boy's, and cleverly danced the two of us away from him as I thanked her silently with my smile. She motioned with her body to a boy not too far away from our dancing zone. I immediately understood her signals; she was going home with this second boy to hook up. I nodded to her, danced away, and easily fell back into my electronic daze, eyes closed, hands in the air, limbs brushing against those by my side.

This brand of intimate encounter, almost devoid of dialogue and instead rich in unspoken norms and the language of gesture, is not just a phenomenon among my small group of friends. Instead, this social spectacle represents a major trend in the college party scene. For undergraduate students throughout the United States, the "hook up" is the new date. Paula England, PhD, a sociologist at Stanford University, baffled by a casual remark by one of her students regarding the death of the dating scene, performed a comprehensive sociological study at eight American institutions. Over 2,500 undergraduate students were interviewed about relationships, romance, and the "hook up" scene. England was shocked by the results. The traditional "date" had been replaced the new and improved hook up, which has taken the youth of America by storm.

Many gender scholars are frantically trying to get to the bottom of the phenomenon. Two articles, "The Decline of the Date and the Rise of the College Hook Up" and "Hooking Up, Hanging Out, and Hoping for Mr. Right," both analyze research and sociological studies that examine the premarital dating phenomenon which has taken place in college settings throughout modern America. The writers of both articles—Paula England and Reuben J. Thomas, and Glenn Norval and Elizabeth Marquardt, respectively—acknowledge how, over time, traditional Platonic dates have been almost replaced, or at least outnumbered, by this new scene called "hooking up."

5　　As far as my personal knowledge extends, and according to sociological research, the hook up is a casual, usually sexual event that occurs privately after social gatherings such as parties. Intoxication and previous acquaintance are optional. Influential historical events such as the sexual revolution of the 1960s, as well as drastic changes in the college setting, have helped sculpt a new sexual college environment.

This setting features recreational sex, sexual freedom, fewer sexual in-hibitions on the part of females, and a heady blend of intoxication and sexual fun.

Although the concurrence of these factors seems to suggest new sexual empowerment of women, men still appear to reap the benefits of this newly sexualized dating scene and, in fact, appear to be on the winning side of the struggle for sexual equaliy. Norval and Mar-quardt's article actually studies the inequities of the hook up further, analyzing outside social norms and how they act as underlying con-stituents of male and female attitudes and reputations in the hook up environment. These outside norms include concepts of marriage, parental divorce, and parental advice. Qualitative and quantitative data from the studies expose the paradox that may leave women dis-satisfied, shamed, ridiculed, and confused at the end of the day—or at the end of a "hook up."

Gender issues certainly factor into this social phenomenon as men and women both appear to have socially outlined expectations in the "hook up" setting. Despite the overall appearance of new sexual freedom and empowerment, many women suffer more sexual obligations and expecta-tions. Women still confront the embarrassing and degrading stigma at-tached to sexual freedom, promiscuity, and recreation. Therefore, women take advantage of the ambiguity of the term "hooking up" because they "are walking a fine line if they choose to be sexually active, particularly when they do so with more than one partner, yet no one can tell them ex-actly where that line is drawn" (Norval and Marquardt). That is, the vague-ness of the term "hooking up," which can include any combination of the actions described in the sexual hierarchy—first base, second base, third base, and home plate (so to speak)—provides women with a kind of safety blanket that masks the details of their actions in order to avoid social dis-approval and demeaning of reputations.

As one male respondent in England and Thomas's research stated, al-though women have gained freedom in their sexual antics in the college hook up scene, "there's still that . . . 'preserve the women' attitude, or de-nounce them . . ." In addition, the sexual freedom that college women at-tempt to embrace in hook ups in fact may be confused results of intoxication and peer pressure. In contrast, men also confront social repu-tations and name-calling; the only difference is that men encounter in-creasingly positive reputations among their peers, in correlation to the number of hook ups in which they engage. While pejorative terms such as *slut, whore, trash*, and *ho* are words used for women who frequently hook up, more socially approving terms such as *player, the man*, and *stud* are used for their male counterparts.

All in all, it seems that the new hook up scene which appeared to lib-erate college women in fact has turned against females by multiplying their social burdens. Sexual competency, coupled with lingering social stigmas attached to sexual promiscuity, only worsens the gender inequality problem. Norval and Marquardt found that the three most common emotions experienced by the college women after a hook up were *desirable*, *awkward*, and *confused*. Women, expected to meet both social criteria (competent and decent), collectively reported mixed emotions regarding their sexual antics. *Triumphant* was the least common emotion these women expressed, which only further emphasizes that females' social awkwardness opposes males' satisfaction and positive reputations in hook ups.

10   Expanding on male satisfaction versus female dissatisfaction, Emily Schafer, a Stanford graduate student who had studied the England and Thomas article, provided this report from a male respondent: "I actually . . . just dropped my level of respect for her. I didn't spend the night in my room with her. I actually said I was going to the bathroom . . ." (qtd. in Schafer 2). This typical personal statement illustrates the gender inequality in the social stigma attached to female sexuality. The male student's loss of respect for the girl and his total lack of attention and attachment to her after the incident were completely logical reactions to his sexual encounter with this female.

The following statement presents a disparaging female perspective on another young woman's emotional involvement after a casual hook up: "One of my suite mates is like that [overly involved; upset] . . . she says, 'Why can't he call me?' and even if she wants to go to the bathroom [she asks,] 'Can you keep an eye on my phone?' I'm like, 'He's not going to call,' [and] she's like, 'Please'" (qtd. in Norval and Marquardt). It seems that men are expected to have recreational attitudes, while women experience confusion and attachment after the hook up event. Therefore, this case study also uncovers male benefits and female detriments in the college casual sex scene. In fact, England, Thomas, Marquardt, and Norval all note how males literally make the decision after a "hook up" whether or not to handle the situation as purely recreational and unattached or as the first step in a meaningful, exclusive relationship. A social process defined as "the talk" coincides with the expectation of females to be relational and the expectation of males to be recreational and more powerful; girls initiate a discussion about the nature and extent of the relationship between the hook up partners, and males act as the final word on what "defines the relationship." In other words, the male holds the power of the woman's body and emotions in his hands. What happened to the sexual freedom and empowerment of women? After doing some research, I began to wonder whether other people felt the same way I did. Who were the "discontents" of the hook-up scene?

In order to find an answer to my questions about the sexual paradox in the college relationship scene, I had some intense discussions with peers regarding the issue, and have noticed an undercurrent of dissatisfaction among both males and females. One male described how he felt that the hook up phenomenon eliminated the need for conversation between potential sexual partners, since the main goal of hooking up is recreation. Because of this lack of communication, he said, disregarding a female's needs and desires has become easier. I asked him whether he felt the hook up scene gave any empowerment or liberation to women at all, and he replied, "No—none at all" (Anonymous male student). I asked the same question to a co-ed. Upon mentioning the topic of discussion, the talk became very heated. In anger, she expressed her disgust with the college hook up. When I proposed that some women believe that they gain more sexual freedom from hooking up rather than getting involved in a cumbersome relationship, she scoffed, "'Hook ups' do the exact opposite! They are a step backwards for women in the feminist movement" (Anonymous female student). She felt that women are more vulnerable in recreational hook up scenes.

In conclusion, as one unwilling to swim towards the shiny "hook" awaiting my capture and submission, I have chosen to distance myself from this increasingly popular yet, at least from a woman's perspective, disturbing social phenomenon. I can only hope that, like many high school and college fads before it, the hook up scene will eventually evolve into something more like ideal male-female relationships that are open, communicative, and relatively free of progressive (or regressive) social norms that tell women and men how they "ought" to behave around members of the opposite sex.

Works Cited

Anonymous female student. Personal Interview. Stanford University. 29 May 2008.

Anonymous male student. Personal Interview. Stanford University. 1 June 2008.

England, P., & Thomas, R. J. (forthcoming). "The Decline of the Date and the Rise of the College Hook Up." *Family in Transition.* 15ᵗʰ ed. Ed. A. S. Skolnich and J. H. Skolnick. Boston: Allyn & Bacon, 2008.

Norval Glenn and Elisabeth Marquardt. *Hooking Up, Hanging Out and Hoping for Mr. Right; College Women on Dating and Mating Today: Report to the Independent Women's Forum.* New York: Institute of American Values, 2001. 26 May 2008 <www.americanvalues.org/Hooking_Up.pdf>.

Schafer, Emily. Personal interview. Stanford University 28 May 2008.

Questions for Discussion

1. Martinez makes a transition from a personal tone, to a more research-based voice, and back to a personal tone towards the end of the essay. Is this effective in presenting the social situation? Why or why not?

2. Discuss the dichotomy or paradox that college-aged females appear to face in the hook up scene.

3. What is the author's reaction to the hook up scene? Do you find this reaction to be logical and reasonable considering the data provided

in the two articles and the interviews she has taken? What is your own reaction?

4. Consider the final, open-ended hope this essay puts forth. Based on social trends outlined by Martinez and modern gender scholars, what do you predict about the next social phenomenon in the college sexual and relationship scene?

Gilberto Jimenez

It's Complicated: Facebook and Modern Youth Relationships

Gilberto Jimenez wrote "It's Complicated" for his first year composition class. He is currently taking classes in chemistry and digital technology, which have always been of special interest to him. In the following essay, Jimenez defines the different features and applications of Facebook, the popular social-networking site, while analyzing the effects of key features of the site on modern approaches to traditional gender roles and the etiquette of dating.

Over 132 million people accessed Facebook pages during the month of June 2008 ("Social Networking"). With its dominance of the college-student demographic, Facebook is the crown jewel of social networking sites, having infiltrated the daily lives of its users to the point that the site mirrors young adult society, especially in regards to gender roles. From the way students present themselves in words and images to the development of relationships, the digital and face-to-face world share many of the same norms for relationships and self-preservation for men and women. These norms are communicated in Facebook through a number of characteristics and applications native to the site itself, which are used in characteristically different ways by male and female users.

The primary foundation for communicating every Facebook personality is the "profile page." Like most social networking sites, profile pages allow users to highlight crucial aspects of their personalities. Essential information can be gathered about a person simply by browsing their profile for a few minutes, which is one reason why many companies use Facebook as a part of their hiring process. Everything from a person's basic information (name, location, gender, sexual orientation, religious and political views) to more personal ideas (favorite movies, quotes, books, TV shows, and music, as well as "interests" and "about me" sections) is available for other users to see. Even images of the user are available in just a few clicks. With so much potential for revelation (or deceit) within a profile, many users distort basic facts about themselves, just as someone might stretch the truth during a job interview or on a date. Some young men display a picture of themselves in their high school football uniform as their default picture, even though some time has passed since they graduated and their only current contact with the game is through the TV set in their dorm room. Likewise, in many pages young women express admiration for and identification with heroines of classic novels and films with which they are most likely only vaguely familiar.

All Facebook users start off with the same basic interactive applications (most importantly the wall and photos applications). The basic Facebook page is essentially gender neutral, with the same minimalist blue and white layout greeting users on every person's page. Although we might assume that males would be most attracted to Facebook because of their technological orientation, female profiles outnumber their male counterparts internationally by a two to one ratio. It is noteworthy that nations with the lowest percentage of female users are Saudi Arabia, Pakistan, the United Arab Emirates, and Egypt, nations where women are frequently repressed in terms of family life, religion, and political rights (Arrington). The many female users of Facebook tend to decorate their pages differently from males, and rely on different applications to express their tastes and personalities.

Imagine the profile of one Pat Doe. The information panel says nothing about Pat's gender; only name, birthday, location, and political affiliation are given. Also, no profile picture is included. If curious users stumble upon the hypothetical Pat Doe, they may be forced to deduce Pat's sex from the applications he/she has added. Quiz applications would be a good place to start. These applications draw from the same think tanks that create the quizzes in teenaged girls' magazines. Add to that the fact that these applications normally have names such as "Which Disney Princess Are You?" and we can see clearly that quiz applications on Facebook target the same demographic as the magazines. On the other hand, women do not carry the burden of reinforcing gender stereotypes alone. Applications such as the various "favorite sports team" widgets can indicate a masculine user. Many males also find themselves drowning their profiles in images of team logos for baseball, football, basketball, hockey, soccer, automotive racing, and many other sports, revealing personalities similar to those rabid fans who seem to have surgically replaced their right hand with an oversized "#1" foam finger.

5   This is not to say that men or women cannot enjoy having both the results of quizzes and declarations of their love of sporting events on their profiles. In fact, many users do cross gender lines in their use of applications and imagery. If Pat Doe is found to employ an equal number of both applications, simply counting the total number of applications used

should be a good indicator of the person's gender. This is because women tend to spend more time on Facebook, perhaps because they devote more attention to social relationships than men do, resulting in more friends and applications used ("Friends"). However, even this tendency is not absolute. Luckily, Facebook's other central applications (the wall, and photos) help to clarify further the genders of users.

For example, one of the best features about Facebook is the "photos" application. Not only does it allow users to upload as many photos as they desire; it also grants them the power to "tag" people in pictures. In a tagged photo, when a user places the cursor over a face in the picture, the name belonging to the face is displayed. As a result, every user has a "view photos of me" link under their profile picture that displays every photo in which the user is tagged. As useful as this may seem, the issue of vanity often makes this feature as frustrating as it is helpful.

Women scrutinize every aspect of their image to a far greater degree than do men . Thus, on Facebook, when a woman finds out she has tagged a photo where she displays a crooked smile or suffers from a bad angle-view, she will most likely "untag" the image so that the photo no longer appears among the block of pictures in the "view photos of me" link. Men, also increasingly vain about their appearance, can also behave in this manner, but relative to women, untagging by men is minimal. Rarely will a male untag himself, lest he be viewed as overly vain or even feminine.

On a related note, many users upload photos that are intentionally crude or risqué. If a woman uploads a photo of herself in a particularly revealing bikini, this is often interpreted as "sexy" behavior. Uploading such a photo on Facebook is almost the same as walking around in such a garment in public. Whether the intention is to garner male attention or simply to show off a great body, a photo of this nature normally leads to the perception that the female is either loose or desperate for love. However, rules for skin-exposing photos change with gender. While some men are shameless enough to show off their bodies online for female attention, far fewer women take the bait than their opposites. Some men even post odd pictures of themselves just for laughs. A male may post a photo of himself posing like a warrior and wearing only leopard print underwear and a bright orange cast, all for the sake of laughter at the expense of dignity. Oddly enough, it seems that anytime somebody posts a revealing photo on Facebook, regardless of gender, the majority of comments on the photo will come from males.

However, this does not mean that men commenting on photos is the only source of flirtatious remarks on Facebook, where every profile comes equipped with a "wall" application, a space where people can write quick public messages to each other for the entire world to see. For the most part, when a user writes on the wall of a user of the same sex, the jargon used is similar to what normal conversation between friends might sound like, with a few emoticons added to clarify the tone of the feelings expressed. As the gender most prone to verbal communication about emotional issues, women tend to write more on-line than men. With the increasing role of social networking in the lives of young people, the mailman no longer takes part in written expressions of love. Instead, a Facebook user with a crush will probably allow their emotions to embody themselves in the form of unprompted and elongated posts on their crush's wall. Many users will find any excuse to write to their crush, no matter how pathetic it seems (these comments usually go along the lines of "Hey, I looked at the sky and it made me think of your blue eyes"). While Facebook's private messaging system (somewhat like email) might be a more proper medium for flirtation, making these expressions public forces a user either to acknowledge the message writer publicly by responding on their wall or to risk being perceived as having no regard for the emotions of others. Because wall posts are public, people who want a bit of gossip can monitor the activities of the person with the crush to see if they are even getting a response from the person fancied. By clicking on the "wall-to-wall" link to see what two people have written on each others' wall, it can become painfully obvious, if conversations seem to be one-sided, that the subject of the crush has no romantic feelings for the suitor. Of course, an ignored lover should not feel too slighted. Relationships have progressively become more complicated due to Facebook.

10   Facebook increasingly affects modern romantic relationships between young men and women. It all begins with a simple friend request. It is safe to assume that any student one meets maintains a Facebook profile. Therefore, any time two people meet, even if it is just for a few minutes, they will often wind up friends on Facebook. Although these friend requests usually mean nothing more than a mutual acknowledgment of existence, there are unwritten laws regarding such desires, especially if the request is to a member of the opposite sex. It is important to note that these rules apply equally to both men and women. To begin with, since this is Twenty-first Century America, it is okay for women to make the first move; a young man no longer needs to agonize over obtaining a lady's phone number. The key to a smooth friend request is timing. It is never acceptable to hunt down a person on Facebook and send a friend request immediately after meeting them, unless one wants to come across as either a flirt or a stalker. After a day or so has passed, attaching a personal message that contains either an inside joke or a single emoticon to the friend request is a good start. The personal message tells the other person that they mean more than just a larger number on the friend counter; it also serves as encouragement to write on a new friend's wall. This will help determine whether or not there is any potential for a relationship.

The wrong way to go about initiating a Facebook friendship is to send a friend request at 3:00 A.M. with a paragraph-long message explaining why he or she should confirm the friend request. For one, this comes across as both overbearing and somewhat unattractive. Furthermore, there is the risk that this potential lover could also be on Facebook at 3:00 A.M. and receive the friend request the moment it is sent, therefore raising several undesirable questions on their part, such as the negative judgment call, "What kind of freak is on Facebook at this hour?" If one plays the friend request cards correctly, there is a chance that the Facebook relationship could bloom into something more.

Of all the information contained within Facebook profiles, few polarize users with joy and/or angst like the "relationship status." Thanks to Facebook, in theory people never have to hit on someone who may or may not have a significant other. One can simply take a quick glance at the relationship status in the information panel of a potential mate's profile for confirmation about their current involvements. While this may seem straightforward and obvious, Facebook has different statuses that can often be misleading or confusing. The two basic ones are "in a relationship" and "single." People who state either of these two statuses are generally being honest, as these are fairly straightforward terms. Going a little further into commitment, there are the terms "engaged" and "married," both of which are a degree or two more serious than "in a relationship," but which are not always accurately described in the limited Facebook categories. Then there are the choices of "in an open relationship" and "it's complicated," which suggest that the person claiming one of these statuses is a liar, or at least emotionally confused and conflicted. Although Facebook users generally carry the correct relationship label on their profile, this does not mean that the "relationship status" is an accurate indicator of a future relationship for correspondents.

First, a large number of users blatantly lie about their relationship status. Specifically, many women will often state that they are "married," "in a relationship," "in an open relationship," or "engaged" with their best girl friend. While these are acceptable statuses for a female user to be engaged in, it does provide agony to the men who desire them. After all, just because a girl has decided to use the "relationship" label to express her love for her best friend does not mean she lacks or does not desire a significant male other. Many women in serious relationships still choose to state that they are "married" to their best girl friend. Thus, many unfortunate male users are forced to continue playing guessing games when they see a feminine name or a gender-ambiguous name like "Pat Doe" in a girl's relationship status. To complicate things further, when someone indicates an actual male-female relationship, it is foolish to believe that the few words used to describe the relationship are accurate. Even when someone is listed as "single," they may actually be in the embryonic stages of a serious relationship, yet there is no convenient label for that status.

The biggest problem in this regard is seen in the common attitude of the male who is afraid of commitment to a serious relationship. A relationship does not become officially listed on Facebook unless both parties are committed. After all, when a user openly states that they are "in a relationship with Person X," they declare to the rest of the online community that their hearts are off-limits. The fact that you have changed your relationship status will show up in many of the user's friends' "newsfeed," which makes changing the relationship status like shouting a lover's name from the top of a mountain. For this reason, many people, especially males, are reluctant to label themselves. Thus, a budding couple must be careful about the timing of the status change. If a young lady sends her lover a status request too soon or before the male even realizes he is in a serious relationship, she risks giving the impression that the relationship is "moving too quickly." This plays to the traditional role of the male as the one who is reluctant to abandon his bachelorhood. Of course men often make the same mistake, perhaps through wanting to brag about a new relationship with a desirable young woman or through failing to communicate deep feelings for her. On the other hand, a relationship that seems to be going well may be sabotaged by the fact that both parties are too afraid to send the official request for a status. Silly as they might seem, these announcement problems are issues that actual or potential couples must deal with nowadays thanks to the emergence of Facebook as a relationship news broadcaster.

15   Despite the relationship and communication problems discussed above, the gender roles of the Twenty-first Century have not changed much because of Facebook. While it seems that the site is responsible for new gender norms, in reality male and female users are simply translating their real-life roles to the digital world. For every romantic wall post and untagged photo in this land of silicon, there is a carbon based love letter and a woman desperately looking into the mirror to perfect her outfit. Perhaps in the future as the average Facebook user becomes older and relationship statuses shift to mostly "married," we will see a more radical shift in the way gender roles are perceived.

WORKS CITED

Arrington, Michael. "Facebok is almost 2/3 Women and Other Stats". *TechCrunch* 2007. 22 Aug. 2008 <http://www.techcrunch.com/2007/ 11/21/Facebook-is-almost-23-women-and-other-stats>.

"Friends of Men vs. Women on Social Networks." *RapLeaf* 2008. 22 Aug. 2008 <http://business.rap!eaf.corn/company_press_2008_04_30.html>.

"Social Networking Explodes Worldwide as Sites Increase their focus on Cultural Relevance," *ComScore* 2008. 22 Aug. 2008 <http://www.comscore.com/press/release.asp?press=2396>.

1. Do you agree or disagree with Jimenez's perspective on the gender roles, flirtation, and "netiquette" used by men and women on social networking sites such as Facebook? Does his essay reveal any gender bias on his part?

2. Jimenez provides several sources and statistics to support and clarify his ideas on Facebook relationships. What other information, studies, or concrete facts might he have presented to make his ideas more convincing and informative?

3. Would it have helped Jimenez in presenting his argument and in making it persuasive to have used more of his own experiences or examples and testimony from his friends or interviewees? Why or why not?

4. Based on your own experience with Facebook, what other applications and features might Jimenez have mentioned in his effort to demonstrate the importance of applications in presenting user self-images and attitudes toward relationships on the site?

Tajamika Paxton

Loving a One-armed Man

After graduating from Georgetown University, Tajamika Paxton held a creative executive position at MTV Films, where she worked on the The Wood *and the Academy Award-nominated* Election. *She was the executive producer of the feature film division of Forest Whitaker's Spirit Dance Entertainment, where she produced* Green Dragon *(2001) and* Chasing Papi *(2003). Paxton is also a member of the Black Women's Network and the Board of Directors of Outfest, a nonprofit organization that exhibits high quality gay, lesbian, bisexual, and transgender-themed films and videos in an annual festival in southern California. Currently, she teaches yoga and writes personal essays that analyze the gender and ethnic issues of her own experiences. The essay included here, "Loving a One-armed Man" (2004), is an examination of her evolving relationship and understanding of her father and his troubled vision of African American manhood.*

JOURNAL

Write about whether you think that the roles played by men today are changing, and how. If you do not think men have accepted a new definition of masculinity, explain why they have not changed.

There's a man coming toward me. Together we're in the middle of a city street: people move hurriedly around us, but he and I don't rush. He walks slowly, almost ambling. He's returning home from a war. He went into battle resilient and optimistic that the world would yield for him and if it didn't he would take it down or die trying, extricating from the struggle a sense of power and self-determination. Instead, he's left "head bloody but unbowed" with his jacket neatly folded over the space where his arm once was. He has stories to tell about how the arm was blown off and other battles fought, but no story can match the intensity of living through it, the lesions the living creates on your soul. This one-armed man is an image I get in a dream. He's the symbol of men being torn apart by the impossible demands of one-dimensional manhood. The real man, fully limbed, is my father, Cassius Paxton.

My father is a veteran not of war, but of life lived within the cage of conflicting expectations particular to Black men born in America. Men who are told to be powerful in spite of economic cycles and discrimination that leave them powerless, and ordered to be rugged when the centuries-old healing they so desperately require demands sensitivity. I remember him as easily threatened, his wrath easily ignited. Self-taught and thus well educated, but lacking the resolve to use that education for his own prosperity. Instead, he chose to become an opportunist, a hustler, someone willing to take from others in a world where Black men go to prison for the same crimes that put White men in office. He spent his youth arrogant. He believed being quite handsome and charming would sustain him, perhaps lead him to the good life he saw in men like Nat King Cole and Sam Cooke.

My daddy is 62 and that man he once was is long gone. Now, he wants to tell other men what he's learned so they can avoid roads paved with personal regrets, the lingering numbness of unrealized dreams or ex-wives and children they never see. He's living with the unanswered question of what to do with those years and the sinking thought that he could have done more. My daddy has prostate cancer and cirrhosis. My daddy is dying. Maybe not today or next year but soon, he thinks, and because no one else in my family speaks to him, I feel like I'm the only one watching. I'm witnessing the transformation of his manhood like a scripted Hollywood film where the debonair leading man comes to some conclusive arc that makes the time watching his character worthwhile.

We're growing closer now. An extension of where we were in the picture I keep on my shelf. Cheek to cheek, his strong amateur middleweight boxing hands wrapped around my tiny three-year-old ones. Closer because we're determined to keep our connection despite the past and because of the future. My mother, his ex-wife of 21 years, talks to him when she must. She makes no pretense of truly caring if he changes or not. My father and I acknowledge the pain of the absence of my brothers. One lives locally and is being ravaged by some of the same addictions that plagued my father. High or sober, it's emotionally difficult for him to face my father, to have a conversation like two adults. He resorts to sickening depictions of his masculinity, bragging about his inability to cook and how his wife prepares meals and how other women respond to him when he's in public. My father usually stares at him pitifully. He probably hears his own father's cryptic words, "One day, son, you'll understand," and wishes that my brother would stand still and engage in a realistic conversation about what it's going to take for him not to die dirty in some hallway.

5   The other brother lives far away with his six children. He thinks having so many children is manly but cries like a baby when he's arrested for not paying his child support. My father sends no money, only admonition. "Son, you made that bed, you lie in it. Don't run from it now. It's not going anywhere." Today his advice is simple, too simple for my psychoanalytic tastes. He says people make two choices: do or don't. It's this simple creed that gave him the resolve to give up narcotics years ago and in 1996, to stop drinking before his habit killed him. So my father is changing and I am alone, listening. Listening to the stories of what life was like for him at 35 and why he sometimes behaved horribly in the name of being a man.

I remember my father as two men, distinct but with the same form. A man-child, he would sit for hours and play Atari Pac-Man with me after school, but a trip to the store that same night could mean a four-day absence. I would walk home wondering if his car was safely back in the driveway, like a friend waiting for me in front of a rickety swing, faithful. When it wasn't there, I suppressed my loss, but it metastasized into a resounding mistrust of all men. I lived, and at times, continue to live, with a sense that I would inevitably be let down, left waiting and alone. When he returned home after those times he offered no explanations and grew sullen when asked. Instead of communicating through the vulnerable places, I learned from my father to get silent and the world will walk away. Not so different from my brothers, I too adapted my father's stoic veneer as protection when I felt emotionally vulnerable.

At a recent birthday lunch, he shared the pain and pressure of the responsibility of parenting when he felt like such a young man, incapable of taking care of himself. He explained and, in his way, apologized for being an inadequate provider; for not having the resilience to consistently raise his children or the patience and understanding to love his wife. When the pressures mounted, he took flight.

I appreciate his candor and experience it as a step toward me. I meet him there, trying to talk to him every day partially because I have so many unanswered questions. Questions like "Why did you get so sad during Christmas?" One Christmas morning we found him in the bathtub obviously high, pupils dilated and stinging from tears. Looking broken and attempting to be coy, he asked what I thought of the gold necklace he had bought and bragged about its cost. He wouldn't respond to our pleading eyes or to my mother's seething resentment. I remember thanking him and wondering what could make a grown man cry at Christmas. To this day I care little for gold.

We don't talk much about the violence. He has taken to believing that he hasn't harmed anyone. It's easier than believing that he's scarred someone beyond repair. I don't pretend to understand this approach but it works for him and after years of tantrums, I've given up the need for blame. Some things must stay in the past so they don't choke the life out of what you're trying to create. But I can't forget. On two occasions, he beat my brothers mercilessly, and I can see clearly the afternoon my mother was cleaning our room and he dragged her out of it by her hair, her leg tearing as the flesh caught ahold of the sharp metal of my brother's bike pedal. Along with horror I was flooded with guilt. Could we have pushed the bike closer to the wall? The sound of her screaming, her open mouth begging, but I can't see his face. I wanted it be someone else, a stranger, not my father. My father who propped me up on the armrest while we rode through the streets of Los Angeles telling me stories of city landmarks and the time he hung out all night with Dinah Washington. My father who played with my hair for hours determined that his baby have an Afro.

10   I found some aspect of this man everywhere I went to look for love. By the grace of God, he was never violent. He was edgy, intelligent, magnetic and usually unavailable. Armed. He was my roughneck, and I was faithful to his type, always wanting to get beneath the armor, to try to make him be gentle with me. They could all be summed up with one. We met at a club dancing to "O.P.P." He knew all the lyrics and recited them through gold teeth emblazoned with his initials as he guided me to the dance floor. Later, I rejoiced when underneath the sagging pants and the heavy New York accent, I uncovered a man who played lacrosse despite the rough inner city upbringing he feigned; a man who talked for hours about growing up mixed race in Long Island. We talked about many subjects but not each other's needs. We exchanged easy childhood stories, more song lyrics, warm laughs and sweaty, disconnected sex. But we quickly tired of playing games the wounded play, neither willing to truly disarm. And I returned to my pattern of reaching for cool, tough men like my father.

The father I know now would not strike out against those he loves. In fact he sits in agony as he hears his neighbors beating each other to signal they're alive. In this new man I see a strong desire to be forgiven and loved. His calls are frequent, usually establishing when we'll spend our next moments together. The attention he wants from his family and the advice he needs to share is urgent to him, his sustenance.

Little of his old masculinity is of use to him now, not much of it can help him fight the diseases inside him. Not the white Cadillac, once a symbol of his street status and now delivering him to frequent doctors' appointments every week. Not the women he allowed to distract him from his marriage. Most of them are dead or just gone. There's a kind one by his side now. She makes it easier to bear but she can't save him. His gold jewelry can't buy him any more time. Not even his once perfect biceps and his right hook. Using our kitchen as a ring, he once showed my brothers and I how to throw and block punches and stay off the ropes. The irony is overwhelming. Even the dominator, the dark side of him, is rendered useless. Age doesn't respond to bullying and there's no one else to rule over. He is left cultivating life-affirming skills he never found relevant. He's relying on spiritual fortitude to keep him grounded and hopeful. He's learning more about the cancer-fighting benefits of an organic diet. He listens to his mother.

Twelve years ago when he was injured in a car accident he joked that he had earned a purple heart from the streets of Oakland: he'd been shot, stabbed with a knife and an ice pick and none of those things could take him out. But I know this illness is different. "It's going to be the fight of my life," he says. Indeed. The harrowing facts about the survival rate for Black men are humbling. The doctors tell him to keep a positive attitude and not to succumb to the fatigue. He says, "My attitude is positive. And I'm tired." In the next hour, he's buoyant again, doing the calisthenics recommended by the doctor to strengthen his body before the radiation begins.

I admire how he now accepts the range of his feelings, not forcing himself into some stoic display of strength. He plans his life in days, maybe weeks if he's feeling optimistic. He says he just simply doesn't want to go yet; there are more days of sunshine, more long drives, boxing on TV every Saturday night, and a longing for creative fulfillment. I talk to him about the summer road trips we'll take together, but it's hard to experience just coming to know someone who could leave so soon.

15   What we have is a return to tenderness. Much is said about returning to the maternal "womb." I consider what we're engaged in now a return to the paternal womb, that place upon my father's chest where as a little girl I would rest comfortably and listen to his heart beating and think it the most melodious sound, comforting and truly strong. I hug this "one-armed man" frequently, and love him for the way he hugs me back generously, and for the meals he prepares for me with care. I love him for the considerate way he sends me home before it gets too late, and for the way I can cry on the phone with him about a thwarted romance and he'll paint a picture of my tomorrows and all the loves I'll have. It reminds me that this part of him was always there, beneath the fury.

I greedily devour him all for me. My brothers don't want to hear him talk about responsibility; they're sharpening their weaponry. During the three years I refused to speak to him, I did the same, but now I relate to him as a disarmed man, not just because that's what he, in the face of aging and death, has finally become, but because I need my own disarmament.

My life had been lacking true openness, an openness that says I am here, love me or not; and if you don't, I have what it takes to tend my own garden. I hadn't tended my garden. I was coping. In the wake of my internal chaos I had embarked on my own nightmare of working hard to achieve success and unconsciously hoping it would fill the neglected spaces in me, the voids created by unprocessed childhood pains and the slashes made by years of broken relationships. I was looking for a fulfillment that came from high-powered salaries and expense accounts. I adapted the masculinity myth for myself, suppressing yin gentility and overdeveloping yang aggression, convincing myself that aggressive people get farther faster and that the same aggression would repel those who might do me harm. I locked away my sense of play and simple pleasure convinced that only "girls" play and get hurt; tough women don't. I presented this armor proudly to the world until I began to suffocate inside the suit.

I loved the same way. Strong and tough but underneath, easily bruised and braced for inevitable disappointment. I was holding onto resentment for the apologies I hadn't received from my father and for all my failed attempts at disarmament. I relied on my relationships to feel that I was wanted, that what I had to offer was valuable. If a potential lover didn't respond to me, I sat dejected, a flood of insecurity overtaking me. From this desperate place I clung tightly to all lovers. When relationships ended, I was broken, trapped in romantic notions that someone could "steal my heart."

I had been avoiding the truth that I am emotionally responsible for delivering my happiness. In these last months I have come to see more clearly that I am responsible for my inner work, for spending quality time with me; for affirming my radiance, for saying yes to those deepest unspoken desires and living a life unbridled by comparisons or the judgments of others. With this awareness, I now see that no amount of protective covering can shield me. That what I needed and am finding is an inner fortification as essential as breath itself.

20   And so at 31, I shed my armor. As I do, I see that remarkable scene from *The Wiz*. After the witch has been killed, her former sweatshop slaves peel off their stifling furry costumes and begin to dance. They clap thunderously, gliding in a criss-cross formation stage left and stage right. They sing with rousing gospel harmonies, "Can you feel a brand-new day? Can you feel a brand-new day? Hello, world, it's like a different way of living now. Thank you, world, we always knew that we'd be free somehow."

It is a brand new day for relating—to my father, to my lovers, to myself. I'm learning to love the men in my life in a place beyond sex and romantic interest, with a genuine closeness that touches the strong and tender beating heart that I once knew. I've decided to love as an act of surrender, not a declaration of war, fighting for my protection and survival. I know now to look for those men disarmed of their own volition, willing to let me touch their soft places and I am willing to let them touch mine, with an understanding of how fragile we all really are. I move closer to a man who can raise his hand in protest to an unjust world and bring it to rest gently on my waist.

I'm one of a collective of people coming home from the same war trying to cross burned bridges with worn-out shoes; we're tired but we have not given up. We're marching forward to a new way of being with and for each other, offering gentleness and attention, exchanging bravado for emotional bravery. Taking responsibility for our individual pasts and sorting through which needs are our own to meet, and which we can expect to be met by others. Willing to offer each other our fidelity not because we're supposed to but because we respect the time it takes to make love in this inundated world. We're creating a space to collectively acknowledge that there has been a war going on and we are committed to the work of rebuilding.

My father and I are doing this work privately, learning how to love each other, to be tender with each other, to put down our guns together. With this newfound freedom, I can finally allow him to make me a promise and believe that he'll keep it, knowing that if he doesn't I can forgive him and he can forgive himself. So much of this has come because we're willing to strain the muscles of trust until they hurt but in the hurting, they expand our mutual compassion and love.

I no longer subscribe to the crippling belief that he, or other men, can't emotionally handle the delicate places in relationships. Perhaps the inner fortification I'm finding is what my father needed long ago to feel safe and truly powerful. He is finding his way to it now. I send grace for his journey and along with it blessings for all of the many men still gasping for air inside their suffocating suits of armor. These men hunger for a new code that will offer them liberation, a code found in books like this one and in nationwide barbershop and boardroom discussions.

25 I'm getting a glimpse of a new dream, different from the one-armed man trudging down the street. I'm imagining a world without battle-scarred soldiers of life who have to be maimed or die in order to become heroic, a world without men who have to wage war to prove their point. This world is full of men who are heroic because they have the courage to nurture their families with a gentle confident strength, to teach children, their own and others, how to be humane, how to live in harmony with those considered different, how to practice spirituality in a world that overvalues the material. Heroic because they know the task of transformation is difficult but they take action anyway because they know it must be done.

Heroic like my father. He is far from perfect and I am farther but together we're reaching. And I'm like a little West African girl going from village to village beating the drum, hailing the sound of the new arrival.

QUESTIONS FOR DISCUSSION

1. What is the significance of the author's dream of a one-armed veteran? Why does she begin the essay with this dream, and how does it related to her own father, a veteran of a different type of war?
2. How would you describe Paxton's father's concept of masculinity? In what sense is it born out of "the cage of conflicting expectations" of black manhood in American? How did Paxton's father's idea of masculinity disconnect him from his family and destroy his health?
3. What advice would Paxton's father like to give his sons? What stories can he now share with his daughter? What influence has he had on her values and choices in men?
4. What does the author mean by "disarming"? Why was her father's disarmament important for her? In what sense had she "adapted the masculinity myth [for herself]"?
5. What does the author mean when she says that she now sees "love as an act of surrender"? Why does this signify a "brand new day for relating" for her?
6. Why does Paxton come to see herself as a veteran returning from war, "exchanging bravado for emotional bravery"? What is the difference between these two terms? How does her "new dream" contrast to the original dream narrated in the introduction?

CONNECTION

Compare the images and ideas of masculinity presented through Paxton's father to those of Dan in "Revising the Boy Code" (p. 317).

IDEAS FOR WRITING

1. Write an essay in which you describe the vision of masculinity presented in this essay. What social and cultural factors cause such a view of masculinity to emerge in an individual, and how is it destructive to family life and relationships? Present examples of such "one-dimensional manhood" from your own experience and reading.
2. Write an essay about a program that can help a man or woman to make the transition from a destructive attitude of "bravado" to a state of "emotional bravery" as described in the final paragraphs of Paxton's essay. Do some research into different types of support groups and/or a series of steps that an individual can take to make such a major life transition.

RELATED WEB SITES

Young Dads

`www.findarticles.com/p/articles/mi_m2248/is_148_37/`
`ai_97723206/pg_3`

This article from the magazine *Adolescence* (2002) examines a program that shows promise for encouraging responsibility for family on the part of urban African American adolescent fathers.

Democrats Find Their Footing on Fatherhood

`http://prospect.org/cs/articles?article=democrats_`
`find_their_footing_on_fatherhood`

This article from *The American Prospect* focuses on the political conversations and controversies between Democrats and Republicans about fatherhood and related public policies. The author also discusses how low-income African American fathers are involved in these issues.

TOPICS FOR RESEARCH AND WRITING

1. Write an essay that defines the gender roles that people accept today. When relevant, show how any of the ideas presented in this chapter help to support your definition of gender roles. To what extent are gender roles based on biological realities, and to what extent on cultural values? Provide examples from your own experiences that help to support your point of view.

2. Discuss what you think are the three most important gender roles that are changing in your own community. Refer to essays in this text and to research to expand on the importance of the change of each gender role that you selected. In what ways are these changes both positive and negative? Use examples to support your ideas. Do not be hesitant to include examples from your own experiences.

3. Write an essay based on readings from the text, research, and your own thoughts and feelings about the role that gender plays in an individual's life, health, and sense of well-being. Do more research in order to compare and contrast the role of gender in another culture.

4. Reread the selection by Freud in this chapter that reflects on the relationships among dreams, the unconscious, and sexuality. Do some further research on this topic, and write your conclusions in the form of a documented essay. To what extent are dreams the product of the unconscious repression of sexual desires, and to what extent are they related more to issues in waking life? Also read through the Table of Contents in *Dreams* to find essays in other chapters that will help you to write your essay.

5. Write an essay about how male and female identities are continuing to change as the result of new opportunities and changes in cyberspace. In addition to doing some outside reading, interview people you know who use the computer frequently. Include conclusions about how you think cyberspace is changing gender roles.

6. The work in this chapter by Sedaris explores societal fears and rejection of gays. Do some research into these fears and their origins, and then write an essay about the causes and effects of homophobia. Consider also the controversies over the legalization of gay marriage. Include your own point of view.

7. Write about a film that portrays an issue of sexuality or gender. How does the film comment on certain issues raised in the readings in this chapter? You can select a film from the following list or one of your own choosing: *Oleanna, The Crying Game, The Wedding Banquet, Orlando, Wilde, Shakespeare in Love, Boys Don't Cry, Chasing Amy, Closer, Sideways, The Stepford Wives, American Beauty, Before Sunset, Talk to Her, Kinsey, What Women Want, Rent, Little Children, Bend It Like Beckham, Juno, Million Dollar Baby*, and *Mamma Mia.*

The Double/The Other

Pablo Picasso (1881–1973)
Girl Before a Mirror (1932)

Write about what you experience when you look at yourself in a mirror. Does what you see look like the self you know, or does it seem like someone else, not entirely familiar or acceptable to you?

Within each one of us there is another whom we do not know. He speaks to us
in dreams and tells us how differently he sees us from how we see ourselves.
                                    CARL JUNG

Our challenge is to call forth the humanity within each adversary, while
preparing for the full range of possible responses. Our challenge is to find a
path between cynicism and naiveté.
                                    FRAN PEAVEY
                                    Us and Them

THEMATIC INTRODUCTION

Many of us are conscious of having an alternate self that, for whatever reasons, we do not make public. We sometimes see glimpses of an alternative or underground personality in a family member, friend, colleague, or even a media figure. From Greek myths to nursery rhymes and fairy tales, from Shakespearean doubles and disguises to Gothic tales of horror and revenge, from Victorian mysteries to the modern psychological short story, images of the double, of twins in spirit or twins in reality, have marked our developing understanding of the workings of the human mind.

The frequent recurrence and popularity of the double in mythology, literature, and popular culture are often attributed to the human need to explore, understand, and perhaps conquer divided feelings that individuals have about the parts of themselves that are in conflict. These conflicts are revealed in many forms: the good versus the evil self, the rational versus the irrational self, the civilized versus the antisocial or criminal self, the masculine self versus the feminine self, the physical self versus the spiritual self, the controlled conventional versus the wild self, and the practical versus the dreamy self.

Although literature and human experiences suggest that inward journeys into the mind's dual nature can lead to confusion or even neurosis or psychosis, there is the possibility of integrating and balancing the opposing parts through developing an increased awareness of the inner self. In this way, through the main character of a poem or story, the writer or a reader can experience a form of rebirth, emerging with a more balanced and confident sense of self and purpose. Your journey through this chapter will provide you with new insights into the dualities within the human personality.

The chapter opens with two selections that explore the double nature of the self. First, in Judith Ortiz Cofer's poem, "The Other," the speaker acknowledges the power of her "other," who is sensual, uninhibited, even dangerous, and more in touch with her cultural roots than her well-behaved public self. The next readings will help you to think about the importance of getting the oppositional sides of your mind and psyche to work together productively. Marie-Louise Von Franz, in an essay on the figure of the double or shadow self, analyses a number of dreams that revolve around such figures. In a selection from his classic novella of divided selves, *The Strange Case of Dr. Jekyll and Mr. Hyde* ("Henry Jekyll's Full Statement of the Case"), Robert Louis Stevenson illustrates through the voice of the doomed Dr. Jekyll the negative consequences of trying to separate the good or civilized side of the human character from its sensual and irrational side.

Our next two essays offer new ways of thinking about how the double-sided nature of social issues can be internalized and affect the development of an individual's self-concept. Maxine Hong Kingston's, "The Silent Girl" (from her memoir *The Woman Warrior*), focuses on the conflict between a Chinese-American girl who struggles to participate in an elementary school where she is part of a minority of immigrant children who have trouble expressing themselves in English and another girl of similar background who refuses to speak at all; the narrator sees the "silent girl" as a culturally Chinese shadow self or double, a threat to the narrator's desire to conform and "fit in." In a related student essay, "Mixed-Up," Susan Voyticky, the daughter of an African-American mother and a white father, discusses some of the difficult decisions she had to make to create an identity that she could call her own.

The next three selections discuss the crucial impact of conflict and duality on social stances and decision-making in the public sphere. In an effort to find some way out of the dilemma of the "other" in society, in her essay "Us and Them," longtime peace activist Fran Peavey suggests a new approach to community organization and political action that avoids dehumanizing and dismissing the opposition. Next, student writer Jessica Rubenstein in her essay "Coed Schools Help Students Excel," attempts to resolve the conflict between single sex schools, currently gaining in popularity, and coed schools, with their negative issues of male-female distraction and dominance in the classroom. She makes positive suggestions for integrating desirable features found in single sex schools in order to revitalize coed schools for both genders. Finally, South African Bishop Desmond Mpilo Tutu presents in his essay, "No Future Without Forgiveness," a concrete example of the need for integrating dualities and making amends to our opposition in the form of the South African Truth and Reconciliation Commission's accomplishments in healing the rift between Afrikaaners and black Africans in the wake of the dismantling of the Apartheid system.

Exploring the duality of the human mind and spirit as reflected in the essays, stories, and poems included in this chapter should prove to be provocative and enlightening. Becoming aware of the voices that exist within you in addition to your dominant voice or persona can help you to understand yourself more fully while providing you with additional resources to draw upon in your writing.

ARGUMENT AND DIALOGUE

Traditional Argument

Traditional argument begins by defining a problem or issue, then taking a position or stance. In this form of argument, the advocate develops a clear thesis and demonstrates its validity through a series of convincing logical arguments, factual supports, and references to authority. Often the major aim of argument is seen as an attack on the ideas and positions of an opponent with the goal of persuading the audience of the correctness of the proponent's position. Arguments that don't quite fit into the debater's viewpoint are sometimes ignored or are introduced as refutation of the principal argument. Such traditional debate is frequently linked to political rhetoric, where only one candidate can be elected. A fundamental part of public life, oppositional argument at its best can be a powerful method of presenting one's own position and beliefs. At its worst, traditional argument can be manipulative and one-sided, leading people to believe that debate is a matter of verbal warfare and that every decision implies an either/or choice rather than an attempt at genuine communication. For examples of oppositional argument that lead to verbal warfare, visit some politically oriented Web sites on the Internet — or read the editorial page of your daily newspaper.

Dialogic Argument

Dialogic argument is based on thoroughly presenting facts and reasons for supporting a position, while acknowledging the importance of creating a bridge between opposing viewpoints that are often rigidly separated in a traditional argument. It may remind you of the literary dialogue between opposites that we see at work in some of this chapter's stories and poems; it is best exemplified in expository form here in Fran Peavey's essay, "Us and Them." The dialogic argument emphasizes the need for discussion and a genuine exchange of ideas, while making a conscious effort to bring together seemingly irreconcilable viewpoints in order to arrive at a synthesis of opposing perspectives and allow the writer and the audience to learn more about themselves. Through the dialogic approach, you can come to a new awareness of positions you may not have understood or considered. Working to understand these opposite positions does not necessarily

imply that you totally accept them, or that you abandon your own
ideas and viewpoints. What it does suggest is that you consider the
possibilities of strong arguments, positions, and value systems that are
different from your own, and that you make a real attempt to integrate
these positions into your thinking.

Dialogue and Prewriting

An effective prewriting strategy for a balanced argument paper
involves engaging your opponent in a dialogue. Begin by creating a
dialogue that explores different positions relative to your subject,
your thesis, and your supporting points. Following is an example of
an excerpt from student dialogue on the subject of reading fairy tales
to small children. We have labeled the two sides in the dialogue "I"
and "Me." "I" stands for the position that the student really wants to
present, while "Me" represents the other side of the argument, perhaps a side of the self that the writer doesn't want to acknowledge
and perceives as the opponent.

I: I think all children should read fairy tales. I always loved hearing them
     as a kid; I liked the scary parts and the adventures. Fairy tales are so
     much more engrossing than the trash on the boob tube.

ME: I can see that you really like fairy tales. But wouldn't a lot of kids
     who get upset easily be frightened by reading stories about mean
     stepmothers and wicked witches, like in "Hansel and Gretel"?

I: I understand what you're saying; fairy tales might frighten some
     children, especially if they were very young or if they had had some
     really horrible things happen in their own lives that the stories
     reminded them of. Still, I think I can handle your objections. Kids
     should be read fairy tales by an adult who makes time to explain the
     issues in the story and who can reassure them if they think the story is
     too scary; after all, a fairy tale is "only a story."

ME: Well, I can see the point in having adults read the stories and explain
     them, but you're wrong about TV. There are some great programs for
     kids, like *Sesame Street* and *Barney*, that teach children to have positive
     values. And what about the values in those fairy tales? *Sesame Street*
     teaches you to love everyone and to give girls equal opportunities to
     succeed! Fairy tales are so old-fashioned and sexist, with all those
     beautiful sleeping princesses waiting around for Prince Charming.

I: I know what you mean. The values in fairy tales aren't always very mod-
     ern. That's why it's really important that the adult who reads the stories
     to the kids discusses the old-fashioned way of life that is being presented
     and compares the world of the tale with our own values and lifestyles.
     I can see letting kids watch TV, too. Fairy tales are only a part of the imag-
     inative experience of childhood, but they're still a very important part!

In this short dialogue, you see the "I" and "Me" positions being brought closer together. "I"'s initial position is now more clearly stated, with some important, commonsense qualifications brought in through the interaction with the "Me."

Prewriting and the Audience

Before you write your essay, try to establish a similar kind of dialogue with your imaginary audience as you did with yourself. As in traditional argument or in any type of writing, this involves trying to determine the interests and values of your audience. For example, the student writing about fairy tales would have to decide if the audience includes cautious parents of school-age children or liberal educators with a progressive philosophy of child rearing. Creating a clear mental image of the audience is essential before appropriate arguments can be selected. Once you have a clear image of the audience in mind, approach your readers directly and respectfully. Make the audience an integral part of your arguments. Do not try to manipulate or dazzle them with your facts and figures; instead, establish a common ground and state the positions you hold in common with them while designating areas of mutual agreement or possible compromise. This approach will remind you to keep your audience's point of view in mind and will facilitate meaningful communication.

Defining Key Terms

As in traditional argument, it is important for dialogic arguers to define their terms. Definitions support clear communication and help develop rapport in an argument. People feel more comfortable in a discussion when they understand what key terms mean. For example, if I am arguing for reading fairy tales to young children and am referring to fairy tales such as those of Hans Christian Andersen while my audience thinks I am discussing modern fantasy children's stories such as those by Maurice Sendak, then we are really thinking about different definitions of a fairy tale and will be unlikely to come to a mutual understanding. When defining your terms, use simple, straightforward definitions; avoid connotative language designed to manipulate or trick your audience.

Evaluating Facts

If you have taken a statistics course or read articles in journals, you know that facts and statistics can be interpreted in a variety of ways. When reading the fact-based studies that will form an important part of the support in any argument paper, you need to consider a number of questions. Have the results of the social scientists or psychologists you are studying been confirmed by other researchers? Are the data current? Was it collected by qualified researchers using thorough and objective methods? Are the results expressed in clear and unambiguous language? These and other questions should be asked about your sources of information so that you can create a sound factual base for the arguments you use in your paper. In doing research for your argument, you might look at Web sites, even extremist ones, to get the feeling for some of the strong sentiments that different groups have about your issue—but don't rely on these partisan, advocacy sites to provide objective information. On the other hand, you do need to mention both widely believed facts and popular misconceptions that may *oppose* the argument you are making. You will need to respectfully show your audience how some of these beliefs are not factual, show how others are not relevant, and concede that some are relevant and either can be dealt with by your proposed argument or cannot within the practical limits of the situation at hand. Present your supporting facts clearly; avoid overstating your conclusions in absolute, unqualified terms or overgeneralizing from limited data.

Feelings in Argument

Emotions play such a significant role in our lives that any argument that tried to be totally rational, pretending that emotional concerns were unimportant and that only facts have significance, would be unrealistic and ineffective. Emotions, both your own and those of your audience, are a central concern in argument. Although you need to present your ideas in ways that won't offend your readers, when feelings are a central issue in the argument itself, emotional issues do need to be directly confronted. For example, it would be impossible to discuss a subject such as abortion without acknowledging your own feelings and those of the audience. In this case, sharing such feelings will help to create an open and trusting relationship with your audience.

However, an important distinction must be made between acknowledging your feelings and exploiting them to manipulate your readers. Often, strong arguments are based on emotions, which can be exaggerated in an attempt to strengthen your position and cause readers to overlook important issues. Avoid language that could ignite emotional fireworks in a discussion. Bringing in irrelevant appeals for pity or fear can obscure the real issues involved in a discussion. Try to use language that is emotionally neutral in describing the positions and ideas taken by the opposition. By doing so, you are more likely to keep the confidence of readers who might otherwise be offended by an overly adversarial position and manipulative language.

Argument can be one of the most satisfying forms of writing, but it can be one of the most difficult. To satisfy the factual, logical, and emotional demands of shaping an effective argument, you can do the following:

- Use inner dialogue as an aid to prewriting and exploring different positions.
- Empathize with and acknowledge the assumptions and needs of your audience.
- Define key terms.
- Evaluate and use relevant factual supports.
- Be honest and direct in your treatment of the emotional aspects of an issue.

All of these strategies will be of use to you in your efforts to find a stance in argument that can build bridges between your inner world and the worlds of others. This type of argument, when thoughtfully developed with an audience in mind, is one of the most effective means of communication that a writer can draw upon, both in academic discourse and in private and community life.

Judith Ortiz Cofer

The Other

(See headnote on Judith Ortiz Cofer in Chapter 2.) As a poet, Cofer often explores issues of cultural identity and heritage. In the following poem, notice how Cofer presents the inner conflict of identity experienced by the speaker through a series of progressively disturbing images.

> **JOURNAL**
>
> Write about a part of yourself that you have difficulty accepting because the "other" in you seems too unconventional, wild, or irresponsible.

A sloe-eyed dark woman shadows me.
In the morning she sings
Spanish love songs in a high
falsetto filling my shower stall
5 with echoes.

She is by my side
in front of the mirror as I slip
into my tailored skirt and she
into her red cotton dress.
10 She shakes out her black mane as I
run a comb through my close-cropped cap.
Her mouth is like a red bull's eye
daring me.
Everywhere I go I must
15 make room for her: she crowds me
in elevators where others wonder
at all the space I need.
At night her weight tips my bed, and
it is her wild dreams that run rampant
20 through my head exhausting me. Her heartbeats,
like dozens of spiders carrying the poison
of her restlessness over the small
distance that separates us,
drag their countless legs
25 over my bare flesh.

QUESTIONS FOR DISCUSSION

1. How would you characterize the "other" that Cofer creates in this poem? Is it anything like your own "other"?
2. Describe the speaker's main self. How does her main self differ from that of the "other"?
3. Which part of the speaker is dominant or will eventually win out in the struggle?
4. Why do you think the two sides of the speaker's personality are in conflict? What different cultural and gender roles does each side reflect?
5. What images help to vividly portray the "other" and to contrast her with the speaker's main self?
6. What dreams and nocturnal fantasies of the speaker help to convey the struggle between the two sides of her personality? What do you think is meant by the fantasy image, "Her heartbeats,/like dozens of spiders carrying the poison/of her restlessness"? In what sense is the restlessness a poison?

CONNECTION

Analyze this poem as a statement of the shadow as defined in the selection by Marie Von Franz (see page 365).

1. Write an essay about an inner struggle you have experienced that reflects a cultural conflict between two of the following: the culture of your parents, your friends, your school, your workplace, or your church. Include examples of ways that your inner conflict is reflected in your dreams and fantasies.

2. Write an essay that could take the form of a dialogue in which you explore inner conflicts that you have about making an important decision in your life. You might want to discuss whether to change your position on political or social issues, or on ways of relating to a marriage partner, friend, parent, supervisor at work, or teacher. After exploring your options, which choice seems preferable?

RELATED WEB SITES

Illuminating the Shadow: An Interview with Connie Zweig
`www.scottlondon.com/insight/scripts/zweig.html`
This online interview with author and psychotherapist Connie Zweig, from a weekly radio series called *Insight & Outlook,* defines the Jungian concept of the shadow and discusses celebrity and public fascination with the idea of the shadow self. The interview also raises the question of how to best integrate the shadow and the self.

Personal Identity
`http://plato.stanford.edu/entries/identity-personal/`
Created by the Stanford University Department of Philosophy, the Stanford Encyclopedia of Philosophy provides insightful and elaborate information on the concept of identity throughout history and from different disciplinary perspectives.

Marie-Louise Von Franz

The Realization of the Shadow in Dreams

Dr. Von Franz (b. 1915), originally from Switzerland, is one of the world's most renowned analysts and a follower of Carl Jung. She has written such works as Shadow and Evil in Fairy Tales, On Dreams and Death, *and* The Way of the Dream, *a book of interviews that Von Franz developed from a film series she made about the psychology of Jung. The following selection, on the psychological archetype of the shadow as it appears in dreams, is from* Man and His Symbols, *a book that Von Franz wrote with Carl Jung.*

JOURNAL

Write about a dream or fantasy that you have had about a stranger.

Whether the unconscious comes up at first in a helpful or a negative form, after a time the need usually arises to re-adapt the conscious attitude in a better way to the unconscious factors—therefore to accept what seems to be "criticism" from the unconscious. Through dreams one becomes acquainted with aspects of one's own personality that for various reasons one has preferred not to look at too closely. This is what Jung called "the realization of the shadow." (He used the term "shadow" for this unconscious part of the personality because it actually often appears in dreams in a personified form.)

The shadow is not the whole of the unconscious personality. It represents unknown or little-known attributes and qualities of the ego— aspects that mostly belong to the personal sphere and that could just as well be conscious. In some aspects, the shadow can also consist of collective factors that stem from a source outside the individual's personal life.

When an individual makes an attempt to see his shadow, he becomes aware of (and often ashamed of) those qualities and impulses he denies in himself but can plainly see in other people—such things as egotism, mental laziness, and sloppiness; unreal fantasies, schemes, and plots; carelessness and cowardice; inordinate love of money and possessions—in short, all the little sins about which he might previously have told himself: "That doesn't matter; nobody will notice it, and in any case other people do it too."

If you feel an overwhelming rage coming up in you when a friend reproaches you about a fault, you can be fairly sure that at this point you will find a part of your shadow, of which you are unconscious. It is, of course, natural to become annoyed when others who are "no better" criticize you because of shadow faults. But what can you say if your own dreams—an inner judge in your own being—reproach you? That is the moment when the ego gets caught, and the result is usually embarrassed silence. Afterward the painful and lengthy work of self-education begins—a work, we might say, that is the psychological equivalent of the labors of Hercules. This unfortunate hero's first task, you will remember, was to clean up in one day the Augean Stables, in which hundreds of cattle had dropped their dung for many decades—a task so enormous that the ordinary mortal would be overcome by discouragement at the mere thought of it.

5   The shadow does not consist only of omissions. It shows up just as often in an impulsive or inadvertent act. Before one has time to think, the evil remark pops out, the plot is hatched, the wrong decision is made, and one is confronted with results that were never intended or consciously wanted. Furthermore, the shadow is exposed to collective infections to a

much greater extent than is the conscious personality. When a man is alone, for instance, he feels relatively all right; but as soon as "the others" do dark, primitive things, he begins to fear that if he doesn't join in, he will be considered a fool. Thus he gives way to impulses that do not really belong to him at all. It is particularly in contacts with people of the same sex that one stumbles over both one's shadow and those of other people. Although we do see the shadow in a person of the opposite sex, we are usually much less annoyed by it and can more easily pardon it.

In dreams and myths, therefore, the shadow appears as a person of the same sex as that of the dreamer. The following dream may serve as an example. The dreamer was a man of 48 who tried to live very much for and by himself, working hard and disciplining himself, repressing pleasure and spontaneity to a far greater extent than suited his real nature.

I owned and inhabited a very big house in town, and I didn't yet know all its different parts. So I took a walk through it and discovered, mainly in the cellar, several rooms about which I knew nothing and even exits leading into other cellars or into subterranean streets. I felt uneasy when I found that several of these exits were not locked and some had no locks at all. Moreover, there were some laborers at work in the neighborhood who could have sneaked in. . . .

When I came up again to the ground floor, I passed a back yard where again I discovered different exits into the street or into other houses. When I tried to investigate them more closely, a man came up to me laughing loudly and calling out that we were old pals from the elementary school. I remembered him too, and while he was telling me about his life, I walked along with him toward the exit and strolled with him through the streets.

There was a strange chiaroscuro in the air as we walked through an enormous circular street and arrived at a green lawn where three galloping horses suddenly passed us. They were beautiful, strong animals, wild but well-groomed, and they had no rider with them. (Had they run away from military service?)

10   The maze of strange passages, chambers, and unlocked exits in the cellar recalls the old Egyptian representation of the underworld, which is a well-known symbol of the unconscious with its unknown possibilities. It also shows how one is "open" to other influences in one's unconscious shadow side, and how uncanny and alien elements can break in. The cellar, one can say, is the basement of the dreamer's psyche. In the back yard of the strange building (which represents the still unperceived psychic scope of the dreamer's personality) an old school friend suddenly turns up. This person obviously personifies another aspect of the dreamer himself—an aspect that had been part of his life as a child but that he had forgotten and lost. It often happens that a person's childhood qualities (for instance, gaiety, irascibility, or perhaps trustfulness) suddenly disappear,

and one does not know where or how they have gone. It is such a lost characteristic of the dreamer that now returns (from the back yard) and tries to make friends again. This figure probably stands for the dreamer's neglected capacity for enjoying life and for his extraverted shadow side.

But we soon learn why the dreamer feels "uneasy" just before meeting this seemingly harmless old friend. When he strolls with him in the street, the horses break loose. The dreamer thinks they may have escaped from military service (that is to say, from the conscious discipline that has hitherto characterized his life). The fact that the horses have no rider shows that instinctive drives can get away from conscious control. In this old friend, and in the horses, all the positive force reappears that was lacking before and that was badly needed by the dreamer.

This is a problem that often comes up when one meets one's "other side." The shadow usually contains values that are needed by consciousness, but that exist in a form that makes It difficult to integrate them into one's life. The passages and the large house in this dream also show that the dreamer does not yet know his own psychic dimensions and is not yet able to fill them out.

The shadow in this dream is typical for an introvert (a man who tends to retire too much from outer life). In the case of an extravert, who is turned more toward outer objects and outer life, the shadow would look quite different.

A young man who had a very lively temperament embarked again and again on successful enterprises, while at the same time his dreams insisted that he should finish off a piece of private creative work he had begun. The following was one of those dreams:

> A man is lying on a couch and has pulled the cover over his face, He is a Frenchman, a desperado who would take on any criminal job. An official is accompanying me downstairs, and I know that a plot has been made against me: namely, that the Frenchman should kill me as if by chance. (That is how it would look from the outside.) He actually sneaks up behind me when we approach the exit, but I am on my guard. A tall, portly man (rather rich and influential) suddenly leans against the wall beside me, feeling ill. I quickly grab the opportunity to kill the official by stabbing his heart. "One only notices a bit of moisture"—this is said like a comment. Now I am safe, for the Frenchman won't attack me since the man who gave him his orders is dead. (Probably the official and the successful portly man are the same person, the latter somehow replacing the formers.)

15   The desperado represents the other side of the dreamer—his introversion—which has reached a completely destitute state. He lies on a couch (i.e., he is passive) and pulls the cover over his face because he wants to be left alone. The official, on the other hand, and the prosperous portly man (who are secretly the same person) personify the dreamer's successful outer responsibilities and activities. The sudden illness of the

portly man is connected with the fact that this dreamer had in fact become ill several times when he had allowed his dynamic energy to explode too forcibly in his external life. But this successful man has no blood in his veins—only a sort of moisture—which means that these external ambitious activities of the dreamer contain no genuine life and no passion, but are bloodless mechanisms. Thus it would be no real loss if the portly man were killed. At the end of the dream, the Frenchman is satisfied; he obviously represents a positive shadow figure who had turned negative and dangerous only because the conscious attitude of the dreamer did not agree with him.

This dream shows us that the shadow can consist of many different elements—for instance, of unconscious ambition (the successful portly man) and of introversion (the Frenchman). This particular dreamer's association to the French, moreover, was that they know how to handle love affairs very well. Therefore the two shadow figures also represent two well-known drives: power and sex. The power drive appears momentarily in a double form, both as an official and as a successful man. The official, or civil servant, personifies collective adaptation, whereas the successful man denotes ambition; but naturally both serve the power drive. When the dreamer succeeds in stopping this dangerous inner force, the Frenchman is suddenly no longer hostile. In other words, the equally dangerous aspect of the sex drive has also surrendered.

Obviously, the problem of the shadow plays a great role in all political conflicts. If the man who had this dream had not been sensible about his shadow problem, he could easily have identified the desperate Frenchman with the "dangerous Communists" of outer life, or the official plus the prosperous man with the "grasping capitalists." In this way he would have avoided seeing that he had within him such warring elements. If people observe their own unconscious tendencies in other people, this is called a "projection." Political agitation in all countries is full of such projections, just as much as the backyard gossip of little groups and individuals. Projections of all kinds obscure our view of our fellow men, spoiling its objectivity, and thus spoiling all possibility of genuine human relationships.

And there is an additional disadvantage in projecting our shadow. If we identify our own shadow with, say, the Communists or the capitalists, a part of our own personality remains on the opposing side. The result is that we shall constantly (though involuntarily) do things behind our own backs that support this other side, and thus we shall unwittingly help our enemy. If, on the contrary, we realize the projection and can discuss matters without fear or hostility, dealing with the other person sensibly, then there is a chance of mutual understanding—or at least of a truce.

Whether the shadow becomes our friend or enemy depends largely upon ourselves, As the dreams of the unexplored house and the French desperado both show, the shadow is not necessarily always an opponent. In fact, he is exactly like any human being with whom one has to get along, sometimes by giving in, sometimes by resisting, sometimes by giving in love—whatever the situation requires. The shadow becomes hostile only when he is ignored or misunderstood.

20   Sometimes, though not often, an individual feels impelled to live out the worse side of his nature and to repress his better side. In such cases the shadow appears as a positive figure in his dreams. But to a person who lives out his natural emotions and feelings, the shadow may appear as a cold and negative intellectual; it then personifies poisonous judgments and negative thoughts that have been held back. So, whatever form it takes, the function of the shadow is to represent the opposite side of the ego and to embody just those qualities that one dislikes most in other people.

It would be relatively easy if one could integrate the shadow into the conscious personality just by attempting to be honest and to use one's insight. But, unfortunately, such an attempt does not always work. There is such a passionate drive within the shadowy part of oneself that reason may not prevail against it. A bitter experience coming from the outside may occasionally help; a brick, so to speak, has to drop on one's head to put a stop to shadow drives and impulses. At times a heroic decision may serve to halt them, but such a superhuman effort is usually possible only if the Great Man within (the Self) helps the individual to carry it through.

The fact that the shadow contains the overwhelming power of irresistible impulse does not mean, however, that the drive should always be heroically repressed. Sometimes the shadow is powerful because the urge of the Self is pointing in the same direction, and so one does not know whether it is the Self or the shadow that is behind the inner pressure. In the unconscious, one is unfortunately in the same situation as in a moonlit landscape. All the contents are blurred and merge into one another, and one never knows exactly what or where anything is, or where one thing begins and ends. (This is known as the "contamination" of unconscious contents.)

When Jung called one aspect of the unconscious personality the shadow, he was referring to a relatively well-defined factor. But sometimes everything that is unknown to the ego is mixed up with the shadow, including even the most valuable and highest forces. Who, for instance, could be quite sure whether the French desperado in the dream I quoted was a useless tramp or a most valuable introvert? And the bolting horses of the preceding dream—should they be allowed to run free or not? In a case when the dream itself does not make things clear, the conscious personality will have to make the decision.

If the shadow figure contains valuable, vital forces, they ought to be assimilated into actual experience and not repressed. It is up to the ego to give up its pride and priggishness and to live out something that seems to be dark, but actually may not be. This can require a sacrifice just as heroic as the conquest of passion, but in an opposite sense.

QUESTIONS FOR DISCUSSION

1. Based on Von Franz's discussion, how would you define the shadow? What inner and outer qualities can the shadow represent?
2. How is the shadow related to reproach and rage?
3. According to Von Franz, why does the shadow usually appear to us in the form of a person of our own sex? Have you ever had a shadow figure appear to you in your dreams? Was the shadow of the opposite sex? What did the shadow figure mean to you?
4. In her essay, Von Franz analyzes two dreams, one by a middle-aged introverted man, one by a younger, "lively" individual. What are the differences between these two dreams? What elements do they share?
5. What role does the shadow play in political conflicts? How is this point illustrated by the second dream that Von Franz analyzes? Can you apply Von Franz's concepts to your own understanding of politics and "party allegiance"?
6. How does Von Franz suggest that the shadow can be made our friend? Does her advice seem sufficient? What more would you like to know about how to befriend and "integrate" your shadow to learn more about him or her?

CONNECTION

Compare Fran Peavey's political ideas in "Us and Them" with Von Franz's ideas about politics and the other (see page 396).

IDEAS FOR WRITING

1. Write a personal essay in which you reflect on the ways that you might try to accommodate or integrate the "shadow" side of your personality. Try creating a dialogue with your shadow or consider some compromises in your lifestyle that might please both sides of your personality.
2. Write an essay in which you argue for or against the concept of the need to integrate the shadow side of the personality as Von Franz proposes. Include examples to support your main ideas.

RELATED WEB SITES

Marie-Louise von Franz
`http://marie-louisevonfranz.com/en/`
This personal Web page of Marie-Louise Von Franz provides links to information about books, films, and essays by the author.

Self-Knowledge
`http://plato.stanford.edu/entries/self-knowledge/`
This entry in Stanford University's Encyclopedia of Philosophy outlines the underlying concepts of the self, self-realization, and personal identity.

Robert Louis Stevenson

Henry Jekyll's Full Statement of the Case from The Strange Case of Dr. Jekyll and Mr. Hyde

Scottish author Robert Louis Stevenson (1850–1894) wrote the short novel The Strange Case of Dr. Jekyll and Mr. Hyde *(1886) at a time when he was very ill with tuberculosis. In the following selection, the conclusion to Stevenson's classic tale of good and evil, the character Henry Jekyll, a highly respected London physician, has chemically altered his own inner nature, constructing a morally depraved "second self," Mr. Hyde. The following statement of Dr. Jekyll, written just before his death, sets forth his reasons for and the fatal consequences of tampering with his inner world. The letter was found by his friends who discovered only the body of Mr. Hyde with a crushed phial of cyanide poison in his hand.*

JOURNAL

Write about experiencing your "other" self, or antiself, through some change in your normal mental state, perhaps from an emotional crisis, chemical stimulation, an illness, or extreme fatigue.

I was born in the year 18__ to a large fortune, endowed besides with excellent parts, inclined by nature to industry, fond of the respect of the wise and good among my fellow-men, and thus, as might have been supposed, with every guarantee of an honourable and distinguished future. And indeed the worst of my faults was a certain impatient gaiety of disposition, such as has made the happiness of many, but such as I found it hard to reconcile with my imperious desire to carry my head high, and wear a more than commonly grave countenance before the public. Hence it came about that I concealed my pleasures; and that when I reached years of reflection, and began to look round me and take stock of my progress and position in the world, I stood already committed to a profound duplicity of life. Many a man would have even blazoned such irregularities as I was guilty of; but from the high views that I had set before me, I regarded and hid them with an almost morbid sense of shame. It was thus rather the exacting nature of my aspirations than any particular degradation in my faults, that made me what I was, and, with even a deeper trench than in the majority of men, severed in me those provinces of good and ill which divide and compound man's dual nature. In this case, I was driven to reflect deeply and inveterately on that hard law of life, which lies at the root of religion and is one of the most plentiful springs of distress. Though so profound a double-dealer, I was in no sense a hypocrite; both sides of me were in dead earnest; I was no more myself when I laid aside restraint and plunged in shame, than when I laboured, in the eye of day, at the furtherance of knowledge or the relief of sorrow and suffering. And it chanced that the direction of my scientific studies, which led wholly towards the mystic and the transcendental, reacted and shed a strong light on this consciousness of the perennial war among my members. With every day, and from both sides of my intelligence, the moral and the intellectual, I thus drew steadily nearer to that truth, by whose partial discovery I have been doomed to such a dreadful shipwreck: that man is not truly one, but truly two. I say two, because the state of my own knowledge does not pass beyond that point. Others will follow, others will outstrip me on the same lines; and I hazard the guess that man will be ultimately known for a mere polity of multifarious, incongruous and independent denizens. I, for my part, from the nature of my life, advanced infallibly in one direction and in one direction only. It was on the moral side, and in my own person, that I learned to recognise the thorough and primitive duality of man; I saw that, of the two natures that contended in the field of my consciousness, even if I could rightly be said to be either, it was only because I was radically both; and from an early date, even before the course of my scientific discoveries had begun to suggest the most naked possibility of such a miracle, I had learned to dwell with pleasure, as a beloved daydream, on the thought of the separation of these elements. If each, I told myself, could be housed in separate identities, life would be relieved of all that was unbearable; the unjust might go his way, delivered from the aspirations and remorse of his more upright twin; and the just could walk steadfastly and securely on his upward path, doing the good things in which he found his pleasure, and no longer exposed to disgrace and penitence by the hands of his extraneous evil. It was the curse of mankind that these incongruous faggots were thus bound together— that in the agonized womb of consciousness, these polar twins should be continuously struggling. How, then, were they dissociated?

I was so far in my reflections when, as I have said, a side light began to shine upon the subject from the laboratory table. I began to perceive more deeply than it has ever yet been stated, the trembling immateriality, the mist-like transience, of this seemingly so solid body in which we walk attired. Certain agents I found to have the power to shake and pluck back that fleshy vestment, even as a wind might toss the curtains of a pavilion. For two good reasons, I will not enter deeply into this scientific branch of my confession. First, because I have been made to learn that the doom and burden of our life is bound for ever on man's shoulders, and when the attempt is made to cast it off, it but returns upon us with more unfamiliar and more awful pressure. Second, because, as my narrative will make, alas! too evident, my discoveries were incomplete. Enough, then, that I not only recognised my natural body from the mere aura and effulgence of certain of the powers that make up my spirit, but managed to compound a drug by which these powers should be dethroned from their supremacy, and a second form and countenance substituted, none the less natural to me because they were the expression, and bore the stamp of lower elements in my soul.

I hesitated long before I put this theory to the test of practice. I knew well that I risked death; for any drug that so potently controlled and shook the very fortress of identity, might, by the least scruple of an overdose or at the least inopportunity in the moment of exhibition, utterly blot out that immaterial tabernacle which I looked to it to change. But the temptation of a discovery so singular and profound at last overcame the suggestions of alarm. I had long since prepared my tincture; I purchased at once, from a firm of wholesale chemists, a large quantity of a particular salt which I knew, from my experiments, to be the last ingredient required; and late one accursed night, I compounded the elements, watched them boil and smoke together in the glass, and when the ebullition had subsided, with a strong glow of courage, drank off the potion.

The most racking pangs succeeded: a grinding in the bones, deadly nausea, and a horror of the spirit that cannot be exceeded at the hour of birth or death. Then these agonies began swiftly to subside, and I came to myself as if out of a great sickness. There was something strange in my sensations, something indescribably new and, from its very novelty, incredibly sweet. I felt younger, lighter, happier in body; within I was conscious of a heady recklessness, a current of disordered sensual images running like a millrace in my fancy, a dissolution of the bonds of obligation, an unknown but not an innocent freedom of the soul. I knew myself, at the first breath of this new life, to be more wicked, tenfold more wicked, sold a slave to my original evil; and the thought, in that moment, braced and delighted me like wine. I stretched out my hands, exulting in the freshness of these sensations; and in the act, I was suddenly aware that I had lost in stature.

5   There was no mirror, at that date, in my room; that which stands beside me as I write, was brought there later on and for the very purpose of these transformations. That night, however, was far gone into the morning—the morning, black as it was, was nearly ripe for the conception of the day—the inmates of my house were locked in the most rigorous hours of slumber, and I determined, flushed as I was with hope and triumph, to venture in my new shape as far as to my bedroom. I crossed the yard, wherein the constellations looked down upon me, I could have thought, with wonder, the first creature of that sort that their unsleeping vigilance had yet disclosed to them; I stole through the corridors, a

stranger in my own house; and coming to my room, I saw for the first time the appearance of Edward Hyde.

I must here speak by theory alone, saying not that which I know, but that which I suppose to be most probable. The evil side of my nature, to which I had now transferred the stamping efficacy, was less robust and less developed than the good which I had just deposed. Again, in the course of my life, which had been, after all, nine tenths a life of effort, virtue and control, it had been much less exercised and much less exhausted. And hence, as I think, it came about that Edward Hyde was so much smaller, slighter and younger than Henry Jekyll. Even as good shone upon the countenance of the one, evil was written broadly and plainly on the face of the other. Evil besides (which I must still believe to be the lethal side of man) had left on that body an imprint of deformity and decay. And yet when I looked upon that ugly idol in the glass, I was conscious of no repugnance, rather of a leap of welcome. This, too, was myself. It seemed natural and human. In my eyes it bore a livelier image of the spirit, it seemed more express and single, than the imperfect and divided countenance I had been hitherto accustomed to call mine. And in so far I was doubtless right. I have observed that when I wore the semblance of Edward Hyde, none could come near to me at first without a visible misgiving of the flesh. This, as I take it, was because all human beings, as we meet them, are commingled out of good and evil: and Edward Hyde, alone in the ranks of mankind, was pure evil.

I lingered but a moment at the mirror: the second and conclusive experiment had yet to be attempted; it yet remained to be seen if I had lost my identity beyond redemption and must flee before daylight from a house that was no longer mine; and hurrying back to my cabinet, I once more prepared and drank the cup, once more suffered the pangs of dissolution, and came to myself once more with the character, the stature and the face of Henry Jekyll.

That night I had come to the fatal crossroads. Had I approached my discovery in a more noble spirit, had I risked the experiment while under the empire of generous or pious aspirations, all must have been otherwise, and from these agonies of death and birth, I had come forth an angel instead of a fiend. The drug had no discriminating action; it was neither diabolical nor divine; it but shook the doors of the prisonhouse of my disposition; and like the captives of Phillipi, that which stood within ran forth. At that time my virtue slumbered; my evil, kept awake by ambition, was alert and swift to seize the occasion; and the thing that was projected was Edward Hyde. Hence, although I had now two characters as well as two appearances, one was wholly evil, and the other was still the old Henry Jekyll, that incongruous compound of whose reformation and improvement I had already learned to despair. The movement was thus wholly toward the worse.

Even at that time, I had not conquered my aversion to the dryness of a life of study. I would still be merrily disposed at times; and as my pleasures were (to say the least) undignified, and I was not only well known and highly considered, but growing toward the elderly man, this incoherency of my life was daily growing more unwelcome. It was on this side that my new power tempted me until I fell in slavery. I had but to drink the cup, to doff at once the body of the noted professor, and to assume, like a thick cloak, that of Edward Hyde. I smiled at the notion; it seemed to me at the time to be humorous; and I made my preparations with the most studious care. I took and furnished that house in Soho, to which Hyde was tracked by the police; and engaged as a housekeeper a creature whom I knew well to be silent and unscrupulous. On the other side, I announced to my servants that a Mr. Hyde (whom I described) was to have full liberty and power about my house in the square; and to parry mishaps, I even called and made myself a familiar object, in my second character. I next drew up that will to which you so much objected; so that if anything befell me in the person of Dr. Jekyll, I could enter on that of Edward Hyde without pecuniary loss. And thus fortified, as I supposed, on every side, I began to profit by the strange immunities of my position.

10   Men have before hired bravoes to transact their crimes, while their own person and reputation sat under shelter. I was the first that ever did so for his pleasures. I was the first that could plod in the public eye with a load of genial respectability, and in a moment, like a schoolboy, strip off these lendings and spring headlong into the sea of liberty. But for me, in my impenetrable mantle, the safety was complete. Think of it— I did not even exist! Let me but escape into my laboratory door, give me but a second or two to mix and swallow the draught that I had always standing ready; and whatever he had done, Edward Hyde would pass away like the stain of breath upon a mirror; and there in his stead, quietly at home, trimming the midnight lamp in his study, a man who could afford to laugh at suspicion, would be Henry Jekyll.

The pleasures which I made haste to seek in my disguise were, as I have said, undignified; I would scarce use a harder term. But in the hands of Edward Hyde, they soon began to turn toward the monstrous. When I would come back from these excursions, I was often plunged into a kind of wonder at my vicarious depravity. This familiar that I called out of my own soul, and sent forth alone to do his good pleasure, was a being inherently malign and villainous; his every act and thought centered on self; drinking pleasure with bestial avidity from any degree of torture to another; relentless like a man of stone. Henry Jekyll stood at times aghast before the acts of Edward Hyde; but the situation was apart from ordinary laws, and insidiously relaxed the grasp of conscience. It was Hyde, after all, and Hyde alone, that was guilty. Jekyll was no worse; he woke again to his good qualities seemingly unimpaired; he would even make haste, where it was possible, to undo the evil done by Hyde. And thus his conscience slumbered.

Into the details of the infamy at which I thus connived (for even now I can scarce grant that I committed it) I have no design of entering; I mean but to point out the warnings and the successive steps with which my chastisement approached. I met with one accident which, as it brought on no consequence, I shall no more than mention. An act of cruelty to a child aroused against me the anger of a passerby, whom I recognised the other day in the person of your kinsman; the doctor and the child's family joined him; there were moments when I feared for my life; and at last, in order to pacify their too just resentment, Edward Hyde had to bring them to the door, and pay them in a cheque drawn in the name of Henry Jekyll. But this danger was easily eliminated from the future, by opening an account at another bank in the name of Edward Hyde himself; and when, by sloping my own hand backward, I had supplied my double with a signature, I thought I sat beyond the reach of fate.

Some two months before the murder of Sir Danvers, I had been out for one of my adventures, had returned at a late hour, and woke the next day in bed with somewhat odd sensations. It was in vain I looked about me; in vain I saw the decent furniture and tall proportions of my room in the square; in vain that I recognised the pattern of the bed curtains and the design of the mahogany frame; something still kept insisting that I was not where I was, that I had not wakened where I seemed to be, but in the little room in Soho where I was accustomed to sleep in the body of Edward Hyde. I smiled to myself, and, in my psychological way, began lazily to inquire into the elements of this illusion, occasionally, even as I did so, dropping back into a comfortable morning doze. I was still so engaged when, in one of my more wakeful moments, my eyes fell upon my hand. Now the hand of Henry Jekyll (as you have often remarked) was professional in shape and size: it was large, firm, white and comely. But the hand which I now saw, clearly enough, in the yellow light of a mid-London morning, lying half shut on the bedclothes, was lean, corded, knuckly, of a dusky pallor and thickly shaded with a swart growth of hair. It was the hand of Edward Hyde.

I must have stared upon it for near half a minute, sunk as I was in the mere stupidity of wonder, before terror woke up in my breast as sudden and startling as the crash of cymbals; and bounding from my bed, I rushed to the mirror. At the sight that met my eyes, my blood was changed into something exquisitely thin and icy. Yes, I had gone to bed Henry Jekyll, I had awakened Edward Hyde. How was this to be explained? I asked myself; and then, with another bound of terror—how was it to be remedied? It was well on in the morning; the servants were up; all my drugs were in the cabinet—a long journey down two pairs of stairs, through the back passage, across the open court and through the anatomical theatre, from where I was then standing horror-struck. It might indeed be possible to cover my face; but of what use was that, when I was unable to conceal the alteration in my stature? And then with an overpowering sweetness of relief, it came back upon my mind that the servants were already used to the coming and going of my second self. I had soon dressed, as well as I was able, in clothes of my own size; had soon passed through the house, where Bradshaw stared and drew back at seeing Mr. Hyde at such an hour and in such a strange array; and ten minutes later, Dr. Jekyll had returned to his own shape and was sitting down, with a darkened brow, to make a feint of breakfasting.

15   Small indeed was my appetite. This inexplicable incident, this reversal of my previous experience, seemed, like the Babylonian finger on the wall, to be spelling out the letters of my judgment; and I began to reflect more seriously than ever before on the issues and possibilities of my double existence. That part of me which I had the power of projecting, had lately been much exercised and nourished; it had seemed to me of late as though the body of Edward Hyde had grown in stature, as though (when I wore that form) I were conscious of a more generous tide of blood, and I began to spy a danger that, if this were much prolonged, the balance of my nature might be permanently overthrown, the power of voluntary change be forfeited, and the character of Edward Hyde become irrevocably mine. The power of the drug had not been always equally displayed. Once, very early in my career, it had totally failed me; since then I had been obliged on more than one occasion to double, and once, with infinite risk of death, to treble the amount; and these rare uncertainties had cast hitherto the sole shadow on my contentment. Now, however, and in the light of that morning's accident, I was led to remark that whereas, in the beginning, the difficulty had been to throw off the body of Jekyll, it had of late gradually but decidedly transferred itself to the other side. All things therefore seemed to point to this: that I was slowly losing hold of my original and better self, and becoming slowly incorporated with my second and worse.

Between these two, I now felt I had to choose. My two natures had memory in common, but all other faculties were most unequally shared between them. Jekyll (who was composite) now with the most sensitive apprehensions, now with a greedy gusto, projected and shared in the pleasures and adventures of Hyde; but Hyde was indifferent to Jekyll, or but remembered him as the mountain bandit remembers the cavern in which he conceals himself from pursuit. Jekyll had more than a father's interest; Hyde had more than a son's indifference. To cast in my lot with Jekyll, was to die to those appetites which I had long secretly indulged and had of late begun to pamper. To cast it in with Hyde, was to die to a thousand interests and aspirations, and to become, at a blow and forever, despised and friendless. The bargain might appear unequal; but there was still another consideration in the scales; for while Jekyll would suffer smart-ingly in the fires of abstinence, Hyde would be not even conscious of all that he had lost. Strange as my circumstances were, the terms of this de-bate are as old and commonplace as man; much the same inducements and alarms cast the die for any tempted and trembling sinner; and it fell out with me, as it falls with so vast a majority of my fellows, that I chose the better part and was found wanting in the strength to keep to it.

Yes, I preferred the elderly and discontented doctor, surrounded by friends and cherishing honest hopes; and bade a resolute farewell to the liberty, the comparative youth, the light step, leaping impulses and secret pleasures, that I had enjoyed in the disguise of Hyde. I made this choice perhaps with some unconscious reservation, for I neither gave up the house in Soho, nor destroyed the clothes of Edward Hyde, which still lay ready in my cabinet. For two months, however, I was true to my determi-nation; for two months, I led a life of such severity as I had never before attained to, and enjoyed the compensations of an approving conscience. But time began at last to obliterate the freshness of my alarm; the praises of conscience began to grow into a thing of course; I began to be tor-tured with throes and longings, as of Hyde struggling after freedom; and at last, in an hour of moral weakness, I once again compounded and swal-lowed the transforming draught.

I do not suppose that, when a drunkard reasons with himself upon his vice, he is once out of five hundred times affected by the dangers that he runs through his brutish, physical insensibility; neither had I, long as I had considered my position, made enough allowance for the complete moral insensibility and insensate readiness to evil, which were the lead-ing characters of Edward Hyde. Yet it was by these that I was punished. My devil had been long caged, he came out roaring. I was conscious, even when I took the draught, of a more unbridled, a more furious propensity to ill. It must have been this, I suppose, that stirred in my soul that tempest of impatience with which I listened to the civilities of my un-happy victim; I declare, at least, before God, no man morally sane could have been guilty of that crime upon so pitiful a provocation; and that I struck in no more reasonable spirit than that in which a sick child may break a plaything. But I had voluntarily stripped myself of all those bal-ancing instincts by which even the worst of us continues to walk with some degree of steadiness among temptations and in my case, to be tempted, however slightly, was to fall.

Instantly the spirit of hell awoke in me and raged. With a transport of glee, I mauled the unresisting body, tasting delight from every blow; and it was not till weariness had begun to succeed, that I was suddenly, in the top fit of my delirium, struck through the heart by a cold thrill of terror. A mist dispersed; I saw my life to be forfeit; and fled from the scene of these excesses, at once glorying and trembling, my lust of evil gratified and stimulated, my love of life screwed to the topmost peg. I ran to the house in Soho, and (to make assurance doubly sure) destroyed my papers; thence I set out through the lamplit streets, in the same divided ecstasy of mind, gloating on my crime, light-headedly devising others in the future, and yet still hastening and still hearkening in my wake for the steps of the avenger. Hyde had a song upon his lips as he compounded the draught, and as he drank it, pledged the dead man. The pangs of transformation had not done tearing him, before Henry Jekyll, with streaming tears of gratitude and remorse, had fallen upon his knees and lifted his clasped hands to God. The veil of self-indulgence was rent from head to foot. I saw my life as a whole: I followed it up from the days of childhood, when I had walked with my father's hand, and through the self-denying toils of my professional life, to arrive again and again, with the same sense of unreality, at the damned horrors of the evening. I could have screamed aloud; I sought with tears and prayers to smother down the crowd of hideous images and sounds with which my memory swarmed against me; and still, between the petitions, the ugly face of my iniquity stared into my soul. As the acuteness of this remorse began to die away, it was succeeded by a sense of joy. The problem of my conduct was solved. Hyde was thenceforth impossible; whether I would or not, I was now confined to the better part of my existence; and O, how I rejoiced to think of it! With what willing humility I embraced anew the restrictions of natural life! With what sincere renunciation I locked the door by which I had so often gone and come, and ground the key under my heel!

20   The next day, came the news that the murder had been overlooked, that the guilt of Hyde was patent to the world, and that the victim was a man high in public estimation. It was not only a crime, it had been a tragic folly. I think I was glad to know it; I think I was glad to have my better impulses thus buttressed and guarded by the terrors of the scaffold. Jekyll was now my city of refuge; let but Hyde peep out an instant, and the hands of all men would be raised to take and slay him.

I resolved in my future conduct to redeem the past; and I can say with honesty that my resolve was fruitful of some good. You know yourself how earnestly, in the last months of the last year, I laboured to relieve suffering; you know that much was done for others, and that the days passed quietly, almost happily for myself. Nor can I truly say that I wearied of this beneficent and innocent life; I think instead that I daily enjoyed it more completely; but I was still cursed with my duality of purpose; and as the first edge of my penitence wore off, the lower side of me, so long indulged, so recently chained down, began to growl for licence. Not that I dreamed of resuscitating Hyde; the bare idea of that would startle me to frenzy; no, it was in my own person that I was once more tempted to trifle with my conscience; and it was as an ordinary secret sinner that I at last fell before the assaults of temptation.

There comes an end to all things; the most capacious measure is filled at
last; and this brief condescension to my evil finally destroyed the balance of
my soul. And yet I was not alarmed; the fall seemed natural, like a return to
the old days before I had made my discovery. It was a fine, clear, January
day, wet under foot where the frost had melted, but cloudless overhead;
and the Regent's Park was full of winter chirrupings and sweet with spring
odours. I sat in the sun on a bench; the animal within me licking the chops
of memory; the spiritual side a little drowsed, promising subsequent penitence, but not yet moved to begin. After all, I reflected, I was like my neighbours; and then I smiled, comparing myself with other men, comparing my
active goodwill with the lazy cruelty of their neglect. And at the very moment of that vainglorious thought, a qualm came over me, a horrid nausea
and the most deadly shuddering. These passed away, and left me faint; and
then, as in its turn faintness subsided, I began to be aware of a change in
the temper of my thoughts, a greater boldness, a contempt of danger, a solution of the bonds of obligation. I looked down; my clothes hung form-
lessly on my shrunken limbs; the hand that lay on my knee was corded and
hairy. I was once more Edward Hyde. A moment before I had been safe of
all men's respect, wealthy, beloved—the cloth laying for me in the dining-
room at home; and now I was the common quarry of mankind, hunted,
house-less, a known murderer, thrall to the gallows.

My reason wavered, but it did not fail me utterly. I have more than
once observed that, in my second character, my faculties seemed sharp-
ened to a point and my spirits more tensely elastic; thus it came about
that, where Jekyll perhaps might have succumbed, Hyde rose to the importance of the moment. My drugs were in one of the presses of my cabinet; how was I to reach them? That was the problem that (crushing my
temples in my hands) I set to myself to solve. The laboratory door I had
closed. If I sought to enter by the house, my own servants would consign
me to the gallows. I saw I must employ another hand, and thought of
Lanyon. How was he to be reached? how persuaded? Suppose that I escaped capture in the streets, how was I to make my way into his presence?
and how should I, an unknown and displeasing visitor, prevail on the
famous physician to rifle the study of his colleague, Dr. Jekyll? Then I
remembered that of my original character, one part remained to me:
I could write my own hand; and once I had conceived that kindling
spark, the way that I must follow became lighted up from end to end.

Thereupon, I arranged my clothes as best I could, and summoning a
passing hansom, drove to an hotel in Portland Street, the name of which I
chanced to remember. At my appearance (which was indeed comical
enough, however tragic a fate these garments covered) the driver could not
conceal his mirth. I gnashed my teeth upon him with a gust of devilish fury;
and the smile withered from his face—happily for him—yet more happily
for myself, for in another instant I had certainly dragged him from his

perch. At the inn, as I entered, I looked about me with so black a countenance as made the attendants tremble, not a look did they exchange in my presence; but obsequiously took my orders, led me to a private room, and brought me wherewithal to write. Hyde in danger of his life was a creature new to me; shaken with inordinate anger, strung to the pitch of murder, lusting to inflict pain. Yet the creature was astute; mastered his fury with a great effort of the will; composed his two important letters, one to Lanyon and one to Poole; and that he might receive actual evidence of their being posted, sent them out with directions that they should be registered. Thenceforward, he sat all day over the fire in the private room, gnawing his nails; there he dined, sitting alone with his fears, the waiter visibly quailing before his eye; and thence, when the night was fully come, he set forth in the corner of a closed cab, and was driven to and fro about the streets of the city. He, I say—I cannot say, I. That child of Hell had nothing human; nothing lived in him but fear and hatred. And when at last, thinking the driver had begun to grow suspicious, he discharged the cab and ventured on foot, attired in his misfitting clothes, an object marked out for observation, into the midst of the nocturnal passengers, these two base passions raged within him like a tempest. He walked fast, hunted by his fears, chattering to himself, skulking through the less frequented thoroughfares, counting the minutes that still divided him from midnight. Once a woman spoke to him, offering, I think, a box of lights. He smote her in the face, and she fled.

25   When I came to myself at Lanyon's, the horror of my old friend perhaps affected me somewhat: I do not know; it was at least but a drop in the sea to the abhorrence with which I looked back upon these hours. A change had come over me. It was no longer the fear of the gallows, it was the horror of being Hyde that racked me. I received Lanyon's condemnation partly in a dream; it was partly in a dream that I came home to my own house and got into bed. I slept after the prostration of the day, with a stringent and profound slumber which not even in the nightmares that wrung me could avail to break. I awoke in the morning shaken, weakened, but refreshed. I still hated and feared the thought of the brute that slept within me, and I had not of course forgotten the appalling dangers of the day before; but I was once more at home, in my own house and close to my drugs; and gratitude for my escape shone so strong in my soul that it almost rivalled the brightness of hope.

I was stepping leisurely across the court after breakfast, drinking the chill of the air with pleasure, when I was seized again with those indescribable sensations that heralded the change; and I had but the time to gain the shelter of my cabinet, before I was once again raging and freezing with the passions of Hyde. It took on this occasion a double dose to recall me to myself; and alas! six hours after, as I sat looking sadly in the fire, the pangs returned, and the drug had to be re-administered. In short, from that day forth it seemed only by a great effort as of gymnastics, and only under the immediate stimulation of the drug, that I was able to wear the countenance of Jekyll. At all hours of the day and night, I would be taken with the premonitory shudder; above all, if I slept, or even dozed for a moment in my chair, it was always as Hyde that I awakened. Under the strain of this continually impending doom and by the sleeplessness to which I now condemned myself, ay, even beyond what I had thought possible to man, I became, in my own person, a creature eaten up and emptied by fever, languidly weak both in body and mind, and solely occupied by one thought: the horror of my other self. But when I slept, or when the virtue of the medicine wore off, I would leap almost without transition (for the pangs of transformation grew daily less marked) into the possession of a fancy brimming with images of terror, a soul boiling with causeless hatreds, and a body that seemed not strong enough to contain the raging energies of life. The powers of Hyde seemed to have grown with the sickliness of Jekyll. And certainly the hate that now divided them was equal on each side. With Jekyll, it was a thing of vital instinct. He had now seen the full deformity of that creature that shared with him some of the phenomena of consciousness, and was co-heir with him to death: and beyond these links of community, which in themselves made the most poignant part of his distress, he thought of Hyde, for all his energy of life, as of something not only hellish but inorganic. This was the shocking thing; that the slime of the pit seemed to utter cries and voices; that the amorphous dust gesticulated and sinned; that what was dead, and had no shape, should usurp the offices of life. And this again, that that insurgent horror was knit to him closer than a wife, closer than an eye; lay caged in his flesh, where he heard it mutter and felt it struggle to be born; and at every hour of weakness, and in the confidence of slumber, prevailed against him, and deposed him out of life. The hatred of Hyde for Jekyll was of a different order. His terror of the gallows drove him continually to commit temporary suicide, and return to his subordinate station of a part instead of a person; but he loathed the necessity, he loathed the despondency into which Jekyll was now fallen, and he resented the dislike with which he was himself regarded. Hence the apelike tricks that he would play me, scrawling in my own hand blasphemies on the pages of my books, burning the letters and destroying the portrait of my father; and indeed, had it not been for his fear of death, he would long ago have ruined himself in order to involve me in the ruin. But his love of life is wonderful; I go further: I, who sicken and freeze at the mere thought of him, when I recall the abjection and passion of this attachment, and when I know how he fears my power to cut him off by suicide, I find it in my heart to pity him.

It is useless, and the time awfully fails me, to prolong this description; no one has ever suffered such torments, let that suffice; and yet even to these, habit brought—no, not alleviation—but a certain callousness of soul, a certain acquiescence of despair; and my punishment might have gone on for years, but for the last calamity which has now fallen, and which has finally severed me from my own face and nature. My provision of the salt, which had never been renewed since the date of the first experiment, began to run low. I sent out for a fresh supply and mixed the draught; the ebullition followed, and the first change of colour, not the second; I drank it and it was without efficacy. You will learn from Poole how I have had London ransacked; it was in vain; and I am now persuaded that my first supply was impure, and that it was that unknown impurity which lent efficacy to the draught.

About a week has passed, and I am now finishing this statement under the influence of the last of the old powders. This, then, is the last time, short of a miracle, that Henry Jekyll can think his own thoughts or see his own face (now how sadly altered!) in the glass. Nor must I delay too long to bring my writing to an end; for if my narrative has hitherto escaped destruction, it has been by a combination of great prudence and great good luck. Should the throes of change take me in the act of writing it, Hyde will tear it in pieces; but if some time shall have elapsed after I have laid it by, his wonderful selfishness and circumscription to the moment will probably save it once again from the action of his ape-like spite. And indeed the doom that is closing on us both has already changed and crushed him. Half an hour from now, when I shall again and forever reindue that hated personality, I know how I shall sit shuddering and weeping in my chair, or continue, with the most strained and fearstruck ecstasy of listening, to pace up and down this room (my last earthly refuge) and give ear to every sound of menace. Will Hyde die upon the scaffold? or will he find courage to release himself at the last moment? God knows; I am careless; this is my true hour of death, and what is to follow concerns another than myself. Here then, as I lay down the pen and proceed to seal up my confession, I bring the life of that unhappy Henry Jekyll to an end.

QUESTIONS FOR DISCUSSION

1. What strengths, faults, and inner divisions of character does Jekyll describe in the first paragraph of the narrative? What compels him to conceal his pleasures?

2. With what fantasy or "beloved daydream" does Jekyll become obsessed? Why does he become so obsessed with this fantasy? What does he invent to make his fantasy a reality? Is his invention a success?

3. What are the differences in appearance, stature, power, and age between Dr. Jekyll and Mr. Hyde? How do these physical distinctions emphasize symbolically the differences in their characters as well as the flaws in Dr. Jekyll's original character and the folly of artificially separating the two parts of the self? Dr. Jekyll honestly believed that he could separate the two parts of himself. How do you feel about his assumption?

4. How does Jekyll first respond to the changes in his character? How do his response and the nature of the control over his double personality gradually change? What difficulty does he experience in deciding which of his sides to finally repress?

5. Why is Jekyll unable to stop himself from transforming into Mr. Hyde? How would you explain the mutual loathing that each side of the divided personality feels for the other?

6. Who was responsible for the death of Dr. Jekyll? From the evidence in the letter, which side of the personality do you think killed Mr. Hyde: Hyde himself, in an act of suicide, or Jekyll, in an act of combined murder/suicide of both sides of his personality? Explain your response using references to the text.

CONNECTION

Compare Stevenson's essay about double identity with Judith Ortiz Cofer's poem "The Other." What different causes for the split self are examined in each work (see page 362)?

IDEAS FOR WRITING

1. After reading the entire text of *The Strange Case of Dr. Jekyll and Mr. Hyde,* write an essay in which you interpret the story as a criticism of rigid social conventions and moral standards of acceptable or unacceptable, or good or bad, behavior. In what ways does the story suggest that such strict standards can heighten the division between an individual's good and bad side, the main self and the double, or shadow self?

2. This story concerns the dual nature of the human psyche, the struggle between our good side and our bad side, between the conscious mind and the unthinking appetites of the body. What do you think can be done to ease such a struggle? Write a paper in which you argue for an approach to life that would help to heal the split between the Jekyll and Hyde personalities within the human psyche.

RELATED WEB SITES

The Robert Louis Stevenson Web site
http://dinamico.unibg.it/rls/rls.htm
This site, maintained by Richard Drury of the University of Bergamo, Italy, contains a biography, criticism, links, images, and bibliographies related to Stevenson and his works.

Doctor Jekyll and Mr. Hyde
www.novelguide.com/dr.jekyllandmr.hyde/
This useful Web site provides a chapter-by-chapter book analysis, character profiles, theme analysis, and author biography.

Maxine Hong Kingston

The Silent Girl

Maxine Hong Kingston (b. 1940) is from Stockton, California, where she grew up listening to the stories her mother would tell about Chinese village life. Hong Kingston graduated from the University of California, Berkeley, and taught high school and college English in Hawaii for a number of years before returning to the San Francisco Bay area to write and teach at the University of California at Berkeley. Her first book, The Woman Warrior: Memories of a Childhood Among Ghosts *(1976), won the National Critics Circle award. Her most widely read books include the historical account of Chinese American life,* China Men *(1980) and the novels* Tripmaster Monkey: His Fake Book *(1989),* To Be the Poet *(2002), and* The Fifth Book of Peace *(2003). In the selection that follows we see one of the consequences of seeing ourselves in another person.*

> **JOURNAL**
>
> Write about an argument or disagreement that you had with someone close to you that awakened one of your inner struggles. Were you changed by the incident? How?

She was a year older than I and was in my class for twelve years. During all those years she read aloud but would not talk. Her older sister was usually beside her; their parents kept the older daughter back to protect the younger one. They were six and seven years old when they began school. Although I had flunked kindergarten, I was the same age as most other students in our class; my parents had probably lied about my age, so I had had a head start and came out even. My younger sister was in the class below me; we were normal ages and normally separated. The parents of the quiet girl, on the other hand, protected both daughters. When it sprinkled, they kept them home from school. The girls did not work for a living the way we did. But in other ways we were the same.

We were similar in sports. We held the bat on our shoulders until we walked to first base. (You got a strike only when you actually struck at the ball.) Sometimes the pitcher wouldn't bother to throw to us. "Automatic walk," the other children would call, sending us on our way. By fourth or fifth grade, though, some of us would try to hit the ball. "Easy out," the other kids would say. I hit the ball a couple of times. Baseball was nice in that there was a definite spot to run to after hitting the ball. Basketball confused me because when I caught the ball I didn't know whom to throw it to. "Me. Me," the kids would be yelling. "Over here." Suddenly it would occur to me I hadn't memorized which ghosts were on my team and which were on the other. When the kids said, "Automatic walk," the girl who was quieter than I kneeled with one end of the bat in each hand and placed it carefully on the plate. Then she dusted her hands as she walked to first base, where she rubbed her hands softly, fingers spread. She always got tagged out before second base. She would whisper-read but not talk. Her whisper was as soft as if she had no muscles. She seemed to be breathing from a distance. I heard no anger or tension.

I joined in at lunchtime when the other students, the Chinese too, talked about whether or not she was mute, although obviously she was not if she could read aloud. People told how *they* had tried *their* best to be friendly. *They* said hello, but if she refused to answer, well, they didn't see why they had to say hello anymore. She had no friends of her own but followed her sister everywhere, although people and she herself probably thought I was her friend. I also followed her sister about, who was fairly normal. She was almost two years older and read more than anyone else.

I hated the younger sister, the quiet one. I hated her when she was the last chosen for her team and I, the last chosen for my team. I hated her for her China doll hair cut. I hated her at music time for the wheezes that came out of her plastic flute.

5   One afternoon in the sixth grade (that year I was arrogant with talk, not knowing there were going to be high school dances and college seminars to set me back), I and my little sister and the quiet girl and her big sister stayed late after school for some reason. The cement was cooling, and the tetherball poles made shadows across the gravel. The hooks at the rope ends were clinking against the poles. We shouldn't have been so late; there was laundry work to do and Chinese school to get to by 5:00. The last time we had stayed late, my mother had phoned the police and told them we had been kidnapped by bandits. The radio stations broadcast our descriptions. I had to get home before she did that again. But sometimes if you loitered long enough in the schoolyard, the other children would have gone home and you could play with the equipment before the office took it away. We were chasing one another through the playground and in and out of the basement, where the playroom and lavatory were. During air raid drills (it was during the Korean War, which you knew about because every day the front page of the newspaper printed a map of Korea with the top part red and going up and down like a window shade), we curled up in this basement. Now everyone was gone. The playroom was army green and had nothing in it but a long trough with drinking spigots in rows. Pipes across the ceiling led to the drinking fountains and to the toilets in the next room. When someone flushed you could hear the water and other matter, which the children named, running inside the big pipe above the drinking spigots. There was one

playroom for girls next to the girls' lavatory and one playroom for boys next to the boys' lavatory. The stalls were open and the toilets had no lids, by which we knew that ghosts have no sense of shame or privacy.

Inside the playroom the lightbulbs in cages had already been turned off. Daylight came in x-patterns through the caging at the windows. I looked out and, seeing no one in the schoolyard, ran outside to climb the fire escape upside down, hanging on to the metal stairs with fingers and toes.

I did a flip off the fire escape and ran across the schoolyard. The day was a great eye, and it was not paying much attention to me now. I could disappear with the sun; I could turn quickly sideways and slip into a different world. It seemed I could run faster at this time, and by evening I would be able to fly. As the afternoon wore on we could run into the forbidden places—the boys' big yard, the boys' playroom. We could go into the boys' lavatory and look at the urinals. The only time during school hours I had crossed the boys' yard was when a flatbed truck with a giant thing covered with canvas and tied down with ropes had parked across the street. The children had told one another that it was a gorilla in captivity; we couldn't decide whether the sign said "Trail of the Gorilla" or "Trial of the Gorilla." The thing was as big as a house. The teachers couldn't stop us from hysterically rushing to the fence and clinging to the wire mesh. Now I ran across the boys' yard clear to the Cyclone fence and thought about the hair that I had seen sticking out of the canvas. It was going to be summer soon, so you could feel that freedom coming on too.

I ran back into the girls' yard, and there was the quiet sister all by herself. I ran past her, and she followed me into the girls' lavatory. My footsteps rang hard against cement and tile because of the taps I had nailed into my shoes. Her footsteps were soft, padding after me. There was no one in the lavatory but the two of us. I ran all around the rows of twenty-five open stalls to make sure of that. No sisters. I think we must have been playing hide-and-go-seek. She was not good at hiding by herself and usually followed her sister; they'd hide in the same place. They must have gotten separated. In this growing twilight, a child could hide and never be found.

I stopped abruptly in front of the sinks, and she came running toward me before she could stop herself, so that she almost collided with me. I walked closer. She backed away, puzzlement, then alarm in her eyes.

"You're going to talk," I said, my voice steady and normal, as it is when talking to the familiar, the weak, and the small. "I am going to make you talk, you sissy-girl." She stopped backing away and stood fixed.

I looked into her face so I could hate it close up. She wore black bangs, and her cheeks were pink and white. She was baby-soft. I thought that I could put my thumb on her nose and push it bonelessly in, indent her face. I could poke dimples into her cheeks. I could work her face around like dough. She stood still, and I did not want to look at her face anymore; I hated fragility. I walked around her, looked her up and down the way the Mexican and Negro girls did when they fought, so tough. I hated her weak neck, the way it did not support her head but let it droop; her head would fall backward. I stared at the curve of her nape. I wished I was able to see what my own neck looked like from the back and sides. I hoped it did not look like hers; I wanted a stout neck. I grew my hair long to hide it in case it was a flower-stem neck. I walked around to the front of her to hate her face some more.

I reached up and took the fatty part of her cheek, not dough, but meat, between my thumb and finger. This close, and I saw no pores. "Talk," I said. "Are you going to talk?" Her skin was fleshy, like squid out of which the glassy blades of bones had been pulled. I wanted tough skin, hard brown skin. I had callused my hands; I had scratched dirt to blacken the nails, which I cut straight across to make stubby fingers. I gave her face a squeeze. "Talk." When I let go, the pink rushed back into my white thumbprint on her skin. I walked around to her side. "Talk!" I shouted into the side of her head. Her straight hair hung, the same all these years, no ringlets or braids or permanents. I squeezed her other cheek. "Are you? Huh? Are you going to talk?" She tried to shake her head, but I had hold of her face. She had no muscles to jerk away. Her skin seemed to stretch. I let go in horror. What if it came away in my hand? "No, huh?" I said, rubbing the touch of her off my fingers. "Say 'No,' then," I said. I gave her another pinch and a twist. "Say 'No.'" She shook her head, her straight hair turning with her head, not swinging side to side like the pretty girls'. She was so neat. Her neatness bothered me. I hated the way she folded the wax paper from her lunch; she did not wad her brown paper bag and her school papers. I hated her clothes—the blue pastel cardigan, the white blouse with the collar that lay flat over the cardigan, the homemade flat, cotton skirt she wore when everybody else was wearing flared skirts. I hated pastels; I would wear black always. I squeezed again, harder, even though her cheek had a weak rubbery feeling I did not like. I squeezed one cheek, then the other, back and forth until the tears ran out of her eyes as if I had pulled them out. "Stop crying," I said, but although she habitually followed me around, she did not obey. Her eyes dripped; her nose dripped. She wiped her eyes with her papery fingers. The skin on her hands and arms seemed powdery-dry, like tracing paper, onion paper. I hated her fingers. I could snap them like breadsticks. I pushed her hands down. "Say 'Hi,'" I said. "'Hi'. Like that. Say your name. Go ahead. Say it. Or are you stupid? You're so stupid, you don't know you own name, is that it? When I say, 'What's your name?' you just blurt it out, O.K.? What's your name?" Last year the whole class had laughed at a boy who couldn't fill out a form because he didn't know his father's name. The teacher sighed, exasperated and was very sarcastic, "Don't you notice things? What does your mother call him?" she said. The class laughed at how dumb he was not to notice things. "She calls him father of me," he said. Even we laughed although we knew that his mother did not call his father by name, and a son does not know his father's name. We laughed and were relieved that our parents had had the foresight to tell us some names we could give the teachers. "If you're not stupid," I said to the quiet girl, "what's you name?" She shook her head, and some hair caught in the tears; wet black hair stuck to the side of the pink and white face. I reached up (she was taller than I) and took a strand of hair. I pulled it. "Well, then, let's honk your hair," I said. "Honk. Honk." Then I pulled the other side—"ho-o-n-k"—a long pull; "ho-o-n-n-nk"—a longer pull. I could see her little white ears, like white cutworms curled underneath the hair. "Talk!" I yelled into each cutworm.

I looked right at her. "I know you talk," I said. "I've heard you." Her eyebrows flew up. Something in those black eyes was startled, and I pursued it. "I was walking past your house when you didn't know I was there. I heard you yell in English and in Chinese. You weren't just talking. You were shouting. I heard you shout. You were saying, 'Where are you?' Say that again. Go ahead, just the way you did at home." I yanked harder on the hair, but steadily, not jerking. I did not want to pull it out. "Go ahead. Say, 'Where are you?' Say it loud enough for your sister to come. Call her. Make her come help you. Call her name. I'll stop if she comes. So call. Go ahead."

She shook her head, her mouth curved down, crying. I could see her tiny white teeth, baby teeth. I wanted to grow big strong yellow teeth. "You do have a tongue," I said. "So use it." I pulled the hair at her temples, pulled the tears out of her eyes. "Say, 'Ow'" I said. "Just 'Ow.' Say, 'Let go.' Go ahead. Say it. I'll honk you again if you don't say, 'Let me alone.' Say, 'Leave me alone,' and I'll let you go. I will. I'll let go if you say it. You can stop this anytime you want to, you know. All you have to do is tell me to stop. Just say, 'Stop.' You're just asking for it, aren't you? You're just asking for another honk. Well then, I'll have to give you another honk. Say, 'Stop.'" But she didn't. I had to pull again and again.

15   Sounds did come out of her mouth, sobs, chokes, noises that were almost words. Snot ran out of her nose. She tried to wipe it on her hands, but there was too much of it. She used her sleeve. "You're disgusting," I told her. "Look at you, snot streaming down your nose, and you won't say a word to stop it. You're such a nothing." I moved behind her and pulled the hair growing out of her weak neck. I let go. I stood silent for a long time. Then I screamed, "Talk!" I would scare the words out of her. If she had had little bound feet, the toes twisted under the balls, I would have jumped up and landed on them—crunch!—stomped on them with my iron shoes. She cried hard, sobbing aloud. "Cry, 'Mama,'" I said. "Come on. Cry, 'Mama.' Say, 'Stop it.'"

I put my finger on her pointed chin. "I don't like you. I don't like the weak little toots you make on your flute. Wheeze. Wheeze. I don't like the way you don't swing at the ball. I don't like the way you're the last one chosen. I don't like the way you can't make a fist for tetherball. Why don't you make a fist? Come on. Get tough. Come on. Throw fists." I pushed at her long hands; they swung limply at her sides. Her fingers were so long, I thought maybe they had an extra joint. They couldn't possibly make fists like other people's. "Make a fist," I said. "Come on. Just fold those fingers up; fingers on the inside, thumbs on the outside. Say something. Honk me back. You're so tall, and you let me pick on you.

"Would you like a hanky? I can't get you one with embroidery on it or crocheting along the edges, but I'll get you some toilet paper if you tell me to. Go ahead. Ask me. I'll get it for you if you ask." She did not stop crying. "Why don't you scream, 'Help'?" I suggested. "Say, 'Help.' Go ahead." She cried on. "O.K. O.K. Don't talk. Just scream, and I'll let you go. Won't that feel good? Go ahead. Like this." I screamed not too loudly. My voice hit the tile and rang it as if I had thrown a rock at it. The stalls opened wider and the toilets wider and darker. Shadows leaned at angles I had not seen before. I was very late. Maybe a janitor had locked me in with this girl for the night. Her black eyes blinked and stared, blinked and stared. I felt dizzy from hunger. We had been in this lavatory together forever. My mother would call the police again if I didn't bring my sister home soon. "I'll let you go if you say just one word," I said. "You can even say 'a' or 'the,' and I'll let you go. Come on. Please." She didn't shake her head anymore, only cried steadily, so much water coming out of her. I could see the two duct holes where the tears welled out. Quarts of tears but no words. I grabbed her by the shoulder. I could feel bones. The light was coming in queerly through the frosted glass with the chicken wire embedded in it. Her crying was like an animal's—a seal's—and it echoed around the basement. "Do you want to stay here all night?" I asked. "Your mother is wondering what happened to her baby. You wouldn't want to have her mad at you. You'd better say something." I shook her shoulder. I pulled her hair again. I squeezed her face. "Come on! Talk! Talk! Talk!" She didn't seem to feel it anymore when I pulled her hair. "There's nobody here but you and me. This isn't a classroom or a playground or a crowd. I'm just one person. You can talk in front of one person. Don't make me pull harder and harder until you talk." But her hair seemed to stretch; she did not say a word. "I'm going to pull harder. Don't made me pull anymore, or your hair will come out and you're going to be bald. Do you want to be bald? You don't want to be bald, do you?"

Far away, coming from the edge of town, I heard whistles blow. The cannery was changing shifts, letting out the afternoon people, and still we were here at school. It was a sad sound—work done. The air was lonelier after the sound died.

"Why won't you talk?" I started to cry. What if I couldn't stop, and everyone would want to know what happened? "Now look what you've done," I scolded. "You're going to pay for this. I want to know why. And you're going to tell me why. You don't see I'm trying to help you out, do you? Do you want to be like this, dumb (do you know what dumb means?), your whole life? Don't you ever want to be a cheerleader? Or a pompon girl? What are you going to do for a living? Yeah, you're going to have to work because you can't be a housewife. Somebody has to marry you before you can be a housewife. And you, you are a plant. Do you know that? That's all you are if you don't talk. If you don't talk, you can't have a personality. You'll have no personality and no hair. You've got to let people know you have a personality and a brain. You think somebody is going to take care of you all your stupid life? You think you'll always have your big sister? You think somebody's going to marry you, is that it? Well, you're not the type that gets dates, let alone gets married. Nobody's going to notice you. And you have to talk for interviews, speak right up in front of the boss. Don't you know that? You're so dumb. Why do I waste my time on you?" Sniffling and snorting, I couldn't stop crying and talking at the same time. I kept wiping my nose on my arm, my sweater lost somewhere (probably not worn because my mother said to wear a sweater). It seemed as if I had spent my life in that basement, doing the worst thing I had yet done to another person. "I'm doing this for your own good," I said. "Don't you dare tell anyone I've been bad to you. Talk. Please talk."

20   I was getting dizzy from the air I was gulping. Her sobs and my sobs were bouncing wildly off the tile, sometimes together, sometimes alternating. "I don't understand why you won't say just one word," I cried, clenching my teeth. My knees were shaking, and I hung on to her hair to stand up. Another time I'd stayed too late, I had had to walk around two Negro kids who were bonking each other's head on the concrete. I went back later to see if the concrete had cracks in it. "Look. I'll give you something if you talk. I'll give you my pencil box. I'll buy you some candy. O.K.? What do you want? Tell me. Just say it, and I'll give it to you. Just say, 'yes,' or, 'O.K.,' or, 'Baby Ruth.'" But she didn't want anything.

I had stopped pinching her cheek because I did not like the feel of her skin. I would go crazy if it came away in my hands. "I skinned her," I would have to confess.

Suddenly I heard footsteps hurrying through the basement, and her sister ran into the lavatory calling her name. "Oh, there you are," I said. "We've been waiting for you. I was only trying to teach her to talk. She wouldn't cooperate, though." Her sister went into one of the stalls and got handfuls of toilet paper and wiped her off. Then we found my sister, and we walked home together. "Your family really ought to force her to speak," I advised all the way home. "You mustn't pamper her."

The world is sometimes just, and I spent the next eighteen months sick in bed with a mysterious illness. There was no pain and no symptoms, though the middle line in my left palm broke in two. Instead of starting junior high school, I lived like the Victorian recluses I read about. I had a rented hospital bed in the living room, where I watched soap operas on TV, and my family cranked me up and down. I saw no one but my family, who took good care of me. I could have no visitors, no other relatives, no villagers. My bed was against the west window, and I watched the seasons change the peach tree. I had a bell to ring for help. I used a bedpan. It was the best year and a half of my life. Nothing happened.

But one day my mother, the doctor, said, "You're ready to get up today. It's time to get up and go to school." I walked about outside to get my legs working, leaning on a staff I cut from the peach tree. The sky and trees, the sun were immense—no longer framed by a window, no longer grayed with a fly screen. I sat down on the sidewalk in amazement—the night, the stars. But at school I had to figure out again how to talk. I met again the poor girl I had tormented. She had not changed. She wore the same clothes, hair cut, and manner as when we were in elementary school, no make-up on the pink and white face, while the other Asian girls were starting to tape their eyelids. She continued to be able to read aloud. But there was hardly any reading aloud anymore, less and less as we got into high school. . . .

QUESTIONS FOR DISCUSSION

1. Why does the narrator hate the silent girl? How does she try to change her?
2. What freedoms does the narrator experience before meeting the silent girl in the lavatory? How might her previous sense of power have affected her attitude toward the silent one?
3. Why does the narrator want the quiet girl to talk? Why does the silent girl refuse to say anything in spite of the narrator's bullying, persecution, and physical attacks? In what sense are both girls struggling against cultural stereotypes of Asian women?
4. Have you ever hated someone for being like a part of yourself that you did not like or accept? Do you think this rejection of a part of oneself as seen reflected in another person is a common cause for interpersonal struggle?
5. Why does the narrator finally start to cry herself? What is she crying about?
6. How do you interpret the narrator's mysterious illness? Why does she eventually get better? How does the final paragraph suggest a permanent split between herself and the "shadow self," the silent girl? What might this split signify?

CONNECTION

Compare the conflict that the narrator has with the silent girl with the inner conflict over the shadow in Von Franz's essay (see page 365).

IDEAS FOR WRITING

1. Write about a relationship that was so intense that you lost perspective on the differences or ego boundaries between yourself and the other person. What did you learn from this struggle?
2. Write an essay about the cultural stereotypes that you have had to struggle against in school. How have these struggles helped you to develop more self-awareness and self-confidence?

RELATED WEB SITES

Powells.com Interviews—Maxine Hong Kingston
`www.powells.com/authors/kingston.html`
The provided URL leads to an interview with author Maxine Hong Kingston by Miel Alegre and Dave Weich of Powell's Books. Kingston reflects on her double identity with both Western culture and Chinese culture.

Voices from the Gaps: Maxine Hong Kingston
`http://voices.cla.umn.edu/vg/Bios/entries/kingston_`
`maxine_hong.html`
Created by the Department of English at the University of Minnesota, Voices from the Gaps caters to an academic community. This specific URL provides bibliographical information on Kingston, as well as resources regarding literary criticism and other related links.

Susan Voyticky

Mixed-Up

Susan Voyticky grew up in Brooklyn, New York. She enjoys traveling, studying genetics, and writing poetry. The following essay was written for her freshman English class in response to a question that asked students to reflect on an aspect of their ethnic heritage about which they have conflicting feelings.

Having parents from different ethnic groups and growing up mixed is not easy in this country; in fact, it can really mix a person up, culturally as well as socially. Often, mixed children are confused about the cultural group to which they belong, and sometimes these children are alienated from half or even all of their cultural background. Other times children exposed to two distinct cultures feel pressured by society to choose one culture and social group to fit into and to define themselves through. However, as a person of mixed background, I try, despite the pressures that society puts on me, to relate to both my European and to my African heritage. I realize that I have a unique and independent cultural identity.

My lack of wanting to identify with a particular culture defines who I am. For instance, I remember going shopping in a store when I was ten years old that had black and white floor tiles. I decided to play with two children, a boy and a girl who were my age. After a while the girl said, "We'll [she and the boy] step on the white tiles, and you [pointing to me] step on the black tiles 'cause you're black." I couldn't believe what she had said. Even at that age, I found the idea insulting to my existence—she was ignoring half of me. I replied indignantly, "You two can step on the white tiles, I'll step anywhere I want because I'm both." Then I quickly returned to my mother.

As a child, I quickly grew to realize that I was not ethnically "identifiable." During recess at my elementary school I often would try to play with the few African American girls at my school. Usually the game was double-dutch, but I didn't know how to play, and the African American kids said I turned the rope "like a white girl." To whites, I was black, and to blacks, I was less than black. I refused to be either; my ethnicity is an entirely different color—gray. If my mother is black and my father is white, then I most certainly must be gray. What else does one get by mixing black and white? Some would consider gray a "drab" color, but often one forgets gray comes in an infinite number of shades.

Because I have not chosen to identify with only one of my parents' cultures, I'll never know the comfort of belonging to a specific group of people with ancient customs and rituals. This society does not recognize my unique cross-cultural heritage of African American, Irish, Russian, Polish, and Czechoslovakian. Few people choose to be mixed, to accept everything about themselves, and sometimes they are not given the choice. I have lost something in not being "white"; I also have lost something in not being "black." However, I have gained something important: my cultural independence. My brother puts it best when he says, "God was making a bunch of cookies. The white people he took out of the oven too soon. The black people he took out too late. We are the perfect cookies. One day everyone will be perfect, like us."

5   I struggle to be accepted in this society for what I am and not for what others would make of me. The longer I live, the more I feel pressured by

society to "label" myself. When standardized forms were handed out in school, I would ask the teachers, "What should I fill out?" Most replied that I could fill whichever I wished. Most of the time that's what I did. One year I was black, the next year I was white, the next year I'd fill out two ovals. In high school, I was told I was black, because the federal government has a rule that if one is one-fourth black, one is black. I ignored this and continued to fill out forms in my usual way.

Finally the true test of my "grayness" arrived—college applications. My mother said that I should fill out African American, for the ethnic question, considering that it would improve my chances of being accepted. I didn't listen to her, for it's not in my nature to lie. How could I not be honest about who I was? On half of my applications I wrote "Black-Caucasian"; on the other half I wrote, "White African-American." My mother was not amused by what seemed to her a completely inane act. She didn't understand that I can't be told what I am, because I know who I am. In my blood run the tears of slaves torn from their homeland and the sweat of poor farmers looking for a better life. Their struggle is part of my identity.

A large part of one's culture is internal and cannot be represented simply by the color of one's skin. In this society it is difficult to be accepted for anything more than face value, but each person must try to be who he or she is within, not simply in the eyes of society. I am proud of my choice of identity with both of my ethnic backgrounds. Although being mixed often means being "mixed-up" through being mistaken for something you are not by people too ignorant to care, identity is more than skin deep.

Questions for Discussion

1. What aspects of her mixed ethnic background cause Voyticky the most difficulty? How has she tried to resolve her problem of identity?

2. Compare Voyticky's view of the consequences of a mixed cultural and ethnic background with that presented in the poem by Judith Ortiz Cofer, "The Other."

3. Do you think that Voyticky should have taken a more serious approach to conveying the meaning of her ethnicity on her college applications?

4. Voyticky illustrates her essay with several examples drawn from her experience of being of mixed heritage at different stages of her life. What does each example add to her essay's persuasiveness and its portrait of the dilemmas faced in our society by individuals from backgrounds similar to Voyticky's? What other kinds of evidence or examples would have helped to persuade you?

Fran Peavey (with Myrna Levy and Charles Varon)

Us and Them

Fran Peavey is a longtime California peace activist, ecologist, and community organizer. Peavey's books include Heart Politics *(1984);* A Shallow Pool of Time: One Woman Grapples with the Aids Epidemic *(1989);* By Life's Grace: Musings on the Essence of Social Change *(1994), (with Radmila Manojlovic Zarkovic); the anthology* I Remember: Writings by Bosnian Women Refugees *(1996); and* Heart Politics Revisited *(2000). Peavey has also written articles for a number of alternative-press publications and has served as a longtime observer of the Balkans struggle and the war in Kosovo. As you read her essay "Us and Them," from* Heart Politics, *consider how the people whom we feel are different from us politically or socially can be mistakenly perceived as alien beings with whom we have nothing in common and how accepting the "other" outside of ourselves is something like accepting the rejected parts of our own identity.*

JOURNAL

Write about someone with whom you have trouble communicating because this individual is different from you in some way. What do you have in common with this person that could form the basis for better communication?

Time was when I knew that the racists were the lunch-counter owners who refused to serve blacks, the warmongers were the generals who planned wars and ordered the killing of innocent people, and the polluters were the industrialists whose factories fouled the air, water and land. I could be a good guy by boycotting, marching, and sitting in to protest the actions of the bad guys.

But no matter how much I protest, an honest look at myself and my relationship with the rest of the world reveals ways that I too am part of the problem. I notice that on initial contact I am more suspicious of Mexicans than of whites. I see that I'm addicted to a standard of living maintained at the expense of poorer people around the world—a situation that can only be perpetuated through military force. And the problem of pollution seems to include my consumption of resources and creation of waste. The line that separates me from the bad guys is blurred.

When I was working to stop the Vietnam War, I'd feel uneasy seeing people in military uniform. I remember thinking, "How could that guy be so dumb as to have gotten into that uniform? How could he be so acquiescent, so credulous as to have fallen for the government's story in Vietnam?" I'd get furious inside when I imagined the horrible things he'd probably done in the war.

Several years after the end of the war, a small group of Vietnam veterans wanted to hold a retreat at our farm in Watsonville. I consented, although I felt ambivalent about hosting them. That weekend, I listened to a dozen men and women who had served in Vietnam. Having returned home only to face ostracism for their involvement in the war, they were struggling to come to terms with their experiences.

5   They spoke of some of the awful things they'd done and seen, as well as some things they were proud of. They told why they had enlisted in the Army or cooperated with the draft: their love of the United States, their eagerness to serve, their wish to be brave and heroic. They felt their noble motives had been betrayed, leaving them with little confidence in their own judgment. Some questioned their own manhood or womanhood and even their basic humanity. They wondered whether they had been a positive force or a negative one overall, and what their buddies' sacrifices meant. Their anguish disarmed me, and I could no longer view them simply as perpetrators of evil.

How had I come to view military people as my enemies? Did vilifying soldiers serve to get me off the hook and allow me to divorce myself from responsibility for what my country was doing in Vietnam? Did my own anger and righteousness keep me from seeing the situation in its full complexity? How had this limited view affected my work against the war?

When my youngest sister and her husband, a young career military man, visited me several years ago, I was again challenged to see the human being within the soldier. I learned that as a farm boy in Utah, he'd been recruited to be a sniper.

One night toward the end of their visit, we got to talking about his work. Though he had also been trained as a medical corpsman, he could still be called on at any time to work as a sniper. He couldn't tell me much about this part of his career—he'd been sworn to secrecy. I'm not sure he would have wanted to tell me even if he could. But he did say that a sniper's work involved going abroad, "bumping off" a leader, and disappearing into a crowd.

When you're given an order, he said, you're not supposed to think about it. You feel alone and helpless. Rather than take on the Army and maybe the whole country himself, he chose not to consider the possibility that certain orders shouldn't be carried out.

10   I could see that feeling isolated can make it seem impossible to follow one's own moral standards and disobey an order. I leaned toward him and said, "If you're ever ordered to do something that you know you

shouldn't do, call me immediately and I'll find a way to help. I know a lot of people would support your stand. You're not alone." He and my sister looked at each other and their eyes filled with tears.

How do we learn whom to hate and fear? During my short lifetime, the national enemies of the United States have changed several times. Our World War II foes, the Japanese and the Germans, have become our allies. The Russians have been in vogue as our enemy for some time, although during a few periods relations improved somewhat. The North Vietnamese, Cubans, and Chinese have done stints as our enemy. So many countries seem capable of incurring our national wrath—how do we choose among them?

As individuals, do we choose our enemies based on cues from national leaders? From our schoolteachers and religious leaders? From newspapers and TV? Do we hate and fear our parents' enemies as part of our family identity? Or those of our culture, subculture, or peer group?

Whose economic and political interests does our enemy mentality serve?

At a conference on holocaust and genocide I met someone who showed me that it is not necessary to hate our opponents, even under the most extreme circumstances. While sitting in the hotel lobby after a session on the German holocaust, I struck up a conversation with a woman named Helen Waterford. When I learned she was a Jewish survivor of Auschwitz, I told her how angry I was at the Nazis. (I guess I was trying to prove to her that I was one of the good guys.)

15   "You know," she said, "I don't hate the Nazis." This took me aback. How could anyone who had lived through a concentration camp not hate the Nazis?

Then I learned that Helen does public speaking engagements with a former leader of the Hitler Youth movement: they talk about how terrible fascism is as viewed from both sides. Fascinated, I arranged to spend more time with Helen and learn as much as I could from her.

In 1980, Helen read an intriguing newspaper article in which a man named Alfons Heck described his experiences growing up in Nazi Germany. When he was a young boy in Catholic school, the priest would come in every morning and say, "Heil Hitler," and then "Good Morning," and finally, "In the name of the Father and the Son and the Holy Spirit . . ." In Heck's mind, Hitler came before God. At ten, he volunteered for the Hitler Youth, and he loved it. It was in 1944, when he was sixteen, that Heck first learned that the Nazis were systematically killing the Jews. He thought, "This can't be true." But gradually he came to believe that he had served a mass murderer.

Heck's frankness impressed Helen, and she thought, "I want to meet that man." She found him soft-spoken, intelligent and pleasant. Helen had already been speaking publicly about her own experiences of the holocaust, and she asked Heck to share a podium with her at an upcoming engagement with a group of four-hundred schoolteachers. They spoke in chronological format, taking turns telling their own stories of the Nazi period. Helen told of leaving Frankfurt in 1934 at age twenty-five.

She and her husband, an accountant who had lost his job when the Nazis came to power, escaped to Holland. There they worked with the underground Resistance, and Helen gave birth to a daughter. In 1940 the Nazis invaded Holland. Helen and her husband went into hiding in 1942. Two years later, they were discovered and sent to Auschwitz. Their daughter was hidden by friends in the Resistance. Helen's husband died in the concentration camp.

20   Heck and Waterford's first joint presentation went well, and they decided to continue working as a team. Once, at an assembly of eight-hundred high school students, Heck was asked, "If you had been ordered to shoot some Jews, maybe Mrs. Waterford, would you have shot them?" The audience gasped. Heck swallowed and said, "Yes. I obeyed orders. I would have." Afterward he apologized to Helen, saying he hadn't wanted to upset her. She told him, "I'm glad you answered the way you did. Otherwise, I would never again believe a word you said."

Heck is often faced with the "once a Nazi, always a Nazi" attitude. "You may give a good speech," people will say, "but I don't believe any of it. Once you have believed something, you don't throw it away." Again and again, he patiently explains that it took years before he could accept the fact that he'd been brought up believing falsehoods. Heck is also harassed by neo-Nazis, who call him in the middle of the night and threaten: "We haven't gotten you yet, but we'll kill you, you traitor."

How did Helen feel about the Nazis in Auschwitz? "I disliked them. I cannot say that I wished I could kick them to death—I never did. I guess that I am just not a vengeful person." She is often denounced by Jews for having no hate, for not wanting revenge. "It is impossible that you don't hate," people tell her.

At the conference on the holocaust and genocide and in subsequent conversations with Helen, I have tried to understand what has enabled her to remain so objective and to avoid blaming individual Germans for the holocaust, for her suffering and for her husband's death. I have found a clue in her passionate study of history.

For many people, the only explanation of the holocaust is that it was the creation of a madman. But Helen believes that such an analysis only serves to shield people from believing that a holocaust could happen to them. An appraisal of Hitler's mental health, she says, is less important than an examination of the historical forces at play and the ways Hitler was able to manipulate them.

25   "As soon as the war was over," Helen told me, "I began to read about what had happened since 1933, when my world closed. I read and read.

How did the 'S.S. State' develop? What was the role of Britain, Hungary, Yugoslavia, the United States, France? How can it be possible that the holocaust really happened? What is the first step, the second step? What are people searching for when they join fanatical movements? I guess I will be asking these questions until my last days."

Those of us working for social change tend to view our adversaries as enemies, to consider them unreliable, suspect, and generally of lower moral character. Saul Alinsky, a brilliant community organizer, explained the rationale for polarization this way:

> One acts decisively only in the conviction that all the angels are on one side and all the devils are on the other. A leader may struggle toward a decision and weigh the merits and demerits of a situation which is 52 percent positive and 48 percent negative, but once the decision is reached he must assume that his cause is 100 percent positive and the opposition 100 percent negative.... Many liberals, during our attack on the then-school superintendent [in Chicago], were pointing out that after all he wasn't a 100-percent devil, he was a regular churchgoer, he was a good family man, and he was generous in his contributions to charity. Can you imagine in the arena of conflict charging that so-and-so is a racist bastard and then diluting the impact of the attack with qualifying remarks? This becomes political idiocy.

But demonizing one's adversaries has great costs. It is a strategy that tacitly accepts and helps perpetuate our dangerous enemy mentality.

Instead of focusing on the 52-percent "devil" in my adversary, I choose to look at the other 48 percent, to start from the premise that within each adversary I have an ally. That ally may be silent, faltering, or hidden from my view. It may be only the person's sense of ambivalence about morally questionable parts of his or her job. Such doubts rarely have a chance to flower because of the overwhelming power of the social context to which the person is accountable. *My* ability to be *their* ally also suffers from such pressures. In 1970, while the Vietnam War was still going on, a group of us spent the summer in Long Beach, California, organizing against a napalm factory there. It was a small factory that mixed the chemicals and put the napalm in canisters. An accidental explosion a few months before had spewed hunks of napalm gel onto nearby homes and lawns. The incident had, in a real sense, brought the war home. It spurred local residents who opposed the war to recognize their community's connection with one of its most despicable elements. At their request, we worked with and strengthened their local group. Together we presented a slide show and tour of the local military-industrial complex for community leaders, and we picketed the napalm factory. We also met with the president of the conglomerate that owned the factory.

We spent three weeks preparing for this meeting, studying the company's holdings and financial picture and investigating whether there were any lawsuits filed against the president or his corporation. And we found out as much as we could about his personal life: his family, his church, his country club, his hobbies. We studied his photograph, thinking of the people who loved him and the people he loved, trying to get a sense of his worldview and the context to which he was accountable.

30   We also talked a lot about how angry we were at him for the part he played in killing and maiming children in Vietnam. But though our anger fueled our determination, we decided that venting it at him would make him defensive and reduce our effectiveness.

When three of us met with him, he was not a stranger to us. Without blaming him personally or attacking his corporation, we asked him to close the plant, not to bid for the contract when it came up for renewal that year, and to think about the consequences of his company's operations. We told him we knew where his corporation was vulnerable (it owned a chain of motels that could be boycotted), and said we intended to continue working strategically to force his company out of the business of burning people. We also discussed the company's other war-related contracts, because changing just a small part of his corporation's function was not enough; we wanted to raise the issue of economic dependence on munitions and war.

Above all, we wanted him to see us as real people, not so different from himself. If we had seemed like flaming radicals, he would have been likely to dismiss our concerns. We assumed he was already carrying doubts inside himself, and we saw our role as giving voice to those doubts. Our goal was to introduce ourselves and our perspective into his context, so he would remember us and consider our position when making decisions.

When the contract came up for renewal two months later, his company did not bid for it.

Working for social change without relying on the concept of enemies raises some practical difficulties. For example, what do we do with all the anger that we're accustomed to unleashing against an enemy? Is it possible to hate actions and policies without hating the people who are implementing them? Does empathizing with those whose actions we oppose create a dissonance that undermines our determination?

35   I don't delude myself into believing that everything will work out for the best if we make friends with our adversaries. I recognize that certain military strategists are making decisions that raise the risks for us all. I know that some police officers will rough up demonstrators when arresting them. Treating our adversaries as potential allies need not entail unthinking acceptance of their actions. Our challenge is to call forth the humanity within each adversary, while preparing for the full range of possible responses. Our challenge is to find a path between cynicism and naiveté.

QUESTIONS FOR DISCUSSION

1. Why does Peavey no longer find it easy to feel clear about the distinctions between the good guys and the bad guys? What elements of the bad guys does she now perceive in herself?
2. What was Peavey's rationale for being angry at soldiers? What did Peavey learn from her experience hosting a group of Vietnam veterans on her farm?
3. What did Peavey learn from the visit with her sister and her sister's husband, a military sniper? Does Peavey feel that the husband should be forgiven? Do you agree?
4. How does Peavey's friendship with Helen Waterford break down the preconceptions Peavey holds about Nazis and concentration camp survivors? Do you agree with Waterford and Peavey's new perspective on Nazis? Why or why not? Explain.
5. Through providing an example of her own successful organizing technique against a napalm factory, Peavey attempts to refute an argument by organizer Saul Alinsky against the folly of qualifying our attacks on our enemies. Is Peavey's argument a convincing one?
6. How effective is Peavey's conclusion in anticipating and resolving objections that readers might have to her position? What point does she concede? Does her concession weaken or strengthen her argument?

CONNECTION

Compare Peavey's view on effective activism that works toward accepting the socially defined "other," or antagonist, with the views of Desmond Tutu on forgiveness and reconciliation (see page 407).

IDEAS FOR WRITING

1. Write an essay on how individuals learn to forgive themselves. Do some research into this topic. Then write about how one might apply these concepts of forgiveness to social and political disagreements and confrontations.
2. Write an essay about an experience in which you separated yourself from another person or group of people because of a difference of opinion, but later were able to understand and identify with his/her or their behavior and accept their differences.

RELATED WEB SITES

Interview with Fran Peavey
`www.jobsletter.org.nz/hpx/fran98.htm`
Interview with Peavey by Australian journalist David Leser from *The Melbourne Age* (1998).

Crabgrass
`http://crabgrassusa.org`
Crabgrass is a small nongovernmental organization based in San Francisco that works globally and locally on environmental, social justice, and human rights issues. The site features articles by Fran Peavey.

Jessica Rubenstein

Coed Schools Help Students Excel

Jessica Rubenstein was born and raised in San Jose, California. After studying at the University of California at San Diego for one year she decided to work as an apprentice on an organic farm in Indiana. Jessica's interests in educational reform brought her back to De Anza college, where she is completing her first-year writing requirements. She plans to transfer to the University of California at Los Angeles, where she will major in Spanish. Currently she is working in a program with teen mothers and their children.

JOURNAL

How would you feel if your parents decided to enroll you in a single-sex school?

Educational reformers are re-thinking the value of same sex education. Author Christine Whelan introduces us to the debate surrounding same-sex education in "Singles," published in the *National Review* (1998). Whelan recounts the story of Cydnee Couch, a student who was not learning in public school because of the conflicts she felt about her academic life at school and relating to boys. She went on to be more successful than she had ever dreamed in a single-sex school. While Cydnee was successful, I can only imagine how my educational life would have been different, and likely less stressful, had I been enrolled in an all-girls school like the one Cydnee Couch was able to attend. Experiences in coed public schools are full of experiences like Cydnee's, but no matter how excruciating it can be to deal with adolescent immaturity, interactions between boys and girls in social and academic settings are important and help shape the men and women they will become. The best argument against same-sex education may well be the simplest: it is not realistic. Although evidence suggests that same-sex education produces successful students, the challenges of coeducational schools are necessary to prepare students for college, the workplace, and beyond. In creating an empowering and mutually respectful environment that mirrors the atmosphere of same-sex schools, coed educators can support students that are just as high-achieving, involved, and satisfied as their peers in same-sex schools.

While some studies indicate that students in same-sex schools perform better than their coed counterparts on many measures, there is no conclusive evidence that suggests this is due purely to the absence of students of the opposite gender. In her article, Whelan notes evidence that students in same-sex schools improve at a higher rate in reading and science tests, have more self-confidence, and are more involved in extra-curricular activities compared to their co-educational counterparts. As the publication "Single-Sex vs. Coed: The Evidence" points out, several foreign studies confirm those claims; and a handful of smaller academic studies of students at same-sex Catholic schools in the United States also point toward the same conclusion, with the most dramatic results noted in students from minority groups, such as the young women served by the Young Women's Leadership School in East Harlem. But quality large-scale studies comparing coeducation and same-sex public schooling are lacking, a fact acknowledged by the United States Department of Education in "Single-Sex Versus Coeducation Schooling: A Systematic Review."

The discrepancies revealed in those studies cannot be explained only by the absence of boys at all-girls schools and vice versa. In her article "Separating the Sexes: A New Direction for Public Education?" Teresa Méndez gives insight into the attitude among students at an all-girls high school. She says the girls "are conscious of the value of their education, and they embrace the expectations that accompany it." That sense of personal responsibility and of taking education seriously is not inherent to same-sex education. Wendy Kaminer, in an article entitled "The Trouble With Single Sex Schools," points to another advantage for the Young Women's Leadership School that is not gender specific: resources. The School is "well-equipped," "well-funded," and has a student population of about 150 students. "There is little if any evidence to suggest," Kaminer argues, "that a small coed school of equal quality would not succeed as well." The nature of these differences suggests that providing the same opportunities and tools for achievement to students at coed schools would yield similar rates of success.

While supporters may emphasize the biological and developmental differences between boys and girls as sufficient reason for separate schools, same-sex schools tend to reinforce damaging gender stereotypes and fail to provide boys and girls the opportunity to socialize with each other in a way that promotes healthy competition and understanding.

Many support same-sex schooling on the grounds that biological differences between boys and girls necessitate separate academic programs that address their different learning styles. Dr. Leonard Sax, executive-director of the National Association for Single Sex Public Education (NASSPE), claims that girls learn better in a friendly environment, while boys tend to succeed in a more formal classroom setting (Méndez). Méndez cites another reason that girls excel in single-sex classrooms. She writes that "teachers tend to call on boys more often, and girls often fall silent in classrooms filled with eager boys." That intimidation, she claims, is absent in all-girl schools.

5   I remember well that feeling of intimidation in the classroom; I never wanted to raise my hand even when I had something to say. Only in the last couple of years I have felt proud of my knowledge and comfortable raising my hand in classroom settings. Despite my experience, I believe that this intimidation would be absent in a coed classroom where highly trained teachers are careful to call on and value all students equally. The high performance and confidence of female students at same-sex schools is compelling, but the nature of their success may be putting those same students at a disadvantage. According to Wendy Kaminer, all-girl schools foster academic achievement, but discourage academic competition with males, which, in turn, encourages females to separate their social and intellectual lives. This schism perpetuates myths of sex difference and reinforces gender stereotypes, suggesting that women are allowed to be intelligent and competitive, but only with other women.

If proponents of same-sex education lack sufficient evidence to support their cause, vivid anecdotes make a very poignant case. Cydnee's reflections on the difficulties of her coed school quickly bring back memories of the majority of American students who were educated alongside their peers of the opposite gender. The teasing and taunting, the ponytail pulling, the spitball shooting, and the constant distractions are difficult things to forget. The potential awkwardness and pain of the school years is often compounded by attention, negative and positive, from the opposite sex. The havoc this can wreak on the emotional and academic life of a young man or woman is not to be taken lightly. Here again, coed schools can learn from the atmosphere established in same-sex schools. A lot is expected of students at same-sex schools; and, in turn, they hold themselves to high standards. Teachers and administrators at coed schools must hold their students to similarly rigorous academic and behavioral standards. Immature and harassing behaviors must simply not be tolerated. Teachers in co-ed schools must emphasize respect and teach their students to value themselves and their own education just as much as same-sex school instructors do. Implementation of school uniforms, common in same-sex schools, should also be considered as an equalizing measure to avoid clothing that may be considered provocative or offensive. All other things being equal, within the coed environment, some separation of genders will still be necessary. Students should be divided where common decency dictates, in locker rooms, for example. They should also be separated where embarrassment or insecurity might lead to dangerous ignorance, specifically in sex education classes. Comprehensive sex education should be mandatory in coeducational schools to further encourage openness, understanding, and respect for peers of all genders and sexualities.

Truly high-achieving, self-motivated, involved, and successful students are not created in a vacuum. Coeducation affords children valuable learning experiences that reflect, and help prepare for, the world they will meet when they graduate. As Kim Gandy, President of the National Organization for Women, emphasizes, coed education is a vital source of collegial relationships between boys and girls that will help them develop into "men and women who understand and respect each other" (qtd. in Méndez). Such men and women will enrich society and become valuable citizens, coworkers, partners, and parents. Coed schools must learn why same-sex schools are so conducive to success and work to create an atmosphere of respect and empowerment where each student is valued and given the tools they need to succeed. If educators can work toward this essential goal, society as a whole will benefit and stories like Cydnee Couch's will happily be a thing of the past.

WORKS CITED

Kaminer, Wendy. "The Trouble With Single-Sex Schools." *The Atlantic*. April 2008. 28 Sept. 2008 <http://www.theatlantic.com/doc/ 199804/single-sex>.

Méndez, Teresa. "Separating the Sexes: A New Direction for Public Education?" Christian Science Monitor. 25 May 2004. 28 Sept. 2008 <http://www.csmonitor.com/2004/ 0525/p11s02-legn.html>.

National Association for Single Sex Public Education. "Single-Sex vs. Coed: The Evidence." June 2005. 28 Sept. 2008 <http://www.singlesexschools. org/evidence.html>.

U.S. Department of Education. "Evaluation of Programs—Single-Sex Versus Coeducation Schooling: A Systematic Review" 30 Sept. 2005. 29 Sept. 2008 <http://www.ed.gov/ rschstat/eval/other/single-sex/index.html>.

Whelan, Christine B. "Singles." National Review. 14 Sept. 1998. 01 Oct. 2008 <http:// findarticles.com/p/articles/mi_m1282/is_n17_v50/ ai_21129274>.

QUESTIONS FOR DISCUSSION

1. How does Rubenstein's opening example help to focus and emotionally enrich the meaning of her argument?
2. Do you think that Rubenstein is always realistic about the potential for change and education reform? Would you disagree with any of her assumptions? Which ones?

3. Rubenstein's essay is a dialogic argument, in which the arguer considers the positions of both sides in a dispute before arriving at a balaced conclusion/solution that brings both sides closer together, much as Fran Prevey proposes in "Us and Them" in this chapter. How effective is her effort to seek a middle ground on this controversial issue? Explain your position.
4. What changes would you like to see made in public education in your community with respect to meeting the needs of male as well as female students?

Desmond Mpilo Tutu

No Future Without Forgiveness

Born in 1931 in a South African mining town, Desmond Tutu suffered from the insults and violence that were a part of every black person's life under apartheid. Ordained as a priest in 1961, in 1976 he was consecrated as a bishop for his continued activism against apartheid and received the Nobel Peace Prize in 1984. His books include Crying in the Wilderness: The Struggle for Justice in South Africa *(1982);* Hope & Suffering: Sermons & Speeches *(1984);* The Rainbow People of God: The Making of a Peaceful Revolution *(1994);* No Future Without Forgiveness *(1999); and* God Has a Dream *(2004). In 1996 Nelson Mandela made Tutu chairman of the Truth and Reconciliation Commission, an organization designed to reduce through testimony and forgiveness the lingering pain and anger over the apartheid years. The essay that follows is a brief account of the important work of the commission and its significance for conflict resolution in a variety of cultural settings.*

JOURNAL

What is your view of the importance of forgiveness? Who benefits the most from the act of forgiveness?

A year after the genocide in Rwanda, when at least half a million people were massacred, I visited that blighted land. I went as the president of the ecumenical body, the All Africa Conference of Churches. In my ten-year, two-term presidency, I had tried to take the AACC to its member churches through pastoral visits, especially to those countries that were experiencing crises of one sort or another. Other officers and I also went to celebrate successes when, for instance, democracy replaced repression and injustice in Ethiopia.

In Rwanda we visited Ntarama, a village near the capital, Kigali. In Ntarama, Tutsi tribespeople had been mown down in a church. The new government had not removed the corpses, so that the church was like a mortuary, with the bodies lying as they had fallen the year before during the massacre. The stench was overpowering. Outside the church building was a collection of skulls, some still stuck with *pangas* (machetes) and daggers. I tried to pray. Instead I broke down and wept.

The scene was a deeply disturbing and moving monument to the viciousness that, as human beings, we are capable of unleashing against fellow human beings. Those who had turned against one another in this gory fashion had often lived amicably in the same villages and spoken the same language. They had frequently intermarried and most of them had espoused the same faith—most were Christians. The colonial overlords had sought to maintain their European hegemony by favoring the main ethnic group, the Tutsi, over the other, the Hutu, thus planting the seeds of what would in the end be one of the bloodiest episodes in modern African history.

A few kilometers from this church, some women had begun to build a settlement which they named the Nelson Mandela Village. It was to be a home for some of the many widows and orphans created by the genocide. I spoke to the indomitable leaders of this women's movement. They said, "We must mourn and weep for the dead. But life must also go on, we can't go on weeping." Over at Ntarama, we might say, there was Calvary, death and crucifixion. Here in the Nelson Mandela Village was Resurrection, new life, new beginning, new hope.

5   I also attended a rally in the main stadium of Kigali. It was amazing that people who had so recently experienced such a devastating trauma could sing and laugh and dance as they did at that rally. Most of the leading politicians were present, from the president on down. I had been asked to preach. I began by expressing the deepest condolences of all their sisters and brothers in other parts of Africa, for people elsewhere had been profoundly shocked at the carnage and destruction.

I said that the history of Rwanda was typical of a history of "top dog" and "underdog." The top dog wanted to cling to its privileged position and the underdog strove to topple the top dog. When that happened, the new top dog engaged in an *orgy* of retribution to pay back the new underdog for all the pain and suffering it had inflicted when it was top dog. The new underdog fought to topple the new top dog, storing in its memory all the pain and suffering it was enduring, forgetting that the new top dog was in its view only retaliating for all that it remembered it had suffered when the underdog had been its master. It was a sad history of reprisal provoking counter reprisal.

I reminded the Tutsi that they had waited for thirty years to get their own back for what they perceived to be the injustices that had been heaped on them. I said that extremists among the Hutu were also quite capable of waiting thirty years or more for one day when they could topple the new government, in which the Tutsi played a prominent role, and in their turn unleash the devastation of revenge and resentment.

I said there was talk about tribunals because people did not want to tolerate allowing the criminals to escape punishment. But what I feared was that, if retributive justice was the last word in their situation, then most Hutu would feel that they had been found guilty not because they *were* guilty but because they were Hutu and they would wait for the day when they would be able to take revenge. Then they would pay back the Tutsi for the horrendous prison conditions in which they had been held.

I told them that the cycle of reprisal and counter reprisal that had characterized their national history had to be broken and that the only way to do this was to go beyond retributive justice to restorative justice, to move on to forgiveness, because without it there was no future.

10   The president of Rwanda responded to my sermon with considerable magnanimity. They were ready to forgive, he said, but even Jesus had declared that the devil could not be forgiven. I do not know where he found the basis for what he said, but he was expressing a view that found some resonance, that there were atrocities that were unforgivable. My own view was different, but I had been given a fair and indeed friendly hearing. Later I addressed the parliamentary and political leadership of that country and I was not shouted down as I repeated my appeal for them to consider choosing forgiveness and reconciliation rather than their opposites.

Why was I not rebuffed? Why did these traumatized people, who had undergone such a terrible experience, listen to an unpopular point of view? They listened to me particularly because something had happened in South Africa that gave them reason to pause and wonder. The world had expected that the most ghastly bloodbath would overwhelm South Africa. It had not happened. Then the world thought that, after a democratically elected government was in place, those who for so long had been denied their rights, whose dignity had been trodden underfoot, callously and without compunction, would go on the rampage, unleashing an orgy of revenge and retribution that would devastate their common motherland.

Instead there was this remarkable Truth and Reconciliation Commission to which people told their heart-rending stories, victims expressing their willingness to forgive and perpetrators telling their stories of sordid atrocities while also asking for forgiveness from those they had wronged so grievously. Was this not a viable way of dealing with conflict? Might those who had been at one another's throats try to live amicably together?

It was courageous leaders who gave the sides hope that negotiations could lead to a good outcome. At that time we were fortunate to have as President F. W. De Klerk, leader of the Nationalist Party. Whatever the reasons may have been that impelled him to do what he did, he deserves his niche in history for having announced those very courageous decisions in February of 1990: amongst them the unbanning of the African National Congress, the Pan African Congress, and the Communist Party and the release of political prisoners. That wasn't done lightly. Had De Klerk been maybe more apprehensive he might not have done it. Had he been his granite-like predecessor, we might still be struggling against a vicious system. It was even more fortunate for us that Mr. De Klerk had, as his opposite number, not someone consumed by bitterness, eager for revenge and retribution, saying we are going to give them the same dose of medicine that they gave us once we come to power.

It was our good fortune that on the other side De Klerk found Nelson Mandela, who despite twenty-seven years of incarceration, instead of being consumed by a lust for revenge, demonstrated an extraordinary magnanimity, a nobility of spirit wishing to be able to forgive. Very many in his constituency were saying "We're going to fight to the last drop of blood." There were many, especially young ones, who felt that they could no longer take what had happened to their people for so long and for their own integrity's sake they really had to clobber the other side. By agreeing to negotiations with the Nationalists, Nelson Mandela was putting his reputation and his life, in a sense, on the line. He knew how to inspire hope.

15   The world could not quite believe what it was seeing. South Africans managed an extraordinary, reasonably peaceful transition from the awfulness of repression to the relative stability of democracy. They confounded everyone by their novel manner of dealing with a horrendous past. They had perhaps surprised even themselves at first by how much equanimity they had shown as some of the gory details of that past were rehearsed. It was a phenomenon that the world could not dismiss as insignificant. It was what enabled me to address my sisters and brothers in Rwanda in a manner that under other circumstances could have been seen as insensitive and presumptuous.

Believers say that we might describe most of human history as a quest for that harmony, friendship, and peace for which we appear to have been created. The Bible depicts it all as a God-directed campaign to recover that primordial harmony when the lion will again lie with the lamb and they will learn war no more because swords will have been beaten into plowshares and spears into pruning hooks. Somewhere deep inside us we seem to know that we are destined for something better than strife. Now and again we catch a glimpse of the better thing for which we are meant—for example, when we work together to counter the effects of natural disasters and the world is galvanized by a spirit of compassion and an amazing outpouring of generosity; when for a little while we are bound together by bonds of a caring humanity, a universal sense of *ubuntu;* when victorious powers set up a Marshall Plan to help in the reconstruction of their devastated former adversaries; when we establish a United Nations organization where the peoples of the Earth can parley as they endeavor to avoid war; when we sign charters on the rights of children and of women; when we seek to ban the use of antipersonnel land mines; when we agree as one to outlaw torture and racism. Then we experience fleetingly that we are made for community, for family, that we are in a network of interdependence.

There is a movement to reverse the awful centrifugal force of alienation, brokenness, division, hostility, and disharmony. God has set in motion a centripetal process, a moving toward harmony, goodness, peace, and justice, a process that removes barriers. Jesus says, "And when I am lifted up from the Earth I shall draw everyone to myself" as he hangs from His cross with outflung arms, thrown out to clasp all, everyone and everything, in a cosmic embrace, so that all, everyone, everything, belongs. None is an outsider—all are insiders, all belong. There are no aliens—all belong in the one family, God's family, the human family.

With all its imperfections, what we have tried to do in South Africa has attracted the attention of the world. This tired, disillusioned, cynical world, hurting so frequently and so grievously, has marveled at a process that holds out considerable hope in the midst of much that negates hope. People in the different places that I have visited and where I have spoken about the Truth and Reconciliation process see in this flawed attempt a beacon of hope, a possible paradigm for dealing with situations where violence, conflict, turmoil, and sectional strife have seemed endemic, conflicts that mostly take place not between warring nations but within the same nation. At the end of their conflicts, the warring groups in Northern Ireland, the Balkans, the Middle East, Sri Lanka, Burma, Afghanistan, Angola, the Sudan, the two Congos, and elsewhere are going to have to sit down together to determine just how they will be able to live together amicably, how they might have a shared future devoid of strife, given the bloody past that they have recently lived through.

God does have a sense of humor. Who in their right minds could ever have imagined South Africa to be an example of anything but the most ghastly awfulness, of how not to order a nation's race relations and its governance? We South Africans were the unlikeliest lot and that is precisely why God has chosen us. We cannot really claim much credit ourselves for what we have achieved. We were destined for perdition and were plucked out of total annihilation. We were a hopeless case if ever there was one. God intends that others might look at us and take courage. God wants to point to us as a possible beacon of hope, a possible paradigm, and to say, "Look at South Africa. They had a nightmare called apartheid. It has ended. Northern Ireland (or wherever), your nightmare will end too. They had a problem regarded as intractable. They are resolving it. No problem anywhere can ever again be considered to be intractable. There is hope for you too."

QUESTIONS FOR DISCUSSION

1. What lesson can be learned through Tutu's contrast between the church building at Ntarama and the new Nelson Mandela Village?
2. How does Tutu's top dog/underdog analogy help explain the slaughter in Rwanda? What vicious circle has been perpetuated in that country?
3. Why does Tutu criticize the idea of "tribunals" to punish the guilty parties in the slaughter? Do you agree with him? Why or why not?
4. What advantage does a truth and reconciliation commission such as the one held in South Africa have over retribution and punishment? How were the personalities of De Klerk and Mandela uniquely qualified to make such a commission work?
5. How does Tutu draw on Christian values in his search for a way to overcome division, hostility, and disharmony? What does he mean by the "centripetal process" set in motion by God? Do you think this kind of faith in Christian values is enough to overcome centuries of hostility and suspicion?
6. Why does Tutu believe that God has chosen South Africa as "a possible beacon of hope, a possible paradigm"? If this is so, why have few divided countries followed the South African example?

CONNECTION

Compare Tutu's ideas on the need for social reconciliation with those of Fran Peavey in this chapter (see page 397).

IDEAS FOR WRITING

1. Write an essay about a warring, divided society that you believe has need for a reconciliation committee. Why has this idea not been put into effect there, and what do you believe it would take to create in this particular society the kind of forgiveness that Tutu would like to see?
2. Write a research essay about the South African Truth and Reconciliation Commission. What did it accomplish for South Africans, in both the short and long term? Do divisions and hostility still linger in that country? Why or why not?

Related Web Sites

The Desmond Tutu Peace Centre
`www.tutu.org/home/default.asp`
The Desmond Tutu Peace Centre is "primarily aimed at using the experience of the South African people and the example of Desmond Tutu to inspire a new generation of visionary peace builders."

Peacejam
`www.peacejam.org/`
Peacejam is a Colorado-based charity active in many parts of the world. Their site features information on their efforts for peace, links to other peace-related sites, and an interview with Desmond Tutu.

TOPICS FOR RESEARCH AND WRITING

1. What struggles are revealed in "Henry Jekyll's Full Statement"? Read a brief summary of the chapters preceding the final statement included in this chapter. Do some research into the Victorian culture in which Dr. Jekyll lived. What does Dr. Jekyll's final statement reveal about the nature of the double? In what ways does Stevenson's portrayal seem relevant to struggles people go through today?

2. Research aspects of the doubled personality as it occurs in popular cultures through heroes and heroines who lead a double life or celebrities who create a false persona that fans mistake for the "real" person. Write an essay in which you analyze the phenomenon of the "doubled self" in the celebrities and hero/heroines of popular culture.

3. In some cases, an inability to incorporate the shadow self into one's dominant personality reveals itself in the form of mental illness and breakdown. Do some research into a type of mental illness such as schizophrenia or multiple personality disorder in which the individual's personality tends to fragment into portions that cannot acknowledge one another or function together as a unified self. What are the causes of the particular disorder you have chosen to study? What treatments have been tried in the past, and which ones are currently available? How did your study help you to understand the concept of the shadow?

4. Although the double is often seen as having a primarily psychological origin, there are often social and practical reasons why someone may choose to lead a literal "double life." Do some research into those who have chosen to pass as the "other," such as women who choose to disguise themselves as men, blacks who choose to pass for white, gays who are "closeted" or pass for "straight," and so on. What are the social causes of this type of self-concealment? What are the psychological effects of having to conceal one's true self in society?

5. Desmond Tutu and Fran Peavey examine the need for an understanding of the "other" through forgiveness and reconciliation as strategies for conflict resolution between individuals and groups. Do further research into programs advocating similar approaches to conflict resolution. Conclude with some assessment and evaluation of the effectiveness of such approaches.

6. People have long been fascinated by identical twins as literal doubles. Do some research into frequent issues that identical twins face. For example, does an identical twin sometimes feel that he or she leads two lives? As their personalities develop, but their appearance remains the same, how do identical twins feel about the constant comparison and contrast of their personalities and appearance? If twins had a close bond in childhood, do they have more trouble separating as they grow into adulthood? Why does one twin often see his or her other as a shadow

self? After considering these questions and doing some research, write about one of the issues raised, or develop your own point of view about how identical twins handle the issues that they face.

7. Write an analysis of a film that dramatically portrays the double or divided personality. How does this film echo insights provided by one or more of the authors in this chapter? You might consider a film such as one of the following: *Three Faces of Eve, Dr. Jekyll and Mr. Hyde* (several versions of this film exist, each with a different view of the double), *Mary Reilly* (still another perspective on Jekyll and Hyde), *The Double Life of Veronique, True Lies, The Dark Knight, Shadow of a Doubt, Tell No One, Interview with a Vampire, Sliding Doors, Multiplicity, Freaky Friday, The Prestige,* and *Being John Malkovich.*

8 Pop Dreams

Jon Ford (b.1943)
Giant Avatars, Hong Kong (2008)

JOURNAL

Write about an experience of creating or using a ready-made video-game avatar. Consider how much of yourself went into the avatar: Did it complement or seem to take the place of your actual personality while you played?

The prevalence of harmful products, the imperative to keep up, and the growth of the materialist attitudes are harming kids.

JULIET SCHOR

It's easy to blame the media. . . . But the real celebrity spinmeister is our own mind, which tricks us into believing the stars are our lovers and our social intimates.

CARLIN FLORA

When we make an avatar, we invent an alternative personality . . . But often the alternative personality that we spend many of our days with can become quite powerful.

MARK STEPHEN MEADOWS

THEMATIC INTRODUCTION

How does popular culture help to shape the content of our dreams and fantasies, our values, even our very identities? The readings in this chapter address these issues. Although it would be naïve to imagine that we could have total control over our own dreams, creating them without being influenced by our culture, many of us aspire to be individualistic, valuing our inner feelings and thoughts while simultaneously forming impressions and evaluations of our social and political worlds. In modern society, however, individualism is often undermined and threatened by forces that seek to mold us into non-questioning citizens, passive consumers, avid fans, and/or productive and compliant workers. Overwhelmed by the power of popular culture, we may allow ourselves to deny the impact that the media and the steady barrage of consumerist and political propaganda can have on the development and integrity of both our public and our private selves. Popular culture does not want us to think critically about the issues or products it promotes. One of our greatest defenses against the power of pop dreams is to try always to think critically and to question the media's messages.

Children and teens may be more vulnerable to the media since they can more easily be caught up in dreams that are for sale, not having the experience and analytical thinking skills that some adults have. Furthermore, children, and you, may be strongly influenced by peer pressure. In the first article in this chapter, the "Decommercialization of Childhood," Juliet Schor analyzes the crucial impact that materialistic dreams can have on young people. She writes about her research, which confirms the problems that growing materialism has both on children and their parents. A parent herself, she knows about resisting the desire to give in to materialistic choices for her children. Her research shows very strongly that parents who spend more time in activity-centered experiences with their children have healthier youngsters who are less addicted to the latest toy or other brand-name product. Have we as parents or children given it to the media's propaganda and stopped believing as firmly in the value of being a family-centered community? Another issue that touches children and youth deeply is presented in "Seeing by Starlight" by Carlin Flora, an editor for *Psychology Today,* who examines recent research by social scientists that indicates how not only the images but also the person-alities of celebrities are internalized by the media audience, who come to mistake celebrities as being a part of their extended family or friendship group. Young people too often see themselves reflected in the models and stars seen in commercials, films, and television shows and often try to model their choices in clothing and lifestyles after those media images.

The impact of media violence is another higly controversial issue. To what extent does the witnessing of countless violent acts on tele-vision or in films, or the fantasy participation in such acts through vio-lent video games, have an effect on young people's tendency to accept or even participate in violence in real life? Eugene F. Provenzo, Jr. in "Impact of Interactive Violence on Children" presents evidence that shows how the many hours children and youths spend in imaginary games or chat groups, where one's real identity and values can be concealed, can easily affect their sense of reality and the natural world. How many hours do youth today spend in front of computers compared to the previous generation? How much time do young people today have to appreciate the natural world with its beauty, logic, and power? Henry Jenkins in "Education, Media, and Violence" argues against blaming the media and proposes a number of ways that children and adults can think critically and talk about the impact of popular culture. His emphasis is on problem solving and creativity rather than media censorship.

A real issue of concern is the deterioration of our environment and global warming. People can no longer deny the devastation that we have created through the abuse of natural resources. Philip Mattera presents an aspect of this issue in "Is Corporate Greenwashing headed for a Fall?" This article discusses the ways that big corporations have acted in a socially irresponsible way by couching their materialistic goals in advertised promises of a "greener future." An implication of Mattera's research is the necessity of making all types of corporations, from those that regulate transportation, education, and health care to entertainment and food production, socially responsible to their customers and to the sustainability of a healthy world.

Two essays comment on the impact of popular music on the choices young people make. Jonathan Cusick in "Do Benefit Concerts Affect Political Decisions?" suggests that musicians as well as politicians may have the power to improve the quality and equality of our lives. Anne Ritchie's essay "Creativity, Drugs, and Rock 'n' Roll" disputes the misconception that musicians are more creative when high, Ritchie provides convincing research on the potential of musicians and their music either to encourage drug use or to empower the public to support values that are socially responsible.

Another essay, appearing just before Anne Richie's, offers a contrast on how popular programs developed for the computer have affected people's ways of communicating and their identities. In "Second Life: Why?" Mark Stephen Meadows raises the real possibility of people becoming more identified with their avatar personalities and lives than the ones that they have in the real world.

Despite the negative impact of many pop dreams, we can shape a future where the technological advances and psychological insights of our new century can make our lives and dreams more vital and rewarding while making communication, education, and quality of life more equal.

RESEARCH WRITING

More so than any other type of writing, the research paper is a journey outward, into the worlds of many other writers past and present who have articulated their thoughts and views on a subject of public interest. The challenge in developing a research paper is in the synthesizing and harmonizing of diverse voices that you encounter and respond to in the course of your research. At the same time, you need to intersperse your own perspective, arguments, and conclusions. This writing process, if successful, can lead to a document that is clearly your own yet properly introduces and fairly credits the ideas and language of your sources.

The new skills needed to integrate and document facts and a variety of intellectual perspectives often overwhelm students as they begin a research paper. To minimize your anxiety, try to maintain a balance between your curious and creative self and your logical and rational self. The steps that follow will provide your rational side with a map to keep you on the main trail, but don't forget to allow your curious and creative mind to explore the many side paths and research possibilities that you will discover as you compose your paper. Above all, start early and pace yourself. A research paper needs to be completed in stages; it takes time to gather, to absorb, and to develop a response to the materials that will be incorporated into your paper.

For many students, being assigned a research paper raises a number of practical questions and issues: "How many sources will I be expected to use?" "What procedure should I follow in taking notes and doing a bibliography?" "How does the computer in the library catalog information?" "How can I access and evaluate information on the Internet?" While these concerns are essential parts of the research paper-writing process, in this text we do not discuss specific techniques of finding, quoting, and documenting source information in the library or on the World Wide Web because these issues are thoroughly covered in most standard writing handbooks. Librarians are also available and willing to help you with your research. We will discuss the process involved in producing a research paper and the importance of maintaining a sense of voice and control over the information and point of view that you are presenting.

Research is more than a catalog of interesting facts and quotations; it also helps writers understand and evaluate their own perspectives and see their topic in relationship to their personal values and to broader issues. Professional writers naturally turn to outside sources to deepen their own personal perspective and to better inform and engage their readers. Because their writing is thoughtfully constructed and thoroughly revised, their source material becomes an integral part of their writer's voice and stance. What was originally the result of research doesn't sound strained, dry, or tacked-on, even though the writers may have used numerous brief quotations and paraphrases of their source material.

While it is natural to think about how your paper will be evaluated, it is more important to remain curious and to enjoy the process of discovering your sources and learning about your subject. It is helpful to keep a regular log of your process, making journal entries as you move through each stage and gather new insights and new understanding about how your mind works under the pressure of research paper deadlines.

Finding a Topic

Spend some time exploring possible topics for your paper. Writing brief summaries of several different topics may help you to decide on the topic that interests you most. The best research papers are produced by students who are thoroughly engaged in their topic and in communicating what they have learned. Their enthusiasm and intellectual interests help them to work through the inevitable frustrations associated with learning how to use a library and tracking down information that may not be easily available.

After you complete some preliminary research, reevaluate and narrow your general topic further, if necessary, so that it can be covered within the scope and limits of the assignment. Notice, for instance, how in her essay in this chapter, Anne Ritchie has narrowed the focus of her essay from the general topic of sex, drugs, and rock-and-roll. She focuses the scope by choosing to examine only the impact of drugs on creativity. She made her paper more manageable by focusing on a particular topic—one that she was concerned and knowledgeable about.

Timetable and Process

Make a timetable for your project and follow it. For example, you might allow yourself two to three weeks to do research and to establish a working bibliography. Then schedule several work sessions to write the first draft and several more days to complete your research and revise the draft, complete the final draft, check your documentation, and do the final proofreading. At every stage in this process, you should seek out as much useful feedback and advice as you possibly can. Tell your family and friends about your topic; they may have ideas about where to find sources. Read your first draft to your friends, and give your teacher a copy. Make sure that your readers clearly understand your paper's purpose and that your writing holds their interest. Don't feel discouraged if you find that you need to do several revisions to clarify your ideas. This is a natural part of the research paper-writing process.

Your Voice and the Voices of Your Sources

Practice careful reading and accurate note-taking as you prepare to write your paper. To avoid becoming bored or overwhelmed by the sources you are working with, treat them as outside voices, as people you want to have a dialogue with. Take every quotation you intend to use in your paper and paraphrase it carefully into your own language to make sure that you really understand it. If you feel confused or intimidated by a source, freewriting may help you to get in touch with your feelings and responses to the authority. Are the assertions of this authority correct, or do your experiences suggest that some comments are questionable? In our study questions throughout this text, we've created models of questions you can ask as you analyze a text. Now it is time for you to begin posing and answering your own questions about your text sources. Undigested sources often produce a glorified book report, a rehash of ideas that you have not fully absorbed and integrated with your own point of view. For further information on evaluating sources and the facts they present, both from print media and from electronic media such as Web sites, newsgroups, and listservs, see the section on argument in Chapter 7 of *Dreams and Inward Journeys* and any of a number of recent texts and Web sites.

Purpose and Structure

Always keep focused on the purpose and structure in your essay. Your research paper should express an original central purpose and have a compelling thesis. Each major idea must be introduced by a clear topic sentence and supported by evidence and examples. While using an outline is very helpful, feel free to revise the outline as you do further research and make changes in your original perspective. A research paper brings together many different ideas into a unified, original vision of a subject that, as the writer, only you can provide.

Language and Style

As you write your first draft, and particularly as you work through later stages of the paper, continue to express your own writer's voice. Your point of view should be communicated in language with which you are comfortable. Your voice should always be your paper's guide. Read your paper aloud periodically. Is it tedious to listen to? Is it interesting? Do you sound like yourself in this essay? Check your vocabulary and compare it with the sense of language in your previous papers. Are you using more multisyllabic words than usual or a specialized jargon that even you can hardly understand, one that is too derivative of your sources? Are your sentences more convoluted than usual? Have you lost touch with your own personal voice? Consider the answers to all of these questions. Make sure that your paper reflects your point of view. Remember that your sources are supporting what you think and believe.

The Computer as a Research Partner

Whether you work on a computer at home or use the computers in your library's resource center, please consider the advantage of using a computer at all stages of your research-writing process. The Internet can help you to identify and refine topics; you also should keep a record of your writing timetable and progress on your computer files. It is helpful to gather and store information from different sources on the computer to save the time of copying information. When it comes time to draft your research paper, you can just start writing and integrating the information you have already saved, moving major portions of the paper around. Fine editing is done more efficiently with the use of a computer. There are computer programs that allow you to search hundreds of libraries and databases and that can help you format your data into different bibliographic styles. As we write this text, more and more new ways to access information for your research paper are being made available.

Writing a research paper is a challenge that provides you with the opportunity to develop, utilize, and integrate your research and writing skills as well as your creativity. A well-written research paper is a genuine accomplishment, a milestone on your inward journey.

Juliet B. Schor

Decommercialization of Childhood

Juliet B. Schor earned her B.A. at Wesleyan University and her Ph.D. in economics from the University of Massachusetts. She taught at Harvard for nine years before joining the faculty at Boston College as a Professor of Sociology. She is best known for her research and writings about family, women's issues, and economic justice. Schor has published articles in Business Week, *the* New York Times, *and the* Boston Globe. *Her books reflect her interest in overworked Americans and the effect of their materialism on family life and society:* The Overworked American *(1993), and* The Overspent American *(1999) are widely read. In the excerpt that follows from her recent book,* Born to Buy: The Commercialized Child and the New Consumer Culture *(2004), Schor argues that parents must help free their children from the culture of consumption, advertising, and the electronic media.*

JOURNAL

Do you think that children and young people have become too involved in material possessions? Provide examples.

Today's most sophisticated children's marketers operate by insinuating themselves into existing social dynamics. They have nuanced understandings of how peer pressure operates; identify trendsetters, influencers, and followers; and target each group with tailored approaches. Fifty-eight percent of nine to fourteen year olds now say that they feel pressure to buy stuff in order to fit in. In addition to the onus of acquiring particular consumer items, social pressures surrounding media content and personal style are of great concern to parents. At what age should kids be permitted to see PG-13 or R movies, use instant messaging, surf the Internet, or get a tattoo? Industry helps popularize these activities.

The more that market-driven trends structure peer interactions, parental restrictions put kids at risk for social exclusion. But basing decisions about what to allow on the basis of other kids' or parents' choices may mean losing control altogether. It's one of the trickiest aspects of parenting today.

The cooperative solution entails adults' and kids' getting together to set limits jointly. This reduces the pressure on kids and keeps the standards from changing more than individuals want. Such collaboration is already occurring with drug and alcohol use, commodities most adults feel should be absolutely forbidden. Around the country, parents have formed Communities of Concern and signed the Safe Homes Pledge, promising that they will supervise gatherings at their home to prohibit minors from using alcohol, drugs, or firearms. The community comes together to create structures that ease the peer pressures on kids and protect them from danger.

A related approach is possible for other consumer practices that involve peer pressure. A first step is community dialogue. Schools and PTAs can sponsor conversations and workshops on topics such as movie ratings, media use, video games, school fashion, spending money—even the customs surrounding birthday parties. As communities come together to work through their attitudes, awareness is created, and common approaches can develop. Sometimes the simple fact of airing a topic contributes to changes in social practices and norms. If the dialogue progresses to the point where people feel more formal action is useful, analogues to the Safe Homes Pledge can be developed. Formalization helps socialize newcomers and maintains standards over time.

5   Smaller-scale cooperation can also be effective. In my research in Doxley, I found that mothers communicate to control consumption choices. Some call before sleepovers to find out what video the kids will be watching. Those who restrict certain types of content make their rules known. Mothers caucus about group dates to the movies. They confer about the acceptability of particular CDs. In some cases, they talk through options and take common responsibility. Occasionally one agrees to play bad cop. The larger point is that to raise children well, adults need to communicate and cooperate and establish safe and healthy environments for them. It's an old-fashioned value that's being lost as neighborhood interaction and community has declined. We owe it to our kids to get it back.

Decommercializing the Household: Evidence from Doxley

Many parents are uncomfortable with aspects of consumer culture. The parents I interviewed in Doxley certainly were, although their likes and dislikes, as well as their rationales, varied widely, from the aesthetic to the practical. Some hate television because its content is junky. Some feel that designer labels aren't good value, and others object to trendiness itself. They worry about sex on the Internet, media violence, adult themes in movies, and excessive attraction to video games. Their attitudes are rather typically middle class, an issue I discuss in some detail in the endnote to this paragraph.

Where the families may be less typical is in their success at controlling and limiting those parts of consumer culture that they object to. Granted, they were mostly financially secure and could afford high levels of maternal involvement. They didn't need television as a baby-sitter. But more than economics is at work. Those who were most successful were thoughtful and consistent in their rules and choices. They spent a lot of time with their children. And perhaps most important, these families' lives were full of engaging alternatives to the corporate offerings.

One perhaps unsurprising finding is the importance of restricting television viewing. My data showed that kids in Doxley watch relatively little television. Virtually every household I interviewed had rules about when, how much, and what kids could watch. Some allowed only minimal viewing. Many opted not to get cable. The restrictions appeared to be relatively effective, in contrast to other research findings with a less affluent sample, among whom there were fewer nonemployed mothers. (See the accompanying note for a fuller discussion of this issue.) In Doxley, the keys to success appeared to be consistency, rules tailored to the needs of individual children, and heavy time commitments to homework, sports, extracurricular activities, and outdoor play.

None of the parents I interviewed prohibited television altogether, but some came close. Their experiences are notable because they contradict widely held views that children need TV. One argument is that prohibiting television will backfire, and children will become avid viewers once parents relinquish control. A second is that children need television knowledge to prevent social exclusion. Some media scholars have also argued that the dominance of electronic media is so strong that prohibition deprives children of basic cultural literacy. The absence of these problems in the households I visited was notable, even allowing for the fact that Doxley is a low-viewing environment.

10   My own experience also supports this view. After our first child was born, we decided not to expose him to television, reasoning that he'd eventually become well versed in electronic media, but that love of reading and the

dying print culture would be more difficult to instill. When people challenged me on this policy, as many did, I responded that we would let him watch television when he started asking for it. I agreed with the common view that we were at risk of forbidden-fruit syndrome if we were too rigid. But a funny thing happened: he never asked. We told him that we didn't think television was good for him, and he accepted that. When he entered first grade, we started watching videos sometimes. He's twelve now, and we do allow occasional viewing of sporting events. We've followed the same policies with our daughter. She doesn't ask either.

I include my story because things turned out so differently than I had expected. A decade ago, I put much more stock in the counterarguments, such as the view that kids need television knowledge to fit in socially and that only by allowing television can parents prevent children from wanting it too much. In my case, neither of these sentiments turned out to be correct. I believe my children have been much better off growing up TV free. I think it's enhanced their creativity, taught them how to amuse themselves, and given them many more hours of beneficial and more satisfying activities such as reading, writing poetry, doing art projects, and getting exercise. Of course, to be successful in restricting television for our kids we had to stop watching it ourselves. So we put our set in a third-floor room, where the temperature is uncomfortable in both winter and summer. Instead of creating a special child-only deprivation, we changed the environment in which we all live. And we're all better for it.

My interview material also suggests that the families who are most successful in keeping the corporate culture at bay are involved with alternatives. Some of the most restrictive mothers are active in their churches. Some of the immigrant families, who tend to be rather strict about commercial influences, come together in each other's homes for regular worship and socializing. I encountered a variety of nonreligious activities as well. One woman started a mother-daughter book club, with discussion of the book and an activity. One household had family movie nights, with row seating, ushers, and popcorn. Another specialized in elaborate but low budget theme parties—Greek mythology, insects, Peter Pan, and Eskimos (complete with a full-scale igloo). Other popular activities were woodworking, playing board games after school, and unorganized sports. The activities they described typically involved parents and kids together. One family makes a yearly pilgrimage to a mine to collect rocks, another took the kids out of school for nearly a year of travel, a third are avid canoeists and campers. These experiences jibe with anecdotal evidence from the downshifter movement, which suggests that many families are rediscovering simple, inexpensive pleasures. Eco-psychologists have also found that disconnection from nature erodes emotional and spiritual well-being. Fostering children's connection to the outdoors serves as a bulwark against excessive involvement with consumer culture.

These kinds of activities require time and energy. My earlier book addressed the inadequacy of free time and the mounting financial pressures on families. Scarcity of time and money is especially acute among low-income and single-parent households, whose members usually have long hours and inflexible jobs, ever-present financial worries, and high-stress lives. But reducing stress and finding time are crucial to engaging with kids in less commercial ways. National survey data suggest that children wish for more of that from their parents, and noncommercial activities remain popular. For example, in their 2003 poll of kids aged nine to fourteen, the Center for a New American Dream found that fewer than a third (32 percent) reported that they spend a lot of time with their parents. Sixty-nine percent of kids said they'd like to spend more time with them, and if granted one wish that would change their parents' job, 63 percent said it would be a job that gave them "more time to do fun things together." Only 13 percent wished their parents made more money. When asked what they would most like to do with their parents, 23 percent chose the three noncommercial outdoor activities offered: building a snow man or a tree house, riding bikes or doing something outside, and gardening. Twenty percent opted for a movie, 18 percent for a ball game, and 13 percent wanted a visit to a zoo or aquarium.

Reducing corporate influences does not entail exorcising money from children's lives. The ideology of childhood sacredness and innocence is frequently counterposed against the profane adult world of money and desire. The moral panic surrounding Pokémon trading cards, and to a lesser extent Beanie Babies and sport cards, revealed the pervasiveness of attitudes that children's play should be motivated by love of the objects themselves rather than acquisitive or speculative desires. Such an attitude pervades the position of the anticommercial Motherhood Project: "We face a conflict of values . . . between the values of the money world and the values of the 'motherworld'—the values of commerce and the values required to raise healthy children."

15   While restricting children from the profanity of the money world has a Superficial appeal, such sacralization unduly deprives children of their fight to be economic agents. Recent ethnographic research shows that children are typically engaged in a variety of productive practices—not only trading cards and toys but also participated in lunchtime food swaps, networks of reciprocal favors, and informal entrepreneurial activities. Indeed, children have far more sophisticated and extensive economic lives than many adults give them credit for. Why should they be deprived of these?

I do not raise this point merely for academic purposes. It is important because it makes a distinction between economic activity per se and the contemporary capitalist marketplace. Big businesses rather than a generic world of money are the forces that children need to be protected from.

In Doxley, I was impressed with how parents were teaching their children to handle money. Most families used allowance systems, and many required that children devote a portion of their allowances to charity or savings, or both. Allowances were also used to teach children the difference between needs and wants and to help them budget for things they wanted. Often kids could save up for items the parents didn't want to buy but wouldn't necessarily forbid, such as video game systems or expensive CD players. Parents developed thoughtful schemes about what they would and would not pay for. Many worried about excessive materialism and tried to teach the value of money by letting the kids manage it. Overall, attitudes toward these money matters were practical, respectful of children's skills and decision-making abilities, and founded on values of balance and prudence. At least among the families I interviewed, the kids were learning valuable lessons about the world of commerce rather than being excluded from it.

I end with an obvious but important point. Parents who are interested in reducing the influence of commercial culture on their children need to walk their talk, especially as children age. Preaching against expensive athletic shoes isn't credible with a closet full of Manolo Blahnik shoes. Restricting television is much harder in households where parents watch a lot. Surveys show that highly materialist kids are more likely to have highly materialist parents. And highly materialist parents are likely to have kids with similar priorities. To transmit values effectively, you need to live them. Parents who desire less commercial lifestyles for their children need to change with them.

Join the Movement to Oppose Corporate-Constructed Childhood

The legislative, cultural, and social changes I have been discussing will be realized only if enough people organize to make them happen. A growing number of groups have begun that work, among them Commercial Alert, Stop the Commercial Exploitation of Children, Obligation Inc., the Center for the Analysis of Commercialism in Education, the Center for Media Education, and the Center for a New American Dream. There are many others. National groups include Daughters and Dads, the Media Education Foundation, Teachers Resisting Unhealthy Children's Entertainment (TRUCE), the New Mexico Media Literacy Project, TV Turn-Off Network, the Alliance for Childhood, and the Motherhood Project. There are numerous local groups, many working on school-related commercialization. (I have put contact information for these organizations in Appendix B.)

20   Although these groups are vastly outmatched in terms of money and personnel, they have managed some impressive successes, especially recently. Daughters and Dads has taken action against offensive commercials, such as a Campbell's soup ad that promoted the product as a diet

aid for young girls. The company pulled the ad. In 2002, Scholastic re-scinded its sponsorship of the Golden Marble awards for the best children's commercials after a coalition of children's advocates questioned the very fact of targeting kids in its "Have you lost your marbles?" counter-awards. Thousands of communities around the country participate in TV Turn-OffWeek. Anticommercialism efforts have made their way into state legislatures and in California led to the passage of two bills. As the public becomes educated about what's going on, it's easier to mobilize support for restricting corporate practices.

The worlds of adults and children are merging. In my mind, that's mainly a good thing. But the commercial aspects of that integration are not working for children. The prevalence of harmful and addictive products, the imperative to keep up, and the growth of materialist attitudes are harming kids. If we are honest with ourselves, adults will admit that we are suffering from many of the same influences. That means our task should be to make the world a safer and more life-affirming place for everyone. Reversing corporate-constructed childhood is a good first step.

QUESTIONS FOR DISCUSSION

1. Why is Schor so concerned about how the media and materialism have infiltrated the homes and schools of young people all over the world? Give examples of children and youth who are addicted to toys, clothes, media games, and computers.
2. What does Schor think is "one of the trickiest aspects of parenting today"? According to Schor's research what types of parents are most successful at limiting their children's dependence on consumption, the Internet, and computer games?
3. Do you think that Schor is completely realistic in thinking that children and youth can be separated from our culture of consumption? Why or why not?
4. How has raising her children affected Schor's thoughts about the extensive infiltration of materialization in our culture?
5. What is more convincing to you: research about materialism, or what you experienced raising your children and being aware of the materialism around you and in your own life? What does each approach add to the strength of an argument?
6. Do you have any suggestions for decommercializing childhood and the teenage years?

CONNECTION

Compare how Schor's essay confronts commercial culture and it's youth impact with the solutions Jenkins offers in his essay in this chapter (see page 442).

IDEAS FOR WRITING

1. Write an essay that develops several negative outcomes of the commercialization of childhood and also positive aspects of the materialization of childhood. Do some research as well as writing from your own experiences.
2. Write an essay that proposes and explains your own solutions (two or three) to controlling the negative effects of our commercialized technological culture.

RELATED WEB SITES

Materialism
`www.allaboutphilosophy.org/Materialism.htm`
This Website presents various perspectives on materialism: philosophical, Biblical, and cultural. Find related articles on American materialism, its consequences, and its impact on society.

National Institute for Media and the Family
`www.mediafamily.org/about/index.shtml`
This Website and its MediaWise programs provide speakers, parent guides, news bulletins, a parent-centered blog, and videos designed to help parents understand how media culture changes the way children learn and who they become, and how parents can intervene positively by monitoring children's media exposure in the home and elsewhere.

Carlin Flora

Seeing by Starlight

An editor and longtime writer for Psychology Today, *Carlin Flora has published many articles over the years on subjects including alternative therapies, memory, indoctrination and brainwashing, marriage and family life, women in the workplace, consumerism, religion, music, psychotropic drugs, obsession, schizophrenia, bipolar disorder, and the narcissistic personality. The essay we have included here, "Seeing by Starlight" (2004), is one of several articles Flora has written that examine the causes and effects of our obsession with celebrities and their lifestyles. Notice how she includes research findings from a variety of social scientists to support her arguments.*

JOURNAL

Write about why people are so fascinated by celebrities. Do you find celebrities intriguing? Why or why not?

Acouple of years ago, Britney Spears and her entourage swept through my boss's office. As she sashayed past, I blushed and stammered and leaned over my desk to shake her hand. She looked right into my eyes and smiled her pageant smile, and I confess, I felt dizzy. I immediately rang up friends to report my celebrity encounter, saying: "She had on a gorgeous, floor-length white fur coat! Her skin was blotchy!" I've never been much of a Britney fan, so why the contact high? Why should I care? For that matter, why should any of us? Celebrities are fascinating because they live in a parallel universe—one that looks and feels just like ours yet is light-years beyond our reach. Stars cry to Diane Sawyer about their problems—failed marriages, hardscrabble upbringings, bad career decisions—and we can relate. The paparazzi catch them in wet hair and a stained T-shirt, and we're thrilled. They're ordinary folks, just like us. And yet . . .

Stars live in another world entirely, one that makes our lives seem woefully dull by comparison. The teary chat with Diane quickly turns to the subject of a recent $10 million film fee and honorary United Nations ambassadorship. The magazines that specialize in gotcha snapshots of schleppy-looking celebs also feature Cameron Diaz wrapped in a $15,000 couture gown and glowing with youth, money and star power. We're left hanging—and we want more.

It's easy to blame the media for this cognitive whiplash. But the real celebrity spinmeister is our own mind, which tricks us into believing the stars are our lovers and our social intimates. Celebrity culture plays to all of our innate tendencies: We're built to view anyone we recognize as an acquaintance ripe for gossip or for romance, hence our powerful interest in Anna Kournikova's sex life. Since catching sight of a beautiful face bathes the brain in pleasing chemicals, George Clooney's killer smile is impossible to ignore. But when celebrities are both our intimate daily companions and as distant as the heavens above, it's hard to know just how to think of them. Reality TV further confuses the picture by transforming ordinary folk into bold-faced names without warning. Even celebrities themselves are not immune to celebrity watching: Magazines print pictures of Demi Moore and "Bachelorette" Trista Rehn reading the very same gossip magazines that stalk them. "Most pushers are users, don't you think?" says top Hollywood publicist Michael Levine. "And, by the way, it's not the worst thing in the world to do."

Celebrities tap into powerful motivational systems designed to foster romantic love and to urge us to find a mate. Stars summon our most human yearnings: to love, admire, copy and, of course, to gossip and to jeer. It's only natural that we get pulled into their gravitational field.

Exclusive: Fan's Brain Transformed by Celebrity Power!

5   John Lennon infuriated the faithful when he said the Beatles were more popular than Jesus, but he wasn't the first to suggest that celebrity culture was taking the place of religion. With its myths, its rituals (the red carpet walk, the Super Bowl ring, the handprints outside Grauman's Chinese Theater) and its ability to immortalize, it fills a similar cultural niche. In a secular society our need for ritualized idol worship can be displaced onto stars, speculates psychologist James Houran, formerly of the Southern Illinois University School of Medicine and now director of psychological studies for True Beginnings dating service. Nonreligious people tend to be more interested in celebrity culture, he's found, and Houran speculates that for them, celebrity fills some of the same roles the church fills for believers, like the desire to admire the powerful and the drive to fit into a community of people with shared values. Leo Braudy, author of *The Frenzy of Renown: Fame and Its History,* suggests that celebrities are more like Christian calendar saints than like spiritual authorities (Tiger Woods, patron saint of arriviste golfers; or Jimmy Carter, protector of down-home liberal farmers?). "Celebrities have their aura—a debased version of charisma" that stems from their all-powerful captivating presence, Braudy says.

Much like spiritual guidance, celebrity-watching can be inspiring, or at least help us muster the will to tackle our own problems. "Celebrities motivate us to make it," says Helen Fisher, an anthropologist at Rutgers University in New Jersey. Oprah Winfrey suffered through poverty, sexual abuse and racial discrimination to become the wealthiest woman in media. Lance Armstrong survived advanced testicular cancer and went on to win the Tour de France five times. Star-watching can also simply point the way to a grander, more dramatic way of living, publicist Levine says. "We live lives more dedicated to safety or quiet desperation, and we transcend this by connecting with bigger lives—those of the stars," he says. "We're afraid to eat that fatty muffin, but Ozzy Osborne isn't."

Don't I know you?! Celebrities are also common currency in our socially fractured world. Depressed college coeds and laid-off factory workers both spend hours watching Anna Nicole Smith on late night television; Mexican villagers trade theories with hometown friends about who killed rapper Tupac Shakur; and Liberian and German businessmen critique David Beckham's plays before hammering out deals. My friend Britney Spears was, in fact, last year's top international Internet search.

In our global village, the best targets for gossip are the faces we all know. We are born to dish dirt, evolutionary psychologists agree; it's the most efficient way to navigate society and to determine who is trustworthy. They also point out that when our brains evolved, anybody with a familiar face was an "in-group" member, a person whose alliances and enmities were important to keep track of.

Things have changed somewhat since life in the Pleistocene era, but our neural hardwiring hasn't, so on some deeper level, we may think NBC's *Friends* really are our friends. Many of us have had the celebrity-sighting mishap of mistaking a minor star—a local weatherman, say, or a bit-part soap opera actor—for an acquaintance or former schoolmate. Braudy's favorite example of this mistake: In one episode of the cartoon show *King of the Hill,* a character meets former Texas Governor Ann Richards. "You probably know me," he says. "I've seen you on TV." That's also why we don't get bored by star gossip, says Bonnie Fuller, editorial director of American Media, which publishes *Star* and *The Enquirer:* "That would be like getting bored with information about family and friends!"

10   The brain simply doesn't realize that it's being fooled by TV and movies, says sociologist Satoshi Kanazawa, lecturer at the London School of Economics. "Hundreds of thousands of years ago, it was impossible for someone not to know you if you knew them. And if they didn't kill you, they were probably your friend." Kanazawa's research has shown that this feeling of friendship has other repercussions: People who watch more TV are more satisfied with their friendships, just as if they had more friends and socialized more frequently. Another study found that teens who keep up to date on celebrity gossip are popular, with strong social networks—the interest in pop culture indicates a healthy drive for independence from parents.

The penchant for gossiping about the stars also plays into our species' obsession with status. Humans naturally copy techniques from high-status individuals, says Francisco Gil-White, professor of psychology at University of Pennsylvania. It's an attempt to get the same rewards, whether that's "attention, favors, gifts, [or] laudatory exclamations." Stars get all kinds of perks and pampering: Sarah Jessica Parker was allowed to keep each of her *Sex in the City* character's extravagant getups; Halle Berry borrowed a $3 million diamond ring to wear to the Oscars. Understandably, we look to get in on the game.

The impulse to copy is behind the popularity of celebrity magazines, says Fuller. Regular women can see what the stars are wearing, often with tips on how to buy cheap knockoffs of their outfits. Taken to extremes—which television is only too happy to do—the urge to copy produces spectacles like the MTV reality show *I Want a Famous Face*. By dint of extensive plastic surgery, ordinary people are made to look more like their famous heroes. In one episode, two gangly 20-year-old twin brothers are molded into Brad Pitt look-alikes. The brothers want to be stars, and they've decided that looking more like Pitt is the fastest road to fame. No wonder makeover shows are so popular, points out Joshua Gamson, an associate professor of sociology at the University of San Francisco. These shows offer drab nobodies a double whammy: simultaneous beauty and celebrity.

The most fascinating measure of status is, of course, sex. "We want to know who is mating with whom," says Douglas Kenrick, professor of psychology at Arizona State University. He speculates that we look to stars to evaluate our own sexual behavior and ethics, and mistake them unconsciously for members of our prospective mating pool. Given this me-too drive to imitate and adore, why are celebrity flame-outs and meltdowns so fascinating? Even though we love to hear about the lavish rewards of fame—remember *Lifestyles of the Rich and Famous?*—we're quick to judge when stars behave too outrageously or live too extravagantly. We suspect some stars are enjoying society's highest rewards without really deserving them, says University of Liverpool anthropologist Robin Dunbar, so we monitor their behavior. "We need to keep an eye on the great-and-the-good because they create a sense of community for us, but also because we need to make sure that they are holding to their side of the bargain."

Diva Alert: Beauty Isn't Everything (Being Nice Helps!)

The beauty bias is well-known. We all pay more attention to good-looking people. Kenrick's eye-tracking research has shown that both men and women spend more time looking at beautiful women than at less attractive women. Babies as young as 8-months-old will stare at an attractive female face of any race longer than they will at an average-looking or unattractive female face. Certain human traits are universally recognized as beautiful: symmetry, regularity in the shape and size of the features, smooth skin, big eyes and thick lips, and an hourglass figure that indicates fertility. Men interpret these features as evidence of health and reproductive fitness. Women's responses are more complex, says psychologist and Harvard Medical School instructor Nancy Etcoff, author of *Survival of the Prettiest*. Women stare at beautiful female faces out of aesthetic appreciation, to look for potential tips—and because a beautiful woman could be a rival worth monitoring.

It's not surprising that gorgeous people wind up famous. What's less obvious is that famous people often wind up gorgeous: The more we see a certain face, the more our brain likes it, whether or not it's actually beautiful. Thanks to what is known as "the exposure effect," says James Bailey, a psychologist at George Washington University, the pleasurable biological cascade that is set off when we see a certain celebrity "begins to wear a neurochemical groove," making her image easier for our brains to process. It begins to explain why Jennifer Aniston—not exactly a classic cover girl—was again named one of *People* magazine's 50 "most beautiful" in the world this year.

15   On the flip side, celebrity overload—let's call it the J.Lo effect—can leave us all thoroughly sick of even the most beautiful celeb. With the

constant deluge of celebrity coverage, says Etcoff, "they at first become more appealing because they are familiar, but then the ubiquity becomes tedious. That is why the stars who reign the longest—Madonna is the best example—are always changing their appearance." Every time Madonna reconfigures her look, she resets our responses back to when her face was recognizable but still surprising.

Just as in pageants, personality plays a part in the beauty contest, too. State University of New York at Binghamton psychology professors Kevin Kniffin and David Sloan Wilson have found that people's perceptions of physical appeal are strongly influenced by familiarity and likeability. "Almost all of the beauty research is based on subjects looking at strangers in photos or computer-generated images—but we don't live in a world of strangers!" Kniffin points out.

In one of Kniffin's experiments, students worked on an archeological dig together toward a shared goal. Those who were deemed cooperative and likable were rated as more attractive after the project was finished than they were at the outset. Conversely, students who were not as hard-working were rated as less attractive after the chore was done.

Kniffin believes this same mechanism is at work in our feelings toward celebrities, who rank somewhere between strangers and intimates. Athletes are an obvious example: Team spirit gives even ugly guys a boost. NBA great Wilt Chamberlain might have been a bit goofy-looking, but his astonishing abilities to propel his team to victory meant that he was a hero, surrounded with adoring—and amorous—fans. Kniffin points to William Hung, the talent-free and homely also-ran on the contest show *American Idol,* as evidence of his theory at work. In part because of his enthusiasm and his good-natured willingness to put up with ridicule, Hung became a bigger star after he was kicked off the show: His album, *Inspiration,* sold more than 37,000 copies in its first week. "William doesn't display the traits of universal attractiveness, but people who have seen the show would probably rate him as more attractive because of nonphysical traits of likeability and courage. He's even received some marriage proposals." Kniffin's theory also explains why models are less compelling objects of fascination than actresses or pop stars. They're beautiful, but they're enigmatic: We rarely get any sense of their personalities.

Saved from Oblivion!

What's the result of our simultaneous yearning to be more like celebrities and our desire to be wowed by their unattainable perfection? We've been watching it for the past decade. Reality television is an express train to fame, unpredictably turning nobodies into somebodies. Reality TV now gives us the ability to get inside the star factory and watch the transition to fame in real time.

20   "The appeal of reality stars is that they were possibly once just like you, sitting on the couch watching a reality TV program, until they leaped to celebrity," says Andy Denhart, blogger and reality TV junkie. "With the number of reality shows out there, it's inexcusable to not be famous if you want to be!" In the past, ambitious young men who idolized a famous actor might take acting lessons or learn to dance. Now, they get plastic surgery and learn to tell their life stories for the camera. In fact, says editor Fuller, the newly minted stars of reality TV are better at the celebrity game than many of the movie and television stars: "They are more accessible, more cooperative. They enjoy publicity. They will open up and offer insight, often more than a 'traditional' celeb, because they want the attention, whereas an actress might have ambivalent feelings about fame and how it is tied in with her 'craft.'" At the same time, shows like *The Simple Life* and *The Newlyweds* (and amateur videotapes like Paris Hilton's) let us gawk at the silly things that stars do in the privacy of their own home. As a result, the distance between celebrity stratosphere and living room couch dwindles even further.

Yet there's still something about that magic dust. A celebrity sighting is not just about seeing a star, author Braudy points out, but is about being seen by a star: "There is a sense that celebrities are more real than we are; people feel more real in the presence of a celebrity." It wasn't just that I saw Britney, it was that Britney saw me.

QUESTIONS FOR DISCUSSION

1. In what sense do celebrities live in a "parallel universe," and why is this a source of their appeal? What examples does Flora give to clarify this concept? What is the "real celebrity spinmeister," according to Flora? Why do we believe that stars are our friends, even our lovers?

2. How does reality TV confuse us further about our relationship to celebrities? Why do these shows make it seem "inexcusable to not be famous if you want to be"? Do you agree?

3. How does celebrity culture fill a spiritual need for worship, community, and guidance? What examples and authorities does Flora present to clarify her ideas on this subject?

4. How is the brain "fooled by TV and movies"? Why do individuals who watch large amounts of television tend to feel "satisfied with their friendships"? Does this "satisfaction" seem healthy to you?

5. Why do celebrities inspire imitation? What is the "exposure effect," and how does it explain why celebrities appear more beautiful than they actually are?

6. What is the significance of the final sentence of the essay: "It wasn't just that I saw Britney, it was that Britney saw me"? How does this sentence refer back to the introduction of the essay and help to explain the "magic dust" of celebrity interaction?

CONNECTION

Compare and contrast the allure of celebrities presented in Flora's essay to positive use of celebrity seen in Cusick's essay (see page 456). How are these distinct responses to celebrities related?

IDEAS FOR WRITING

1. Write an analysis of a reality TV show that tries to create "instant celebrities" from its ordinary contestants. What is the source of popularity for this show? Make reference to Flora's article as well as your own experiences and those of your friends who have viewed the show.

2. Select one of the psychological effects that celebrities have on the public, according to one or more of the social scientists that Flora cites in her essay, and write an essay in which you evaluate their views based on your own reading and experience.

RELATED WEB SITES

Celebrity Links
www.celebrity-link.com
This giant celebrity links and photo Web site is ideal for studying the complex relationship between fans and celebrities. Contains links to many fan sites for particular celebrities, television shows, and bands.

Poppolitics
www.poppolitics.com
This thought-provoking Web site with a political outlook contains reviews, interviews, and in-depth criticism on celebrities, popular entertainment, and culture.

Eugene F. Provenzo, Jr.

The Impact of Interactive Violence on Children

Eugene F. Provenzo, Jr. (b. 1949) received a Ph.D. from the Graduate Institute of Education in the Philosophy and History of Education in 1976. He has taught social sciences at the secondary level and has been a full professor in the School of Education at the University of Miami, Coral Gables, Florida, since 1985. He is particularly concerned with the social and cultural aspects of education, with a special focus on the ways that computers influence children, culture, and education. His books include Video Kids: Making Sense of Nintendo, The Educator's Brief Guide to the Internet and the World Wide Web *(1998), and* Critical Literacy: What Every American Needs to Know *(2006). He is currently completing a new book entitled* Computing, Scholarship and Learning: The Transformation of American Higher Education. *Provenzo has testified twice before U.S. Senate committees related to the impact of violent video games: in 1993 and again in March of 2000 before the Senate Transportation and Commerce Committee on issues of children and violent interactive technology. The following selection is taken from his 2000 testimony.*

JOURNAL
_____

Do you think that violence on television, news stories, and video games plays a role in the escalating violence enacted by adolescence and youth? Why or why not?
_____

My comments this morning must be brief. Much of what I will discuss is found in a new book I am working on entitled *Children and Hyperreality: The Loss of the Real in Contemporary Childhood and Adolescence.* It continues a line of inquiry I began in 1991 with *Video Kids: Making Sense of Nintendo,* as well as in a number of articles and book chapters. In this work, I am arguing that children and teenagers are spending much of their time in simulations, rather than in the natural or "real" world. It is an argument, which if true, has serious implications for not only our children, but also for the future of our society. Essentially, I believe that the unreal, the simulation, the *simulacra* has been substituted for the real in the lives of our children. This occurs at many different levels: in the video games that are so much a part of the experience of contemporary childhood; in the shopping malls and "commercial civic spaces" where our children spend so much of their time; in television programs, advertisements and movies; in the theme parks where we vacation; in the online chat rooms and discussion programs through which we communicate and exchange information; and finally, in the images of beauty and sexuality that run as a powerful undercurrent through much of our culture and the lives of our children, game controller. The effect is one of literally stepping into the action of the game as a participant holding the weapon. Lieutentant Colonel David Grossman, a former Professor of Psychology at West Point, argues that first person shooter video games "are murder simulators which over time, teach a person how to look another person in the eye and snuff their life out."

Games like *Doom* are, in fact, used by military and police organization to train people. The Marine Corps, for example, has adapted *Doom* to train soldiers in the Corps. Some critics claim that there is little difference between what goes on in a first-person shooter and playing a game of Paintball, where players divide up on teams and hunt each other in a wood or elaborately constructed game room. To begin with, Paintball is acting that takes place in the real world. You run around a little, get tired and winded, bumped and scrapped. There are serious consequences for getting out of control as you play—in other words—the fact that the game is physical and tangible means that it has limits. These limits not only include your own endurance, but the rules and procedures followed by your fellow players.

In a first-person shooter like *Quake* there are no boundaries or limits. The more "extreme" you are (a terminology often used in describing the action of the games), the more likely you are to win. Paul Keegan explains that in John Romero's recently released first-person shooter game *Daikatana:*

> Physical reality suggests that you are sitting in a chair operating a mouse and a keyboard. But with the computer screen replacing your field of vision, you believe you're actually creeping around a corner, causing your breath to shorten. Afraid an enemy is lying in wait, you feel your pulse quicken. When the monster jumps out, real adrenaline roars through your body. And few things in life are more exhilarating than spinning around and blowing the damn things to kingdom come, the flying gibs so lifelike you can almost feel wet blood.

What is going on here is clearly different than just a game of Paintball or "Cowboys and Indians." However, the creators of first-person shooters just don't understand that there is a problem. John Carmack, the main creator of *Quake,* for example, considers the game nothing more than "playing Cowboys and Indians, except with visual effects."[5] In a recent interview, Carmack was reminded that in the past kids playing Cowboys and Indians weren't able to blow their brothers' heads off. His response was to laugh and say: "But you wished you could."

Keep in mind this important face: in first-person shooter games, players are not responsible for what they do. There are no consequences for other children, for families, or for society. As Mark Slouka explains in reference to the CD-ROM video game *Night Trap,* the game allows its players: "To inflict pain. Without responsibility. Without consequences. The punctured flesh will heal at the touch of a button, the scream disappear into cyberspace."

Games that employ a first-person shooter model represent a significant step beyond the tiny cartoon figures that were included in *Mortal Kombat* in the mid-1990s. In fact, there has been a continuous evolution of the realism of these games as computing power has increased and become cheaper. Much of this has to do with the enormous increase in computing power. A moderately fast desktop computer . . . that could be purchased for under $1,000 today has the speed of a $20 million Cray supercomputer from the mid-1980s.

Even more interesting is the availability of inexpensive game consoles. Sony's dominance of this market has recently been challenged by Sega's game machine. It will soon be superseded by Microsoft's X-Box, which is designed specifically for interactive gaming. . . . The X-Box will cost less than $500 and will allow players to go online to play games. The machine and the programs that will drive it represent what is potentially an extraordinary virtual reality simulator.

Larry Smarr, director of the National Center for Supercomputer Applications in Champaign-Urbana, Illinois, believes that systems like these represent "the transition from people playing video games to a world where we will create our own fantasies in cyberspace."

In many respects, the content of violent video games represents a giant social and educational experiment. Will these ultra violent games actually teach children to behave and view the world in markedly different ways? To repeat an earlier argument, video and computer games are, in fact, highly effective teaching machines. You learn the rules, play the game, get better at it, accumulate a higher score, and eventually win. As Mark Slouka argues, the implications of new technologies like video games "are social: the questions they pose, broadly ethical; the risks they entail, unprecedented. They are the cultural equivalent of genetic engineering, except that in this experiment, even more than the other one, we will be the potential new hybrids, the two-pound mice."

10   It is very possible, that the people killed in the last few years as the result of "school shootings" may in fact be the first victims/results of this experiment. If this is indeed the case, it is an experiment *we* need to stop at once. Some things are too dangerous to experiment with.

QUESTIONS FOR DISCUSSION

1. What is the focus of Provenzo's remarks to the Senate Committee on the "Impact of Interactive Violence on Children"? What is his opening thesis?

2. What activities does Provenzo list as detrimental to children and adolescents? How doe he support his claims?

3. How do you think the deaths of the students at Littleton High School are related to Klebold and Harris's obsession with interactive, violent video games? How did virtual reality video games motivate these youths to murder their classmates?

4. Why does Provenzo think that first person games such as "Quake" or "Doom" are more dangerous than earlier games that featured cartoon characters?

5. Why does Provenzo think that the availability and use of games with a first-person character will affect the future if not stopped?
6. Do you think that violent video games are as serious a problem as Provenzo does? Why or why not?

CONNECTION

Integrate what you think are the best ideas of Provenzo and Jenkins. On what might they agree (see page 442)?

IDEAS FOR WRITING

1. Write an argument that supports or refutes Provenzo's point of view. Do research and draw on your experiences to support your conclusions.
2. Write an imaginary dialogue between Jenkins and Provenzo that presents each one's point of view and develops a controversy on the issue.

RELATED WEB SITES

Media Violence, Video Game Violence, TV Violence, Movie Violence, Music Violence–Research and Reports
`www.commonsensemedia.org/resources/violence.php`
Common Sense Media provides links to all the latest research regarding mediaviolence. Also find archived stories relating to this topic.

Media Violence debates
`www.media-awareness.ca/english/issues/violence/`
`violence_debates.cfm`
The Media Awareness Network presents perspectives on the media violence debate. Viewpoints include media violence as art, as a public health issue, and as free speech.

Henry Jenkins

Education, Media, and Violence

Henry Jenkins III (b. 1958), professor of humanities and co-director of the MIT Comparative Media Studies program, earned his M.A. in Communication Studies from the University of Iowa and his Ph.D. in Communication Arts from the University of Wisconsin-Madison.

He views media culture as active and participatory, with a focus on what he terms "media convergence," which holds that fans/participants combine insights in a complex manner that could be termed reforming, creative, and political. He has explored these issues in his 2006 anthology, Fans, Bloggers, and Gamers: Exploring Participatory Culture, *as well as in his work with the Convergence Culture Consortium at MIT that led to his recent book Convergence Culture (2008). The selection below from his 1999 testimony before a Senate committee on the Littleton, Colorado school killings reveals some of Jenkins's ideas on the complex, participatory role of media in the culture of modern youth and argues against demonizing this culture as a result of recent acts of school violence.*

JOURNAL

Do you think parents need to take a stronger stance on the amount of media violence that their children are exposed to?

Media effects research typically starts from the assumption that we know what we mean by "media violence," that we can identify and count violent acts when we see them, that we can choose or construct a representative example of media violence and use it as the basis for a series of controlled experiments. Under most circumstances, our children don't experience violent images abstracted from social or narrative contexts. Exposing children to such concentrated doses of decontextualized violence focuses their attention on the violent acts and changes the emotional tone which surrounds them. Storytelling depends upon the construction of conflict; and in visual based media, conflict is often rendered visible by being staged through violence. Stories help to ascribe meaning to the violent acts they depict. When we hear a list of the sheer number of violent acts contained on an evening of American television, it feels overwhelming. But, each of these acts occurs in some kind of a context and we need to be attentive to the specifics of those various contexts. . . . Some works depict violence in order to challenge the culture that generates that violence; other works celebrate violence as an appropriate response to social humiliation or as a tool for restoring order in a violent and chaotic culture or as a vehicle of patriotism. Some works depict self-defense; others acts of aggression. Some make distinctions between morally justifiable and morally unjustifiable violence; some don't. We know this, of course, because we are all consumers of violent images. We read murder mysteries; we watch news reports; we enjoy war movies and westerns; we go to operas and read classic works of western literature. So many of the films, for example, which have been at the center of debates about media violence—*A Clockwork Orange, Pulp Fiction, Natural Born Killers, The Basketball Diaries,* and now *The Matrix*—are works that have provoked enormous critical debates because of their thematic and aesthetic complexity, because they seem to be trying to say something different about our contemporary social environment and they seem to be finding new images and new techniques for communicating their meanings. Depicting violence is certainly not the same thing as promoting violence. Cultural studies research tells us we need to make meaningful distinctions between different ways of representing violence, different kinds of stories about violence, and different kinds of relationships to violent imagery.

Media-effects research often makes little or no distinction between the different artistic conventions we use to represent violent acts. At its worst, media effects research makes no distinction between violent cartoons or video games that offer a fairly stylized representation of the world around us and representation of violence that are more realistic. Other researchers, however, show that children learn at an early age to make meaningful distinctions between different kinds of relationships between media images and the realm of their own lived experience. These studies suggest that children are fairly adept at dismissing works that represent fantastic, hyperbolic, or stylized violence and are more likely to be emotionally disturbed by works that represent realistic violence and especially images of violence in documentary films (predator-prey documentaries, war films) that can not be divorced from their real world referents. Such research would suggest that children are more likely to be disturbed by reports of violent crimes on the evening news than representations of violence in fictional works.

One of the most significant aspects of play is that play is divorced from real life. Play exists in a realm of fantasy that strips our actions of their everyday consequences or meanings. Classic studies of play behavior among primates, for example, suggest that apes make basic distinctions between play fighting and actual combat. In some circumstances, they seem to take pleasure wrestling and tousling with each other and in other contexts, they might rip each other apart in mortal combat. We do things in our fantasies that we would have no desire to do in real life, and this is especially true of fantasies that involve acts of violence. The pleasure of play stems at least in part from escapism. The appeal of video game violence often has more to do with feelings of empowerment than with the expression of aggressive or hurtful feelings. Our children feel put down by teachers and administrators, by kids on the playground; they feel like they occupy a very small space in the world and have very limited ability to shape reality according to their needs and desires. Playing video games allows them to play with power, to manipulate reality, to construct a world through their fantasies in which they are powerful and can exert control. The pleasure stems precisely from their recognition of the contrast between the media representations and the real world. It is not the case that media violence teaches children that real world violence has no consequence. Rather, children can take pleasure in playing with power precisely because they are occupying a fantastic space that has little or no direct relationship to their own everyday environment. Fantasy allows children to express feelings and impulses that have to be carefully held in check in their real world interactions. Such experiences can be cathartic, can enable a release of tension that allows children to better cope with their more mundane frustrations. The stylized and hyperbolic quality of most contemporary entertainment becomes one of the primary markers by which children distinguish between realistic and playful representations of violence.

Let us be clear: while I am questioning both the methodology and the conclusions employed by a central tradition of media effects research, I am not arguing that children learn nothing from the many hours they spend consuming media; I am not arguing that the content of our culture makes no difference in the shape of our thoughts and our feelings. Quite the opposite. Of course, we should be concerned about the content of our culture; we should be worried if violent images push away other kinds of representations of the world. The meanings youths weave into their culture are at least partially a product of the kinds of fantasy materials they have access to and therefore we should subject those materials to scrutiny. We should encourage children to engage critically with the materials of their culture. But, popular culture is only one influence on our children's fantasy lives. As the Littleton case suggests, the most powerful influences on children are those they experience directly, that are part of their immediate environment at school or at home. In the case of Harris and Klebold, these influences apparently included a series of social rejections and humiliations and a perception that adult authorities weren't going to step in and provide them with protection from the abuse directed against them from the "in crowd."

5   We can turn off a television program or shut down a video game if we find what it is showing us ugly, hurtful, or displeasing. We can't shut out the people in our immediate environment quite so easily. Many teenagers find going to school a brutalizing experience of being required to return day after day to a place where they are ridiculed and taunted and sometimes physically abused by their classmates and where school administrators are slow to respond to their distress and

can offer them few strategies for making the abuse stop. Media images may have given Harris and Klebold symbols to express their rage and frustration, but the media did not create the rage or generate their alienation. What sparked the violence was not something they saw on the internet or on television, not some song lyric or some sequence from a movie, but things that really happened to them. When we listen to young people talk about the shootings, they immediately focus on the pain, suffering, and loneliness experienced by Harris and Klebold, seeing something of their own experiences in the media descriptions of these troubled youths, and struggling to understand the complex range of factors which insure that they are going to turn out okay while the Colorado adolescents ended up dead. If we want to do something about the problem, we are better off focusing our attention on negative social experiences and not the symbols we use to talk about those experiences.

Some of the experts who have stepped forward in the wake of the Littleton shootings have accused mass media of teaching our children how to perform violence—as if such a direct transferal of knowledge were possible. The metaphor of media as a teacher is a compelling but ultimately misleading one. As a teacher, I would love to be able to decide exactly what I want my students to know and transmit that information to them with sufficient skill and precision that every student in the room learned exactly what I wanted, no more and no less. But, as teachers across the country can tell you, teaching doesn't work that way. Each student pays attention to some parts of the lesson and ignores or forgets others. Each has their own motivations for learning. Whatever "instruction" occurs in the media environment is even more unpredictable. Entertainers don't typically sec themselves as teaching lessons. They don't carefully plan a curriculum. They don't try to clear away other distractions. Consumers don't sit down in front of their television screens to learn a lesson. Their attention is even more fragmented; their goals in taking away information from the media are even more personal; they aren't really going to be tested on what they learn. Those are all key differences from the use of video games as a tool of military training and the use of video games for recreation. The military uses the games as part of a specific curriculum with clearly defined goals, in a context where students actively want to learn and have a clear need for the information and skills being transmitted, and there are clear consequences for not mastering those skills. None of this applies to playing these same or similar games in a domestic or arcade context.

So far, the media response to the Littleton shootings has told us a great deal more about what those symbols mean to adults than what they mean to American youth, because for the most part, it is the adults who are doing all of the talking and the youth who are being forced to listen.

Three key factors have contributed to the current media fixation on the role of popular culture in the shootings . . .: our generational anxiety about the process of adolescence, our technophobic reaction about our children's greater comfort with digital technologies, and our painful discovery of aspects of our children's play and fantasy lives which have long existed but were once hidden from view. Read in this context, the materials of youth culture can look profoundly frightening, but much of what scares us is a product of our own troubled imaginations and is far removed from what these symbols mean to our children.

All of the above suggests a basic conclusion: banning specific media images will have little or no impact on the problem of youth crime, because doing so gets at symbols, not at the meanings those symbols carry and not at the social reality that gives such urgency to teens' investments in those cultural materials. . . . The best way to do that is to create opportunities for serious conversations about the nature of our children's relationships with popular culture. One project which sets a good example for such discussions is the Superhero TV Project conducted by Ellen Seiter at the University of California-San Diego. Seiter recognized the centrality of superhero cartoons, games, comics, and action heroes to preschool children and recognized the recurring concerns parents and teachers had about the place of those materials in the children's lives. [18] Seiter and her graduate students worked with teachers to encourage classroom activities that center around these superhero myths. Students were encouraged to invent their own superheroes and to make up stories about them. Students discussed their stories in class and decided that they would collaborate in the production of a superhero play. Through the classroom discussions about what kinds of physical actions could be represented in their play, teachers and students talked together about the place of violence in the superhero stories and what those violent images meant to them. Through such conversations, both students and teachers developed a much better understanding of the role of violent imagery in popular entertainment.

Writing for the slashdot.com website, journalist Jon Katz has described a fundamentally different reaction to popular culture in high schools across America in the wake of the Littleton shootings. Schools are shutting down student access to the net and the web. Parents are cutting their children off from access to their on-line friends or forbidding them to play computer games. Students are being suspended for coming to school displaying one or another cultural symbol (black trench coats, heavy metal T-shirts). Students are being punished or sent into therapy because they express opinions in class discussions or essays that differ from the views about the events being promoted by their teachers. Guidance counselors are drawing on checklists of symptoms of maladjustment to try to ferret out those students who are outsiders and either force them into the mainstream or punish them for their dissent. Rather than teaching students to be more tolerant of the diversity they encounter in the contemporary high school, these educators and administrators are teaching their students that difference is dangerous, that individuality should be punished, and that self expression should be curbed. In this polarized climate, it becomes impossible for young people to explain to us what their popular culture means to them without fear of repercussion and reprisals. We are pushing this culture further and further underground where it will be harder and harder for us to study and understand it. We are cutting off students at risk from the lifeline provided by their on-line support groups.

10   We all want to do something about the children at risk. We all want to do something about the proliferation of violent imagery in our culture. We all want to do something to make sure events like the Littleton shootings do not occur again. But repression of youth culture is doomed not only to fail but to backfire against us. Instead, we need to take the following steps:

1. We need to create contexts where students can form meaningful and supportive communities through their use of digital media. Sameer Parekh, a 24-year-old software entrepreneur, has offered one such model through his development of the High School Underground website (http://www.hsunderground.com). His site invites students who feel ostracized at school to use the web as a means of communicating with each other about their concerns, as a tool of creative expression and social protest, as the basis for forming alliances that leads to an end of the feelings of loneliness and isolation. We need to have more spaces like High School Underground that provide a creative and constructive direction for children who are feeling cut off from others in their schools or communities. A number of websites have been built within the goth subculture to explain its perplexing images to newcomers, to challenge its representation in the major media, and to rally support for the victims of the shootings.

2. We also need to work on building a more accepting and accommodating climate in our schools, one which is more tolerant of difference, one which seeks to understand the cultural choices made by students rather than trying to prohibit them open expression. A core assumption behind any democratic culture is that truth is best reached through the free market of ideas, not through the repression of controversial views. Popular culture has become a central vehicle by which we debate core issues in our society. Our students need to learn how to process and evaluate those materials and reach their own judgments about what is valuable and what isn't in the array of media entering their lives. They need to do this in a context that respects their right to dignity and protects them from unreasoned and unreasonable degrees of abuse.

What should have rang alarm bells for us in the aftermath of the Littleton shooting is how alone and at risk students can feel in their schools and how important it is for us to have a range of different activities, supported by caring and committed teachers, which can pull all of our students into the school community and not simply those the school values because of their good grades, good sports skills, or good conduct. All signs are that Harris and Klebold were enormously talented and creative kids who never found an outlet where they could get respect for what they created from the adults in their community.

3. We need to provide more support for media education in our schools. Given the centrality of media in contemporary life, media issues need to be integrated into all aspects of our K-12 curriculum, not as a special treat, but as something central to our expectations about what children need to learn about their environment. Most contemporary media education is designed to encourage children to distance themselves from media culture. The governing logic is "just say no to Nintendo" and "turn off your television set." Instead, we need to focus on teaching children how to be safe, critical, and creative users of media. Research suggests that when we tell students that popular culture has no place in our classroom discussions, we are also signaling to them that what they learn in school has little or nothing to say about the things that matter to them in their after school hours.

4. For this new kind of media literacy to work, our teachers and administrators need to be better informed about the nature of popular culture and their students' investments in media imagery. Such understanding cannot start from the assumption that such culture is meaningless or worthless, but has to start from the recognition that popular culture is deeply significant to those who are its most active consumers and participants. The contents of that culture shift constantly and so we need to be up to date on youth subcultures, on popular music, on popular programs.

5. We need to provide fuller information to parents about the content of media products so that they can make meaningful and informed choices about what forms of popular culture they want to allow into their homes. . . . But the ratings system for games and for television needs to be more nuanced, needs to provide more specific information. We also need to create more websites where parents respond to the games and other media products they have purchased and share their insights and reactions with other parents.

6. We need to challenge the entertainment industry to investigate more fully why violent entertainment appeals to young consumers and then to become more innovative and creative at providing alternative fantasies that satisfy their needs for empowerment, competition, and social affiliation.

QUESTIONS FOR DISCUSSION

1. Why, according to Jenkins, is it impossible to pin down one significant media-influenced event or symbol that motivated the Columbine killers? What is the significance of his remark that "When it comes to popular culture, we all 'roll our own.'"

2. Is the evidence Jenkins presents to support his thesis relative to the complexity of our relationship to the "hyper-mediated culture" convincing or relevant to the case of the Columbine killers? Why or why not?

3. What solutions does Jenkins present to make children less fearful of violence in schools, thus reducing the kind of conditions that led the Columbine killers to massacre their classmates? How do his solutions differ from those Jon Katz notes as current school responses?

4. Do you think the solutions presented by Jenkins are adequate? Which of his solutions do you think would be most effective? Explain your position.

5. How are you affected by media violence? Provide examples.

6. What solutions do you have for decreasing the amount of media violence to which children are exposed?

CONNECTION

Compare and contrast the causes of youth violence and media as discussed by Jenkins and Provenzo (see page 439).

IDEAS FOR WRITING

1. Write an argument in response to Jenkins. To what extent do you agree or disagree with his ideas on the solution's for "mediated" youth violence?

2. Do research into media violence, and write your own argument about its effects on young people.

RELATED WEB SITES

SafeYouth.org—Media Violence Facts and Statistics
www.safeyouth.org/scripts/faq/mediaviolstats.asp
The National Youth Violence Prevention Resource Center provides media violence facts and statistics, as well as links to related resources and the articles cited in this article.

The Lion & Lamb Project
www.lionlamb.org/media_violence_video_games.htm
A parent organization created in opposition of "the marketing of violence to children," the Lion & Lamb Project Web site offers research, toy lists, toy alternatives, and other resources for parents, psychologists, teachers, and other groups.

Phil Mattera

Is Corporate Greenwashing Headed for a Fall?

Phil Mattera, a former writer for Fortune Magazine, *is research director of* Good Jobs First, *"a national policy resource center for grassroots groups and public officials, promoting corporate and government accountability in economic development." He is head of Good Jobs's* Corporate Research Project, *which assists labor and environmental organizations through "identifying the information activists can use as leverage to get business to behave in a socially responsible manner." Mattera has contributed many articles to Alternet. In the article that follows, Mattera defines and traces the increasing public disillusionment with the process of "greenwashing," which involves corporate efforts to convince consumers that businesses are doing great things to improve environmental conditions and combat global warming—when, in fact, the opposite may be true.*

JOURNAL

Write about why you do or do not purchase products that are "good for the environment."

Imagine you are a communication technician on a planet in another solar system that is facing an ecological disaster and is looking for new solutions. One day you suddenly pick up broadcast signals from Earth that happen to include a man talking to a group of children sitting beside a hulking vehicle he is describing as a "vegetarian" because it uses a fuel called ethanol. The segment ends with the statement: "Chevy: from gas-friendly to gas-free. That's an American revolution."

Then you get a transmission from something called BP that is talking about going beyond—beyond darkness, beyond fear, beyond petroleum. Another from Toyota shows a vehicle being put together like a grass hut and then disintegrating back into nature without a trace. The messages keep coming—from General Electric ("eco-imagination"), Chevron (celebrating the miraculous power of "human energy") and so on.

As you receive more of these signals, you rush to your superiors and announce the good news: Planet Earth has wonderful entities called corporations that can solve all our environmental problems.

Residents of our planet may be tempted to jump to the same conclusion. These days we are bombarded with advertisements that want us to believe that major oil companies, automakers and other large corporations are solving the environmental and energy problems facing the earth. Fear not global warming, peak oil, polluted air and water—big business will take care of everything.

5   In the late 1990s we saw a hyped-up dot com boom that came crashing down. In the past year or so, we have seen a hyped real estate boom turn into a credit crunch and an unprecedented number of home foreclosures. Are we now seeing a green business boom that will also turn out to be nothing more than hot air?

The "Green Con"

Today's surge of corporate environmentalism is not the first time business has sought to align itself with public concerns about the fate of the Earth. Two decades ago, marketers began to recognize the benefits of appealing to green consumers. This revelation first took hold in countries such as Britain and Canada. For example, in early 1989 the giant British supermarket chain Tesco launched a campaign to promote the products on its shelves that were deemed "environmentally friendly." That same year, Canadian mining giant Inco Ltd. began running ads promoting its effort to reduce sulfur emissions from its smelters, conveniently failing to mention it was doing so under government orders.

In 1990 the green business wave spread to the United States in time to coincide with the 20th annual Earth Day celebration. Large U.S. companies such as DuPont began touting their environmental initiatives and staged their own Earth Tech environmental technology fair on the National Mall. General Motors ran ads emphasizing its supposed concern about the environment, despite its continuing resistance to significant increases in fuel efficiency requirements.

Such exercises in corporate image-burnishing did not have a great deal of impact. For one thing, environmental groups wasted no time debunking the ads. In 1989 Friends of the Earth in Britain gave "Green Con" awards to those companies that made the most exaggerated and unsubstantiated environmental claims about their products. First prize went to British National Fuels for promoting nuclear power as friendly to the environment.

Greenpeace USA staged a protest at the 1990 corporate Earth Tech fair, denouncing companies such as DuPont for trying to whitewash their poor environmental record with green claims. Greenpeace's invented term for this practice—greenwashing—immediately caught on, and to this day is a succinct way of undermining dubious corporate claims about the environment.

10   The general public was also not taken in by the corporate environmental push of 1989–1990. It was just a bit too obvious that these initiatives were meant to deflect attention away from recent environmental disasters

such as the Exxon Valdez oil spill in Alaska and Union Carbide's deadly
Bhopal chemical leak. It also didn't help that many of the claims about
green products turned out to be misleading or meaningless.

'Little Green Lies'

The question today is whether people have become more receptive to
corporate environmental hype. One thing business has going for it in
the United States is that the Bush Administration has pursued environmental policies so retrograde that even the most superficial green measures by the private sector shine in comparison. Another is that some
environmental groups have switched from an outside adversarial strategy
to a more collaborative approach that often involves forming partner-
ships with companies. Such relationships serve to legitimize business initiatives while turning those groups into cheerleaders for their corporate
partners. Former Sierra Club president Adam Werbach took it a step further and joined the payroll of Wal-Mart.

On the other hand, the use of the term "greenwashing" is enjoying a
resurgence and has entered the mainstream. A search of the Nexis news
archive turns up more than 700 mentions of the term in the past six months
alone. Even that bible of the marketing world—*Advertising Age*—recently
published a list titled "The Green and the Greenwashed: Ten Who Get It
and 10 Who Talk a Good Game." Among the latter were General Motors,
Toyota, ExxonMobil, Chevron, Wal-Mart, General Electric and Ikea, though
Toyota, Wal-Mart and Ikea were also put on the green list for other reasons.

Other business publications have also been taking a more critical approach to green claims. Last September, the *Wall Street Journal* looked behind GE's eco-imagination campaign and found all was not well. For one
thing, there was significant resistance even within GE's managerial ranks
and among many of the conglomerate's major industrial customers.
Then there was the fact that GE was still pushing big-ticket products such
as coal-fired steam turbines that were significant contributors to global
warming. Finally, the paper pointed out that the campaign was motivated in substantial part by a desire to increase sales of existing GE products such as wind turbines that could be promoted as eco-friendly.

In October, *Business Week* published a cover story titled "Little Green
Lies." It began with the declaration: "The sweet notion that making a company environmentally friendly can be not just cost-effective but profitable
is going up in smoke." The piece featured Auden Schendler of Aspen Ski-
ing Company, a pioneer in adopting environmentally friendly practices.
After showing off his company's energy-efficient facilities, he was described as having turned to the *Business Week* reporter and said: "Who are
we kidding?" He then acknowledged that the growth of the company necessarily means burning more power, including the ever-increasing energy

needed to create artificial snow during warmer winters. "How do you really green your company? It's almost f------impossible."

The Six Sins

15 Another factor working against corporate hype is that critics are becoming more systematic in their critique of greenwashing. In November, a marketing firm called TerraChoice did an analysis of more than 1,000 products bearing environmental claims. After finding that all but one of those claims were false or misleading in some respect, TerraChoice issued a paper called *The Six Sins of Greenwashing* that analyzed the various forms of deception.

The most common shortcoming found by TerraChoice is the "sin of the hidden trade-off," in which a single positive attribute of a product is promoted while ignoring the detrimental environmental impact of the whole manufacturing process. For example, paper that has some recycled content but is produced in a way that causes serious air and water pollution as well as entailing a large amount of greenhouse gas emissions. The other sins listed by TerraChoice are no proof, vagueness, irrelevance, lesser of two evils and fibbing.

Do-it-yourself greenwashing criticism is now possible through a website recently launched by EnviroMedia Social Marketing. Its Greenwashing Index site allows users to post ads—usually video footage taken from YouTube—and rate them on a scale of 1 (good ad) to 5 (total greenwashing).

More troubling, from the corporate perspective, are signs that government regulators and industry-established watchdog groups are giving more scrutiny to green claims. Last month, the UK's Advertising Standards Authority found that a series of television ads being run around the world by the Malaysian Palm Oil Council contained misleading statements about the environmental benefits of its product. Several months ago, government regulators in Norway banned automobile ads from stating that any cars are environmentally friendly, given their contribution to global warming.

Even in the United States there are signs that regulators may be getting concerned about greenwashing. The Federal Trade Commission, which in 1992 issued national guidelines for environmental marketing claims but has done little on the subject since then, announced in November that it was beginning a review of its guidelines.

Unclean Hands and Excessive Size

20 Corporations, no doubt, will not give up their environmental claims without a fight. Perhaps the hardest nut to crack will be Wal-Mart. For the past couple of years, the giant retailer has depicted itself as being on a crusade to address global warming and other environmental issues—a

crusade it wants its suppliers, its workers and its customers to join. In October 2005 CEO Lee Scott gave a speech in which he embraced sweeping goals to reduce greenhouse gas emissions and raise energy efficiency. Last month he gave another speech that reaffirmed those goals and upped the ante by envisioning a future in which Wal-Mart customers would drive to the store in electric cars that could be recharged in the parking lot using power generated by wind turbines and solar panels.

Wal-Mart's greenwashing involves sins beyond those listed by Terra-Choice. First there is the sin of unclean hands. It is difficult to avoid thinking that the company is using its environmental initiatives to draw attention away from its widely criticized labor practices—both in its own stores and in the factories of its low-wage suppliers abroad. Until the company provides decent working conditions, respects the right of its employees to unionize and ceases to sell goods made by sweatshop labor, Wal-Mart cannot expect to be a paradigm of social responsibility.

Then there's the sin of size. A company as large as Wal-Mart will inevitably have a negative effect on the countries from which it obtains its goods, the agricultural areas from which it gets it food products, and the communities where it locates its big-box localism and moderate-size enterprise. That rules out Wal-Mart, no matter what its CEO professes.

Wal-Mart's problem may be the problem of big business as a whole. As hard as they try to convince us, huge profit-maximizing transnational corporations may never be true friends of the environment. Let's hope this message also gets through to those listening in distant worlds.

QUESTIONS FOR DISCUSSION

1. Why are the opening series of paragraphs in Mattera's essay set on another planet that listens to transmissions of ads from Earth? Is this fanciful approach an effective way to begin this essay on greenwashing? Why or why not?

2. Do you think ecologically oriented publications and/or magazine exposés would be effective in the effort to combat greenwashing-style advertising campaigns? Why or why not?

3. Consider other forms of action that could be taken against greenwashing. For instance, could laws be changed to make such deceptive practices illegal?

4. How do Wal-Mart and other international mega-corporations go beyond the original six sins of greenwashing?

5. Does Mattera find any hope for or credence in corporations as "true friends of the environment"? Do you agree with his skeptical perspective?

CONNECTION

Compare Phil Mattera's article with one of the other essays in this chapter that is critical of how the media helps corporations to undermine and harm the lives of citizens.

IDEAS FOR WRITING

1. What are the "Six Sins of Greenwashing" as written and distributed by the ecological marketing firm TerraChoice? Can you think of other problems caused by greenwashing? What are they?

2. Write an essay in which you propose ways to stop greenwashing. You can select a specific company or product that uses greenwashing and develop a solution to stop the corporation's unethical behavior. You might find companies that have been caught greenwashing and apply some of the regulations that have been used effectively before in similar situations.

RELATED WEB SITES

The EnviroMedia Greenwashing Index
www.greenwashingindex.com
This Web site offers up-to date information on how to evaluate greenwashing and offers foundational cases as well as important up-to-date cases.

Stop Greenwash
www.stopgreenwash.org
Launched in 2008 by the environmental group Greenpeace, the site is designed to "confront deceptive greenwashing campaigns, engage companies in debate, and give consumers and activists and lawmakers the information and tools they need to . . . hold corporations accountable for the impacts their core business decisions and investments are having on our planet."

Jonathan Cusick

Do Benefit Concerts Affect Political Decisions?

Jonathan Cusick is a reporter for the Sunday Herald Tribune, *a Scottish independent newspaper. Cusick's writing frequently focuses on political and governmental issues such as Britain's role in the War in Iraq, conflicts within the government, and race-hate legislation. In the following article from the* Tribune, *he argues about the ability of large, political rock concerts like the* Live8 *concert in the summer of 2005 to change politicians' minds and to convince them to act on global problems such as AIDS, starvation, and genocide.*

Do you often attend large fundraising concerts, or do you find them artificial and uninspiring?

"**K**eep your eyes wide. The chance won't come again."

The time is 1963. The voice is Bob Dylan. The wider message is stark and threatening for politicians who aren't listening to a new generation that thinks it knows the answers and warns those who don't not to "stand in the doorway" or block up the hall.

Four decades on our politicians are again being warned not to get in the way; warned to listen . . . or else. Four decades on we still prefer to put our faith in the simple gospels of pop star missionaries like Bob Geldof or Bono. We applaud basic questions such as, "How many ears do we need before we can hear people cry?", rather than bother ourselves with the market obstacles that need to be overcome in implementing a successful economic growth model for Africa. We prefer our would-be saints and stars to be raw, youthful and accessible, rather than elected and stuffed with shirt and stripped club tie.

Put Geldof on a platform alongside an establishment politician and it's obvious which is which. Geldof is the deliberate antithesis of city smart. He looks as though he's borrowed Dylan's worried hair—and much else; his message is the same, only the poetry is of a lower caliber. Last week, Dylan's final "chance" had changed into a "unique opportunity"—to permanently end poverty in Africa. So 20 years after Live Aid there will be a rerun, Live8, to coincide with next month's G8 summit.

5   We elect the politicians who will travel to Gleneagles and tell us Africa's problems are complex. But we'll follow, and we prefer to believe, Geldof: the popstar who tells us to "just do it." Why? What place is occupied in our collective psyche by the Dylans, the Joan Baezes and the latter-day pop pulpiteers? And can they actually change the world?

Dylan, almost by accident, found himself the emblem of the fight against Washington's political elite. He was a rag-tag jean-clad youth: a slight figure who looked incapable of finding his next meal on the streets of New York's Greenwich Village, never mind creating unease among powerful senators and congressmen. But he had what the establishment didn't have—and still don't. He possessed what today's pop prophets and campaigners have inherited and continue to use: youthful energy and rawness and the confidence not to rely on pretence. When pop prophets speak, followers believe they "speak to me," and so they are listened to.

Marshal McLuhan, the early guru of media culture, said The Beatles' secret was that they spoke with Liverpool accents and flaunted their low-rent, working-class roots.

American writer and social commentator Tom Wolfe thought The Beatles brought stardom down to the level of their lowliest audience. There was no longer a class barrier, no air of superiority. The illusionary show of wealth and elegance had gone. And in its place? Youth and a willingness to abandon the safety of all rules.

Geldof's "Give us your f**king money" is his badge of authority and energy, his ditching of the rules. It makes him sound like he's made sense of the world—on our terms.

10   Those at the rock industry's epicenter aren't surprised that people trust pop stars more than politicians. "With pop stars, at least you know who's paying them and what their sins are, " argues Joe Levy, deputy managing editor of *Rolling Stone* magazine in New York. "There's less false morality and they are less beholden to special interest groups." For Levy, it doesn't even come down to preferring a pop idol over a politician. "Wouldn't we rather have individuals making these decisions rather than massive corporations?" Levy believes pop stars hold a kind of unique democratic office. "They stand for election every time they put out a single, rather than every four years. I think it's better to trust people who haven't made a career out of getting elected. Pop stars have nothing to fear from speaking from their hearts." For Levy, there is a complexity about the solutions offered by politicians: questions about who they need to keep onside; who they might offend; who they trade with.

"Bono doesn't worry about this stuff. He can operate from a more humanistic perspective." Although Live8 is a complex business, for people like Bono "it will be less subject to compromise. In fact," argues Levy, "their clarity comes from a lack of compromise: so they pay attention to the real lives that are on the line here." Here in Britain, Richard Holloway, retired Anglican bishop of Edinburgh and chair of the Scottish Arts Council, offers an alternative, almost religious, perspective on why pop apostles command our trust. He believes simple "recognition and celebrity" helps us listen and believe. "John Lennon once said he thought The Beatles were more popular than Jesus. He had put his finger on something, because The Beatles carried more clout in the world than religious figures—and that continues today." Holloway doesn't seem overly concerned that today's preachers might be packaged, not in sacred vestments or clerical collars, but in jeans and wrap-round dark sunglasses. Bono and others simply have "high recognition" combined with openness and a seeming lack of self-regard. This pits them against politicians who are regarded with suspicion because they lack either quality.

But there's a caveat for Holloway. "What pop stars have is celebrity, not power." But don't our pop choirmasters hold the illusion of power: the notion that things can be changed, that the officially impossible can become possible?

Ted Honderich, Emeritus Professor of Mind and Logic at University College London, argues that judgments about what can and can't be changed "are a matter of the greatest importance," and what is conceivable, possible and even necessary, needs a lot more reflection. Honderich believes there is a "paralyzing ideology" of what we can't do, more influenced by governments than by pop stars.

He thinks we have accepted that there are limitations on what is possible, almost as a matter of convention. "The convention is owes more to fundamental distributions of political power and influence in a society." Politicians, he says, have more power than pop stars, and so does the media. The ultimately optimistic Honderich argues that the matter of what will happen is more open than we think.

15 Honderich is "delighted" that a million people have been invited to demonstrate in Edinburgh, but seems unsure of what they will achieve. "They may be making a move, a start in the right direction, but then there's what happens after that. What happens at the World Bank over the next 10 years? What happens when Tony Blair actually faces paying a price for things he's talked about?" But it is governments that worry about the long term. Pop prophets want action now. And "now" is easier to understand and battle for than a distant future.

Nicholas Bayne, of the London School of Economics' International Trade Policy Unit, identifies a relationship between what pop stars bring to the table, and what politicians learn from their campaigns. "The great merit of involving celebrities . . . is that they bring these issues to the attention of a far wider circle than governments can reach. Their involvement can help governments judge how far their aid and development policies have popular support—or whether they should do more."

Bayne, whose new book on recent G8 summits is published later this month, accepts that popular campaigns like Geldof's can oversimplify the issues or back proposals that would do more harm than good. But if the pop prophets are engaged in the business of blue-skies dreaming, Bayne thinks it then becomes the job of governments to point out the flaws, to effectively deal with the dangers of a short-term focus on what might essentially be a long-term problem.

The pop apostle as economic sounding board seems a nice idea. But it can't explain our continuing belief in pop-driven protest. So if we've lost faith in politicians and prefer the short-term passion offered by rock stars, how do we recognize where simple trust should end and hard-faced pragmatism should kick in?

Here, Holloway thinks we are guided by an almost natural antenna of trust: "When a pop star says something, they may be right or they may be wrong. But it is their opinion, it's not an official line." Geldof, Bono and other informed pop apostles are characterized by what Holloway dubs "raw passion," linked to a deeper understanding of what they are trying to do and what grand gestures are required to achieve it. Geldof is what Holloway calls a "technical authority" who is still seen as a "tortured soul" and therefore capable of generating empathy with his cause. Geldof and Bono belong to a tradition that goes back to Pete Seeger, Joan Baez and the anti-war protest singers of the 1960s whose genuine moral passion came through in their songs. Holloway is romantic, quasi-religious even, about such connectivity. "It is a kind of apostolic succession—a DNA handed down." He seems to be saying that the Geldofs and Bonos will retain our faith and belief as long as they remain off to one side of formal power, "as long as they don't get sucked into too many dinners at Downing Street." Yet that is precisely what Bono and Geldof have done. They have gone to the enemy, the lion's den, but refused to be eaten; they haven't been turned to the dark side.

20   At last year's Labour conference in Brighton, Bono even joked to the audience about the irony of the place in which he found himself. "Listen, I know what this looks like, a rock star standing up here, shouting imperatives others have to fulfill. But that's what we do, rock stars. Rock stars get to wave flags, shout at the barricades, and escape to the south of France. We're unaccountable. We behave accordingly. But not you. You can't. We're counting on you."

Geldof is different from Bono. And he's different from Dylan. As a pop star he had no poetry to offer. As an activist he lacks subtlety. Instead he offers anger and impatience—two things we all recognize, because we deal with anger, we live with impatience.

Twenty years after Live Aid, it strikes Geldof as "morally repulsive and intellectually absurd that people die of want in a world of surplus." He was a driving force in getting Blair to set up and deliver the recently published Commission for Africa report. It recommended debt cancellation, increased aid and fairer trade laws. But having dined at Downing Street to get the report, Saint Bob said it was "gathering dust on the shelf." Now he wants the public pressure generated from the Live8 concerts to get it off the shelf and implemented.

The consistency of Geldof's passion to solve Africa's economic problems has given him, according to Stirling University's film and media professor, Simon Frith, "a stronger moral voice on Africa than the Archbishop of Canterbury." But Frith is wary about seeing all would-be pop apostles in the same light as Geldof; wary about the assumption that we place our faith in anything a pop preacher says or does. "We only put our trust in some pop stars." So Geldof might be a one-off, a pop missionary who we recognize as achieving huge success, even though his success is measured by "media achievement" and not by the reality of his impact on Africa. Geldof, claims Frith, understands the media and works it to his advantage. If that sounds intentionally manipulative, it is.

Geldof knows that the culture of the pop world is all about the ability to mobilize large crowds—and that's what he's done. Music didn't drive the success of Live Aid in 1985; big crowds and known names did. The same strategy is driving Live8. Live Aid highlighted the potential global reach of music to the television industry. Live8 simply builds on the audiences that have grown up, and grown with, MTV and the hybrid music/TV culture born since the mid-1980s.

25   But having created the stage, and the audience: what to do with it? Politicians today—unlike those of the late 19th or early 20th century—are incapable of sustaining lengthy moral rhetoric to mass audiences. During the general election, Blair not only avoided large crowds, he avoided meeting anyone who hadn't first been vetted by his party organizers.

Filling the vacuum left by politicians, unable or unwilling to address crowds in the way Martin Luther King did in the 1960s, are crusading pop stars. For Frith a better personal comparison for Geldof's appealing and clear moral rhetoric is the last pope. "The pope offered a moral certainty and perhaps a simple-mindedness in his objectives. But he did it on the world's largest stages. The same is true for Geldof. And there is no point in criticizing his moral voice—because that is the only voice he has," says Frith.

So Geldof's nickname of Saint Bob is appropriate. However, for the NGOs (non governmental organizations) who have to deliver the aid, and the sweat, where it counts, after the Blessed Bob has banged the table for cash or demanded a march to Edinburgh's castle mount, it matters little. Their troubled job is getting people to listen and pop apostles— with a stage and audience—are able to do what they can't.

John Coventry at War On Want says the NGOs have to "bang on and on. Then a pop star or celebrity comes along, says something and everyone listens. They don't usually look to them for a political steer, it's usually a cultural steer they're after. And it seems amazing that here are these famous people giving up time, energy and money to help this great cause." The fact rock stars don't normally "bang on" about aid and power is what gives them their power.

"Bob speaks and everyone listens"—fantastic. But what of the detractors? What of those who believe we've put our faith in the wrong place, the wrong people; that the problems are too complex, too important to be left to the pop apostles?

30   Clare Short, the former international development secretary, who used to have responsibility for Africa, expressed concern last week that

Live8 would end in disillusionment and cynicism. "My fear is there will be all these people wearing the wrist bands [Make Poverty History] and thinking they are helping, when nothing is agreed to stop the killing on the ground, and Africa goes on getting poorer." Short was in Blair's government in 2001 when he said: "Africa is a scar on the conscience of the world. But if the world as a community focused on it, we could heal it. And if we don't it will become deeper and angrier." Richard Holloway thinks the reason we believe Geldof when he says much the same thing, is that professional politicians' "narcissism and self-righteousness" get in the way. "People just don't respond to their pleas in the same way." Dylan had advice for the dissenters. It still stands. "Don't criticize what you can't understand." So for Geldof and perhaps those who come after him, we have to at least hope that the times are changing.

QUESTIONS FOR DISCUSSION

1. Why are people more inclined to listen to a celebrity singing or speaking on behalf of a social cause than they are to a politician?
2. What differing views on this subject does Cusick examine in the essay?
3. How important do politicians believe concerts like Live Aid and Live8 to be, in Cusick's opinion? Why does Cusick contrast Geldof, Bono, and Dylan? Why is Geldof's nickname, "Saint Bob," appropriate?
4. Why do you think most people attend such concerts as Live8, for the music or because of their concern for the cause? Does it make any difference why they attend?
5. How do NGOs (nongovernmental organizations) feel about rock stars' contributions to helping raise money for impoverished people? How do NGOs value their jobs in contrast to how rock stars value their contributions?
6. Discuss Cusick's style in writing and his tone. How do they affect his point of view?

CONNECTION

Compare ways celebrities are presented in Cusick's essay and that of Carlin Flora in this chapter (page 450). Does Flora's article shed any light on how celebrities could promote a cause effectively?

IDEAS FOR WRITING

1. Argue your own point of view on the power of large social issue concerts to bring about social change as opposed to the ordinary political process. Take into account the reservations expressed by Nicholas Bayne and Claire Short, whose research is included in this essay.
2. Write an essay about a recent fundraising concert to help people to support issues or communities in need. Then, argue for who made the greater contribution, rock stars or politicians?

Mark Stephen Meadows

Second Life: Why?

*Mark Stephen Meadows earned a B.A. degree from St. John's College in Santa
Fe and studied at a variety of other colleges including The San Francisco Art
Institute, the University of Colorado, and Harvard University. He helped design one of the first commercial websites (WELL.com) in 1993 and went on to
found several hi-tech companies and to register a number of software patents.
He was a researcher/artist in residence at Xerox-PARC for 15 years and has
consulted for many companies. In 1996 he was a designer on the first multi-
user 3-D virtual reality environment and has continued his interest in designing artifacts for such environments ever since. His designs and models have
been used by such media corporations as Lucasfilm, Sony Pictures, Microsoft,
and Second Life. He is also a successful artist who has sold his work in the
United States and Europe since 1987 and has won awards for his work.
Meadows lectures internationally on a broad range of technical and cultural
subjects; his books include* Pause & Effect: The Art of Interactive Narrative *(2002) and* I, Avatar: The Culture and Consequences of Having a
Second Life *(2008), from which the following essay on the uses and abuses
of the Second Life interactive virtual reality environment is taken.*

JOURNAL

Write about an experience you have had playing or participating in a video
or virtual reality game in which you become a character in the game. How
did it feel to immerse yourself in your character or "avatar"? Did this immersion have any impact on your self-perception or sense of time?

My second life was much like my first, only accelerated, smaller, and
more dramatic. People married, money moved, wars began, king-
doms crumbled. Noses and lips and hair and clothes shifted like tiny
weather systems, raining images and emotions onto the computer

screens of people around the world. Little programs that animated your avatar to kiss another avatar were handed around during Valentine's Day, along with perfume and embarrassment and gossip and more romance. Mood swings and conversation shifts and grand promises and tiny lies. Leather and lace and flowers and swords decorated this Harlequin Romance world, this world of social exchange.

A day in Second Life lasts for four hours. These thin, short days flickered by like a movie, whirring and chattering with the events in this faraway place that had colonized my skull. The sun spun around me as I went through 24-hour cycles in the real world that were punctuated only by biobreaks. Sometimes I completely lost track of what time it was, as the Second Life days dictated my rhythm more than the real days. I continued to dive deep, Carmen was always a few levels deeper, and as we swam it became darker and colder and stranger.

> Eventually, my health deteriorating, I was confronted with a decision: Which world did I prefer?

It's a potentially dangerous decision, and many arguments warn against, shall we say, *going native*. Avatars present a danger of isolation from not only the real world, but from ourselves. If an avatar is used too much, it can remove us from our real-world society. We lose touch with reality. The Stanford Institute for the Quantitative Study of Society points out that with only five hours per week of Internet use, 15 percent of people interviewed reported a decrease in real-life social activities. They spent, for example, 25 percent less time talking on the phone to friends and family. Many American adults spend more time than that—an average of more than seven hours a week—playing games, and kids twice that much. This seems like a good reason to start looking more closely at what is going on.

Most of us have had the experience of trying to talk to someone while they're more engaged with their avatar, or zippered down into their fantasy world or game and reluctant to come out. Kids yell, "Be right there, Mom!" as they furiously pump the console to get leveled up before unplugging. Adults mumble half-replies to their kids as they coordinate their guild for the next raid. Roommates refuse to answer the phone. Friends don't IM back as quickly as they used to. People simply get lost in their avatar.

5   When we make an avatar, we invent a personality. In some cases, it may be the same personality, or a similar one, that we spend most of our days being. But often the alternative personality—the personality of the avatar—can become quite powerful. Part of the danger lies in how we control our avatar and how our avatar controls us. As people become more involved in the roles and rules of their avatar, they can also lose control of their alternative personality they have invented for that system. The alternative personality can become predominant and begin to take over the primary, daily one. This is the situation that most concerns parents. When

they see their kid playing hours upon hours of World of Warcraft or Second Life or Lineage or Webkinz they become concerned that their child will lose touch with the real-world society that is more important.

People sometimes prefer their avatar personas to their 'real' ones.

Your role as an avatar can take control of your life as a person. This was true long before online games and avatars. The classic example is the corporate executive who comes home and treats his children like employees. Or the marine who comes home and treats his family like recruits. The role has overcome the person and the context in which a person moves.

Losing control of one's life as a person, and therefore losing control of an alter-ego, can endanger others. One day in 2006, several Second Life avatars were having a roll in the virtual hay. A pretty normal day in Second Life—but when it was noticed that a few of them had been designed to look like prepubescents, many an eyebrow was raised. Avatars pretending to have sex with kids? Was this pedophilia? It wasn't clear. After all, an avatar that looks like an old woman may be driven by a young boy, and vice versa. The Second Life Teen Gird had been opened up for those under eighteen, so it was assumed the coast was clear enough and adult play could be allowed in the adult grid.

Emily Semaphore, one of the owners of Jailbait, an age-play region in Second Life, was quoted by the *Second Life Herald* as saying, "Being able to 'play' a kid in a 'safe' environment can be very healing for many people." Child-pornography prosecutors in the Netherlands disagreed and brought the case to court. It was later dropped because "the children avatars were not 'realistic enough.'" But this debate, as well as pressure from groups such as Familles de France, eventually contributed to Linden Lab hiring a company named Integrity-Aristotle to oversee identity verification in Second Life. Linden Lab made it clear that it would do nothing with the personal data, but Integrity-Aristotle made no such claim. The end result was the beginning of a kind of driver's license. Avatars needed authentic identities that could be traced to a real human. People were furious about this enforced identity tracking, as well as with the company chosen to do it. They wanted their avatar to remain separate from their real identity, or at least to be able to decide themselves whether to be officially connected to them. Some users left. And although this "driver's license" reduced the ability to keep a psychological division and allowed for prosecution of the rampant alter-ego's owner, it could really do nothing to address the situation's cause. After all, what could Linden Lab do? Ban child avatars from the adult grid? What, then, would happen to the Harry Potter Fan Club?

Other anti-avatar arguments include the antisocial ones, which claim that spending social time online is less valuable and valid than spending time, with people in the real world. People, and kids in particular, become shut-ins, pale, maggoty versions of their former selves. By spending too much time online they avoid spending time with anyone different from themselves. They start to lose their ability to interpret signs such as body language and intonation—important social signals that allow navigation through real, human society. They start to smell, and their hair becomes messy. They turn geeky and lose any social skills they may have had.

10   There are the arguments that claim video games are violent media that lead to violent behavior, and that exposure to violent media creates violent people. Parents cry danger, teachers see distraction, ministers warn of devil worship, and politicians makes speeches about corruption of the young. There's not much new about this argument. Parents, politicians, and pedagogues have always been afraid for our safety, and they have always made the same objections about each medium.

> "The free access which many young people have to romances, novels, and plays has poisoned the mind and corrupted the morals of many a promising youth; and prevented others from improving their minds in useful knowledge. Parents take care to feed their children with wholesome diet; and yet how unconcerned about the provision for the mind, whether they are furnished with salutary food, or with trash chaff; or poison?"
>
> —Reverend Enos Hitchcock, *Memoirs of the Bloomsgrove Family,* 1790.

> "The indecent foreign dance called the Waltz was introduced . . . at the English Court on Friday last . . . It is quite sufficient to cast one's eyes on the voluptuous intertwining of the limbs, and close com-pressure of the bodies . . . to see that it is far indeed removed, from the modest reserve which has hitherto been considered distinctive of English females. So long as this obscene display was confined to prostitutes and adulteresses, we did not think it deserving of notice; but now that it is . . . forced on the respectable classes of society by the evil example of their superiors, we feel it a duty to warn every parent against exposing his daughter to so fatal a contagion."
>
> —The *Times* of London, 1816

> "This new form of entertainment has gone far to blast maidenhood. . . . Depraved adults with candies and pennies beguile children with the inevitable result. The Society has prosecuted many for leading girls astray through these picture shows, but GOD alone knows how many, are leading dissolute lives begun at the 'moving-pictures.'"
>
> —The Annual Report of the New York Society for the Prevention of Cruelty to Children, 1909

> "Does the telephone make men more active or more lazy? Does [it] break up home life and the old practice of visiting friends?"
>
> —Survey conducted by the Knights of Columbus Adult Education Committee, San Francisco Bay Area, 1926

"Delinquencies formerly restricted to adults are increasingly committed by young people and children. . . . All child drug addicts, and all children drawn into the narcotics traffic as messengers, with whom we have had contact, were inveterate comic-book readers. This kind of thing is not good mental nourishment for children!"

—Fredric Wertham, *Seduction of the Innocent,* 1954

"The effect of rock and roll on young people, is to turn them into devil worshippers; to stimulate self-expression through sex; to provoke lawlessness; impair nervous stability and destroy the sanctity of marriage. It is an evil influence on the youth of our country."

—Minister Albert Carter, 1956

"The disturbing material in Grand Theft Auto and other games like it is stealing the innocence of our children and it's making the difficult job of being a parent even harder. . . . I believe that the ability of our children to access pornographic and outrageously violent material on video games rated for adults is spiraling out of control."

—U.S. Senator Hillary Rodham Clinton, 2005

"In traveling through Second Life one quickly perceives that 'reality' in this universe is quite different. Actual photos and videos of pornography are pasted around certain regions. Users have the option to mimic sexual intercourse, themselves becoming scenes of rape, of bondage, bestiality, and scatophilia. . . . [This is] a simple question of ethics, but, having given to minors the unrestricted ability to access these sites, the question becomes more important."

—French Conservative Organization, Famillies de France, 2007

What horror! Some find avatars to be gateways into a kind of hell. The avatar user becomes a schizophrenic personality, a hyper-violent, hyper-sexual, child-molesting psychopath, an outsider squinting out at the world, trapped inside an unhealthy body, abusing others, ultimately alone and unable to determine what is important.

Would I become this person if I continued to spend the majority of my waking hours in a geeky little fictional world inhabited by dressed-up strangers driving around in weird doll-machines? Would I continue to let my own life fall to die side and slide away? These are not uncommon questions. Millions have to make the same decisions every day.

I considered these questions thoroughly, slipped on my mask, and dove back in.

But why?

15   The more than 50 million people who choose to spend time as their avatars in virtual worlds probably think about such questions, or at least some of them do. Which gives us many millions of different answers.

For me, it's what I do. I travel, I paint, and I write. So I went back because flying around in a visual world of symbols and social interaction is where I live, what I live to build, and where I love to live. For me it was just a sensible decision. After all, I prefer to live the way I want as much as I can. Where I can fly. Where there is no such thing as scarcity or tragedy. Where I can stretch out my hand and create carpets, trees, castles, and mountains. Where—most of all—I can easily make smiles on the screen-lit faces of my far-flung friends as we dwell, laughing together, in the same dream. That is beautiful. That is a blending of the things in my life that I love most. I'm lucky I can experience this kind of travel.

Different people, of course, have different motivations, and patterns have been noted. Richard Bartle is an internationally recognized authority on virtual worlds, a pioneer of the MMORPG industry, and co-creator of the first text-based virtual World, MUD, back in 1979. He divides user motivations into four primary categories: the Explorers, the Socializers, the Achievers, and the Controllers. Explorers like to uncover beauty and show it to others. Socializers like to form groups, build social infrastructure, and throw parties. Achievers enhance the abilities of their avatars, increasing their power, wealth, and reputation, gaining social respect while doing it. Controllers are there to dominate, compete, and defeat. But whatever people use their avatars for, the avatars allow them to become more like what they want to be.

For some users, virtual worlds provide an alternative, online social life and actually provide access to more social living in real life. In August 2007, in the U.S. journal *CyberPsychology and Behavior,* researchers at Nottingham Trent University published a study called, "Social Interactions in Massively Multiplayer Online Role-Playing Gamers." Of the 1,000 gamers they interviewed, three quarters had made good friends online, half had met in real-life situations, a third had found themselves attracted to another gamer, and a tenth of them had developed physical relationships. So, it's not just that spending time as your avatar allows you to make new friends online; it opens the door for more social interaction in the real world.

Some would argue that sports are challenging and social and that playing them allows you to be competent and self-confident. When I was growing up, playing a lot of video games, adults often told me I should go out and play more sports. American football was the popular recommendation. But which, really, is more violent? Shooting pixels on a screen or breaking real bones on a football field from some kid jumping on your back because his dad's screaming from the bleachers?

20   Which really allows for increased social interaction? Which initiates group problem-solving and collaborative thinking?

Many spend time as their avatar not because they are addicted to a new thrill but because they are satisfying an old need. World of Warcraft, Second Life, and other role-playing games are engaging because they serve the primary human drives of socializing and being competent at a skill set. This has been confirmed by several researchers over the years. In 2006, the University of Rochester (N.Y.) and researchers at Immersyve

Inc. interviewed 1,000 gamers in various MMOs. According to Richard Ryan, a motivational psychologist at the University, ". . . the psychological 'pull' of games is largely due to their capacity to engender feelings of autonomy, competence, and relatedness."

When someone slips into an avatar, they slip into the ability to be competent, to be who they want, and to spend time with a community that they choose. Being able to do all three things at once is a rare experience for many people—perhaps because of appearance, gender, race, sexuality, age, or simply the fact that they want more friends of different sorts, or more enemies, or for any of a million different reasons and justifications. For example, one wheelchair-bound 19-year-old man says, "I really love gaming. I love gaming because I can't really do what other people do because of my own problems as you see. But in games, I am just like everybody else, it's like I live my life there, and I'm not different, and I like that."

Everyone experiences some discomfort among their fellow humans; everyone has some way in which they would like a fantasy, or an improvement, or even just a break. Everyone is, on some level, fighting a great battle, and everyone finds life a bit difficult at times.

> Avatars can give us an alternative, a break from daily hardships, and a space to practice for another try.

The first avatars and indeed the first large-scale virtual environment built for multi-user operation were built for this very reason. Chip Morningstar and F. Randall Farmer developed Lucasfilm's Habitat specifically so that hospitalized children could have an alternative, and a break from a limbo life in a hospital bed. The system, built on Commodore 64s, gave the kids a chance to go on quests together when they couldn't even get out of a hospital bed. Morningstar adopted the term "avatar" from Hindu mythology to describe the graphical representation of a user. This happened in California, in 1985.

25   The avatar is a Californian invention that uses computer software. It is a technological, automated American Dream. This is important for understanding why people use avatars.

The "American Dream" tells us that we can become who we want, and we can profit by doing so. It is the dream of independence and success and that core ability to make yourself into who and what you want. During the population explosion of Los Angeles, in 1931, James Adams published a book titled *The Epic of America* and in it he describes The American Dream as, "that dream of a land in which life should be better and richer and fuller for every man, with opportunity for each according to his ability or achievement." This dream of profit and social mobility via industry wasn't, nor is it now, particularly *American*. The immigrants to L.A. were pre-industrial nomads, rootless and willing to give up their homes, friends, and families back East or in Europe in exchange for a promise of a world they could build themselves. It was a "My land, my imagination" mentality. These were people who didn't fit within a community of strict rules, who didn't recognize themselves as members of that community and because they were nomadic they were also community builders. So they built a new kind of community that allowed them to be freer, and more recognized as individuals with less social pressure. They packed their bags, walked away from their past, and started on an ambitious and strange project that we now call Los Angeles.

The same thing has happened in Second Life. These two sets of immigrants were not only demographically similar, as I've pointed out, but they were also moved by many of the same motivations as immigrants to Second Life and other virtual worlds. In 2007, I surveyed, either via form or interview, more than 300 virtual-world residents. Some interviews were with the ten percent who had been spending about as much time in-world as a full-time job. What I found made a kind of grim sense: These people had assembled their own synthetic communities because they had none on hand in the real world. Most of them came from small families, had no siblings, came from small communities, traveled a great deal. Eighty percent of these users lived in cities more than 100 miles from where they were born. More than a third moved to a new city every four years. About a third were Asian, a little over half were male, and all had a desire to leave a system they disliked. Avatars had allowed them to create their own community.

Avatars also give these same people an opportunity to explore a place that is safer than what the modern world seems to afford. If I believe the media I notice around me, the world seems to be getting a lot more dangerous. Compared to a decade ago the danger level in the United States is probably not higher, but the fear level certainly is. Parents are less inclined to let their children play alone in the streets. Governments are less inclined to advise their citizens to travel abroad. Gangs roam in front of your home, terrorists lurk in your neighborhood alley, danger supposedly hides under every bridge. Living in Los Angeles, I hear an awful lot of noise about how dangerous it is outside. Newspapers, radios, televisions, and airport ceiling-robots scream about the dangers nearby. We are pushed by our media to risk less. We are told by our police force to avoid strangers. We are told to be afraid. We are told to stay at home. And so we go into the virtual world.

> Avatars offer an alternative to the "American Dream" of decentralized cities full of anonymous faces, depersonalized living, mass media, and fear.

Avatars, self-assembled constellations of the individual and the community, allow a way to return to something that is central to the human experience. They bring us back to a smaller society of people whom we know and care about and trust.

> Ironically, avatars offer a return to pre-industrial, pre-automated societies; to small groups of families and friends that once existed only in villages.

30   As my friend, the novelist William Kowalski, writes: "Is this an attempt for us to get back to the life that really matters—the symbolic life? Is this our weird American version of waking up and saying that the world we actually live in, the world we've created for ourselves—strip malls, pollution, racism, meaningless jobs—is absolute bullshit, and not worth living?"

Carmen's take on it is similar: "One of the things that fuels synthetic worlds is that the society we live in is so rigid and the roles are so over-determined, yet none of them works. People are rebuilding western society inside these worlds, just as they did in the Renaissance."

Simply put, avatars fill in the social blanks of contemporary society and in doing so, if used too much, offer real dangers.

People get more and more deeply involved, passing more and more heartbeats, exploring broader landscapes with their avatars, playing these "games" and letting what may be an unsatisfying or potentially unconnected lives—their first lives—fade and fall to the side in favor of something that often feels like a cross between a movie and a dream, perhaps because their real lives are a nightmares. It only makes sense that another life offering greater engagement might start to compete with one that, for many people, is not what they'd hoped. They have another option.

Virtual worlds are the American Dream, second edition—a response to the American Dream, first edition.

Questions for Discussion

1. How similar and how different are the virtual or "second " life of Mark Meadows and his "real" life? How does Second Life impact his outside life and his health?

2. What has the Stanford Institute for the Qualitative Study of Society found about the relationship between time spent in Internet use and playing video games and time spent in "real-life social activities"? What are the implications of such studies?

3. What dangers does Meadows see in creating and emotionally engaging with the "alternative personality" of the avatar? What examples does he provide of such dangers? How can such engagement and subsequent online behavior lead to immoral and illegal behavior?

4. How does Meadows explain the dispute over avatar "driver's licenses" for Second Life participants? What were the causes for requiring such licenses and why did many participants object? With which side would you agree in this dispute and why?

5. How does Meadows respond to the series of historic anti-media quotations he provides? What concessions does he make? How does he attempt to answer the question "Why?" that is the title of his essay; i.e., *why* persist in being part of virtual reality online communities despite the psychological and sociological risks involved? Do you think he answers the question adequately? Why or why not?

6. Why and where did the first avatars originate? Why does Meadows consider the avatar a "technological, automated American Dream"? Do his argument and the evidence he provides from American history seem convincing?
7. What impact do the perceived dangers and alienation of modern American communities have on the development of avatars and the need to create virtual worlds, according to Meadows? Why does he end his essay by referring to virtual worlds as "The American Dream, second edition"? How is this new edition "a response to the original American Dream"? Can you think of other reasons for the recent interest in virtual avatar-based communities?

CONNECTION   •

Compare the function of avatars in Meadows' essay with that of the shadow self in dreams as described in marie Von Franz's essay in (Chapter 7 (see page 364).

IDEAS FOR WRITING

1. Do some research into Second Life and the values expressed within the community of players. What seems typically American about the avatar activities engaged there, and what seems other-wordly, fantasy, or dream-like? How do your conclusions coincide with or differ from those of Meadows?
2. Write an essay in which you consider areas in virtual worlds where "law and order" might be needed, as in the issuing of avatar "drivers' licenses." Consider what gamers and corporations can do to promote civilized and nonexploitive online behavior. Consult the following essay for a discussion of these issues: Dan Hunter and F. Gregory Lastowka, "To Kill an Avatar," *Legal Affairs* July|August 2003. <http://www.legalaffairs.org/issues/July-August-2003/feature_hunter_julaug03.msp>.

RELATED WEB SITES

My Virtual Life
www.businessweek.com/magazine/content/06_18/b3982001.htm
This article, featured in *BusinessWeek* Magazine, discusses the business opportunities in virtual living. Also featured are related articles dealing with online virtual worlds.

Hot Virtual Reality Sites
http://ovrt.nist.gov/hotvr.html
A government agency, the National Institute of Standards and Technology, provides a long list of virtual reality Web sites, divided into academia, commercial, cyberspace, and government categories.

Anne Ritchie

Creativity, Drugs, and Rock 'n' Roll

Anne Ritchie, a native Californian, wrote this research paper for her first-semester Writing and Rhetoric course at Stanford University in a section that focused on social and rhetorical issues in rock 'n' roll music. She is contemplating a career in journalism. Because of her love for the rock music of the 1960s and 1970s, she was interested in investigating the mythical correlation between drugs and rock 'n' roll.

We all know the scene: the show is over, the audience has left, the band has packed up the instruments, and back at the hotel, the musicians are celebrating another successful performance. On goes the music, in come the girls, and out come the drugs: cocaine, heroin, methamphetamines, LSD, marijuana, and, of course, alcohol. A common societal image of a rock star is that of a young performer addicted to drugs and sex, living the glorified lifestyle of a musician-celebrity. Through movies like Cameron Crowe's *Almost Famous,* the media illustrate the strong interdependence of sex, drugs, and rock 'n' roll. The recording industry bombards listeners with songs about smoking joints; "driving that train, high on cocaine" (Grateful Dead); and, for rap enthusiasts, "keepin' it real, packin' steel, gettin' high/Cause life's a bitch and then you die" (Nas). To the casual fan, drugs appear to be everywhere in pop music.

What, then, is the basis for this alleged necessary connection between drugs and rock 'n' roll? As social and political activist Abbie Hoffman put it, "[I]f you don't have sex and you don't do drugs, your rock 'n' roll better be awfully good" (qtd. in Driver xiii). Is this really the "truth" that drives the music industry? Do musicians need drugs to be successful? Many musicians and fans believe that drug use positively affects musical ability and creativity. As technological innovations allowed for the creation of more and more advanced drugs in the twentieth century, rock music evolved correspondingly, lending slight credence to this idea. However, despite the myths that link rock music and illegal drugs, musicians use drugs primarily for social reasons, and often find that drugs adversely affect their musical creativity. Thus, drugs are by no means necessary for a group's success, and can even have a detrimental effect on a single member of a band or the entire group.

A historical reason for the mythical connection between popular music and drugs lies with the advent of patent medicines in pre–World War I America. Patent medicines were tonics and elixirs containing opium, morphine, heroin, and cocaine, sold to cure any and all of the ills that plagued the general public (Shapiro 9). However, simple word-of-mouth popularity was not a good enough advertisement for the cure-alls, and so "medicine shows" were born (12). Designed to bring attention to the tonics, in the medicine shows, a salesman enthusiastically described the products' attributes while men who referred to themselves as doctors reassured the crowd that the "medicines" were safe and effective. A group of traveling entertainers, which included musicians, lured people to the shows and helped to build excitement for the products. As Harry Shapiro, author of *Waiting for the Man: The Story of Drugs and Popular Music,* observes, "[M]usic played an important part in the medicine show, which enabled those struggling to earn a living as musicians to find regular work and gave them a chance to travel" (14). In fact, most of the best blues musicians of the time worked in the medicine shows at one point or another, including "the King of Rock 'n' Roll, Little Richard" (16). These shows were the first significant events to connect music and drugs in the United States, to the extent that the traveling musicians were exposed to and often paid in drugs.

Traveling medicine shows ended with the Harrison Narcotics Act of 1914, which required the registration of all doctors, pharmacists, and vendors involved in drug transactions. Marijuana then became the drug of choice for musicians, as U.S. Treasury agents often used the new legislation to arrest anyone engaged in any way with the narcotic tonics. Thus, drug transactions through medicine shows came to an end, and musicians changed their focus to marijuana (Shapiro 17). With Prohibition in full swing, alcohol was only available illegally; three-quarters of all jazz clubs were Mob controlled during the 1920s (30). This connection with the underworld not only provided musicians with bootlegged alcohol, but also aligned them with a man named Milton "Mezz" Mezzerow, an instrumental figure in combining marijuana with jazz. Mezzerow was a central figure in a group of "marijuana musicians" who believed that marijuana smoking was crucial to producing good music. Although, as Shapiro explains, "it was widely felt among the jazz community that marijuana helped the creation of jazz by removing inhibitions and providing stimulation and confidence," not all musicians felt that way (32). Many musicians resented being associated with drugs; they shared clarinet player Artie Shaw's view that "during the twenties and thirties, a lot of good jazz went down in spite of marijuana rather than because of it" (qtd. in Shapiro 33). In the 1930s, the *Chicago Tribune* reported that marijuana addiction was "common among local musicians," marking the first time that concern was expressed regarding the intimate relationship between musicians and marijuana (qtd. in Shapiro 47). Furthermore, this connection to drugs gave birth to the idea of musicians as outlaw figures, rebelling against the norm. Since then, the media have played a large part in persuading the public about the link between musicians and drugs.

5   Music began to change dramatically in the 1950s, as did the drugs
with which it was associated. Jazz musicians moved on from marijuana
and became involved with heroin, which had become more accessible
since its limited availability during World War II (Shapiro 64). Musicians
took heroin and other drugs socially in order to become closer to other
members of the band. One jazzman of the time noted that "it became
such a habit with so many [musicians] that it was almost expected for any
new man in the band to show his sense of brotherhood by sticking that
needle into his arm, just like his buddies would" (qtd. in Shapiro 70).
Many were taking heavier drugs because everyone else was, not because
they made them any better at playing music. Once the heroin cycle began, musicians often would not be able to play gigs without the drug because their tolerance was so high that what they were once able to play
sober now required the help of the illicit substance (67). Musical talent
did not markedly improve with heroin usage, and the belief that jazz genius Charlie "Bird" Parker's heroin addiction somehow made heroin essential to jazz genius is illogical, because the correlation between one
man's genius and his drug habit does not imply causation (78). Even
though heroin did not contribute to the creation of music, the musician
lifestyle, with its insecurities, temporary fame, high expectations, and
constant, fatigue-inducing travel, led to the need for the drug and continues to support the illegal use of drugs today (Collins 19).

The social and political atmosphere of the 1950s deepened the role
of rock music as a form of rebellion against the establishment. Elvis Presley's pelvis thrusting was controversial enough for the new genre, which
developed out of a white appreciation for black rhythm and blues music.
According to John Orman, professor of politics at Fairfield University in
Connecticut and author of *The Politics of Rock Music,* the controversy of
rock was compounded by the introduction of many new types of drugs
to the United States' pop culture (3). The Central Intelligence Agency
developed LSD in this time period, and the U.S. Army's mass distribu-
tion of performance-enhancing amphetamines to its troops spread their
influence to the populace throughout the 1950s and 1960s (102). Elvis
himself was exposed to amphetamines for the first time while on guard
duty in the Army as a means to stay awake (104). Once the drugs had
reached the general population through their introduction in the military, musicians promoted the substances through their lyrics, interviews,
and onstage behavior. In the 1960s the drug lifestyle was popularized by
a new set of rock songs and stars, from Eric Clapton's "Cocaine" to
Rolling Stones guitarist Keith Richard's open discussions of his heroin
addiction (57). Additionally, the psychedelic music genre acted as an advertisement for psychedelic drugs, and still does to this day (58). Pink
Floyd's album *Dark Side of the Moon* can be found on Amazon.com under
the subheading "Music Best Heard Under the Influence of Psychedelic

Drugs" (Malone). The proliferation of songs about drugs and rock stars' lifestyles firmly cemented the connection between rock 'n' roll music and drugs.

The question of whether or not these drugs, from marijuana to cocaine to heroin to LSD to amphetamines, were necessary for the creation of good music and the success of bands can be answered in part by a case study of the Rolling Stones. The Rolling Stones established themselves as rock stars in 1965 with the release of "(I Can't Get No) Satisfaction," which, according to John Orman, is "perhaps the best rock song ever recorded" (91). They are also considered to have one of the worst reputations for on-the-road antics and drug abuse (Shapiro 216). The Rolling Stones not only are extremely successful, but also have a long history of drug use and abuse. The drug abuse, however, did not create the success.

Richards's addiction to heroin is so well known that he has become an iconic figure in association with the drug. In an interview with Jann Wenner for *Rolling Stone* magazine in 1995, Stones front man Mick Jagger discussed his bandmate's addiction: "Anyone taking heroin is thinking about taking heroin more than they're thinking about anything else. That's the general rule about most drugs. If you're really on some heavily addictive drug, you think about the drug and everything else is secondary" (qtd. in Wenner). Richards's focus was on his drug use, not on his music. Additionally, when asked about how Richards's heroin use affected the band, Jagger responded, "I think that people taking drugs occasionally are great. I think there's nothing wrong with it. But if you do it the whole time, you don't produce as good things as you could. It sounds like a puritanical statement, but it's based on experience . . . when Keith was taking heroin, it was very difficult to work. He was still creative, but it took a long time" (qtd. in Wenner). Clearly, Jagger thinks that drug use has a hindering effect on a band's ability to produce music. Although they may not completely destroy creativity, drugs slow the creation process. Jagger's authority on the subject of drugs is undeniable; as he himself puts it, "[I]t's based on experience" (qtd. in Wenner).

Many would disagree with Jagger's critical comments regarding drug use and creativity. In 1969, the Valentines were the first band to get arrested for possession of marijuana in Australia. In their defense, their lawyer, William Lennon, claimed that "under the influence of marijuana they became more perceptive to musical sounds . . . they could distinguish more clearly various instruments and how they were being played" (qtd. in Walker 154). When analyzing this idea, though, the context of the situation becomes extremely important. Who wouldn't say that drug use augmented their creativity when faced with jail time? Lennon's reasoning is obviously suspect. Often, drugs are thought to help capture the essence of the music, and, as Australian rock critic Clinton Walker believes, "the music sounds like its drug of choice. Psychedelia—acid rock—sounds like, well, acid. Australian pub music sounds like beer. . . . Reggae sounds like da'erb. Disco was the sound of amyl nitrate, or 'poppers.' Punk sounds like speed, as did the first wave of fifties rock 'n' roll and early 'beat' music" (154). This, however, is not necessarily a positive attribute for popularity and success. Many of the Grateful Dead's psychedelic rock songs are considered impossible to listen to unless one is in an altered state of consciousness (Shapiro 142). Thus, much of the population which does not approve of or does not partake of drugs, but still enjoys rock music, may feel alienated from the group's music. As a result, an extreme focus on drugs can be detrimental to a band's success. Fewer fans are attracted, and those who are interested may be involved with drugs themselves.

So funny

10   In the 1960s, some groups were able to enjoy mainstream musical success despite extensive drug use and drug references in their songs. In terms of success, the Beatles are incomparable. Often thought of as "opinion leaders" in the late 1960s, the Beatles were responsible for establishing much of what is known as "rock culture" (Orman 106). As the leaders of their generation of musicians, the Beatles' interactions with drugs reflect the general drug trend of the 1960s. Many of their songs contain drug references, including "Lucy in the Sky with Diamonds," which refers in the initials of its title to LSD, and "Day Tripper," which, according to Beatle member Paul McCartney, also is about acid. The image created by these songs, in conjunction with the Beatles' trip to India and their appreciation of marijuana and hashish, paints a drug-heavy picture. However, despite the prominence of drugs in the group's music, McCartney recently told the London *Daily Mirror* that although drugs did influence some of their songs, "[I]t's easy to overestimate the influence of drugs on the Beatles' music. Just about everyone was doing drugs in one form or another and we were no different, but the writing was too important for us to mess it up by getting off our heads all the time" ("McCartney"). In this interview, McCartney admits that using drugs is detrimental to creativity ("the writing"); thus, he is in agreement with Jagger of the Stones that too much drug use is detrimental to a group's production of original music. Rather than enhancing creativity, as drugs are thought to do, they most often impede it.

A discussion of individual bands' and groups' opinions regarding the effects of drug use on creativity, originality, and overall success (as more creative bands generally are more popular and successful) can help to demonstrate that drugs are not necessary for musical success. Even more effective, and quite graphic in illustrating the detrimental effects of drug use, is this list of names: Jimi Hendrix, Brian Jones, Janis Joplin, Jim Morrison, Elvis Presley, Sid Vicious, Hank Williams, Kurt Cobain, Brad Nowell (Driver ix). These musicians, and countless others, died from drug overdoses or drug-related incidents. Many of the deaths are still surrounded by mystery, like Morrison's sudden death in the bath of his Paris hotel and, of course, that of Presley, who, according to certain conspiracy theorists, still lives (Driver 592). More recently, in November 2004, rapper Ol' Dirty Bastard (O.D.B.) died from an overdose of cocaine mixed with the painkiller Tramadol. As a member of the Wu-Tang Clan rap group, O.D.B. had been working on a solo album at the time of his death and was creating a reality TV show, *Stuck on Dirty,* which is yet to be released on television (Devenish). These youthful performers would have had great potential had they lived. Each overdose contributed to a great loss in musical innovation.

A 1995 poll conducted for the Massachusetts Mutual Life Insurance Company found "the sixties drug mentality to be the most negative societal development of the past forty years" (Bozell 28). Even worse than the hindering of creativity that drug use causes is overdosing. The risk of overdose is there with every hit, every injection, and every swallowed pill. Even doing drugs once can kill. Assuming that narcotics do not kill the musicians, the negative effects of the chemicals can be detrimental to their creative ability and overall health.

The threats to musicians' well-being caused by substance abuse are evidenced by the recent change of heart in music industry executives, who now are looking to get their performers off of drugs. The leaders of Capitol, MCA, Virgin, and Revolution record labels have agreed to supervise an industry antidrug program. The president of the National Academy of Recording Arts and Sciences, Michael Greene, has said that "anyone who profits off an artist has the obligation to stop whatever was going on—touring, recording—and put that individual into treatment" (qtd. in Bozell 28). Additionally, Sony Music Entertainment and Dreamworks Records have given their support to Road Recovery, a nonprofit organization comprised of music industry professionals who seek to share a substance-free message with the youth of the United States. Gene Bowen, Road Recovery's founder, is a former tour manager who once was responsible for supplying his bands with drugs. After realizing the dangers of substance abuse, Bowen switched his focus to Road Recovery in order to educate musicians as well as other young adults about addiction, and to publicize treatment options for addicts in the industry ("Who We Are"). MusiCares Foundation, established in 1989, is a group devoted to providing musicians with all kinds of support, from drug treatment to psychological therapy ("MusiCares"). When the industry executives, whose jobs require that they focus on the monetary success of their bands, begin to focus on treatment programs for their musicians, the evidence is clear: using drugs not only does not enhance musical creativity and overall band success; in contrast, it can be extremely detrimental to a band, and in extreme cases can effectively end a group or a musician's career.

Despite the obvious health risks of drug use, many people still believe that music is better with drugs as part of the package. Nick Cave, an Australian singer, produced several albums while in the throes of drug addiction. According to Australian rock critic Clinton Walker, "These albums have a special magic, an all-consuming ambience, that is sadly, it seems, in part a result of the drugs in which they were pickled" (154). Drugs affected the music created under their influence. While this can be good, as it is in some of Cave's work, it does not mean that it is the best. Cave finally reached his potential once he checked into rehab in 1988 and cleaned himself up. As Walker describes it, "[A]t the same time, Cave has confounded the stereotypes, since his early 'clean' albums such as *The Good Son* of 1990 and *Let Love In* of 1994 are perhaps his pinnacle" (154). Cave could only reach his peak when he had removed drugs from the creative process.

15   In conclusion, musical creativity is not dependent on drug use. Although the history of drugs is intertwined with the history of rock music, the connection is mainly a social one. The music industry is one of the only realms of American society in which drug use is condoned, expected, and even encouraged. While the legal system has sentenced musicians to jail time for drug violations, socially, it still is acceptable for musicians to use, abuse, and become addicted to drugs, and the legal repercussions are outweighed by the reputation gained by brushes with the law. According to Shapiro, "[D]rugs . . . have always been part of the social grease of the industry" (203). Although they may be socially acceptable, the myth that drugs enhance musical ability, creativity, and overall group success is simply untrue. True genius lies in the musician, and cannot be found in any drug.

Works Cited

Bozell, L. Brent III. "When Rock 'n' Roll Finally Says 'No.'" *Insight on the News* 29 Jul. 1996. 7 Mar. 2005 {http://www.findarticles.com/p/articles/mi_m1571/is_n28_v12/ai_18524894}.

Collins, Tim. "Everybody Must Not Get Stoned." *New York Times* 20 Jul. 1996, late ed.: 19.

Devenish, Colin. "ODB Died of Drug Overdose." *Rolling Stone* 14 Dec. 2004. 18 Apr. 2005 {http://www.rollingstone.com/news/story/_/ id/6769257}.

Driver, Jim. *The Mammoth Book of Sex, Drugs & Rock 'n' Roll.* New York: Carroll & Graf, 2001.

Grateful Dead. "Casey Jones." *Steal Your Face* 1976. *LyricsXP.* 28 Feb. 2005 {http://www.lyricsxp.com/lyrics/c/casey_jones_grateful_dead. html}.

Malone, Jo Jo. "Music Best Heard Under the Influence of Psychedelic Drugs." *Amazon.com* Apr. 2005. 15 Apr. 2005 {http://www.amazon. com}.

"McCartney: Of Course Those Songs Were About Drugs." *Washington Post* 3 Jun. 2004. 22 Feb. 2005 {http://www.washingtonpost.com/wp-dyn/articles/A11258-2004Jun2.html}.

"MusiCares Foundation: Programs and Services." *Grammy* 2005. 18 Apr. 2005 {http://www.grammy.com/musicares/programs_services. aspx}.

Nas (Nasir Jones). "Life's a Bitch." *Illmatic* 1994. *LyricsXP* 4 May 2005 {http://www.lyricsxp.com/lyrics/l/life_s_a_bitch_nas.html}.

Orman, John. *The Politics of Rock Music.* Chicago: Nelson-Hall, 1984.

Shapiro, Harry. *Waiting for the Man: The Story of Drugs and Popular Music.* New York: William Morrow, 1988.

Walker, Clinton. "Codependent: A Potted History of Drugs and Australian Music." *Meanjin* 61.2 (2002). 7 Mar. 2005 {http://www.findarticles.com/p/articles/mi_hb200/is_200206/ai_n5785729}.

Wenner, Jann. "Jagger Remembers." *Rolling Stone* 14 April 1995. 7 Mar. 2005 {http://www.rollingstone.com/news/story/_/id/5938037}.

"Who We Are." *Road Recovery Foundation* 2005. 18 Apr. 2005 {http://www.roadrecovery.com}.

QUESTIONS FOR DISCUSSION

1. What is the main point or thesis of Anne Ritchie's essay on rock musicians and drug use? Do you think she is successful at making her point and refuting possible counterarguments on the subject? Why or why not?

2. To what audience does this essay seem to be directed? If the article were being sent around to periodicals for publication, what kind of publication would be most likely to accept it? Give examples to support your position.

3. How effectively does Ritchie make use of source materials to support her argument? Do the sources she relies upon seem to you relevant and credible? Why or why not?

4. Ritchie uses a broad definition of "drugs" in her introduction. Do you agree that substances like marijuana, LSD, alcohol, heroin, and cocaine should all be placed in the same general category of substances? How might drawing distinctions between these substances and their effects have changed the focus or direction of her paper?

5. Although Ritchie's paper deals with the impact of drugs on musicians, very little emphasis is placed on the influence of the music on fans' patterns of drug use. Do you think raising such issues would have helped the paper to communicate its antidrug message more forcefully? Why or why not?

TOPICS FOR RESEARCH AND WRITING

1. Many critics have commented that mass communications media often portray a biased or stereotyped image of minority groups and women, sometimes excluding certain groups altogether. Research the media coverage of one or more minority groups, and write your conclusions in the form of a documented research essay. Refer to the readings in this chapter to support your ideas and point of view.

2. Write an essay on the media's coverage of an event in your neighborhood or in your community. Research several different points of view. Then draw conclusions about the influence of the media on the outcome of the event. Do you think that the media impacted people's understanding of the event? How often do you think that news coverage stereotypes an event? How reliable, then, is the information that we get from the media?

3. After doing some outside reading and Internet research, write an essay that focuses on the ways that the Internet and the electronic environment can influence one's self-concept. What types of communication through the World Wide Web do you think are positive, and which ones are negative? Focus on several issues to make your point.

4. Examine the current television schedule (cable as well as network TV) for programs that you think encourage imagination, creativity, and a concern for the inner life; then read some reviews of these programs in print media or the Internet. After considering the media critiques, write an evaluative review of several such programs, trying to draw some conclusions about the potential the television medium has for improving the quality of modern life, as well as the ways it often fails to achieve its potential.

5. Considering the ideas of writers such as Jenkins, Schor, Cusick, Provenso, and Mattera, write a research paper that addresses the negative, positive, or ambiguous impact of a particular aspect of pop culture on the identity and mental health of citizens in our society. You might consider popular music, children's TV programs, gaming on the Internet, MTV, commercials, branding, or sex and violence in films or on television.

6. Write a research essay that discusses the impact of celebrities on youth throughout the world. Along with researching this question, refer to articles in this chapter to support your point of view.

7. Write about a film that examines issues of advertising, propaganda, or mass media on society, politics, and the inner life of the individual. Watch the film and take notes on the dialogue and any other details that can be used to support the conclusions you draw; also read some critical responses to the film, both in popular journals and in specialized magazines that critique films. You might select a film from the following list: *Network, Broadcast News, The Kiss of the Spider Woman, Pulp Fiction, The Matrix, The Truman Show, Walk the Line, Ray, Pleasantville, Mean Girls, Crash, The Devil Wears Prada, Sex and the City, Lost in Translation*, and *Be Cool*.

Voyages in Spirituality

Jon Ford (b.1943)
Boudhanath Stupa, Kathmandu (2008)

JOURNAL

Write about a spiritual place that is especially meaningful to you, and the values/ experiences it offers for you and for others.

*Holiness is a force, and like the others can be resisted. It was given, but
I didn't want to see it, God or no god.*

ANNIE DILLARD

*With this faith we will be able to hew out of the mountain of despair a
stone of hope. With this faith we will be able to transform the jangling
discords of our nation into a beautiful symphony of brotherhood.*

MARTIN LUTHER KING, JR.

*Do you have the patience to wait?
Till your mud settles and the water is clear?
Can you remain unmoving
till the right action arises by itself?*

LAU-TZU

THEMATIC INTRODUCTION

From ancient times to the present, people have discovered solutions to personal, aesthetic, social, and scientific problems through spiritual messages brought to them from their dreams, their intuitions, and the religious communities of which they are a part. The selections in this chapter reflect the spiritual experiences of people from different cultures, denominations, generations, and social classes. They present a range of issues and experiences, all of which speak about a unique quality of spirituality. While many people connect their spirituality to a particular religion, in this chapter we present spirituality more broadly, as being capable of embracing all religions and including all people, even those who have spiritual experiences and vocations that exist outside of any ordinary religious context.

The chapter begins with a poem by Linda Gregg, "God's Places," in which she finds traces of God and religious inspiration in the most ordinary events that seem products of pure chance or grace, yet she yearns for a human love that can match the power of these momentary insights. "In the Forests of Gombe" tells of Jane Goodall's mystical experience of the interconnectedness of scientific and spiritual knowledge after returning to the place in Africa that was her home with the chimpanzees she came to study and to love.

In contrast, Donna Lovong's "Are You Joining a Cult?" focuses on her Laotian family's response to her daily meditations and Buddhist practice, which her parents perceive as a form of cult-like behavior compared to the traditional, temple-based observances that constitute their idea of religion. Similar to Lovong, Norman Yeung Bik Chung, student author of "A Faithful Taoist," rejected the pious traditional

Taoism of his father, yet is struck by how his father's faith helps him to make important decisions about his health that allows his family to better cope with his death.

Our next group of selections discusses ways that spiritual beliefs and social activism can be joined. Jessie van Eerden's essay. "The Soul Has Six Wings," focuses on the female religious mystical group The Beguines, who roamed Europe in the thirteenth century, surviving from the land and helping one another out despite persecution from church authorities. Van Eerden draws a parallel between an informal spiritual community of women she belongs to and the Beguines. Spiritual teacher Noah Levine, a former addict and punk rocker, in his memoir, "Death Is Not the End My Friend," describes his own spiritual regeneration after the death by overdose of a close friend, resulting in Levine's renewed dedication to service for incarcerated youth.

In his powerful sermon "A Christmas Sermon on Peace," the minister and civil rights leader Martin Luther King, Jr. develops a politically charged spiritual argument that uses both modern and biblical language to create a plea for a future free of racial injustice and exploitation. King's essay is followed by Jim Wallis's "Taking Back the Faith," in which Wallis, whose activist ministry is dedicated to helping the poor, discusses ways in which many modern denominations have strayed from their mission by focusing on political issues and moralism rather than on doing good works. Our final student essay, Karen Methot-Chun's "Living Spirituality," defines active spirituality in daily life and discusses issues of morality and service.

Each of the essays in this chapter captures a sense of the meaning and importance of spirituality. We hope that these readings will encourage you to think and reflect more deeply on the enduring qualities of spiritual life. Although spirituality has an individual meaning for each person, we can all strive to cherish our spiritual lives, both in the public world and in our inner worlds. Our dreams and visions will create the future.

CREATIVITY, PROBLEM SOLVING, AND SYNTHESIS

Creativity and spirituality have many similar qualities. Both involve a new way of seeing—going beyond the surface appearance of things to find deeper and more complex meanings. These new insights may include a combination of information and experience into a new synthesis that solves problems and/or produces something that a person can value and respect. In the case of writing, that new product may be a poem, story, or nonfiction work that is humanely and aesthetically satisfying, both to you and to others. While many people are inspired by the examples of creative visionaries in different fields and can learn from studying their techniques, creativity is in large part a generative rather than an imitative and technical process, a process of discovery that often originates in the unconscious mind, sometimes without a clear goal or defined product in mind—at least at the beginning. An open, receptive mental attitude encourages the initiation of the creative process.

Everyone is potentially creative; in fact, all people are creative when they dream, whether or not they are consciously aware of the process. As author John Steinbeck noted, a problem is often "resolved in the morning after the committee of sleep has worked it out." In waking life people are creative in a more conscious, directed manner, seeking solutions to problems in order to survive and to make their lives more comfortable and rewarding. For example, when you redecorate your room, look for a better job, or select a new course of study in school, you are working on creative solutions for the problems that you have recognized in your life, just as you are when you write a proposal for your job or for one of your classes at school. You may see what you are doing at work or school as competing for a raise or completing a course requirement—but there is also an element of creativity in every new solution and usually the creative ideas that get the most attention.

Although it is true that everyone exercises some degree of creativity, it is equally true that most people have the potential to be far more creative in many aspects of their lives than they actually are. Writers, psychologists, and social scientists have identified patterns of behavior that are likely to block an individual's creativity. Understanding how these mental traps work may help you find a way to release yourself from nonproductive behavior and to become more creative.

Habit Versus Risk

Habit and self-image can be major blocks to creativity. If your inner self-image is that of a person stuck in a round of repetitive daily tasks and rituals, it is unlikely that you will feel that you can be a creative person. You may have come to believe that you really need to follow a ritualized pattern in performing your job, relating to people, or writing. This type of thinking also protects you from taking risks: the risk of an original expression of a feeling or situation, the risk of a controversial solution to a problem, the risk of not being understood by others.

Furthermore, creative risk-taking approaches to problem solving can be quite time consuming. Many people convince themselves that they don't have the time to explore a new and creative approach and that it is more efficient to follow a method that has worked (or sort-of worked) in the past. This inclination to play it safe and to be overly concerned with time management is typical of workers, managers, students, teachers, and writers who fear change and are wary of embarking on a new direction in their lives. Even if you see yourself as a non-risk-taking person, it is never too late to change. Fantasizing about new approaches and thinking about alternatives are positive first steps toward finding creative solutions. Try to develop your alternative fantasies, as do many of the writers in this chapter.

Reason Versus Intuition

You may be building another obstacle to uncovering your creativity if you value a linear, rational approach to handling problems to the extent that you ignore the imaginative, emotional, and intuitive side of the mind and the solutions that your imagination might suggest. Did you know that many landmark solutions to creative problems, both in the arts and in the sciences, were born in the unconscious mind and some specifically in dreams? Some examples include Descartes' philosophical system, the invention of the sewing machine needle, and the pattern of the benzene ring, as well as the basic concepts for classic works of literature such as Mary Shelley's *Frankenstein*, Samuel Taylor Coleridge's "Kubla Khan," and Robert Louis Stevenson's *The Strange Case of Dr. Jekyll and Mr. Hyde*.

We do not want you to think that all you have to do is to take a nap and allow your problems to solve themselves, or that if you sleep long enough, you will discover the seeds of great art and great ideas. We do encourage you though to look to your dream mind for ideas and feelings and to allow your unconscious mind to have time to process and integrate ideas that are being developed by your rational mind. For example, after you have finished the first draft of a paper, go for a walk or a swim, listen to some music, or take a nap. Let your unconscious mind have a chance to think about what you have written. When you return refreshed to your first draft, you may find that your unconscious mind has sent you new ideas to work with or that you have a solution to a problem in your paper that was frustrating you.

Developing Self-Confidence: Learning to Trust Your Own Processes

Another barrier to the creative process can come from trying too hard to please an authority such as a teacher or employer. If you focus your energy on trying to please your teacher at the expense of what you think or believe, an inner conflict may keep you from writing your paper altogether. If you become too reliant on your instructor's assignment and approval, you will not be developing your own working style and sense of independence, which every writer must possess. Finally, if you rush to produce a finished paper in one draft, you will miss the excitement of discovery, the potential for personal involvement that is an essential part of the writing process; furthermore, it is always preferable to relax and work within a writing project rather than to become too focused on what it is supposed to be.

Evaluation and Application

The creative problem-solving process does include evaluation and application—but only after you give free expression to a range of imaginative solutions and ideas. Once you have finished the creative or generative part of your writing project, you will want to think about whether or not you have accomplished your goals. To evaluate your work, you need to establish clear standards so that you can compare your work with that of others. Always try to formulate standards that are challenging and yet realistic.

Peer sharing can be a useful comparative and evaluative process that will help you to create realistic standards for assessing your own writing in relationship to that of your classmates. Through sharing your work as well as reading and editing the work of your classmates, you will begin to develop realistic standards for the style, structure, and content of your writing. Learn to ask questions of yourself and of your peers. Develop criteria for evaluating papers as you go along. Soon you will find that you have established a vocabulary that allows you to talk about one another's papers and that you have defined standards for effective writing.

Synthesis

Synthesis, the final step in the creative process, involves bringing a number of different ideas or solutions, which you may have considered separately, together to form an integrated solution. For example, if you are trying to decide on a method for presenting an essay on "How to Make Your Dreams Work for You," you will need to evaluate and then synthesize or integrate the different points of view of experts—as well as your own—on the subject of dream power. Synthesis is an excellent metaphor for the gathering and unifying of information from diverse sources that can produce a lively research proposal. In a sense, synthesis also defines the writing process itself, as writing involves bringing together a number of different skills to solve a variety of problems: engaging your reader's interest, persuading your reader, developing an overall structure and pattern, supporting your main ideas, and using language that is both appropriate and creative. The student essay by

Karen Methot-Chun ("Living Spirituality") in this chapter includes examples of synthesis writing in her development of a complex philosophical definition that mediates between ideas and quotations from different writers while also employing strategies of illustration and contrast to build and support her argument.

Writing is a rewarding activity that can help you discover your thoughts and feelings and combine them in new ways. In any type of writing, you work through the stages and difficulties inherent in the creative process as a whole.

Linda Gregg

God's Places

Linda Gregg was born in New York in 1942 and spent her childhood in Northern California. She received her M.A. from San Francisco State College in 1972 and has taught creative writing and poetry at the University of Iowa, Columbia University, the University of California at Berkeley, and, most recently, at Princeton University. She has received many awards for her poetry, including a Guggenheim Fellowship, a Lannan Literary Foundation Fellowship, and a National Endowment for the Arts grant. Her work has been praised by such noted poets as Joseph Brodsky, Czeslaw Milosz, and W. S. Merwin. Linda Gregg gains inspiration for her work from her travels, particularly to Greece, where she has lived and returned to on many occasions. Her poems have appeared in poetry reviews and in national magazines such as The New Yorker *and* The Atlantic. *Her books include* The Sacraments of Desire *(1991),* Things and Flesh *(1999), and* All of It Singing: New and Selected Poems *(2008). The following poem about loss and places of spiritual illumination is from* Chosen by the Lion *(1994).*

JOURNAL

Write about a moment of spiritual insight or higher sense of place that has come to you from noticing something unexpected or new in your daily environment.

Does the soul care about the mightiness
of this love? No. The soul is a place
and love must find its way there.

A fisherman on his boat swung a string
5   of fish around his head and threw it
across the water where it landed at my feet.
That was a place. One day I walked into
a village that was all ruins. It was noon.
Nobody was there, the roofs were gone,
10   the silence was heavy. A man came out,
gradually other people, but no one spoke.
Then somebody gave me a glass of water
with a lump of jam on a spoon in it.
It was a place, one of God's places,
15   but love was not with me. I breathed
the way grape vines live and give in
to the whole dream of being and not being.
The soul must be experienced to be achieved.
If you love me as much as you say you
20   love me, stay. Let us make a place
of that ripeness the soul speaks about.

QUESTIONS FOR DISCUSSION

1. What is the meaning of the title of the poem, "God's Places"? How does the title prepare us for the issues and examples provided in the poem?

2. Linda Gregg begins her poem with a rhetorical question about whether the soul "care[s] about the mightiness of this love"—Why doesn't the soul care? Why is it significant that "this love" is ambiguous, that we're confused as to whether "this" refers to the mightiness of the love of God for the soul, the love of the speaker in the poem for God, or the love of the speaker for some human lover (or of the lover for her)?

3. What is the purpose of the vivid example that follows about the fish thrown "across the water" to the speaker's feet? Why does the speaker comment on this event with the line "That was a place"? How might this be considered one of "God's places," a sacred moment in time?

4. The second example the speaker provides of a "God's place" is a dreamlike narrative about visiting a "ruined village" where she is offered water and jam, but not spoken to. Why is it significant that she is totally alone in her experience and that "love was not with me"?

5. How is the speaker's breathing transformed in this experience? What is the significance of this transformation? How does her experience parallel the "achievement" of the soul mentioned in line 18?

6. Who is the "you" the speaker addresses in the poem's final lines? How does she present the idea of making a "place of that ripeness the soul speaks about" as a solution for the problems related to love and the "God's places" she has examined throughout the poem?

CONNECTION

Compare and contrast Linda Gregg's and Jane Goodall's experiences of spirituality (see page 490).

IDEAS FOR WRITING

1. Develop your journal writing assignment for this section into a reflective essay about how finding a "God's Place" in your own daily life has taught you a lesson about yourself and your personal/spiritual values.
2. Linda Gregg has written that "The art of finding in poetry is the art of marrying the sacred to the world, the invisible to the human." Apply this insight about the "art of finding" to the poem "God's Places" and the issues it raises about spirituality, creativity, and human love.

RELATED WEB SITES

Linda Gregg

`www.poets.org/poet.php/prmPID/931`

This page from the Academy of American Poets features a biography on Linda Gregg, as well as links to some of her poetry, prose, and to related poets.

Spiritual Poets

`www.writespirit.net/spiritual_poets`

This Web site, dedicated to "sharing ancient wisdom and modern inspiration," provides links to spiritual poets. In addition, links to spiritual poets of specific religions or schools of thought are also presented.

Jane Goodall

In the Forests of Gombe

Jane Goodall was born in London, England, in 1934. Dr. Louis Leakey, a paleontologist and anthropologist, chose Goodall to begin a study of wild chimpanzees on the shore of Lake Tanganyika. In 1960 she observed a chimpanzee using and making tools to fish for termites, a discovery that challenged the view of humans as being the only toolmakers in the animal kingdom. Although Jane Goodall did not complete a formal education, she was awarded a Ph.D. at Cambridge University. She is a spokesperson for the conservation of chimpanzee habitats and for the humane treatment of captive primates. Her most recent books include Great Apes and Humans:

The Ethics of Coexistence *(2001) and* The Ten Trusts: What We
Must Do to Care for the Animals We Love *(2002). In the following se-*
lection from her memoir, A Reason for Hope *(1999), Goodall writes*
about a mystical experience in the forest of Gombe that helped her to recover
from the death of her husband and gave her life a new spiritual perspective.

JOURNAL

Discuss a time that you spent in a forest, at the seashore, or in any natural
setting. Did the time you spent in this natural setting rejuvenate your mind
and spirit? In what ways?

I was taught, as a scientist, to think logically and empirically, rather than
intuitively or spiritually. When I was at Cambridge University in the
early 1960s most of the scientists and science students working in the
Department of Zoology, so far as I could tell, were agnostic or even atheist. Those who believed in a god kept it hidden from their peers.

Fortunately, by the time I got to Cambridge I was twenty-seven years
old and my beliefs had already been molded so that I was not influenced
by these opinions. I believed in the spiritual power that, as a Christian,
I called God. But as I grew older and learned about different faiths
I came to believe that there was, after all, but One God with different
names: Allah, Tao, the Creator, and so our God, for me, was the Great
Spirit in Whom "we live and move and have our being." There have been
times during my life when this belief wavered, when I questioned—even
denied—the existence of God. At such times I felt there can be no
underlying meaning to the emergence of life on earth.

Still, for me those periods have been relatively rare, triggered by a variety of circumstances. One was when my second husband died of cancer. I was grieving, suffering, and angry. Angry at God, at fate—the
unjustness of it all. For a time I rejected God, and the world seemed a
bleak place.

It was in the forests of Gombe that I sought healing after Derek's
death. Gradually during my visits, my bruised and battered spirit found
solace. In the forest, death is not hidden—or only accidentally, by the
fallen leaves. It is all around you all the time, a part of the endless cycle
of life. Chimpanzees are born, they grow older, they get sick, and they
die. And always there are the young ones to carry on the life of the
species. Time spent in the forest, following and watching and simply
being with the chimpanzees, has always sustained the inner core of my
being. And it did not fail me then.

5   One day, among all the days, I remember most of all. It was May 1981
and I had finally made it to Gombe after a six-week tour in America—six

weeks of fund-raising dinners, conferences, meetings, and lobbying for various chimpanzee issues. I was exhausted and longed for the peace of the forest. I wanted nothing more than to be with the chimpanzees, renewing my acquaintance with my old friends, getting my climbing legs back again, relishing the sights, sounds, and smells of the forest. I was glad to be away from Dar es Salaam, with all its sad associations—the house that Derek and I had shared, the palm trees we had bought and planted together, the rooms we had lived in together, the Indian Ocean in which Derek, handicapped on land, had found freedom swimming among his beloved coral reefs.

Back in Gombe. It was early in the morning and I sat on the steps of my house by the lakeshore. It was very still. Suspended over the horizon, where the mountains of the Congo fringed Lake Tanganyika, was the last quarter of the waning moon and her path danced and sparkled toward me across the gently moving water. After enjoying a banana and a cup of coffee, I was off, climbing up the steep slopes behind my house.

In the faint light from the moon reflected by the dew-laden grass, it was not difficult to find my way up the mountain. It was quiet, utterly peaceful. Five minutes later I heard the rustlings of leaves overhead. I looked up and saw the branches moving against the lightening sky. The chimps had awakened. It was Fifi and her offspring, Freud, Frodo, and little Fanni. I followed when they moved off up the slope, Fanni riding on her mother's back like a diminutive jockey. Presently they climbed into a tall fig tree and began to feed. I heard the occasional soft thuds as skins and seeds of figs fell to the ground.

For several hours we moved leisurely from one food tree to the next, gradually climbing higher and higher. On an open grassy ridge the chimps climbed into a massive mbula tree, where Fifi, replete from the morning's feasting, made a large comfortable nest high above me. She dozed through a midday siesta, little Fanni asleep in her arms, Frodo and Freud playing nearby. I felt very much in tune with the chimpanzees, for I was spending time with them not to observe, but simply because I needed their company, undemanding and free of pity. From where I sat I could look out over the Kasakela Valley. Just below me to the west was the peak. From that same vantage point I had learned so much in the early days, sitting and watching while, gradually, the chimpanzees had lost their fear of the strange white ape who had invaded their world. I recaptured some of my long-ago feelings—the excitement of discovering, of seeing things unknown to Western eyes, and the serenity that had come from living, day after day, as a part of the natural world. A world that dwarfs yet somehow enhances human emotions.

As I reflected on these things I had been only partly conscious of the approach of a storm. Suddenly, I realized that it was no longer growling in the distance but was right above. The sky was dark, almost black, and the rain clouds had obliterated the higher peaks. With the growing darkness came the stillness, the hush, that so often precedes a tropical downpour. Only the rumbling of the thunder, moving closer and closer, broke this stillness; the thunder and the rustling movements of the chimpanzees. All at once came a blinding flash of lightning, followed, a split second later, by an incredibly loud clap of thunder that seemed almost to shake the solid rock before it rumbled on, bouncing from peak to peak. Then the dark and heavy clouds let loose such torrential rain that sky and earth seemed joined by moving water. I sat under a palm whose fronds, for a while, provided some shelter. Fifi sat hunched over, protecting her infant; Frodo pressed close against them in the nest; Freud sat with rounded back on a nearby branch. As the rain poured endlessly down, my palm fronds no longer provided shelter and I got wetter and wetter. I began to feel first chilly, and then, as a cold wind sprang up, freezing; soon, turned in on myself, I lost all track of time. I and the chimpanzees formed a unit of silent, patient, and uncomplaining endurance.

10   It must have been an hour or more before the rain began to ease as the heart of the storm swept away to the south. At four-thirty the chimps climbed down, and we moved off through the dripping vegetation, back down the mountainside. Presently we arrived on a grassy ridge overlooking the lake. I heard sounds of greeting as Fifi and her family joined Melissa and hers. They all climbed into a low tree to feed on fresh young leaves. I moved to a place where I could stand and watch as they enjoyed their last meal of the day. Down below, the lake was still dark and angry with white flecks where the waves broke, and rain clouds remained black in the south. To the north the sky was clear with only wisps of gray clouds still lingering. In the soft sunlight, the chimpanzees' black coats were shot with coppery brown, the branches on which they sat were wet and dark as ebony, the young leaves a pale but brilliant green. And behind was the backcloth of the indigo sky where lightning flickered and distant thunder growled and rumbled.

Lost in awe at the beauty around me, I must have slipped into a state of heightened awareness. It is hard—impossible, really—to put into words the moment of truth that suddenly came upon me then. It seemed to me, as I struggled afterward to recall the experience, that *self* was utterly absent: I and the chimpanzees, the earth and trees and air, seemed to merge, to become one with the spirit power of life itself. The air was filled with a feathered symphony, the evensong of birds. I heard new frequencies in their music and also in the singing insects' voices—notes so high and sweet I was amazed. Never had I been so intensely aware of the shape, the color of the individual leaves, the varied patterns of the veins that made each one unique. Scents were clear as well, easily identifiable: fermenting overripe fruit; waterlogged earth; cold, wet bark; the damp odor of chimpanzee hair and, yes, my own too, I sensed a new presence, then saw a bushbuck, quietly browsing upwind, his spiraled horns gleaming and chestnut coat dark with rain.

Suddenly a distant chorus of pant-hoots elicited a reply from Fifi. As though wakening from some vivid dream I was back in the everyday world, cold, yet intensely alive. When the chimpanzees left, I stayed in that place—it seemed a most sacred place—scribbling some notes, trying to describe what, so briefly, I had experienced.

Eventually I wandered back along the forest trail and scrambled down behind my house to the beach. Later, as I sat by my little fire, cooking my dinner of beans, tomatoes, and an egg, I was still lost in the wonder of my experience. Yes, I thought, there are many windows through which we humans, searching for meaning, can look out into the world around us. There are those carved out by Western science, their panes polished by a succession of brilliant minds. Through them we can see ever farther, ever more clearly, into areas which until recently were beyond human knowledge. Through such a scientific window I had been taught to observe the chimpanzees. For more than twenty-five years I had sought, through careful recording and critical analysis, to piece together their complex social behavior, to understand the workings of their minds. And this had not only helped us to better understand their place in nature but also helped us to understand a little better some aspects of our own human behavior, our own place in the natural world.

Yet there are other windows through which we humans can look out into the world around us, windows through which the mystics and the holy men of the East, and the founders of the great world religions, have gazed as they searched for the meaning and purpose of our life on earth, not only in the wondrous beauty of the world, but also in its darkness and ugliness. And those Masters contemplated the truths that they saw, not with their minds only but with their hearts and souls also. From those revelations came the spiritual essence of the great scriptures, the holy books, and the most beautiful mystic poems and writings. That afternoon it had been as though an unseen hand had drawn back a curtain and, for the briefest moment, I had seen through such a window.

15 How sad that so many people seem to think that science and religion are mutually exclusive. Science has used modern technology and modern techniques to uncover so much about the formation and the development of life forms on Planet Earth and about the solar system of which our little world is but a minute part. Alas, all of these amazing discoveries have led to a belief that every wonder of the natural world and of the universe—indeed, of infinity and time—can, in the end, be understood through the logic and the reasoning of a finite mind. And so, for many, science has taken the place of religion. It was not some intangible God who created the universe, they argue; it was the big bang. Physics,

chemistry, and evolutionary biology can explain the start of the universe and the appearance and progress of life on earth, they say. To believe in God, in the human soul, and in life after death is simply a desperate and foolish attempt to give meaning to our lives.

But not all scientists believe thus. There are quantum physicists who have concluded that the concept of God is not, after all, merely wishful thinking. There are those exploring the human brain who feel that no matter how much they discover about this extraordinary structure it will never add up to a complete understanding of the human mind—that the whole is, after all, greater than the sum of its parts. The big bang theory is yet another example of the incredible, the awe-inspiring ability of the human mind to learn about seemingly unknowable phenomena in the beginning of time. Time as we know it, or think we know it. But what about before time? And what about beyond space? I remember so well how those questions had driven me to distraction when I was a child.

I lay flat on my back and looked up into the darkening sky. I thought about the young man I had met during the six-week tour I had finished before my return to Gombe. He had a holiday job working as a bellhop in the big hotel where I was staying in Dallas, Texas. It was prom night, and I wandered down to watch the young girls in their beautiful evening gowns, their escorts elegant in their tuxedos. As I stood there, thinking about the future—theirs, mine, the world's—I heard a diffident voice:

"Excuse me, Doctor—aren't you Jane Goodall?" The bellhop was very young, very fresh-faced. But he looked worried—partly because he felt that he should not be disturbing me, but partly, it transpired, because his mind was indeed troubled. He had a question to ask me. So we went and sat on some back stairs, away from the glittering groups and hand-holding couples.

He had watched all my documentaries, read my books. He was fascinated, and he thought that what I did was great. But I talked about evolution. Did I believe in God? If so, how did that square with evolution? Had we really descended from chimpanzees?

20   And so I tried to answer him as truthfully as I could, to explain my own beliefs. I told him that no one thought humans had descended from chimpanzees. I explained that I did believe in Darwinian evolution and told him of my time at Olduvai, when I had held the remains of extinct creatures in my hands. That I had traced, in the museum, the various stages of the evolution of, say, a horse: from a rabbit-sized creature that gradually, over thousands of years, changed, became better and better adapted to its environment, and eventually was transformed into the modern horse. I told him I believed that millions of years ago there had been a primitive, apelike, humanlike creature, one branch of

which had gone on to become the chimpanzee, another branch of which had eventually led to us.

"But that doesn't mean I don't believe in God," I said. And I told him something of my beliefs, and those of my family. I told him that I had always thought that the biblical description of God creating the world in seven days might well have been an attempt to explain evolution in a parable. In that case, each of the days would have been several million years.

"And then, perhaps, God saw that a living being had evolved that was suitable for His purpose. *Homo sapiens* had the brain, the mind, the potential. Perhaps," I said, "that was when God breathed the Spirit into the first Man and the first Woman and filled them with the Holy Ghost."

The bellhop was looking considerably less worried. "Yes, I see," he said. "That could be right. That does seem to make sense."

I ended by telling him that it honestly didn't matter how we humans got to be the way we are, whether evolution or special creation was responsible. What mattered and mattered desperately was our future development. How should the mind that can contemplate God relate to our fellow beings, the other life forms of the world? What is our human responsibility? And what, ultimately, is our human destiny? Were we going to go on destroying God's creation, fighting each other, hurting the other creatures of His planet? Or were we going to find ways to live in greater harmony with each other and with the natural world? That, I told him, was what was important. Not only for the future of the human species, but also for him, personally. When we finally parted his eyes were clear and untroubled, and he was smiling.

25   Thinking about that brief encounter, I smiled too, there on the beach at Gombe. A wind sprang up and it grew chilly. I left the bright stars and went inside to bed. I knew that while I would always grieve Derek's passing, I could cope with my grieving. That afternoon, in a flash of "outsight" I had known timelessness and quiet ecstasy, sensed a truth of which mainstream science is merely a small fraction. And I knew that the revelation would be with me for the rest of my life, imperfectly remembered yet always within. A source of strength on which I could draw when life seemed harsh or cruel or desperate. The forest, and the spiritual power that was so real in it, had given me the "peace that passeth understanding."

QUESTIONS FOR DISCUSSION

1. Why did Goodall return to the forest? How did it heal her?
2. Goodall says that living in the natural world "dwarfs yet somehow enhances human emotions." Explain her assertion within the context of her experience in the forest.

3. What precipitates Goodall's mystical experience? Why and how is her sense of reality altered? When does her mystical experience end? What insights does Goodall take away from this moment?

4. Describe Goodall's writing style. Does her style help to engage you in her experiences and beliefs? Give examples of effective use of time and unusual shifts of perspective in the essay.

5. How and why does Goodall contrast her Eastern mystical experience to her Western scientific and analytical study of the complex social behaviors of chimpanzees? What conclusions does she make?

6. How does Goodall help the bellhop and her readers to understand how both scientific and religious thinking can help us to find meaning in life? Do you agree or disagree with Goodall's perspective? Explain.

CONNECTION

Compare and contrast Jane Goodall's views on the connection between the spiritual and scientific experiences of the world with those of Marcelo Gleiser (Chapter 4, see page 178).

IDEAS FOR WRITING

1. After the rainstorm Goodall looks over a ridge to see the lake in a new way. Write a descriptive narrative about an experience in the natural world that helped you develop a new perspective on your life. In what ways was this experience spiritual or mystical? Explain how you felt about this event.

2. Write an analysis of Goodall's conversation with the young hotel employee about the space for both spiritual and scientific explanations of the world to coexist. Do you agree with her reasoning here? Why or why not?

RELATED WEB SITES

The Jane Goodall Institute
www.janegoodall.org
The mission of the Jane Goodall Institute is to advance the power of individuals to take informed and compassionate action to improve the environment. Find out more about the institute, Jane Goodall's life and work, and how to get involved at this Web site.

Gombe National Park, Tanzania
http://weber.ucsd.edu/~jmoore/apesites/Gombe/Gombe.html
Learn about Gombe National Park, where Jane Goodall began her research on chimpanzees, at this Web site from the University of California, San Diego. The site also features a link to UCSD's "African Ape Study Site."

Donna Lovong

Are You Joining a Cult?

Born in Thailand near the border with Laos, Donna Lovong has lived most of her life in the United States. She earned a B.A. in sociology and is involved with public health work and research. Although her parents are Laotian refugees with strong traditional Buddhist beliefs centered on temple rituals, she has been involved with a less formal type of Buddhist-derived meditation in recent years. The following essay, published in The Best Buddhist Writing *of 2007, examines the way her meditation practice helped Lovong to reconcile herself with the tensions and cultural misunderstandings within her family.*

JOURNAL

What do you know about the practice of Zen meditation? If you are not familiar with the practice, learn something about it through research.

"A re you joining a cult?" my mother asked, her eyebrows furrowing. My mom looked anxious as I told her that I would be going to a Buddhist meditation retreat the next weekend. I laughed. "No, Mom, this isn't a cult. Don't you remember what the monks did back when you lived in Laos? I'm doing meditation." She wasn't reassured. Even though our family frequently went to the local Buddhist temple, meditation by laypeople was as foreign to her as offering sticky rice to monks was to me. Mom continued, "Be careful. Don't let them brainwash you." She proceeded to tell me about people at her workplace who followed some kind of group. "I know these Asian women at work who stopped eating meat altogether . . . I think they are being brainwashed."

At first, I couldn't believe that my mother, herself an avowed Buddhist, would think that my meditation practice was weird. I have since come to appreciate the big cultural gap between my mom's Asian past and my American upbringing, and between her ethnic Buddhism and my Western Buddhism. Looking for ways to bridge our differences, I've probed deeper into my family, my community, and myself.

My parents grew up in Southeast Asia during the 1950s, '60s, and early '70s. In those decades, the region was in constant war and conflict. When the Communist regime expanded into my parents' country in 1975, my mother—pregnant with me at the time—and my father fled and became refugees. We took shelter at a Buddhist temple temporarily, and there I was born. We emigrated to the United States, bringing with us generations of suspicion, mistrust, and anger. I suspect that my parents' experience of being uprooted and of witnessing their own country being "brainwashed" by the Communists is why my mom felt apprehensive when I joined a meditation group.

My mother grew up in a traditional ethnic Chinese family, which had Confucian and Taoist sensibilities mixed in with spirit and nature worship. She told me that no one in her family was Buddhist. She started going to the local Lao Buddhist temple as a teen simply because her friends went there and because the temple taught English classes. She told me that she was drawn to the peaceful grounds of the temple, the sounds of the temple bells, and the chanting of the monks in their colorful robes. My father's side of the family is not Buddhist either. He comes from an ethnic minority group who perform rituals to appease the spirit world. Thus my mother and father were the first ones in their families to partake in Buddhism. Similarly, I am embarking on a path never practiced by anyone in my family—a path of Zen meditation and mindfulness practice.

5   But the Buddhism I grew up with is very different. The Thai and Lao Buddhist temples in the Theravada tradition are centered on community events like Lao and Thai New Year celebrations. Monks performed blessings for a new house or for a sick person. At home, we celebrated Chinese New Year and gave offerings to the spirits of our ancestors at the ancestor altar. My parents and I were never taught meditation. We thought that only monastics meditated and that we laypeople were supposed to earn merit by donating money to the temple, making offerings to the Buddha, and cooking for the monks.

Despite being a Buddhist family, our home was actually filled with anger, violence, and hurtful speech. I remember trying to protect my siblings from my father's uncontrollable rage. The bathroom became our shelter, a place to retreat and find safety. There are many dents and scars in our home, evidence of unskillful actions. Like my father, and his mother before him, I also tried to discipline and control my younger siblings by instilling fear in them. I would be in my room reading alone quietly when I would hear my siblings making a ruckus outside. Instantly, I would lose my patience. I would yell, "Be quiet! Why are you being so loud? You are driving me crazy." I would come out and threaten to beat them if they did not shut up. One time, I lost control and threw a glass at my sister. Another time, I melted my brother's glasses in the microwave.

In high school, I sought ways to control my anger and keep myself sane at home. I asked a teacher how to find quiet time amid the busyness of life. He told me that he dedicated at least ten to fifteen minutes every day to doing nothing. He would sit or lie down in silence and relax, or gaze outside his window and see what was going on outdoors, in the skies and in the yard. He also suggested eating raisins slowly, one at a time, chewing each fifteen to twenty times, while breathing in and out, concentrating on tasting the raisin. I was not aware then that this was my first instruction on mindfulness and meditation—eating meditation, that is.

When I left home for college, I rebelled against my family and its traditions. I didn't want anything to do with the anger and instability of my parents' home, just as I didn't want anything to do with the Buddhist cultural practices of my parents. I felt that my family and my community were just using the Buddhist temple as a filling station. I felt that they partook in the many rituals just to accumulate merit and temporarily relieve their anxieties about life. But afterward, they went right back to their harmful habits of hurting their families, their community, and themselves. People prayed in front of the Buddha for a new car or to win the lottery, as if the Buddha were Santa Claus.

During my college years, I began reading books by Thich Nhat Hanh and Buddhist magazines. I learned about mindfulness, engaged Buddhism, and other Buddhist traditions. I thought to myself, "Wow, there is so much I am not aware of!" I started attending meditation sessions and retreats offered by a local Zen group, composed of mostly non-Asians. I felt a connection to this group of people who, like me, were all trying to cross over to the other shore of freedom and truth, where lies our true home. I began rediscovering the Buddha, dharma, and sangha in a new light, not through my ethnic Buddhist temple, but through Western culture and American Buddhist teachers. I found a Buddhism that spoke to me as a young, Asian American woman, opening my heart and mind. This path began to heal my wounds, and through mindfulness, I cultivated some sense of patience and compassion.

10　　After eight years away from home, I recently returned to live with my parents. It's a little less chaotic now than when I was growing up, but there are still plenty of times I feel myself really challenged—in a way that living on my own didn't challenge me—to practice compassion, mindfulness, and patience. Still, things feel different. One night, a huge fight broke out between my sister and father. It started because my sister thought that my father was refusing to give her some documents that she needed for school. There was screaming, angry faces and words, hearts racing faster, and misery. An object went flying toward my sister. In that moment, I realized that as much as I tried to stop what was happening, I could not control the situation. I could not control the fear that arose within me. I certainly could not control another human being, whether it was my father, sister, or mother. Although I was scared, I also felt an indescribable sense of calm and stability in letting go of this desire for control.

After my father left the room, I walked past my other sister's room and saw that she was sitting on her bed, her body shaking from listening to the whole incident. When our eyes met, we both started to cry. I knew that this cycle of anger and violence needed to stop, because we were passing this on to younger generations. Somehow I sensed that our own family's cycle had an extended effect on the well-being of the Earth itself. I felt our unskillful actions reverberating through the past, present, and future—the consequences going far beyond what we can comprehend.

That night, I urged everyone in the household to practice noble silence (silence of body, speech, and mind) for the rest of the night. I said that unkind words were hurting us all. More than ever, I voiced that we need this quiet time now to calm down and heal and that we must try and refrain from hurting each other further. Amazingly, everyone gave it a try. The next morning, my father gave my sister the documents that she thought he was keeping from her.

Things are getting better at home. The teachings of the Buddha have provided me with the tools to look deeply and understand why my family and I say and do what we do. The study and practice of Buddhism has also helped me to look deeply and understand where my parents are coming from. I am now aware that my anger and hot temper were passed down from my parents and my parents' parents, many generations ago. I feel I am also absorbing the karma of my own country's violence and anger, and that of the world.

A few weeks ago, I came home late one night from a long day at work and was starting to prepare dinner for myself. My mom, who was washing dishes, suddenly asked, "When are you going to finish your thesis so that you can get another job that pays more? Hurry up and finish. My friend's son just finished his bachelor's and got a job starting at $60,000. . . ."

15 In the past, I would have instantly lost my patience and reacted defensively. "Stop getting on my case. I'll finish when I finish. And I've told you before that in my field of work, I won't make that high of a salary." She would respond, "Then why did you pick that field to study? Why didn't you pick doctor or lawyer?" We would argue some more and then I wouldn't even feel like eating my dinner, so I would storm upstairs to my room. These days, though, I'm less bothered by what my mom says. This time around, I responded, "I understand that you want the best for me and our family, but don't worry, I'll finish soon and get another job." I played along and avoided getting excessively involved. Then I said, "OK, I am going to eat dinner now. Let's talk about this another time." I ate peacefully as my seeds of anger didn't arise. These days, I can be patient for much longer periods.

Each day, I learn that all these barriers, problems, negative habits, anger, and jealousies are all part of my path—they are me. They are gifts too, gifts that provide me with opportunities to practice wholesome ways. For the first time, I feel I am being intimate with my fears by not running away anymore.

My father still asks me occasionally why I meditate. My parents do not understand my meditation practice fully, but they no longer call it a "cult." They seem to have come to some degree of acceptance of my practice. I still participate in the local Lao temple activities, but now I am not blindly following what others are doing.

Just recently, my mother came home from work one evening and asked if I could give her information on meditation places in town. She wanted to give it to her coworker who had inquired about it. Her coworker told her that she had a very good daughter because I practiced meditation. Having someone tell her this altered the way she thought about me and the practice of meditation—I am less odd now. A week later, my mother asked me how she could meditate herself, to calm her mind and be free of worries. The seeds of dharma are beginning to grow.

QUESTIONS FOR DISCUSSION

1. Why does Lovong's mother warn her daughter not to be brainwashed at the Zen Buddhist meditation retreat she is going to attend? What fuels the mother's fears?
2. What are the differences between Western Buddhism and the ethnic spirituality that Lovong's parents practiced in Southeast Asia and continue to practice in the United States?
3. In spite of her parents' spiritual practices, why was there so much anger in Lovong's family? Why does Lovong finally rebel against her family's values? Why does she object to their sense of family life?
4. How does learning the practice of Zen Buddhism and meditation help Lovong to control her anger? After eight years of practice, why can't she finally come home and remain separate from the anger and fighting that still rages in her family? How does what she has learned from meditation eventually help her brothers and sisters and mother gain more control over their anger?
5. Talk with friends and/or read about Zen masters to find out more about meditation and how it can help you to find inner peace. Are you convinced that the practice of Zen meditation could help you to know yourself better? Why or why not?
6. As the essay closes, we learn: "Just recently my mother came home from work . . . and asked if I could give her information on meditation places in town." What do you think caused Lovong's mother and her family to change? How do you imagine your family would change if family members started to practice meditation?

CONNECTION

Both Lovong and Chung believe that some rituals are a part of any spiritual or religious practice. How do they both differ from their parents' customs (see page 502)?

IDEAS FOR WRITING

1. Assume a persona that does not know anything about Zen meditation and is not interested in learning about it. Have your persona
   write a long letter to Lovong explaining how he or she feels about
   what has happened in her family.
2. Do some research to learn about how Eastern philosophies and spirituality such as Zen Buddhism came to be popular in the West. Why
   do you think Westerners have become seriously interested in many
   of the values associated with Eastern spirituality? Develop your
   views in a documented essay.

RELATED WEB SITES

The Zen Site
`www.thezensite.com`
The Zen Site, dedicated to promoting knowledge and insight into Zen
Buddhism, gives links to resources such as teachings, translations,
essays, history, and book reviews.

Zen Guide: The Comprehensive Guide to Zen & Buddhism
`www.zenguide.com`
Created and updated by Alan Do and Chon Tri, Zen Guide outlines the
principles and practice of Zen Buddhism in contemporary times. Links
to media, a discussion forum, and organizations are also provided.

Norman Yeung Bik Chung

A Faithful Taoist

*Born in Hong Kong and raised in a traditional Chinese family, Norman
Yeung left home to study abroad in England at 17. After immigrating to the
United States, he worked in the high-tech industry as a software manager
for many years before returning to school at De Anza College in Cupertino,
California. He wrote the following essay for an English composition class to
demonstrate the role that Taoist beliefs and rituals played in his father's
capacity for hope in the face of life-threatening illness.*

Faith is an important part of every religion. A strong belief in a higher
order or power can help people in their daily life and gives many individuals a sense of purpose in this world. Because I grew up with both
Eastern culture and Western religion, I have a difficult time accepting
one main truth system; I have also come to believe that there are both
good and evil aspects to every religion. Although I am not going to try to

explain away the supernatural aspect of the spiritual experiences I have had, I can at least recollect them and reflect on how they happened and on how they helped my family and my father in particular.

Because my father was a strong believer of Taoism, an Eastern philosophy and religion that has many followers in Hong Kong, we had an altar in my home ever since I was very little. A beautifully painted portrait of Lao Tzu riding his ox hung on the wall by the altar along with some calligraphy. A small pot to hold the incense that filled the room with whatever fragrance my father chose was placed on a table in front of Lao Tzu. He devoted at least ten minutes twice a day, morning and evening, to meditation. He would light up three sticks of incense, bow three times, and chant, never missing a day until he had to go into the hospital. At that point he asked one of us to do the ritual for him, a practice that my older brother followed religiously until my father passed away.

In addition to the private ritual that he carried out at home, there was also a place of worship where he went to pray and to meditate. My father was among the many frequent visitors to a Taoist temple on the east side of Hong Kong. The first time I visited that temple with him, I was eighteen years old; and, having just come back from London for a summer vacation, I wanted to spend some time with him. Because my father was such a generous donor, I had always considered the temple as a place where con artists made money from the believers. The altar at this temple was very similar to the one I used to see at home, except it was bigger and has more space, enough room for forty to fifty people to stand in front of Lao Tzu's picture, chanting and meditating together.

On the first and fifteenth of each month, Taoist followers gathered at the temple to pray and ask for spiritual advice. On one side of the hall was a large table with a Chinese painting brush hanging from the ceiling. Like the ouija board that people use to seek spiritualistic or telepathic messages in the West, the "brush" composed and wrote poems and verses on large piece of papers in response to the believers' questions. Of course there was a person who helped to guide the brush, and my brothers, who visited the temple often with my father, told me that they often saw the priests there practicing the writing and composing of the poem beforehand—yet this knowledge had never altered my father's faith in Taoism.

5   My father was one of the few patients in Hong Kong in the early 1960s to have had heart surgery and to have had a pacemaker implanted. However, after twenty years, the battery inside his pacemaker stopped working. Considering his age and health condition, he was faced with a choice of having surgery to replace his battery, which would have necessitated a long and difficult period of recovery, or of letting nature take its course. No one in the family wanted to be responsible for that choice; after all, my father was a hardhearted person who usually had the last word in our domestic decisions.

On the evening of the first of July, 1982, my father and I went to the temple, where it was my first time to witness the "ghost painting" ritual. After the grand ceremony, the few people who wanted to ask for the gods' wisdom gathered around the table. In turn, each one lit three sticks of incense and said a prayer in private. Then the brush, assisted by a man who worked there, moved for each of them. Most of the worshippers got a symbol of luck, health or prosperity; only a few received a verse or a poem. Soon it was my father's turn. As he walked up to the altar, lit the sticks, and bowed down to pray, I knew he must be very worried; yet he never showed any emotions. As I eagerly watched close by, the pen began to move for him.

The verses that my father received gave him the answer he needed to hear: "Go and he will be healed." Taking this message as a sign of the need for surgery, he contacted the surgeon the next day and had the operation soon after. He lived for another fifteen years while he saw my mother gradually deteriorate with Alzheimer's disease. Just before he died, my mother lost consciousness, so she did not have to moan and suffer the loss of her dear husband. For two years, she had lain in bed with great physical pain, yet I think her devotion to my father for over sixty years brought them together in spirit from the day he died. We could feel my father's presence in the weeks that followed his death.

In Taoism, one believes that the spirit of the dead comes home every seventh day for seven weeks before it moves on permanently. Our family put fruit and food at the altar to honor my father every day during that period. On the first seventh day, a hummingbird came into our house and landed quietly on my sister-in-law's shoulder. "He" then went over to the altar and picked on the apple, which was my father's favorite fruit. A bat, which in Chinese rhymes with the word "blessing," came into our house on the second seventh day. It flew all over the room and stopped at the altar. Both creatures were taken as a sign of my father's presence. They symbolized my father who brought luck to our family. I would like to note that this happened in the city of Hong Kong in an apartment among many high-rise buildings; to have a bird or a bat come inside the house was unheard of in that area.

After a year abroad, I went back to Hong Kong for a visit. My family and I went to meet my brothers in their office, a place where my father had worked for over twenty years. As we entered the lift, we realized that no one remembered which floor the office was on; so we decided to go up to the top, the twentieth floor, and to walk back down, looking for the right level. Mystically, the lift opened on the eighth floor; I looked outside and found that we were just outside my father's office. I can only relate this happening to the fact that his presence was still so strong within the building.

10   It is possible for me to dismiss all the events described above as coincidence or even as the work of my imagination. However, it is not important whether I think that the "ghost painting" was the result of the

people who worked at the temple or not. What is important is that those few words in calligraphy strengthened my father's willpower to live and to seek the medical care he needed, and I will always be grateful to those who gave him the hope none of us in our family could offer. For someone with a strong faith, the spirit will continue to live on; to me, the spirit of my father remains, continually looking over those whom he loved and worked for all his life, until one day we will meet again.

QUESTIONS FOR DISCUSSION

1. What is Chung's position on religion and faith in supernatural events? How does his position differ from that of his father?
2. In what way and for what reasons did the author change his initial view of the temple and those who worked there? Point out particular places in the essay where his spiritual perceptions and beliefs seem to shift and grow.
3. How do specific observed details and Chung's interpretations of them add to the mystery and emotional power of the essay? Give examples.
4. Comment on the title of the essay. How does his father's Taoism differ from what most Western people think Taoism means as a spiritual philosophy? Would it have been helpful for readers if Chung had discussed this distinction? Why or why not?

Jessie van Eerden

The Soul Has Six Wings

Essayist Jessie van Eerden is originally from the Whetsell Settlement in northern West Virginia. She received her B.A. in English in 2001 from West Virginia University and her M.F.A. in nonfiction from the University of Iowa in 2007. From 2007–2008 she was a Milton Center Fellow in Seattle, WA, teaching creative writing at Seattle Pacific University. She currently teaches at The Oregon Extension in Ashland, Oregon. She has published her creative non-fiction essays in the Oxford American, North Dakota Quarterly, Riverteeth, Portland, *and the* Bellingham Review. *The essay that follows, which draws a parallel between van Eerden's own informal spiritual community of women and the Thirteenth Century European Beguine communities of female mystics, was published originally in* Portland *and reprinted in* The Best American Spiritual Writing *of 2006.*

JOURNAL

What is your concept of a mystic?

The way I see it, a mystic takes a peek at God and then does her best to show the rest of us what she saw. She'll use image-language, not discourse. Giving an image is the giving of gold, the biggest thing she's got. Mysticism suggests direct union, divine revelation, taking a stab at the Unknown with images, cryptic or plain, sensible or sensory. A mystic casts out for an image in whatever is at her disposal and within reach, like a practiced cook who can concoct a stew from the remaining carrots and a bruised potato, or like a musician improvising with buckets and wooden spoons. She does not circumvent; she hammers a line drive. A mystic is a kid finding kingdom in ash heap.

The thirteenth-century Beguine mystics were women with their eyelids licked open by God, like those of monkey-faced puppies. These women seemed slipped into history, or in between histories. Though their only options were marriage or the cloister, they carved out a new option by forming quirky spiritual communities, out from under the rule of men or monastic structure. They spanned about a hundred years and covered some ground circulating a few manuscripts before they were married off or shuffled into approved orders. The lay women's movement spread like a brushfire over northern Europe. Women grouped into Beguinages, small cities within cities. Some of the larger ones, like the Beguinage of Ghent hosting a thousand women, had a church, cemetery, hospital, streets. They cropped up on the outskirts of cities in the Netherlands, Belgium, Germany. The women took no conventional vows. They were free to leave the community to marry; some brought along their children. They retained private property; they didn't beg; they did manual work for pay. They had no founder, no common rule that dictated community life. And no signing or changing your name.

Wars of the thirteenth century left a surplus of solitary women, and they also made way for a pop religion upsurge: meetings dotted the hillsides like Baptist tent revivals. Women made up the majority of the penitent, and many sought a full-time religious life, flocking to the doors of Cistercian Orders, but denied access. This huge batch of proselytes was sniffing out a Way beyond a doctrine. In 1175 Lambert le Bègue, a sympathetic priest of Liège in Belgium, encouraged a group of lay women to form an independent religious community. Their main tenets were voluntary poverty and freedom. They held fast to the Eucharist and the humanity of Jesus; they were chaste and charitable and unpopular with most parish priests. They came to be known as the Beguines.

The surviving texts of the Beguine mystics deliver image-language in the form of allegory and dialogue and lyric. A Beguine named Margaret Porette wrote the controversial text *The Mirror of Simple Souls* in the French vernacular, personifying Love, the Soul, and Reason. She claimed that a human soul can be joined at the hip with God through love: This Soul, says Love, has six wings, just as the Seraphim. She no longer wishes for anything which comes by an intermediary, for that is the proper state of being of the Seraphim; there is no intermediary between their love and God's love. She taught the soul's annihilation: that the soul, in Holy Church the Greater, might have no will of her own, that it serve only as a mirror for God's image and will. Porette's book was burned publicly by the Bishop of Cambrai, but she made no concessions. In fact, she added seventeen more chapters, moved her allegory forward, spruced up her characters. She was burned at the stake in 1310.

5　Another main text came out of Germany: *Flowing Light of the Godhead,* by Mechthild of Magdeburg. Her first manuscript is in the low-German dialect and draws on images from courtly love, a secular tradition. Mechthild admits: I do not know how to write nor can I, unless I see with the eyes of my soul and hear with the ears of my eternal spirit and feel in all the parts of my body the power of the Holy Spirit. And, to convey the Spirit, she uses what's available, what she sees out her window, touches to her lips, knows in her body.

A mystic is unapologetic for a lack of theological education, a scholar's explanations. (Porette: You must let Love and Faith together be your guides to climb where Reason cannot come.) The Beguines' writings play out scenes in common tropes of spiritual literature: a bride, a desert, a bed of pain. These images trigger something in me. What if I cast about for my own, for things that have caught my attention the way a fence barb does a loose shirt? What if that's all you have? Just the images? Perhaps images leave room or make room for mystery. Image as a felt truth for the weak who need more than doctrine. You struggle for an image; it wriggles into life and is born.

Is there a place for the contemporary mystic? Can someone try again to crawl into the big shell of mystical tradition and holler and hear her small voice echo back? Can she reclaim it in some way?

The way I see it, a mystic simply believes that God visits.

A mystic stays with what's striking: out the windshield, in between the intermittent wipers, a shadow, a flash of light, color, a face. She sees something, she sees and then she runs to show and tell, or at least she practices speeches in her head. She mulls over her images, arranges her sermon in a picture book—it's like a touch-and-feel kids book, furry cloth for monkey feet, a bit of rubber ball for bear nose. She wants her images vivid.

10　The Beguines had two main takes on the image of the desert. Some references pointed to the wilderness where the Old Testament children of Israel wandered for forty years, in exile, in desperation, trying to make it to the Promised Land of Milk and Honey. Life is exile, according to these writings, life is the trial to be endured, the soul's desolate journey home to God. The other manifestation of the desert image is an encounter: the desert isn't the thing to be endured for the goal; it is the goal; it is the landscape of union. It is, from the Book of Hosea, the place where God will allure her, bring her into the wilderness, and speak comfort to her. It's where you learn how to love.

A burned-down trailer is a desert of ash, silt, secrets. It is exposure, down to the ground, to wind to sun to rain. Brought to nothing. A melted photograph here, a charred unfastened locket there. A blackened mirror.

A fencerow, attended by walnut and hickory trees and underbrush, separated my house from Christy Gribbles's trailer. Before the trailer burned, Christy and I made a break in the fence so she could come to my side and I could go to hers.

A grease fire on the stove started the fire. It was in late fall. My brother Luke and I were just returning from a walk. We'd seen a deer close-up, licking water from the streambed. We had been silent with it and after it quenched its thirst, it picked its way through the underbrush into the cloak of the pines. We were heading back when we saw the huge piles of black smoke stacking on top of the bare trees. The trailer seemed to burn clear to the ground in minutes. Nobody was caught inside, and they even got some of the clothes out. But Christy and her younger brother G.W. were standing outside, close to the fence, with smoky blank faces. They seemed exposed there to the wind and the bits of ash flaking down like dirty snow. From my front porch, I stood watching her home become nothing.

What happens, Christy, when you lose everything? I picture that charred trailer-desert in my head now, remembering how they stayed for a time up at Nolan Wilson's old place and how we gave bags of clothes and a Glow Worm that lit up when you pressed him, trying to fill their new Nothing. In the beginning, there was a home with rooms and maybe not plenty but at least something, and then there was wasteland, No-place, No-home.

15 What happens when you lose everything? When you slip out, down the chainlink fire escape ladder and leave all evidence of self behind in the rubbish? I think sometimes: I could throw my day, my lifework out a window. And try to learn emptiness, a trailer-desert, a sigh in the soul.

Why speak in images? In trailer fire? What's the point when they leave you winded? Well, you don't know what else to say or how else to say it, like holding the hand of someone who's lost everything. It is an inexplicable being-with, a fleshing, a new Way.

Is a mystic anyone who realizes a truth and flashes it like a strong poker hand? She is the checkout lady at the Dollar General, talking on the phone to her husband who's trying to get the title for the truck but can't, and she has to go, there are customers. And she realizes and she says, This is all too much. On her face you see clearly where her weeping goes. You remember exactly what she looks like.

A neighbor calls in early evening about the double rainbow in the sky. Another and another calls, Judy, my aunt Kathy from town. From the porch, we can see the full arc of one, the marvelous ghost of the other. We have not lost this need to tell, to show, to point.

Sometimes you see nothing in the sky, no promises or mark of Jesus's feet, no sign that he's coming back to bring you home—so you write down the Nothing and the No-place, too.

20 Beguines weren't recluses. Uncloistered, they grouped their small cabins together into their Beguinages on the outskirts of cities where they worked making lace or gardens, teaching or nursing, managing shelters for urban women and kids who worked in textiles. Their cabins made a half-circle; one could see the other's light from her stoop, could string together two tin cans, window to window. Out from this half-circle shelter, Beguine mystics attracted the urban faithful, with their penchant for heresy and the use of the vernacular, the tongue of fire making sense. They gathered in the exiled and wandering. They had a context for dealing with suffering.

I gather with a group of women in Philadelphia, all of us assembling around Jesus, perked for evangel like girls hovering around a radio. But as you hover in a circle, you brush arms with each other. Liz Lopez was a woman among us whose husband was incarcerated, and she had three boys and a tiny frame; she looked like she could blow away. And still, she beautifully braced herself under her heavy beam of a dadless series of days that bore down with the weight of her boys' birthdays, street hockey games, piss-the-bed nights. Nobody skirted around her; we entered in as best we could, catching her insides as she spilled out, ready, at any moment, to spill ourselves.

We met in Susan's house in Hunting Park. We ate and then sang a few choruses and discussed sermons. One night the sermon was on James's epistle in the New Testament: Count it all joy, he says, when you fall into various trials, knowing that the testing of your faith produces patience. We cried onto our plates of Spanish rice and chicken that Blanca had brought, because the trials were various: Wendy's husband left her and the kids, another husband had cancer, Celeste and her girls lost their row house.

Often a woman takes tentative steps toward another, shy about the magnetic pull of this other's wounds. A raw, undisguised wound pulls you out of your own general okayness: your safe bed, your comfort. There is something about her uncontained and spilling-out life, a doll losing its fiber-fill, the dazed hungry look of one knocked off course. You want to zip up the back of her dresses, paint your lips with Bonnie Bell Cranberry or Smolder, and borrow her wakefulness that came the moment she was left. You feel that you've been drawn away from your life till you missed it with a fresh homesickness, so you can see it and take off its walls and shiver, alive again, as though you've taken a dip in icy cold water.

But is it a longing for laceration? That extreme mystical asceticism or mortification of flesh and the wakefulness it affords? Or is it maudlin, sentimental, like a rhyming couplet in a sympathy card?

25   I don't think so. I don't think that's what it was for most of the Beguines. It's just the fact of suffering, the dealing with it, making meaning out of it, and if there is no meaning, just to share it.

Here's my image: a gathering on a porch stoop, maybe some of the women smoking, maybe some just watching the door to the neighboring convenience store, but a group surely bound to each other. The image goes as follows: a girl alone, hugging her knees on the stoop—she's missed a period, or she's lost her baby, or her husband's left, or she simply couldn't get out of bed till two in the afternoon—the fire hydrant shooting out streams in the July heat and kids galloping this way and that, and she suffers, and the others come around, from other porches. They bring Spanish rice and chicken, boiled milk for coffee. And the gathered women stay there, through the early fall, into November. They are entering winter together out there, pointing, Look: how gentle the snow.

I wonder if mystical life is really about visions, or if it's about looking again at the pieces you've already got: of a rocky marriage, a job at Dollar General, a double rainbow. And if you see the kingdom of God there if you stare long enough. I wonder if it's about holding yourself still as a mirror. Or just about making a big old scene, waving your arms wildly.

What's dangerous about a mystic?

Held suspect from the beginning for their disregard for ecclesiastical hierarchy, the unschooled Beguines fell out of favor with the clerics. The women fueled the Church's disapproval by reading biblical texts to everyday folks in their native tongue. In 1274 the Council of Lyons banned any new spiritual orders from forming; new groups had to operate within an existing, approved order. There were rumors of prostitution, sexual license. The Inquisition wasn't kind. In 1312 the Council of Vienne officially declared the Beguines heretical, accusing them of association with antinomian adherents of the Free Spirit. Their property was confiscated; many women had to marry. Many were forced to sign up with a convent.

30   But what's dangerous about a mystic? Hurling and wielding the best stuff she can imagine, insisting on an unmediated Way of Wakefulness. A mild heretic with dyed pink hair and a threadbare T-shirt with the slogan *Take me seriously.*

Today I don't suppose she fears the Inquisition and its fire—just dullness, just missing it. She fears dismissal. She wrestles, she squints the eyes of her soul. Perhaps she doesn't ditch tradition as much as take it for its word and peer inside its cavernous shell. There must still be something worth saying, worth pointing to.

QUESTIONS FOR DISCUSSION

1. Why does a mystic use image language rather than discourse to communicate? Van Eerden begins with the lives of Beguine mystics in the thirteenth century. What two images of the desert represent the goals of mysticism for them?
2. Explain why Beguine mystics formed "quirky spiritual communities out from under the rule of men or monastic structure." Why did Beguine mysticism form in communities all over Northern Europe? What were the rules of these communities?
3. How did Margaret Porette in *The Mirror Simple* define the relationship between humans and gods? Her book was controversial, and she was burned at the stake. Mary Mechthild of Magdedburg wrote a mystical text *Flowing Light of the God-Head*. How was her book different from Porette's, and why did she not suffer the same fate?
4. Why does van Eerden believe that mysticism can be a part of contemporary society? How does she think mysticism can be reborn? How would contemporary mystics connect with God? Why is her use of personal mystical experiences effective? How did they help you to understand Beguine mysticism?
5. Van Eerden shows different ways that Beguine women (or similar modern communities) help one another. Why does she explain these activities as mystical? Why do Beguine women form communities to communicate? Why are mystics still considered dangerous?
6. What is your reaction to "The Soul Has Six Wings"? Did you find yourself interested in the little- known form of Beguine religion, or were you skeptical about its history and continuing existence?

CONNECTION

Compare van Eerden's idea of a spiritual community with that of Donna Lovong in *Are You Joining a Cult* (see page 499).

IDEAS FOR WRITING

1. Research the history of the Beguine mystics and write a paper that explains their relationship to Christianity. Include information and details that will help your reader to better understand this mystic religion.
2. Do research into mystic communities similar to the Beguines today. Where are they? How do these mystics support themselves? Why do they continue to thrive? Write up your findings and responses to these groups.

RELATED WEB SITES

Mysticism

`http://plato.stanford.edu/entries/mysticism/`

Provided by the Stanford University Encyclopedia of Philosophy, this entry provides insight, history, and elaborate examples of the concept of mysticism. In addition, the encyclopedia article gives links to related resources on spirituality and mysticism.

Mysticism Resources

`www.religiousworlds.com/mystic/index.html`

This Web site presents a list of mysticism resources, by geographical region and ethnicity, as well as links to forums, journals, and text collections on the topic of mysticism.

Noah Levine

Death Is Not the End My Friend

Noah Levine was born in 1971 and grew up in a New Age spiritual family in northern California. His father was Stephen Levine, a Buddhist convert and author of books on meditation and coping with loss. Angry at social injustice and troubled after the divorce of his parents, Noah Levine was arrested 17 times as a juvenile and was involved with punk rock culture, alcohol, and drugs. After achieving sobriety, Levine attended the California Institute of Integral Studies and trained at the Spirit Rock Meditation Center in Woodacre, California. He also has studied with the Dalai Lama, Thich Nhat Hanh, and many other spiritual teachers. He is the cofounder and director of the Mind Body Awareness Project, a nonprofit organization serving incarcerated young people. Levine now lives in San Francisco, where he teaches Buddhist meditation techniques and counsels young prisoners. He writes regularly for online Buddhist publications. The following selection, excerpted from Dharma Punx: A Memoir *(2003), reveals how meditation and service helped Levine to develop a spiritual self and to overcome deep anger, fear, and grief.*

JOURNAL

Write about the death of a friend or relative. In what sense did this loss change the direction of your life or give you new insights?

Driving fast with the music up loud, as usual, I didn't even hear my cell phone ring. Seeing that I had missed a call, I picked up the phone and checked my messages. I could tell by the sound of Alicia's voice that something terrible had happened; all she said was, "Noah, call me as soon as you get this, it's an emergency." Dialing her number, I could feel my belly get really tight, like I was bracing myself for a hard blow. When she answered the phone I heard the desperation in her voice. I said, "It's Noah, what happened?" and all she replied was, "Toby's dead." Everything became fuzzy and dark for a moment and I felt like my chest was being smashed, like a heavy weight was crushing my sternum. I didn't even reply. I couldn't speak; only a deep guttural sigh came out followed by a flood of tears. I started saying, "Fuck. What the fuck? Why? What happened? Fucking Toby." I had to pull my car to the side of the road and just cry and scream for a while. Alicia told me that she and Jerilyn, Toby's mom, had found him that morning, sitting up in bed, his skin cold and blue. They called the paramedics but it was too late—he had stopped breathing several hours earlier. She thought he probably overdosed but didn't really know; they hadn't found any dope or needles.

Alicia asked me to come down to Santa Cruz and be with her and Gage, Toby's son. I was crying so hard that I couldn't think. I was on my way to work at Spirit Rock, where I was supposed to meet with someone, but I couldn't remember whom. I was also supposed to be leading a weekend for a rites-of-passage boys' group at Tassajara Zen Center, but it didn't look like I was going to be able to make it to either commitment. I couldn't even think about trying to teach or work, my mind was foggy and confused, every cell in my body was in anguish.

I told Alicia that I would be there as soon as possible. After I got off the phone with her I immediately made several calls: to my dad and Ondrea in New Mexico, to my mom in Santa Cruz, to Vinny, Joe, and Micah. Mostly I just left messages telling them what had happened and asking for some support. I talked to Vinny for a little while and he was very supportive—it was so nice to just hear a friendly voice. I felt so alone, so overwhelmed and distraught.

My heart felt like it had just been torn from my chest. I couldn't believe it. I wasn't ready for this, not now. Toby had been doing so well. He had been out of prison and going to recovery meetings and counseling, and as far as I knew he had been sober for almost a year. He was so in love with his son, and every time I talked to him he spoke about wanting to start helping kids like I was doing. He was trying to volunteer at some teen counseling programs in Santa Cruz and going to church every week with his family.

5 Not now! There was a time a few years ago when he was on the streets and I was just waiting for the call to come, but not now. He had just spent the weekend with me a few weeks ago in the city and had come to a teen

retreat that I was leading at Spirit Rock. I had led a day of meditation and a sweat lodge in the afternoon. Toby had been great, sharing his life's experience with the teens and expressing his hope that they would never have to experience what he had. The kids had really loved him and it was so great to be sharing my role of Buddhist teacher with my oldest friend in the world.

Just the day before I had gotten an e-mail from him, something about being a spiritual porn star, another one of his punk rock fantasies. I wrote back telling him of my love for him and encouraging his continued commitment to the steps and spiritual practice. I said that I had been thinking about him a lot lately because of the meditation groups that I was doing in San Quentin. Thinking of the time he spent there, I was so glad he was back in my life and I never wanted him to have to go back to prison. I said that above everything else I hoped he was putting his recovery first, because without staying clean it seemed inevitable that he, that I, that we all would end up back in a cell, if not physically then at least spiritually.

He probably never even got it. Or maybe he did and since he was already relapsing it made him feel so bad that he had killed himself. I would never know.

My whole body was flushed with guilt and the tears flowed out of my empty eyes, soaking my face and sweatshirt. I made a quick stop at work to let them know that I would probably be out the rest of the week and drove directly to Santa Cruz to be with Alicia and Jerilyn and all the rest of our friends and family. I tried turning my stereo up so that it would be louder than my mind, but every song, every chord, and each beat reminded me of Toby.

It felt like nothing had prepared me for this; no amount of meditation, no amount of therapy, none of the spiritual practices or experiences I'd had, prepared me to lose my best friend. I felt like without him nobody in the world really knew me. It seemed like when I was ten years old I had left home and found my real family. The day I met Toby I finally felt understood. We had been through everything together. When we were kids on the streets getting high, chasing girls, when we couldn't relate to our parents and they couldn't understand us, we always had each other. The first time I had sex Toby was there—the first punk rock show, first acid trip, first fucking everything. We fought together and stole together, we shared bottles, crack pipes, and needles. We did it all. Even when I got sober and turned into a fucking self-righteous Straight Edge asshole, Toby was still there. When he was strung out on the streets and needed somewhere to stay, my door was always open. Even when he ripped me and everyone else off and ended up in prison, our connection was still too strong and nothing could break our friendship; we were brothers. I sent him books in prison, he sent me letters. When he got out and met back up with Alicia and she got pregnant he asked me if I would be godfather.

10   We spent twenty years together, longer than with anyone else. My oldest friend in the world was dead. And with him died the only witness to see me both shoot dope and teach meditation. Now I was all alone, surrounded by people who I could tell about my past but who would never really know what it was like.

No amount of spiritual understanding or faith could make that feeling go away. I knew he was okay wherever he was, be it outside of his body or on to the next realm. But I wasn't okay. I was left behind to deal with his skeleton. I wished I believed that he was resting in peace, but I didn't. I knew that whatever his work was, it would be done, either this time or the next, in this realm or another.

When I finally spoke to my father he said that he felt that Toby might be feeling lost and confused and that what he really needed was my forgiveness. He suggested that I do as much forgiveness practice as possible to help set Toby free and guide him on his journey. I didn't even realize that I hadn't forgiven him, or that maybe I had but he just needed to hear it to help him navigate his strange journey, feeling confused and afraid. I hope my prayers and meditations touched him and helped him to let go and go back into the essence and into the next distressing disguise. I offered any merit that I might have accumulated to him, that he might take rebirth in a realm where he will come into contact with the Dharma.

In Santa Cruz I had to do everything for the funeral. Toby's mom was too overwhelmed with grief, his dad wasn't around, and Alicia had her hands full with taking care of Gage and getting them both out of the apartment where Toby had died. Lola was with Alicia when I arrived. Lola had been sober since just after that night in the hospital three years earlier. She was Alicia's sponsor. We had been in touch off and on and had been able to establish somewhat of a friendship. It was great to see her. I was in so much pain, her hug felt incredibly comforting. She just wanted to know what she could do to help.

We set up the funeral and got the word out as best we could, in the newspaper and by word of mouth. About two hundred people showed up, overflowing St. John's Church, the little chapel on the hill in Capitola where we grew up. People, some of whom I hadn't seen in fifteen years, lined the aisles and spilled out into the streets.

15   I stood at the pulpit in the front of the church. Pictures of Toby hung on the walls, and a large pile of flowers was being laid on the altar we had created. It was the most important talk I would ever give, remembering Toby and honoring his life and his search for freedom. Looking out over the gathering of his family and friends, feeling inadequate and afraid, I spoke of his love for his family and friends, his son and his girlfriend, his humor, his style, and his struggle with addiction. I told the story of how our friendship had been one of the most important things in my life, how I might not have made it through some of the more difficult times without him. How

he'd saved my life so many times by just being understanding and support-ive, by just listening when we couldn't relate to our parents or anyone else.

I spoke of how we met at Little League, of our first punk shows and our first sexual experiences. I shared with the gathering of punks and parents, skaters and surfers, what I knew of Toby's life journey, of his search for love and happiness that led instead to addiction and confu-sion. Of his many loves and his son, of the honor I felt to be godfather to his child. Through my own tears and the tears of a church filled to the brim with love and grief, I did my best to memorialize Toby's life, his in-credible sense of humor, and his uncanny ability to make anyone feel comfortable in any situation.

Before we ended the service I led the whole gathering in a short medi-tation of forgiveness and gratitude and we all offered our love and forgive-ness, ending the period of reflection with a funny sound that Toby was famous for making. Everyone was laughing and crying at the same time.

I took some more time off from work and spent a lot of it just crying and reflecting on how lucky I had been to have such a good friend for so long, how rare and wonderful it was to ever connect with someone in such a deep way.

I kept coming back to the feeling of being lost, like a part of me had died, and it began to hit me that all of our other friends were dead also: Shooter, Mark, Darren, and even Toby's old girlfriend Jamie. My mind started swimming upstream, asking the useless question of "Why?" Why them and not me? Why was I surrounded by such wonderful spiritual teachers, all only a phone call away, all available to me? All of them help-ing me on the spiritual path.

20   After some time I realized that I was experiencing survivor's guilt. It was as if I had lived through a war and was one of the only ones left. And on some level it was true.

Talking to my parents and my teachers about my grief process, al-though helpful, also seemed to compound my feeling of guilt. There I was, being supported by some of the most wonderful teachers in the world, and all my friends were dying alone in ghetto apartments, shoot-ing some more dope so that they wouldn't have to deal with the suffer-ing for one more minute. That was me and where I came from, and I felt like I was somehow betraying them by surviving.

The guilt and doubt began to fade fairly quickly and were replaced by the realization that it was for Toby and all my other friends, all of the punks and kids who didn't make it, that I was continuing my spiritual quest, and for them that I had committed my life to sharing what I was finding with others—to teaching the simple meditation techniques that had so profoundly altered the course of my life.

Toby's death became the next teaching, opening my heart to the floods of grief and despair that we all hold at bay. No longer able to keep myself together, I fell apart and stumbled into a deeper understanding of what it means to be human. I began to see Toby's death and all of my life's experiences as teachings and tools to offer to others who will surely walk a similar path. I saw all of it as an opportunity for awakening, as grist for the mill.

Still processing all that had happened, I put one foot in front of the other and showed up for my life's work, using the grief and even the feelings of guilt and confusion over having escaped from a life of addiction and crime as the basis of my teachings. My heart was ripped open, raw and tender—I offered it to others so that they might benefit from my suffering.

25   A short time later Jack Kornfield invited me to join a small Buddhist teachers' training group that he was offering. I humbly accepted, knowing that it was the appropriate next step in actualizing my intention to share the Dharma with others. I decided that my time would be better spent working in juvenile halls and prisons, gave notice at Spirit Rock, and with a couple of friends started our own nonprofit organization to teach meditation to inmates, called the Mind Body Awareness project.

QUESTIONS FOR DISCUSSION

1. How would you interpret the title of this essay? Does Levine seem to believe in a literal afterlife, or is the statement true on another level? Explain your response.
2. Why is it significant that Levine receives his notification of his friend Toby's death via cell phone, while "[d]riving fast with the music up loud, as usual"? What is his immediate response to the news? What metaphors does he use to describe his response?
3. From whom does Levine ask for support? Why does he feel guilty about Toby's death, despite the fact that he sent warnings about the risks of returning to drugs and prison to his friend by e-mail?
4. What memories of his relationship with Toby does Levine share with his readers and with the many friends in attendance at the hastily organized funeral? Which details seem particularly vivid and poignant? Why does Levine consider this address "the most important talk I would ever give"?
5. In what sense was Toby's death "the next teaching"? What new insights about the meaning of Toby's death come to Levine in the days after the funeral?
6. To what active spirituality does Levine dedicate himself after his mourning for Toby and period of guilt and doubt? How does his new spiritual direction suggest both growth and leadership ability?

CONNECTION

Compare Levine's approach to spirituality and service with that of Jim Wallis in this chapter (see page 528).

IDEAS FOR WRITING

1. Write an essay about an abrupt change of direction in your life and/or about spiritual awareness that came to you through some form of trauma, crisis, or loss. As Levine does, try to capture both the physical and emotional impact of your loss as well as the type of reflection that it prompted in you. How did you change?

2. Do some research into meditation and recovery groups in prisons, and write an essay on your findings. How effective do such groups seem to be in helping inmates adjust to life in prison while maintaining hope and confidence that they can do something productive and rewarding with themselves, both in and out of incarceration?

RELATED WEB SITES

End of Life and Dharma Talks
`www.aniccahouse.org/htm/buddhist_hindu_mp3_talks_`
`hospice_dharma.htm`
The Anicca House site presents talks and guided meditations in MP3 format by Noah Levine, Stephen and Ondrea Levine, and Ajahn Amaro.

Buddha was a Punk Rocker: Interview With Noah Levine
`www.satyamag.com/oct03/levine.htm`
In his interview with the e-magazine *Satya,* Noah Levine discusses his Buddhist/punk ethic and his classes in meditation and psychotherapy with inmates at San Quentin Prison.

Martin Luther King, Jr.

A Christmas Sermon on Peace

Martin Luther King, Jr. (1928–1968), who came from a family of ministers, graduated from Morehouse University and received a Ph.D. in theology from Boston University. After graduation, King became a pastor and founded the Southern Christian Leadership Conference, developing the concept, derived from the teachings of Henry David Thoreau and Mahatma Gandhi, that nonviolent civil disobedience is the best way to obtain civil rights and to end segregation. King won the Nobel Peace Prize in 1964. Although his life ended in a tragic assassination, King wrote many speeches and essays on race and civil rights, which are collected in books such as I Have a Dream: Writings and Speeches That Changed the World *(1992) and* The Papers of Martin Luther King, Jr. *(1992).*

JOURNAL

Write about a time when you have thought about the phrase "Peace on Earth, Good Will Towards Men" not as a Christmas card slogan but as an urgent necessity in a time of war and international conflict.

Peace on Earth . . .

This Christmas season finds us a rather bewildered human race. We have neither peace within nor peace without. Everywhere paralyzing fears harrow people by day and haunt them by night. Our world is sick with war; everywhere we turn we see its ominous possibilities. And yet, my friends, the Christmas hope for peace and good will toward all men can no longer be dismissed as a kind of pious dream of some utopian. If we don't have good will toward men in this world, we will destroy ourselves by the misuse of our own instruments and our own power. Wisdom born of experience should tell us that war is obsolete. There may have been a time when war served as a negative good by preventing the spread and growth of an evil force, but the very destructive power of modern weapons of warfare eliminates even the possibility that war may any longer serve as a negative good. And so, if we assume that life is worth living, if we assume that mankind has a right to survive, then we must find an alternative to war—and so let us this morning explore the conditions for peace. Let us this morning think anew on the meaning of that Christmas hope: "Peace on Earth, Good Will toward Men." And as we explore these conditions, I would like to suggest that modern man really go all out to study the meaning of nonviolence, its philosophy and its strategy.

We have experimented with the meaning of nonviolence in our struggle for racial justice in the United States, but now the time has come for man to experiment with nonviolence in all areas of human conflict, and that means nonviolence on an international scale.

Now let me suggest first that if we are to have peace on earth, our loyalties must become ecumenical rather than sectional. Our loyalties must transcend our race, our tribe, our class, and our nation; and this means we must develop a world perspective. No individual can live alone; no nation can live alone, and as long as we try, the more we are going to have war in this world. Now the judgment of God is upon us, and we must either learn to live together as brothers or we are all going to perish together as fools.

5　　Yes, as nations and individuals, we are interdependent. I have spoken to you before of our visit to India some years ago. It was a marvelous experience; but I say to you this morning that there were those depressing moments. How can one avoid being depressed when one sees with one's own eyes evidences of millions of people going to bed hungry at night?

How can one avoid being depressed when one sees with ones own eyes thousands of people sleeping on the sidewalks at night? More than a million people sleep on the sidewalks of Bombay every night; more than half a million sleep on the sidewalks of Calcutta every night. They have no houses to go into. They have no beds to sleep in. As I beheld these conditions, something within me cried out: "Can we in America stand idly by and not be concerned?" And an answer came: "Oh, no!" And I started thinking about the fact that right here in our country we spend millions of dollars every day to store surplus food; and I said to myself: "I know where we can store that food free of charge? in the wrinkled stomachs of the millions of God's children in Asia, Africa, Latin America, and even in our own nation, who go to bed hungry at night."

It really boils down to this: that all life is interrelated. We are all caught in an inescapable network of mutuality, tied into a single garment of destiny. Whatever affects one directly, affects all indirectly. We are made to live together because of the interrelated structure of reality. Did you ever stop to think that you can't leave for your job in the morning without being dependent on most of the world? You get up in the morning and go to the bathroom and reach over for the sponge, and that's handed to you by a Pacific islander. You reach for a bar of soap, and that's given to you at the hands of a Frenchman. And then you go into the kitchen to drink your coffee for the morning, and that's poured into your cup by a South American. And maybe you want tea: that's poured into your cup by a Chinese. Or maybe you're desirous of having cocoa for breakfast, and that's poured into your cup by a West African. And then you reach over for your toast, and that's given to you at the hands of an English-speaking farmer, not to mention the baker. And before you finish eating breakfast in the morning, you've depended on more than half of the world. This is the way our universe is structured, this is its interrelated quality. We aren't going to have peace on earth until we recognize this basic fact of the interrelated structure of all reality.

Now let me say, secondly, that if we are to have peace in the world, men and nations must embrace the nonviolent affirmation that ends and means must cohere. One of the great philosophical debates of history has been over the whole question of means and ends. And there have always been those who argued that the end justifies the means, that the means really aren't important. The important thing is to get to the end, you see.

So, if you're seeking to develop a just society, they say, the important thing is to get there, and the means are really unimportant; any means will do so long as they get you there? they may be violent, they may be untruthful means; they may even be unjust means to a just end. There have been those who have argued this throughout history. But we will never have peace in the world until men everywhere recognize that ends are not cut off from means, because the means represent the ideal in the making, and the end in process, and ultimately you can't reach good ends through evil means, because the means represent the seed and the end represents the tree.

It's one of the strangest things that all the great military geniuses of the world have talked about peace. The conquerors of old who came killing in pursuit of peace, Alexander, Julius Caesar, Charlemagne, and Napoleon, were akin in seeking a peaceful world order. If you will read Mein Kampf closely enough, you will discover that Hitler contended that everything he did in Germany was for peace. And the leaders of the world today talk eloquently about peace. Every time we drop our bombs in North Vietnam, President Johnson talks eloquently about peace. What is the problem? They are talking about peace as a distant goal, as an end we seek, but one day we must come to see that peace is not merely a distant goal we seek, but that it is a means by which we arrive at that goal. We must pursue peaceful ends through peaceful means. All of this is saying that, in the final analysis, means and ends must cohere because the end is preexistent in the means, and ultimately destructive means cannot bring about constructive ends.

10   Now let me say that the next thing we must be concerned about if we are to have peace on earth and good will toward men is the nonviolent affirmation of the sacredness of all human life. Every man is somebody because he is a child of God. And so when we say "Thou shalt not kill," we're really saying that human life is too sacred to be taken on the battlefields of the world. Man is more than a tiny vagary of whirling electrons or a wisp of smoke from a limitless smoldering. Man is a child of God, made in His image, and therefore must be respected as such. Until men see this everywhere, until nations see this everywhere, we will be fighting wars. One day somebody should remind us that, even though there may be political and ideological differences between us, the Vietnamese are our brothers, the Russians are our brothers, the Chinese are our brothers; and one day we've got to sit down together at the table of brotherhood. But in Christ there is neither Jew nor Gentile. In Christ there is neither male nor female. In Christ there is neither Communist nor capitalist. In Christ, somehow, there is neither bound nor free. We are all one in Christ Jesus. And when we truly believe in the sacredness of human personality, we won't exploit people, we won't trample over people with the iron feet of oppression, we won't kill anybody.

There are three words for "love" in the Greek New Testament; one is the word "eros." Eros is a sort of esthetic, romantic love. Plato used to talk about it a great deal in his dialogues, the yearning of the soul for the realm of the divine. And there is and can always be something beautiful about eros, even in its expressions of romance. Some of the most beautiful love in all of the world has been expressed this way.

Then the Greek language talks about "philia," which is another word for love, and philia is a kind of intimate love between personal friends. This is the kind of love you have for those people that you get along with well, and those whom you like on this level you love because you are loved.

Then the Greek language has another word for love, and that is the word "agape." Agape is more than romantic love, it is more than friendship. Agape is understanding, creative, redemptive good will toward all men. Agape is an overflowing love which seeks nothing in return. Theologians would say that it is the love of God operating in the human heart. When you rise to love on this level, you love all men not because you like them, not because their ways appeal to you, but you love them because God loves them. This is what Jesus meant when he said, "Love your enemies." And I'm happy that he didn't say, "Like your enemies," because there are some people that I find it pretty difficult to like. Liking is an affectionate emotion, and I can't like anybody who would bomb my home. I can't like anybody who would exploit me. I can't like anybody who would trample over me with injustices. I can't like them. I can't like anybody who threatens to kill me day in and day out. But Jesus reminds us that love is greater than liking. Love is understanding, creative, redemptive good will toward all men. And I think this is where we are, as a people, in our struggle for racial justice. We can't ever give up. We must work passionately and unrelentingly for first-class citizenship. We must never let up in our determination to remove every vestige of segregation and discrimination from our nation, but we shall not in the process relinquish our privilege to love.

I've seen too much hate to want to hate, myself, and I've seen hate on the faces of too many sheriffs, too many white citizens' councilors, and too many Klansmen of the South to want to hate, myself; and every time I see it, I say to myself, hate is too great a burden to bear. Somehow we must be able to stand up before our most bitter opponents and say: "We shall match your capacity to inflict suffering by our capacity to endure suffering. We will meet your physical force with soul force. Do to us what you will and we will still love you. We cannot in all good conscience obey your unjust laws and abide by the unjust system, because non-cooperation with evil is as much a moral obligation as is cooperation with good, and so throw us in jail and we will still love you. Bomb our homes and threaten our children, and, as difficult as it is, we will still love you. Send your hooded perpetrators of violence into our communities at the midnight hour and drag us out on some wayside road and leave us half-dead as you beat us, and we will still love you. Send your propaganda agents around the country, and make it appear that we are not fit, culturally and otherwise, for integration, and we'll still love you. But be assured that we'll wear you down by our capacity to suffer, and one day we will win our freedom. We will not only win freedom for ourselves; we will so appeal to your heart and conscience that we will win you in the process, and our victory will be a double victory."

15   If there is to be peace on earth and good will toward men, we must finally believe in the ultimate morality of the universe, and believe that all reality hinges on moral foundations. Something must remind us of this as we once again stand in the Christmas season and think of the Easter season simultaneously, for the two somehow go together. Christ came to show us the way. Men love darkness rather than the light, and they crucified him, and there on Good Friday on the cross it was still dark, but then Easter came, and Easter is an eternal reminder of the fact that the truth-crushed earth will rise again. Easter justifies Carlyle in saying, "No lie can live forever." And so this is our faith, as we continue to hope for peace on earth and good will toward men: let us know that in the process we have cosmic companionship.

In 1963, on a sweltering August afternoon, we stood in Washington, D.C., and talked to the nation about many things. Toward the end of that afternoon, I tried to talk to the nation about a dream that I had had, and I must confess to you today that not long after talking about that dream I started seeing it turn into a nightmare. I remember the first time I saw that dream turn into a nightmare, just a few weeks after I had talked about it. It was when four beautiful, unoffending, innocent Negro girls were murdered in a church in Birmingham, Alabama. I watched that dream turn into a nightmare as I moved through the ghettos of the nation and saw my black brothers and sisters perishing on a lonely island of poverty in the midst of a vast ocean of material prosperity, and saw the nation doing nothing to grapple with the Negroes' problem of poverty. I saw that dream turn into a nightmare as I watched my black brothers and sisters in the midst of anger and understandable outrage, in the midst of their hurt, in the midst of their disappointment, turn to misguided riots to try to solve that problem. I saw that dream turn into a nightmare as I watched the war in Vietnam escalating, and as I saw so-called military advisors, sixteen thousand strong, turn into fighting soldiers until today over five hundred thousand American boys are fighting on Asian soil. Yes, I am personally the victim of deferred dreams, of blasted hopes, but in spite of that I close today by saying I still have a dream, because, you know, you can't give up in life. If you lose hope, somehow you lose that vitality that keeps life moving, you lose that courage to be, that quality that helps you go on in spite of all. And so today I still have a dream.

I have a dream that one day men will rise up and come to see that they are made to live together as brothers. I still have a dream this morning that one day every Negro in this country, every colored person in the world, will be judged on the basis of the content of his character rather than the color of his skin, and every man will respect the dignity and worth of human personality. I still have a dream that one day the idle industries of Appalachia will be revitalized, and the empty stomachs of Mississippi will be filled, and brotherhood will be more than a few words at the end of a prayer, but rather the first order of business on every legislative agenda. I still have a dream today that one day justice will roll down like water, and righteousness like a mighty stream. I still have a dream today that in all of our state houses and city halls men will be elected to go there who will do justly and love mercy and walk humbly with their God. I still have a dream today that one day war will come to an end, that men will beat their swords into plowshares and their spears into pruning hooks, that nations will no longer rise up against nations, neither will they study war any more. I still have a dream today that one day the lamb and the lion will lie down together and every man will sit under his own vine and fig tree and none shall be afraid. I still have a dream today that one day every valley shall be exalted and every mountain and hill will be made low, the rough places will be made smooth and the crooked places straight, and the glory of the Lord shall be revealed, and all flesh shall see it together. I still have a dream that with this faith we will be able to adjourn the councils of despair and bring new light into the dark chambers of pessimism. With this faith we will be able to speed up the day when there will be peace on earth and good will toward men. It will be a glorious day, the morning stars will sing together, and the sons of God will shout for joy.

QUESTIONS FOR DISCUSSION

1. Why does King believe that "war is obsolete" and must be stopped, and that international nonviolence in an "ecumenical" world is the solution to armed conflicts? Do you agree with the reasons he gives? Why or why not?

2. What is the point of King's example about the Indian people? How does he suggest that we could help solve some of their problems? How does King demonstrate that "all life is interrelated?" Are his examples effective?

3. What is King's argument about the importance of the relationship between "means and ends" in the quest for peace? How does this argument serve as a demonstration of the need for universal nonviolence?

4. What is the significance of King's discussion of the three kinds or levels of love? How does this discussion help to emphasize the principle of the "sacredness of all human life," and how does it lead into his argument for the necessity of love and nonviolence within the struggle for civil rights in order to obtain "a double victory"?

5. What is King's view of the "ultimate morality of the universe"? How do the two sacred seasonal celebrations, Christmas and Easter, help us to have faith that "No lie can live forever"?

6. King revisits his famous "I Have a Dream" speech, delivered in 1963 to a huge crowd at the Lincoln Memorial in Washington, D.C., in the final two paragraphs of this essay. Why does King believe that his dream (which was optimistic and idealistic in its view of the future of racial harmony and equality in the United States) had become a "nightmare" by the end of 1967? Examine some of the important social and historical crises and struggles that took place during this four-to five-year period.

7. Despite his feelings about the nightmarish qualities of the age, King ends his essay by evoking and repeating with variation some of the visionary language found in the "I Have a Dream" speech. Why does he remain hopeful despite the setbacks of recent years? Give examples of inspiring rhetoric of hope and faith in the future found in the final paragraph of the essay.

CONNECTION

How do Wallis's and King's beliefs in spiritual social activism complement each other (see page 528)?

IDEAS FOR WRITING

1. This essay was written only four months before King's assassination at the hands of a white racist. Compare the spiritual state of black people and our nation then and now. What progress have black Americans made in terms of political and economic rights and social acceptance?

2. King's essay makes a strong argument for the importance of pacifism and nonviolence during a time of war. Sum up the reasons King gives for his position and argue either in favor of or in dissent from his views on war.

RELATED WEB SITES

The Martin Luther King, Jr. Research and Education Institute
www.stanford.edu/group/King/
Directed by Clayborne Carson, the Martin Luther King, Jr. Research and Education Institute conducts research and hosts educational programs in order to provide a better understanding of King's peaceful philosophy. This Web site provides links to the King Papers Project, public programs, news, publications, and other resources.

Martin Luther King Speeches
www.mlkonline.net/speeches.html
This Web site provides a list of complete famous speeches by Dr. King. Other links lead to pictures, quotes, and videos pertaining to Dr. King and his social philosophy.

Jim Wallis

Taking Back the Faith

Jim Wallis (b. 1948) was raised in a midwestern evangelical family and spent his student years involved in the civil rights and antiwar movements. Wallis founded and continues to edit Sojourners, *a magazine for Christian activists working for justice and peace. In 1995, Wallis was instrumental in forming the Call to Renewal, a national federation of faith-based organizations from across the theological and political spectrum working to overcome poverty. He teaches a course on faith and politics at Harvard University and frequently speaks at conferences and meetings around the country. Wallis writes for major newspapers and has written several books, including* Who Speaks for God? A New Politics of Compassion, Community, and Civility *(1996), and* Faith Works *(2000). The selection that follows is taken from* God's Politics: Why the Right Gets It Wrong and the Left Doesn't Get It *(2005).*

JOURNAL

Write about your ideas of the place of religious faith in the area of politics. Do you believe that politics and religion should be intertwined? Why or why not?

Many of us feel that our faith has been stolen, and it's time to take it back. In particular, an enormous public misrepresentation of Christianity has taken place. And because of an almost uniform media misperception, many people around the world now think Christian faith stands for political commitments that are almost the opposite of its true meaning. How did the faith of Jesus come to be known as pro-rich, pro-war, and pro-American? What has happened here? And how do we get back to a historic, biblical, and *genuinely* evangelical faith rescued from its contemporary distortions? That rescue operation is even more crucial today, in the face of a deepening social crisis that literally cries out for more prophetic religion.

Of course, nobody can steal your personal faith; that's between you and God. The problem is in the political arena, where strident voices claim to represent Christians, when they clearly don't speak for *most* of us. It's time to take back our faith in the public square, especially in a time when a more authentic social witness is desperately needed.

The religious and political Right gets the public meaning of religion mostly wrong—preferring to focus only on sexual and cultural issues while ignoring the weightier matters of justice. And the secular Left doesn't seem to get the meaning and promise of faith for politics at all—mistakenly dismissing spirituality as irrelevant to social change. I actually happen to be conservative on issues of personal responsibility, the sacredness of human life, the reality of evil in our world, and the critical importance of individual character, parenting, and strong "family values." But the popular presentations of religion in our time (especially in the media) almost completely ignore the biblical vision of social justice and, even worse, dismiss such concerns as merely "left-wing."

It is indeed time to take back our faith.

5 Take back our faith from whom? To be honest, the confusion comes from many sources. From religious right-wingers who claim to know God's political views on every issue, then ignore the subjects that God seems to care the most about. From pedophile priests and cover-up bishops who destroy lives and shame the church. From television preachers whose extravagant lifestyles and crass fund-raising tactics *embarrass* more Christians than they know. From liberal secularists who want to banish faith from public life, and deny spiritual values to the soul of politics. And even from liberal theologians whose cultural conformity and creedal modernity serve to erode the foundations of historic biblical faith. From New Age philosophers who want to make Jesus into a non-threatening spiritual guru. And from politicians who love to say how religious they are but utterly fail to apply the values of faith to their public leadership and political policies.

It's time to reassert and reclaim the gospel faith—especially in our public life. When we do, we discover that faith challenges the powers that be to do justice for the poor, instead of preaching a "prosperity gospel" and supporting politicians that further enrich the wealthy. We remember that faith hates violence and tries to reduce it, and exerts a fundamental presumption against war, instead of justifying it in God's name. We see that faith creates community from racial, class, and gender divisions, [that it] prefers international community over nationalist religion, and that "God bless America" is found nowhere in the Bible. And we are reminded that faith regards matters such as the sacredness of life and family bonds as so important that they should never be used as ideological symbols or mere political pawns in partisan warfare.

The media likes to say, "Oh, then you must be the religious left." No, not at all, and the very question is the problem. Just because a religious right has fashioned itself for political power in one utterly predictable ideological guise does not mean that those who question this political seduction must be their opposite political counterpart. The best public contribution of religion is precisely *not* to be ideological predictable nor a loyal partisan. To always raise the moral issues of human rights, for example, will challenge both left and right-wing governments who put power above principles. Religious action is rooted in a much deeper place than "rights"—that being the image of God in every human being.

Similarly, when the poor are defended on moral or religious grounds it is certainly not "class warfare," as the rich often charge, but rather a direct response to the overwhelming focus on the poor in the Scriptures which claims they are regularly neglected, exploited, and oppressed by wealthy elites, political rulers and indifferent affluent populations. Those Scriptures don't simply endorse the social programs of the liberals or the conservatives, but make clear that poverty is indeed a religious issue, and the failure of political leaders to help uplift the poor will be judged a moral failing.

It is precisely because religion takes the problem of evil so seriously that it must always be suspicious of too much concentrated power—politically *and* economically—either in totalitarian regimes or in huge multi-national corporations which now have more wealth and power than many governments. It is indeed our theology of evil that makes us strong proponents of both political and economic democracy—not because people are so good, but because they often are not, and need clear safeguards and strong systems of checks and balances to avoid the dangerous accumulations of power and wealth.

10   It's why we doubt the goodness of *all* superpowers and the righteousness of empires in any era, *especially* when their claims of inspiration and success invoke theology and the name of God. Given the human tendencies of military and political power for self-delusion and deception, is it any wonder that hardly a religious body in the world regards the ethics of unilateral and pre-emptive war as "just"? Religious wisdom suggests that the more overwhelming the military might, the more dangerous its capacity for self and public deception. If evil in this world is deeply human and very real, and religious people believe it is, it just doesn't make spiritual sense to suggest that the evil all lies "out there" with our adversaries and enemies, and none of it "in here" with us—imbedded in our own attitudes, behaviors, and policies. Powerful nations dangerously claim to "rid the world of evil," but often do enormous harm in their self-appointed vocation to do so.

The loss of religion's prophetic vocation is terribly dangerous for any society. Who will uphold the dignity of economic and political outcasts? Who will question the self-righteousness of nations and their leaders? Who will question the recourse to violence and rush to wars, long before any last resort has been unequivocally proven? Who will not allow God's name to be used to simply justify ourselves, instead of calling us to accountability? And who will love the people enough to challenge their worst habits, coarser entertainments, and selfish neglects?

Prophetic religion always presses the question of the common good. Indeed, the question, "Whatever became of the common good?" must be a constant religious refrain directed to political partisans whose relentless quest for power and wealth makes them forget the "commonwealth" again and again. That common good should always be constructed from the deepest wells of our personal *and* social responsibility and the absolute insistence to never separate the two.

I am always amazed at the debate around poverty, with one side citing the need for changes in personal behaviors and the other for better social programs, as if the two were mutually exclusive. Obviously, both personal and social responsibility are necessary for overcoming poverty. When this absurd bifurcation is offered by ideological partisans on either side, I am quickly convinced that both sides must never have lived or worked anywhere near poverty or poor people. That there are behaviors that further entrench and even cause poverty is undisputable, as is the undeniable power of systems and structures to institutionalize injustice and oppression. Together, personal and social responsibility create the common good. Because we know these realities as *religious* facts, taught to us by our sacred Scriptures, religious communities can teach them to those still searching more for blame than solutions to pressing social problems.

But recovering the faith of the biblical prophets and Jesus is not just about politics; it also shapes the way we live our personal and communal lives. How do we live a faith whose social manifestation is compassion, and whose public expression is justice? And how do we raise our children by those values? That may be the most important battle of spiritual formation in our times, as I am personally discovering as a new father. Our religious congregations are not meant to be social organizations that merely reflect the wider culture's values, but dynamic counter-cultural communities whose purpose is to reshape both lives and societies. That realization perhaps has the most capacity to transform both religion and politics.

15 We contend today with both religious and secular fundamentalists, neither of whom must have their way. One group would impose the doctrines of a political theocracy on their fellow citizens, while the other would deprive the public square of needed moral and spiritual values often shaped by faith. In a political and media culture that squeezes everything into only two options of left and right, religious people must refuse the ideological categorization and actually build bridges between people of good will in both liberal and conservative camps. We must insist on the deep connections between spirituality and politics, while defending the proper boundaries between church and state which protect religious and non-religious minorities, and keep us all safe from state-controlled religion. We can demonstrate our commitment to pluralistic democracy *and* support the rightful separation of church and state without segregating moral and spiritual values from our political life.

QUESTIONS FOR DISCUSSION

1. Why do many people believe that religious faith needs to be taken back from those who have "stolen" it? Why does Wallis believe that people around the world now think that Christian faith is "pro-rich, pro-war, and pro-American"? Do you think that this is an accurate perception of world opinion?
2. How, according to Wallis, does the "political Right" misunderstand the "public meaning of religion"? How does the "secular Left" also misunderstand or underestimate the nature and power of faith? Do you agree with Wallis's assertions here?
3. What are some other mistaken attitudes toward religion that make it necessary to "take back" faith? Is it necessary for Wallis to list so many mistaken views? Is it perhaps inevitable that people will perceive and relate to religion differently in a secular society?
4. What positive suggestions for reclaiming true faith and authentic religious practice does Wallis begin to make in his sixth paragraph? How and why does he believe that "faith creates community"? How does faith heal divisions and go beyond "nationalist religion"? Why does an awareness of human evil make necessary a firm theological support for "political and economic democracy"?
5. What does Wallis believe to be the importance of helping the poor through religion, and why does he believe that no distinction or separation should be made between "personal and social responsibility" in order to advance "the common good"?
6. Despite his religious convictions, why does Wallis believe so strongly in the need for separation of church and state? Why does he believe that religious congregations should function as "dynamic counter-cultural communities"?

CONNECTION

Compare Jim Wallis's ideas and actions about religion, service, and politics with Martin Luther King's views and actions as found in his "Christmas Sermon" (see page 520).

IDEAS FOR WRITING

1. Write an essay about a religious group or denomination in which you have participated. How well would this group measure up to Wallis's vision of the ideal spiritual community? How could it become more dynamic, more "counter-cultural"?
2. Write a response to Wallis's ideas about the importance of the separation between church and state. Do you agree or disagree with Wallis's position? Why or why not?

Sojourners: Faith, Politics, Culture
www.sojo.net
The *Sojourners* site (founded by Jim Wallis) features an electronic version of the group's magazine; a study guide to Jim Wallis's new book, *God's Politics;* news; and editorial articles.

God's Politics: An Interview With Jim Wallis
www.motherjones.com/news/qa/2005/03/gods_politics_jim _wallis.html
In this interview with *Mother Jones* magazine, Jim Wallis clarifies his critique of the Republican Party, the religious Right, the Democrats, and the "secular fundamentalists."

Karen Methot-Chun

Living Spirituality

Student writer Karen Methot-Chun works in human resources at a large computer company in Silicon Valley and attends classes at De Anza College in Cupertino, California, where she is working toward a degree in nursing. She comes from a nondenominational Christian household and has studied massage, meditation, Tai Chi, and yoga. In the following paper, Karen draws together ideas from several different texts and a television interview to help develop her definition of "living spirituality."

The term "spirituality" encompasses a very broad spectrum of definitions, emotions, and reactions. Although the *American Heritage Dictionary* defines "spiritual" as "not tangible or material; of, concerned with, or affecting the soul; of, from or relating to God; deific, sacred, supernatural," and "spirit" as "the vital principle or animating force within living beings," when we describe people who are engaged with a living spirituality, we generally assume that their lifestyle is moral, that they are conscious of a greater being or guiding force in life, and that they are in harmony with their surroundings and in communication with their inner being or soul. Most importantly, however, the word "living" implies that they are involved in putting their spirituality into action through living in a highly conscious and aware manner, in touch with the life inside them and around them, while maintaining a consistent desire to improve the way in which they live and interact with the people and the world around them.

Often the term "living spirituality" is used interchangeably with "morality," but morality can sometimes be confused with narrowly dogmatic and inflexible beliefs that might better be termed "dying spirituality." For instance, the emphasis on dogma in fundamentalist religions and in the Catholic Church often seeks to extinguish the lively debate over moral issues in today's society over subjects such as the role of women in the church, abortion, and gay marriage. In the selection of the new pope, Catholics seem to desire to move the church back to the strict conservative tradition of Roman Catholicism; however, a significant number of modern Catholics, particularly those in America and Western Europe, seek to push the Church forward to accept more modern concepts, such as allowing priests to marry, permitting women to lead the church, considering the needs of the impoverished, and welcoming gays and lesbians into the Church community without judgment. As people who practice a living spirituality, we need to be aware of each other's differences in order to accept and acknowledge them, and to recognize that common spiritual ground that binds us to one another and to our shared humanity.

Living spirituality can be tarnished and deadened by extreme political agendas. Jim Wallis writes in "Taking Back the Faith" that Christianity has been stolen from the Christians and redefined by the New Right's political, media, and social agenda. Wallis poses the question "How did the faith of Jesus come to be known as pro-rich, pro-war, and pro-American?" Here Wallis is arguing that political extremists often use God and religion to support their own agenda. Wallis goes on to argue that both the left- and right-wing politicians have a very limited view of religion: "[R]ight-wingers . . . ignore the subjects that God seems to care the most about . . . [f]rom pedophile priests and cover-up bishops who destroy lives and shame the church . . . [f]rom television preachers whose extravagant lifestyles and crass fund-raising tactics *embarrass* more Christians than they know." On the other end of the spectrum, Wallis states that the "liberal secularists . . . want to banish faith from public life, and deny spiritual values to the soul of politics."

Frustrated by the lack of understanding of our media and politicians in the area of religious and spiritual values, Wallis "support[s] the rightful separation of church and state [but] without segregating moral and spiritual values from our political life." Politics neglects to see religion and spirituality for what they truly are—a set of guiding principles with which we should model our lives and our interactions with one another in order to give us a moral and spiritual "safe haven" when we can no longer cope with the world around us, and to provide us with motivation, through living spirituality, to help the less fortunate.

5   Summing up the concept of religious manipulation and the need for a living spirituality, Wallis states, "It is precisely because religion takes the

problem of evil so seriously that it must always be suspicious of too much concentrated power—politically *and* economically—either in totalitarian regimes or in huge multi-national corporations which now have more wealth and power than many governments." It is this kind of "suspicious" theology that Wallis believes "makes us strong proponents of both political and economic democracy—not because people are so good, but because they often are not, and need clear safeguards and strong systems of checks and balances to avoid the dangerous accumulations of power and wealth."

Living spirituality is a structure that provides an emotional and sometimes a physical haven to the downtrodden. When people encounter difficulties or struggles in life, their spiritual faith and guidance become the rock in which they find their stability, coping, and endurance. Ironically many people in their time of suffering turn and blame their religion or spiritual leader for not protecting them, only later to discover the path to healing is through living, active spiritual faith. In his memoir *Dharma Punx,* Noah Levine writes about his experience as a recovering drug user who has devoted his life to teaching meditation and counseling youth prisoners and drug abusers. When Levine loses his best friend to an overdose he "felt like nothing had prepared [him] for this; no amount of meditation, no amount of therapy, none of the spiritual practices or experiences . . . prepared [him] to lose [his] best friend" (237). Levine felt a sense of guilt and remorse for having a plethora of spiritual guidance in his own life, while his friend did not. Although he suffered from "survivor guilt," he used these emotions to further engage with his "spiritual quest . . . [to] teach the simple meditation techniques that had so profoundly altered the course of [his] life" (240). Levine discovered a new strength within himself through spiritual awareness, and then used this gift to guide others to do the same.

Although spirituality relates to the belief in a higher power and the concept of a greater harmony or energy among us, so that each of us is a part of a bigger whole. For instance, when Natascha McElhone, an actress on the television series *Revelations,* was asked during an interview with the *Today Show* about the issues of religion and spirituality, she stated, "I think the whole issue of whether we're religious and spiritual or not is kind of confusing, because it's more in the practice of living that that stuff comes out than in what we say we believe." In her life and in the process of filming *Revelations,* she came to realize that people may believe a certain way, yet their lifestyle often is inconsistent with their claims. She now feels that society is "looking for something more spiritual that can't necessarily be bought . . . religious or otherwise." McElhone clearly sees the need to dig deep within ourselves in order to find another method of fulfilling our emotional needs, and for many, this spiritual void is filled by a living spirituality rather than through the mechanism of religion.

McElhone's suspicion of religious moralism is echoed in many of the works of Duane Michals, an accomplished photographer. Michals has a controversial work titled *Salvation*, in which a person is being held figuratively at gunpoint where the "gun" is a crucifix and the gunman is a collared priest. In an interview with *Photo/Design* magazine, Michals states that he is a "fallen-away Catholic [and that he] never confuse[s] religiosity with spirituality." He further claims, "I hate organized religions . . . there is no bigger bigot than a professionally religious person." Michals believes that self-discovery is the essence of spirituality: we must be able to discover our self in order to understand spirituality, and to do so, we must be able to "let go" of everything, for by doing this we can capture the essence of what it means to possess living spirituality by abandoning selfishness and materiality.

In conclusion, we can see that a person can be spiritual and not be religious, or highly "religious" and not truly spiritual at all. Living spirituality is something within us that sees the innocence in the laughter of a child, the familiarity and comfort in the eyes of a loved one, the allure of the clouds of an afternoon sunset, the natural beauty in the wilderness. The beauty in life itself is a spiritual reality, and an artist with living spirituality may seek to capture that beauty in his or her work, in order to share it with others and inspire them on their own spiritual quest, much as Noah Levine brought his abilities as a spiritual healer through meditation to the prisoners of San Quentin Prison, a place where the inmates are truly in need of spiritual hope and rebirth. When people find the ability to grasp that which is in front of them, they can see the beauty in everyone and everything and can see beyond face value, depression, and confusion to a solution for the problems of others. This is spiritual growth and enlightenment. This is living spirituality.

WORKS CITED

Levine, Noah. "Death Is Not the End My Friend." *Dharma Punx: A Memoir*. New York: HarperCollins, 2003.

McElhone, Natascha. Interview with Katie Couric. *Today Show*. NBC. KNTV, San Francisco. 27 Apr. 2005.

Michals, Duane, and Joel-Peter Witkin. "Theater of the Forbidden." *Photo/Design* Jan./Feb. 1989. 25 Apr. 2005 {http://lestblood.imagodirt.net/ uploads/pictures/DuaneMichals_Salvation.jpg}.

"Spirit," "Spiritual." *American Heritage Dictionary*. 4th ed. 2000.

Wallis, Jim. "Taking Back the Faith." *God's Politics* Jan. 2005. 6 May 2005 {http://www.beliefnet.com/story/159/story_15987_1.html}.

QUESTIONS FOR DISCUSSION

1. How clear is Methot-Chun's initial definition of "living spirituality"? How does she contrast her definition of this complex term to the dictionary definitions for "spiritual" and "spirit"? Is this contrast effective? Why or why not?

2. How do Methot-Chun's comments on the Catholic Church's movement to reaffirm traditional positions on issues such as gay marriage and women in the clergy help or detract from her core definition of living spirituality? Would citations of opinion on these issues from different authorities within the Church have helped make her positions clearer or more powerful? Are they necessary?

3. How do the position statements on religion versus spirituality from Jim Wallis and Noah Levine help to support Methot-Chun's definition and position on living spirituality? What makes these "authorities" credible?

4. Later in the essay, Methot-Chun brings in testimony from an actress and a photographer on the issue of living spirituality. How do these individuals' positions as artists provide a new and thought-provoking insight into the issue in question? Are their statements as convincing as those of the more spiritually committed authorities, Wallis and Levine? Why or why not?

TOPICS FOR RESEARCH AND WRITING

1. Describe a conflicting desire for authentic religious experience combined with doubt about some of the more traditional forms of religious belief and practice. Do some further research into the place of religion in modern life. Do other writers whom you have encountered express similar views of doubt and confusion about religion?

2. Jane Goodall addresses the relationship between science and religious practices as does Marcello Gleiser in "The Myths of Science (see Chapter 4). Also do further research into modern relations between science and religion, and write an essay in which you discuss ways that science and religion can reinforce and shed light on one another.

3. Reflect on the essays in this chapter that discuss prayer in religious and secular devotion. Then do research on this topic. Write a research paper that discusses the reasons why people pray and why they find this practice meaningful.

4. Do some further research on the importance of ritual observances such as those described in Norman Chung's essay in both religious and secular life, and write an essay in which you consider what purpose such observances serve for people and for society.

5. Jessie van Eerden and Jane Goodall describe religious experiences that could be described as mystical. After doing some further research into this subject, write an essay in which you define and discuss what it means to have a mystical experience and what the positive effects of such experiences might be.

6. King, Wallis, Methot-Chun, and Levine discuss the ways that spiritual love and service can be used to effect social change. Do some further research into spiritual social activism and service. What is particularly effective about social activist movements that use love and kindness as their source of energy?

7. The following films portray spiritual leaders (positive and negative) and elements of spirituality in action. Pick one of these films—*The Seventh Seal, Little Buddha, The Last Temptation of Christ, Gandhi, The Last Wave, Seven Years in Tibet, Kundun, The Passion of Christ,* or *The Himalayas*—and write an essay in which you analyze the film and its spiritual message. Research critical reviews and contextual information to combine with your own analysis. What makes this film memorable?

Credits

Text Credits

Marc Ian Barasch, "What is a Healing Dream?" from Healing Dreams. Copyright © 2000 by Marc Ian Barasch. Used by permission of Riverhead Books, an imprint of Penguin Putnam Inc.

Melissa Burns, "The Best Seat in the House." Reprinted by permission of the author.

Joseph Campbell, Quotations from *The Mythic Dimension: Selected Essays 1959–1987.* Copyright © 1997, 2007; reprinted by permission of the Joseph Campbell Foundation (jcf.org).

Joyce Chang, "Drive Becarefully." Reprinted by permission of author.

Norman Chung, "A Faithful Taoist." Reprinted by permission of the author.

Judith Ortiz Cofer "The Other" from *Reaching for the Mainland & Selected New Poems* by Judith Ortiz Cofer, Bilingual Press/Editorial Bilingüe, 1995, Tempe, Arizona (Arizona State University, Tempe, AZ).

Judith Ortiz Cofer, "Silent Dancing" from *Silent Dancing: A Partial Remembrance of a Puerto Rican Childhood.* © 1990 Arte Público Press - University of Houston. Reprinted with permission from Arte Público Press - University of Houston.

James Cusick, "Politicians Might Hear, but Does Popular Culture Have the Power to Actually Make Them Listen?" from *Sunday Herald,* June 5, 2005, Glasgow (UK). Reproduced with the permission of the Herald & Times Group.

Carrie Demers, M.D., from *Yoga International,* March 2004. The author is the Medical Director of the Total Health Center at the Himalayan Institute in Honesdale, Pennsylvania. This article first appeared in this edition of *Yoga International* magazine.

Jessie van Eerden, "The Soul has Six Wings" from The Best American Spiritual Writing of 2006 (published originally in Portland Autumn, 2005). Reprinted by permission of the author.

Carlin Flora, "Seeing by Starlight" from Psychology Today, July/August 2004. Copyright © 2004 Psychology Today. Reprinted by permission of Psychology Today.

Sigmund Freud, "Erotic Wishes and Dreams" from On Dreams by Sigmund Freud, translated by James Strachey. Copyright © 1952 by W.W. Norton & Company, Inc., renewed © 1980 by Alix S. Strachey. Used by permission of W.W. Norton & Company, Inc.

Sigmund Freud, "Erotic Wishes and Dreams" from The Standard Edition of the Complete Psychological Works of Sigmund Freud translated and edited by James Strachey. © Copyrights, The Institute of PsychoAnalysis and The Hogarth Press for permission to quote from Reprinted by permission of The Random House Group Ltd.

Marcelo Gleiser, "The Myths of Science - Creation" from *The UNESCO Courier,* May 2001, www.unesco.org/en/courier. Copyright © 2001 UNESCO. Reprinted by permission from UNESCO.

Natalie Goldberg, "On the Shores of Lake Biwa" from the July 2006 issue of the *Shambhala Sun.* Copyright © 2006 Natalie Goldberg. Reprinted by permission of the author.

Jane Goodall, "In the Forests of Gombe" from *Reason For Hope.* Copyright © 1999 by Soko Publications Ltd. and Phillip Berman. Reprinted by permission of Grand Central Publishing.

Robert Graves, "The Pelasgian Creation Myth" from *The Greek Myths,* Copyright © 1955. Used by permission of Carcanet Press Limited.

Photo Credits

Index